THE OXFORD HANI

POLICE AND POLICING

THE OXFORD HANDBOOKS IN CRIMINOLOGY AND CRIMINAL JUSTICE

GENERAL EDITOR: MICHAEL TONRY

The *Oxford Handbooks in Criminology and Criminal Justice* offer authoritative, comprehensive, and critical overviews of the state of the art of criminology and criminal justice. Each volume focuses on a major area of each discipline, is edited by a distinguished group of specialists, and contains specially commissioned, original essays from leading international scholars in their respective fields. Guided by the general editorship of Michael Tonry, the series will provide an invaluable reference for scholars, students, and policy makers seeking to understand a wide range of research and policies in criminology and criminal justice.

OTHER TITLES IN THIS SERIES

THE OXFORD HANDBOOK OF

POLICE AND POLICING

Edited by

MICHAEL D. REISIG

and

ROBERT J. KANE

OXFORD

UNIVERSITY PRESS

Oxford University Press is a department of the University of Oxford. It furthers
the University's objective of excellence in research, scholarship, and education
by publishing worldwide. Oxford is a registered trade mark of Oxford University
Press in the UK and certain other countries.

Published in the United States of America by Oxford University Press
198 Madison Avenue, New York, NY 10016, United States of America.

Library of Congress Cataloging-in-Publication Data
The Oxford handbook of police and policing/edited by Michael D. Reisig and Robert J. Kane.
pages cm
Includes bibliographical references and index.
ISBN 978-0-19-984388-6 (hardcover : alk. paper); 978-0-19-094731-6 (paperback : alk. paper)
1. Police—United States—Handbooks, manuals, etc.   2. Police—Europe—Handbooks, manuals, etc.
I. Reisig, Michael Dean, 1968–
II. Kane, Robert J.
HV8139.O94 2014
363.2–dc23 2013027011

Contents

PART III POLICE AUTHORITY

PART IV RACE/ETHNICITY AND POLICING

PART V VARIETIES OF POLICE RESEARCH

PART VI   POLICING INTO THE FUTURE

LIST OF CONTRIBUTORS

Ben Bradford is a Career Development Fellow at the University of Oxford.

Anthony A. Braga is the Don M. Gottfredson Professor of Evidence-based Criminology in the School of Criminal Justice at Rutgers University and a Senior Research Fellow in the Program in Criminal Justice Policy and Management at Harvard University.

Rod K. Brunson is an Associate Professor of Criminal Justice at Rutgers University.

Mark Button is a Professor of Criminology at the University of Portsmouth.

Derek M. Cohen is a Policy analyst at the Texas Policy Foundation.

Gary Cordner is a Professor of Criminal Justice at Kutztown University.

Scott H. Decker is a Foundation Professor of Criminology and Criminal Justice at Arizona State University.

Robin S. Engel is a Professor of Criminal Justice at the University of Cincinnati and Director of the Institute of Crime Science.

Brian Forst is a Professor in the Department of Justice, Law and Criminology at American University.

Jacinta M. Gau is an Assistant Professor of Criminal Justice at the University of Central Florida.

Jack R. Greene is a Professor of Criminology and Criminal Justice at Northeastern University.

Steve Herbert is a Professor of Geography and Law, Societies, and Justice at the University of Washington.

Matthew J. Hickman is an Associate Professor of Criminal Justice at Seattle University.

Mike Hough is a Professor of Criminal Policy at the University of London.

Jonathan Jackson is a Senior Lecturer in Research Methodology at the London School of Economics.

Lallen T. Johnson is an Assistant Professor of Criminal Justice at Drexel University.

Sanja Kutnjak Ivković is a Professor of Criminal Justice at Michigan State University.

Paul G. Lewis is an Associate Professor in the School of Politics and Global Studies at Arizona State University.

Willem de Lint is Professor of Criminal Justice in the School of Law at Flinders University.

Branko Lobnikar is an Associate Professor of Security Organization Management at the University or Maribor.

Cynthia Lum is an Associate Professor in the Department of Criminology, Law and Society at George Mason University.

Edward R. Maguire is a Professor in the Department of Justice, Law, and Criminology at American University.

Peter K. Manning is the Elmer V. H. and Eileen M. Brooks Chair in the School of Criminology and Criminal Justice at Northeastern University.

Lorraine Mazerolle is a Research Professor in the Institute for Social Science Research at the University of Queensland.

Sarah J. Mclean is Associate Director and Director of Research and Technical Assistance at the John F. Finn Institute for Public Safety.

Gorazd Meško is a Professor of Criminology at the University of Maribor.

Melissa Schaefer Morabito is an Assistant Professor of Criminal Justice and Criminology at the University of Massachusetts at Lowell.

Doris M. Provine is a Professor in the School of Social Transformation at Arizona State University.

Wesley G. Skogan is a Professor of Political Science at Northwestern University.

Andrej Sotlar is an Associate Professor of Security Sciences at the University of Maribor.

Justice Tankebe is a University Lecturer and Fellow of Fitzwilliam College at University of Cambridge.

Melanie A. Taylor is an Assistant Professor of Criminal Justice at the University of Nevada at Reno.

William Terrill is an Associate Professor of Criminal Justice at Michigan State University.

David Thacher is an Associate Professor of Public Policy and Urban Planning at the University of Michigan.

Monica W. Varsanyi is an Associate Professor of Political Science at John Jay College of Criminal Justice.

Alison Wakefield   is a Senior Lecturer of Security Risk Management at the University of Portsmouth.

Ronald Weitzer   is a Professor of Sociology at George Washington University.

Michael D. White   is an Associate Professor of Criminology and Criminal Justice at Arizona State University.

James J. Willis   is an Associate Professor in the Department of Criminology, Law and Society at George Mason University.

Robert E. Worden   is an Associate Professor of Criminal Justice at the University at Albany, Suny, and the Director of the John F. Finn Institute for Public Safety.

John L. Worrall   is a Professor of Criminology at the University of Texas at Dallas.

THE OXFORD HANDBOOK OF

POLICE AND POLICING

PART I

POLICING CONTEXTS

CHAPTER 1

··

A RECENT HISTORY OF
THE POLICE

··

JAMES J. WILLIS*

LIKE many other political and social institutions, the police have been the focus of many reform efforts aimed at improving what they do and how they do it. This essay sketches some of the major efforts at changing local police organizations in the United States over the last thirty years. In doing so, it takes occasion to make comparisons to policing developments in other countries (mostly other Western democracies). Its purpose is to identify some broad patterns and trends as a context for interpreting the essays that follow.

Following Weisburd and Braga (2006a), its point of departure is Everett Rogers's (2003, 137) notion that social change is often driven by a perceived problem or crisis to an existing social system that demands an innovative response. Not only may this generate new approaches; it can also influence their form and character. As Hans Toch (1980, 55) writes, "The premise here is not that crises inevitably lead us to new ideas, but that crises permit us to evolve new ideas by unsettling old ones." The late 1960s in the United States was such a period of crisis, when racial tensions and concerns about crime and disorder revealed the limitations of the existing policing model. Not long after, urban riots in Britain exposed the police to similar scrutiny (Brain 2011). The government inquiries and ensuing reports on both sides of the Atlantic identified a host of challenges facing the criminal justice system including the police.[1] Key among these was improving public safety though effective crime strategies and repairing the fraught relationship between the police and its publics (particularly with minorities living in inner-city neighborhoods).

This essay suggests that some recent and important innovations in the policing environment can be regarded as new or continued adaptations to the problems of public safety and police legitimacy first identified in the United States in the 1960s and 1970s, and in Britain in the early 1980s. Thus, in the decades since community policing emerged as a coherent reform, we have witnessed its evolution in response to developments in police research and practice and in response to larger social, economic, and political forces. At the same time, other innovations, such as Compstat, have appeared as new attempts to improve the police capacity to fight crime and strengthen public accountability for performance. In addition, the structure of policing in the United States and elsewhere has been influenced by a new shock to the policing environment that in turn has presented a set of new challenges to the way police operate—the threat of terrorism. Thus this essay is structured around developments in the following key and overlapping areas: strategic innovations, accountability and legitimacy, and policing terrorism.

Reform efforts rarely work as intended, and so it is important to distinguish the desires and recommendations of reformers and reform movements from actual police operations in order to get an accurate historical portrait. This essay will also offer a brief assessment of the nature and degree of change over this reform period. Finally, just as the President's Commission on Law Enforcement and Administration of Justice (1967, x) recognized research as a "powerful force for change," some trends in police scholarship are also considered.

The essay is organized as follows: Section 1.1 discusses some key strategic innovations to have emerged in policing over the last few decades; Section 1.2 examines recent efforts to strengthen police accountability and enhance legitimacy; Section 1.3 explores how local police have adapted to the new challenge of terrorism since the attacks of September 11, 2001; and Section 1.4 concludes by offering some comments about continuity and change over this period and by noting opportunities for future research.

A number of conclusions can be drawn:

- Police scholarship has significantly advanced understanding about the effectiveness of a variety of police strategies for reducing crime and disorder.
- It has become generally accepted that the police role extends beyond crime control to include a wide range of citizen concerns and neighborhood problems.
- New systems have emerged for holding police organizations accountable for their crime control efforts, for improving oversight of individual police officer performance, and for increasing public confidence in these processes.
- Despite attempts to improve police community relations, most notably through the continued development of community policing, studies still show that African Americans are less supportive of the police than whites.
- A growing body of research suggests that treating people in procedurally just ways enhances the legitimacy of the police and delivers important crime control benefits.
- Local police are regarded as playing a key role in anti-terrorist activities, but by and large their organizational priorities, structures, and practices have been little affected by the attacks of September 11, 2001.
- Routine and reactive patrol work remain at the core of policing and yet little is still known about whether or how often patrol officers make the best choice in using their discretion in their encounters with the public.

1.1 STRATEGIC REFORMS

The focus in this section is on strategic innovations whose lineage can be traced back to the crises of the 1960s and 1970s and that continue to shape the contemporary police role and function: community policing and order maintenance policing,[2] problem-oriented policing (POP), and hot spots policing. These are obviously not the only important reforms to have emerged over the intervening period (these exclude, for example, legal, administrative, and technological changes), but they have generated considerable discussion among police scholars and practitioners and can be thought of as "strategic" because their doctrines, if implemented faithfully, promise to transform the means and ends of policing (Moore, Sparrow, and Spelman 1997, 278; Weisburd and Braga 2006a). Moreover, examining the context in which these "big reform ideas" emerged helps to highlight aspects of the policing environment that lie at the core of other attempts to change police (Bayley 2008, 8).

1.1.1 The Standard Model of Policing

In order to make any meaningful assessment of recent reform efforts, it is first necessary to establish some kind of benchmark for measuring change. What is policing purportedly changing *from*? Regarding this question, it is worth bearing in mind that assessments of police reform, including the one here, are more often based on interpretations of case histories from big city police departments than on rigorous scholarly analysis (see Lane 1967; Fogelson 1977). While models identifying different reform eras provide a helpful framework for considering general historical trends (Kelling and Moore 1988), to what degree they accurately capture the diverse workings of thousands of police departments over several decades is an empirical question that needs to be tested. For example, when a study of two large police departments in the United States from the 1990s shows that "general patrol, administrative activities, and personal breaks accounted for the majority of the [patrol] officer's self-directed time," is this significantly different from how patrol officers spent their time twenty or even a hundred years ago? (Mastrofski 2004, 114). If not, what does this say about claims that the last three decades have been "remarkable" in terms of police innovation (Committee to Review Research on Police Policy and Practice 2004, 82)?

Accurate comparisons over time eschew impressions for hard empirical evidence, whose absence brings to mind what Marcel Duchamp called "the delightful fantasy of history" (Tomkins 2011, 69). What is needed is a more reliable basis for making judgments about how extensive changes in policing have or have not been. Longitudinal field studies could help fill this lacuna in existing police scholarship, but this would require the implementation of a research infrastructure very different from the current model where individual projects are funded over short two-to-three-year periods rather than being sustained over decades (Willis and Mastrofski 2011, 327). Fortunately, the National Institute of Justice is currently testing a long-term research platform that would allow researchers in the United States to collect data indefinitely on hundreds of police departments across the country (Rosenbaum et al. 2011). Such an approach would allow for more meaningful assessments of police reform, including the historical factors promoting stability and change.

Putting this caveat aside, the conventional wisdom is that up until the crises of the 1960s, police operational strategies in the United States were primarily reactive, focused on serious crime, and applied generally across a jurisdiction (Committee to Review Research on Police Policy and Practice 2004). Referred to as the "standard" policing model, the primary police methods of routine preventive patrol, rapid response to calls for service, and retrospective investigations were influenced by ideas about general deterrence and incapacitation (Weisburd and Eck 2004, 44). It was thought that maintaining a visible presence in communities, responding promptly to individual emergency calls (especially those that were crime related), and increasing the risk of apprehension could reduce crime because arresting some offenders and deterring others would give the impression of police omnipresence. Furthermore, consistent with the assumption that the police exercise of legal-rational authority should be protected from arbitrary political interests, subject to rules, and applied uniformly by well-trained professionals, police organization took the form of a "legalistic and technocratic bureaucracy whose members are committed to an occupational community with norms of subordination and service that set it apart from the community that it policed" (Reiss 1992, 57).

Rising crime rates from the late 1960s to the mid-1980s (Bayley and Nixon 2010, 3), and a series of high-profile research studies questioning the effectiveness of standard police practices (Kelling et al. 1974; Greenwood, Petersilia, and Chaiken 1977; Spelman and Brown 1981), presented serious challenges to the strategic assumptions of a policing model that had dominated for much of the twentieth century. Additionally, the Civil Rights Movement, race riots, and increasing citizen alienation from government (Mastrofski 2006, 44) revealed a tense and distrusting police-citizen relationship (Fogelson 1968). The form and character of ensuing police reform strategies were influenced by the nature of this performance gap between current practices and public expectations for what the police should be doing and how they should be doing it in a democratic society (Weisburd and Braga 2006a, 3).

In this context, community policing and broken windows policing can be considered police departments' attempts to foster closer working relationships with communities and to respond to a broader range of public safety concerns than just serious crime; problem-oriented policing developed to reorient policing from a bureaucratic focus on internal management concerns and "one-size-fits-all" responses to individual incidents; and lastly, hot spots policing emerged in the wake of evidence challenging the effectiveness of crime control strategies involving the uniform application of police resources across jurisdictions. It is to these reforms that I now turn.

1.1.2 Community Policing and Order Maintenance Policing

When it comes to the development of strategic innovations, it is important to recognize their evolutionary and hybrid nature. Attempts to improve policing rarely emerge as fully-formed packages like a phoenix that arises from the ash heap of its past. Conceiving of innovation in this way leads to misunderstandings about "the genesis of reform" and its significance to the development of innovations (Willis and Mastrofski 2011, 313). With the benefit of hindsight, commentators generally agree that the roots of community policing and order maintenance policing lie in a milieu of new ideas and practices (including team policing, community crime prevention, and foot patrol) that were implemented in a few cities in the 1970s and early 1980s in response to perceived failures of the standard policing model (Moore 1992). Rather than being a purposeful effort at widespread police reform, these collectively "morphed" over time into more coherent policing strategies (Skogan and Roth 2004, xix). In light of this, thinking of reforms as waves that simply wash away the efforts that preceded them is not particularly insightful. A more useful analogy is one of sedimentary rock, where new innovations are transposed onto "the core service-oriented structures and operations that have long sustained American police" and are, in turn, powerfully shaped by them (Mastrofski and Willis 2010, 117).

1.1.2.1 Community Policing

Perhaps the most popular of the strategies to have emerged over the last three decades, both in the United States and abroad, is community policing (Brogden and Nijhar 2005), which is now a global commodity that can be found on virtually every continent (Mastrofski, Willis, and Kochel 2007, 223). International organizations (such as the United Nations, European Union, and World Bank) encourage developing democratic nations to adopt community policing projects (Brogden 2005), and whereas most innovations fail (Rogers 2003), community policing has shown impressive resilience. In the most recent federal survey conducted in 2007, 56 percent of all police agencies in the United States reported having a mission statement that included community policing, and 44 percent of departments, employing 70 percent of all officers, trained all new recruits in community policing (Bureau of Justice Statistics 2010, 26–27).

The roots of community policing in the United States can be traced back to the limitations of the standard policing model where the primary functions of motorized patrol (any department's largest resource) were to maintain a visible presence, respond to 911 calls, and suppress serious crime. Over time, these practices conspired to alienate the police from local communities and helped to foster an image of the police as unresponsive to the needs and desires of those they were supposed to serve. More troubling was that many minority citizens, especially African Americans living in inner-city neighborhoods, felt marginalized and treated "differentially under color of law" (Greene 2004, 35). A wave of race riots between 1964 and 1968 were almost all sparked by incidents involving the police and black citizens, leading the Kerner Commission to report: "The atmosphere of hostility and cynicism is reinforced by a widespread belief among Negroes in the existence of police brutality and in a "double standard" of justice and protection—one for Negroes and one for whites" (National Advisory Commission on Civil Disorders 1968, 10). Similarly, the community policing movement in Britain emerged in the 1970s and 1980s in the aftermath of riots exposing hostilities between the police and minority communities (Newburn and Reiner 2007, 929). A similar crisis-driven adoption pattern can be seen in developing democracies where reforms implemented in response to challenges to government authority often include the adoption of community policing initiatives to help recapture lost legitimacy (Pino and Wiatrowski 2006).

In response to this crisis of confidence in the United States, the police began to experiment with ways to reconnect with the public, such as the long-term assignment of teams of officers to small geographic areas, the establishment of community relations units, and the implementation of community crime prevention programs (Moore 1992). These strategies helped to establish the value of two-way communication between the police and community and of collaborative partnerships to improve public safety in local neighborhoods. By pooling their collective resources and working together, the idea was that local police departments and community organizations could respond more effectively to crime and neighborhood problems than the police acting on their own (Rosenbaum 1986). Thus these early reform efforts can be regarded as important precursors to the current community policing model whose defining element is making police responsive "to citizen input concerning both the needs of the community and the best ways by which police can help meet those needs" (Skogan 2006, 28).

From this perspective, politics has been a powerful factor contributing to the origins and development of community policing in the United States (Skogan 1995), particularly when one considers that community policing's other core dimensions help enhance powerful ideals about participatory democracy (Sklansky 2008, 83). Consider the second key element of community policing—changes to "organizational structures." Central to this approach is the decentralization of decision making to patrol officers at the beat level in order to foster positive exchanges with citizens that help to create trust and cooperation. Moreover, community policing's proponents identify a third key element, or "problem solving." This process encourages communities to work with the police in identifying and responding to a variety of public safety concerns that communities themselves (and not just the police) identify as important. In doing so, it broadens the traditional police mandate beyond serious crime to include fear of crime, minor offenses (e.g., vandalism, public drinking), and social and physical disorders (Skogan and Hartnett 1997). In addition to engaging with local communities to set priorities, problem solving also involves police and citizens working together as co-producers of public safety.

Politics also helps to account for the *diffusion* of community policing. The Executive Session on Policing held at the Kennedy School of Government (1985–1991) and supported by the Department of Justice was instrumental to promoting community policing, and in 1994 under Title I of the Violent Crime Control and Law Enforcement Act (the Crime Act) Congress authorized an appropriation of $8.8 billion to state and local police agencies to advance community policing across the United States (Roth, Roehl, and Johnson 2004). According to the Department of Justice's Office of Community Oriented Policing Services (COPS Office), between 1994 and 2011 over thirteen thousand law enforcement agencies received grants (James 2010). The COPS Office has also funded approximately thirty Regional Community Policing Institutes to provide training in community policing and problem solving. Whether or not a department actually needed to implement community policing during this period as a rational response to pressures of crime and community discord in its environment (Mastrofski 1998), the promise of a reform endorsed by politicians and progressive police leaders and backed by billions in federal money has been a powerful incentive for its adoption (Ritti and Mastrofski 2002; Helms and Gutierrez 2007). Similar pressures for conformity are at work in the international arena, where police consultants, think tanks, national governments, and non-governmental agencies promote community policing as a cure for rising crime rates and a lack of public support for government authorities, including local police (Brogden 2005).

Focusing on community policing's political appeal should not diminish the influence of other factors that have influenced its development during this period. Crime reduction may not be community policing's primary goal (Skogan 2006), but it is so central to the police mandate that community policing has had to justify itself at least partly in these terms (Klockars 1988). An extensive review by the National Academies on community policing's effectiveness published in 2004 was cautious and equivocal regarding its capacity to reduce crime, disorder, and fear of crime (Committee to Review Research on Police Policy and Practice 2004, 246), but a later assessment is also more optimistic (Reisig 2010). The basis for the latter's conclusion can be attributed to a body of empirical research that draws on recent theoretical developments in social disorganization theory (Kubrin and Weitzer 2003). These studies suggest that complex processes involving relational networks and social resources help mediate the effects of poverty, residential mobility, and ethnic heterogeneity on neighborhood crime (Sampson and Raudenbush 1999). One of the most important of these factors is collective efficacy, or the conditions of trust and solidarity among neighbors that lead them to share similar expectations and work with one another toward their common good. The direct effects of community policing on collective efficacy are unknown (Reisig 2010, 38), but some scholars claim that community policing's focus on building healthy partnerships can help promote greater social cohesion and shared responsibility to reduce crime (Sampson 2004). To the extent that community policing can be shown to strengthen collective efficacy and the U.S. trend toward declining crime rates begins to reverse, departments may well seek to strengthen their existing community policing programs.

In sum, even in the face of a global economic crisis and the formidable challenges to full and effective implementation (particularly in terms of the police capacity to establish partnerships in disadvantaged communities where minorities are deeply suspicious of government authorities) (Weitzer and Tuch 1999), community policing continues to resonate powerfully with communitarian and democratic ideals about responsive

government (Bayley and Nixon 2010, 7). Coupled with these cultural and political sentiments is a small but significant body of evidence that community policing may be able
to reduce crime and disorder and significantly improve police-community relations
(Reisig 2010; Gill et al. 2011). Given the promise it holds for good government and the
expectations it has helped to create among the public for "client-oriented, service-style
policing" (Mastrofski 2006, 45), news of community policing's demise, to paraphrase
Mark Twain, would seem to be greatly exaggerated (Kerlikowske 2004). Community
policing might not be the revolution envisioned by its early supporters, but many of its
precepts appear to have become institutionalized in police organization and practice.

1.1.2.2 Order Maintenance Policing

Order maintenance or broken windows policing is another innovation that emerged in
response to what were seen as limitations of the standard policing model. Similar to
community policing it has endured and has become recognized internationally (Ismaili
2003), and its development has been influenced by social, political, and intellectual currents of the past few decades. Variations in how these forces have been interpreted and
adapted have led to the evolution of different policing strategies that share the common
goal of broadening the police role beyond serious crime to address citizens' fear of crime
and physical and social disorder.

The origins of order maintenance policing lie in the recognition among researchers in
the 1970s and 1980s that residents' fears of crime were largely unrelated to their risk of
victimization and in the reemergence of foot patrols in several American cities (Skogan
and Roth 2004). In addition to concerns about crime, residents were more often worried
about urban blight and behavior that was disruptive to the quality of life in their neighborhoods (Taylor 2006, 99). Meanwhile, foot patrol experiments in Flint, Michigan and
Newark, New Jersey suggested that foot patrol might not always reduce crime but it did
reduce citizens' fears and increase their levels of satisfaction with police services.

The idea of broken windows policing developed from an *Atlantic Monthly* article by
James Q. Wilson and George Kelling (1982) that suggested that physical and social disorder were linked to serious crime. Illustrating their perspective with examples from
the Newark Foot Patrol Experiment (Kelling et al. 1981), Wilson and Kelling surmised
that graffiti, trash-strewn lots, loitering, rowdy teenagers, and aggressive panhandlers
were examples of physical deterioration, disorderly behaviors, and minor crimes often
referred to as quality-of-life offenses. If left untended these "broken windows" signaled
that no one cared about a neighborhood which in turn could lead to fear, neighborhood
withdrawal, weakening community controls, and eventually serious crime. The implication was that the police should play a role in fixing these windows, a rationale that has
since given rise to a range of operational strategies that fall under the umbrella of order
maintenance policing.

One version involves the police deciding on what problems to address and how to
address them while virtually ignoring community concerns in the process. Under a zero
tolerance strategy the police operate largely exclusively in targeting disorderly behaviors, which are thought to offend community standards, or minor offenses. Police tactics

can incorporate a range of responses from issuing citations, dispersing loiterers, increasing surveillance, and conducting field interrogations, but typically include the strict enforcement of public order and nuisance laws through fines or arrest (Mastrofski 1988, 53). The New York City Police Department popularized this approach in the 1990s when then-Mayor Rudolph Giuliani and Commissioner William Bratton targeted quality-of-life offenders such as "fare-beaters" who jumped subway turnstiles, and "squeegee people" who approached stopped motorists to clean their windshields and then aggressively demanded payment (Bratton 1998, 213). An important justification for this strategy was the assertion that those engaging in seemingly minor offenses were often guilty of more serious crimes, such as illegally concealing weapons, or the subject of an outstanding warrant. Giuliani, Bratton, and many others associated the ensuing drop in serious crime and fear in New York City throughout the 1990s with the suppression of these behaviors (although, like George Kelling, they reject the term "zero tolerance"). Such support contributed to zero tolerance policing's face validity among police leaders, politicians, and the public despite empirical studies raising doubts about its crime reduction benefits (Eck and Maguire 2000).

More broadly, the movement toward the selective enforcement of incivilities over the last twenty years or so has been attributed to the rise of neoconservative politics and a diverse blend of social, economic, and cultural changes associated with late-twentieth-century modernity (Taylor 2006). In this context, zero tolerance policing is seen as representative of a major transformation in the entire criminal process from the traditional goals of punishing and rehabilitating individuals toward managing the risks presented by certain threatening groups through crime prevention and fear reduction (Garland 2001, 19). It is worth noting, however, that some studies that have tried to apply this theoretical framework to police innovations other than zero tolerance policing have found only a loose fit with actual police practice (Willis and Mastrofski 2012).

An alternative order maintenance approach is demonstrated by Chicago's community policing or Chicago Alternative Policing Strategy (CAPS), one located squarely in the developments in social disorganization theory discussed earlier (Skogan and Hartnett 1997). Under CAPS the police mandate includes working closely with local communities to address problems of both physical and social disorder. Unlike New York's zero tolerance model, this approach is more consistent with the early foot patrol experiments whose goals included promoting face-to-face communication with local residents, developing trust, identifying local problems, and establishing effective crime prevention partnerships (Pate 1986; Trojanowicz 1986). In Chicago, the police partner with local communities to clean up trash in vacant lots and remove graffiti and other signs of urban blight. Moreover, residents are responsible for strengthening social control in their own neighborhoods. So, for example, they may conduct "stand-ups" in front of problem businesses or engage in "positive-loitering" to challenge prostitutes and their potential customers (Skogan et al. 2004, 91).

A third-order maintenance strategy has emerged in England in the past decade under the moniker of reassurance policing. Impetus for this reform came from the British government's concern that anxiety about crime remained high during the mid-1990s while several waves of the British Crime Survey revealed that crime rates were falling (Skogan 2009, 303). The explanation for this disconnect, and one that led to the development of signal crimes theory (Innes 2004), was that some crime and disorder incidents mattered more than others in shaping individuals' assessments of risk (Bottoms 2008, 571). Thus residents might perceive the sudden appearance of graffiti or litter in their neighborhood as significantly more threatening to their safety than, for example, a sudden increase in auto thefts, which might be less visible to the public. The policy response, which was developed as the National Reassurance Policing Programme (NRPP), was for the police to respond to signs of disorder with a "control signal" that communicated law enforcement's attempt to increase order and thus provide a reassurance effect (Innes 2007). The key elements of the NRPP, tested in 16 experimental areas around Britain in 2003, were to assign police teams to neighborhoods where they could engage with local residents and work jointly with them in a problem-solving process to resolve those signal crimes that were the cause of greatest concern (Barnes and Eagle 2007). An evaluation of these trials was positive, showing that residents were less worried about crime and victimization when police were visible and accessible and worked alongside the community (Skogan 2009, 303).

Whatever form the order maintenance response might take, and despite ongoing debates about whether disorder causes crime or both are manifestations of the same conditions of structural disadvantage, the idea that the management of minor offenses and disorderly behaviors is an essential function of public police has become well established since the 1980s.

1.1.3 Problem-Oriented Policing

In his article on problem-oriented policing (POP), Herman Goldstein (1979, 242) called for a paradigm shift in policing from a primarily reactive, incident-driven model toward one where police proactively targeted a wide range of "troublesome situations that prompt citizens to turn to the police" and developed a systematic process for analyzing and resolving these problems. According to Goldstein, not only had research revealed the limitations of standard crime strategies, but local police agencies had become so preoccupied with internal management issues of efficiency, administrative procedure, and staffing that they had lost sight of the important social goals they were supposed to accomplish. His original POP model highlighted the need for more precise definitions of problems than general crime categories, careful inquiry into the nature of a specific problem and its underlying causes, and a willingness to explore a wide range of alternative responses than merely arrest. Goldstein (1990) later expanded on these basic elements, including their relationship to one another and their relevance to police organizations. Key to this approach was the attempt to identify and address the underlying conditions that gave rise to clusters of problems that on the surface appeared to be unrelated.

Since its initial conceptualization, the evolution of POP has been influenced by the institutional support it has received from the U.S. government, the creation of analytical frameworks for its operationalization, and scholarly developments in environmental criminology. Problem solving is a key element of community policing, and so when the COPS Office was formed in 1994, it adopted POP as a key strategy and funded the Center for Problem-Oriented Policing (www.popcenter.org). Moreover, through the Problem-Solving Partnerships Program, it funded 470 police agencies to apply a POP approach to a significant community crime or disorder problem (Scott 2000, 39). Police professional associations, such as the Police Executive Research Forum (PERF), annual POP conferences, and national awards for problem solving excellence have further contributed to POP's visibility and adoption both in the United States, other Western countries, and even in more authoritarian and militarized regimes such as in the former Soviet bloc where the police have historically operated autonomously from the public (Boba and Crank 2008; Weisburd et al. 2010, 141).

The challenges of translating research into practice are well documented (Lum 2009), and so the creation of basic models for aiding POP's implementation has helped market it nationally and internationally. The SARA assessment model, which has become widespread in police circles, identifies four steps that police should take when engaging in POP (scanning, analysis, research, and assessment), and the problem analysis crime triangle links incidents based on three key elements, each represented by a side of the triangle—common offenders, victims, or locations—and tailoring responses accordingly (Eck and Spelman 1987). Both models reveal POP's relationship to environmental criminology, a school of thought that provides the theoretical underpinnings to POP. Environmental criminologists seek to understand criminal events in the specific settings where they occur in in order to prevent them. Guidance on reducing crime from a POP perspective is provided by routine activities and rational choice theories which focus on reducing criminal opportunities by changing features of the immediate environment and by increasing offenders' perceptions of risk.

According to one commentator, along with community policing, problem-oriented policing has "probably done more to shape the debate over the role of the American police than anything since the introduction of the patrol car and two-way radio" (Reisig 2010, 42–43). In addition to the factors already mentioned, its rise has been facilitated by the efforts of its supporters to engage practitioners and the influence of a new environmental perspective that "has emerged to become arguably the fastest growing approach in criminology and criminal justice" (Wortley and Mazzerole 2008, 14).

1.1.4 Hot Spots Policing

While police have long known that crime was spread unevenly across jurisdictions, hot spots policing can be traced back to theoretical, empirical, and technological innovations that emerged in the 1980s and 1990s (Committee to Review Research on Police Policy and Practice 2004, 237). Its theoretical basis lies in some of the developments in problem-oriented policing and environmental criminology discussed above. These brought attention to place or location as a key factor in understanding and preventing crime and disorder. Empirically, hot spots policing was influenced by the Kansas City Patrol Experiment conducted from 1972 to 1973 that suggested that changing levels of patrol in a jurisdiction seemed to have little effect on crime (Weisburd and Braga 2006b, 230). In a subsequent study conducted in 1989 (the Minneapolis Hot Spots Patrol Experiment), Sherman and Weisburd (1995) sought to challenge the assumption that police patrol delivered few crime prevention benefits by determining whether patrol would be more effective if it were focused on small discrete places where crime and disorder were concentrated. Using an experimental design, their findings indicated that hot spots that received two to three times the level of preventive patrol compared to the control sites experienced a significant reduction in crime calls to the police and lower levels of disorder. Subsequent research has continued to support the crime control benefits of hot spots policing and challenge the commonplace wisdom that crime merely moves to nearby areas (Braga 2008). This led the National Research Council to conclude that hot spots policing is probably the most promising crime control strategy to have emerged since 1968.

Given the strength of this evidence, it is unsurprising that hot spots policing has become popular on the policing landscape over the last thirty years. There are at least two additional reasons for why police have been quick to adopt a hot-spots approach. First, it demands little change to existing police practices and organizational structures. Research suggests that police can produce significant crime control benefits while still using traditional police interventions, such as directed patrols and proactive arrests, as long as these strategies are focused on high-risk times and places (Weisburd and Braga 2006b). Crime prevention approaches that are tailored to the underlying causes of specific problems and involve collaborations with other city and community organizations might be more effective, but they are also more challenging to implement, often requiring the kinds of institutional support (e.g., officer skills and organizational resources) that police departments lack particularly during a time of declining budgets.

Technological advances since the 1980s in computing and crime mapping have also facilitated the adoption of hot-spots policing. Information from official police reports and calls for service can easily be culled from police databases, mapped, and made quickly available to patrol officers and their superiors. Large police departments began to use crime mapping in the 1990s and according to a survey conducted by the Police Foundation at the end of that decade, 7 in 10 U.S. police departments reported using crime mapping to identify crime hot spots (Braga 2008).

Perhaps one of the most notable features regarding the historical progress of hot spots policing during this period is the central role played by criminological theory and research evidence (Weisburd and Braga 2006b). Unlike other reforms, such as community policing, that diffused rapidly before rigorous evaluation, hot spots policing can be used as an example of the power of science to influence police practice and an illustration of the advances that have been made in police-researcher partnerships over the last two decades (Weisburd and Neyroud 2011).

1.2 POLICE ACCOUNTABILITY AND LEGITIMACY

These innovations in police strategies demonstrate the continuing importance of the police mandate to control crime and to bring offenders to justice. Crime in the United States and in many European nations has declined dramatically since 1990 (Baumer 2011), and unlike the policing environment in the 1970s, there is now general consensus among police scholars and practitioners that current crime control efforts are more effective than those that preceded them (Weisburd and Braga 2006a). There are probably few, if any, that would agree fully with James Q. Wilson's (1978, 63) statement made about a generic police administrator over 40 years ago: "If he knew how to prevent crime, of course he would, but he is in the unhappy position of being responsible for an organization that lacks a proven technology for achieving its purpose."

These increasing expectations about police capacity to reduce crime have been accompanied by interest in establishing more exacting standards for judging institutional performance. In addition to subjecting police crime control efforts to closer scrutiny, the periods of significant social unrest experienced in the United States (during the 1960s and 1970s) and United Kingdom (in the 1980s) also illuminated the power of public judgments about *how* the police go about their work, particularly when it comes to incidents of serious police misconduct or brutality. Citizens expect that individual officers will be held accountable for using their coercive authority in ways that are consistent with laws, administrative standards, and ideas about justice. A relatively new line of research shows that citizens make judgments of police officers and the organizations they work for based on their perceptions of fairness and impartiality and that there is a profound gap between minorities and whites in their trust and confidence in the police (Ivkovich 2011). This section addresses attempts to enhance accountability structures and recent empirical and theoretical advances in a major area of police research, namely police legitimacy.

1.2.1 Institutional Accountability for Police Performance

In the United States the emergence of Compstat demonstrates the growing visibility of a government wide movement toward embracing "accountability as a tool for good governance in both the public and private sectors" (Stone 2007, 247). According to its doctrine, Compstat is a strategic management system that embraces both internal and external accountability. Timely crime data are used to hold middle managers directly responsible for reducing crime and to provide stakeholders with accurate and timely information about how well the police agency is accomplishing its official crime control mission. Compstat originated in the New York City Police Department in 1994 under then-Commissioner William Bratton who articulated specific crime reduction goals— such as reducing crime by 10 percent in a year—for which the organization and its leaders could then be held accountable (Bratton 1998). Taking accountability for crime outcomes a step further, a leading police scholar in the United States has called for police agencies to measure their performance in relation to predictions about crime rates that take into account economic and socio-demographic factors and risks of recidivism. Big-city departments could then be ranked against one another in a league table according to their actual results (Sherman 1998, 10–11).

Since its inception Compstat has diffused rapidly across the United States, although agencies have tended to favor more modest and flexible crime control goals than those called for by the NYPD model (Willis, Kochel, and Mastrofski 2010). In a national survey of large (>100 sworn) police departments in the United States administered by the Police Foundation in 2000, a third of agencies reported they had implemented a Compstat-like program with a quarter claiming they were intending to do so. Only six years later this figure had doubled, with 60 percent of large police departments in the United States reporting on a national survey conducted in 2006 that they had implemented Compstat or a Compstat-like program (Willis, Kochel, and Mastrofski 2010). Moreover, Compstat's appeal has not been limited to North America: politicians, delegates and police leaders from a host of democratic nations have flocked to New York City (Gootman 2000). Many countries, including England and Australia, have since adapted methods for assessing police performance from the NYPD model.

Unlike the United States, where the structure of policing is highly decentralized, the adoption of performance measurement to enhance accountability in other countries has occurred at the national level. For example, the last two decades in England and Wales have witnessed the arrival of the Audit Commission and managerial techniques adopted from the private sector to enhance accountability for the quality of police service. These changes have resulted in the establishment of performance criteria mandated by the national government to measure budget and crime control priorities. Over time the Audit Commission's focus on Britain's police forces meeting strict targets and making these public has become "an embedded part of police performance and culture" (Neyroud 2008, 343). Recently the British government's push toward making police agencies increasingly responsible for the services they deliver to the public has led to the proposal of a new governance model where directly-elected police commissioners replace police authorities (Herbert et al. 2007; Johnson 2012). The powers of these 41 Police and Crime Commissioners (PCC) include appointing and firing chief constables, holding them accountable for their performance, and setting the police budget. Although it is designed to devolve greater control of the police to local communities, a key element of this approach is the continuance of national level standards for measuring police performance.

1.2.2   Oversight of Individual Officer Behavior

Another recent trend in accountability has taken the form of attempts to revamp administrative structures to help prevent misconduct and increase public confidence in the process of policing, particularly when it comes to use of force against citizens (Stone

2007). It is well established that police officers exercise a great deal of leeway in making decisions, a feature of their daily work which affords ample opportunity for potential abuses of authority. These abuses might take the form of any number of improper behaviors which can provoke a powerful public reaction, including bribery, brutality, and the misuse of deadly force. National and international outrage in response to the 1991 beating of a Rodney King, an unarmed black motorist, by officers in the Los Angeles Police Department recalled memories from the Civil Rights era and revitalized interest in developing internal strategies for strengthening oversight of officers' behavior, and for disciplining officers who behaved improperly while on duty.

1.2.2.1 *Early Intervention Systems*

As data-based management tools for identifying and correcting officer misconduct, Early Intervention Systems (EIS) share Compstat's focus on collecting and using data to address problems and holding managers accountable for doing so (Walker 2003). In 1981, the U.S. Commission on Civil Rights recommended that all police departments put mechanisms in place to help identify officers who appeared to have performance problems, and in 1994 the Violent Crime Control and Law Enforcement Act empowered the Civil Rights Division of the Department of Justice to investigate and bring civil suits against police agencies where there was a pattern or practice of abuse of citizens' "rights, privileges, or immunities secured or protected by the Constitution" (Committee to Review Research on Police Policy and Practice 2004, 280–81). As part of any ensuing settlement, it is common for a consent decree or memorandum of understanding to include the implementation of an early intervention system (Walker and Alpert 2004). The Department of Justice identifies early intervention systems as among its "best practices" for enhancing accountability, and in the United States, the Commission on Accreditation for Law Enforcement Agencies requires an early intervention system in all large agencies (Walker 2003). In 1999, 39 percent of all local law enforcement agencies serving jurisdictions with more than 50,000 people either had an EIS or were planning to implement one (Walker, Alpert, and Kenney 2001).

Although there is significant variation across departments, early intervention systems share three basic principles: selection, intervention, and post-intervention monitoring (Walker, Alpert, and Kenney 2001). The identification of problem officers is based on a number of indicators, which can include citizen complaints, use-of-force reports, official reprimands, and firearm discharges collected over a specified period. The Miami Police Department in Florida which has one of the oldest continuously operating EISs uses these four categories of behavior over a period of two to five years (depending on the category) to identify problem officers to supervisors and managers (Walker and Alpert 2004, 25). Because these systems are designed to identify officers before their actions warrant official disciplinary action, interventions are generally non-punitive and educative and include peer-review counseling and training. Finally, many EISs include a post-intervention strategy for monitoring officers' performance that can be conducted informally by their supervisors or through a more formal observation and evaluation process. The overall purpose of an EIS is to promote a culture of accountability within a police department. The little research currently available suggests that they can be effective in reducing complaints and other indicators of problem performance against officers, but more rigorous tests are still needed (Walker, Alpert, and Kenney 2001).

1.2.2.2 *Citizen Oversight*

Recent police history has also seen the growth of citizen oversight as a new accountability mechanism with the potential to change the policing landscape (Walker 2001). In the United States, the notion of special agencies staffed by nonpolice and responsible for investigating and disposing of complaints against sworn officers originated in the Civil Rights Movement, but it has gained momentum nationally and internationally over the last twenty-five years (De Angelis and Kupchik 2007). In 1975, for example, there were only seven citizen oversight agencies in operation in the United States, but now there are over a hundred in law enforcement agencies that cover as much as one-third of the U.S. population (Walker 2001, 6). Other English-speaking democracies have shown similar interest in creating external bodies to oversee police, including Britain which in 2004 established a new model for dealing with serious complaints of police misconduct, the Independent Police Complaints Commission (IPCC) (Seneviratne 2004).

In the United States, the police historian Samuel Walker (2001, 34) traces the increasing support for civilian oversight to a number of historical trends including an increase in the political power of African Americans in cities and towns through the election of mayors and city council members and the movement toward community policing with its emphasis on police-community partnerships. Both in the United States and abroad, calls for strengthening citizen oversight are often precipitated by events of police misconduct that challenge police credibility.

Proponents claim that compared to a complaints system administered solely by the police, citizen oversight improves the overall quality of the process by making it more objective, thorough, and transparent; provides greater satisfaction for individual complainants; and increases public confidence in the police (De Angelis and Kupchik 2007). Most citizen oversight models might share these goals, but their structural and power arrangements vary widely with as many as six different models being identified in the literature (Prenzler and Ronken 2001, 156). David Bayley provides a useful typology for making comparisons between different forms of civilian oversight by distinguishing between the degree to which nonpolice play a role in investigating complaints and in deciding on an appropriate punishment (Bayley 1995). In the United States and in the United Kingdom, departments generally rely on a civilian review model where police are responsible for both stages of the complaints process and civilians are primarily limited to a monitoring role. This can be considered a compromise that tries to balance police interest in the autonomy and self-governance of their organizations with calls from outsiders for a fully independent complaints process. In comparison, a citizen control model operates with much greater independence from the police (Prenzler and Ronken 2001). Northern Ireland, for example, adopted a police ombudsman model for addressing civilian complaints in 1998 (the Police Ombudsmen for Northern Ireland, or PONI). Characterized by some as one of the most progressive models for police

oversight in the world, it has its own staff for conducting investigations, can make recommendations on disciplinary matters, and can be easily accessed by any member of
the public at any time (Seneviratne 2004).

1.2.3 Police Legitimacy

These attempts to reshape the structures and processes of accountability and control
between the police and the community illuminate the importance of the degree to which
the public perceives the police as legitimate. Despite the advances in police-community
relations that have been made since the 1960s, tensions between the police and racial
and ethnic minorities continue to make front-page headlines. Over the last twenty
years, perhaps no single issue in the United States has brought the police under more
intense scrutiny than racial profiling. Widespread alarm about police officers using race
or ethnicity as a factor when deciding to stop, search, or arrest people reemerged in the
1990s. In 1999, for example, 59 percent of the American public perceived racial profiling by the police as "widespread," and in 2000, 75 percent viewed it as a problem in the
United States (reported in Gallagher et al. 2001). Blacks are much more likely to perceive
racial profiling as a common practice, and this contributes to their lowered perceptions
of police legitimacy compared to whites (Tyler and Wakslak 2004). Blacks are also consistently less likely than whites to report that they are treated well in their interactions
with police officers and more likely than whites to express general dissatisfaction with
the police (Weitzer and Tuch 2006).

The Committee to Review Research on Police Policy and Practice's (2004, 291) definition of legitimacy as "the judgments that ordinary citizens make about the rightful-
ness of police conduct and the organizations that employ and supervise them" suggests
at least two different police approaches for building legitimacy and support among the
public. Adopting this definition here helps illustrate several noteworthy developments
in the recent history of police.

At the broad organizational level, police agencies can demonstrate that they are
responsive to their constituents by implementing programs, policies, and procedures
designed to meet their expectations or needs. Doing so promises significant financial,
political, and community support in the form of tax revenues, crime control legislation
(e.g., gun, curfew, or trespass laws), or community members' participation in crime
prevention programs (Mastrofski 2000). At the level of individual encounters with the
public, officers can enhance citizens' perceptions of legitimacy by treating them in ways
perceived as fair and respectful. Research suggests that people who regard the law and
legal authorities as legitimate are more likely to obey the law, defer to an officer's directives, support the crime fighting efforts of the police by identifying criminals and reporting crimes, and even to appear as witnesses at criminal court trials (Reisig, Bratton,
and Gertz 2007; Tyler 2004, 2009; Robinson, Goodwin, and Reisig 2010). Since the
1990s a large body of research, much of it conducted by Tom Tyler and his colleagues,
has emerged on the process-based elements that lead people to obey the law or legal

authorities voluntarily (see Tyler 2003 for a review), while less is known about how and how much any changes to organizational structures contribute to public perceptions of police legitimacy.

Given the popular notion that the primary responsibility of the police is to fight crime, police organizations can build legitimacy by adopting programs that either professional norms or scientific research suggest are most effective and efficient in promoting the goal of public safety (Committee to Review Research on Police Policy and Practice 2004, 308–09). Compstat is a good example of the former as it has become widely accepted among police administrators, policy makers, and police professional associations (e.g, PERF) as a cutting-edge crime control program despite little rigorous research on its effectiveness (Willis, Mastrofski, and Weisburd 2007). Although it is still in its early stages, predictive policing, which has suddenly emerged in the United States, might be taking a similar path toward professional validation. Regarded by its supporters as an extension of Compstat's focus on using analyses of timely crime data to drive police strategies, predictive policing combines crime and non-crime data (e.g., economic data on housing foreclosures) with forecasting, modeling, and sophisticated statistics to help make predictions about where crime is likely to occur in the future so that it can be prevented. To date, anecdotal evidence of its crime control effectiveness has been positive although its legitimacy-conferring potential might be hampered by concerns that it will be used to profile specific groups and treat them unfairly (Ferguson 2011).

At the same time, there is reason to believe that the police are paying increasing attention to what works in reducing crime when making decisions (Bayley 2008). An important development in this regard, and one that has gained momentum since the late 1990s, is the "evidence-based policing" movement whose origins lie in the 1997 University of Maryland report evaluating the effectiveness of various crime control approaches (Sherman et al. 1997). Drawing repeatedly on the analogy of medical research (Thacher 2001), evidence-based policing has become largely synonymous, although not exclusively, with a scientific approach that promotes the use of randomized controlled trials to measure the effects of different crime control "treatments" on reducing crime and disorder (Sherman 1998; Welsh 2006). Today a growing number of researchers as well as the federal government embrace the assessment of different crime strategies through controlled experiments and systematic research reviews. Not only has this approach led to calls for a new model of police-practitioner partnerships, one where the police take ownership of science and researchers participate more actively in the daily operations of police (Weisburd and Neyroud 2011), but the degree to which evidence-based policing is becoming recognized as a "best practice" suggests a relatively new and potentially powerful source of police legitimacy for those agencies with the will and skill to adopt its tenets.

Although assessments of police effectiveness in fighting crime affect people's perceptions of police legitimacy, research suggests that a more important factor in many, but not all situations, is judgments about whether the police treat them in fair and considerate ways (McCluskey 2003; Sunshine and Tyler 2003). That is, public evaluations of the legitimacy of the police are powerfully influenced by procedural justice judgments that occur both at a general institutional level and at the level of personal interactions with the police as victims, offenders, witnesses, bystanders, or persons reporting crimes (Tyler and Huo 2002).

Tyler identifies four key elements of procedural justice: (1) participation (people are more satisfied with procedures that allow them to give input before a decision is made about how to handle a problem); (2) neutrality (people desire evenhandedness and objectivity or police officers putting aside their personal views when making decisions); (3) dignity and respect (people care about being treated with politeness and having their rights acknowledged); and (4) motives (people are more likely to see procedures as fair when they trust the motives of the police officer) (Tyler 2004). The fact that procedural justice judgments are equally important to blacks, whites, and Hispanics has important policy implications (Tyler 2000). It suggests that a procedural-justice based approach to policing, one that officers could be trained in, could help improve police-minority relations in the United States. At the same time, it is unclear whether these dynamics of procedural justice would have similar effects on police legitimacy in other nations, particularly in those places where people feel considerably alienated from police authorities. In Ghana, for example, a study showed that public cooperation with the police was influenced by perceptions of police effectiveness in fighting crime rather than considerations of procedural fairness (Tankebe 2009).

Finally, procedural justice is closely tied to another innovation that has reemerged over the last thirty years and that has implications for the police (Braithwaite 1999; Shapland 2003). Restorative justice presents a different moral vision than the current criminal justice system's emphasis on deterrence and retribution—one that is based on reconciliation and persuasion (Sherman 2003). It is multifaceted, but a key feature of some programs is the use of specially trained police officers to manage victim-offender conferences. The purpose of these conferences is to help repair the harm caused by a particular offense and to prevent the commission of future crimes by victims, offenders, and others who have been harmed. Restorative justice has emerged across the world as a powerful movement for reform (Braithwaite 1999), although its influence in the United States remains fairly limited compared to other nations, such as Northern Ireland and New Zealand, where it has been implemented on a larger scale (McGarrell et al. 2000; Shapland 2003).

1.3 POLICING TERRORISM

As police organizations have striven to improve crime strategies and police-public relations, they have also been forced to confront a new set of challenges that have implications for both. In the aftermath of the terrorist attacks of September 11, 2001 on the World Trade Center and the Pentagon, much attention has focused on America's political and organizational response in waging wars against Iraq and Afghanistan and in retooling different federal agencies to more effectively attack, prevent, and respond to terrorist threats. Regarding responses to the new threat, one of the most important changes of the last decade has been the creation of the Department of Homeland Security in October 2001 under which many federal agencies have been regrouped (including the Transportation Security Administration and U.S. Immigration and Customs Enforcement) (Maguire and King 2011, 328–29).

At the same time, the 9/11 attacks have resulted in concerted efforts to mobilize local and state police as a vital resource on the war on terror. As many have observed, given the economy of scale of local compared to federal law enforcement, local police agencies are a vital resource for preventing, planning for, and responding to terrorist attacks. In 2007, there were an estimated 693,346 full-time sworn officers working in state and local law enforcement agencies (Bureau of Justice Statistics 2010). Compare this to the roughly 13,000 special agents working for the Federal Bureau of Investigation, the federal agency whose primary responsibility is "to prevent acts of terrorism before they happen" (Federal Bureau of Investigation 2012). As part of this movement, structures such as the Joint Terrorism Task Forces (JTTFS) have been rapidly expanded to try and coordinate intelligence-sharing and investigations among federal, state, and local law enforcement representatives (Kelling and Bratton 2006; Lum et al. 2009). There have also been significant developments in research in this area, including the establishment of the National Consortium for the Study of Terrorism and Responses to Terrorism (START) at the University of Maryland for the scientific study of the causes and consequences of terrorism.

What precise role local police agencies should play in combating the threat of terrorism, as well as its implications for crime prevention and police-community relations, is unclear. Part of this ambiguity can be explained by the sheer number and diversity of activities that fall under the guise of counterterrorism. Some of these are closely aligned to the traditional role of the police, such as identifying suspicious persons and activities. Vehicle stops or foot patrols, for example, are opportunities to identify suspects that are on federal watch-lists or to spot activities that might be related to plans for a terrorist attack (Mastrofski and Willis 2010). Of course, the effectiveness of these tactics depends a great deal on the quality of the information that the police are able to gather and how easily it can be shared with other agencies, especially at the federal level, to return accurate and actionable "hits." Prevention also includes local police routinely mobilizing the community to provide information and developing a capacity to perform risk analyses of potential targets and finding ways to make these less vulnerable to attack. In a post-9/11 world, local police, along with other emergency services, are also expected to play a key role in response and recovery operations and to develop investigative expertise on terrorism through their participation in regional networks and JTTFs (Maguire and King 2011, 341–42). The extent to which police engage in surveillance and covert operations (e.g., using undercover agents or informants) to collect intelligence represents the most radical change to a traditional law enforcement model based on visibility and transparency and thus the change most likely to provoke resistance (Bayley and Weisburd 2009, 82; Mastrofski and Willis 2010, 121).

In some large agencies, such as the New York Police Department, there is evidence of significant transformations to existing police organizational structures and practices in response to the threat of terrorism. The NYPD, for example, has established a large and sophisticated counterintelligence division with detectives who can speak Pashto and Arabic stationed throughout the world, and Chicago has recently announced plans to follow suit, albeit on a smaller scale (Dickey 2009; Lepeska 2011). However, these changes are not representative of most local police agencies in the United States. The little research that has been done suggests that local police have preferred to emphasize interagency coordination, training, and general preparedness rather than adopting new terrorist-oriented "on-the-ground" tactics (Lum et al. 2009). In a 2007 survey administered to police agencies in the United States that asked about 63 counterterrorism activities, 80 percent of large police departments reported cooperating regularly with other state or local law agencies and having received training on biological or chemical hazards, with 70 percent having engaged in terrorism-focused emergency drills. In comparison, 22 percent reported checking the residency/immigration status of arrestees and 15 percent had a database for terrorism information (Lum et al. 2009, 112–19). The kinds of covert and proactive surveillance and investigative activities associated with "high policing" were also among the least implemented (Bayley and Wiesburd 2009): only 17 percent of large departments reported using video cameras in public places and 6.5 percent conducted random searches in these places. Only 11 percent had increased the number of personnel assigned to counterterrorism duties (Lum et al. 2009, 112–19). These findings are consistent with other surveys, leading some to conclude that "little has changed in the policing of Mayberry post-9/11" (Schafer, Burress, and Giblin 2009, 283). While the events of 9/11 have undoubtedly impacted local law enforcement (Bayley and Weisburd 2009, 86), most departments remain committed to their traditional responsibilities of controlling crime and disorder and providing services to their local communities while pushing terrorist-oriented activities to the periphery of daily operations (Mastrofski and Willis 2010, 123).

One key reason for the reluctance of police leaders to make counterterrorism activities central to their operations, especially when it comes to engaging in the most intrusive and disruptive activities, is their potential for undermining police-community relations. Hard-fought improvements in trust and transparency have been won over the last few decades, and so it is unsurprising that many police leaders are reluctant to jeopardize the collaborations and problem-solving efforts that they have developed with local residents and business owners (Thacher 2005). This threat to police legitimacy is especially pronounced among those Arab or Muslim American communities that are most likely to be the focus of counterterrorism attention from the police. In a recent survey conducted by the Pew Research Center (2011, 48), 52 percent of Muslim Americans believe the U.S. government's anti-terrorism policies single them out for increased surveillance and monitoring with 38 percent saying this bothers them "a lot or some." While there is a general lack of research on the impact of anti-terror efforts by local law enforcement agencies on Muslim Americans, some evidence indicates that members of these communities are most likely to cooperate with the police to combat terrorism and to report specific terror-related activities when they perceive them to be legitimate. Key to these perceptions are the extent to which local police authorities seek and consider the views of these segments of the community when making policies to combat terrorism and whether these are policies are implemented fairly (Tyler, Schullhofer, and Huq 2010, 368, 377).

Thus, despite the social, political and historical significance of the events of 9/11, it appears that local police have not been quick to adopt a new style of "homeland security" policing (Oliver 2006). In contrast to terrorism, everyday crime remains the core concern of the police, and local agencies continue to devote the lion's share of their resources to their traditional functions of uniformed patrol and answering calls for service and to engaging with local communities to prevent it.

1.4 CONCLUSION

Change, like beauty, tends to lie in the eye of the beholder. To some this recent history of police can be interpreted as a period of significant reform. Indeed, if one were to imagine what police work looked like to a patrol officer in 1982 compared to an officer working in 2012, there are some notable differences. For instance, today's officer may not have full knowledge of the scholarship that has advanced understanding about crime control during this period, but she would surely feel the effects. Perhaps she has been temporarily assigned to a problem-solving project or to patrolling a street block during certain times to address a recent spate of burglaries that have been electronically mapped and delivered via her patrol car's laptop computer. Moreover, she might be required to use her unassigned time to tackle physical and social disorder in her beat in order to improve its quality-of-life and also to enhance police-community relations. Her patrol sergeant might also ask that she attend a community meeting to discuss recent crime strategies, listen and respond to problems raised in this context, and make suggestions for how residents might assist the police in their crime prevention efforts. If she were employed by a large police department, it is likely that she will know about what transpired at the agency's recent Compstat meeting, including whether or not the chief was satisfied by a recent decline in assaults over the previous reporting period. At the same meeting, the top brass may also have discussed changes in the number of citizen complaints against the department or the status of problem officers identified as part of a revamped early-warning system. Throughout all of this, technological advances in computing and communications would be especially visible.

However, much would also have remained the same, and were our two fictional officers to have a conversation, they would probably find they have much more in common than not despite the years between them. It is probably fair to say that the adoption of more strategic approaches for patrolling does more to illustrate the willingness of U.S. police agencies to try new crime control methods over the last 30 years than to fundamentally change what they do and how they do it (Mastrofski and Willis 2011, 83).

Much of the research suggests that while police have been generally receptive to these innovations, they have adapted them in ways that are minimally disruptive to the core police technology of routine and reactive patrol that has distinguished the police for the last seventy years, never mind the last thirty (Cordner and Biebel 2005; Mastrofski 2006; Willis, Mastrofski, and Weisburd 2007; Braga and Bond 2008).

Similar to the patrol officer in 1982, the main responsibility of our 2012 officer would be to engage in preventive/reactive patrol while making herself available to all manner of citizen requests through the department's 911 system. The patrol methods informed by recent scholarship on reducing crime and disorder and supported with federal monies might consume part of her day, but they would no doubt remain peripheral to her traditional patrol function. More importantly, perhaps, research would continue to offer her little in the way of guidance in terms of helping her figure out what constitutes good police performance in her encounters with the public. The emergence of legitimacy-based policing has drawn attention to the importance of the process-based actions of police officers to citizen assessments of police fairness and concern, but the majority of this research has not focused on what this actually means for those patrol officers working the street and who are charged with turning policy into practice. Indeed, this is a criticism that can be leveled more generally at police scholarship from this period under review; it has done a far better job of addressing the concerns of policy makers and police managers than the interests and perspectives of front-line workers (Thacher 2008). Thus the evidence-based research movement has made an important contribution to our understanding of effective policing, but it has generally focused on assessing what does and does not work in reducing crime and disorder than on whether or how often police "do the right thing" or make the best choice in using their discretion. As of yet, we do not have any standards for assessing the quality (rather than quantity) of patrol officer performance (Mastrofski 1996, 2004). In light of this lacuna, future research should consider ways that social science can advance knowledge about the craft of patrol work and engage with its essential normative dimensions since improvements in policing ultimately rest on the shoulders of those who do the work at the "coal face" and the judgments they make about what qualifies as good or bad policing (Bayley 2008, 13; Willis 2012).

NOTES

* The author is very grateful to Stephen Mastrofski for his advice and encouragement during the writing of this essay.
1. In the United States, the commissions and their reports were the President's Commission on Law Enforcement and Administration of Justice (1967) and the National Advisory Commission on Social Disorders (1968). In the United Kingdom, the Home Secretary appointed Lord Scarman (1981) to lead a local inquiry into the Brixton riots.
2. Although distinct in important ways, order maintenance, or Broken Windows policing, is conmonly associated with community policing (see Mastrofski 1988; Weisburd and Braga 2006a; Reisig 2010).

References

Barnes, Ian, and Tania Eagle. 2007. "The Role of Community Engagement in Neighborhood Policing." *Policing: A Journal of Policy and Practice* 1(2): 161–72.

Baumer, Eric P. 2011. "Crime Trends." In *The Oxford Handbook of Crime and Criminal Justice*, edited by Michael Tonry, 26–59. Oxford: Oxford University Press.

Bayley, David H. 1995. "Police Brutality Abroad." In *Police Violence: Understanding and Controlling Police Abuse of Force*, edited by William A. Geller and Hans Toch, 273–291. JNew Haven, CT: Yale University Press.

——. 2008. "Police Reform: Who Done It?" *Policing and Society* 18(1): 7–17.

Bayley, David H., and Christine Nixon. 2010. *The Changing Environment for Policing, 1985–2008*. New Perspectives on Policing, Program in Criminal Justice Policy and Management, John F. Kennedy School of Government, Harvard University. Washington, DC: U.S. Department of Justice.

Bayley, David H., and David Weisburd. 2009. "Cops and Spooks: The Role of the Police in Counterterrorism." In *To Protect and Serve: Policing in An Age of Terrorism*, edited by David Weisburd, Thomas E. Feucht, Idit Hakimi, Lois Felson Mock, and Simon Perry, 81–99. New York: Springer.

Boba, Rachel, and John P. Crank. 2008. "Institutionalizing Problem-Oriented Policing: Rethinking Problem Solving, Analysis, and Accountability." *Police Practice and Research* 9:379–93.

Bottoms, Anthony E. 2007. "Place, Space, Crime, and Disorder." In *The Oxford Handbook of Criminology*, edited by Mike Maguire, Rod Morgan, and Robert Reiner, 528–574. Oxford: Oxford University Press.

Braga, Anthony A. 2008. *Crime Prevention Research Review No. 2: Police Enforcement Strategies to Prevent Crime in Hot Spot Areas*. Washington, DC: U.S. Department of Justice, Office of Community-Oriented Policing Services.

Braga, Anthony A., Brenda J. Bond. 2008. "Policing Crime and Disorder Hot Spots: A Randomized Controlled Trial." *Criminology* 47(3): 577–607.

Brain, Timothy. 2011. *A History of Policing in England and Wales from 1974: A Turbulent Journey*. Oxford: Oxford University Press.

Braithwaite, John. 1999. "Restorative Justice: Assessing Optimistic and Pessimistic Accounts." In *Crime and Justice: A Review of Research*, vol. 25, edited by Michael Tonry, 1–127. Chicago: University of Chicago Press.

Bratton, William J. (with Peter Knobler). 1998. *Turnaround: How America's Top Cop Reversed the Crime Epidemic*. New York: Random House.

Brogden, Mike. 2005. "'Horses for Courses' and 'Thin Blue Lines': Community Policing in Transitional Society." *Police Quarterly* 8(1): 64–98.

Brogden, Mike, and Preeti Nijhar. 2005. *Community Policing: National and International Models and Approaches*. Cullompton, Devon: Willan.

Bureau of Justice Statistics. 2010. *Local Police Departments, 2007*. Washington, DC: U.S. Department of Justice.

Committee to Review Research on Police Policy and Practices. 2004. *Fairness and Effectiveness in Policing: The Evidence*. Washington, DC: The National Academies Press.

Cordner, Gary, and Elizabeth Perkins Biebel. 2005. "Problem-Oriented Policing in Practice." *Criminology and Public Policy* 4(2): 155–80.

De Angelis, Joseph, and Aaron Kupchik. 2007. "Citizen Oversight, Procedural Justice, and Officer Perceptions of the Complaint Investigation Process." *Policing: An International Journal of Police Strategies and Management* 30(4): 651–71.

Dickey, Christopher. 2009. *Securing the City: Inside America's Best Counterterror Force—The NYPD*. New York: Simon and Schuster.

Eck, John E., and Edward R. Maguire. 2000. "Have Changes in Policing Reduced Violent Crime? An Assessment of the Evidence." In *The Crime Drop in America*, edited by Alfred Blumstein and Joel Wallman, 207–265. Cambridge: Cambridge University Press.

Eck, John E., and William Spelman. 1987. "Who Ya Gonna Call? The Police as Problem-Busters." *Crime and Delinquency* 33(1): 31–52.

Federal Bureau of Investigation. 2012. *Investigative Programs and Working for the FBI*. http://www.fbi.gov/stats-services/publications/facts-and-figures-2010-2011/investigative-programs#counterterrorism and http://www.fbi.gov/stats-services/publications/facts-and-figures-2010-2011/working-for-the-fbi.

Ferguson, Andrew Guthrie. 2011. "Predictive Policing and the Fourth Amendment." *American Criminal Law Review* (January 3). http://www.americancriminallawreview.com/Drupal/blogs/blog-entry/%E2%80%9Cpredictive-policing%E2%80%9D-and-fourth-amendment-11-28-2011.

Fogelson, Robert M. 1968. "From Resentment to Confrontation: The Police, the Negroes, and the Outbreak of the Nineteen-Sixties Riots." *Political Science Quarterly* 83(2): 217–47.

——. 1977. *Big-City Police*. Cambridge, MA: Harvard University Press.

Gallagher, Catherine, Edward R. Maguire, Stephen D. Mastrofski, and Michael D. Reisig. 2001. *The Public Image of the Police*. Final Report to The International Association of Chiefs of Police. Washington DC: IACP. http://www.theiacp.org/PoliceServices/ProfessionalAssistance/ThePublicImageofthePolice/tabid/198/Default.aspx.

Garland, David. 2001. *The Culture of Control: Crime and Social Order in Contemporary Society*. Chicago: University of Chicago Press.

Gill, Charlotte, David Weisburd, Trevor Bennett, Cody Telep, and Zoe Vitter. 2011. "Community-Oriented Policing: Effects of Crime and Disorder, Legitimacy, and Citizen Satisfaction." Paper presented at the annual meeting of the *American Society of Criminology*, Washington, DC, November.

Goldstein, Herman. 1979. "Improving Policing: A Problem-Oriented Approach." *Crime and Delinquency* 25:236–58.

Goldstein, Herman. 1990. *Problem-Oriented Policing*. New York: McGraw-Hill.

Gootman, Elissa. 2000. "A Police Department's Growing Allure; Crime Fighters From Around the World Visit for Tips." *New York Times* (October 24). http://www.nytimes.com/2000/10/24/nyregion/a-police-dept-s-growing-allure-crime-fighters-from-around-world-visit-for-tips.html?pagewanted=all&src=pm.

Greene, Jack R. 2004. "Community Policing and Organization Change." In *Community Policing (Can it Work?)*, edited by Wesley G. Skogan, 30–53. Belmont, CA: Wadsworth/Thomson Learning.

Greenwood, Peter W., Joan Petersilia, and Jan Chaiken. 1977. *The Criminal Investigation Process*. Lexington, MA: D.C. Heath.

Helms, Ronald, and Ricky S. Gutierrez. 2007. "Federal Subsidies and Evidence of Progressive Change: A Quantitative Assessment of the Effects of Targeted Grants on Manpower and Innovation in Large U.S. Police Agencies." *Police Quarterly* 10(1): 87–107.

Herbert, Nick, Oscar Keeble, Adain Burley, and Blair Gibbs. 2007. *Policing for the People: Interim Report of the Police Taskforce*. Brentford: TPF Group.

Innes, Martin. 2004. "Signal Crimes and Signal Disorders: Notes on Deviance as Communicative Action." *British Journal of Sociology* 55(3): 335–55.

———. 2007. "The Reassurance Function." *Policing: A Journal of Policy and Practice* 1(2): 132–41.

Ismaili, Karim. 2003. "Explaining the Cultural and Symbolic Resonance of Zero Tolerance in Contemporary Criminal Justice." *Contemporary Justice Review* 6(3): 255–64.

Ivković, Sanja Kutnjak. 2011. "Legitimacy and Lawful Policing." In *The Oxford Handbook of Crime and Criminal Justice*, edited by Michael Tonry, 577–624. Oxford: Oxford University Press.

James, Nathan. 2010. *Community Oriented Policing Services (COPS): Current Legislative Issues*. Washington, DC: Congressional Research Service. http://www.fas.org/sgp/crs/misc/R40709.pdf.

Johnson, Jayme. 2012. "Police and Crime Commissioners: Learning from the United States." Presentation at George Mason University, Virginia (January 26).

Kelling, George L., and William J. Bratton. 2006. *Policing Terrorism*. New York: The Manhattan Institute.

Kelling, George L., and Mark H. Moore. 1988. *The Evolving Strategy of Policing*. Perspectives on Policing, No. 5, Program in Criminal Justice Policy and Management, John F. Kennedy School of Government, Harvard University. Washington, DC: U.S. Department of Justice.

Kelling, George L., Antony Pate, Duane Dieckman, and Charles E. Brown. 1974. *The Kansas City Preventive Patrol Experiment: A Summary Report*. Washington, DC: The Police Foundation.

Kelling, George L., Antony Pate, Amy Ferrera, Mary Utne, and Charles E. Brown. 1981. *The Newark Foot Patrol Experiment*. Washington, DC: The Police Foundation.

Kerlikowske, Gil, R. 2004. "The End of Community Policing: Remembering the Lessons Learned." *Law Enforcement News* April, 6–10.

Klockars, Carl. 1988. "The Rhetoric of Community Policing." In *Community Policing: Rhetoric or Reality*, edited by Jack R. Greene and Stephen D. Mastrofski, 239–270. New York: Praeger.

Kubrin, Charis E., and Ronald Weitzer. 2003. "New Directions in Social Disorganization Theory." *Journal of Research in Crime and Delinquency* 40(4): 373–402.

Lane, Roger. 1967. *Policing the City: Boston 1822–1885*. Cambridge, MA: Harvard University Press.

Lepeska, David. 2011. "Preparing for 2012, Police Create Counterterrorism Unit." *New York Times* (September 8).

Lum, Cynthia. 2009. *Translating Police Research Into Practice*. Ideas in American Policing Lecture Series. Washington, DC: Police Foundation.

Lum, Cynthia, Maria (Maki) Haberfeld, George Fachner, and Charles Lieberman. 2009. "Police Activities to Counter Terrorism: What We Know and What We Need to Know." In *To Protect and Serve: Policing in An Age of Terrorism*, edited by David Weisburd, Thomas E. Feucht, Idit Hakimi, Lois Felson Mock, and Simon Perry, 101–141. New York: Springer.

Maguire, Edward R., and William R. King. 2011. "Federal-Local Coordination in Homeland Security." In *Criminologists on Terrorism and Homeland Security*, edited by Brian Forst, Jack R. Greene, and James P. Lynch, 322–356. Cambridge: Cambridge University Press.

Mastrofski, Stephen D. 1988. "Community Policing as Reform." In *Community Policing: Rhetoric or Reality*, edited by Jack R. Greene and Stephen D. Mastrofskii, 47–67. New York: Praeger.

———. 1996. "Measuring Police Performance in Public Encounters." In *Quantifying Quality in Policing*, edited by Larry T. Hoover, 207–241. Washington, DC: Police Executive Research Forum.

——. 1998. "Community Policing and Police Organization Structure." In *Community Policing and the Evaluation of Police Service Delivery*, edited by Jean-Paul Brodeur, 161–189. Thousand Oaks, CA: Sage.

——. 2000. "The Police in America." In *Criminology*, edited by Joseph F. Sheley, 405–445. Belmont, CA: Wadsworth/Thomson.

——. 2004. "Controlling Street-Level Police Discretion." *The Annals of the American Academy of Political and Social Science* 593:100–18.

——. 2006. "Community Policing: A Skeptical View." In *Police Innovation: Contrasting Perspectives*, edited by David L. Weisburd and Anthony A. Braga, 44–73. Cambridge: Cambridge University Press.

Mastrofski, Stephen D., and James J. Willis. 2010. "Police Organization: Continuity and Change." In *Crime and Justice: A Review of Research*, vol. 39 edited by Michael Tonry. Chicago: University of Chicago Press.

Mastrofski, Stephen D., James J. Willis, and Tammy Reinhart Kochel. 2007. "The Challenges of Implementing Community Policing in the United States." *Policing: A Journal of Policy and Practice* 1(2): 223–34.

McCluskey, John D. 2003. *Police Requests for Compliance: Coercive and Procedurally Justice Tactics.* El Paso, TX: LFB Scholarly Publishing.

McGarrell, Edmund F., Kathleen Olivares, Kay Crawford, and Natalie Kroovand. 2000. *Returning Justice to the Community: The Indianapolis Juvenile Restorative Justice Experiment.* Indianapolis, IN: Hudson Institute.

Moore, Mark H. 1992. "Problem-Solving and Community Policing." In *Modern Policing*, edited by Michael Tonry and Norval Morris, 99–158. Vol. 15 of *Crime and Justice: A Review of Research*. Chicago: University of Chicago Press.

Moore, Mark H., Malcolm Sparrow, and William Spelman. 1997. "Innovations in Policing: From Production Lines to Jobs Shops." In *Innovation in American Government: Challenges, Opportunities, and Dilemmas*, edited by Alan A. Altshuler and Robert D. Behn, 274–298. Washington, DC: Brookings Institution Press.

National Advisory Commission on Civil Disorders (The Kerner Report). 1968. Washington, DC: U.S. Government Printing Office. http://www.eisenhowerfoundation.org/docs/kerner.pdf.

Newburn, Tim, and Robert Reiner. 2007. "Policing and the Police." In *The Oxford Handbook of Criminology*, edited by Mike Maguire, Rod Morgan, and Robert Reiner, 910–952. Oxford: University of Oxford Press.

Neyround, Peter. 2008. "Past, Present and Future Performance: Lessons and Prospects for the Measurement of Police Performance." *Policing: A Journal of Policy and Practice* 2(3): 340–48.

Oliver, Willard M. 2006. "The Fourth Era of Policing: Homeland Security." *International Review of Law Computers and Technology* 20(1–2): 49–62.

Pate, Antony. 1986. "Experimenting with Foot Patrol: The Newark Experience." In *Community Crime Prevention: Does it Work?*, edited by Dennis Rosenbaum, 137–156. Beverly Hills, CA: Sage.

Pew Research Center. 2011. *Muslim Americans: No Sign of Growth in Alienation or Support for Extremism.* http://www.people-press.org/files/legacy-pdf/Muslim-American-Report.pdf.

Pino, Nathan, and Michael D. Wiatrowski. 2006. *Democratic Policing in Transitional and Developing Countries.* Aldershot, England: Ashgate.

Prenzler, Tim, and Carol Ronken. 2001. "Models of Police Oversight: A Critique." *Policing and Society* 11(2): 151–80.

President's Commission on Law Enforcement and Administration of Justice. 1967. *The Challenge of Crime in a Free Society*. Washington, DC: United States Government Printing Office.

Reisig, Michael. 2010. "Community- and Problem-Oriented Policing." In *Crime and Justice: A Review of Research*, vol. 39, edited by Michael Tonry, 1–53. Chicago: University of Chicago Press.

Reisig, Michael D., Jason Bratton, and Marc G. Gertz. 2007. "The Construct Validity and Refinement of Process-Based Policing Measures." *Criminal Justice Behavior* 34(8): 1005–28.

Reiss, Albert J., Jr. 1992. "Police Organization in the Twentieth Century." In *Modern Policing*, edited by Michael Tonry and Norval Morris, 51–97. Vol. 15 of *Crime and Justice: A Review of Research*. Chicago: University of Chicago Press.

Ritti, Richard R., and Stephen D. Mastrofski. 2002. *The Insitutionalization of Community Policing: A Study of the Presentation of the Concept in Two Law Enforcement Journals*. Manassas, VA: Administration of Justice Program, George Mason University.

Robinson, Paul H., Geoffrey P. Goodwin, and Michael D. Reisig. 2010. "The Disutility of Injustice." *New York University Law Review* 85:1940–2033.

Rogers, Everett M. 2003. *Diffusion of Innovations*. New York: Free Press.

Rosenbaum, Dennis. P. 1986. "Community Crime Prevention: A Review and Synthesis of the Literature." *Justice Quarterly* 5(3): 324–95.

Rosenbaum, Dennis P., Wesley G. Skogan, Lorie Fridell, Stephen D. Mastrofski, Susan Hartnett, Gary Cordner, and Jack McDevitt. 2011. *Measuring Police Organizations and their "Life-Course": The National Police Research Platform*. NPRP Report, January. http://www.nationalpoliceresearch.org/.

Roth, Jeffrey A., Jan Roehl, and Calvin C. Johnson. 2004. "Trends in the Adoption of Community Policing." In *Community Policing (Can It Work?)*, edited by Wesley G. Skogan, 3–29. Belmont, CA: Wadsworth/Thomson Learning.

Sampson, Robert. 2004. "Neighborhood and Community: Collective Efficacy and Community Safety." *New Economy* 11:106–13.

Sampson, Robert J., and S. W. Raudenbush. 1999. "Systematic Social Observation of Public Spaces: A New Look at Disorder in Urban Neighborhoods." *American Journal of Sociology* 105(3): 603–51.

Scarman, Lord J. 1981. *The Brixton Disorders, 10–12th April*. London: HMSO.

Schafer, Joseph, George W. Burruss, Jr., and Matthew J. Giblin. 2009. "Measuring Homeland Security Innovation in Small Municipal Agencies: Policing in a Post—9/11 World." *Police Quarterly* 12(3): 263–88.

Scott, Michael S. 2000. *Problem-Oriented Policing: Reflections on the First 20 Years*. Washington, DC: U.S. Department of Justice, Office of Community-Oriented Policing Services.

Seneviratne, Mary. 2004. "Policing the Police in the United Kingdom." *Policing and Society* 14(4): 329–47.

Shapland, Joanna. 2003. "Restorative Justice and Criminal Justice: Just Responses to Crime." In *Restorative Justice and Criminal Justice: Competing or Reconcilable Paradigms?*, edited by Andrew Von Hirsch, Julian Roberts, Anthony Bottoms, Kent Roach, and Mara Schiff, 195–217. Portland, OR: Hart Publishing.

Sherman, Lawrence W. 1998. *Evidence-Based Policing*. Ideas in American Policing Lecture Series. Washington, DC: Police Foundation.

——. 2003. "Reason for Emotion: Reinventing Justice with Theories, Innovations, and Research—The American Society of Criminology 2002 Presidential Address." *Criminology* 41(1): 1–38.

Sherman, Lawrence W., and David L. Weisburd. 1995. "General Deterrence Effects of Police Patrol in Crime "Hot-Spots:" A Randomized Controlled Trial." *Justice Quarterly* 12:626–48.

Sherman, Lawrence W., Denise Gottfredson, Doris MacKenzie, John Eck, Peter Reuter, and Shawn Bushway. 1997. *Preventing Crime: What Works, What Doesn't, What's Promising.* Washington, DC: National Institute of Justice.

Sklansky, David Alan. 2008. *Democracy and the Police.* Stanford, CA: Stanford University Press.

Skogan, Wesley G. 1995. "Community Policing in the United States." In *Comparisons in Policing: An International Perspective*, edited by J-P Brodeur, 86–112. Aldershot: Avebury Publishing Company.

———. 2006. "The Promise of Community Policing." In *Police Innovation: Contrasting Perspectives*, edited by David L. Weisburd, David and Anthony Braga, 27–43. Cambridge: Cambridge University Press.

———. 2009. "Concern About Crime and Confidence in the Police: Reassurance or Accountability?" *Police Quarterly* 12(3): 301–18.

Skogan, Wesley G., and Susan M. Hartnett. 1997. *Community Policing, Chicago Style.* Oxford: Oxford University Press.

Skogan, Wesley G., and Jeffrey A. Roth. 2004. Introduction to *Community Policing (Can It Work?)*, edited by Wesley G. Skogan. Belmont, CA: Wadsworth/Thomson Learning.

Skogan, Wesley, G., Lynn Steiner, Claudia Benitez, Jason Bennis, Sarah Borchers, Jill DuBois, Rita Gondocs, Susan Hartnett, So Young Kim, and Sarah Rosenbaum. 2004. *Community Policing in Chicago, Year Ten.* Illinois: Illinois Criminal Justice Authority. http://www.ipr.northwestern.edu/publications/policing_papers/Yr10-CAPSeval.pdf.

Spelman, William, and Dale K. Brown. 1981. *Calling the Police: Citizen Reporting of Serious Crime.* Washington, DC: U.S. Government Printing Office.

Stone, Christopher. 2007. "Tracing Police Accountability in Theory and Practice." *Theoretical Criminology* 11(2): 245–59.

Sunshine, Jason, and Tom R. Tyler. 2003. "The Role of Procedural Justice and Legitimacy in Shaping Public Support for Police." *Law and Society Review* 37(3): 513–47.

Tankebe, Justice. 2009. "Public Cooperation with the Police in Ghana: Does Procedural Fairness Matter?" *Criminology* 47(4): 1265–93.

Taylor, Ralph. 2006. "Incivilities Reduction Policing, Zero Tolerance, and the Retreat from Coproduction: Weak Foundations and Strong Pressures." In *Police Innovation: Contrasting Perspectives*, edited by David L. Weisburd and Anthony A. Braga, 98–114. Cambridge: Cambridge University Press.

Thacher, David. 2001. "Policing is not a Treatment." *Journal of Research in Crime and Delinquency* 38(4): 387–415.

———. 2005. "The Local Role in Homeland Security." *Law and Society Review* 39(5): 635–76.

———. 2008. "Research for the Front Lines." *Policing and Society* 18(1): 46–59.

Toch, Hans. 1980. "Mobilizing Police Expertise." *The Annals of the American Academy of Political and Social Science* 452:53–62.

Tomkins, Calvin. 2011. "The Materialist: Carl Andre's Eminent Obscurity." *The New Yorker* (December 5).

Trojanowicz, Robert C. 1986. "Evaluating a Neighborhood Foot Patrol Experiment: The Flint, Michigan, Project." In *Community Crime Prevention: Does it Work?*, edited by Dennis Rosenbaum, 157–178. Beverly Hills, CA: Sage.

Tyler, Tom R. 2000. "Social Justice: Outcome and Procedure." *International Journal of Psychology* 35(2): 117–25.

——. 2003. "Procedural Justice, Legitimacy, and the Effective Rule of Law." *Crime and Justice: A Review of Research*, vol. 30 edited by Michael Tonry. Chicago: University of Chicago Press.

——. 2004. "Police Legitimacy." *The Annals of the American Academy of Political and Social Science* 593:84–99.

——. 2009. "Legitimacy and Criminal Justice: The Benefits of Self-Regulation." *Ohio State Journal of Criminal Law* 7:307–59.

Tyler, Tom R., and Yuen J. Huo. 2002. *Trust in the Law: Encouraging Public Cooperation with the Police and Courts*. New York: Russell Sage.

Tyler, Tom R., Stephen Schullhofer, and Aziz Z. Huq. 2010. "Legitimacy and Deterrence Effects in Counterterrorism Policing: A Study of Muslim Americans." *Law and Society Review* 44(2): 365–402.

Tyler, Tom R., and Cheryl J. Wakslak. 2004. "Profiling and Police Legitimacy: Procedural Justice, Attribution of Motives, and Acceptance of Police Authority." *Criminology* 42(2): 253–81.

Walker, Samuel. 2001. *Police Accountability: The Role of Citizen Oversight*. Belmont, CA: Wadsworth/Thomson.

——. 2003. *Early Intervention Systems for Law Enforcement: A Planning and Management Guide*. Washington, DC: U.S. Department of Justice, Office of Community-Oriented Policing Services.

Walker, Samuel, and Geoffrey P. Alpert. 2004. "Early Intervention Systems: The New Paradigm." In *Police Integrity and Ethics*, edited by Matthew Hickman, Alex R. Piquero, and Jack R. Greene, 21–35. Belmont, CA: Wadsworth/Thomson.

Walker, Samuel, Geoffrey P. Alpert, and Dennis J. Kenney. 2001. *Early Warning Systems: Responding to the Problem Officer*. Research in Brief. Washington, DC: U.S. Department of Justice, National Institute of Justice.

Weisburd, David L., and Anthony A. Braga. 2006a. "Introduction: Understanding Police Innovation." In *Police Innovation: Contrasting Perspectives*, edited by David L. Weisburd and Anthony A. Braga,1–23. Cambridge: Cambridge University Press.

Weisburd, David L., and Anthony A. Braga. 2006b. "Hot Spots Policing As a Model for Police Innovation." In *Police Innovation: Contrasting Perspectives*, edited by David L. Weisburd and Anthony A. Braga, 225–244. Cambridge: Cambridge University Press.

Weisburd, David L., and John Eck. 2004. "What Can Police Do To Reduce Crime, Disorder and Fear?" *The Annals of the American Academy of Political and Social Science* 593:42–65.

Weisburd, David L., and Peter Neyroud. 2011. *Police Science: Toward a New Paradigm*. Kennedy School Program in Criminal Justice Policy and Management. Washington, DC: National Institute of Justice.

Weisburd, David L., Cody W. Telep, Joshua C. Hinkle, John E. Eck. 2010. "Is Problem-Oriented Policing Effective In Reducing Crime and Disorder? Findings from a Campbell Systematic Review." *Criminology and Public Policy* 9(1): 139–72.

Weitzer, Ronald, and Steven A. Tuch. 1999. "Race, Class, and Perceptions of Discrimination by the Police." *Crime and Delinquency* 45:494–507.

——. 2006. *Race and Policing in America: Conflict and Reform*. Cambridge: Cambridge University Press.

Welsh, Brandon C. 2006. "Evidence-Based Policing for Crime Prevention." In *Police Innovation: Contrasting Perspectives*, edited by David L. Weisburd and Anthony A. Braga, 305–321. Cambridge: Cambridge University Press.

Willis, James J. 2012. "The Craft of Policing." Presentation for the Ideas in Policing Lecture Series (February 23). Washington, DC: Police Foundation.

Willis, James J., Tammy Rinehart Kochel, and Stephen D. Mastrofski. 2010. *The Co-Implementation of Compstat and Community Policing: A National Assessment.* Washington DC: Department of Justice, Office of Community-Oriented Policing Services.

Willis, James J., and Stephen D. Mastrofski. 2011. "Innovations in Policing: Meanings, Structures, and Processes." *Annual Review of Law and the Social Sciences* 7:309–34.

——. 2012. "Compstat and the New Penology: A Paradigm Shift in Policing?" *British Journal of Criminology* 52(1): 73–92.

Willis, James J, Stephen D. Mastrofski, and David L. Weisburd. 2007. "Making Sense of Compstat: A Theory-Based Analysis of Organizational Change in Three Police Departments." *Law and Society Review* 41(1): 147–88.

Wilson, James Q. 1978. *Varieties of Police Behavior: The Management of Law and Order in Eight Communities.* Cambridge, MA: Harvard University Press.

Wilson, James Q., and George L. Kelling. 1982. "Broken Widows: The Police and Neighborhood Safety." *Atlantic Monthly* 249:29–38.

Wortley, Robert, and Lorraine Mazzerole. 2008. "Environmental Criminology and Crime Analysis Situating the Theory, Analytic Approach, and Application." In *Environmental Criminology and Crime Analysis*, edited by Richard Wortley and Lorraine Mazzerole, 1–15. Cullompton. Devon: Willan.

CHAPTER 2

··

POLICING URBAN DRUG MARKETS

··

LALLEN T. JOHNSON

THINKING ecologically, it is important to theorize on the extent to which shifting community dynamics shape the role and effects of policing urban drug crime. In particular, scholarship must draw connections at the intersection of drug crime, policing, and social demographics. An analysis bereft of the above severely limits our understanding of drug offending, and appropriate responses to such offending. Notwithstanding the above, drug abuse and distribution adversely affects American society in a myriad of ways and is extremely costly. According to the Office of National Drug Control Policy (2004), in 2002 drug related costs totaled $180.9 billion. "This value represents both the use of resources to address health and crime consequences as well as the loss of potential productivity from disability, death and withdrawal from the workforce" (Office of National Drug Control Policy 2004, vi). The public health consequences of drug abuse are equally dire. In 2010 alone, over 1 million individuals were admitted to hospital emergency departments for illicit drug abuse (Substance Abuse and Mental Health Administration 2012).

Social concerns about drug and drug-related crime abound, in particular drug-related violence. Considering the criminalization of drug use and distribution, actors in illicit markets suffer from a poverty of options in addressing market disputes—the result of which may be violence (Goldstein 1985). In turn, the prevailing assumption of drug crime (and drug-related crime) is that it is associated with those residing in communities of low socioeconomic status, with high minority populations, and in the inner city (Saxe et al. 2001). Research, however, has cast much doubt on assumptions of minorities and drug use (Johnston, O'Malley, Bachman, and Schulenberg 2010), and community level drug crime-violence linkages (Lum 2008).

In response, law enforcement has engaged in a number of militaristic (and generally ineffective) tactics to address drug crime, much of which was encouraged by top-down propaganda developed from the federal government (C-Span 1989) and media (Brownstein 1991; Gilliam and Iyengar 2000). Such approaches tend to be focused on inner-city, poor, minority environments, calling into question the equity of the drug war

(Provine 2011). It should come as no surprise, therefore, that as of January 2013, 90,394 or 47 percent of federal inmates were serving time for a drug offense (Federal Bureau of Prisons 2013), and that blacks are significantly more likely to be arrested and incarcerated for drug offenses than their white counterparts (Austin and Allen 2000). In spite of structural shifts, as well as existing social conditions such as economic isolation, poverty, and hyper-segregation that facilitate offending (Peterson and Krivo 2010), the nature of drug enforcement within poor urban communities is predicated on the idea of punishment (Provine 2011).

This essay describes the development of urban drug markets and the ensuing enforcement strategies designed to reduce drug crime in structurally disadvantaged communities. Section 2.1 highlights the changing social and economic conditions during post-war America, as well as the resulting effects of concentrated disadvantage and social/racial isolation. This section also traces the development of illicit drug markets in urban communities characterized by racially-concentrated economic disadvantage. Section 2.2 focuses on the evolving drug economy as a replacement for a legal economy, and addresses the extreme violence that came with the introduction of crack cocaine into American urban centers. This section also discusses the role of gangs, as well as the concept of "self-help" with respect to social control in drug markets. Section 2.3 describes the racial stereotypes often invoked to symbolize urban drug markets, and the evolving federal policies designed to help federal and local police fight the so-called drug war. This section highlights the disproportionate consequences of drug enforcement strategies experienced by many urban communities of color. Finally, Section 2.4 draws several conclusions regarding both the past and future of policing urban drug markets. In particular, this section argues that policing should rely less on legalistic interventions, while working with community partners to create drug reduction solutions based more on cooperation than coercion.

A number of conclusions can be drawn:

- Declines in manufacturing and factory production in post-World War II America led to the creation of racially-concentrated structurally disadvantaged communities in many large cities, and the subsequent development of drug markets as a response to sustained joblessness and poverty in these communities.
- As addiction rates have increased in urban drug markets, violent crime has also increased due to drug-related robberies, as well as conflict over turf.
- Communities characterized by extreme structural disadvantage are least able to mobilize in ways that protect against the development and operation of illicit drug markets; and as a result they suffer from both the effects of high addiction rates, as well as the violence that accompanies drug corners.
- The creation of federally funded drug enforcement task forces has concentrated drug policing in structurally disadvantaged, racially isolated, communities—in many cases, exacerbating rates of local violence as police and drug dealers engage in armed conflict.

- Despite that many, if not most, residents of disadvantaged communities of color do not support the illicit drug market, they often hold even less favorable attitudes toward police due to the real or perceived abuses of authority that often accompany police interventions.
- Evolving police interventions should deemphasize purely legalistic approaches to drug enforcement, while attempting to leverage community resources, participation, and support for alternative police strategies to not rely exclusively on coercion to achieve results.

2.1 STRUCTURAL SHIFTS, OPPORTUNITY STRUCTURES, AND DRUG CRIME

Ecological shifts post-World War II have set in motion a series of socio-economic setbacks for urban, economically distressed, minority communities. Crime, and drug crime in particular, is a byproduct of such shifts. Massey and Denton (1993) argue that the loss of low-skill manufacturing positions in the inner city contributed to the jobs-skills mismatch common in many post-industrial American cities, which in turn created new pockets of poverty in urban centers.

Federal post-war policies led to highway development which also opened up suburban tracts for residential and industrial development (Kasarda 1989). Around that same time the Home Owners' Loan Corporation (HOLC) and Federal Housing Administration (FHA) developed redlining practices that further isolated blacks to inner city neighborhoods and limited racial integration. Additionally, the Housing Acts of 1949 and 1954 provided urban renewal grants to demolish low-income blighted neighborhoods for the development of public works projects and public housing (Massey and Denton 1993).

Collectively, these practices contributed to the isolation of poor minorities in the inner city while allowing the middle class to relocate and reallocate their tax dollars to suburban jurisdictions. But, because blacks are segregated to a small number of neighborhoods, black poverty is also confined to those neighborhoods. Whites are not as spatially confined; therefore, white poverty is more able to evenly distribute itself across space, resulting in white poverty not being as spatially concentrated as black poverty (Massey and Denton 1993; Massey and Fischer 2000).

2.2 DRUGS, VIOLENCE, AND COMMUNITY DISADVANTAGE

Absent legitimate opportunities, some residents of economically distressed communities may find themselves seeking employment outside of the legitimate economy. One such illicit economy is that of the drug trade. The arrival of the 1980s crack-cocaine era presented unique yet illicit opportunities for inner-city black males to acquire money and status through drug sales (Anderson 1999). Yet the nature of such exchanges places participants in complicated situations. Because both sellers and buyers are breaking the law and neither desires arrest, they must make a personal connection that indicates they are not police officers. Further, drug buyers seek reassurances that dealers will not rip them off. While, conversely, dealers seek reassurances that buyers will not try to steal their money. With all of these constraints in place, these actors must converge in time and space in such a way that sellers can profit and buyers satisfy narcotic dependencies. Furthermore, such micro-level interactions within a socio-economically deprived context have implications for community violence.

Concentrated disadvantage appears to be strongly related to drug market activity, with drug market activity in turn having a strong causal connection with robbery rates (Bursik and Grasmick 1993; Berg and Rengifo 2009). Such communities tend to be socially disorganized and unable to regulate drug crime and the related violence that it engenders (Berg and Rengifo 2009). However, even controlling for sociodemographic factors such as instability, heterogeneity, and deprivation, drug activity still has a significant positive effect on assault and robbery rates (Martínez, Rosenfeld, and Mares 2008). Other research has explored the possibility that the drugs/violence nexus is contingent upon sociodemographics. Ousey and Lee (2002) found that increases in drug arrest rates were positively related to homicide rates; however, that relationship is contingent on the preexisting level of resource deprivation. In other words, when the level of resource deprivation is at or above the average, drug crime rates are positively related to homicide rates, but when the level of preexisting deprivation is less than the average the relationship is negative.

The risk of homicide is likely due to the association of outdoor drug markets with the use of guns (Mieczkowski 1992; Messner et al. 2007), as young minority males seek protection while engaging in the risks of drug dealing (Blumstein 1995). Not only are guns instrumental in protecting inner-city dealers from the risks of the drug trade, but carrying guns and being prepared to use them as necessary is a symbol of status; and, ideally such presentations self-serve to protect dealers from their rivals (Anderson 1999).

Research has also found the above relationships among drugs and violent crime to demonstrate spatial dependency (Zhu, Gorman, and Horel 2006). Using data from Houston, Gorman, Zhu, and Horel (2005) found that drug crime accounted for 72 percent of the variation in violent crime, with significant spatial lag effects. Spatial research has also revealed that not all drug markets are violent, suggesting that research should consider the systemic factors by which they vary (Lum 2008). Such considerations are explored below.

The systemic model is rooted in Donald Black's (1976) theory of law and self-help (Ousey and Lee 2004; Jacques and Wright 2008; Jacques 2010). According to Black, social groups may employ a number of methods to address conflict; however, the decision to resort to violence depends on a social group's relative position on the social ladder. "In other words, as people or groups gain status, their access to law increases and, in turn their involvement in retaliation decreases" (Jacques 2010, 188). Because of this, marginalized groups may be more likely than more highly-positioned, wealthier groups to resort to violence, or what Black describes as "self-help," to settle disputes.

In turn, lower status or less "respectable" groups such as drug offenders are subject to additional social control by the law, even though they cannot use the law to their benefit. The perceived threat by higher-status members of drug dealers and buyers may allow higher-status members to use their social positions to apply strict penalties to drug offending. This would further increase the isolation of drug offenders from legal remedies, leading their problem-solving solutions to be centered around violence (Black 1976).

Gang drug-dealing organizations, operating in an extra-legal paradigm, are exemplary of the self-help concept. Gangs typically have a set space where they carry out leisure and "business-related" activity which essentially serves as a node or base within their routine activities (Tita, Cohen, and Engberg 2005). Drug selling and shots fired calls to the police appear to concentrate within and near such areas, which may be suggestive of conflict between rival gangs or at least between the gang in question and the community (Tita and Ridgeway 2007). Other research has shown that corners that are a part of gang drug selling territory are associated with about two times higher counts of violent crime events than corners that are not a part of gang set space (Taniguchi, Ratcliffe, and Taylor 2011). Furthermore, corners where multiple gangs have sold or those under dispute experience violent crime counts almost three times higher than non-gang corners.

Additional environmental features are significant for systemic drug violence. Goldstein (1985) argues that the nature of drug market areas is such that they provide a substantial number of robbery targets. Fixed-site drug distribution and use locations such as crack houses and shooting galleries present opportunities for robbery victimization (Brownstein, Spunt, Crimmins, and Langley 1995). The following quote from a drug robber respondent interviewed by Brownstein and colleagues illustrates this point:

> I had noticed one of the guys that had been standing behind the scale went for his pocket, and I was always told, "Never allow anybody to move after the specific orders were given." So when he went to go, I pistol-whipped him. When I pistol-whipped him, the bullet hit the next guy.... Actually, the one I took his life, it wasn't called for. The bullet wasn't meant for him. The bullet wasn't meant for either of them. It was to show [that] when orders are given, don't do nothing but what you are supposed to do. (490)

A significant aspect of drug market violence overlooked by Goldstein (1985) is that which may take place between the community and buyers and/or dealers. Law abiding residents living in drug market areas may become violent against users and dealers if they feel the criminal justice system is ineffective in addressing the problem. Such vigilante justice, however, places law-abiding residents at risk of bodily harm, as well as sanctioning by the criminal justice system (Brownstein et al. 1995). To a lesser extent, residents may also become verbally hostile and condemn drug dealing in their communities, but even this has the potential to lead to violent confrontations if a dealer sees the area as profitable (St. Jean 2007).

Although the above provides examples of systemic forms of violence, it is important to remember that such violence is situated within the ecological shifts of urban
settings. In other words, urban drug markets are in part a reflection of an inner city
devoid of employment opportunities and institutions that facilitate them. Again,
urban race and class segregation is determinative in terms of access to upward mobility (Briggs 2005). When segregation takes place in the form of income and race, not
only are African Americans isolated to a few select communities, but the outcomes
of African Americans in terms of poverty, joblessness, education, and inequality
are also disproportionately focused in such neighborhoods, making them subject
to random economic shifts (such as the loss of low-skill jobs) (Massey and Denton
1993). Much criminological research has shown that opportunity structures such
as access to poverty (or lack thereof), education, and employment are strong predictors of deviant behavior (Hipp 2007; McCord and Ratcliffe 2007; Uggen 2000).
Peterson and Krivo's (2010) study of over 9,000 neighborhoods grouped by race
across 91 cities is particularly telling. Not only are communities of color likely to be
subject to conditions of disadvantage; they are more likely than their white counterparts to demonstrate multiple forms of disadvantage. Fifty-six percent of African
American neighborhoods and 51 percent of Latino neighborhoods demonstrated at
least four distinct forms of extreme disadvantage, compared to 1 percent of white
neighborhoods.

Such conditions may undermine the ability of residents to regulate illicit drug sales
(Bursik and Grasmick 1993; Bursik 1999). In turn, communities suffering from multiple
forms of disadvantage may find it difficult to regulate crime through informal and formal mechanisms (Peterson and Krivo 2010). The question here is whether the highly
raced and classed context of inner city neighborhoods conditions law enforcement
responses to drug crime. Are the responses of law enforcement to drug markets conditioned by *who* versus *what* is being policed?

2.3 POLICING DRUG MARKETS: COMMUNITY RACE AND STATUS

The 1980s brought about substantial changes in the way the American criminal justice system dealt with drug abuse, through the Anti-Drug Abuse Acts of 1986 and 1988.
Around the same time, media reports suggested that the pharmacological effects of
crack were more dangerous than its powdered form (Baum 1996), and that middle-class
whites were at risk of victimization by inner-city crack-addicted minorities (Brownstein
1991). Yet even prior to the 1980s, people of color have been used to exploit fears of illicit
drugs. Examples include media articles depicting cocaine-addicted African Americans
as resistant to bullets (Williams 1914) and sexually violating white women (Schatzman
1975), federal statutes exclusively prohibiting Chinese immigrants from smoking and

importing opium (Latimer and Goldberg 1981), and more recently criminal justice responses to the "crack baby" epidemic targeting minority women (Logan 1999).

Research clearly violates the above stereotypes. For example, findings by Saxe and colleagues (2001) indicate that African Americans and Latinos are more likely than their white counterparts to report witnessing drug sales in their neighborhoods. Yet, while residents of high-minority communities are more likely to witness drug sales, they are less likely to engage in drug use or become dependent than residents in low-minority communities.

In spite of competing and convincing evidence of the extent of minority drug use, one must consider the extent to which criminal justice actors and policymakers consciously or subconsciously internalize racist and classist stereotypes about drug crime. One would be naïve to assume that such individuals, who also live in a society highly structured by race, would be insulated from such ideologies (Bonilla-Silva 2001). In particular, research has indicated that the presence of physical racial cues associated with African Americans can lead to bias in the criminal justice system. Controlling for offense type and race, Florida defendants with Afrocentric facial features tended to receive lengthier sentences than those with fewer Afrocentric features (Blair, Judd, and Chapleau 2004). These findings suggest two things: 1) Some criminal justice actors, too, may associate criminal behavior with African Americans, and 2) deviant behavior by African Americans in the criminal justice system is more likely to be seen as a cultural, rather than individual failure (Muhammad 2010). Furthermore, findings demonstrate that overt racist policies are unnecessary for bias to occur in criminal justice decisions. Unchecked discretion throughout the criminal justice system leaves room for those in marginalized positions to be exploited without the need for racial justifications (Alexander 2012).

Turning specifically to law enforcement, federal funding programs such as the Edward Byrne Memorial State and Local Law Enforcement Assistance Program have proven particularly problematic in the targeting of racial minorities for drug offending. The program, established in 1988 and administered by the U.S. Department of Justice, provides funds for state and local criminal justice agencies in multiple focus areas. Among these areas is the establishment and operation of multi-jurisdictional drug task forces. From the program's inception in 1989 to 1991, $738.4 million has been allocated to such task forces (Dunworth, Haynes, and Saiger 1997). Yet, in spite of such lofty expenditures toward task forces, research suggests that task force member agencies are not necessarily more productive than non-member agencies (Novak, Hartman, Holsinger, and Turner 1999).

Egregious abuses of authority have occurred under drug task forces, through race-based arrest policies. Over a fifteen-year period residents of Hearne, TX have experienced drug sweeps targeted at the African American community. In a court petition noting the most recent sweep, complainants noted that the task force engaged in a number of warrantless searches, violating Fourth and Fourteenth Amendment rights. Further, the director of the task force based sweeps on information derived from a coerced burglary and drug offender with mental health issues. The informant was instructed to purchase illicit drugs from a number of predetermined individuals and note that such purchases occurred within a school zone. He was also provided with drugs that were to be used to implicate the suspects. The informant was threatened such that if he failed to comply he would be sentenced to prison for at least 60 years with a cellmate that would repeatedly sexually violate him. In November of 2000 alone, 28 individuals were arrested in a single raid and held in jail for periods of up to 5 months. Lacking credible evidence, charges for the vast majority of individuals were subsequently dismissed (*Kelly v. Paschall*, 124 Fed. Appx. 259 [2005]).

A study of Seattle drug offenders found that while 79 percent of those arrested for crack cocaine dealing were African American, survey data indicated that only 47 percent of crack dealers were of the same race (Beckett, Nyrop, and Pfingst 2006). In addition, findings revealed that geographic targeting has implications for arrests rates by race. Researchers noted during observation that while hundreds of outdoor drug transactions occurred in the mostly white Capitol Hill neighborhood, arrests were uncommon. By comparison, the more racially diverse downtown drug market experienced 25 times the amount of drug arrests as Capitol Hill, even though drug transactions in downtown exceeded those in Capitol Hill by only 4 times. And, blacks represented 70 percent of downtown arrestees. Overt or not, tactical deployment decisions have clear implications for racial disproportionality and call into question whether deployment tactics are a response to a perceived racial threat (for more on racial threat hypothesis see Kane (2003) and Kane, Gustafson, and Bruell (forthcoming)).

Another perceptively biased law enforcement tactic is that of asset forfeiture. The Comprehensive Drug Abuse Prevention and Control Act of 1970 allows federal law enforcement agencies to seize property and proceeds associated with or derived from drug transactions (Office of the Inspector General 2012). Seizures are derived from joint federal, state, and/or local efforts, and profits may be divided on a 20 percent (federal), 80 percent (state and/or local) scale (Alexander 2012). Since most seizures occur without criminal proceedings (because the property, not the person is deemed guilty), defendants are left to seek and pay for their own legal assistance (Alexander 2012). Such an approach has a disparate impact on low-income individuals, rather than the wealthy drug kingpins who are the law's intended targets. Disinterest in addressing the class-based issues of asset forfeiture may be attributed to the reliance of law enforcement departments on the proceeds. In a survey of 383 large police departments, Worrall (2001, 179)) found that 46 percent of law enforcement executives agree with the statement that "[c]ivil forfeiture is necessary as a budgetary supplement." At the very least, forfeiture calls into question issues of fairness among defendants, and ethics in policing.

As a result, one must consider the extent to which prior contact with the justice system may undermine perceptions of law enforcement in minority communities. Militarized tactics, such as the Los Angeles Police Department's use of a battering ram vehicle to tear through the walls of suspected drug houses in the 1980s, called into question not only issues of safety and constitutionality but of the department's broader image (Hager

1986). Indeed research has shown that negative contact with law enforcement officers in minority and poor neighborhoods may undermine police legitimacy (Gau and Brunson 2009); and such police legitimacy has implications for neighborhood crime rates (Kane 2005). Perceptions of minority officers by urban minority residents appear to be situated in an ecological framework (Brunson and Gau forthcoming). That is, the quality and nature of policing is conditioned, in part, by chronic underfunding and macro-level economic shifts. Additional research has shown that residents of disadvantaged neighborhoods tend to be more cynical about and dissatisfied with law enforcement than residents of wealthier neighborhoods (Sampson and Bartusch 1998).

Residents of some disadvantaged communities feel that reporting rogue officers may do more harm than good (Venkatesh 2008), which may also explain why many Fourth Amendment search violations are unnoticed by the courts (Gould and Mastrofski 2004). In a study of a medium-sized American city, Gould and Mastrofski (2004) found that 30 percent of police searches were in violation of the Constitution. And the odds of an unconstitutional search occurring increased substantially when an officer was motivated to find drugs, even though unconstitutional searches were no more likely than constitutional ones to reveal illicit drugs. In New York, stops and searches for illicit drugs and weapons occur largely at the expense of the city's African American and Hispanic neighborhoods, in spite of producing no real crime reduction benefit (Fagan, Geller, Davies, and West 2010).

Even when urban minority residents are knowledgeable and concerned about drug crimes in their neighborhoods, structural factors and social ties may make them reluctant to involve the police. Research in a poor Chicago neighborhood indicates that residents agree that even though drug dealing is a problem, they are empathetic with drug dealers due to the lack of legitimate job opportunities available (St. Jean 2007). Additionally, it is important to remember that the social networks of drug offenders and law-abiding residents are inextricably linked, and in turn, drug offenders are able to draw social capital from both groups (Browning, Feinberg, and Dietz 2004). For example, residents have been reluctant to report illicit drug dealing due to social ties with relatives of drug offenders (St. Jean 2007); or because gang drug organizations, while contributing to crime, also serve as a protective element and are civically engaged (Pattillo 1998; Venkatesh 2008).

2.4 DISCUSSION AND CONCLUSIONS

The above reveals that a myriad of historical, social, and policy issues have shaped drug crime interdiction in urban communities. Structural changes have left inner cities without legitimate opportunities for a low-skill workforce. Consistent flight from such communities has drained them of investment and has redistributed wealth to suburban areas. In turn, access to neighborhoods providing greater opportunities for upward mobility has historically been conditioned by race. Further undermining opportunities for inner city community enhancement was the arrival of crack, and the ensuing war on drugs. In light of the historically racialized and classist approach to drugs in American society, poor minorities, while clearly not the most likely to engage in drug use, appear to be unfairly targeted by drug enforcement.

In spite of the inherently legalistic approach to illicit drug use and dealing, there have been a number of approaches that have attempted to involve community stakeholders, representing a step in the right direction. Among these include the pulling levers strategy, which identifies problem drug offenders and attempts to provide them with access to services in lieu of strict law enforcement (Corsaro, Brunson, and McGarrell 2010). The Nashville approach included a multi-stage strategy involving multiple stakeholders. Law enforcement identified and met with known offenders to communicate a message of strict enforcement if offenders choose to continue deviant behavior. Most importantly, each individual was met with a series of supports to assist with prosocial behavior including, but not limited to, job training skills and treatment. Evaluations indicated significant reductions in drug crime in the target community. The pulling levers approach has also proven a viable strategy in High Point, NC (Hunt, Sumner, Scholten, and Frabutt 2008) as well as Boston (Braga, Kennedy, Waring, and Piehl 2001).

Other policing strategies have involved landlords, which stand in a unique position to regulate illicit drug activities occurring on their properties. An evaluation on the role of place managers in reducing crime and disorder and increasing civil behavior on one hundred street blocks randomly assigned to Oakland, California's Beat Health Program or typical patrol yielded positive results (Mazerolle, Kadleck, and Roehl 1998). Stakeholders of the experimental group were more likely to report decreases in the number of males selling drugs over time, and increased signs of civil behavior. Even written communication from law enforcement to landlords of nuisance properties has proven effective in reducing drug crime (Eck and Wartell 1998).

Considering what appears to be differential treatment of drug crime in poor and minority neighborhoods, researchers and policymakers must continue to question how policing can avoid exacerbating dire conditions in urban low-income minority communities. The above approaches represent a step in the right direction, but a number of additional perspectives merit consideration as well. First, we must call into question the inherent fairness of asset forfeiture programs. The fundamental ideas of justice and fairness are questioned when indigent individuals are unable to seek justice because of their socioeconomic status. Furthermore, law enforcement agency funding should not be dependent upon the seizure of private property, as such policies have the potential to invite corruption. Second, stop and frisk policies should be aborted. Research demonstrates not only that they are racially biased, but they are also an inefficient approach to crime reduction (Fagan et al. 2010). Third, there is ample reason to reconsider the use of aggressive arrest policies of low-level non-violent drug offenders in urban communities. The removal of drug dealers may create a vacuum effect, whereby more violence is created by new dealers competing for newly available turf (Resignato 2000). Also drug arrest sets in motion a number of subsequent biased justice approaches at later stages of the criminal justice system (Belenko, Fagan, and Chin 1991) and may exclude individuals from housing, education, and voting opportunities, thus perpetuating poor social outcomes (Alexander 2012). Finally, it is important that more socially oriented responses to social problems be developed. Drug offending is not a social issue that will subside due to drug laws' enforcement. Policies must address the social conditions that indicate why offenders engage in drug dealing in the first place, as well as the treatment of addicted individuals.

Policing research and policy must continue to examine drug offending through the lenses of race and class. As the consequences of inner-city drug crime are (in part) attributed to structural shifts, and as policing has historically taken on punitive approaches to drug interdiction in racially defined geographies, failing to recognize the significance of race and class leaves us with an incomplete understanding of causes and solutions. None of this is to suggest that policing should not have a role in drug interdiction, but that the viability of economically depressed and minority communities depend on a re-conceptualization of the nature of drug enforcement.

References

Alexander, Michelle. 2012. *The New Jim Crow: Mass Incarceration in the Age of Colorblindness.* New York: New Press.

Anderson, Elijah. 1999. *Code of the Street: Decency, Violence, and the Moral Life of the Inner City.* New York: W. W. Norton and Company.

Austin, Roy L., and Mark D. Allen. 2000. "Racial Disparity in Arrest Rates as an Explanation of Racial Disparity in Commitment to Pennsylvania's Prisons." *Journal of Research in Crime and Delinquency* 37:200–20.

Baum, Dan. 1996. *Smoke and Mirrors: The War on Drugs and the Politics of Failure.* Boston: Little, Brown and Company.

Beckett, Katherine, Kris Nyrop, and Lori Pfingst. 2006. "Race, Drugs, and Policing: Understanding Disparities in Drug Delivery Arrests." *Criminology* 44:105–37.

Belenko, Steven, Jeffrey Fagan, and Ko-Lin Chin. 1991. "Criminal Justice Responses to Crack." *Journal of Research in Crime and Delinquency* 28:55–74.

Berg, Mark T., and Andres F. Rengifo. 2009. "Rethinking Community Organization and Robbery: Considering Illicit Market Dynamics." *Justice Quarterly* 26:211–37.

Black, Donald. 1976. *The Behavior of Law.* New York: Academic Press.

Blair, Irene V., Charles M. Judd, and Kristine M. Chapleau. 2004. "The Influence of Afrocentric Facial Features in Criminal Sentencing." *Psychological Science* 15:674–79.

Blumstein, Alfred. 1995. "Youth Violence, Guns, and the Illicit-drug Industry." *Journal of Criminal Law and Criminology* 86:10–36.

Bonilla-Silva, Eduardo. 2001. *White Supremacy and Racism in the Post-Civil Rights Era.* Boulder, CO: Lynne Reinner.

Braga, Anthony A., David M. Kennedy, Elin J. Waring, and Anne Piehl. 2001. "Problem-oriented Policing, Deterrence, and Youth Violence: An Evaluation of Boston's Operation Ceasefire." *Journal of Research in Crime and Delinquency* 38:195–225.

Briggs, Xavier de Souza. 2005. "More Pluribus, Less Unum? The Changing Geography of Race and Opportunity." In *The Geography of Opportunity: Race and Housing Choice in Metropolitan America*, edited by Xavier de Souza Briggs, 17–41. Washington, DC: Brookings.

Browning, Christopher R., Seth L. Feinberg, and Robert Dietz. 2004. "The Paradox of Social Organization: Networks, Collective Efficacy and Violent Crime in Urban Neighborhoods." *Social Forces* 83:503–34.

Brownstein, Henry H. 1991. "The Media and the Construction of Random Drug Violence." *Social Justice* 18:85–103.

Brownstein, Henry H., Barry J. Spunt, Susan M. Crimmins, and Sandra C. Langley. 1995. "Women Who Kill in Drug Market Situations." *Justice Quarterly* 12:473–98.

Brunson, Rod K., and Jacinta M. Gau. Forthcoming. "Officer Race Versus Macro-level Context: A Test of Competing Hypotheses about Black Citizens' Experiences with and Perceptions of Black Police Officers." *Crime and Delinquency*, doi:10.1177/0011128711398027.

Bursik, Robert J. 1999. "The Informal Control of Crime through Neighborhood Networks." *Sociological Focus* 32:85–97.

Bursik, Robert J., and Harold G. Grasmick. 1993. *Neighborhoods and Crime: The Dimensions of Effective Community Control*. Lanham, MD: Lexington Books.

C-Span. 1989. *Presidential Address on National Drug Policy*. Washington, DC: C-Span.

Corsaro, Nicholas, Rod K. Brunson, and Edmund F. McGarrell. 2010. "Evaluating a Policing Strategy to Disrupt an Illicit Street-level Drug Market." *Evaluation Research* 34:513–48.

Dunworth, Terence, Peter Haynes, and Aaron J. Saiger. 1997. *National Assessment of the Byrne Formula Grant Program*. Washington, DC: National Institute of Justice.

Eck, John, and Julie Wartell. 1998. "Improving the Management of Rental Properties with Drug Problems: A Randomized Experiment." *Crime Prevention Studies* 9:161–85.

Fagan, Jeffrey, Amanda Geller, Garth Davies, and Valerie West. 2010. "Street Stops and Broken Windows Revisited: The Demography and Logic of Proactive Policing in a Safe and Changing City." In *Race, Ethnicity, and Policing: New and Essential Readings*, edited by Stephen Rice and Michael White, 309–348. New York: New York University Press.

Federal Bureau of Prisons. 2013. *Quick Facts about the Bureau of Prisons*. Washington, DC: U.S. Department of Justice.

Gau, Jacinta M., and Rod K. Brunson. 2009. "Procedural Justice and Order Maintenance Policing: A Study of Inner City Young Men's Perceptions of Police Legitimacy." *Justice Quarterly* 27:255–79.

Gilliam, Franklin D., and Shanto Iyengar. 2000. "Prime Suspects: The Influence of Local Television News on the Viewing Public." *American Journal of Political Science* 44:560–73.

Goldstein, Paul J. 1985. "The Drugs/Violence Nexus: A Tripartite Conceptual Framework." *Journal of Drug Issues* 15:493–506.

Gorman, Dennis M., Li Zhu, and Scott Horel. 2005. "Drug 'Hot-Spots,' Alcohol Availability and Violence." *Drug and Alcohol Review* 24:507–13.

Gould, Jon B., and Stephen D. Mastrofski. 2004. "Suspect Searches: Assessing Police Behavior under the U.S. Constitution." *Criminology and Public Policy* 3:315–62.

Hager, Philip. 1986. "ACLU Asks Court to Bar LAPD's Battering Ram." *Los Angeles Times* (May 13).

Hipp, John R. 2007. "Income Inequality, Race, and Place: Does the Distribution of Race and Class within Neighborhoods Affect Crime Rates?" *Criminology* 45:665–97.

Hunt, Eleazer D., Marty Sumner, Thomas J. Scholten, and James M. Frabutt. 2008. "Using GIS to Identify Drug Markets and Reduce Drug-related Violence." In *Geography and*

Drug Addiction, edited by Yonette F. Thomas, Douglas Richardson, and Ivan Cheung, 395–413. New York: Springer.

Jacques, Scott. 2010. "The Necessary Conditions for Retaliation: Toward a Theory of Nonviolent and Violent Forms in Drug Markets." *Justice Quarterly* 27:186–205.

Jacques, Scott, and Richard Wright. 2008. "The Relevance of Peace to Studies of Drug Market Violence." *Criminology* 46:221–54.

Johnston, Lloyd D., Patrick M. O'Malley, Jerald G. Bachman, and John E. Schulenberg. 2010. *Monitoring the Future: National Survey Results on Drug Use, 1975–2009*, vol. 1. Rockville, MD: National Institute on Drug Abuse.

Kane, Robert J. 2003. "Social Control in the Metropolis: A Community-level Examination of the Minority Group-threat Hypothesis." *Justice Quarterly* 20:265–95.

——. 2005. "Compromised Police Legitimacy as a Predictor of Violent Crime in Structurally Disadvantaged Communities." *Criminology* 43:469–98.

Kane, Robert J., Joseph L. Gustafson, and Christopher Bruell. Forthcoming. "Racial Encroachment and the Formal Control of Space: Minority Group-threat and Misdemeanor Arrests in Urban Communities." *Justice Quarterly*.

Kasarda, John D. 1989. "Urban Industrial Transition and the Underclass." *Annals of the American Academy of Political and Social Science* 501:26–47.

Latimer, Dean, and Jeff Goldberg. 1981. *Flowers in the Blood: The Story of Opium*. New York: F. Watts.

Logan, Enid. 1999. "The Wrong Race, Committing Crime, Doing Drugs, and Maladjusted for Motherhood: The Nation's Fury over 'Crack Babies.'" *Social Justice* 26:115–38.

Lum, Cynthia. 2008. "The Geography of Drug Activity and Violence: Analyzing Spatial Rrelationships of Non-homogenous Crime Event Types." *Substance Use and Misuse* 43:179–201.

Martínez, Ramiro, Richard Rosenfeld, and Dennis Mares. 2008. "Social Disorganization, Drug Market Activity, and Neighborhood Violent Crime." *Urban Affairs Review* 43:846–74.

Massey, Douglas S., and Nancy A. Denton. 1993. *American Apartheid: Segregation and the Making of the Underclass*. Cambridge, MA: Harvard University Press.

Massey, Douglas S., and Mary Fischer. 2000. "How Segregation Concentrates Poverty." *Ethnic and Racial Studies* 23:670–91.

Mazerolle, Lorraine Green, Colleen Kadleck, and Jan Roehl. 1998. "Controlling Drug and Disorder Problems: The Role of Place Managers." *Criminology* 36:371–403.

McCord, Eric S., and Jerry H. Ratcliffe. 2007. "A Micro-spatial Analysis of the Demographic and Criminogenic Environment of Drug Markets in Philadelphia." *Australian and New Zealand Journal of Criminology* 40:43–63.

Messner, Steven F., Sandro Galea, Kenneth Tardiff, Melissa Tracy, Angela Bucciarelli, Tinka Piper, Victoria Frye, and David Vlahov. 2007. "Policing, Drugs, and the Homicide Decline in New York City in the 1990s." *Criminology* 45:385–413.

Mieczkowski, Tom. 1992. "Crack Dealing on the Street: The Crew System and the Crack House." *Justice Quarterly* 9:151–63.

Muhammad, Khalil Gibran. 2010. *The Condemnation of Blackness: Race, Crime and the Making of Modern Urban America*. Cambridge, MA: Harvard University Press.

Novak, Kenneth J., Jennifer Hartman, Alexander Holsinger, and Michael Turner. 1999. "The Effects of Aggressive Policing of Disorder on Serious Crime." *Policing: An International Journal of Police Strategies and Management* 22:171–90.

Office of National Drug Control Policy. 2004. *The Economic Costs of Drug Abuse in the United States 1992–2002*. Washington, DC: Executive Office of the President.

Office of the Inspector General. 2012. *Audit of the Drug Enforcement Administration's Adoptive Seizure Process and Status of Related Equitable Sharing Requests*. Washington, DC: U.S. Department of Justice.

Ousey, Graham C., and Matthew R. Lee. 2002. "Examining the Conditional Nature of the Illicit Drug Market-homicide Relationship: A Partial Test of the Theory of Contingent Causation." *Criminology* 40:73–102.

——. 2004. "Investigating the Connections between Race, Illicit Drug Markets, and Lethal Violence, 1984–1997." *Journal of Research in Crime and Delinquency* 41:352–83.

Pattillo, Mary E. 1998. "Sweet Mothers and Gangbangers: Managing Crime in a Black Middle-class Neighborhood." *Social Forces* 76:747–74.

Peterson, Ruth D., and Lauren J. Krivo. 2010. *Divergent Social Worlds: Neighborhood Crime and the Racial-Spatial Divide*. New York: Russell Sage Foundation.

Provine, Doris Marie. 2011. "Race and Inequality in the War on Drugs." *Annual Review of Law and Social Science* 7:41–60.

Resignato, Andrew J. 2000. "Violent Crime: A Function of Drug Use or Drug Enforcement?" *Applied Economics* 32:681–88.

Sampson, Robert J., and Dawn J. Bartusch. 1998. "Legal Cynicism and (Subcultural?) Tolerance of Deviance: The Neighborhood Context of Racial Differences." *Law and Society Review* 32:777–804.

Saxe, Leonard, Charles Kadushin, Andrew Beveridge, David Livert, Elizabeth Tighe, David Rindskopf, Julie Ford, and Archie Brodsky. 2001. "The Visibility of Illicit Drugs: Implications for Community-based Drug Control Strategies." *American Journal of Public Health* 91:1987–94.

Schatzman, Morton. 1975. "Cocaine and the 'Drug Problem.'" *Journal of Psychoactive Drugs* 7:7–17.

St. Jean, Peter K. B. 2007. *Pockets of Crime: Broken Windows, Collective Efficacy, and the Criminal Point of View*. Chicago: University of Chicago Press.

Substance Abuse and Mental Health Administration. 2012. *Highlights of the 2010 Drug Abuse Warning Network (DAWN) Findings on Drug-related Emergency Department Visits*. Rockville, MD: Center for Behavioral Health Statistics and Quality.

Taniguchi, Travis A., Jerry H. Ratcliffe, and Ralph B. Taylor. 2011. "Gang Set Space, Drug Markets, and Crime: Violent and Property Crimes Around Drug Corners in Camden." *Journal of Research in Crime and Delinquency* 48:327–63.

Tita, George E., Jacqueline Cohen, and John Engberg. 2005. "An Ecological Study of the Location of Gang 'Set Space.'" *Social Problems* 52:272–99.

Tita, George, and Greg Ridgeway. 2007. "The Impact of Gang Formation on Local Patterns of Crime." *Journal of Research in Crime and Delinquency* 44:208–37.

Uggen, Christopher. 2000. "Work as a Turning Point in the Life Course of Criminals: A Duration Model of Age, Employment, and Recidivism." *American Sociological Review* 65:529–46.

Venkatesh, Sudhir. 2008. *Gang Leader for a Day: A Rogue Sociologist Takes to the Streets*. New York: Penguin Press.

Williams, Edward Huntington. 1914. "Negro Cocaine 'Fiends' are a New Southern Menace." *New York Times* (February 8).

Worrall, John L. 2001. "Addicted to the Drug War: The Role of Civil Asset Forfeiture as a Budgetary Necessity in Contemporary Law Enforcement." *Journal of Criminal Justice* 29:171–87.

Zhu, Li, Dennis M. Gorman, and Scott Horel. 2006. "Hierarchical Bayesian Spatial Models for Alcohol Availability, Drug 'Hot Spots' and Violent Crime." *International Journal of Health Geographics* 5:54–65.

CHAPTER 3

....

THE POLITICS OF POLICING

....

JOHN L. WORRALL

POLICING is as political as any government function—and not necessarily in a pejorative sense. The word "political" can be defined, simply, as "pertaining to, or incidental to, the exercise of the functions vested in those charged with the conduct of government" (Black 1990, 1158). Though "political" often connotes dysfunction, favoritism, and influence, it can also be regarded as an essential element of government. If politics is *incidental* to the functioning of government, then there can be no politics without government. And if politics *pertains* to government, then government and politics are basically the same thing. The same extends to policing. Being a government function, it cannot be—and perhaps should not be—divorced from politics.

What, then, is meant by the "politics of policing?" At the risk of simplification, it is the extent to which the policing function is connected with the multitude of actors involved in the conduct of government. Such actors are found, foremost, in the three main branches of government. Yet insofar as American government is a representative democracy, the activities of those outside the halls of government—concerned citizens, marginalized groups, civic leaders, and others—are also considered political.

From the organization of the first formal department up to the present day, law enforcement has both been shaped by and influenced the American political landscape. Perhaps the simplest example is its position in the executive branch; policing is political because it executes laws enacted by legislatures and interpreted by courts. More controversially, policing is political not just because it occupies a governmental post but because, through dramaturgy, the police posture and perform for the public they serve (e.g., Manning 2001). Image promotion and maintenance are essential for gaining public support, appearing effective, and maintaining self-protection.

Politics and policing have gone hand in hand for more than one hundred years. In the early days of American law enforcement, the "shady" side of politics was realized. Executive political influence was subsequently used to improve policing through professionalism, but that movement backfired to some degree. Pressures for reform soon hailed from *outside* police departments. Disenchanted groups and civic leaders called for fair treatment and improved relations. This movement never completely let up. By the 1970s, the police were besieged on all sides by political pressures from within government and beyond. This trend continued through the 1980s and into the 1990s.

The politics of policing throughout the 1990s and into the twenty-first century have taken a decidedly federal turn. In other words, the federal government, more than local governments, has made the largest imprint on the direction of law enforcement in the United States. Traditional crimes persist and uniquely local problems continue to rear their heads, but terrorism, community policing, and a concern with evidence-based justice have set local agencies on something of a predictable course.

These observations, which are developed more fully in the sections that follow, highlight a number of key points:

- The relationship of politics to policing can be both beneficial and harmful.
- The "shady" side of politics in policing manifests when selfish interests, rather than the common good, are pursued.
- Political influence in policing is a moving target, moving from a local focus in the early days to, more recently, a federal focus.
- As time goes on, the police are confronted with an increasing number of (often conflicting) demands, while being forced to operate with fewer and fewer resources.

This essay begins in Section 3.1 with an examination of the role of politics in policing, including the sources and consequences of political influence. Section 3.2 presents a historical look at the role of politics in policing, organized into four eras: policing in the political era, early reform efforts, the limitations of professionalism, and politics of policing during a time of crisis running through the 1960s and 1970s. In Section 3.3 attention turns to the period from the 1980s to the present, including the era of war on crime, the community-policing era, and the modern era. Section 3.4 speculates about future directions for policing.

3.1 POLITICS IN POLICING

The police, perhaps more than any other government entity, function in a complex political environment. Sources of political influence range from citizens to interest groups, from professional associations to other departments, and from the media to other governmental actors. This array of sometimes competing interests makes law enforcement a difficult, sometimes contradictory, and above all else, political profession. Since this essay's definition of "political" dwells on governmental function, the focus will be primarily on sources of political influence that are governmental in nature. Yet since community sources are also important (Bass 2000), their influence will be touched on from time to time as the need arises.

3.1.1 Sources of Political Influence

Sources of (governmental) political influence in policing can be organized into two categories. One concerns the level at which such influence manifests. The other concerns the person or parties responsible.

America's system of cooperative federalism blurs some of the lines between levels of government. In theory, federal, state, and local governments perform distinct functions, as does law enforcement at each of those levels. In reality, those functions often overlap, are duplicative, and may even work against one another. Local government invariably has the greatest effect on local law enforcement, as most agencies are local in nature (Reaves 2010), but federal and state governments, through the power of the purse, also exert their share of power and control (more on this later).

Notwithstanding the varying degrees of political power across different levels of government, it is also important to consider the degree to which distinct government actors shape the politics of policing. We can organize these officials into their respective branches: executive, legislative, and judicial (Tunnell and Gaines 1996). Depending on the form of local government in a particular jurisdiction, the mayor, city council, or a combination of each is directly influential in policing, such as by choosing the chief (e.g., Mastrofski 1988) or by making police resource decisions (e.g., Stucky 2005). Moving into the legislative arena, officials there typically dole out funds and enact laws that directly influence the form and function of everyday law enforcement. Finally, judicial influence is just as important, as courts serve as checks on policing activities (such as by releasing the wrongfully-arrested) and, at the appellate level and beyond, by issuing decisions that dictate what officers can and cannot do during the course of their daily affairs.

The executive, legislative, and judicial branches of government have made indelible imprints on policing throughout history. At the risk of simplification, a continuum ranging from pure self-interest to pure altruism helps explain this tradition. At the self-interested extreme, early police departments often served at the disposal of political machines whose foremost concerns were to remain in power (e.g., Walker 1998, 60). To some degree these traditions continue, though perhaps not as blatantly as they once did. At the altruistic extreme, some political initiatives have been undertaken with what seems, on the face, a genuine motivation to improve fairness and equal treatment. The results of these initiatives include the scores of U.S. Supreme Court cases dealing with the civil liberties of criminal suspects (e.g., *Tennessee v. Garner*, 471 U.S. 1 [1985]; *Miranda v. Arizona*, 386 U.S. 436 [1966]). The norm, though, is for most "politics" in policing to occupy something of a middle ground between the purely selfish and the purely altruistic. This notion is explained further in the sections that follow.

3.1.2 How Police Agencies Respond to Political Pressure

Two broad theoretical perspectives have been drawn on to explain a wide range of polic-ing phenomena: structural contingency theory and institutional theory (King 2009). According to the former, law enforcement organizations interact with a rational envi-ronment that rewards effectiveness and efficiency: "Administrators exercise control over the organizational environment in which the police operate; they plan strategy in such a way that the environment changes or is modified in response to changes in the allocation of resources, personnel, and equipment" (Manning 1997, 184). Institutional theory *also* posits that organizations interact with an external environment, but it also claims that the environment is not rational and is instead characterized by myth, tradi-tion, symbolism, and the like. In this view, organizations make changes "not as ratio-nal adaptations to their contingencies in the technical-instrumentalities mode, but by reference to normative suasion, imposition, legitimation requirements, myths, beliefs, thought-ways and such non-technical instrumental factors" (Donaldson 1995, 80). In short, both perspectives regard the environment as important, but they part ways when it comes to the mechanisms at work.

According to King (2009), both contingency and institutional perspectives fall short in terms of explaining law enforcement change over the long term. What is needed, he argues, is a life course perspective on police organizations, one that accounts for changes *over time*. This is in contrast to a so-called "life-cycle" approach, which claims that all entities pass through more or less similar stages (e.g., Kimberly 1980). Instead, a life course perspective claims that while key stages in organizational development exist, not all organizations pass through every stage, nor do they do so at the same times. As Whetten (1987, 337) observes, these "'stages' are simply clusters of issues or problems that social systems must resolve, and that the inherent nature of these problems suggest a roughly sequential ordering." King (2009, 221) then applies this line of theorizing to police organizational development over time, calling attention to six stages that agen-cies may or may not encounter at varying points in time: organizational birth and death, early founding effects, growth, decline, and crisis.

While relatively few law enforcement organizations disband or disappear, it is not difficult to agree that they all proceed to varying degrees through the other five stages. The birth of the modern police agency, for example, is itself an interesting avenue of inquiry; police departments burst on the scene at different times and for different rea-sons. Likewise, their formative years were quite distinct from their later years, as char-acterized by the so-called "political era" of policing. And every law enforcement agency has gone through varying periods of growth and decline. As city populations grew in the 1880s, so did their police departments. As budgets have become constrained in recent years, police departments have limited hiring and, in some rare cases, laid off officers in droves. Finally, police departments, like organizations in general, face vary-ing degrees of crisis. It is thus useful to keep this framework in mind, as this essay begins with American law enforcement's formative years and then discusses growth, decline, and crisis over time—with a focus on the political impetus for change at each key turning point.

3.2 POLITICS IN EARLY POLICING

Policing has at all times been politicized, but at no point in history was the seedy underbelly of politics more apparent than in American law enforcement's early days. The period between approximately 1838 and the turn of the twentieth century provides plenty of ammunition to make the case that politics and policing go hand in hand. Of course, the year 1900 was not a magic turning point. Law enforcement remained political and, by some accounts, became even more politicized during throughout the 1900s—and even up to the present. This section of the essay offers a cursory overview of this progression.

3.2.1 Protecting Selfish Interests: 1838–1900

In response to riots, growing disorder, and violence in early American cities, modern law enforcement organizations were formed. Boston created in 1838 what is widely considered the first organized police department in America (Lane 1971). The department failed, though, to break with traditions; it basically placed existing law enforcement institutions (watches, constables) under a single umbrella. Slave patrols had developed some years earlier in the south, but Boston's eight-officer force arguably became the first to perform contemporary policing functions, such as preventive patrol (Walker 1998, 520). A number of other cities around the country promptly emulated the Boston approach.

It was at this early point in American history that officials were wary of politics in policing. People were still nervous about the prospect of overreaching government. There was concern over how to *pay* for organized police forces. Politicians also feared that, once created, police departments could be controlled by their rivals. Many stakeholders chose to rely on their own private security forces, which underscores the concern there was with making police work governmental. Public policing eventually took hold, however, once it was realized that not even the best private security apparatus could curb problems like civic disorder (Schneider 1980).

The London Metropolitan Police, formed in 1829, served as the primary model for American police departments. Yet greater democratization in the states gave rise to a unique brand of domestic law enforcement. Coupled with the right to vote, people had greater control over their local governments than was the case in London (Miller 1977). This, as Walker (1998, 54) observed, "quickly proved to be a mixed blessing for policing." Citizens had considerable control over their police departments, but they often used the police to perform decidedly non-law enforcement functions—and political ones at that.

There was more concern with getting friends jobs and soliciting bribes than control-ling or preventing crime. As August Vollmer noted, this was "an era of incivility, igno-rance, brutality, and graft" (Vollmer and Schneider 1917, 877). The situation was made worse by the facts that police officers were not formally trained, enjoyed little in the way of job security (entire forces were occasionally fired in times of political upheaval), and were often left to their own devices with little supervision due to the lack of communica-tion technology.

The role of politics in policing during the time was in some ways more bottom-up than top-down. This was made evident in von Hoffman's (1992) portrayal of Boston police officer, Stillman S. Wakeman, whose diary revealed details about the "day in the life" of a policeman in 1895. Since his work was relatively unsupervised and because the police presence was spread very thin, Stillman acted more like a "roving local magis-trate" than a police officer as we understand them today. His role was "defined as much from below as above" (322), meaning he did more to serve the interests of citizens in the community than his superiors. This observation was echoed in the remarks of another historian: "Policemen came to reflect the values of those members of the neighborhood with whom they had ongoing social contacts" (Haller 1976, 308). The "politics" of polic-ing were thus more community-oriented in nature during this time than they were con-nected with government.

Tammany Hall, the Democratic Party machine that played a major role in New York City government during the mid-1800s, offers perhaps the best example of the role poli-tics played in early American policing. As was common, election to political office was paid back with promises of employment. Various positions within government, includ-ing police departments, were used to repay supporters. The newly-appointed officers, intent on keeping their jobs, thus focused more on keeping their "bosses" in power. There are many accounts of police officers being assigned to polling stations, influ-encing the vote. They were also involved, with the likes of then-Tammany Hall leader, William M. "Boss" Tweed, in a wide range of corrupt and illegal activities. Some rogue officers profited handsomely from criminal activity. Others used an "iron fist" to control their beats.

If the politics of policing in the early to mid-1800s were characterized by corruption and incompetence, then the tide shifted as the twentieth century drew near. In 1892, Reverend Charles Parkhurst, a prominent religious figure in New York City, described the mayor and his aides as "a lying, perjuring, rum-soaked, and libidinous lot of polluted harpies" (Parkhurst 1970, 5). He was also upset with the police department and used his church as a forum to begin crusading for reform in all aspects of city governance. He and other like-minded reformers galvanized a movement that culminated in 1895 with the appointment of Theodore Roosevelt, who later became a U.S. president, as commis-sioner of the city's police department.

Once Roosevelt took charge, he forced corrupt officers out of the police depart-ment, conducted unannounced inspections, and launched disciplinary proceedings against wayward officers. He resigned in 1897, claiming that the police department had been successfully reformed. In reality, little had changed, but his actions set in motion a chain of events that led to reforms in a number of other police departments around the country. Most such reforms were aimed at transferring control over police departments from local politicians to commissions appointed by state governors or legislators. Unfortunately, this, too, did little to improve policing. As Walker (1998, 65) observed, "commission members had no new ideas about how to manage police departments. They were just as partisan as the mayors and city council members they replaced." Real and substantial improvements were not realized until 1900 and beyond.

In summary, policing between 1838 and 1900 was "political" in every unsavory sense of the term. Law enforcement agencies served at the pleasure of local politicians who, through their own selfish interests, acted in a corrupt fashion, largely indifferent to crime. Ironically, democracy in America was partly responsible for this chain of events. Whereas government in London was nominally democratic, control over its police force was more centralized, thus helping it maintain a greater measure of control. The centralized and admittedly more "democratic" London police model was all but abandoned in early American police departments, breeding the problems just reviewed. Lane (1992, 18) has called this the "central paradox" of modern policing.

Though America's governmental structure has not changed markedly over the years, control over the police became more centralized between the nineteenth century and the present. This is evident in the police professionalism movement and subsequent reforms, to which we now turn.

3.2.2 Signs of Reform: The Early 1900s

Police reforms gained steam in the early 1900s, in concert with other public sector reforms aimed at divorcing politics from administration (e.g., Wilson 1887). A number failed miserably; others were institutionalized and successful. The Philadelphia experience serves as an example of the former. A new mayor, Rudolph Blankenburg, was elected in 1912, in response to frustrations with a corrupt political machine that dominated city politics for years before. He appointed a new police chief, James Robinson, who revised the department's patrol manual, reorganized patrol, ordered new uniforms, implemented exercise programs, emphasize military drills, and the like. But the Blankenburg administration was soon swept out of office, a new chief was appointed, and by most accounts the department returned to its old ways (Walker 1998, 133). Other cities, such as Milwaukee, Chicago, New York City, experienced similar failures.

One lasting reform was the creation of the International Association of Chiefs of Police (IACP). Initially formed as the National Police Chief's Union in 1893, the organization eventually grew and matured in the early twentieth century. Annual meetings offered a forum for law enforcement leaders to debate law enforcement strategy, social policy, and issues of political influence in policing.

At his address to the IACP in 1919, August Vollmer, the first police chief in Berkeley, California, argued that policing should be professionalized and focused on improving society. He further claimed that the police had "far greater obligations than the mere apprehending and prosecution of lawbreakers" (Vollmer 1971). He also called for organizational reforms in policing, increased recruitment standards, and the adoption of modern management techniques, among other changes. Indeed, Vollmer did more than just call for a new style of policing; he implemented many of the same reforms in Berkeley. He became the first police leader of note to hire college graduates. He implemented novel patrol tactics. He was among the first police executives to utilize fingerprinting in criminal investigations. He even took his ideas beyond Berkeley and consulted for a number of other departments around the country, including the LAPD. Finally, he was eventually elected president of the IACP.

If policing in the 1800s served the selfish interests of select politicians (and the officers themselves), Vollmer pushed it in the opposite direction. Policing, in his view, should *serve* the community and perform a loftier function than simply apprehending law-breakers. He argued, again in his address to the IACP, that policing should go "upstream a little further" and work with other institutions (families, schools, etc.) to make communities safer. This signaled a marked shift in the politics of policing.

Vollmer was also one of several individuals who authored the 1929 Illinois Crime Survey, a series of influential reports on the administration of justice in Chicago. He criticized "the corrupt political influence exercised by administrative officials and corrupt politicians" (Illinois Association for Criminal Justice 1929, 359). He was also the lead consultant for the National Commission on Law Observance and Enforcement, also known as the Wickersham Commission, named after its head, George W. Wickersham. The commission, which was appointed by then-President Herbert Hoover to investigate operations of the criminal justice system, once again called attention to excessive political meddling, poor leadership, ineffective recruitment practices, inadequate training, and so on. Its *Lawlessness in Law Enforcement* report found, for example, that "the inflicting of pain, physical or mental, to extract confessions or statements" was commonplace in policing at the time (National Commission on Law Observance and Enforcement 1931, 4).

Vollmer and other like-minded reformers called for a professional model of policing, one that was centralized, oriented toward crime fighting, and above all else, followed the letter of the law. The government function of policing was to be *freed* of as much political influence as possible.

This era also marked the centralization of certain law enforcement functions in Washington, DC. In 1908, Roosevelt created the Bureau of Investigation, which later became the Federal Bureau of Investigation (FBI). Congress was initially opposed to the idea of a national law enforcement organization, but it eventually relented. States also followed suit. Between 1900 and 1915, more than twenty-five states created some version of their own law enforcement agency. These developments were important for the politics of policing.

Race riots in 1919 revealed the failure of certain reforms to take hold. A Chicago police officer's failure to arrest white assailants prompted a four-day race riot. The mayor eventually had to call in the militia to quell the violence. Similar incidents erupted in Omaha,

Knoxville, and Washington, DC. As Walker (1998, 149) observed, "The Chicago police were guilty of blatant race discrimination, often standing by as whites attacked African Americans." Rioting died down, but race relations remained strained. It would not be until 1949 that an African American was promoted to the rank of sergeant in that city (Dulaney 1996, 21–22). Political pressures police faced during this time thus emanated from outside the halls of government.

In the same year as the Chicago race riots, officers in Boston went on strike. Their decision to walk out on the job was prompted in part by stagnant pay and rampant war-time inflation. Crime promptly surged, but the governor called in the militia and the strike ended within five days. A police union was formed, but it was soon disbanded. Grievances between administrators and the rank and file festered for decades and unions eventually took a stronger foothold in the 1960s.

Yet another development occurring at around the same time was the increased power and presence of J. Edgar Hoover's Federal Bureau of Investigation. Partly in response to President Roosevelt's call for "immediate suppression" of crime, a series of federal laws were enacted that expanded the organization's jurisdiction. Moreover, Hoover took professionalism to another level, promoting an image of his agents as highly educated and trained crime fighters. He highlighted contrasts between them and local officers, partly by winning over Hollywood screenwriters who made a number of movies glorifying the FBI's exploits, including *G-Men, Public Hero No. 1,* and *Show Them No Mercy.*

Hoover's aggressive public relations campaign hid other shadier activities occurring within the agency. He was authoritarian and often capricious in his personnel decisions. He also became obsessed with spying on prominent U.S. citizens, including alleged Communists. These practices turned back the clock in some respects, making the FBI resemble nineteenth-century police agencies intent on meddling in political affairs. Recall that Congress initially rejected the idea of an FBI-like federal law enforcement agency. Its chief concern was that such an agency would become overly politicized, as it most definitely had become.

3.2.3 The Limitations of Professionalism: Approaching the 1960s

The police professionalism movement made great strides, but its limitations were quickly revealed. Community relationships with the police remained strained. Additional race riots broke out in a number of big cities as police turned a blind eye to unequal treatment. For example, in 1943, police in Los Angeles stood by while white sailors and marines assaulted a number of Mexican American men. The resulting "Zoot Suit" riot lasted for more than seven days. More serious riots erupted in New York City and Detroit. The riots began as small inter-race altercations coupled with little or no police intervention.

In contrast to their reactions to the 1919 race riots, officials this time around felt there was a definite need to improve race relations, particularly between minorities and the police. This ushered in a police-community relations movement, but it took considerable time before much progress was made.

Meanwhile, the limits of Vollmer's professional model were being revealed in other ways. His protégé, O. W. Wilson, picked up where Vollmer left off, first as police chief in Wichita, Kansas, where he resigned after facing resistance to reform, and eventually as superintendent in the Chicago Police Department, where the managerial style he adopted did little to please minority communities. In the interim, he became a professor of police administration at the University of California and authored his popular 1950 text, *Police Administration*. He also argued for the allocation of patrol according to calls for service, encouraged one-officer instead of two-officer patrols, and otherwise continued his mentor's tradition of improving policing through professionalism. But he also continued to encounter resistance to his ideas.

Among the most resistant to Wilson was LAPD chief William Parker, who was appointed in 1950. He adopted a Hoover-like authoritarian leadership style in that agency. He cleaned up the corrupt department but also adopted an aggressive crime-fighting stance, which as Walker (1998, 174) notes, "left him utterly insensitive to race relations problems." Brutality persisted and police-community relations remained strained. The same occurred in most other large law enforcement agencies around the country. It soon became apparent that the chief political issue in policing was not the preferred managerial strategy, but the need to turn attention outward and improve relationships with minority communities.

3.2.4 Crisis Mode: The 1960s and 1970s

Criminal justice entered crisis mode during the 1960s and 1970s (Uchida 2010, 29). Race relations were at an all time low. Crime increased at a dramatic rate, doubling from 1960 to 1970. Anti-war sentiments prevailed. Riots once again erupted. Police were, in a sense, victims of their own creation. The emphasis on crime fighting prompted people to blame the police for rising crime. When it was apparent there was only so much they could do, their image was tarnished all the more. And the civil rights movement did not help matters for the police, as they became visible symbols of a government that failed to treat people fairly.

In response to a surge in rioting, President Lyndon Johnson appointed the National Advisory Commission on Civil Disorders, also dubbed the Kerner Commission. It identified institutional racism as a driving force behind rioting and resistance. It also found a number of problems in police departments around the country, including brutality, abuse of power, corruption, inadequate supervision, poor police-community relations, and inadequate minority representation in America's police departments. President Johnson then created the President's Commission on Law Enforcement and the Administration of Justice (to further study problems in the criminal justice system) and Congress authorized federal assistance for local criminal justice agencies, first with the Office of Law Enforcement Assistance (1965–1968) and later with the Law Enforcement

Assistance Administration (LEAA). Both efforts solidified the government's resolve to improve policing and improve strained relations with minority groups. The limits of a "professional" crime-fighting model were revealed and a new set of reforms was ushered in.

Up until the 1960s, the politics of policing were decidedly confined to executive branch politics. In the pre-1900 period, the chief problem in policing was the "cozy" relationships police departments enjoyed with local mayors and political machines. The professional movement sought to centralize policing and internalize reforms, which strained the relationship between subordinates and superiors. Though to some extent the legislative branch was brought to the table in the context of early crime commissions, its role in American policing was relatively marginal up until its creation of the Law Enforcement Assistance Administration and eventually the LEAA. The judiciary, too, remained relatively quiet until the 1960s, but this changed when the U.S. Supreme Court issued a number of key civil rights decisions, many of which had critical implications for American criminal justice—and especially policing.

Two key cases, *Mapp v. Ohio* (367 U.S. 643 [1961]) and *Miranda v. Arizona* (384 U.S. 436 [1966]), made indelible imprints on American law enforcement. *Mapp* for the first time mandated that evidence obtained in violation of the Constitution be inadmissible in court to prove guilt. *Miranda* required police to advise suspects of the Fifth Amendment privilege against compelled self-incrimination. These and other influential decisions forced police departments to improve their training and revise policy manuals. The Supreme Court, rather than police reformers, made perhaps the clearest case that law enforcement officials should be held to the highest standards of professionalism and equal treatment. The Supreme Court continues to this day to issue important criminal justice-related decisions, which keeps law enforcement on its toes. The Court's civil rights decisions also signaled an increasing concern with police accountability, which carries over to the present day as well.

The police reacted to these developments by a number of means. First, they rekindled the union movement. Many were tired of having become a lightning rod for criticism. They also felt that the Supreme Court decisions hampered their abilities to fight crime; key civil rights decisions were roundly criticized in a number of popular outlets (e.g., Cipes 1966; Wilson 1966). Moreover, their salaries and benefits also continued to fall short of those in related occupations (President's Commission on Law Enforcement and Administration of Justice 1967). By the 1970s, many large-city police departments were working under collective bargaining agreements (Juris and Feuille 1973). This afforded police officers a greater "say" in law enforcement administration, extended to them due process protections during disciplinary proceedings, and eventually improved salaries and benefits. Against this backdrop, minority officers also began to assert themselves, forming their own interest groups, among them the Afro-American Patrolmen's League in Chicago (Dulaney 1996). Women also made great strides during this period. In 1968, Betty Blankenship and Elizabeth Coffal became the first two female officers assigned to patrol duty (Schulz 1995, 126). In short, officers themselves became a formidable force in the politics of American policing.

3.3 POLITICS FROM THE 1980S TO THE PRESENT

Not only did the politics of policing retain a multidimensional character going into the 1980s, but the problems the police were called on to address continued to increase. Drugs, domestic violence, and disorder become top priorities. This period began with a "tough on crime" era, followed by the ushering in of community policing, and it continues to evolve in the wake of 9/11.

3.3.1 Tough on Crime: The 1980s

As crime continued to rise throughout the 1970s, America embarked on an aggressive "get tough" mission. Prison populations quadrupled in two decades (e.g., Mauer 1992). Reagan's election in 1980 also led to an increase in Republican-appointed justices on the U.S. Supreme Court, which later issued a number of pro-law enforcement decision, fueling the get-tough mentality. For example, the 1984 *United States v. Leon* (468 U.S. 897 [1984]) decision created the so-called "good faith" exception to the exclusionary rule, making it easier for evidence that was unconstitutionally but mistakenly seized to be admitted in court. Preventive detention, the practice of denying bail to high-risk defendants, not only gained popularity, but was sanctioned by the Supreme Court in *United States v. Salerno* (481 U.S. 739 [1987]).

Liberal critics were frustrated with the new hard-line stance on crime, but they were soon drowned out in a veritable cacophony of frustration over the rising drug problem. Crack cocaine burst on the scene in the mid-1980s, presenting new challenges for the police. Law enforcement initiated scores of crackdowns, many of which while initially effective did not yield lasting results. As Walker (1998, 229) observed, these "were mainly exercises in public relations, designed to convince the media and the general public that the police were 'doing something' about drugs and gangs." The nation's first "drug czar" was appointed and called upon to coordinate the national and international response to illicit drugs (Trebach 1987). In 1989, then-President Bush formally announced a "war" on drugs. His approach consisted of everything from stepped-up local law enforcement to cooperative agreements with other nations. Tougher sentencing laws were enacted, and anti-drug publicity campaigns were launched and became visible symbols of an aggressive anti-drug mentality.

On one hand, the police were forced in the 1980s to take an aggressive stance with respect to drugs. On the other, they were also called upon to educate the public and, ideally, dissuade people from trying drugs in the first place. Drug Abuse Resistance Education (DARE) began in Los Angeles and quickly spread around the country. Though researchers were unable to show the program worked, it at least cast law enforcement in a favorable light and made inroads in the public relations arena (Worrall 2008a, 289–90).

The drug war, coupled with a get-tough stance on crimes, did not make a significant dent in the crime problem, nor did it do much to improve the police's image. The number of police shootings grew substantially between the 1960s and the 1980s (Fyfe 1982; Geller and Scott 1992). Moreover, African Americans were shot at a seven-to-one rate over whites (Geller and Scott 1992, 503). Symptomatic of this problem was the Supreme Court's decision in *Tennessee v. Garner* (471 U.S. 1 [1985]), which for the first time enacted strict limitations on police use of deadly force; it would be a Fourth Amendment violation to shoot an unarmed fleeing felon, absent an imminent threat to others. Allegations of police brutality again surfaced, leading to a surge in citizen complaints and eventual improvements in citizen complaint review procedures (Walker and Wright 1995).

The police were also called upon during the 1980s to tackle the ever-sensitive issue of domestic violence. Prompted in part by lawsuits filed on behalf of female victims against the police, mandatory arrest policies took hold. Women's groups, such as Sally Cooper's National Assault Prevention Center, the New York State Coalition Against Sexual Assault, and the New York Asian Women's Center, also called attention to the failure of police to routinely arrest perpetrators and prosecutors to move forward with criminal charges. A popular Police Foundation study (Sherman and Berk 1984) found that repeat domestic violence was deterred if the defendant was arrested rather than counseled or simply released. The study encouraged a number of other jurisdictions to enact their own mandatory arrest laws. Subsequent studies cast doubt on the utility of mandatory arrest (Sherman 1992), which then prompted a retreat from the approach, but important for this essay's purpose is the political tone to the whole process; police found themselves forced into a particular course of action (stripped of their discretion, in essence), partly because of litigation in the courts and partly because of vocal (mostly female) critics of their actions.

As all this was occurring, the seeds of a community-oriented policing movement were being sown. Public relations damage from the war on crime forced police to adopt a more customer-friendly approach. Strained race relations, a familiar refrain in American law enforcement, also prompted police to go out into neighborhoods and attempt to regain the support of disenfranchised groups. A growing awareness of the failed wars on crime and drugs also called for a new set of strategies. Finally, critics of centralized law enforcement management called for giving line-level officers more authority to make important decisions, thereby improving their abilities to fight crime—and even their morale (e.g., Angell 1971; Kelling 1996).

To sum up, law enforcement agencies the 1980s was not unlike small boats being tossed around in rough seas. A range of external pressures, stemming from federal influence in the drug war to disgruntled citizens calling for improved responsiveness, made for a volatile mix of multiple responsibilities. Such was also characteristic of policing in the 1970s, and, indeed, the problem persists: As Manning (1978, 100) put it, "The police in modern society are in agreement with their audiences—which include their professional interpreters, the American family, criminals and politicians—in at least one respect: they have an 'impossible' task."

3.3.2 Community Policing Takes Hold: The 1990s

Community policing came of age during the 1990s, particularly with the establishment of the Office of Community-Oriented Policing Services (COPS Office) in the U.S. Justice Department, as part of the 1994 Violent Crime Control and Law Enforcement Act. Since its inception, the COPS Office has granted over $11 billion to local police departments around the country to promote community policing strategies. The bulk of that spending occurred between 1995 and 2000, with some $8.8 billion in grants (Government Accountability Office 2005).

Prior to the creation of the COPS program, community policing gained something of a philosophical foothold around the United States. Many agencies espoused the ideals of a citizen-oriented, customer service-based approach to policing, but actual changes to administrative structures (true decentralization, for example) were minimal (e.g., Maguire 1997). The COPS program, by infusing funding into the community policing movement, took perhaps the most significant step toward solidifying reform. For departments to receive money under the Universal Hiring Program (the largest of the COPS funding streams), it was necessary for them to demonstrate precisely how community policing functions would be performed. This was perhaps the most significant step by the federal government to shape local law enforcement. For comparison's sake, the LEAA's enabling legislation called for $7 million in appropriations. Even adjusted for inflation, COPS funding dwarfed that of the LEAA.

The COPS program funded local agencies through a number of other competitive and formula grant programs, including Making Officer Redeployment Effective (MORE), Accelerated Hiring, Education, and Deployment; Funding Accelerated for Smaller Towns, the Youth Firearms Violence Initiative; the Anti-Gang Initiative; and others. It also spawned a number of federal funding initiatives during the 1990s, include the Local Enforcement Block Grant (LLEBG) program (e.g., Bauer 2004) and Operation Weed and Seed (Dunworth and Mills 1999).

Whether these programs, particularly COPS, altered the face of policing is not entirely clear. Structural changes to local law enforcement agencies since the heyday of the COPS program have not been explored. A number of studies have examined the effects of these programs on crime (e.g., Dunworth and Mills 1999; Evans and Owens 2007; Worrall and Kovandzic 2008; Worrall 2008b; Zhao, Scheider, and Thurman 2002), but the jury is still out. The point, however, is that the politics of policing became decidedly community-oriented in the 1990s, not just out of some noble effort to improve police relations, but because there was considerable funding available for doing so.

At the same time community policing was in full swing, a seemingly contradictory movement (but see Peak and Barthe 2009) was afoot. CompStat (short, usually, for Computer Statistics) imported a private business-based managerial model into policing, one that emphasized, among other things, strict accountability for top administrators; those who failed to bring crime down in their respective domains of control would, on some occasions, be demoted or possibly even fired. Not all versions of CompStat necessarily put top-level administrators' jobs on the line, but most fit within a frame-work of performance-based management, reliance on clear goals and objectives, thoughtful and thorough crime analysis, and implementation of problem-solving strat-egies (Dabney 2010, 29).

The CompStat approach to law enforcement management seems at least partially at odds with the more outward-looking nature of community policing. If it is not fully at odds with community policing, it can at least operate independently of it (Mastrofski, Willis, and Kochel 2010).

What makes CompStat interesting from a politics of policing standpoint is its origins. Whereas community policing, as manifested in the COPS Program, emanated from Washington, DC, under the Clinton Administration, CompStat began in New York City with William Bratton as commissioner of the NYPD (Silverman 1999) and then spread interdepartmentally across the United States as word was spread of New York's precipi-tous drop in violent crime during the 1990s (e.g., Bratton 1997). By 1999, hundreds of police departments around the country reported adherence to at least some CompStat principles (Weisburd et al. 2003).

3.3.3 Policing in the Modern Era: The Early 21st Century

An evidence-based justice movement was set in motion with the University of Maryland's *Preventing Crime* report, published in 1997 (Sherman et al. 1997). Commissioned by the National Institute of Justice, the report categorized crime preven-tion strategies by whether they "worked," did not work, or remained unclear in terms of their effectiveness. Its intent was to inform practitioners of effective crime prevention and crime control strategies so they could put them in place rather than take shots in the dark. It was also intended to prompt additional research into the so-called "promising" strategies that lacked sufficient evidence.

Books devoted to all aspects of evidence-based criminal justice were published soon thereafter (Wilson and Petersilia 2002; Sherman et al. 2002). The Campbell Collaboration, the University of Colorado's Blueprints program, and other efforts were also launched to identify effective strategies for combating crime. The evidence-based justice movement remains in full swing, particularly with the recently-activated crime-solutions.gov website, "intended to be a central, reliable, and credible resource to help practitioners and policy makers understand what works in justice-related programs and practices" (Office of Justice Programs 2011).

September 11, 2001 then ushered in one of the more dramatic structural changes in American law enforcement. The most marked changes occurred at the federal level, with the creation of the Department of Homeland Security. Federal agencies that moved to the new cabinet-level agency included the Secret Service, Customs and Border Protection (formerly the U.S. Customs Service), and Immigration and Customs Enforcement (formerly the Immigration and Naturalization Service). The missions of other fed-eral agencies, including most notably that of the Federal Bureau of Investigation, also changed considerably, making the prevention of additional terrorist acts a top national priority. Most state and local law enforcement agencies also made similar changes, prioritizing antiterrorism. On some levels, the war on terror is at odds with the more community-oriented strategies adopted throughout the 1980s and 1990s, but researchers have found that the two are not fundamentally at odds with one another (e.g., Lee 2010).

Clearly a hallmark of this period is the weight of federal influence in local law enforcement. This is not to suggest, however, that federal priorities have dramatically altered the *structure* of local law enforcement agencies. Evidence suggests that political culture is only weakly linked to such organizational characteristics as centralization, formalization, and occupational differentiation (Zhao, Ren, and Lovrich 2010), but law enforcement priorities have nonetheless been significantly shaped by what the federal government feels is important.

3.4 MOVING FORWARD

Where law enforcement in the United States is headed is anyone's guess, but three priorities will likely remain front and center. One is of course the fiscal constraints that continue to grip governments across the country. Law enforcement agencies will need to continue to protect themselves and creatively cope with budgetary shortfalls. Some creative initiatives, such as asset forfeiture, have become more common in recent years, but they are not without a measure of public relations fallout; any impressions that policing is for profit are bane for policing agencies that continually struggle to gain public support.

Moving forward, agencies will also need to build additional collaborative relationships. The war on terror has made this abundantly clear, but crime prevention in general cannot occur as intended without some measure of cooperation between agencies across jurisdictions and between levels of government. Relating to both this and fiscal constraints is the inevitable mainstreaming of evidence-based policing—and criminal justice in general. More than ever before, law enforcement agencies will need to work together to implement effective crime prevention and control strategies. Remaining political barriers will need to be broken down. And to the extent that occurs, law enforcement may soon adhere to a more or less single set of principles and priorities. If taken to the extreme, police agencies across the United States may, in some respects, resemble a single national-level force.

REFERENCES

Angell, John E. 1971. "Toward an Alternative to the Classic Police Organizational Arrangements: A Democratic Model." *Criminology* 9:185–206.

Bass, Sandra. 2000. "Negotiating Change: Community Organizations and the Politics of Policing." *Urban Affairs Review* 36:148–77.

Bauer, Lynn. 2004. *Local Law Enforcement Block Grant Program, 1996–2004*. Washington, DC: U.S. Department of Justice, Office of Justice Programs.

Black, Henry Campbell. 1990. *Black's Law Dictionary*, 6th ed. St. Paul, MN: West.

Bratton, William J. 1997. "Crime is Down in New York City: Blame the Police." In *Zero Tolerance Policing in a Free Society*, edited by Norman Dennis, 29–43. London: IEA Health and Welfare Unit.

Cipes, Robert. 1966. "Crime, Confessions, and the Court." *The Atlantic* 218:51–58.

Dabney, Dean. 2010. "Observations Regarding Key Operational Realities in a CompStat Model of Policing." *Justice Quarterly* 27:28–51.

Donaldson, Lex. 1995. *American Anti-Management Theories of Organization: A Critique of Paradigm Proliferation*. Cambridge, UK: Cambridge University Press.

Dulaney, W. Marvin. 1996. *Black Police in America*. Bloomington, IN: University of Indiana Press.

Dunworth, Terence, and Gregory Mills. 1999. *National Evaluation of Weed and Seed*, Research in Brief. Washington, DC: U.S. Department of Justice, National Institute of Justice.

Evans, William M., and Emily Owens. 2007. "COPS and Crime." *Journal of Public Economics* 91:181–201.

Fyfe, James J. 1982. "Blind Justice: Police Shootings in Memphis." *Journal of Criminal Law and Criminology* 73:707–22.

Geller, William A., and Michael S. Scott., eds. 1992. *Deadly Force: What We Know*. Washington, DC: Police Executive Research Forum.

Government Accountability Office. 2005. *Community Policing Grants: COPS Grants Were a Modest Contributor to Declines in Crime in the 1990s* (Report GAO-06-104). Washington, DC: Government Accountability Office.

Haller, Mark. 1976. "Historical Roots of Police Behavior: Chicago, 1890–1925." *Law and Society Review* 10:303–23.

Illinois Association for Criminal Justice. 1929, repr. 1968. *Illinois Crime Survey*. Montclair, NJ: Patterson Smith.

Juris, Hervey A., and Peter Feuille. 1973. *Police Unionism*. Lexington, MA: Lexington Books.

Kelling, George L. 1996. "Police and Communities: The Quiet Revolution." In *Criminal Justice in America: Theory, Practice, and Policy*, edited by Barry W. Hancock and Paul M. Sharp, 134–144. Upper Saddle River, NJ: Prentice Hall.

Kimberly, John R. 1980. "The Life Cycle Analogy and the Study of Organizations: Introduction." In *The Organizational Life Cycle: Issues in the Creation, Transformation, and Decline of Organizations*, edited by John R. Kennedy, Robert H. Miles, and Associates, 1–17. San Francisco, CA: Jossey-Bass.

King, William R. 2009. "Toward a Life-Course Perspective of Police Organizations." *Journal of Research in Crime and Delinquency* 46:213–44.

Lane, Roger. 1971. *Policing the City: Boston, 1822–1885*. New York: Atheneum.

——. 1992. "Urban Police and Crime in Nineteenth-Century America." In *Crime and Justice: An Annual Review of Research*, vol. 15, edited by Michael Tonry and Norval Morris, 1–50. Chicago: University of Chicago Press.

Lee, Jason. 2010. "Policing After 9/11: Community Policing in an Age of Homeland Security." *Police Quarterly* 13:347–66.

Maguire, Edward R. 1997. "Structural Changes in Large Municipal Police Organizations during the Community-Policing Era." *Justice Quarterly* 14:547–76.

Manning, Peter K. 1997. *Police Work: The Social Organization of Policing*. Prospect Heights, IL: Waveland.

———. 2001. "Theorizing Policing: The Drama and Myth of Crime Control in the NYPD." *Theoretical Criminology* 5:315–44.

———. 1978, repr. 1999. "The Police: Mandate, Strategy, and Appearances." In *The Police and Society: Touchstone Readings,* 2d ed., edited by Victor E. Kappeler, 94–122. Prospect Heights, IL: Waveland.

Mastrofski, Stephen D. 1988. "Varieties of Police Governance in Metropolitan Areas." *Politics and Policy* 8:12–31.

Mastrofski, Stephen D., James J. Willis, and Tammy Rinehart Kochel. 2010. "Co-Implementation of CompStat and Community Policing." *Journal of Criminal Justice* 38:969–80.

Mauer, Marc. 1992. *Americans Behind Bars: One Year Later.* Washington, DC: Sentencing Project.

Miller, Wilbur. 1977. *Cops and Bobbies: Police Authority in New York and London, 1830–1870.* Chicago: University of Chicago Press.

National Commission on Law Observance and Enforcement. 1931. repr. 1968. *Report on Lawlessness in Law Enforcement.* Montclair, NJ: Patterson Smith.

Office of Justice Programs. 2011. *About CrimeSolutions.gov.* Washington, DC: U.S. Department of Justice. Accessed September 20, 2011. http://www.crimesolutions.gov/about.aspx.

Parkhurst, Charles H. (1895; reprint ed.) 1970. *Our Fight With Tammany.* New York: Arno Press.

Peak, Ken, and Emmanuel P. Barthe. 2009. "Community Policing and CompStat: Merged or Mutually Exclusive?" *Police Chief* 76:72–84.

President's Commission on Law Enforcement and Administration of Justice. 1967. *Task Force Report: The Police.* Washington, DC: Government Printing Office.

Reaves, Brian A. 2010. *Local Law Enforcement, 2007.* Washington, DC: Bureau of Justice Statistics.

Schneider, John C. 1980. *Detroit and the Problem of Order, 1830–1880.* Lincoln, NE: University of Nebraska Press.

Schulz, Dorothy Moses. 1995. *From Social Worker to Crimefighter: Women in United States Municipal Policing.* Westport, CT: Praeger.

Sherman, Lawrence W. 1992. *Policing Domestic Violence.* New York: Free Press.

Sherman, Lawrence W., and Richard A. Berk. 1984. *The Minneapolis Domestic Violence Experiment.* Washington, DC: Police Foundation.

Sherman, Lawrence W., Denise Gottfredson, Doris MacKenzie, John Eck, Peter Reuter, and Shawn Bushway. 1997. *Preventing Crime: What Works, What Doesn't, What's Promising.* Washington, DC: U.S. Department of Justice, National Institute of Justice.

Sherman, Lawrence W., David P. Farrington, Brandon C. Welsh, and Doris L. MacKenzie. 2002. *Evidence-Based Crime Prevention.* New York: Routledge.

Silverman, Eli B. 1999. *NYPD Battles Crime: Innovative Strategies in Policing.* Boston: Northeastern University Press.

Stucky, Thomas D. 2005. "Local Politics and Police Strength." *Justice Quarterly* 22:139–69.

Trebach, Arnold S. 1987. *The Great Drug War.* New York: Macmillan.

Tunnell, Kenneth D., and Larry K. Gaines. 1996. "Political Pressures and Influences on Police Executives." In *Managing Police Organizations,* edited by Gary Cordner and Dennis Kenney, 5–18. Cincinnati: Anderson.

Uchida, Craig D. 2010. "The Development of the American Police: An Historical Overview." In *Critical Issues in Policing: Contemporary Readings,* 6th ed., edited by Roger G. Dunham and Geoffrey P. Alpert, 14–30. Long Grove, IL: Waveland.

Vollmer, August. 1971. "Predelinquency." In *Proceedings*, 1919, ed., International Association of Chiefs of Police, 77–80. New York: Arno Press.

Vollmer, August, and Albert Schneider. 1971. "School for Police as Planned at Berkeley," *Journal of Criminal Law and Criminology* 7:877–98.

von Hoffman, Alexander. 1992. "An Officer of the Neighborhood: A Boston Patrolman on the Beat in 1895." *Journal of Social History* 26:309–30.

Walker, Samuel. 1998. *Popular Justice: A History of American Criminal Justice*, 2d ed. New York: Oxford University Press.

Walker, Samuel, and Betsy Wright. 1995. *Citizen Review of the Police, 1994: A National Survey*. Washington, DC: Police Executive Research Forum.

Weisburd, David, Stephen D. Mastrofski, A.M. McNalley, Rosann Greenspan, and James J. Willis. 2003. "CompStat and Organizational Change: Findings from a National Survey." *Criminology and Public Policy* 2:421–56.

Whetten, David. A. 1987. "Organizational Growth and Decline Processes." *Annual Review of Sociology* 13:335–58.

Wilson, James Q., and Joan Petersilia. 2002. *Public Policies for Crime Control*. Oakland, CA: Institute for Contemporary Studies.

Wilson, O. W. 1966. "Crime, the Courts, and the Police." *The Journal of Criminal Law, Criminology, and Police Science* 57:291–300.

Wilson, Woodrow. 1887. "The Study of Administration." *Political Science Quarterly* 2:197–222.

Worrall, John L. 2008a. *Crime Control in America: What Works?* 2d ed. Boston: Allyn and Bacon.

Worrall, John L. 2008b. "The Effects of Local Law Enforcement Block Grants on Serious Crime." *Criminology and Public Policy* 7:325–50.

Worrall, John L., and Tomislav V. Kovandzic. 2008. "COPS Grants and Crime Revisited." *Criminology* 45:159–90.

Zhao, Jihong, Ling Ren, and Nicholas Lovrich. 2010. "Wilsons' Theory of Local Political Culture Revisited in Today's Police Organizations." *Policing: An International Journal of Police Strategies and Management* 33:287–304.

Zhao, Jihong, Matthew C. Schneider, and Quint C. Thurman. 2002. "Funding Community Policing to Reduce Crime: Have COPS Grants Made a Difference?" *Criminology and Public Policy* 2:7–32.

CHAPTER 4

POLICE ORGANIZATIONS AND THE IRON CAGE OF RATIONALITY

EDWARD R. MAGUIRE*

POLICING varies. Police scholarship examines variations in policing at multiple levels. For instance, there is substantial variation between individual police officers—in their demographics, their levels of experience, their assignments, their predispositions, and their behaviors—and a long line of scholarship has explored the nature and effects of these variations. Similarly, encounters between police and citizens are fundamentally important and, in the aggregate, shape the character of policing as experienced by citizens. A rich tradition of scholarship has examined variations in the nature of these encounters. Much of the research on criminal investigations concentrates at the case level, typically seeking to determine what factors influence whether cases are resolved successfully. Another long line of scholarship has focused on police organizations as a unit of analysis. The modal type of research in this genre focuses on variations between police organizations, either seeking to explain why these variations exist or whether they influence agency behavior or performance.

This essay examines police organizations from an alternative perspective. It views police agencies through the lens of classic literature from the sociology of organizations and focuses on some of the ways in which they are becoming more alike over time. It also asks an important normative question: Are these changes in police organizations desirable?

From the industrial revolution to the digital revolution, the idea that organizations can be impersonal or dehumanizing has been a common theme in popular culture. The eminent German sociologist Max Weber (1864–1920) once wrote that modern life was beginning to resemble an "iron cage" as a result of society's growing quest for rationalization and bureaucratic efficiency. The iron cage is a metaphor for the anonymity and despair felt by workers and consumers in an increasingly capitalist, bureaucratized, technocratic, and impersonal world. The metaphor of the iron cage is often invoked in analyses of organizations, particularly larger organizations with more highly elaborated structures. The metaphor has also been invoked by some analysts seeking to understand the nature of police organizations (e.g., Maguire and King 2004, 2007; Manning 2008; Heslop 2011). This essay examines theory and research on whether the notion of the iron cage is a useful or accurate way of thinking about modern police organizations.[1]

Police agencies are experiencing slow, deliberate changes on a number of important dimensions that are likely to alter the character of policing over time. This essay examines four types of changes. First, police agencies are becoming larger, both in absolute terms and relative to the size of the populations they serve. Second, police agencies are adopting more mechanistic and inflexible structures. Third, police agencies are becoming more dependent on technology. Fourth, police agencies are becoming more militarized. These are not small changes. Together, they foretell a fundamental and profound shift in the character of policing. Though some of these changes are occurring slowly, it is vital to consider how they might alter the future of policing.

This essay is organized into six main sections. Section 4.1 provides a review of the iron cage metaphor, from its inception in Weber's work to its application and extension in organization theory and policing. Section 4.2 examines changes in the size of police organizations. Section 4.3 explores changes in the formal structures of police organizations. Section 4.4 discusses the role of information technologies in police organizations. Section 4.5 examines changes in the militarization of policing. Section 4.6 ties together the earlier sections by discussing the importance of these various themes for the nature and character of policing. One key theme running throughout the essay is an emphasis on whether the police research industry—the world in which I work—currently has sufficient capacity to detect, measure, track, and reflect on these glacial but potentially profound changes in the social organization of policing.

This essay draws a number of conclusions:

- Although contingency theory predicts that organizations will act in rational ways, sometimes police departments, like other types of organizations, act in irrational ways.
- Police organizations are shaped to some extent by concerns with performance, efficiency and goals, but other social forces also appear to play an important role.
- An emerging line of scholarship applies institutional theory to police organizations. This theory, which that organizations act partly out of the need to preserve and enhance legitimacy, helps explain the profusion of special units in police agencies—even if workloads do not support the need such units.
- Since 1990, police agencies across the United States have increased in both absolute numbers, as well as per capita; and this growth is not readily explained by rational choice or contingency theories.
- Growth has likely occurred in response to police departments attempting to maintain their legitimacy and respond to public demands. This has likely led them to become more technologically proficient and para-militaristic over time.
- It is unclear if the evolving focus on IT and para-militarization will ultimately dehumanize police organizations, much in the tradition of Weber's "iron cage" of rationality.

4.1 RATIONALITY, BUREAUCRACY, AND THE IRON CAGE

Weber has often been called one of the founding fathers of modern sociology and social science more generally. Though Weber made scholarly contributions in many areas of social inquiry, he is perhaps best known for his thinking about organizations. His work on bureaucracy and authority is widely considered foundational in organizational theory. Though much of Weber's work examines organizations, bureaucratization, and the nature of authority within society, his arguments about the iron cage of rationality first appeared in his 1904 essay, *The Protestant Ethic and the Spirit of Capitalism* (Weber 1904/1930). Weber wrote in German; therefore the English language world must rely on translations of his work.[2]

Weber was a sociologist of grand scope and vision, taking on the massive social changes that occurred as a result of Protestant asceticism and the growth of capitalism in western civilization. These changes included an inexorable drive toward bureaucratic rationality and efficiency, which Weber viewed as impersonal and dehumanizing. The iron cage metaphor focuses on bureaucratization and rationalism as fundamental and potentially harmful aspects of modern life. Under capitalism, modern people are driven by a need to achieve economic autonomy. Capitalism leads to the development of complex organizations with an ever increasing focus on rationality, technical superiority, and efficiency. The rigidity and impersonality of these complex organizations can imprison people in an iron cage of rationality and thus serve as potent symbols of the dark side of modernization. According to Weber:

> This passion for bureaucracy... is enough to drive one to despair. It is as if in politics... we were deliberately to become men who need "order" and nothing but order, who become nervous and cowardly if for one moment this order wavers, and helpless if they are torn away from their total incorporation in it. That the world should know no men but these: it is in such an evolution that we are already caught up, and the great question is therefore not how we can promote and hasten it, but what can we oppose to this machinery in order to keep a portion of mankind free from this parceling-out of the soul, from this supreme mastery of the bureaucratic way of life. (Weber 1909/1944, 127–128)

At the same time, Weber viewed bureaucracies as better than alternative organizational forms. One of his most widely cited contributions was his articulation of the nature and sources of authority in society. Authority is a means by which one person or institution gains the voluntary compliance of another. Weber (1947) argued that authority derives from three principal sources. Charismatic authority derives from the personal attributes of extraordinary leaders able to generate loyalty through their virtuosity, heroism, vision, religious inspiration, or ability to connect with people. Charismatic leaders—some wicked and some benevolent—are evident throughout history, from Adolph

Hitler and Mao Zedong to Mahatma Gandhi and Martin Luther King, Jr. Some organizations have charismatic leaders whose personal attributes inspire others to view them as a source of authority. Traditional authority, commonly seen in families, churches, and premodern societies, is woven into culture and social mores. Traditional authority is vested in elders, parents, priests, tribal chiefs, and others who, by virtue of history and tradition, occupy positions worthy of trust and compliance. Rational-legal authority is based on codified, impersonal, rational rules that are enacted by law or established by contract. It is the principal source of authority in modern society and in bureaucracies such as police organizations.

Certain organizational forms are associated with each type of authority. According to Scott (1991, 38), "traditional authority gives rise to the particularistic and diffuse structures exemplified by patrimonialism and its various manifestations, including gerontocracy, patriarchalism, and feudalism." These types of structures are common in the developing world (Riggs 1964). Charismatic authority inheres in the individual, not in the office. It is a deeply personal form of authority associated with structures that link "an impressive leader with his or her devoted coterie of followers or disciples" (Scott 1991, 39). Rational-legal authority inheres in the office, not in the individual. It is the basis of the modern bureaucracy (Scott 1991). Weber viewed bureaucracies—built on rational-legal authority, as opposed to traditional or charismatic authority—as having the greatest chance of achieving rationality and efficiency:

> [A] bureaucracy is capable of attaining the highest degree of efficiency, and is in this sense formally the most rational known means of exercising authority over human beings. It is superior to any other form in precision, in stability, in the stringency of its discipline, and in its reliability. It thus makes possible a particularly high degree of calculability of results...It is finally superior both in intensive efficiency and in the scope of its operations. (Weber 1921/1968, 223)

Although Weber is often cited as the principal architect or proponent of bureaucratic forms of organization, he was clearly ambivalent about bureaucratization and saw both its strengths and weaknesses. He viewed bureaucracies as the most stable and efficient organizational form, but he was also concerned about their capacity to imprison workers and consumers in an overly routinized, impersonal, and dehumanized iron cage of rationality.

4.1.1 The Influence of Legitimacy

Though Weber focused primarily on capitalism and competitive markets as the driving force behind the increasing power of rationalism, efficiency, and dehumanization, DiMaggio and Powell (1983) argue that other forces are now also responsible for driving these social changes. They note that organizations are strongly influenced by the need to sustain legitimacy, not just efficiency. According to DiMaggio and Powell (1983, 147), "structural change in organizations seems less and less driven by competition or by the need for efficiency. Instead…bureaucratization and other forms of organizational change occur as the result of processes that make organizations more similar without necessarily making them more efficient."

The notion that organizations are influenced by legitimacy concerns, and not just performance, is a central theme in the "institutional school" of organizations. The institutional school derives in part from the work of sociologist Philip Selznick, who described institutionalization as the process by which organizations develop an organic character and become "infused with value beyond the technical requirements of the task at hand" (Selznick 1957, 17; Perrow 1986). Selznick was fascinated by the paradox that organizations are created for rational action, but they are never really able to escape irrationality because they are "inescapably embedded in an institutional matrix" (Selznick 1948, 25). Selznick's perspective is part of an earlier generation of institutional theory, in contrast with the "new institutionalism" as outlined by Meyer and Rowan (1977), Zucker (1977), DiMaggio and Powell (1983), and others. In Meyer and Rowan's conception, organizations are heavily influenced by cultural pressures to conform to belief systems about what they ought to look like. According to Meyer and Rowan (1977, 343), organizational structures "are manifestations of powerful institutional rules which function as highly rationalized myths that are binding on particular organizations." The key challenge for institutional theory scholarship is determining how legitimacy is conferred on organizations and how the quest for legitimacy influences organizational forms.

According to DiMaggio and Powell (1983, 147), "the engine of rationalization and bureaucratization has moved from the competitive marketplace to the state and the professions." They argue that three isomorphic forces lead organizations within a particular organizational field to resemble one another more and more over time, a process called homogenization.[3] The three isomorphic forces described by DiMaggio and Powell—coercive, normative, and mimetic—derive from the power of governments and professions to shape the nature and character of organizations through subtle pressures toward conformity and homogeneity. Coercive isomorphism results from regulation, political pressure and oversight, often by the state. For instance, organizations may be compelled to adopt a certain policy, procedure, or structural element to comply with federal or state regulations. Normative isomorphism results from widely shared conceptions about how organizations within the field should look or how they should behave. These forces often emerge from the professions, whether formally from professional associations or informally through professional subcultures. For instance, though certification or accreditation may or may not be associated with increased effectiveness in certain industries, these official stamps of approval come to be regarded as symbols of professional competence. Mimetic isomorphism results when organizations copy the structures or practices of others. It is the organizational equivalent of what happens when individuals attempt to "keep up with the Joneses" by purchasing certain goods or services to maintain appearances.[4] A key contribution of institutional theory is that these three isomorphic forces may lead organizations within the same field to resemble one another more and more over time.

DiMaggio and Powell (1983, 148) argue that organizational fields exhibit consider-able diversity in structure and behavior during the early part of the field's existence, but once the field evolves, "there is an inexorable push toward homogenization." Research evidence from various organizational fields—including textbook publishing, hospi-tals, schools, and public agencies more generally—is consistent with this hypothesis (e.g., Tyack 1974; Katz 1975; Coser, Kadushin, and Powell 1982; Starr 1984; Frumkin and Galaskiewicz 2004). The idea of homogenization within an organizational field applies to many aspects of organizations, including their formal structures, policies and proce-dures, styles and activities, outward appearances, and patterns of innovation adoption. For instance, research suggests that early adopters of innovation within an organiza-tional field are concerned with improving performance. Yet later adopters are often motivated by the desire to reduce external pressure and increase legitimacy (e.g., Tolbert and Zucker 1983; Zattoni and Cuomo 2008). Thus innovations implemented by later adopters often serve primarily symbolic purposes.

The body of research I have just reviewed is large and dates back more than a cen-tury. It applies to organizations of all types and covers a wide range of organizational phenomena, including behavior, style, structure, policies and procedures, innovative-ness, and others. While it is impossible to do justice to the complexity of this work in such a short space, three points are most salient for this essay. First is Weber's notion that organizations become more bureaucratized over time and can become so heavily focused on the development and maintenance of rationalized structures and practices that these human artifacts take on lives of their own. Means and ends become confused, and certain structures and practices become taken for granted as the only "right" way of doing things. In this way, organizations dehumanize their workers and clients in irratio-nal structures that are cloaked in rationality. Second is Selznick's notion that although organizations attempt to achieve goal-oriented rationality, their efforts are often con-strained by the institutional environments in which they are embedded. Third is the idea that institutional environments exert multiple forms of pressure on organizations. In the aggregate, these pressures encourage conformity and homogeneity in organiza-tional fields. Most importantly for this essay, the homogeneity in organizational forms that results from these institutional forces may lead organizations closer and closer to the iron cage.

4.1.2   Applying These Ideas to Police Organizations

A long tradition of research has applied theories of organizations to the study of police. Much of this research is rooted in structural contingency theory, which is essentially a rational choice theory that views organizations as adaptive entities seeking to conform to the demands of their work and their environment to maximize performance and efficiency. Contingency theory represents an optimistic perspective on organizations—that they are rational, goal-seeking entities that adjust to the contingencies presented by their work and their environment to achieve the best fit. Evidence suggests that some of contingency theory's propositions hold true for police organizations, but the theory's explanatory power overall is weak (e.g., Langworthy 1986; Maguire 2003; Zhao, Ren, and Lovrich 2010). Understanding police organizations means viewing them as something more than just goal-oriented entities seeking only to maximize their performance. Put differently, if police agencies are so rational, why do they end up behaving so irrationally sometimes? Police organizations are shaped to some extent by concerns with performance, efficiency and goals, but other social forces also appear to play an important role.

Because contingency theory provides an incomplete explanation for the structures and practices of police organizations, scholars have turned to other theories. One promising line of scholarship on police organizations has examined the nature and influence of institutional environments. The first comprehensive application of these ideas to policing was an article by Crank and Langworthy (1992, 338) which argued that police agencies are "highly institutionalized organizations and should be studied in terms of how their formal structure and activities are shaped by powerful myths in their institutional environments." Crank and Langworthy observed that police organizations are not driven merely by a rational quest to achieve their stated goals, but also by the need to achieve legitimacy and the stability it engenders. Crank and Langworthy emphasized that "a police department's organizational structure, policies and organizational strategies have a great deal to do with institutional values in its environment and very little to do with production economies or technical capabilities" (342).

Testing institutional theory's propositions empirically in organizations is challenging because the theory focuses not just on observable structures and practices, but on the motivations for these phenomena. According to contingency theory, organizations adapt to maximize their performance, but according to institutional theory, organizational phenomena result instead from a quest for legitimacy. Parsing the motivations for particular organizational characteristics—as resulting from a quest for high performance or for legitimacy—represents a serious analytical challenge. Qualitative and historical studies can provide rich detail and are useful for investigating subtle institutional dynamics. However they tend to rely on case studies or small samples, thus raising concerns about generalizability. Quantitative research relies on larger samples but may struggle to capture the nuance and complexity of institutional processes.

A growing body of scholarship has applied institutional theory to policing. For instance, Crank (1994) argues that community policing, one of the most important strategic innovations in policing over the past four decades, emerged largely out of concerns with legitimacy. Crank shows how community policing resulted from the confluence of two myths: the myth of community and the myth of the police officer as watchman. Joining these myths together into the idea of community policing served as a legitimating mechanism that enabled police organizations to "ceremonially regain the legitimacy" they lost in the 1960s (Crank 1994, 347). Crank's suspicions about the symbolic nature of community policing receive some support from qualitative case studies. For instance, Lyons (1999, XXX) concluded that community policing in Seattle was a symbolic ploy that rearranged "the power to punish" and helped the police achieve greater power and control over communities. Similarly, Reed (1999, xii) concluded that community policing teams in Seattle "were highly symbolic and political rather than meaningful agents of crime control and prevention." The findings from qualitative research in several other American cities are consistent with institutional theory (e.g., Maguire and Wells 2009).

Some quantitative research that relies on larger samples of police agencies also supports institutional theory. For instance, Burruss and Giblin (2009) find that "centrist forces—including publications, the professionalization of law enforcement, and other law enforcement agencies" influenced the adoption of community policing. Several studies highlight the powerful effect of federal government funding in stimulating either the actual or symbolic adoption of community policing in American police agencies (Maguire and Mastrofski 2000; Roth and Ryan 2000; Worrall and Zhao 2003). Based on findings from a national study, Maguire and Katz (2002) speculate that larger police agencies might incur higher legitimacy costs and endanger their eligibility for federal grants unless they claim to do community policing.

Institutional theory has also been applied to other policing practices. For instance, Willis, Mastrofski, and Weisburd (2007) found that the implementation of CompStat in three agencies was largely motivated by a desire to appear more progressive to constituents, not to improve performance. Willis and Mastrofski (2012, 86) note that "the display of crime statistics and electronic maps at regular Compstat accountability meetings sent a powerful message that the organization was taking crime seriously whether or not these data had a significant influence on the selection of effective crime prevention strategies." Institutional pressures have also been found to exert a significant influence on police homeland security practices (Burruss, Giblin, and Schafer 2010), drunk driving enforcement (Mastrofski, Ritti, and Hoffmaster 1987), and paramilitarism (Jiao, Lao, and Lui 2005). Though this body of research is still in its infancy and faces a variety of methodological and conceptual challenges, institutional theory has succeeded in highlighting the many ways in which concerns about legitimacy shape police organizations.

One of the easiest ways for police agencies to demonstrate conformity with the demands placed upon them by their institutional environments is to adopt specialized units. Special units do not alter the "core technology" of policing, but they provide a clear sign to an agency's constituents that it is taking certain problems seriously.[5] Crank and Langworthy (1992) argue that the adoption of special units is sometimes ceremonial, serving to confer legitimacy rather than to improve performance. A useful line of research on institutional theory in policing focuses on special units. For instance, Katz's (2001) ethnographic study of a gang unit in a Midwestern police agency found that the community did not have much of a gang problem. Though specialized police gang units once represented an important innovation for police agencies facing serious problems with gangs and gang violence, late adopters often jump on the bandwagon for symbolic reasons. Katz (2001, 37) concluded that the police department established the gang unit to reduce external pressure from influential community figures and was driven largely by the need "to achieve and maintain organizational legitimacy." Webb and Katz (2003) observed these same types of institutional processes in five of the six police gang units they studied. Similarly, Giblin (2006) found that the adoption of crime analysis units was based in part on institutional concerns. Agencies that were accredited were more likely to have crime analysis units than agencies that were not accredited. Though accreditation standards did not require agencies to have a crime analysis unit, the standards did require agencies to have a policy on crime analysis. Giblin concludes that having a special unit served as a symbol of compliance with accreditation standards, which he interprets as an example of normative isomorphism.

Though a rich body of scholarship looks at the policing industry through the lens of organizational theory, none of it has considered the iron cage hypothesis in a direct way. Existing research supports the notion that police organizations are not simply governed by a rational or technical quest to improve performance and meet the agency's substantive goals. They are also influenced heavily by institutional pressures that can confer, withhold, or withdraw legitimacy. Institutional theory suggests that these social forces may be generating a slow but deliberate homogenization process among police organizations, leading them to resemble one another more and more over time. Those organizations that fail to keep up with the herd will face mounting legitimacy costs. Because homogenization is antithetical to the kinds of customized and contextual forms of policing that form the basis of the community policing movement, these changes are likely to result in more distant relationships between police and the communities they serve. This chapter examines four major changes in police organizations—in size, structure, technology, and militarization—that have the potential to lead them toward these more distant relationships and closer to the iron cage described by Weber.

4.2 SIZE OF POLICE ORGANIZATIONS

Police organizations in the United States have been growing for many years, not only in absolute terms, but also relative to the size of the populations they serve. Some research also suggests that this growth may be a worldwide phenomenon (Maguire and Schulte-Murray 2001). Unfortunately, data and measurement issues make it somewhat difficult to track changes in the size of American police organizations. More than a decade ago, Maguire and his colleagues documented the serious difficulties they encountered in estimating the number of police agencies and police officers in the United States (Maguire et al. 1998). They identified two major issues that made their job of "counting cops" difficult. First, they found quality control problems in the two major national data sets on police, including data entry errors, duplicate database entries, missing information, and inconsistent information across databases. Second, they encountered classification problems associated with certain types of police agencies.[6] Due to these and other data and measurement issues, this section of the essay relies on a patchwork quilt of evidence.

4.2.1 Evidence of Growth

The Bureau of Justice Statistics (BJS) has carried out national censuses of law enforcement agencies in the United States six times since 1986. Changes in agency type classifications in 1996 and again in 2004 make it difficult to draw clear inferences about change over time, though data for some agency types appear more reliable than for others.[7] In spite of these challenges, BJS data show that the number of sworn officers increased steadily throughout every wave of their estimates, for a total increase of about 33.4 percent from 1986 to 2008. Due to data quality issues and the narrow range of years, it is useful to examine several additional sources of evidence on changes in the sizes of police organizations in the United States.[8]

First, according to the FBI's *Police Employees* data, the mean number of police officers per 1,000 population in the United States increased from 1.66 officers in 1975 to 1.95 in 2009.[9] During this time, 18.3 percent of agencies decreased their total number of sworn officers, 1.4 percent retained the same number of officers, and 80.3 percent increased their number of officers. The total number of sworn officers in these agencies grew by 35.3 percent from 1975 to 2009. The growth in the total number of civilian employees working in police agencies is even more striking, increasing by 93.5 percent over this 34-year period.

Second, an analysis of police staffing from 1937 to 2009 shows that 7.4 percent of American police agencies decreased in size, less than half a percent remained the same size, and about 92 percent increased in size.[10] The total number of sworn officers increased by about 132 percent during this period, while the total number of civilian employees increased by nearly 850 percent.[11] Combining both employee types, the number of police employees rose by more than 175 percent during this period. Unfortunately, the earlier data set does not contain populations so it is not possible to compute changes in the ratio of officers to citizens for these specific agencies. However, census data reveal that the U.S. population as a whole rose by about 137 percent during this period.[12]

Third, the periodic *Law Enforcement Management and Administrative Statistics* (LEMAS) surveys carried out by BJS show that the number of municipal police agencies with 100 or more sworn officers increased steadily from 387 in 1990 to 538 in 2007, a 39 percent increase. LEMAS samples agencies with 100 or more sworn officers with certainty during every wave and obtains a probability sample of smaller agencies. Officer to citizen ratios increased from 2.12 in 1990 to 2.34 in 1999. They then began to decrease, reaching 2.17 in 2007. Other scholars have pointed out some of the reasons for this phenomenon, including budget cuts, baby boomer retirements, and diminished applicant pools (Wilson et al. 2011; Wilson 2012; Wilson and Grammich 2012; Wilson and Weiss 2012).[13]

The patchwork evidence presented here provides solid support for the hypothesis that police agencies are growing in both absolute and relative terms. There is some evidence of a recent downturn in police-citizen ratios due most likely to the economic crisis and other factors.

4.2.2 Discussion of Growth

Why are police agencies growing? Rational/technical explanations like contingency theory provide the most straightforward account, suggesting that police agencies grow in response to environmental imperatives like increased workload, higher crime rates, or greater demand for police services. While it is appealing to attribute the growth in police organizations to rational/technical explanations, research shows that the causes of police strength are more complex (e.g., Loftin and McDowall 1982; Chamlin and Langworthy 1996; Nalla, Lynch, and Leiber 1997; Koper, Maguire, and Moore 2001; Maguire and Schulte-Murray 2001). For instance, a long line of conflict theory research suggests that police agencies grow in response to the size of minority or economically marginalized populations that are perceived as threatening, independent of actual crime rates (e.g., Jacobs 1979; Jackson and Carroll 1981; Kent and Jacobs 2005). Another line of research emphasizes the role of internal organizational processes, finding that police agencies regularly seek their own incremental growth, often independent of their actual workload (Nalla 1992). For instance, Nalla, Lynch, and Leiber (1997, 120) note that members of an organization "may lobby for funding and personnel increases, whether or not these additional resources are needed." Another emerging line of research draws on theories of urban politics in examining the influence of local political arrangements on police strength (Sever 2001). Stucky (2005), for instance, finds that cities with partisan elections and district based city council elections (as opposed to "at large" elections) have more police employees per capita. Maguire and King (2007, 355) invoke institutional theory in noting that both the police and the public tend to equate larger agencies with greater quality. They argue that smaller police agencies emulate their larger peers, and that "this process of peer emulation is driven by a desire to copy reputable agencies and that in the absence of more detailed information, size and legitimacy become intertwined." While rational or technical explanations for the growth of police organizations may appear to be the most plausible, research evidence provides support for a number of alternative explanations.

Larger police organizations offer many potential benefits, including more efficient use of personnel, greater functional specialization, improved economies of scale, and greater promotional opportunities for personnel. At the same time, there is little evidence that they perform better than smaller agencies. An ambitious set of studies by Nobel laureate Elinor Ostrom and her colleagues found that "small and medium-sized police departments perform more effectively than large police departments serving similar neighborhoods.... Citizens served by small departments tend to receive better services at lower costs than their neighbors living in the center city" (Ostrom 2000, 36; also see Ostrom and Parks 1973; Ostrom, Parks, and Whitaker 1973; Ostrom and Whitaker 1974; Whitaker 1983). Other research has reached similar conclusions (Mastrofski, Ritti and Hoffmaster, 1987; Cordner 1989).

Though American police agencies are currently facing severe budget crises, they have grown steadily throughout the twentieth century. Some research also reports that the number of agencies may be diminishing, thus raising the prospect of a smaller number of larger police agencies.[14] Research suggests that different communities want different styles of policing and make unique demands of their police (Dunham and Alpert 1988). It seems reasonable to question whether the growing number of large police agencies will be able to customize their service delivery to meet the needs of their many unique communities. Slack and Bird (2012, 85) note that small government units "play an important role in ensuring adequate local 'voice' and accountability." If the future involves a smaller number of larger agencies, policing is likely to become more routinized and homogeneous and less customized and personalized.

4.3 POLICE ORGANIZATIONAL STRUCTURE

Police organizations also appear to be experiencing changes in their formal structures. Analyzing the precise nature of these changes means first articulating the various components that comprise an organization's structure. Maguire (2003) drew on seven generic structural components derived from organization theory in his study of American police agencies. He distilled these into two categories: structural complexity, and structural coordination and control. The four primary types of structural complexity (also referred to as "differentiation") are vertical, functional, spatial, and occupational (Langworthy 1986; Maguire 2003). Organizations become more complex vertically when they add layers of command or supervision; they become more complex functionally when they add new bureaus, divisions, or units; they become more complex occupationally when they hire employees having different specialties, skills, or occupations; and they become more complex spatially when they open new sites in different geographic locations (Maguire and King 2007). The three primary types of structural coordination and control are formalization, centralization, and administrative intensity. Formalization is the extent to which an organization's rules and processes are codified in formal written rules and policies. Centralization is the extent to which decision-making in an organization is concentrated as opposed to being shared throughout the organization. Administrative intensity is the relative proportion of workers in an organization whose work involves administrative functions (e.g., overseeing accreditation) as opposed to production functions (e.g., working on patrol or investigations). All of these structural characteristics have been measured in American police organizations, including many of them over time, thus making it possible to explore changes in the formal structures of these organizations.

American police agencies have come under great pressure in recent decades to alter their formal organizational structures as part of the shift toward community policing, a reform movement focused primarily on improving relationships between police and citizens and solving community problems (Greene 2000). The flexible, organic structures and non-routine policing strategies associated with the implementation of community policing are intended to facilitate more collaborative relationships between police and communities (Greene 2000; Maguire and Mastrofski 2000). These adaptive organizational forms differ from the mechanistic, paramilitary organizational forms that police agencies have traditionally embraced (Jermier and Berkes 1979; Maguire 1997). Traditional police organizational structures can insulate police from the communities they are intended to serve and, in the extreme, resemble Weber's notion of the iron cage. Of primary interest here is the extent to which American police organizations have altered their formal structures in ways that are concordant with community policing ideals.

During the community policing movement, American police agencies were encouraged by reformers to reduce their vertical complexity, eliminating unnecessary layers of command that make decision-making more cumbersome; and to reduce their functional complexity, slashing boxes in the organizational chart, empowering patrol officers to become "uniformed generalists,"[15] and providing them the latitude and support to handle some of the tasks previously handled by special units. At the same time, police departments were under pressure to increase their occupational and spatial complexity, hiring a more diverse mix of employees with different skills and qualifications and opening new precinct houses and mini-stations in neighborhoods (Maguire 1997). Police agencies were also urged to decentralize and deformalize, allowing officers greater discretion to design creative solutions to community problems. Finally, agencies were encouraged to reduce the size of their administrative apparatus to focus their resources on the streets. It is well established that American police agencies experienced dramatic alterations in formal structure throughout the twentieth century, and that these changes led to a more impersonal style of policing and more distant relationships between police and communities (Fogelson 1977; Kelling and Moore 1988; Reiss 1992). A key contemporary question is whether the community policing era was successful in reversing some of these structural shifts.

Research suggests that American police organizations adopted some of these structural changes but not others. For instance, two studies found no changes in vertical differentiation, or the depth of the hierarchy, in police organizations (Maguire et al. 2003; Zhao, Ren, and Lovrich 2010). The authors of one study note that there may actually have been an increase, but data problems limited their ability to draw clearer inferences (Maguire et al. 2003). The evidence was sufficient to conclude that American police agencies did not adopt the shallower rank structures promulgated by community policing reformers. Guyot (1979) once likened changing the police rank structure to "bending granite," a characterization that appears apropos today.

Three studies reported increases in functional differentiation over the past twenty-five years (Maguire 1997; Maguire et al. 2003, 259; Zhao, Ren, and Lovrich 2010). Specialized units can provide greater expertise on complex matters but the proliferation of specialized units often means greater fragmentation in service delivery. The increases in functional differentiation are interesting because they illustrate one of the tensions faced by police administrators. Special units have strong symbolic appeal for an organization. Therefore, in spite of the pressure community policing advocates place on police leaders to despecialize, there are strong countervailing pressures not to heed that advice.

No skillful police administrator in agencies of sufficient size is likely to buck the trend of establishing a specialized gang unit, an emergency response team, or a child abuse unit. Sometimes agencies adopt specialized units for the right reasons and sometimes they do so for symbolic purposes. An increase in functional differentiation suggests that American police have not fully embraced the notion of the patrol officer as uniformed generalist as called for by community policing reformers.

While one study found no change in occupational differentiation from 1987 to 1993, two later studies detected a significant increase in occupational differentiation (Maguire 1997; Maguire et al. 2003; Zhao, Ren, and Lovrich 2010). Police agencies expanded their hiring of civilians having a diverse mix of educational backgrounds and specialties. It is unclear if this change was motivated by a shift to community policing or if it was due to other causes. During this period, police agencies augmented their technical capacity, including information technology, forensic evidence processing, and other specialties likely to attract civilian employees. The U.S. Department of Justice also provided an infusion of federal funding to state and local police agencies under the COPS MORE program to increase civilianization.[16]

Evidence suggests that spatial differentiation also increased, with police agencies opening new precinct stations and mini-stations (Maguire et al. 2003; Zhao, Ren, and Lovrich 2010). This pattern is consistent with community policing ideals. At the same time, Maguire (2003) found that the main predictor of spatial differentiation in police organizations is their size; thus it is unclear whether increases in spatial differentiation were due to increases in agency size, the adoption of community policing, or other factors.

Two studies found no change in the level of formalization in police organizations in the 1990s (Maguire 1997; Maguire et al. 2003). Though community policing reformers called for police agencies to become more flexible and less formal, these prescriptions came at a time when litigiousness in the United States was increasing (Johnston 2007), and police agencies presumably felt the need to manage their risk through the elaboration of formal written policies and procedures (Archbold 2005). Administrative intensity did not experience any significant changes from 1987 to 1997 but then decreased significantly from 1997 to 1998 (Maguire 1997; Maguire et al. 2003). Like the changes in occupational differentiation, the most direct explanation for this finding may be funding under the COPS MORE program to redeploy officers from administrative support to field positions. Unfortunately, more recent data are not available to determine whether this reduction persisted. Finally, one study showed that centralization decreased during the 1990s, though there are some reasons to question the adequacy of the methodology used to reach this finding (Maguire et al. 2003).[17] Decentralization is consistent with the community policing movement, though it is also a common consequence of increases in spatial differentiation.

In the early 1970s, Angell (1971, 187) described American police agencies as a "firmly established, impersonal system in which most of the employees and clients are powerless to initiate changes or arrest the system's motions." Community policing reformers sought to alter this state of affairs by recommending a wide range of changes in the formal structures of police organizations. Zhao, Ren, and Lovrich (2010, 222) conclude that there was a "remarkable stability of structural arrangements in American police organizations over this important period of reform in policing philosophy." The evidence reviewed here suggests that American police organizations adopted some elements of structural reform recommended by community policing advocates, and not others. Police agencies appear to embrace reforms that call for increases in structural complexity, but not those that call for decreases. This finding is consistent with Maguire's (2003) structural elaboration hypothesis, which suggests that organizations tend to adopt more complex structures over time. The findings reported in this section also suggest that federal funding may have stimulated certain structural changes, though there is no empirical research to test this hypothesis. Occupational differentiation may have increased due to federal support for local police agencies to hire more civilians, and administrative intensity may have decreased due to federal grants to redeploy sworn officers from administrative support functions back to field assignments. Unfortunately, data on structural change in American police agencies are sparse and inconsistent, thus research has filled in only a few pieces of the puzzle.

4.4 TECHNOLOGY

Police agencies have begun to adopt a variety of new technologies over the past two decades. These technologies are influencing the way police communicate, conduct surveillance, gather and analyze data, learn and adapt, use force, and other vital elements of the police role. Research has barely kept up with the profound changes in the application of new technologies in policing. While acknowledging the importance of many types of technological innovation, here I focus primarily on information technologies, which one observer has called "the most important and influential kinds of technology" in policing (Manning 1992, 350).

A fundamental question for research on police use of information technology (IT) is whether or how it has altered the core work performed by police officers on the streets. Do new IT tools simply enable police to perform their usual tasks more efficiently or have these tools altered the nature and effectiveness of core police activities? More generally, it is not clear how the IT revolution has altered the goals, boundaries, and activity systems of modern police organizations. The most important question for this essay is how IT is influencing both those who deliver police services, as well as the recipients or clients of those services.

The most consistent voice on these matters is sociologist Peter K. Manning, whose decades of research and reflection on police organizations have often considered the role of IT. For instance, Manning (1992, 350) notes that information technologies "have been constrained by the traditional structure of policing and by the traditional role of the officer." In a later reflection, Manning (2003, 125) argues that IT tends to be grafted on "to the extant structure and traditional processes of the police organization, and these organizations have little changed." He concludes more generally that three decades of technological innovation have not "produced much change in police practice or effectiveness" (Manning 2003, 136). While a scattered and incomplete body of research evidence lends plausibility to Manning's sweeping conclusion, data on the nature, extent, and consequences of technological innovation in police organizations are not yet sufficient to provide empirically precise or policy-relevant findings.

Some of Manning's more recent reflections and research focus on the role and effects of crime mapping and crime analysis in police organizations. For instance, Manning (2005, 231) observes a tendency among police to use crime maps "for short-term tactical interventions" rather than more analytical and meaningful problem-solving efforts. Based on a study of three American police agencies, Manning (2008) concluded that crime analysis and crime mapping have not yet had the dramatic effect on police organizations that some observers expected. He found that crime analysis and crime mapping had become icons of "scientific, crime-focused police work" (21). These tools and practices "dramatized and elevated those aspects of policing most appealing to police themselves—their capacity to intervene and reduce officially recorded crime," but ultimately did very little to change police organizations. Manning's observations about the symbolic and dramatic value of these technologies is consistent with institutional theory's focus on the quest for legitimacy as one of the primary driving forces for organizational change. His findings are not inconsistent with those of Chan (2001, 156), whose case study of an Australian police agency found that officers were beginning to appreciate the tactical and strategic value of information technology, but "the dominance of traditional policing styles and values remains." Similarly, Harris (2007, 181) concludes there is "little evidence that IT has revolutionized policing" relative to earlier technological innovations and that it "appears to have largely enhanced traditional practices."

The dire conclusions of these analysts stand in sharp contrast to the drumbeat of more optimistic assessments found in the police practitioner literature, where technology is often seen as the cure to many of the problems thought to ail police organizations. These conclusions are also inconsistent with research findings from other scholars who report that IT is having a profound impact on police organizations. For instance, Flanagin (2002, 88) reports that communication and information technologies are altering police organizational forms: "by facilitating coordination tasks once performed by middle managers, electronic technologies result in the 'flattening' of the organizational hierarchy." Similarly, Ericson and Haggerty (1997, 388) report that "communication technologies...radically alter the structure of police organization by leveling hierarchies, blurring traditional divisions of labor, dispersing supervisory capacities, and limiting individual discretion. In the process, traditional rank structures of command and control are replaced by system surveillance mechanisms for regulating police misconduct." Garicano and Heaton (2007), on the other hand, report that IT in policing promotes *greater* bureaucratization without any improvement in productivity. It is difficult to reconcile these wildly conflicting findings. Does IT have a fundamental impact on police organizations or is it simply grafted onto existing structures without disturbing the core of policing? Does it make police organizations less or more bureaucratic? Research on the effects of IT in policing has not reached a consensus and much more work is clearly necessary.

One area in which IT has allegedly influenced police organizations is CompStat, an innovation developed in the New York Police Department that then spread around the world. CompStat is credited with reducing crime in several jurisdictions and is one of the major police innovations of the 1990s (e.g., Bratton and Malinowski 2008). Fortunately, CompStat has been studied in a number of locations and it is now possible to consider its strengths and weaknesses on the basis of research evidence rather than just anecdotes or untested assumptions. Dabney's (2010, 44–45) research in a large southeastern city found that officers misunderstood CompStat and its underlying principles, perceived the analyses and statistics as "serving an auditing function rather than that of precision diagnosis of crime patterns," and didn't see clear linkages between data analysis and operational tactics and strategies. Dabney (2010, 44–45) also found unintended consequences associated with CompStat, including "heightened competition among tactical units" which led to "an erosion of information sharing and cooperation between these units." All of these issues taken together "undermined the crime fighting goals and decentralized structure that underlies the Compstat model" (Dabney 2010, 44–45). Similar findings have been reported from research in other agencies (e.g., Willis, Mastrofski, and Weisburd 2007; Eterno and Silverman 2010; Willis and Mastrofski 2012).

The findings reported in this section highlight the tension between new IT and existing processes and structures. While nearly every police agency is adopting some type of new IT, the extent to which these technologies penetrate the "technical core" of police agencies probably varies widely. Qualitative analyses can provide useful details about the nature and effects of IT, however the generalizability of these "small-n" studies may be limited. A quantitative study of thousands of American police agencies by Garicano and Heaton (2010) did not find a statistically significant relationship between IT and police effectiveness in general, but the authors found that "productivity improvements become relatively large" when IT is adopted as part of a "package of organizational changes.... Police departments, like firms, appear likely to enjoy the benefits of computerization only when they identify the specific ways in which new information and data availability interact with existing organizational practices and make adjustments accordingly" (Garicano and Heaton 2010, 196). A simplistic interpretation of these findings is that some agencies adopt IT in ways that align clearly with structures and practices, while others adopt IT in less integrated ways, perhaps due to symbolic or haphazard implementation. An ongoing research agenda using both quantitative and qualitative methods is necessary to achieve more a nuanced and generalizable understanding of the effects of IT on police organizations.

Given that research on the nature and effects of IT in policing is still in its infancy, many important research questions remain unanswered. A key unknown is the nature of the linkages between legitimacy and technology. Snow (2007) argues that when technology is used to solve high-profile cases, it assumes an aura of infallibility. At that point, "good" police departments must have that technology to retain legitimacy. Similarly, Corbett and Marx (1991) note: "New technology is inherently attractive to an industrial society. It's risky to be against new technology, however mysterious its operations or recondite its underlying engineering. Technical innovation becomes synonymous with progress. To be opposed to new technology is to be a heretic, to be old-fashioned, backwards, resistant to change, regressive, out of step." Unfortunately, the idea that legitimacy concerns can lead police agencies to adopt new technologies is still speculative since research has not tested this hypothesis in a comprehensive way.

Similarly, little is known about how IT might generate unintended consequences. For instance, Byrne and Marx (2011) argue that risk assessment technologies can institutionalize race and class disparities. Similarly, police chief Tom Casady (2011) notes that "predictive policing" strategies can result in overzealous policing in areas police identify as risky. He advises police agencies to be thoughtful in how they use the information resulting from predictive analytics. Katz (2003) found that officers in one agency did a poor job of maintaining accurate information in their gang database, resulting in "serious social consequences" for youth listed in the database. Much remains to be learned about how the IT revolution in policing might infringe upon civil liberties, generate procedural injustices, or produce other unintended consequences.

Little is also known about how technology undermines, preserves, or enhances the nature of people's interactions with police. Policing is a human service industry, and technology has the capacity to dehumanize policing, to make it more actuarial and impersonal (Byrne and Marx 2011). Snow (2007, 156) worries that technology will take the place of old-fashioned police work, noting that the core job of policing is still "finding the right people to talk to and getting the people to talk to you." Similarly, Manning (2008, 252) argues that verbal skills are still the "the primary technology of policing." The National Institute of Justice notes that "technology cannot make up for poor judgment, compensate for inadequate or nonexistent training, substitute for poor officer screening and selection processes, replace competent leadership, or usurp the basic skills and street smarts of seasoned police officers" (Seaskate 1998, 8). In short, technology is not a replacement for the human skills of a police officer.

We want our police to be equipped with the best available technologies that enable them to maintain order, preserve public safety, and do their jobs most efficiently. Technology can enhance, enable, and enlighten, but it can also take us in the wrong direction. It can be used for symbolic value when grafted onto existing practices without genuine change. It can generate unintended and undesirable consequences. Even worse, technology can lead police to engage in practices that harm their relationships with communities and undermine their own legitimacy.

4.5 MILITARIZATION

Policing has often been described as a quasi-military institution that relies on many of the trappings of military organizations, including formal ranks, insignias, uniforms, codes of discipline, structures, equipment, doctrine, and culture (Bittner 1970; Jermier and Berkes 1979; for a counterargument, see Cowper 2000). Militarism has always been present to some degree in policing, but research suggests that it is expanding in the United States and other nations (Kraska 1996; Kopel and Blackman 1997; Weber 1999; McCulloch 2001; Rizer and Hartman 2011). Four themes are apparent from the literature on militarization in policing.

First, federal law regulating military involvement in domestic law enforcement operations in the United States has become less restrictive over the past three decades. The Posse Comitatus Act (PCA) of 1878 (18 U.S.C. 1385) prohibits the United States military from enforcing domestic laws. The Insurrection Act (10 U.S.C. 331–333) is a narrow exception to Posse Comitatus that allows the president to deploy the U.S. military to perform domestic law enforcement functions "where an insurrection has arisen within a state, and where the local and state law enforcement agents are incapable of quelling the insurrection" (McGrane 2010, 1312). Congress has chipped away at both acts, enabling increased military involvement in civilian law enforcement efforts.[18, 19] American police organizations now work more closely with the military than ever.

Second, police paramilitary units (like SWAT teams) are becoming more common and now carry out a wider range of law enforcement activities. Researchers have documented an increase in the number of agencies with police paramilitary units, from 59 percent in 1982, to 78 percent in 1990, to 89 percent in 1995 (Kraska and Cubellis 1997; Kraska and Kappeler 1997). Moreover, the units are now more active than they were in the past. From 1982 to 1995, their activity levels more than quadrupled (Kraska and Kappeler 1997). Once used primarily for high-risk emergencies like barricaded suspect or hostage situations, these units are now also used for mainstream policing activities, including patrol.

Third, police are now more heavily armed than ever. Maguire (2010, 205) argues that three events served as "environmental jolts" that led to significant increases in the level of police armament in the United States: a 1986 shootout between FBI agents and bank robbery suspects in Miami, a 1997 shootout between LAPD officers and bank robbery suspects in North Hollywood, and the 1999 shootings at Columbine High School in Colorado. Maguire (2010, 206) concludes that in the aftermath of these incidents, "police agencies have replaced revolvers with semiautomatic pistols with greater capacity and often with larger-caliber bullets; they have also armed themselves with more high-powered weapons including automatic weapons." Since 9/11, these trends have accelerated, with police agencies now routinely gaining access to military hardware, including armored vehicles, automatic weapons, grenade launchers, and other surplus military equipment (e.g., Rizer and Hartman 2011; Whitehead 2012).

Finally, police are also beginning to rely on a host of nonlethal military technologies intended to augment their communication, surveillance, and computational capacities (Wright 1978; Haggerty and Ericson 1999; Andreas and Price 2001). These technologies include robots, surveillance drones, night vision equipment, and other tools that extend the level of police surveillance and control over the populace (Becker and Schulz 2011).

These four themes point to an overall increase in the militarization of police agencies. Research suggests that the war on terrorism is enhancing this ongoing trend

(McCulloch 2001) as local agencies draw on military strategies, tactics, training, and equipment as part of their homeland security efforts. Rizer and Hartman (2011) argue that "the most serious consequence of the rapid militarization of American police forces... is the subtle evolution in the mentality of the 'men in blue' from 'peace officer' to soldier. This development is absolutely critical and represents a fundamental change in the nature of law enforcement." This trend was particularly evident in 2011 and 2012 when some police agencies responded in overly militarized ways to protesters in the Occupy movement. Americans observed news coverage of police officers dressed like soldiers and using unreasonable force against people participating in mostly nonviolent protests. For example, after police cracked down on an Occupy Oakland protest in October 2011, the agency's independent monitor criticized the police for their "overwhelming military-type response" (Warshaw 2012, 81). A reporter wrote that the police launched their assault "on a legitimate political demonstration" and concluded that "something is dangerously out of control here.... Police officers are public servants. They are not soldiers, facing down enemies. This is not a war. This is America" (Pierce 2011).

The current preoccupation with militarization is understandable. We do not want our police to be outgunned, or to endanger themselves without proper training or equipment. We want to make sure they have everything they need to keep our communities safe and secure. At the same time, there are good reasons for a bright line between internal and external defense forces. Throughout their history, police have become increasingly skilled in the precision with which they apply force; thus their embrace of militarization is not surprising. A primary imperative for soldiers is to kill the enemy; but police have a very different mission than the military. Some level of militarization makes sense, but too much takes police in the wrong direction. The widespread militarization of the police is a compelling reminder of the power of the state and the need to be judicious and thoughtful in regulating that power.

4.6 Conclusion

This essay began by outlining a general perspective useful for thinking about police organizations. The metaphor of the "iron cage" of rationality depicts the increasingly mechanical, actuarial, and impersonal modes by which modern organizations seem to operate. Police organizations are prone to many of the same pressures and constraints facing other modern organizations. However, as vital institutions for maintaining order and security in communities, they have a unique capacity to insert themselves into people's lives. One of the major drivers influencing the quest for rationality in police organizations is a dedication to doing better; to improving efficiency and effectiveness and ensuring that communities are orderly and secure. However, another major driver of the quest for rationality is legitimacy—the need for organizations to appear successful and to win the support of powerful individuals and groups inside and outside of police organizations. Legitimacy helps to establish autonomy, generate additional political and civic support, and maximize the flow of resources. This primal concern with legitimacy also leads police agencies to adopt policies, practices, and structures considered *de rigueur* in the policing industry. These features may not suit their unique contexts or needs; yet adopting them enables the agency to appear progressive. Failing to adopt them may incur legitimacy costs. This tension between genuine rationality and the need to appear rational is a common theme in organizational studies dating back to the birth of institutional theory in the 1940s and 1950s. This tension plays out in each of the major subsections in this essay.

The notion that legitimacy concerns can have a powerful influence on organizations emerged as a counterpoint to rational choice or contingency theories. These theories view organizations in much more straightforward terms, as rational entities, engaged in goal-directed behavior, that adapt as needed to maximize their performance. While research suggests that legitimacy is clearly important, many other social forces also play a role in shaping police organizations. This essay made reference to several such alternative explanations.

Though severe budget crises are currently hampering the police in many nations, American police agencies have a long and essentially linear pattern of growth throughout the twentieth century. This growth is often independent of their actual workload. American police agencies have long been viewed as having increasingly mechanistic and paramilitary structures that are at odds with their human services mission. The community policing reform movement sought to reverse this trend. Police organizations appear to have embraced some of these structural reforms but not others. Police are now heavily dependent on information technologies for carrying out their work. The extent to which these technologies have influenced the nature and effectiveness of policing is not well understood. IT and other technologies can generate unintended consequences, including more actuarial and impersonal modes of policing. Police agencies are also becoming increasingly militarized, drawing heavily on military training, equipment, doctrine, and worldview in carrying out domestic policing functions. These changes are useful in some ways for keeping our communities safe, but excessive militarization can dramatically alter the relationships between police and citizens.

The iron cage metaphor provides a useful perspective for thinking about modern police organizations. As these organizations become larger, more complex, more technocratic, and more militaristic, policing runs the risk of becoming more mechanical, actuarial, and impersonal. Human beings are the raw material of service organizations like the police, but human service organizations vary widely in the time and energy they invest in processing and helping each person with whom they come into contact. Size, structure, technology, and militarization can all contribute to a set of conditions in which people matter less, in which they are categorized and processed more quickly with less humanity and greater rigidity. Large, complex, formal, technocratic, and militaristic police organizations may lose sight of the community policing principles that formed the cornerstone of police reform in the 1980s and 1990s.

Existing research is currently insufficient to judge the extent to which these concerns are valid. Throughout this essay I have pointed out substantively important questions that we cannot answer due to insufficient data and gaps in the research. Scattered and inconsistent research on these issues makes it difficult to draw firm conclusions. But if these concerns are valid, as some research suggests, then the iron cage may be upon us.

Notes

* I am grateful to Maya Barak at American University, William R. King at Sam Houston State University and Jeremy Wilson at Michigan State University for their comments on an earlier version of this essay.

1. The essay focuses primarily on police organizations in the United States, though some of the patterns discussed here also apply to police organizations in other nations.

2. Just as constitutional scholars debate the original intent of the founding fathers, Weberian scholars continue to debate whether English language translations of Weber's work are consistent with his intended meaning. Some commentators have taken issue with Parsons's translation of Weber's words "*stahlhartes Gehäuse*" as meaning "iron cage." They argue that other translations are more likely accurate, including "casing as hard as steel" (Kent 1983), "shell as hard as steel" (Chalcraft 1994; Baehr 2001), or "steel shell" (Chalcraft 1994).

3. "Isomorphic" means having similar form or structure; thus isomorphic forces are those that encourage similarity in form or structure. An "organizational field" is a set of organizations that are similar in purpose, like police agencies. The terminology used to describe organizational fields and similar phenomena can be confusing. Scott (1991) differentiates between four levels of organizational environments: the organizational set, the organizational population, the areal organizational field, and the functional organizational field. DiMaggio and Powell's (1983) use of the term "organizational field" corresponds most closely with Scott's definition of organizational populations ("organizations that are alike in some respect") and functional organizational fields (organizations linked by "functional rather than geographic criteria") (Scott 1991, 127–30).

4. Scott (2001) later outlined a more general conceptual scheme for thinking about the elements of institutional environments. He argued that institutions are comprised of regulative, normative, and cultural/cognitive forces.

5. Here the term "core technology" is used in the organizational theory sense to refer to the primary methods by which an organization accomplishes its work.

6. For instance, sheriffs' agencies employ sworn officers who engage in functions outside the traditional scope of policing (serving civil process, providing courtroom security, or serving as jail guards). Sheriffs are responsible for traditional policing functions in some states but not others. Similarly, counting county, regional, and state police agencies poses an additional challenge when one attempts to compute officer-to-citizen ratios since the true populations served by these agencies are often unknown. Police officers in these agencies may have arrest authority in the whole jurisdiction, but some communities within these jurisdictions have their own police agencies. Computing accurate officer-to-citizen ratios for county, regional, or state agencies involves subtracting the populations of jurisdictions with their own police agencies. Finally, special police agencies pose the most challenging data issues, and estimates of the number and size of these types of agencies are especially prone to measurement error.

7. For instance, from 1986 to 2008, the number of sheriffs' agencies changed little. The number of municipal police agencies dropped by 6.1 percent in 1992 and then increased by

6.5 percent in 1996. These changes might have signaled the demise and resurgence of approximately 700 American police agencies, but a more likely explanation is quality control issues in the 1992 data. The greatest fluctuations occur for special police agencies. Interpreting these fluctuations is made more difficult by changes in the classification scheme used by BJS, but the number of special police agencies ranges from a low of 707 in 2004 to a high of 1,721 in 2008.

8. Due to quality control issues in government databases, some scholars rely on a private data source to develop sampling frames of American police agencies (e.g., Taylor et al. 2006; Wilson, Rostker, and Fan 2010; Wilson and Heinonen 2011). The *National Directory of Law Enforcement Administrators* (NDLEA) is updated annually (www.safetysource.com/directories).

9. The FBI's *Police Employees* data are only available in a public archive for the years 1975 to 2009 (Federal Bureau of Investigation 1975–2009). The findings reported here are based on data from 1,047 municipal police agencies serving populations of at least 25,000 in 1975 that I was able to match with agencies also reporting data in 2009. This analysis excludes smaller agencies due to the well-known statistical problems associated with outlier values in data on sworn officers, populations, and ratios and change scores computed from these quantities in small agencies and communities.

10. The FBI's *Police Employees* data are only available in electronic form in a public archive going back to 1975. Professor William King at Sam Houston State University has digitized older versions of the data going back to 1937. I obtained the data from Professor King, which covers the 390 police agencies surveyed by the FBI in 1937–1938. I merged the 1937–1938 data with the most recent year available in a public archive (2009) and examined changes in police strength from 1937 to 2009. I was able to match data from these two years for 377 agencies.

11. The number of sworn officers increased from 84,963 to 197,007 (131.9 percent). The number of civilian employees increased from 5,913 to 56,055 (848 percent). Combining both employee categories, the number of police employees increased by 178.5 percent.

12. According to the United States Census Bureau, the U.S. population was 128,824,829 in 1937 and 305,529,237 in 2009, an increase of approximately 137 percent.

13. The denominator (population) in police officer-to-citizen ratios is an imprecise proxy for police workload. These ratios provide only a crude estimate of police size relative to demand (e.g., Wilson and Weiss 2012).

14. Maguire and King (2004, 2007) argue that mergers, consolidations, and various contract policing arrangements are reducing the number of police agencies in the United States. While police agencies are often thought of as permanent, King (2009) argues that they disband "with appreciable regularity." A survey in three states showed that deaths of existing police agencies outpaced births of new agencies (King 1999). Unfortunately, current national data are insufficient to determine whether the patterns observed in these three states are similar in the remaining states.

15. The first use of this term that I could find in the published literature was by Hansen (1983).

16. The COPS MORE (Making Officer Redeployment Effective) program provided funding for police agencies to purchase technology or hire civilians that would enable them to redeploy sworn officers assigned to administrative functions back onto the streets. In 1995 and 1996, COPS MORE distributed more than $530 million to state and local police agencies (U.S. Department of Justice, Office of Community Oriented Policing Services 2012).

17. The study developed an innovative composite measure of centralization that had two shortcomings. First, it relied on one respondent to act as an informant for the whole organization. Second, the temporal analysis was somewhat artificial because it asked respondents to recall the level of centralization three years before filling out the survey.

18. For instance, in 2006, Congress modified the Insurrection Act to include not only insurrections, but natural disasters, epidemics, or other serious public health emergencies, terrorist attacks, and other types of incidents. Similarly, the Military Cooperation with Law Enforcement Officials (MCLEO) Act of 1981 (10 U.S.C. 18) created several exceptions to the PCA to enable the military to "to help enforce drug, immigration, and tariff laws" (Kealy 2003, 409). The MCLEO Act "expanded the powers of the military to cooperate with law enforcement by providing equipment, research facilities, and information; by training and advising police on the use of loaned equipment; and by assisting law enforcement personnel in keeping drugs from entering the country" (Kealy 2003, 409). Since then, a number of presidential directives and administrative rulings, often associated with the war on drugs, have further blurred the lines between civilian law enforcement and the military (Weber 1999).

19. Some critics, especially after 9/11, argue that these laws need to be relaxed to allow for greater cooperation between the military and state and local police. Many argue that state and local law enforcement agencies are poorly equipped to deal with certain types of issues, like "well-trained foreign terrorist cells equipped with military ordnance" (Klinger and Grossman 2002). Critics were especially incensed that the spirit of the PCA and the Insurrection Act prevented the president from deploying U.S. troops to New Orleans after Hurricane Katrina. State and local officials were unable to stop the widespread looting and violence, yet the Governor of Louisiana did not request help from the U.S. military under the Insurrection Act. Military personnel were already in the area providing rescue and relief services, but they were not called upon to provide law enforcement services (McGrane 2010). The general theme posed by critics of the PCA and the Insurrection Act is that state and local officials may not have the capacity to deal with large-scale, rapidly unfolding threats to public safety, and that structures need to be put in place for deploying federal troops much more quickly and easily in such instances.

References

Andreas, Peter, and Richard Price. 2001. "From War Fighting to Crime Fighting: Transforming the American National Security State." *International Studies Review* 3:31–52.

Angell, John E. 1971. "Toward an Alternative to the Classic Police Organizational Arrangements: A Democratic Model." *Criminology* 9:185–206.

Archbold, Carol A. 2005. "Managing the Bottom Line: Risk Management in Policing." *Policing: An International Journal of Police Strategies and Management* 28(1): 30–48.

Baehr, Peter. 2001. "The 'Iron Cage' and the 'Shell as Hard as Steel': Parsons, Weber, and the Stahlhartes Gehäuse Metaphor in the Protestant Ethic and the Spirit of Capitalism." *History and Theory* 40(2): 153–69.

Becker, Andrew, and G. W. Schulz. 2011. "Local Police Stockpile High-Tech Combat-Ready Gear." http://americaswarwithin.org/articles/2011/12/21/local-police-stockpile-high-tech-combat-ready-gear.

Bittner, Egon. 1970. *The Functions of the Police in Modern Society*. Washington, DC: U.S. Department of Health, Education and Welfare.

Bratton, William J., and Sean W. Malinowski. 2008. "Police Performance Management in Practice: Taking COMPSTAT to the Next Level." *Policing* 2(3): 259–65.

Burruss, George W., and Matthew J. Giblin. 2009. "Modeling Isomorphism on Policing Innovation: The Role of Institutional Pressures in Adopting Community-Oriented Policing." *Crime and Delinquency*, doi: 10.1177/0011128709340225.

Burruss, George W., Matthew J. Giblin, and Joseph A. Shafer. 2010. "Threatened Globally, Acting Locally: Modeling Law Enforcement Homeland Security Practices." *Justice Quarterly* 21(1): 77–101.

Byrne, James M., and Gary T. Marx. 2011. "Technological Innovations in Crime Prevention and Policing: A Review of the Research in Implementation and Impact." *Cahiers Politiestudies* 20(3): 17–40.

Casady, Tom. 2011. "Police Legitimacy and Predictive Policing." *Geography and Public Safety* 2(4): 1–2.

Chalcraft, David. 1994. "Bringing the Text Back In: On Ways of Reading the Iron Cage Metaphor in the Two Editions of 'The Protestant Ethic.'" In *Organizing Modernity: New Weberian Perspectives on Work, Organization and Society*, edited by Larry J. Ray and Michael Reed, 16–45. New York: Routledge.

Chamlin, Mitchell B., and Robert H. Langworthy. 1996. "The Police, Crime, and Economic Theory: A Replication and Extension." *American Journal of Criminal Justice* 20:165–82.

Chan, Janet B. L. 2001. "The Technological Game: How Information Technology is Transforming Police Practice." *Criminology and Criminal Justice* 1(2): 139–59.

Corbett, Ronald, and Gary Marx. 1991. "Critique: No Soul in the New Machine: Technofallacies in the Electronic Monitoring Movement." *Justice Quarterly* 8(3): 359–414.

Cordner, Gary. 1989. "Police Agency Size and Investigative Effectiveness." *Journal of Criminal Justice* 17:145–55.

Coser, Lewis, Charles Kadushin, and Walter W. Powell. 1982. *The Culture and Commerce of Book Publishing*. New York: Basic Books.

Cowper, Thomas J. 2000. "The Myth of the 'Military Model' of Leadership in Law Enforcement." *Police Quarterly* 3:228–48.

Crank, John P. 1994. "Watchman and Community: Myth and Institutionalization in Policing." *Law and Society Review* 28(2): 325–52.

Crank, John P., and Robert H. Langworthy. 1992. "An Institutional Perspective of Policing." *Journal of Criminal Law and Criminology* 83(2): 338–63.

Dabney, Dean A. 2010. "Observations Regarding Key Operational Realities in a Compstat Model of Policing." *Justice Quarterly* 27(1): 28–51.

DiMaggio, Paul J., and Walter W. Powell. 1983. "The Iron Cage Revisited: Institutional Isomorphism and Collective Rationality in Organizational Fields." *American Sociological Review* 48(2): 147–60.

Dunham, Roger G., and Geoffrey P. Alpert. 1988. "Neighborhood Differences in Attitudes Toward Policing: Evidence for a Mixed-Strategy Model of Policing in a Multi-Ethnic Setting." *Journal of Criminal Law and Criminology* 79(2): 101–20.

Ericson, Richard V., and Kevin D. Haggerty. 1997. *Policing the Risk Society*. Toronto: University of Toronto Press.

Eterno, John A., and Eli B. Silverman. 2010. "The NYPD's Compstat: Compare Statistics or Compose Statistics?" *International Journal of Police Science and Management* 12(3): 426–49.

Federal Bureau of Investigation. 1975–2009. *Uniform Crime Reporting Program Data: Police Employee (LEOKA) Data* (computer files). Ann Arbor, MI: Inter-University Consortium for Political and Social Research.

Flanagin, Andrew J. 2002. "The Impact of Contemporary Communication and Information Technologies on Police Organizations." In *Law Enforcement, Communication, and Community*, edited by Howard Giles, 85–105. Amsterdam: John Benjamins.

Fogelson, Robert M. 1977. *Big-City Police*. Cambridge, MA: Harvard University Press.

Frumkin, Peter, and Joseph Galaskiewicz. 2004. "Institutional Isomorphism and Public Sector Organizations." *Journal of Public Administration Research and Theory* 14(3): 283–307.

Garicano, Luis, and Paul Heaton. 2007. *Information Technology, Organization, and Productivity in the Public Sector: Evidence from Police Departments*. CEP Discussion Papers. London: Centre for Economic Performance, London School of Economics.

——. 2010. "Information Technology, Organization, and Productivity in the Public Sector: Evidence from Police Departments." *Journal of Labor Economics* 28(1):167–201.

Giblin, Matthew J. 2006. "Structural Elaboration and Institutional Isomorphism: The Case of Crime Analysis Units." *Policing: An International Journal of Police Strategies and Management* 29(4): 643–64.

Greene, Jack R. 2000. "Community Policing in America: Changing the Nature, Structure, and Function of the Police." In *Criminal Justice 2000: Policies, Processes, and Decisions of the Criminal Justice System*, edited by Julie Horney, 299–370. Washington, DC: National Institute of Justice.

Guyot, D. 1979. "Bending Granite: Attempts to Change the Rank Structure of American Police Departments." *Journal of Police Science and Administration* 7:253–84.

Haggerty, Kevin, and Richard Ericson. 1999. "The Militarization of Policing in the Information Age." *The Journal of Military and Political Sociology* 27 (Winter): 233–45.

Hansen, E. B. 1983. "Uniformed Generalist—One Approach to Police Professionalism." *FBI Law Enforcement Bulletin* 52(6): 6–10.

Harris, Christopher J. 2007. "Police and Soft Technology: How Information Technology Contributes to Police Decision Making." In *The New Technology of Crime, Law and Social Control*, edited by James M. Byrne and Donald J. Rebovich, 153–183. New York: Criminal Justice Press.

Heslop, Richard. 2011. "British Police Service: Professionalisation or McDonaldization." *International Journal of Police Science and Management* 13(4): 312–21.

Jackson, Pamela I., and Leo Carroll. 1981. "Race and the War on Crime: The Socio-Political Determinants of Municipal Police Expenditures in 90 Non-Southern Cities." *American Sociological Review* 46(3): 290–305.

Jacobs, David. 1979. "Inequality and Police Strength: Conflict and Coercive Control in Metropolitan Areas." *American Sociological Review* 44(6): 913–24.

Jermier, John, and Leslie J. Berkes. 1979. "Leader Behavior in a Police Command Bureaucracy: A Closer Look at the Quasi-Military Model." *Administrative Science Quarterly* 24(1): 1–23.

Jiao, Allan Y., Raymond W. K. Lau, and Percy Lui. 2005. "An Institutional Analysis of Organizational Change: The Case of the Hong Kong Police." *International Criminal Justice Review* 15(1): 38–57.

Johnston, Michael D. 2007. "The Litigation Explosion, Proposed Reforms, and their Consequences." *Brigham Young University Journal of Public Law* 21:179–207.

Katz, Charles M. 2001. "The Establishment of a Police Gang Unit: An Examination of Organizational and Environmental Factors." *Criminology* 39(1): 37–74.

——. 2003. "Issues in the Production and Dissemination of Gang Statistics: An Ethnographic Study of a Large Midwestern Police Gang Unit." *Crime and Delinquency* 49(3): 485–516.

Katz, Michael B. 1975. *Class, Bureaucracy, and Schools: The Illusion of Educational Change in America.* New York: Praeger.

Kealy, Sean J. 2003. "Reexamining the Posse Comitatus Act: Toward a Right to Civil Law Enforcement." *Yale Law and Policy Review* 21:383–94.

Kelling, George L., and Mark H. Moore. 1988. "The Evolving Strategy of Policing." *Perspectives on Policing*, vol. 4, 1–16. Washington, DC: National Institute of Justice.

Kent, Stephen A. 1983. "Weber, Goethe, and the Nietzschean Allusion: Capturing the Source of the 'Iron Cage' Metaphor." *Sociological Analysis* 44(4): 297–319.

Kent, Stephanie L., and David Jacobs. 2005. "Minority Threat and Police Strength From 1980 to 2000: A Fixed-Effects Analysis of Nonlinear and Interactive Effects in Large U.S. Cities." *Criminology* 43:731–60.

King, William R. 1999. "Notes on the Demise of Ohio Police Departments: 105 Disbanded and Counting." Paper presented at the annual meeting of the Midwestern Criminal Justice Association, Chicago, IL, October.

King, William R. 2009. "Toward a Life-Course Perspective of Police Organizations." *Journal of Research in Crime and Delinquency* 46:213–44.

Klinger, David A., and David Grossman. 2002. "Who Should Deal with Foreign Terrorists on US Soil? Socio-Legal Consequences of September 11 and the Ongoing Threat of Terrorist Attacks in America." *Harvard Journal of Law and Public Policy* 25:815–34.

Kopel, David, and Paul Blackman. 1997. "Can Soldiers be Peace Officers? The Waco Disaster and the Militarization of American Law Enforcement Period." *Akron Law Review* 30:619–59.

Koper, Christopher S., Edward R. Maguire, and Gretchen E. Moore. 2001. *A National Study of Police Hiring and Retention Issues in Police Agencies.* Washington, DC: Urban Institute.

Kraska, Peter B. 1996. "Enjoying Militarism: Political/Personal Dilemmas in Studying US Police Paramilitary Units." *Justice Quarterly* 13(3): 405–29.

Kraska, Peter B., and Louis J. Cubellis. 1997. "Militarizing Mayberry and Beyond: Making Sense of American Paramilitary Policing." *Justice Quarterly* 14(4): 607–29.

Kraska, Peter B., and Victor E. Kappeler. 1997. "Militarizing American Police: The Rise and Normalization of Paramilitary Units." *Social Problems* 44(1): 1–18.

Langworthy, Robert H. 1986. *The Structure of Police Organizations.* New York: Praeger.

Loftin, Colin, and David McDowall. 1982. "The Police, Crime, and Economic Theory: An Assessment." *American Sociological Review* 47(3): 393–401.

Lyons, William. 1999. *The Politics of Community Policing: Rearranging the Power to Punish.* Ann Arbor: University of Michigan Press.

Maguire, Edward R. 1997. "Structural Change in Large Municipal Police Organizations During the Community Policing Era." *Justice Quarterly* 14(3): 701–30.

Maguire, Edward R. 2003. *Organizational Structure in American Police Agencies: Context, Complexity, and Control.* Albany: State University of New York Press.

Maguire, Edward R. 2010. "Conclusion: A Journey Through the World of Police Use of Force." In *Police Use of Force: A Global Perspective*, edited by Joseph B. Kuhns and Johannes Knutsson, 199–211. Santa Barbara, CA: Praeger.

Maguire, Edward R., and Charles Katz. 2002. "Community Policing, Loose Coupling, and Sensemaking in American Police Agencies." *Justice Quarterly* 19(3): 501–34.

Maguire, Edward R., and William R. King. 2004. "Trends in the Policing Industry." *The Annals of the American Academy of Political and Social Science* 593(1): 15–41.

———. 2007. "The Changing Landscape of American Police Organizations." In *Policing 2020: Exploring the Future of Crime, Communities, and Policing*, edited by Joseph A. Schafer, 337–371. Washington, DC: Federal Bureau of Investigation.

Maguire, Edward R., and Stephen D. Mastrofski. 2000. "Patterns of Community Policing in the United States." *Police Quarterly* 3(1): 4–45.

Maguire, Edward R., and Rebecca Schulte-Murray. 2001. "Issues and Patterns in the Comparative International Study of Police Strength." *International Journal of Comparative Sociology* 42(1–2): 75–100.

Maguire, Edward R., Yeunhee Shin, Jihong Zhao, and Kimberly D. Hassel. 2003. "Structural Change in Large Police Agencies During the 1990s." *Policing: An International Journal of Police Strategies and Management* 26(2): 251–75.

Maguire, Edward R., Jeffrey B. Snipes, Craig D. Uchida, and Margaret Townsend. 1998. "Counting Cops: Estimating the Number of Police Departments and Police Officers in the USA." *Policing: An International Journal of Police Strategies and Management* 21(1): 97–120.

Maguire, Edward R., and William H. Wells. 2009. *Implementing Community Policing: Lessons from 12 Agencies*. Washington, DC: Office of Community Oriented Policing Services.

Manning, Peter K. 1992. "Information Technologies and the Police." In *Modern Policing*, edited by Michael Tonry and Norval Morris, 349–398. Chicago: University of Chicago Press.

———. *Policing Contingencies*. Chicago: University of Chicago Press.

———. 2005. "Environment, Technology, and Organizational Change: Notes from the Police World." In *Information Technology and the Criminal Justice System*, edited by April Pattavina, 221–241. Newbury Park, CA: Sage.

———. 2008. *The Technology of Policing: Crime Mapping, Information Technology, and the Rationality of Crime Control*. New York: NYU Press.

Mastrofski, Stephen D., R. Richard Ritti, and Debra Hoffmaster. 1987. "Organizational Determinants of Police Discretion: The Case of Drinking-Driving." *Journal of Criminal Justice* 15(5): 387–402.

McCulloch, Jude. 2001. *Blue Army: Paramilitary Policing in Australia*. Carlton South, Victoria, Australia: Melbourne University Press.

McGrane, Sean. 2010. "Katrina, Federalism, and Military Law Enforcement: A New Exception to the Posse Comitatus Act." *Michigan Law Review* 108:1309–40.

Meyer, John, and Brian Rowan. 1977. "Institutionalized Organizations: Formal Structure as Myth and Ceremony." *American Journal of Sociology* 83:340–63.

Nalla, Mahesh K. 1992. "Perspectives on the Growth of Police Bureaucracies, 1948-1984: An Examination of Three Perspectives." *Policing and Society* 3:51–61.

Nalla, Mahesh K., Michael J. Lynch, and Michael J. Leiber. 1997. "Determinants of Police Growth in Phoenix, 1950-1988." *Justice Quarterly* 14(1):115–43.

Ostrom, Elinor. 2000. "The Danger of Self-Evident Truths." *PS: Political Science and Politics* 33(1): 33–44.

Ostrom, Elinor, and Roger B. Parks. 1973. "Suburban Police Departments: Too Many and Too Small?" In *The Urbanization of the Suburbs*, edited by Louis H. Masotti and Jeffrey K. Hadden, 367–402. Beverly Hills: Sage.

Ostrom, Elinor, and Gordon P. Whitaker. 1974. "Community Control and Governmental Responsiveness: The Case of Police in Black Neighborhoods." In *Improving the Quality of Urban Management*, edited by Willis D. Hawley and David Rogers, 303–334. Beverly Hills: Sage.

Ostrom, Elinor, Roger B. Parks, and Gordon P. Whitaker. 1973. "Do We Really Want to Consolidate Urban Police Forces?" *Public Administration Review* 33:423–33.

Perrow, Charles. 1986. *Complex Organizations: A Critical Essay.* New York: Random House.

Pierce, Charles P. 2011. "Occupy Oakland and the Militarization of America's Police." *Esquire.*

Reed, Wilson E. 1999. *The Politics of Community Policing: The Case of Seattle, Washington.* New York: Garland.

Reiss, Albert J., Jr. 1992. "Police Organization in the Twentieth Century." In *Modern Policing*, edited by Michael Tonry and Norval Morris, 51–97. Chicago: University of Chicago Press.

Riggs, Fred. 1964. *Administration in Developing Countries: The Theory of Prismatic Society.* Boston: Houghton Mifflin.

Rizer, Arthur, and Joseph Hartman. 2011. "How the War on Terror has Militarized the Police." *The Atlantic.* http://www.theatlantic.com/national/archive/2011/11/how-the-war-on-terror-has-militarized-the-police/248047/.

Roth, Jeffrey A., and Joseph F. Ryan. 2000. *The COPS Program After 4 Years—National Evaluation.* Washinton, DC: National Institute of Justice.

Scott, W. Richard. 1991. *Organizations: Rational, Natural and Open Systems*, 3d ed. Englewood Cliffs, NJ: Prentice Hall.

——. 2001. *Institutions and Organizations*, 2d ed. Thousand Oaks, CA: Sage Publications.

Seaskate, Inc. 1998. *The Evolution and Development of Police Technology.* Report prepared for the National Committee on Criminal Justice Technology, National Institute of Justice.

Selznick, Philip. 1948. "Foundations of the Theory of Organization." *American Sociological Review* 13:25–35.

——. 1957. *Leadership in Administration.* New York: Harper and Row.

Sever, Brion. 2001. "The Relationship Between Minority Populations and Police Force Strength: Expanding our Knowledge." *Police Quarterly* 4:28–68.

Slack, Enid, and Richard Bird. 2012. *Merging Municipalities: Is Bigger Better?* Helsinki, Finland: Government Institute for Economic Research (VATT).

Snow, Robert L. 2007. *Technology and Law Enforcement: From Gumshoe to Gamma Rays.* Westport, CT: Praeger.

Starr, Paul. 1984. *The Social Transformation of American Medicine: The Rise of a Sovereign Profession and the Making of a Vast Industry.* New York: Basic Books.

Stucky, Thomas D. 2005. "Local Politics and Police Strength." *Justice Quarterly* 22:139–69.

Taylor, Bruce, Bruce Kubu, Lorie Fridell, Carter Rees, Tom Jordan, and Jason Cheney. 2006. *Cop Crunch: Identifying Strategies for Dealing with the Recruiting and Hiring Crisis in Law Enforcement.* Washington, DC: Police Executive Research Forum.

Tolbert, Pamela S., and Lynne G. Zucker. 1983. "Institutional Sources of Change in the Formal Structure of Organizations: the Diffusion of Civil Service Reform, 1880–1935." *Administrative Science Quarterly* 28(1): 22–39.

Tyack, David. 1974. *The One Best System: A History of American Urban Education.* Cambridge, MA: Harvard University Press.

U.S. Department of Justice. [multiple years]. *Census of State and Local Law Enforcement Agencies.* Washington, DC: Bureau of Justice Statistics.

U.S. Department of Justice. [multiple years]. *Law Enforcement Management and Administrative Statistics.* Washington, DC: Bureau of Justice Statistics.

U.S. Department of Justice, Office of Community Oriented Policing Services. 2012. "COPS MORE (Making Officer Redeployment Effective)." http://www.cops.usdoj.gov/default. asp?item=55.

Warshaw, Robert S. 2012. *Ninth Quarterly Report of the Independent Monitor for the Oakland Police Department*. Dover, NH: Police Performance Solutions.

Webb, Vincent J., and Charles M. Katz. 2003. "Policing Gangs in an Era of Community Policing." In *Policing Gangs and Youth Violence*, edited by Scott H. Decker, 17–50. Belmont, CA: Wadsworth.

Weber, Diane C. 1999. *Warrior Cops: The Ominous Growth of Paramilitarism in American Police Departments*. Washington, DC: Cato Institute Briefing Papers.

Weber, Max. 1904/1930. *The Protestant Ethic and the Spirit of Capitalism*. Translated by Talcott Parsons. New York: The Citadel Press.

——. 1909/1944. "Max Weber on Bureaucratization in 1909." In *Max Weber and German Politics*, edited by Jacob Peter Mayer, 125–131. London: Faber and Faber.

——. 1921/1968. *Economy and Society*. Translated and edited by Guenther Roth and Claus Wittich. New York: Bedminster Press.

——. 1947. *The Theory of Social and Economic Organization*. Translated by Alexander Morell Henderson and Talcott Parsons. New York: Free Press.

Whitaker, Gordon. 1983. "Police Department Size and the Quality and Cost of Police Services." In *The Political Science of Criminal Justice*, edited by S. Nagel, E. Fairchild, and A. Champagne, 185–196. Springfield, IL: Charles C. Thomas.

Whitehead, John W. 2012. "Tanks on Mainstreet: The Militarization of Local Police." *Huffington Post* (January 4). http://www.huffingtonpost.com/john-w-whitehead/police-militarization_b_1180875.html.

Willis, James J., and Stephen D. Mastrofski. 2012. "Compstat and the New Penology: A Paradigm Shift in Policing?" *British Journal of Criminology* 52(1): 73–92.

Willis, James, Stephen D. Mastrofski, and David Weisburd. 2007. "Making Sense of Compstat: A Theory-based Analysis of Organizational Change in Three Police Departments." *Law and Society Review* 41:147–88.

Wilson, Jeremy M. 2012. "Articulating the Dynamic Police Staffing Challenge: An Examination of Supply and Demand." *Policing: An International Journal of Police Strategies and Management* 35(2): 327–55.

Wilson, Jeremy M., Erin Dalton, Charles Scheer, and Clifford Grammich. 2011. *Police Recruitment and Retention for the New Millennium: The State of Knowledge*. Washington, DC: U.S. Department of Justice, Office of Community Oriented Policing Services.

Wilson, Jeremy M., and Clifford Grammich. 2012. *Police Consolidation, Regionalization, and Shared Services: Options, Considerations, and Lessons from Research and Practice*. Washington, DC: U.S. Department of Justice, Office of Community Oriented Policing Services.

Wilson, Jeremy M., and Justin Heinonen. 2011. "Advancing a Police Science: Implications from a National Survey of Police Staffing." *Police Quarterly* 14(3): 277–97.

Wilson, Jeremy M., Bernard Rostker, and Cha-Chi Fan. 2010. *Recruiting and Retaining America's Finest: Evidence-Based Lessons for Police Workforce Planning*. Santa Monica, CA: Rand.

Wilson, Jeremy M., and Alexander Weiss. 2012. *A Performance-Based Approach to Police Staffing and Allocation*. Washington, DC: U.S. Department of Justice, Office of Community Oriented Policing Services.

Worrall, John L., and Jihong Zhao. 2003. "The Role of the COPS Office in Community Policing." *Policing: An International Journal of Police Strategies & Management* 26(1): 64–87.

Wright, Steve. 1978. "New Police Technologies: An Exploration of the Social Implications and Unforeseen Impacts of Some Recent Developments." *Journal of Peace Research* 15:305–22.

Zattoni, Alessandro, and Francesca Cuomo. 2008. "Why Adopt Codes of Good Governance? A Comparison of Institutional and Efficiency Perspectives." *Corporate Governance: An International Review* 16(1): 1–15.

Zhao, Jihong, Ling Ren, and Nicholas Lovrich. 2010. "Police Organizational Structures during the 1990s: An Application of Contingency Theory." *Police Quarterly* 13(2): 209–32.

Zucker, Lynne G. 1977. "The Role of Institutionalization in Cultural Persistence." *American Sociological Review* 42:726–43.

PART II

POLICING STRATEGIES

CHAPTER 5

··

PROBLEM-ORIENTED POLICING: PRINCIPLES, PRACTICE, AND CRIME PREVENTION

··

ANTHONY A. BRAGA

MOST police departments have historically engaged in incident-driven crime prevention strategies. In dealing with crime, these departments were aimed at resolving individual incidents instead of addressing recurring crime problems (Eck and Spelman 1987). Officers responded to repeated calls and never looked for the underlying conditions that may be causing like groups of incidents. Officers often became frustrated because they answered similar calls and seemingly made no real progress. Citizens also became dissatisfied because the problems that generated their repeated calls still existed (Eck and Spelman 1987). In a seminal article that challenged existing police policy and practice, Herman Goldstein (1979) proposed an alternative; he felt that police should go further than answering call after call and should instead search for solutions to recurring problems that generate the repeated calls. Goldstein described this strategy as the "problem-oriented approach" and envisioned it as a department-wide activity. Problem-oriented policing is now a common police crime prevention and control strategy.

Problem-oriented policing seeks to identify the underlying causes of crime problems and to frame appropriate responses using a wide variety of innovative approaches (Goldstein 1979). Using a basic iterative approach of problem identification, analysis, response, assessment, and adjustment of the response, this adaptable and dynamic analytic approach provides an appropriate framework to uncover the complex mechanisms at play in crime problems and to develop tailor-made interventions to address the underlying conditions that cause crime problems (Eck and Spelman 1987; Goldstein 1990). Since the publication of Goldstein's article, many police departments have experimented with the approach and the available evaluation evidence suggests that problem-oriented policing is a fundamentally sound approach to controlling crime and disorder problems (Skogan and Frydl 2004; Braga 2008; Weisburd et al. 2010).

This essay examines the principles, practice, and crime prevention effects of problem-oriented policing. Section 5.1 discusses the emergence of problem-oriented policing, key stages in the process, theoretical underpinnings, and its relationship to situational crime prevention and community policing. Problem-oriented policing as practiced in the field is the topic of Section 5.2. The available evaluation evidence on the crime control benefits of the approach is reviewed in Section 5.3. Section 5.4 concludes the essay by briefly reflecting on the current state of problem-oriented policing. Key observations and conclusions include:

- Traditional police crime control strategies, such as preventive patrol, rapid response to calls for service, and follow-up investigations, did not produce the desired crime reduction impacts.
- Problem-oriented policing is an alternative approach to crime reduction that challenges police officers to understand the underlying situations and dynamics that give rise to recurring crime problems and to develop appropriate responses to address these underlying conditions.
- Problem-oriented policing is often given operational structure through the well-known SARA model that includes a series of iterative steps: Scanning, Analysis, Response, and Assessment.
- Police officers often find it difficult to implement problem-oriented policing properly, with deficiencies existing in all stages of the process.
- The existing evaluation evidence shows that problem-oriented policing generates noteworthy crime and disorder reduction impacts.
- These crime reduction impacts are generated even when problem-oriented policing is not fully implemented; this confirms the robustness of the problem-oriented approach in addressing crime and disorder problems.

5.1 THE PRINCIPLES OF PROBLEM-ORIENTED POLICING

Beginning in the 1940s and continuing through the emergence of community policing, police departments followed what many have come to call the "standard" or "professional" model of policing (see, e.g., Skogan and Frydl 2004) that was characterized by rigorous professional standards, militaristic organizational structures, the use of technology, and other important historical reforms. Under this model, police departments attempted to prevent serious crimes by advancing three operational strategies: preventive patrol, rapid response, and investigation of more serious cases by specialized detective units. The limits of these strategies are, by now, well known. Research studies found that varying levels of preventive patrol did not reduce crime (Kelling et al. 1974), rapid response to calls for service did not increase the probability of arrest as very few crimes are reported in progress (Spelman and Brown 1984), and follow-up investigations solved only a relatively small proportion of reported crimes (Greenwood, Chaiken, and Petersilia 1977).

The findings of these studies had a strong impact on a generation of police scholars and practitioners. By the early 1990s, there was a broad consensus among criminologists and police scholars that crime was a product of larger social forces, and the police could do little if anything to impact crime or crime rates (Gottfredson and Hirschi 1990; Bayley 1994). The police as "crime fighters" might have been a popular idea in the media and among the public, but the idea that the police could do something about crime had little credence in the universities or research institutes that were concerned with policing.

In 1979, Herman Goldstein, a respected University of Wisconsin law professor and former aide to Chicago police chief O. W. Wilson, made a simple and straightforward proposition that challenged police officers to address problems rather than simply respond to incidents. According to Goldstein (1979, 1990), behind every recurring problem there are underlying conditions that create it. Incident-driven policing never addresses these conditions; therefore incidents are likely to recur. Answering calls for service is an important task and still must be done, but police officers should respond systematically to recurring calls for the same problem. In order for the police to be more efficient and effective, they must gather information about incidents and design an appropriate response based on the nature of the underlying conditions that cause the problem(s) (Goldstein 1990).

It is important to note here that Herman Goldstein (1979, 1990) intended problem-oriented policing to be a general approach that could be applied to a wide range of police business problems. This includes non-crime problems such as personnel issues, budgetary concerns, and police-community relations. Most problem-oriented policing research and practical experience, however, has focused on applying the approach to addressing crime and disorder problems. As such, this essay examines our existing knowledge base on police use of the problem-oriented approach to tackle recurring crime and disorder problems.

5.1.1 The Process of Problem-Oriented Policing

The problem-oriented policing approach was given an operational structure in Newport News, Virginia. Researchers from the Police Executive Research Forum (PERF) and a group of officers selected from the various ranks of the Newport News Police Department crystallized the philosophy into a set of steps known as the SARA model (Eck and Spelman 1987). The SARA model consists of these stages: *Scanning*—the identification of an issue and determining whether it is a problem; *Analysis*—data collection on the problem to determine its scope, nature, and causes; *Response*—information from the analysis is used to design an appropriate response which can involve other agencies outside the normal police arena; and *Assessment*—the response is evaluated and the results can be used to re-examine the problem and change responses or maintain positive conditions (Eck and Spelman 1987). In practice, it is important to recognize that the development and implementation of problem-oriented responses do not always follow the linear, distinct steps of the SARA model (Capowich and Roehl 1994; Braga 2008). Rather, depending on the complexity of the problems to be addressed, the process can be characterized as a series of disjointed and often simultaneous activities. A wide variety of issues can cause deviations from the SARA model, including identified problems needing to be re-analyzed because initial responses were ineffective and implemented responses sometimes revealed new problems (Braga 2008).

5.1.1.1 Scanning

The process of scanning involves the identification of problems that are worth looking at because they are important and amenable to solution. Herman Goldstein (1990) suggests that the definition of problems be at the street-level of analysis and not be restricted by preconceived typologies. Goldstein defines a problem as "a cluster of similar, related, or recurring incidents rather than a single incident; a substantive community concern; or a unit of police business" (1990, 66).

There are many ways a problem might be nominated for police attention. A police officer may rely upon his or her informal knowledge of a community to identify a problem that he or she thinks is important to the well being of the community. Another possibility is to identify problems from the examination of citizen calls for service coming into a police department or crime incident reports. This approach is implicitly recommended by those who advocate the identification of "hot spots" (Sherman, Gartin, and Buerger 1989). With the proliferation of computerized mapping technology in police departments, there has been a strong movement in police departments to use these techniques in the identification of crime problems (Weisburd and McEwen 1997). Problems can also be identified by examining the distribution of crime incidents at specific public or private places such as stores, bars, restaurants, shopping malls, ATM locations, apartment buildings, and other facilities (Clarke and Eck 2007).

Another approach to identifying problems is through consultation with community groups of different kinds, including other government agencies. This differs from analyzing individual calls for service because the demands come from groups, rather than individuals. If the police are interested in forging partnerships with groups as well as individuals, then it is important to open up channels through which groups can express their concerns, such as community advisory councils or regular meetings held by the police to which all members of a community are invited (Skogan and Hartnett 1997). This approach has the advantage of allowing the community's views about what is important shape the police's views about what is important rather than leaving the nomination of problems to police analysts.

The best approach to identifying problems would be to combine these efforts. Police officers know the locations within their beats that tend to be trouble spots and also are often very sensitive to signs of potential crimes across the places that comprise their beats (see, e.g., Bittner 1970). Problem identification through examination of official data can ensure that police departments are appropriately focusing their resources on the small number of places, offenders, victims, and products that comprise the bulk of crime and disorder problems (Braga 2008). Community engagement approaches can identify problems that may elude official statistics and also yield the added benefit of improving police-community relations through building cooperative relationships and empowering citizens (Reisig 2010). A blended problem identification approach best positions police departments to ensure public safety.

5.1.1.2 *Analysis*

The analysis phase challenges police officers to analyze the causes of problems behind a string of crime incidents or substantive community concern. Once the underlying conditions that give rise to crime problems are known, police officers develop and implement appropriate responses. The challenge to police officers is to go beyond the analysis that naturally occurs to them; namely, to find the places and times where particular offenses are likely to occur, and to identify the offenders that are likely to be responsible for the crimes. Although these approaches have had some operational success, this type of analysis usually produces directed patrol operations or a focus on repeat offenders. The idea of analysis for problem solving was intended to go beyond this. Goldstein (1990) describes this as the problem of "ensuring adequate depth" in the analysis.

Situational crime prevention has further developed the methodology of analyzing problems and provided important examples of how crime problems may be closely analyzed. Situational crime prevention measures are tailored to highly specific categories of crime. As Clarke (1997) describes, distinctions must be made not between broad crime categories such as burglary and robbery, but between the different kinds of offenses that comprise each of these categories. For example, in their analysis of domestic burglary in a British city, Poyner and Webb (1991) revealed that cash and jewelry burglaries tended to occur in older homes near the city center, while burglaries of electronic goods, such as TVs and VCRs, generally occurred in newer homes in the suburbs. Analysis further revealed that offenders on foot committed cash and jewelry burglaries. In the electronic goods burglaries, offenders used cars that had to be parked near to the house, but not so close that they would attract attention. The resulting crime prevention strategies differed accordingly. To prevent cash and jewelry burglaries in the city center, Poyner and Webb (1991) recommended improving security and surveillance at the burglar's point of entry; in contrast, to prevent electronic goods burglaries in the suburbs, they suggested improving the natural surveillance of parking places and roadways in the area.

Beyond providing important theoretical and conceptual insights on the dynamics of crime problems, environmental criminology has developed a number of data collection methodologies that can greatly enrich the understanding of crime problems and, in turn, result in more effective responses (Clarke 1998). Environmental criminology, also known as crime pattern theory, explores the distribution and interaction of targets, offenders, and opportunities across time and space (Brantingham and Brantingham 1991). Most police agencies usually don't analyze data beyond the information contained in their official systems—typically arrests, crime incidents, and citizen calls for service. These alternative data collection methods include (Clarke 1998, 324):

- Victimization surveys, which provide more detail about the impact of the problem on people's everyday lives;
- Crime audits, where interviewers walk around a neighborhood with people who live there or around a park with regular users, and record where they report being afraid; and
- Structured interviews with offenders to find out more about their motives and their methods of committing crimes.

5.1.1.3 Response

After a problem has been clearly defined and analyzed, police officers confront the challenge of developing a plausibly effective response. The development of appropriate responses is closely linked with the analysis that is performed. The analysis reveals the potential targets for an intervention, and it is at least partly the idea about what form the intervention might take that suggests important lines of analysis. As such, the reason police often look at places and times where crimes are committed is that they are already imagining that an effective way to prevent the crimes would be to get officers on the scene through directed patrols. The reason they often look for the likely offender is that they think that the most effective and just response to a crime problem would be to arrest and incapacitate the offender. However, the concept of problem-oriented policing, as envisioned by Goldstein (1990), calls on the police to make a much more "uninhibited" search for possible responses and not to limit themselves to getting officers in the right places at the right times, or identifying and arresting the offender (although both may be valuable responses). Effective responses often depend on getting other people to take actions that reduce the opportunities for criminal offending, or to mobilize informal social control to drive offenders away from certain locations.

The responses that problem-oriented police officers develop may be close to current police practices or, in some instances, quite different. Goldstein (1990, 102–47) offers the following suggestive list of general alternatives police may consider in developing responses to neighborhood crime problems:

- Concentrating attention on those individuals who account for a disproportionate share of the problem
- Connecting with other government and private services through referral to another agency, coordinating police responses with other agencies, correcting inadequacies in municipal services, and pressing for new services
- Using mediation and negotiation skills to resolve disputes

- Conveying information to reduce anxiety and fear, to enable citizens to solve their own problems, to elicit conformity with laws and regulations that are not known or understood, to warn potential victims about their vulnerability and warn them of ways to protect themselves, to demonstrate to individuals how they unwittingly contribute to problems, to develop support for addressing a problem, and to acquaint the community with limitations on the police and define realistically what may be expected of the police
- Mobilizing the community and making use of existing forms of social control in addition to the community
- Altering the physical environment to reduce opportunities for problems to recur
- Increased regulation, through statutes or ordinances, of conditions that contribute to problems
- Developing new forms of limited authority to intervene and detain
- Using civil law to control public nuisances, offensive behavior, and conditions contributing to crime

5.1.1.4 Assessment

The crucial last step in the practice of problem-oriented policing is to assess the impact the intervention has had on the problem it was supposed to solve. Assessment is important for at least two different reasons. The first is to ensure that police remain accountable for their performance and for their use of resources. Citizens and their representatives want to know how the money and freedom they surrendered to the police are being used, and whether important results in the form of less crime, enhanced security, or increased citizen satisfaction with the police has been achieved. A second reason that assessment is important is that it allows the police to learn about what methods are effective in dealing with particular problems. Unless the police check to see whether their efforts produced a result, it will be hard for them to improve their practices.

The assessment of responses is key in facilitating an active exchange of what works in crime prevention among police departments. As Clarke (1998, 319) suggests, "if law enforcement agencies do not have a mechanism to learn from others' mistakes and assist others to learn from their experiences, they will always be reinventing the wheel." The degree of rigor applied to the assessment of problem-oriented initiatives will necessarily vary across the size and overall importance of the problems addressed (Braga 2008). Serious, large, and recurrent problems such as controlling gang violence or handling domestic disputes deserve highly rigorous examinations. Other problems that are less serious, or common, such as a lonely elderly person making repeat calls to the police for companionship, are obviously not worth such close examinations. To meet the demands of measuring accountability and performance, problem-oriented police should, at a minimum, describe the scanning, response, and assessment phases by measuring inputs, activities, outputs, and whatever can be said about the outcomes of their initiatives.

In general, problem-oriented police should strive to conduct more rigorous assessments of their responses with due consideration to time and resource constraints. Depending on the availability of funds, police departments should consider partnering up with independent researchers to conduct systematic evaluations of their efforts. In the absence of such a partnership, Clarke (1998) suggests that police should take care to relate any observed results to specific actions taken, develop assessment plans while outlining the project, present control data when available and reasonably comparable to the subject(s) of the intervention, and, as will be discussed further, measure crime displacement. While the degree of rigor applied to the assessment of responses may vary, what must not be sacrificed is the goal of measuring results. This will keep the police focused on results rather than means, and that is one of the most important contributions of the idea of problem-oriented policing.

5.1.2 Community Policing and "Problem Solving"

During the late 1980s and throughout the 1990s, problem-oriented policing and community policing were heralded as revolutionary alternatives to the professional model. The terms are sometimes referred to as essentially the same strategy (Walker 1992; Kennedy and Moore 1995); however, others maintain a distinct separation between the two concepts (Eck and Spelman 1987; Goldstein 1990; Reisig 2010). Problem-oriented policing is typically defined as focusing police attention on the underlying causes of problems behind a string of crime incidents, while community policing emphasizes the development of strong police-community partnerships in a joint effort to reduce crime and enhance security (Moore 1992). Indeed, community-oriented police officers use problem solving as a tool and problem-oriented departments often form partnerships with the community.

Community policing is not a specific set of programs. Rather, communities with different problems and varied resources to bring to bear against them will implement different strategies. However, as an organizational strategy, the community policing *process* leaves setting priorities and the means of achieving them largely to residents and the police that serve in the neighborhood. The three core, and densely interrelated, elements of community policing are *citizen involvement* in identifying and addressing public safety concerns, the *decentralization* of decision-making down the police organizational hierarchy to encourage development of local responses to locally-defined problems, and *problem solving* to respond to community crime and disorder concerns (Skogan 2006). The iterative problem-oriented policing process is commonly used as an important framework in dealing with local community concerns proactively.

The term "problem solving" is often conceptualized as what an officer does to handle small, recurring beat-level problems, and it is distinguished from problem-oriented policing based on its rudimentary analysis of the problem and lack of formal assessment (see, e.g., Cordner 1998). In short, some observers suggest the term "problem solving" does not adequately capture the substance of problem-oriented policing as envisioned by Goldstein (1990). Scott (2000) reports that Goldstein himself has been especially careful to avoid the term "problem solving" because many, if not most, problems the police confront are too complex for anything approaching a final solution; reducing harm, alleviating suffering, and/or providing some measure of relief are ambitious enough aims for the police.

5.1.3 Situational Crime Prevention and Supporting Theoretical Perspectives

The field of situational crime prevention has supported the problem-oriented policing movement since its genesis in the British Government's Home Office Research Unit in the early 1980s (Clarke 1997). Instead of preventing crime by altering broad social conditions such as poverty and inequality, situational crime prevention advocates changes in local environments to decrease opportunities for crimes to be committed. Situational crime prevention techniques comprise opportunity-reducing measures that are: "(1) directed at highly specific forms of crime (2) that involve the management, design, or manipulation of the immediate environment in as systematic and permanent way as possible (3) so as to increase the effort and risks of crime and reduce the rewards as perceived by a wide range of offenders" (Clarke 1997, 4). Like problem-oriented policing, the situational analysis of crime problems follows an action-research model that systematically identifies and examines problems, develops solutions, and evaluates results. Applications of situational crime prevention have shown convincing crime prevention results to a variety of problems ranging from obscene phone callers (Clarke 1990) to burglary (Pease 1991) to car radio theft (Braga and Clarke 1994). This simple but powerful perspective is applicable to crime problems facing the police, security personnel, business owners, local government officials, and private citizens.

Problem-oriented policing and situational crime prevention draw upon theories of criminal opportunity, such as rational choice and routine activities, to analyze crime problems and develop appropriate responses (Clarke 1997; Braga 2008; Reisig 2010). Most criminological research focuses on why some people become persistent offenders (Felson and Clarke 1998). However, as Eck (2000) observes, by the time a problem comes to the attention of the police, the questions of why people offend are no longer relevant. The most pressing concerns are why offenders are committing crimes at particular places, selecting particular targets, and committing crimes at specific times (Eck 2000). While police officers are important entry points to social services for many people, they are best positioned to prevent crimes by focusing on the situational opportunities for offending rather than attempting to manipulate socio-economic conditions that are the subjects of much criminological inquiry and the primary focus of other governmental agencies (Braga 2008). Theories that deal with the "root causes" of crime focus on interventions that are beyond the scope of most problem-oriented policing projects. Theories that deal with opportunities for crime and how likely offenders, potential victims, and others make decisions based on perceived opportunities have greater utility in designing effective problem-oriented policing interventions (Felson and Clarke 1998; Eck 2000).

The rational choice perspective assumes that "crime is purposive behavior designed to meet the offender's commonplace needs for such things as money, status, sex, and excitement, and that meeting these needs involves the making of (sometimes quite rudimentary) decisions and choices, constrained as these are by limits of time and ability and the availability of relevant information" (Clarke 1995, 98; see also Cornish and Clarke 1986). Rational choice makes distinctions between the decisions to initially become involved in crime, to continue criminal involvement, and to desist from criminal offending, as well as the decisions made to complete a particular criminal act. This separation of the decision-making processes in the criminal event from the stages of criminal involvement allows the modeling of the commission of crime events in a way that yields potentially valuable insights for crime prevention.

The emphasis of the rational choice perspective on concepts of risk, reward, and effort in criminal decision making has been used to inform the development of problem-oriented policing and situational crime prevention strategies that seek to change offender appraisals of criminal opportunities (Clarke 1997; Braga 2008). Of particular importance, the decision processes and information utilized in committing criminal acts can vary greatly across offenses; ignoring these differences and the situational contingencies associated with making choices may reduce the ability to effectively intervene (Clarke 1995). For example, a robber may choose a "favorite" spot because of certain desirable attributes that facilitate an ambush, such as poor lighting and untrimmed bushes. One obvious response to this situation would be to improve the lighting and trim the bushes.

Rational choice is often combined with routine activity theory to explain criminal behavior during the crime event (Clarke and Felson 1993). Rational offenders come across criminal opportunities as they go about their daily routine activities and make decisions whether to take action. The source of the offender's motivation to commit a crime is not addressed (it is assumed that offenders commit crimes for any number of reasons); rather, the basic ingredients for a criminal act to be completed are closely examined. Routine activity posits that a criminal act occurs when a likely offender converges in space and time with a suitable target (e.g., victim or property) in the absence of a capable guardian (e.g., property owner or security guard) (Cohen and Felson 1979).

The routine activity approach was used to demonstrate that increases in residential burglary in the United States between 1960 and 1970 could be largely explained by changes in the routine activities of households (Cohen and Felson 1979). During this time period, the number of empty homes during the day increased as the number of single-person households and female participation in the workforce grew. At the same time, households increasingly contained attractive items to steal, such as more portable televisions and other electronic goods. Burglary increased, as fewer capable guardians were present in the home to protect the new suitable targets from burglars. These kinds of analytical insights on the nature of crime problems are very valuable to problem-oriented police officers seeking to develop appropriate responses.

5.2 THE PRACTICE OF PROBLEM-ORIENTED POLICING

Although the problem-oriented approach has demonstrated much potential value in improving police practices, research has also documented that it is very difficult for police officers to implement problem-oriented policing strategies (Eck and Spelman 1987; Clarke 1998; Braga and Weisburd 2006). Cordner (1998) identifies a number of challenging issues in the substance and implementation of many problem-oriented policing projects. These issues include: the tendency for officers to conduct only a super-ficial analysis of problems and rushing to implement a response, the tendency for offi-cers to rely on traditional or faddish responses rather than conducting a wider search for creative responses, and the tendency to completely ignore the assessment of the effectiveness of implemented responses (Cordner 1998). Indeed, the research literature is filled with cases where problem-oriented policing programs tend to lean towards tra-ditional methods and where problem analysis is weak (Eck and Spelman 1987; Buerger 1994; Capowich and Roehl 1994; Read and Tilley 2000). In his review of several hundred submissions for the Police Executive Research Forum's Herman Goldstein Award for Excellence in Problem-Oriented Policing, Clarke (1998) laments that many examples of problem-oriented policing projects bear little resemblance to Goldstein's original defi-nition and suggests this misrepresentation puts the concept at risk of being pronounced a failure before it has been properly tested.

Deficiencies in current problem-oriented policing practices exist in all phases of the process. During the scanning phase, police officers risk undertaking a project that is too small (e.g., the lonely old man who repeatedly calls the police for companionship) or too broad (e.g., gang delinquency) and this destroys the discrete problem focus of the project and leads to a lack of direction at the beginning of analysis (Clarke 1998). Some officers skip the analysis phase or conduct an overly simple analysis that does not ade-quately dissect the problem or does not use relevant information from other agencies (such as hospitals, schools, and private businesses) (Clarke 1998). Based on his exten-sive experience with police departments implementing problem-oriented policing, Eck (2000) suggests that much problem analysis consists of a simple examination of police data coupled with the officer's working experience with the problem. In their analysis of problem-oriented initiatives in forty-three police departments in England and Wales, Read and Tilley (2000) found that problem analysis was generally weak with many ini-tiatives accepting the definition of a problem at face value, using only short-term data to unravel the nature of the problem, and failing to adequately examine the genesis of the crime problems.

Given the limited analysis that many crime problems receive, it is not surprising that the responses of many problem-oriented policing projects rely too much on traditional police tactics (such as arrests, surveillance, and crackdowns) and neglect the wider range of available alternative responses. Read and Tilley (2000) found, in addition to a number of other weaknesses in the response development process, that officers selected certain responses prior to, or in spite of, analysis; failed to think through the need for a sustained crime reduction; failed to think through the mechanisms by which the response could have a measurable impact; failed to fully involve partners; and narrowly focused responses, usually on offenders. Finally, Scott and Clarke (2000) observed that the assessment of responses is rare and, when undertaken, it is usually cursory and limited to anecdotal or impressionistic data.

Reflecting on these practical issues, Eck (2000) comments that the problem-oriented policing that is practiced by many police departments diverges significantly from the original concept that was envisioned by Goldstein. Cordner and Biebel (2005) found that, despite fifteen years of national promotion and a concerted effort at implementation within the San Diego Police Department, problem-oriented policing as practiced by ordinary police officers fell far short of the ideal model. Cordner and Biebel suggest that it may be unreasonable to expect every police officer to continuously engage in full-fledged problem-oriented policing. Braga and Weisburd (2006), however, find value in the imperfect implementation of problem-oriented policing. They argue that there is much evidence that what might be called "shallow" problem solving responses can be effective in combating crime problems. Apparently, weak problem-oriented policing is better than none at all. This being the case, Braga and Weisburd (2006) question whether the pursuit of problem-oriented policing, as it has been modeled by Goldstein and others, should be abandoned in favor of the achievement of a more realistic type of problem solving. While less satisfying for scholars, it is what the police have tended to do, and it has been found to lead to real crime prevention benefits.

5.2.1 Ideal Applications of Problem-Oriented Policing

Herman Goldstein (1979, 1990) originally suggested that problem-oriented policing efforts should be located within a headquarters unit rather than assigned to police officers in operational units. The decentralization of the approach to street police officers may have reduced the quality of routine problem-oriented policing efforts as busy officers handled too many problems and had little time to conduct the extensive analysis and search for appropriate responses (Eck 2006). Ideal applications of problem-oriented policing tend to involve larger scale problems, the involvement of academic researchers and crime analysis units, and the solid support of the police command staff to implement alternative responses. Two examples of these types of "ideal" problem-oriented projects are briefly reviewed here: The Boston Police Department's Operation Ceasefire intervention to prevent gang violence (Braga et al. 2001) and the Charlotte-Mecklenburg

Police Department's program to reduce theft from construction sites (Clarke and Goldstein 2002).

The Boston Gun Project was a problem-oriented policing enterprise expressly aimed at taking on a serious, large-scale crime problem—homicide victimization among young people in Boston. Like many large cities in the United States, Boston experienced a large sudden increase in youth homicide between the late 1980s and early 1990s. The Boston Gun Project proceeded by: (1) assembling an interagency working group of largely line-level criminal justice and other practitioners; (2) applying quantitative and qualitative research techniques to create an assessment of the nature of, and dynamics driving, youth violence in Boston; (3) developing an intervention designed to have a substantial, near-term impact on youth homicide; (4) implementing and adapting the intervention; and (5) evaluating the intervention's impact (Kennedy, Piehl, and Braga 1996). The Project began in early 1995 and implemented what is now known as the "Operation Ceasefire" intervention, which began in the late spring of 1996.

The trajectory of the Boston Gun Project and of Operation Ceasefire is by now well known and extensively documented (see, e.g., Kennedy 1997). Briefly, the working group of law enforcement personnel, youth workers, and researchers diagnosed the youth violence problem in Boston as one of patterned, largely vendetta-like ("beef") hostility amongst a small population of chronic offenders, and particularly among those involved in some 61 loose, informal, mostly neighborhood-based groups. These 61 gangs consisted of between 1,100 and 1,300 members, representing less than 1 percent of the city's youth between the ages of 14 and 24. Although small in number, these gangs were responsible for more than 60 percent of youth homicide in Boston.

Operation Ceasefire's "pulling levers" strategy was designed to deter violence by reaching out directly to gangs, saying explicitly that violence would no longer be tolerated, and backing up that message by "pulling every lever" legally available when violence occurred (Kennedy 1997). Simultaneously, youth workers, probation and parole officers, and later churches and other community groups offered gang members services and other kinds of help. The Ceasefire Working Group delivered this message in formal meetings with gang members, through individual police and probation contacts with gang members, through meetings with inmates at secure juvenile facilities in the city, and through gang outreach workers. The deterrence message was not a deal with gang members to stop violence. Rather, it was a promise to gang members that violent behavior would evoke an immediate and intense response. If gangs committed other crimes but refrained from violence, the normal workings of police, prosecutors, and the rest of the criminal justice system dealt with these matters. But if gangs hurt people, the Working Group concentrated its enforcement actions on their members.

A large reduction in the yearly number of Boston youth homicides followed immediately after Operation Ceasefire was implemented in mid-1996. A U.S. Department of Justice (DOJ)-sponsored evaluation of Operation Ceasefire revealed that the intervention was associated with a 63 percent decrease in the monthly number of Boston youth homicides, a 32 percent decrease in the monthly number of shots-fired calls, a 25 percent decrease in the monthly number of gun assaults, and, in one high-risk police district given special attention in the evaluation, a 44 percent decrease in the monthly number of youth gun assault incidents (Braga et al. 2001). The evaluation also suggested that Boston's significant youth homicide reduction associated with Operation Ceasefire was distinct when compared to youth homicide trends in most major U.S. and New England cities (Braga et al. 2001).

To many observers, the analysis phase is the critical step in the problem-oriented policing process as it unravels the nature of recurring problems and points police towards innovative responses that go beyond traditional enforcement activities. Clarke and Goldstein (2002) document the vital role played by innovative crime analysis in a problem-oriented policing project undertaken by the Charlotte-Mecklenburg Police Department to address a sharp increase in the number of kitchen appliances stolen from new houses under construction. A detailed analysis of security practices and risks for theft among twenty-five builders in one police service district was conducted. The analysis led to the recommendation that the installation of appliances should be delayed until the new owners moved into the residence. Removing the targets of theft was found to be an effective response, as appliance theft declined markedly in the police service district and there was no evidence of displacement to surrounding district (Clarke and Goldstein 2002).

A key moment in the analysis of the theft problem occurred when the crime analyst discovered that a "certificate of occupancy" had to be issued by the county before a new owner could move into the residence. Compared to the building permits that had been used in earlier iterations of the problem analysis, these certificates provided a better measure of when a house was ready to be occupied and, therefore, a timelier basis for calculating the risk of theft. Building permits measured only planned construction. Builders may obtain a hundred permits to build houses, but only actually build a few in a given year. That is why building permit data could not be used to accurately assess the stage when a house was completed and, thus, at-risk for theft of newly installed appliances.

5.3 CRIME PREVENTION EFFECTS OF PROBLEM-ORIENTED POLICING

There is a growing body of evaluation evidence that problem-oriented policing generates noteworthy crime control gains. The U.S. National Academy of Sciences' Committee to Review Research on Police Policy and Practices concluded that problem-oriented policing is a promising approach to deal with crime, disorder, and fear and recommended that additional research was necessary to understand the organizational arrangements that foster effective problem solving (Skogan and Frydl 2004; Weisburd and Eck 2004). This conclusion contrasts with an earlier review by Sherman (1991) that suggested there was little rigorous evaluation evidence in support of Herman Goldstein's (1990) contention that problem-oriented policing was privileged over traditional policing methods in preventing crime. Several published volumes on problem-oriented policing case studies provide a good sense for the work being done as well as the strengths and weaknesses of some of the better problem-oriented efforts (see, e.g., O'Connor Shelly and Grant 1998; Sole Brito and Allan 1999; Sole Brito and Gratto, 2000; Sampson and Scott 2000). Indeed, the widespread use of problem-oriented policing as a central crime prevention and control strategy in police agencies across the world is a strong indicator of the practical value of the approach.

However, the strongest empirical evidence available in support of problem-oriented policing comes from three Campbell Collaboration systematic reviews. Formed in 2000, the Campbell Collaboration Crime and Justice Group aims to prepare and maintain systematic reviews of criminological interventions and to make them electronically accessible to scholars, practitioners, policy makers and the general public (Farrington and Petrosino, 2001; see also www.campbellcollaboration.org). The Crime and Justice Group requires reviewers of criminological interventions to select studies with high internal validity such as randomized controlled trials and quasi-experiments (Farrington and Petrosino, 2001).

David Weisburd and his colleagues (2010) recently completed a Campbell Collaboration systematic review of the crime prevention effects of problem-oriented policing on crime and disorder. Despite reviewing a very large number of empirical studies on the approach, they identified only ten problem-oriented policing studies that used more rigorous randomized experimental and quasi-experimental evaluation designs. Given the popularity of problem-oriented policing, Weisburd et al. (2010) were surprised by the small number of rigorous evaluations studies that examined the crime prevention benefits of the approach. A meta-analysis of these ten evaluations revealed that problem-oriented policing programs generated a modest but statistically-significant impact on crime and disorder outcomes. These results were consistent when Weisburd et al. (2010) examined randomized experiments and quasi-experiments separately.

The Campbell problem-oriented policing review also reported on the crime prevention effects of simple pre/post-comparison evaluation studies. While these studies did not include a comparison group and were less methodologically rigorous, Weisburd et al. (2010) found that they were far more numerous, identifying forty-five pre/post-evaluations. Forty-three of these forty-five evaluations reported that the approach generated beneficial crime prevention effects. These studies also reported much larger crime reduction impacts associated with problem-oriented policing when compared to the effects reported by the more rigorous research designs.

Policing crime hot spots represents an important advance in focusing police crime prevention practice (Braga 2001; Braga and Weisburd 2010). Since crime hot spots generate the bulk of urban crime problems (Sherman, Gartin, and Buerger 1989; Weisburd et al. 2004), it seems commonsensical to address the conditions and situations that give rise to the criminal opportunities that sustain high-activity crime places. The available evaluation evidence also suggests that problem-oriented policing holds great promise in addressing the criminogenic attributes of specific places that cause them to be crime hot spots. A recently updated Campbell Collaboration review of nineteen rigorous evaluation studies found that hot spots policing generates modest crime reductions and these crime control benefits diffuse into areas immediately surrounding targeted crime hot spots (Braga, Papachristos, and Hureau 2011). A moderator analysis of the types of hot spots policing programs found that problem-oriented policing interventions generate larger crime control impacts when compared to interventions that simply increase levels of traditional police actions in crime hot spots.

The Campbell hot spots policing review also reported that problem-oriented policing interventions generated larger diffusion of crime control benefits into areas immediately surrounding the targeted hot spot areas (Braga, Papachristos, and Hureau 2011). Many of the problem-oriented policing interventions used to control crime hot spots were described as suffering from superficial problem analyses, a preponderance of traditional policing tactics, and limited situational crime prevention responses. However, these generally "shallow" problem-oriented policing programs still generated crime reduction gains. This finding supports the assertion made earlier by Braga and Weisburd (2006) that limited problem-oriented policing, also known simply as "problem solving," is a stronger approach to crime prevention when compared to traditional police crime prevention strategies.

A number of U.S. jurisdictions have been experimenting with new problem-oriented policing frameworks, generally known as pulling levers focused deterrence strategies, to understand and respond to serious crime problems generated by chronically offending groups, such as gun violence among gang-involved offenders (Kennedy 2008). These approaches include the well-known Boston Gun Project and its Operation Ceasefire intervention (Braga et al. 2001) discussed earlier in this essay and typically represent carefully implemented problem-oriented policing projects. Another recently completed Campbell Collaboration systematic review of focused deterrence strategies found that ten out of eleven rigorous evaluations reported significant crime reduction effects associated with this problem-oriented approach (Braga and Weisburd 2012). A meta-analysis of these programs reported that focused deterrence strategies were associated with an overall statistically-significant, medium-sized crime reduction effect. This review provides additional evidence that the general problem-oriented policing approach can inform innovative violence reduction strategies and generate impressive crime control gains.

5.4 CONCLUSION

Problem-oriented policing represents an important innovation in American policing. Indeed, the advocates of this young and evolving approach have accomplished much since Herman Goldstein first presented the concept in 1979. The early experiences in Madison, Wisconsin (Goldstein and Susmilch 1982), London (Hoare, Stewart, and Purcell 1984), Baltimore County, Maryland (Cordner 1986), and Newport News,

Virginia (Eck and Spelman 1987) demonstrated that police officers could greatly improve their handling of crime problems by taking a problem-oriented approach. Since then, many police agencies in the United States, the United Kingdom, Canada, Scandinavia, Australia, and New Zealand have continued to implement problem-oriented policing, to apply it to a wide range of crime and disorder problems, and to change their organizations to better support problem-oriented policing (www.popcenter.org).

Problem-oriented policing seems well positioned to remain a central crime prevention strategy for police departments in the future. Eck (2006, 118–19) summarized problem-oriented policing as having three core principles: 1) the *empirical principle* that states that the public demands that the police handle a wide range of problems; 2) the *normative principle* that claims that police are supposed to reduce problems rather than simply respond to incidents and apply the relevant criminal law; and 3) the *scientific principle* that asserts that police should take a scientific approach to crime problems that applies analytical approaches and interventions based on sound theory and evaluation of evidence. While knowledge and practice will continue to evolve, the core principles of the approach that drive its popularity seem likely to remain constant. There seems to be consensus among police leaders, scholars, and the public that police agencies should be focused on problem reduction—that is, ensuring fewer, less serious, and less harmful crime and disorder problems (Eck 2006).

The practice of problem-oriented policing sometimes falls short of the principles suggested by Herman Goldstein (1979, 1990). While the approach is more than thirty years old, it is important to recognize that problem-oriented policing is still in its formative stages and its practice is still developing. Progress in policing is incremental and slow, and that does not make problem-oriented policing unrealistic. Police departments should strive to implement problem-oriented policing properly but recognize that even weak problem solving can be beneficial when applied to recurring crime problems. Within police departments, it seems like a balanced problem-oriented policing agenda would include both a commitment among officers in the field to apply problem solving techniques to address problems that they encounter on a routine basis and a commitment to maintaining a centralized problem-oriented policing unit capable of conducting high-quality analyses of larger and more persistent problems and developing more creative responses to reduce them.

In closing, it also seems important to point out that the demonstrated crime reduction efficacy of problem-oriented policing is a striking result considering the large body of research that shows the ineffectiveness of many police crime prevention efforts (Visher and Weisburd 1998). The robustness of problem-oriented policing is underscored by the observation that, even when it is not implemented properly, the approach still generates noteworthy crime reduction gains (Braga and Weisburd 2006). It is tantalizing to think that had the police more fully implemented the problem-oriented approach and took a more specific, more focused approach to crime and disorder problems, crime control benefits might have been greater. Of course, this requires the development of such skills from both trial and error experience of problem solving on the street and additional training in the problem-oriented model, particularly in the area of problem analysis. The investment in the acquisition of these skills could be well worth the effort.

References

Bayley, David. 1994. *Police for the Future*. New York: Oxford University Press.

Bittner, Egon. 1970. *The Functions of the Police in Modern Society*. New York: Aronson.

Braga, Anthony A. 2001. "The Effects of Hot Spots Policing on Crime." *Annals of the American Academy of Political and Social Science* 455:104–25.

——. 2008. *Problem-Oriented Policing and Crime Prevention*, 2d ed. Boulder, CO: Lynne Rienner.

Braga, Anthony A., and Ronald V. Clarke. 1994. "Improved Radios and More Stripped Cars in Germany: A Routine Activities Analysis." *Security Journal* 5:154–59.

Braga, Anthony A., David M. Kennedy, Elin J. Waring and Anne M. Piehl. 2001. "Problem-Oriented Policing, Deterrence, and Youth Violence: An Evaluation of Boston's Operation Ceasefire." *Journal of Research in Crime and Delinquency* 38:195–225.

Braga, Anthony A., Andrew V. Papachristos, and David M. Hureau. 2011. *The Effects of Hot Spots Policing on Crime: An Updated Systematic Review and Meta-Analysis*. Unpublished manuscript. Cambridge, MA: Harvard University.

Braga, Anthony A., and David L. Weisburd. 2006. "Problem-Oriented Policing: The Disconnect Between Principles and Practice." In *Police Innovation: Contrasting Perspectives*, edited by David L. Weisburd and Anthony A. Braga, 133–154. New York: Cambridge University Press.

——. 2010. *Policing Problem Places: Crime Hot Spots and Effective Prevention*. New York: Oxford University Press.

——. 2012. "The Effects of Focused Deterrence Strategies on Crime: A Systematic Review and Meta-Analysis of the Empirical Evidence." *Journal of Research in Crime and Delinquency* 49(3):323–358.

Brantingham, Paul J., and Patricia L. Brantingham, eds. 1991. *Environmental Criminology*, 2d ed. Prospect Heights, IL: Waveland Press.

Buerger, Michael. 1994. "The Problems of Problem-Solving: Resistance, Interdependencies, and Conflicting Interests." *American Journal of Police* 13:1–36.

Capowich, George, and Jan Roehl. 1994. "Problem-Oriented Policing: Actions and Effectiveness in San Diego." In *The Challenge of Community Policing: Testing the Promises*, edited by Dennis Rosenbaum, 127–146. Thousand Oaks, CA: Sage.

Clarke, Ronald V. 1990. "Deterring Obscene Phone Callers: Preliminary Results of the New Jersey Experience." *Security Journal* 1:143–48.

Clarke, Ronald V. 1995. "Situational Crime Prevention." In *Building a Safer Society: Strategic Approaches to Crime Prevention*, edited by Michael Tonry and David Farrington, 91–150. Chicago: University of Chicago Press.

Clarke, Ronald V., ed. 1997. *Situational Crime Prevention: Successful Case Studies*, 2d ed. Albany, NY: Harrow and Heston.

Clarke, Ronald V. 1998. "Defining Police Strategies: Problem Solving, Problem-Oriented Policing and Community-Oriented Policing." In *Problem-Oriented Policing: Crime-Specific Problems, Critical Issues, and Making POP Work*, edited by Tara O'Connor and Anne C. Grant, 315–330. Washington, DC: Police Executive Research Forum.

Clarke, Ronald V., and John E. Eck. 2007. *Understanding Risky Facilities.* Problem-Oriented Guides for Police, Problem Solving Tools Series 6. Washington, DC: U.S. Department of Justice, Office of Community Oriented Policing Services.

Clarke, Ronald V., and Marcus Felson. 1993. "Introduction: Criminology, Routine Activity, and Rational Choice." In *Routine Activity and Rational Choice,* edited by Ronald V. Clarke and Marcus Felson, 1–14. New Brunswick, NJ: Transaction Press.

Clarke, Ronald V., and Herman Goldstein. 2002. "Reducing Theft at Construction Sites: Lessons from a Problem-Oriented Project." In *Analysis for Crime Prevention,* edited by Nick Tilley, 89–130. Monsey, NY: Criminal Justice Press.

Cohen, Lawrence E., and Marcus Felson. 1979. "Social Change and Crime Rate Trends: A Routine Activity Approach." *American Sociological Review* 44:588–605.

Cordner, Gary. 1986. "Fear of Crime and the Police: An Evaluation of a Fear Reduction Strategy." *Journal of Police Science and Administration* 14:223–33.

——. 1998. "Problem-Oriented Policing Vs. Zero Tolerance." In *Problem-Oriented Policing: Crime-Specific Problems, Critical Issues, and Making POP Work,* edited by Tara O'Connor and Anne C. Grant, 303–314. Washington, DC: Police Executive Research Forum.

Cordner, Gary, and Elizabeth P. Biebel. 2005. "Problem-Oriented Policing in Practice." *Criminology and Public Policy* 4:155–80.

Cornish, Derek, and Ronald V. Clarke, eds. 1986. *The Reasoning Criminal: Rational Choice Perspectives on Offending.* New York, NY: Springer-Verlag.

Eck, John E. 2000. "Problem-Oriented Policing and Its Problems: The Means Over Ends Syndrome Strikes Back and the Return of the Problem-Solver." Unpublished manuscript. Cincinnati, OH: University of Cincinnati.

Eck, John E. 2006. "Science, Values, and Problem-Oriented Policing: why Problem-Oriented Policing?" In *Police Innovation: Contrasting Perspectives,* edited by David L. Weisburd and Anthony A. Braga, 117–132. New York: Cambridge University Press.

Eck, John E., and William Spelman. 1987. *Problem-Solving: Problem-Oriented Policing in Newport News.* Washington, DC: National Institute of Justice.

Farrington, David P., and Anthony Petrosino. 2001. "The Campbell Collaboration Crime and Justice Group." *Annals of the American Academy of Political and Social Science* 578:35–49.

Felson, Marcus, and R.V. Clarke. 1998. *Opportunity Makes the Thief: Practical Theory for Crime Prevention.* Crime Prevention and Detection Series Paper 98. London, UK: Home Office.

Goldstein, Herman 1979. "Improving Policing: A Problem-Oriented Approach." *Crime and Delinquency* 25:236–58.

Goldstein, Herman. 1990. *Problem-Oriented Policing.* Philadelphia, PA: Temple University Press.

Goldstein, Herman, and Susan Susmilch. 1982. *Experimenting with the Problem-Oriented Approach to Improve Police Service: A Report and Some Reflections on Two Case Studies.* Madison: University of Wisconsin Law School.

Gottfredson, Michael, and Travis Hirschi. 1990. *A General Theory of Crime.* Stanford, CA: Stanford University Press.

Greenwood, Peter, Jan Chaiken, and Joan Petersilia. 1977. *The Investigation Process.* Lexington, MA: Lexington Books.

Hoare, M. A., G. Stewart, and C. M. Purcell. 1984. *The Problem-Oriented Approach: Four Pilot Studies.* London: Metropolitan Police, Management Services Department.

Kelling, George, Tony Pate, Duane Dieckman, and Charles Brown. 1974. *The Kansas City Preventive Patrol Experiment: A Technical Report.* Washington, DC: Police Foundation.

Kennedy, David M. 1997. "Pulling Levers: Chronic Offenders, High-Crime Settings, and a Theory of Prevention." *Valparaiso University Law Review* 31:449–84.

——. 2008. *Deterrence and Crime Prevention*. London and New York: Routledge.

Kennedy, David M., and Mark H. Moore. 1995. "Underwriting the Risky Investment in Community Policing: What Social Science Should Be Doing to Evaluate Community Policing." *Justice System Journal* 17:271–90.

Kennedy, David M., Anne M. Piehl, and Anthony A. Braga. 1996. "Youth Violence in Boston: Gun Markets, Serious Youth Offenders, and a Use-Reduction Strategy." *Law and Contemporary Problems* 59:147–97.

Moore, Mark H. 1992. "Problem-Solving and Community Policing." In *Modern Policing*, edited by Michael Tonry and Norval Morris, 99–158. Chicago: University of Chicago Press.

O'Connor Shelly, Tara, and Anne Grant, eds. 1998. *Problem-Oriented Policing: Crime-Specific Problems, Critical Issues, and Making POP Work*. Washington, DC: Police Executive Research Forum.

Pease, Kenneth 1991. "The Kirkholt Project: Preventing Burglary on a British Public Housing Estate." *Security Journal* 2:73–7.

Poyner, Barry, and Barry Webb. 1991. *Crime Free Housing*. Oxford, UK: Butterworth-Architecture.

Read, Timothy, and Nick Tilley. 2000. *Not Rocket Science? Problem-Solving and Crime Reduction*. Crime Reduction Series Paper 6. London, UK: Policing and Crime Reduction Unit, Home Office.

Reisig, Michael D. 2010. "Community and Problem-Oriented Policing." In *Crime and Justice: A Review of Research*, vol. 39, edited by Michael Tonry, 1–53. Chicago: University of Chicago Press.

Sampson, Rana, and Michael Scott. 2000. *Tackling Crime and Other Public-Safety Problems: Case Studies in Problem Solving*. Washington, DC: Office of Community Oriented Policing Services, U.S. Department of Justice.

Scott, Michael. 2000. *Problem-Oriented Policing: Reflections on the First 20 Years*. Washington, DC: Office of Community Oriented Policing Services, U.S. Department of Justice.

Scott, Michael, and Ronald V. Clarke. 2000. "A Review of Submission for the Herman Goldstein Excellence in Problem-Oriented Policing." In *Problem Oriented Policing: Crime-Specific Problems, Critical Issues, and Making POP Work*, vol. 3, edited by Corina Sole Brito and Eugenia Gratto, 213–230. Washington, DC: Police Executive Research Forum.

Sherman, Lawrence. 1991. "Herman Goldstein: Problem-Oriented Policing [book review]." *Journal of Criminal Law and Criminology* 82:693–702.

Sherman, Lawrence, Patrick Gartin, and Michael Buerger. 1989. "Hot Spots of Predatory Crime: Routine Activities and the Criminology of Place." *Criminology* 27:27–56.

Skogan, Wesley. 2006. *Police and Community in Chicago: A Tale of Three Cities*. New York: Oxford University Press.

Skogan, Wesley, and Kathleen Frydl, eds. 2004. *Fairness and Effectiveness in Policing: The Evidence*. Committee to Review Research on Police Policy and Practices. Washington, DC: The National Academies Press.

Skogan, Wesley, and Susan Hartnett. 1997. *Community Policing, Chicago Style*. New York: Oxford University Press.

Sole Brito, Corina, and Tracy Allan, eds. 1999. *Problem-Oriented Policing: Crime-Specific Problems, Critical Issues, and Making POP Work*, vol. 2. Washington, DC: Police Executive Research Forum.

Sole Brito, Corina, and Eugenia Gratto, eds. 2000. *Problem-Oriented Policing: Crime-Specific Problems, Critical Issues, and Making POP Work,* vol. 3. Washington, DC: Police Executive Research Forum.

Spelman, William, and Dale Brown. 1984. *Calling the Police: Citizen Reporting of Serious Crime.* Washington, DC: U.S. Government Printing Office.

Visher, Christy, and David L. Weisburd. 1998. "Identifying What Works: Recent Trends in Crime Prevention Strategies." *Crime, Law and Social Change* 28:223–42.

Walker, Samuel. 1992. *The Police in America,* 2d ed. New York: McGraw-Hill.

Weisburd, David L., Shawn Bushway, Cynthia Lum, and Sue-Ming Yang. 2004. "Trajectories of Crime at Places: A Longitudinal Study of Street Segments in the City of Seattle." *Criminology* 42:283–322.

Weisburd, David L., and John E. Eck. 2004. "What Can Police Do to Reduce Crime, Disorder, and Fear?" *Annals of the American Academy of Political and Social Science* 593:42–65.

Weisburd, David L., and J. Thomas McEwen, eds. 1997. *Crime Mapping and Crime Prevention.* Monsey, NY: Criminal Justice Press.

Weisburd, David L., Cody W. Telep, Joshua C. Hinkle, and John E. Eck. 2010. "Is Problem-Oriented Policing Effective in Reducing Crime and Disorder? Findings from a Campbell Systematic Review." *Criminology and Public Policy* 9:139–72.

CHAPTER 6

··

ORDER MAINTENANCE
POLICING

··

DAVID THACHER*

Public spaces are shared spaces, and the people who share them often disagree about how they can legitimately be used. Their complaints range from the petty gripes of thin-skinned people unhappy with the hustle and bustle of urban life to the desperate pleas of the seriously aggrieved—complaints about raucous protestors in the city square trying to effect political change, about hookers and drug pushers selling their vices on the sidewalks, about teenagers trying to impress their friends in the park, about street musicians collecting tips, about gang members trying to assert control over turf, about families drinking beer on the beach, about misogynists harassing women from their front steps, about immigrants roasting cuy in city parks, about hawkers selling bootlegged videos on the sidewalk, about skateboarders practicing kickflips on the softball bleachers, about mentally ill people yelling at friends and strangers in city plazas, about business owners dumping trash in the gutter, about homeless men sleeping on bus stop benches, and about college students milling around on the sidewalk clutching plastic cups while Lady Gaga blasts from the fraternity speakers an hour before kickoff. Some of the targets of these complaints are exercising socially-sanctioned rights that legally *cannot* be infringed, while others are exercising important personal freedoms worth protecting as far as possible. At the same time, all of them make use of the public realm—the sidewalks, parks, airwaves, beaches, plazas, and bus stops that the members of our dense and interdependent society share—in ways that other people using those spaces consider excessive and impolitic, crowding out (they say) their legitimate claims to use those spaces themselves. Order maintenance involves attempts to resolve these conflicts over the use of that shared environment; it is the police role in defining and regulating the fair use of public spaces.

That is a revisionary definition. It has to be, for our current understanding of order maintenance is in shambles. The contemporary use of the term "order maintenance" apparently began with James Q. Wilson, who defined it alternatively as the regulation of behavior "that disturbs or threatens to disturb the public peace or that involves face-to-face conflict among two or more persons" (Wilson 1968, 16) or as "handling disputes... among citizens who accuse each other of being at fault" (as opposed to law enforcement work focused on the victimization of innocents) (Wilson 1969, 131), but those definitions have long since faded from view.[1] Today order maintenance usually gets defined by enumeration, as the enforcement of a wide range of quality of life standards including rules against public drinking, noise pollution, public indecency, verbal harassment, aggressive panhandling, and obstruction. (Wesley Skogan recently complained that such things "constitute an untidy list" united by no principle other than that "legislators do not like them" [Skogan 2008, 401].) It is often treated as a residual category that refers to most of the things police do besides enforcing the core elements of the criminal law.

This ambiguity has allowed the order maintenance function to degenerate. Most important, it has increasingly become identified with a form of aggressive policing aimed at providing more opportunities for police to question, search, and detain people they encounter on the street (Fagan and Davies 2000; Harcourt 2001; Gau and Brunson 2010). That meaning of "order maintenance" is hardly new. The police have always used the broad discretion that public order laws grant them as a covert tool to monitor and control suspicious and unpopular people in circumstances when doing so overtly would be forbidden. Disorderly conduct and vagrancy laws have been used to harass labor agitators like the Wobblies and the peaceful protesters of the civil rights era, to banish tramps from city limits ("if you ever come back to Philadelphia we'll arrest you"), and to round up people suspected of crimes that can't be proven (Foote 1956; Douglas 1960; Dubber 2001). These pretextual uses of public order law continue today, as many cities encourage police to enforce public drinking and loitering rules not out of any intrinsic concern about the behaviors they regulate but to give police more opportunity to search for guns and fugitives. Those practices have been the most significant lightning rod for controversy about order maintenance policing, and there is a danger that its abuse will drag down its legitimate uses as well.

This essay aims to pry apart the order maintenance function proper from the morally-ambiguous shadows it has always cast. Section 6.1 begins historically, clarifying the central place of order maintenance in the earliest modern police agencies and the evolution of that role up through the present. Section 6.2 then turns to the rationale for order maintenance policing today, and Sections 6.3 and 6.4 discuss two major complexities involved in carrying it out. Section 6.5 sketches some key questions for police scholarship about this topic in the future.

This essay emphasizes several conclusions:

- The heart of the order maintenance function involves regulating the fair use of public spaces by the members of a diverse public, who often have conflicting standards about how those spaces should be used.
- Order maintenance has been part of the police mandate since the inception of modern police agencies. Because public order is a collective good, the rise of full-time professional police was an essential step in providing it.

- The abuse of the order maintenance function to round up and harass suspicious and unpopular people has also been present from the start, as the ambiguity and flexibility of this role have repeatedly tempted police to hijack it for ulterior aims.
- The "broken windows" thesis may or may not be correct, but it is far less important for the justification of order maintenance than commonly appreciated.
- Order maintenance is best understood as a branch of problem-oriented policing concerned with a particular type of community problem called "disorder."
- A major frontier for order maintenance practice involves the development and wider use of more restrained forms of police authority short of arrest, including prevention tactics, persuasion, civil penalties, and temporary detention.

6.1 THE RISE AND FALL OF ORDER MAINTENANCE

The modern police arose as a byproduct of nineteenth-century urbanization, and that connection clarifies the deep roots of their order maintenance role. Police historians often suggest that the establishment of full-time public police represented an attempt to substitute formal social control for the informal controls that urban life had eroded (Lane 1967, 2; Richardson 1970, 16; Miller 1977, 5; Monkkonen 1981b, 65; Walker 1998, 27), but urbanization had another implication for social control as well. In the city people made their homes in dense mixed-use environments that had not yet been sorted out and segregated along the lines of the modern metropolis, and when they ventured out of those homes they came together in the crowded streets, squares, and parks that began to proliferate in the nineteenth century. This complex environment made new demands on their behavior, as conduct that would have bothered no one in sparse rural spaces became problematic in the densely shared environments of the city (Lane 1968, 163; Schneider 1980).

The largely-mercenary system of law enforcement that preceded the modern police was badly-suited to enforce those demands, relying as it did on crime victims to detect and prosecute their own cases. The trouble was that disorder worth worrying about usually affects *many* people rather a single individual, so none of its "victims" has the right incentive to combat it. The American colonies did pass laws designed to protect the public realm—rules against grazing cattle or removing trees from public lands, rules prohibiting disruptive behavior near the town meetinghouse, rules requiring homeowners to keep their chimneys clean, rules prohibiting the obstruction of roads and highways or riding horses on those designed for pedestrians—but enforcement was at best uneven (e.g., Smith 1961, 110–14, 124–26; Flaherty 1972, ch. 7). Like other jobs targeting offenses against intangible or diffuse victims (such as risk management, crime prevention, and morals policing), order maintenance only gets vigorous attention from professional police; it is a collective good, so only collective institutions can provide it effectively. Roger Lane (1968) put the point memorably: "Private citizens may initiate the processes of justice when injured directly, but professionals are usually required to deal with those whose merely immoral or distasteful behavior hurts no one in particular. It takes real cops to make drunk arrests" (160).

6.1.1 The Roots of Order Maintenance: 1829–1900

In fact, drunk arrests skyrocketed after the arrival of the first modern police agencies, and other forms of order maintenance did too (Phillips 1977, 84–87). In Boston, home of one of the oldest police department in the United States, officers spent most of their time maintaining order in public spaces—regulating traffic, rounding up stray animals, controlling public drunkenness, forcing property owners to clean up ice and obstructions from adjacent sidewalks, and arresting would-be poachers from Boston Common, among other jobs (Lane 1967). Police in other cities did similar work. In the most extensive overview of nineteeth-century American police, Eric Monkkonen (1981b, 103) found that almost two-thirds of arrests in eighteen large cities fell into order maintenance categories like public drunkenness, disorderly conduct, and loitering. In London, more than 80 percent of arrests in 1838 invoked order maintenance charges (Ignatieff 1979).

It is hard to tell what exactly all this order maintenance work involved. On paper, it aimed to clarify and enforce the new standards of public behavior demanded by the urban environment, but in practice it often served other aims. The old vagrancy statutes, in particular, usually get categorized as "public order" rules, but police mainly used them to control and harass unpopular people. In the 1880s Christopher Tiedeman, one of the leading legal commentators of the era, explicitly advocated the use of vagrancy laws to detain and punish suspicious outsiders when police could not prove the crimes they were sure they had committed; and in the postbellum South, vagrancy rules were sometimes used to exert control over free blacks—even returning them to a version of slavery by pressuring them to enter exploitative labor contracts (Dubber 2001, 911–12). Some evidence suggests that the use of public order statutes for harassment increased over the course of the nineteenth century, as the share of public order arrests dismissed without prosecution grew (Monkkonen 1981b, 85).

In other cases, order maintenance degenerated into morals enforcement. By the end of the century, New York police used public order statutes so extensively to harass homosexuals that their internal records soon began noting which arrests for "disorderly conduct" fell into the subcategory of "degeneracy" (Chauncey 1995, 185), and Victorian moralists pressed the police to enforce middle-class standards of virtue on immigrant and working-class life. That last application of order maintenance inspired Sidney Harring's memorable comment that "the criminologist's definition of 'public order crimes' comes perilously close to the historian's description of 'working-class leisure-time activity'" (Harring 1983, 198).

It would be a mistake, however, to conclude that nineteenth-century order maintenance never went beyond morals policing. In many cities the police resisted pressures to convert their public order role into morals enforcement because they were too embedded in the communities they policed to enforce any outsiders' moral code (Walker

1998, 58–59; von Hoffman 1992, 318). In the 1860s London police and the British parliament pushed back against calls from influential Londoners to clamp down on noisy street musicians, insisting (as one member of parliament put it) that street music "was about the only innocent recreation the poor and powerless had left to them" (Winter 1993, 74–79). London police commissioners also refused to enforce the comprehensive ban on Sunday trading the Sabbatarians demanded, directing police "to prevent street cries which disturbed church services but to ignore quiet selling" (Miller 1977, 133). They handled the Sunday blue laws similarly, trying to prevent the disorderly drunks who spilled out of nearby gin palaces and taverns from disrupting church services but opposing a complete ban on alcohol sales (Miller 1977). In conflicts like these, the advocates of public order were not just prudes concerned with whether other people conformed with their own ideals of personal virtue. At least some of them plausibly claimed that the other side's use of public space disrupted their own.

6.1.2 Retrenchment: 1900–1980

In the century that followed, the police role began to change in fundamental ways that transformed and narrowed the order maintenance function. Eric Monkkonen's (1981a) detailed compendium of police statistics for large American cities over more than a century plots a steady decline in order maintenance arrests, from about 50 per 1,000 population in 1860 to one-fifth that number by 1980, leading him to conclude that "as arrest categories, drunkenness and disorderly conduct continue to diminish and may be destined to virtually disappear" (543). Elsewhere Monkkonen (1981b, ch. 4) suggests that this decline was part of a narrowing of the police function to focus on the control of serious crime, which had already begun by the final decades of the 19th century and was largely complete by 1920. Other historians date the timing of this shift somewhat later but argue even more strongly that it reflected a deliberate movement "away from public order offenses towards the more urgent task of protecting lives and property" (Wertsch 1987, 448; cf. Watts 1983, 357). In their eyes order maintenance is a relic of an older model of policing, one that institutional progress has rightfully left behind.[2]

The evidence for this common view is more fragmentary and ambiguous than commonly appreciated. When Eugene Watts (1983, 355) writes that the police department he studied "completed its transition to a primarily crime-fighting agency by the later 1940s," one wonders how he accounts for the large body of ethnographic research in the 1960s and 1970s that documented how little of *any* police agency's workload focused on "crime-fighting" even at those late dates. Progressive reformers at the beginning of the twentieth century did try mightily to refocus police attention on serious crime, but as Robert Fogelson (1977) has shown those reforms often failed.

As some of Watts's own work suggests, two factors make the broad decline in order maintenance arrests over the twentieth century hard to interpret. First, public order arrests cover a hodgepodge of different kinds of events, including not just order maintenance proper but also the many distortions of that task that have appeared throughout history—particularly its use as a pretext to detain, question, and punish the suspicious and despised. Some of the decline in order maintenance arrests may reflect a decline in the share that fell into these degenerate categories rather than a decline in police regulation of public spaces. That seems particularly likely after the 1960s, when the share of all police arrests that involved drunkenness, disorderly conduct, and vagrancy fell dramatically (from 44 percent in 1965 to 9 percent in 2005). Near the beginning of this period Supreme Court Justice William Douglas (1960, 9) worried that police made widespread use of order maintenance statutes to "as a cloak or cover for arresting and convicting people for some other crime that cannot be proved or for conduct that is not a crime," but a decade later Douglas authored the Court's opinion in *Papachristou v. City of Jacksonville*, 405 U.S. 156 (1972), which struck down one of the most important statutory foundations of that practice. As Watts (1983) himself found in a different context, when police abandon the use of such catch-all statutes for crime control and investigation, the number of order maintenance arrests plummets while arrests for the crimes they had been used to target surge. *Papachristou* was only part of a broader legal revolution during the 1960s and 1970s that transformed the legal basis for order maintenance. As the courts struck down many state laws and local ordinances for vagueness and infringement on constitutionally-protected freedoms, they were replaced by more narrowly-tailored public order statutes (Livingston 1997). As Douglas's role in *Papachristou* suggests, one motivation for this legal transformation was precisely to rein in the pretextual use of order maintenance authority. To the extent that it succeeded, the drop in public order arrests since the 1960s may reflect a purification of the order maintenance function rather than its demise.

Second, order maintenance does not always or even usually end in arrest, so a declining number of public order arrests may reflect a shift in order maintenance tactics rather than a decline in its prevalence. Once again Watts himself provides an apt illustration. In 1912, the St. Louis Police Commissioners empowered officers to issue court notices for many public order violations rather than arresting the perpetrators, and order maintenance arrests immediately began a steep decline, falling 75 percent over the next decade (Watts 1983, 347). Four years earlier Cleveland police chief Fred Kohler had announced a policy encouraging officers to avoid arrests whenever possible for less-serious violations of the law, including most public order offenses. Instead he directed police to issue warnings or (in the case of juveniles) escort the offender home to his or her parents for discipline. Drunkenness and disorderly conduct arrests immediately dropped by two-thirds (Walker 1977, 95–96). Changes like these did reflect a judgment that arrest was often an inappropriate response to public disorder, but in each case police officials called for alternative tactics rather than no response at all.

Finally, insofar as the priority of order maintenance did decline over the course of the twentieth century, the decline may not reflect more enlightened police attitudes as much as it reflects social changes that many people regard with ambivalence. Over the past century the dense and relatively unsegregated cities of the nineteenth century gave way to sprawling and fragmented metropolitan areas with much less street life than their predecessors, and cultural ideals have increasingly directed Americans to the private home rather than the public realm for fulfillment (Sennett 1977; Schneider 1978). Monkkonen (1981a, 555–57) once analyzed in considerable detail whether the steep decline in arrests for public drunkenness over the course of the twentieth century might be connected with the relatively modest changes in overall per capita alcohol consumption, but the proportion of alcohol consumed *at home* changed much more dramatically during this period. According to Ray Oldenberg (1999, 166) (who views the neighborhood tavern as an important social institution that once helped to bind many communities together), the share of alcohol consumed in public places like bars fell from around 90 percent in the first half of the twentieth century to somewhere between 10 and 30 percent by its end. Part of the decline in public order arrests may be the result of a decline in public life itself. As our social and recreational lives have increasingly retreated to the private home, the conflicts they generate fade out of the public realm and reappear, to some degree, in the domestic sphere.

6.1.3   Revival: 1980 to the Present

After decades of effort to rein in the order maintenance function, the 1980s saw a revival of enthusiasm in some quarters for expanding it. The watershed was clearly Wilson and Kelling's "Broken Windows" essay, which more than anything was a reaction to the transformation of public order law that had just transpired. After two decades of court decisions striking down many of the legal tools police had used to maintain order, Wilson and Kelling (1982, 35) argued that "this wish to 'decriminalize' behavior that 'harms no one'— and thus remove the ultimate sanction police can employ to maintain neighborhood order" was "a mistake." By the time "Broken Windows" appeared, disorder had already become a major public issue in cities like New York, where city officials had already begun to develop aggressive new strategies to tackle graffiti in the subways and streetwalking in Times Square (Vitale 2008). The accelerating deinstitutionalization of the mentally ill through the 1970s (Jencks 1992) probably contributed to the revival of attention to public order; in many cities the call to "restore order" to public spaces emphasized problems like aggressive panhandling, verbal harassment, public sleeping, and public urination commonly associated with the homeless mentally ill. For many critics, that focus made the revival of order maintenance look like an exclusionary and possibly mean-spirited attack on the disadvantaged (e.g., Waldron 1991; Beckett and Herbert 2010).

A few years after "Broken Windows" appeared, police agencies around the country embarked on new aggressive order maintenance strategies. Most had given patrol officers no direction at all in this area, and several of them hired Kelling as a consultant to develop enforcement guidelines and disorder reduction programs. The most prominent was the New York City Transit Police, where Kelling worked with a transit system task force to develop a tailored strategy for restoring order. (A one-time student of Herman Goldstein, Kelling viewed this task as an application of problem-oriented policing to the "problem" of public order, and he circulated material from a draft of Goldstein's forthcoming book to some of the task force members.)

(Kelling 1997; Kelling and Coles 1996). Other cities soon followed suit throughout the country and elsewhere in the world; Britain's "Anti-Social Behavior" initiative, in particular, was often presented as an adaptation and extension of Broken Windows policing (Tonry and Bildsten 2009). Back in the United States, national agencies like the communitarian American Alliance for Rights and Responsibilities (AARR) began to develop and support legal tools designed to facilitate more vigorous order maintenance efforts, such as aggressive panhandling, curfew, and gang loitering ordinances (e.g., Teir 1993). More recently, the National Center for Problem-Oriented Policing (CPOP) has contributed to the development of order maintenance policing through guides focused on a wide variety of specific "disorder" problems, from disorder at day labor sites (Guerette 2006) to loud car stereos (Scott 2001). CPOP's work, in particular, has helped to move the revival of order maintenance beyond the narrow focus on the homeless where it has frequently become mired.

6.2 THE RATIONALE FOR ORDER MAINTENANCE

The history of the order maintenance function, filled as it is with controversy and abuse, invites the question of why the police should bother with it at all. Today the most widely-debated answer comes from Wilson and Kelling (1982), who argued (among other things) that vigorous order maintenance may reduce serious crime, as unchecked disorder drives law-abiding residents indoors and emboldens would-be criminals by signaling that the neighborhood is out of control. The debate about this hypothesis will be familiar to students of the police, and it makes little sense to provide a comprehensive review here.[3] (The literature it inspired has grown so large that a full review would make it impossible to discuss anything else in this essay. As Gary Sykes [1986] already lamented four years after "Broken Windows" appeared, that tendency to crowd out more substantive discussion of the order maintenance function has been the most unfortunate byproduct of the disorder-causes crime hypothesis.) Instead I will try to explain why this approach to the study of order maintenance policing may matter less than the attention it has gotten suggests.

6.2.1 The Limits of Broken Windows

First, many of the most significant order maintenance debates are debates about the kinds of behavior the police can and cannot legitimately regulate, and the disorder-causes-crime thesis could not resolve them even if it were correct. If public behavior like panhandling causes crime in the way that Wilson and Kelling suggested, the effect is too indirect to provide a reason for criminalizing it. We rarely hold people criminally responsible for the indirect effects that their otherwise-innocuous behavior has on the voluntary actions of others; for example, we do not hold moviemakers liable for the copycat crimes their films inspire (Thacher 2004; von Hirsch 1996). Our reluctance to do that makes good sense, for abandoning these moral limitations on the extent of personal responsibility would threaten to undermine any principled limits to police authority. If a public behavior (or private, for that matter) can be shown to raise the odds of crime down the road, police can put a stop to it—regardless of the intrinsic character of the behavior, the motives underlying it, the attitude of the person engaged in it towards the crime it causes, or other factors that normally help to define the outer limits of moral responsibility. These are not academic worries. Many recent abuses of the order maintenance function seem to result from a sense that the ends justify the means, as police press order maintenance authority as hard as possible for the sake of crime control (Fagan and Davies 2000).

In principle, the effect of disorder on crime might still play a legitimate role in determining the priority that police assign to enforcing the public order standards that have been justified on other grounds, but it turns out to be much more difficult to determine what that effect *is* than either advocates or critics of the broken windows hypothesis usually acknowledge.[4] (The fact that they still disagree about the basic question of whether order maintenance has *any* effect on serious crime after thirty years of research seems to illustrate that difficulty.) My own sense, probably not shared by most criminologists, is that the most compelling experimental studies of order maintenance have identified significant effects on neighborhood crime in the initiatives they studied, though none of these studies is beyond reproach and others find no direct causal link between disorder and crime. Regardless, order maintenance can take so many different forms and play out in so many different neighborhood contexts that it seems unlikely that there is any one answer—or any manageable family of answers—to the question of whether it "works" to reduce serious crime.

The drive to arrive at that kind of answer reflects the influence of the program evaluation paradigm on recent police research, but there are other ways to study the link between disorder and crime. In particular, we might look for more robust scientific understanding through abstract studies of basic causal mechanisms (Heckman 2005; Cartwright and Pemberton 2011)—an approach illustrated by a recent Dutch experiment that demonstrated how disorder undermines the commitment to abide by social norms in favor of a "hedonistic" psychology of self-interest (Keizer, Lindenberg, and Steg 2008). (In one of the study's three experiments, for example, the researchers left an envelope containing a visible 5-Euro note sticking out of a mailbox. On days when the researchers left litter in the area or painted graffiti on the walls, a quarter of those who passed by stole the envelope, while only one-eighth did when the litter and graffiti were gone.) The study has been justly described as a major contribution to our understanding of the Broken Windows hypothesis. Unfortunately, when work like this does generate reliable knowledge of basic psychological mechanisms, that knowledge can be difficult to apply in the uncontrolled environments we ultimately want to intervene in because even when we can be sure those mechanisms operate, other forces may overwhelm them in particular cases (Cartwright 1999). After the Dutch study appeared, critics complained that the contrived and relatively trivial nature of the scenarios it examined make it foolhardy to apply its results to the serious crime problems of troubled neighborhoods (Kaplan 2008; Reisig 2010, 34).

Taken together, these two challenges pose a dilemma for complex interventions like order maintenance—interventions that take many forms and play out differently in different contexts. On one hand, program evaluations of realistic order maintenance interventions often do not generalize, while on the other hand, basic science focused on fundamental causal mechanisms that *do* operate fairly consistently across a wide range of contexts can be difficult to apply. This dilemma makes it hard to base policy decisions on the kinds of long-term and indirect effects that "Broken Windows" proposed, at least when the intervention that is supposed to bring them about is as variable and sensitive to context as order maintenance policing. Such effects may simply be too uncertain to provide a firm basis for policy choice (Rein and Winship 1998; Thacher 2004).

6.2.2 Beyond Broken Windows

Ironically, one of the most important legacies of "Broken Windows" may have been to entrench a mode of thought that Wilson and Kelling themselves lamented. Criticizing the decriminalization movements of the 1960s and 1970s, these authors complained about "a growing and not-so-commendable utilitarianism" that held that law should never restrict behavior "that does not 'hurt' another person" (1982, 35). The argument Broken Windows became famous for and thrived on exactly this utilitarian perspective. As Bernard Harcourt (2001, 207) put it, the theory aimed to "transform these quality-of-life offenses from mere nuisances or annoyances into *seriously harmful conduct*—conduct that in fact contributes to serious crimes." Instead of a challenge to the utilitarian perspective on police work, "Broken Windows" may be its most significant recruit.

In the process, the essay may have reinforced precisely the view of the police role that Wilson and Kelling meant to contest—the view that the one and only mission of policing is to combat serious crime. Over and over the most sophisticated police scholarship has shown that the image of the police as "crime-fighters" is an oversimplification or even a deliberate mystification, demonstrating that police perform a wide variety of tasks including crowd management, traffic patrol, accident investigation, and dispute resolution (Goldstein 1977; Manning 1977; Bittner 1990; Ericson and Haggerty 1997; Kleinig 1996). To think about these tasks only in terms of their relationship with serious crime is to flatten the police function gratuitously. A full appreciation for the complexity and breadth of the police role will remain elusive until we have developed a rationale for these tasks that goes beyond their derivative significance for crime control.

6.2.3 Order Maintenance and Problem-Oriented Policing

The threats to public spaces at the center of the order maintenance function are community problems in their own right, regardless of the indirect effects they may or may not have on other problems like serious crime; they are *substantive police problems* in

Herman Goldstein's (1990) sense of that term. Earlier I noted how George Kelling relied explicitly on Goldstein's work to develop one of the most influential order maintenance initiatives a few years after "Broken Windows" appeared, conducting interviews and undertaking detailed observation of conditions in the New York City subway system to define the nature of the problem the transit police faced and develop tailored strategies for resolving it. In that sense the contemporary revival of order maintenance can be viewed as a particular application of problem-oriented policing.

More surprising, there is a case to be made that the relationship works the other way—that problem-oriented policing descends from order maintenance policing, as a generalization of the remarkable but neglected analysis of the order maintenance function published forty years ago by Tulane law professor Robert Force (1972). In *Problem-Oriented Policing* (1990) Goldstein credited Force with the central criticism that underlay his own reconceptualization of the police role, that "police are often responding to little more than the most overt, one-time symptom or manifestation of a problem rather than to the problem itself" (20), and he went on to assert that Force's work "still provides the best exploration" of how and why the police need to search for creative alternatives to arrest to resolve the problems they face (131). A major purpose of Force's essay was to develop a clearer understanding of the nature of public disorder as a community problem and to develop new strategies to control it.

As a problem-solving enterprise, one of the distinctive features of order maintenance work is that many of its most pressing questions focus on ends rather than means—on what kind of public behavior should be prohibited, rather than how exactly to put a stop to it once we know what it is. Of course, all problem-oriented policing efforts must spend time defining and redefining the nature of the condition police aim to establish (Goldstein 1990, ch. 6), and questions about means are hardly absent from order maintenance work. Nevertheless, the moral ambiguity and conflict surrounding "disorder" make this normative task loom especially large.

Force (1972, 406) himself argued that the historical legacy of the order maintenance function weighed it down with illegitimate efforts to control the "diversions and morals of the poor," insisting that a new morally-defensible conception needed to be developed to rein these abuses in. In that respect, the most pressing task in the analysis of disorder as a substantive community problem lies in clarifying the moral basis of the standards of public behavior that define it. The conception of disorder as unfair use of public space provides that basis.

6.2.4 Disorder as Unfair Use of Shared Space

As the history of order maintenance illustrates, the kind of rules a society needs depends on the kind of society it is. To the extent that a society is mainly a collection of individuals who live side by side in private homes, coming together in privately-run offices and stores to work and shop but scattering to their individual enclaves to consume and live (Lofland 1998, 196), it needs rules that protect their individual interests and safeguard the boundaries that define the private spheres where they carry out their lives. A police focused entirely on protecting life and property may be all this sort of society needs. But if a society is more collective than that, so that its members live important parts of their lives together, sharing some of their resources and their environment rather than carving everything up into individual portions for private use, then it needs rules defining how they are going to regulate the sharing. If their children play on public playgrounds as well as in their backyards; if they shop in public bazaars as well as private stores and mail-order shops; if they engage with politics on the sidewalks as well as in commercial media; if they move from place to place on public roads, sidewalks, buses, and subways; if they invest wealth and cultural meaning in collective enterprises like public parks and monuments rather than private consumption alone; then they need to clarify terms of use for these collective assets that will ensure everyone fair access and safeguard the purposes for which the public has created them. A society with ambitious hopes for its public realm needs an equally ambitious conception of the police role.[5]

It is often difficult to determine what counts as unfair or inapt use of a public space—this ideal describes an approach to analysis rather than an unambiguous principle—but clear examples exist. Many fall into the category of "accumulative harms" (Feinberg 1984, 225–32), acts that are trivial in isolation but make up part of a larger whole that *does* pose a significant danger. (Wesley Skogan [2008, 196] observes that residents experience such transgressions as "conditions" rather than "incidents.") It is a serious mistake to ignore such harms simply because each seems so minor on its own (Glover 1975; Parfit 1984, ch. 3; Kagan 2011). The clearest examples are littering and (further afield) pollution: Each individual act of littering or pollution is a minor annoyance rather than the sort of serious harm that typically justifies criminal justice intervention, but if *everyone* littered or drove cars with dirty engines then important shared resources would be destroyed. To prevent that we agree to fair terms of cooperation that will keep the accumulated damage below the crucial threshold where inconvenience fades into harm—for example, by prohibiting littering altogether and requiring everyone to follow strict emissions standards—and then back those restrictions up with legal sanctions. This basic model captures many instances of disorder, such as prohibitions on amplified music, lying down in transit stations, soliciting on crowded sidewalks, and even trampling the grass or picking flowers in public parks. Whether or not such things cause more crime and disorder, they are wrong because these individually-trivial acts would destroy the livability of our public spaces if everyone engaged in them. As a matter of fairness, everyone ought to share the burdens of self-restraint (with some exceptions discussed in Thacher 2004).

In other cases, a single disorderly act may unacceptably burden other users of public space on its own; public lewdness and verbal harassment of pedestrians are examples. Such actions may not "harm" anyone in the sense that our most familiar crimes do, but they frighten, disgust, anger, worry, or humiliate their unwilling targets and onlookers in indefensible ways—in other words, they *offend* them in the idiosyncratic sense of that word defined by legal philosopher Joel Feinberg (1985). In a diverse society we all need to have thick skins, but tolerance has limits; it just is unreasonable to expect to indulge our most offensive whims in public places that we share with others. The people using sidewalks, buses, plazas, parks, and beaches are taking advantage of collective assets designed to be used by everyone, and when needless offense crowds them out they have a legitimate complaint.[6] Of course, not all offenses are proper subjects for government regulation. If an offensive action serves a vital purpose or only offends the skittish, then the police have no business putting a stop to it. But if the action is maliciously *designed* to offend, or if it could easily be performed somewhere else less disruptively, police action may well be appropriate.[7] It can be difficult both in theory and practice to draw these distinctions—one attempt comes from First Amendment law, which allows government to regulate the time, place, and manner of offensive speech but not eliminate it entirely—and police constantly find themselves caught between demands to crack down and to lay off. Feinberg (1985) himself made the most substantial effort to develop criteria for isolating true "offenses" that plausibly warrant criminal justice intervention (ch. 8), believing that this line of thought provided the most defensible basis for breach of the peace statutes and similar public order rules (46).

There are other ways of using public spaces unfairly, but these two categories suffice to demonstrate that the justification for order maintenance does not depend on its uncertain link to crime control. Legal decisions about order maintenance tactics rarely if ever turn on the indirect consequences of disorder for crime; instead they focus on more immediate offenses and harms (Thacher 2004, 388–89). "Broken Windows" itself has become too closely identified with one of many arguments Wilson and Kelling (1982, 29, 31) made. Their essay began with a call to "understand what most often frightens people in public places," insisting that "outside observers should not assume that they know how much of the anxiety now endemic in many big city neighborhoods stems from fear of 'real' crime and how much from a sense that the street is disorderly, a source of distasteful, worrisome encounters." Not everything that scares other people warrants police intervention, and there are ways to make unfair claims on public space other than instilling fear, but this central theme of "Broken Windows" makes most sense as a discussion of *offense*. To go on to speculate that these worrisome encounters might generate crime added an interesting hypothesis for social scientists to investigate but nothing essential for the justification of order maintenance.

Of course, many of the existing rules that govern public spaces do not reflect any principle of fairness but instead bear the imprint of illicit moralism, political power, and prejudice. Rules regulating street vendors often reflect the protectionist interests of fixed-location businesses and nativism more than real concerns about traffic, safety, and the fair allocation of tax burdens (Bluestone 1991; Kettles 2004); gang injunctions and loitering rules sometimes reflect racist overreaction rather than legitimate concerns about public intimidation (Roberts 1999; Sampson and Raudenbush 2004); and youth curfews and skateboard bans may reflect cultural anxieties about youth and their political disenfranchisement rather than any actual danger posed by their activity (Valentine 2004). When public order rules do target disruptive uses of public space, they sometimes ignore the significant personal freedoms those uses involve, enforcing a sterile homogeneity that undermines a central purpose of public space—the room it makes for experimentation, diversity, and surprise (Sennett 1970; Lynch 1990). They may also ignore inequality in access to *private* space, which influences the share of their lives different groups must live out in the public realm (Stinchcombe 1963). At the extreme, homelessness is defined by the fact that the homeless person has no unconditional access to private space, so the rules of behavior in public spaces mark out the extent of his freedom. Beginning from this simple observation, Jeremy Waldron (1991) mounted a powerful attack on many recent public order laws, arguing that they represent a dramatic incursion into the freedom of the homeless to take care of a variety of basic human needs. "What is emerging," Waldron warned, "is a state of affairs in which a million or more citizens have no place to perform elementary human activities like urinating, washing, sleeping, cooking, eating, and standing around" (301).

Those who believe that public order should be a major police priority ought to advocate not the enforcement of existing public order standards but their reconstruction to make them worth enforcing. Legitimate order maintenance only targets public behaviors that really do use public spaces unfairly, such as accumulative harms and Feinberg's "offenses," and it does so equitably and with due respect for personal freedom, particularly for the homeless and others with limited access to private space. The task is undoubtedly difficult and complex, but most sophisticated agencies have risen to the challenge (Kelling 1997; Livingston 1997; Thacher 2004).

6.3 Matching Means to Ends

The job of maintaining order in subways, parks, and sidewalks is no more dispensable than the physical maintenance of these public assets is, but *individual* acts of disorder often seem too trivial to warrant the time and effort it takes to combat them. For that reason police and their critics alike often argue that their time would be spent better fighting serious crime (Bratton 1995, 450; Kelling and Coles 1996, 131; Zimring and Hawkins 1997, 14); it is the trivial nature of many instances of disorder that led Albert Reiss (1985) to dub them "soft" crimes.

These objections contain an element of truth, but often they are overblown. In practice, the main task that competes with order maintenance is not crimefighting but response to 911 calls (Moskos 2008, 109), which only rarely have much to do with serious crime, and which tend to skew police effort towards private priorities (no matter how trivial) rather than public problems. It also bears remembering that the impact of a single act of public disorder is typically felt by many people, so the aggregate harm or offense may be more substantial than it appears to any one "victim" in particular. (Wilson and Kelling [1982, 38] were right to conclude that "public drunkenness, street prostitution, and pornographic displays can destroy a community more quickly than any team of professional burglars" even if such incivilities have no effect on crime itself.) Finally, the prospects for deterrence may be especially encouraging for many public disorder crimes compared with the most familiar *mala in se* wrongs covered by the criminal law; in this area internal moral restraints are often weak and "nearly all of us are potential criminals" (Andenaes 1974, 10–11). To ascertain what rules of conduct govern a public place we often take our cues from the way other people behave. In that respect disorderly conduct often arises from imitation or precedent, so that (in a more modest version of the Broken Windows thesis) putting a stop to the first act of disorder may prevent much more than the harm of that act alone (Thacher 2011). A single arrest for farebeating costs the police more than the $2 fare to process, but if it is an arrest for the *first* act of farebeating in what otherwise would become an epidemic it may make sense in purely financial terms.

All of that said, arrest and prosecution often still seem like grossly disproportionate responses to a single merely offensive act, or to the tiny fraction of an accumulative harm contributed by one transgression. An important frontier in order maintenance theory and practice involves the development of responses and tactics proportionate to the venial harms associated with individual incidents of disorder. The earlier examples of Cleveland and St. Louis illustrate how progressive police agencies have pursued that task for at least a century.

6.3.1 Preventing Disorder

Ideally order maintenance can be accomplished without police enforcement at all. The users of public spaces regulate each other with subtle stares and mild rebukes (Goffman 1966), and recognized public figures like newsstand operators, transit station managers, and respected elders step in when those least formal sanctions fail (e.g., Jacobs 1961; Whyte 1988). These informal efforts provide the bulk of order maintenance in most public spaces. Nevertheless, they may be discounted and lose their effectiveness unless everyone implicitly recognizes that the police can be called in as backup, and by themselves they risk worse forms of intolerance and discrimination than the police themselves are likely to mete out (Thacher 2009).

When community members and institutions do complain to the police about disorder, the police have a wide range of responses to draw from. As an application of problem-oriented policing, order maintenance has often searched for ways to reduce opportunities for disorder rather than simply enforce the rules against it. Public drunkenness has been reduced through controls on alcohol sales (Björ, Knuttson, and Kühlhorn 1992), disruptive gatherings of youth have been alleviated by staggering the end of the school day or arranging transportation as soon as a popular roller rink closes (Scott 2004, 16–17; Eck and Spelman 1987), careful zoning rules prevent conflicts over noise and other nuisance complaints (Garnett 2010, ch. 4), public urination can be prevented by improving public restroom facilities (Duneier 1999, 173–87), neighborhood disruption caused by feeding the hungry and homeless in parks has been alleviated by moving these programs indoors (Zeveloff 2008), and in many contexts simply clarifying and publicizing rules of conduct may help restore public order (Clarke 1997, 23–24). On George Kelling and Catherine Cole's account, New York's influential effort to restore order in the subways began in 1984 with Transit president David Gunn's "Clean Car Program," which tackled rampant graffiti by rolling out new clean subway cars one-by-one and then immediately removing them from service for rapid repainting as soon as graffiti struck. By depriving graffiti artists of the visibility and fame they sought, the program succeeded where arrest and deterrence had failed (Sloan-Howitt and Kelling 1990). Kelling and Coles (1996, 117) conclude approvingly that transit agency succeeded "because the Gunn administration abandoned the use of a law-enforcement strategy in dealing with graffiti."

6.3.2 The Educational Role of the Police

When prevention fails and patrol officers come across or get summoned to disorderly conduct, reminders and admonitions may be enough to put a stop to it. Precisely because disorder's harms can be so hard to detect and the rules that define it so complex and variable, disorder often results from thoughtlessness rather than malice.

In that respect the police role in regulating the use of public spaces often has more to do with teaching and reminding people about appropriate standards of conduct than with the enforcement of clear-cut rules that everyone already understands. This is a very different role for the police than the more familiar one of controlling malicious wrongdoing; its central tool is education rather than deterrence. Its best and earliest exponent was Frederick Law Olmsted, who directed the Central Park Police force at its inception in 1858. Where municipal police focused on crime control aimed to "overawe, outwit, and bring to punishment the constant enemies of society," as Olmsted put it, the park police focused on order maintenance had a very different aim—to "respectfully aid" the users of public space "toward a better understanding of what is due to others, as one gentlemen might manage to aid another who was a stranger to him" (Thacher 2011). Olmsted's quaint Victorian language sounds antiquated today, but it has important contemporary echoes. One comes from the order maintenance guidelines for the New Haven, Connecticut Police Department, which call on officers first and foremost to "educate the public about civility, the consequences of incivility, and the laws that oblige citizens to behave in particular ways" on the assumption that "some citizens do not fully understand their obligations, and if those obligations—for example, regarding a noisy car or public drinking in parks—are patiently explained, they will adhere to the law"; only when these efforts at persuasion fail should they resort to citations or arrest (Kelling 1997, 50).

Recognizing this educative role for police is crucial in the order maintenance context. When we conceive of the police's job in the more familiar way, as focused on the control of deliberate predation through deterrence and incapacitation, hamfisted responses to disorder like the "zero tolerance" approach that gained currency over the past two decades seem to follow naturally.

6.3.3 Enforcement

The harder questions come when, despite our best efforts to prevent disorder and control it informally, serious and debilitating problems still plague our public spaces. When prevention and persuasion fail, how can police respond?

They can and sometimes they should resort to arrest, but they may have more appropriate sources of authority to draw from as well. Police handle a wide range of minor infractions like public drinking, unlicensed vending, obstructing traffic, and public urination using citations and court summonses that do not carry the same severe consequences as misdemeanor arrests; indeed those severe consequences make it hard to justify the continuing practice of cities that *do* customarily arrest people for such things. Other sanctions short of arrest may exist depending on where disorder occurs. One factor that makes order maintenance easier in quasi-public spaces like subway systems and stadiums is the legal possibility of simply ejecting disruptive people for short periods rather than arresting them (e.g., Wilson and Kelling 1982, 38). Some cities have extended this kind of authority to a much wider range of true public spaces for much longer periods, but that strategy has received incisive criticism (von Hirsch and Shearing 2000; Beckett and Herbert 2010). Police have also used asset forfeiture, liquor license suspensions, and "padlock laws" that allow them to temporarily close nuisance properties as order maintenance tools (Bratton 1995), though again these interventions raise civil liberties concerns that call for careful safeguards and limits.

Legal innovation continues to add to these alternative sanctions. Forty years ago Robert Force (1972, 407) worried that "one reason for the great number of arrests and prosecutions for petty offenses today is that, in many cases, those are the only authorized governmental responses," and he proposed giving police authority to take a variety of less intrusive steps to maintain order depending on the circumstances—including forcibly escorting the violator to his home, a hospital, or a social welfare agency; detaining him temporarily on the street; or taking him into custody in police lockup for up to four hours with no intention of filing charges, housing him separately from people charged with criminal offenses, and protecting him from interrogation and most searches. Force's proposals were never enacted in full (Goldstein 1993, 50), but many states have authorized police to detain disruptive drunks and drive them home or to detox facilities (Goldstein 1990, 130–31), and shortly after Force wrote, the Swedish legislature empowered police in that country to detain disorderly people for up to six hours (Kühlhorn 1978). This kind of police authority raises obvious concerns. Detentions without prosecution lack an important opportunity for judicial oversight, and the very fact that they seem less intrusive may encourage police to overuse them. Force and others have argued that the first concern may be more apparent than real—it is possible to provide legal safeguards for temporary detention, and a very large share of order maintenance arrests *already* end with no prosecution (Force 1972, 403; Goldstein 1990, 137–38)—and an evaluation of the Swedish law found no evidence of net-widening (Kühlhorn 1978, 8). Nevertheless, such concerns deserve serious attention.

A major challenge facing all of these less-intrusive sanctions for disorderly conduct is the possibility that offenders will just disregard them. The most important role for arrest and prosecution may be to serve as a last resort in the face of such defiance. New York City's famous "squeegiemen" had received citations for years but rarely appeared in court to pay or contest them; police finally put a stop to the problem by rigorously serving arrest warrants for those who ignored their summons (Kelling and Coles 1996,

141–43). In cases like these, the severe sanction of arrest is not used to punish disorderly conduct itself but to punish defiance of less intrusive sanctions—a serious offense that threatens the very possibility of a moderate but effective system of justice.

None of this is to deny that arrest and prosecution may sometimes be appropriate responses to disorderly conduct, but an ideal approach to order maintenance strives to craft more measured responses—responses that are proportionate to the often venial character of the offenses involved, reserving more serious sanctions like arrest as last resorts to deal with extreme cases and defiance. Significant organizational barriers may stand in the way of this ideal; in particular, performance measurement and supervision systems often demand arrest statistics and therefore get them. Because of those barriers, reorienting order maintenance practice along these lines will require organizational innovations that go beyond front-line practice. The effort is worthwhile, though, and not only because of the intrinsic fairness of responding to minor offenses with mild sanctions. It may also provide a bulwark against some of the pretextual uses of order maintenance authority I have repeatedly returned to. If a disorderly person *does* move along when the police ask her, then the police may not search her (Livingston 1999, 187), and neither citations nor even temporary detention provide police with as much scope for harassment and investigatory fishing expeditions as arrests for disorderly conduct do (Force 1972, 422–23).

6.4 Regulating Police Discretion

Pretextual uses of order maintenance authority represent only one example of the potential for police to abuse it. Even when police do invoke their order maintenance authority to regulate the fair use of public spaces, they may do so selectively, cracking down on disorder more zealously when the guilty party is a poor minority (Roberts 1999). Order maintenance may also serve exclusionary purposes, aiming to eject undesirable people from elite neighborhoods and business districts rather than instilling standards of conduct designed to allow different groups to coexist (Beckett and Herbert 2010; Waldron 1991, 314). In each case police become, as Wilson and Kelling (1982, 35) themselves put it, "the agents of neighborhood bigotry." That danger is an inherent part of the order maintenance function: Empowering police with the legal tools to maintain order almost inevitably means enhancing their discretion, with all the potential for abuse and inequity that unchecked discretion involves.

The legal transformation of the 1960s and 1970s made progress on this front, putting an end to the nearly unrestricted authority police once had to maintain order however they saw fit (Livingston 1997, 595). Today police must focus on a person's behavior rather than her status; they must respect her constitutional rights to free speech, assembly, and travel; and the rules they enforce must be clear enough to inform her of what is forbidden (e.g. *Robinson v. California*, 370 U.S. 660 [1962]; *Gooding v. Wilson*, 405 U.S. 518 [1972]; *Coates v. Cincinnati*, 402 U.S. 611 [1971]). These new standards forced police to stay within the boundaries of increasingly delimited public order rules—for example, rules against "aggressive" solicitation that includes touching or following (as opposed to broad bans on any panhandling whatsoever), rules against *intending* to annoy passersby (as opposed to acting in any manner that happens to have that effect), and rules against loitering for the purpose of prostitution or other vices (as opposed to broad bans on standing on the sidewalk with no apparent purpose).

This legal transformation eliminated some of the worst abuses of order maintenance authority, but Debra Livingston (1997, 1999) has made a compelling argument that scrutiny of public order authority by the courts may have reached a point of diminishing returns—and that in some cases it has actually become counterproductive. The central thrust of this legal transformation aimed to restrict police discretion by forcing legislatures to eliminate vague public order standards, but the demand for clarity often drives legislators to pass precise but extremely broad laws that no one expects the police to enforce consistently, such as comprehensive youth curfews in place of vague "youth loitering" laws. Such broad laws hand officers at least as much discretion as the vaguely-worded statutes they replaced (Livingston 1999, 172–73).

Livingston herself argues that legal oversight should increasingly give way to organizational measures for reining in abuse, and she points to many efforts that the most progressive police agencies have carried out. Police agencies should develop formal guidelines for the use of their discretion (Kelling 1997), improve order maintenance training (Bittner 1967, 715), provide greater accountability by "auditing" officer practice through community surveys and peer review (Kelling, Wasserman, and Williams 1988), and increase the role of community members and democratic representatives in police decision-making (Goldstein 1990, 21–27), among other reforms (Livingston 1997, 650–67).

All of these strategies hold promise, but they are generic. They describe the task of management in general—the management of human resources, information systems, accountability and control, and external relations—rather than that of managing order maintenance work in particular. The key task of guiding the use of *order maintenance* discretion will be accomplished or not depending on how well these generic management strategies are guided by a sense of the order maintenance mission—by a sense of the public value this aspect of police work aims to create (Moore 1995). The bulk of this essay has tried to provide a general account of that mission, drawing out its implications both for the nature of the substantive problems police should attend to and for the tactics they can legitimately rely on.

6.5 FUTURE RESEARCH

The most important frontiers in order maintenance policing involve the further clarification of these two aspects of its practice—of how police should understand the concept of "public order" they ultimately aim to defend, and of the tactics they should use to accomplish that goal. Real progress on these tasks will require a different approach to the study of policing than the narrowly social scientific model that has dominated police research over the past three decades.

Most important, a robust research agenda about order maintenance policing needs to turn away from the nearly-exclusive emphasis on the disorder-causes-crime thesis that has dominated this topic for three decades. The question of whether order maintenance policing is worthwhile and what form it should take cannot be reduced to the question of whether it reduces serious crime in the long run. The tendency to try do just that over the past three decades has flattened our understanding both of what "disorder" is and of the tactics police should use to regulate it, corroding important moral restraints on the practice of this delicate police function along the way. "Order" and "order maintenance" are essentially moral concepts, and when we view them through the lens of social scientific study we risk distorting them (Thacher forthcoming). At minimum, if further research into the disorder-causes-crime thesis proves irresistible to social scientists, it should rely on a much more sophisticated concept of "disorder" than most of the survey research and observational studies so far.[8]

Critics who have complained about the conceptual confusion surrounding order maintenance (Harcourt 2001; Thacher 2004; Kubrin 2010) are surely right that future research and practice in this area badly need to clarify what "disorder" means. That task of conceptual clarification represents one of the most important avenues for advancing practice in this area. It is a task, however, that requires something more than familiar approaches to social science provide. For example, turning over the definition of "disorder" more wholeheartedly to neighborhood residents through intensive survey research, as Kubrin (2010) seems to recommend, may actually move us further away from a morally-legitimate conception of disorder because the police have no business regulating many things that neighborhood residents find objectionable. Real progress in our understanding of how police should conceptualize the crucial concept of "disorder" requires moral and legal analysis, not just social science. In that respect, this area is one of many where interpretive fields like philosophy, history, and law would have much to contribute to advancing the practice of policing. Best of all would be a morally-informed approach to ethnographic research about order maintenance practice that draws simultaneously from social science and the humanities (Thacher 2001, 2004, 2006).

A second major avenue for future research and practice would aim to broaden the range of tactics that police can use to maintain order and scrutinize their worth. Wesley Skogan recently lamented that the scholarly discussion of order maintenance policing has often been remarkably stilted, treating "order maintenance policing" as a homogenous "policy intervention" that police are free to adopt or not, and that researchers typically identify it with a focus on strict enforcement that they rightfully reject in other contexts (Skogan 2008, 403–06). As a branch of problem-oriented policing, order maintenance should draw from a much wider range of tactics than that. I have tried to illustrate throughout this essay how legal scholarship and policing practice have made important contributions in this area for more than a century. Social science could contribute more than it typically has to this alternative tradition through close study and scrutiny of the variations in practice that sophisticated practitioners have adopted (Thacher 2004, 2008). Evaluation efforts should stop treating order maintenance as a homogenous intervention that "works" or "doesn't work" and turn to more nuanced studies of the components of an agency's practice that show the most promise (e.g., Braga and Bond 2008). Those evaluations, moreover, need to study the intrinsic fairness of policing practice at least as much as they study their long-term consequences, which may prove inscrutable in any event (Thacher 2001).

More broadly, future scholarship and practice related to order maintenance policing should recognize the moral significance of order maintenance practice more than most recent scholarship has. Order maintenance is not just a neutral tool that can be used arbitrarily to manipulate neighborhood outcomes. It involves the exercise of police authority against people who are often vulnerable and despised, and who in any case should not be treated simply as means to the achievement of other people's ends. None of that is to say that order maintenance is never justified. At its best, order maintenance vindicates the fair terms of cooperation our common spaces require, and in that respect it can claim a moral justification separate from any instrumental consequences it may or may not produce. Spelling out what those fair terms of cooperation are and how police can fairly and effectively enforce them has not been the central focus of recent scholarship about order maintenance policing, but it can and should be in the future.

NOTES

* Thanks to Bob Axelrod, Jeff Fagan, George Kelling, and Michael Reisig for helpful discussion and comments.
1. Wilson drew heavily from Michael Banton's (1964) and Egon Bittner's (1967) idea of "peace-keeping," and like them he stressed the fact that order maintenance work often did not culminate with an arrest (Wilson 1968, 18). For Banton, that was its defining feature, but that definition is unsatisfactory partly because police may intervene in situations without knowing whether an arrest will result; and while informal intervention surely dominates the police response to disorder, the most venerable "public order" offenses have always figured prominently in police arrest statistics too. Wilson's later defense of order maintenance in "Broken Windows" seems to abandon his earlier definitions.
2. Monkkonen's own view is more complex. He apparently saw the decline in order maintenance arrests partly as a result of a real decline in public disorder (1981a) and partly as an unintended consequence of police bureaucratization (1981b, 143–46).
3. One thorough, balanced, and recent review is Reisig (2010, 24–35).
4. The first wave of observational research on the disorder-causes-crime hypothesis culminated with Sampson and Raudenbush's (1999, 638) widely-cited study of Chicago, which found that neighborhoods with high levels of daytime disorder do not generally have higher crime rates than we would expect given their other measured characteristics; on that basis they concluded that the enthusiasm for using order maintenance to reduce crime was "simplistic and largely misplaced." More recent studies have turned to experimental designs. Two field experiments led by Anthony Braga (Braga et. al. 1999; Braga and Bond 2008) both found that crime fell substantially in neighborhoods where police had been

randomly assigned to conduct aggressive order maintenance compared to the control neighborhoods where they had not—though critics have argued that the crime reduction in the first study may have resulted simply from heightened police presence, and the same concern may apply to the second. (It is worth noting that the second of Braga's studies, which concluded that order maintenance has the greatest impact on crime when it targets identified hot spots and relies on broad situational crime prevention strategies rather than a narrow focus on misdemeanor arrests, is the only study in this literature I am aware of that attempts to address the concern expressed at the end of the paragraph in the text.)

5. For example, when New York City removed 700 acres from private ownership to create an elaborate rural park that would serve as a respite from the crowded commercial city surrounding it, it had to develop rules that would protect the physical and social environment that its residents had invested so much to create—rules against vending and commercial traffic to insulate it (as Walt Whitman put it) from "the hand of Mammon," rules against clipping flowers and feeding the swans to protect the park's elaborate and delicate natural environment, rules against verbal harassment to safeguard the park's tranquility, and many others. The task of defining and enforcing those rules fell to the nascent park police, whose work differed fundamentally from that of the municipal police charged with controlling serious crime (Thacher 2011). The history of controversy surrounding Central Park's rules (e.g., Rosensweig and Blackmar 1992) also vividly illustrates the challenges involved in determining what counts as unfair use of public spaces.

6. Feinberg himself set his scenes of offensive conduct on a crowded city bus, and other authors who discuss the offense principle also emphasize shared spaces (e.g., Simester and von Hirsch 2002, 274, 292).

7. A telling example comes from an 1864 petition asking the English parliament to strengthen the laws regulating street musicians in residential areas. The petition alleged that many of the musicians were after extortion rather than entertainment, as they staked out spots outside the homes of wealthy families until the owner sent a servant out to pay them to leave. The petition is telling because one of its signatories was John Stuart Mill (Winter 1993, 73–74), who five years earlier had published the decisive statement of the idea that the state should only regulate behavior if it positively harms other people (Mill 1978 [1859]). Apparently this kind of (allegedly) gratuitous offense qualified as a "harm" in Mill's eyes.

8. For example, in the most prominent social scientific study of the link between disorder and crime, the measure of "social disorder" in each neighborhood essentially amounts to the number of groups of three or more people on the street (Sampson and Raudenbush 1999; Thacher forthcoming). The most such a study can tell us about social disorder is that neighborhoods with many groups of people on the sidewalks generally do not have higher crime rates than we would expect given their other measured characteristics. That conclusion tells us nothing about the impact of any legitimate form of order maintenance policing on crime because order maintenance policing does not aim to eliminate groups of people from sidewalks; it aims to ensure that they abide by defensible norms of order.

References

Andenaes, Johannes. 1974. *Punishment and Deterrence*. Ann Arbor: University of Michigan Press.
Banton, Michael. 1964. *The Policeman in the Community*. New York: Basic Books.

Beckett, Katherine, and Steven Herbert. 2010. *Banished*. New York: Oxford University Press.

Bittner, Egon. 1967. "The Police on Skid Row." *American Sociological Review* 32:699–715.

——. 1990. *Aspects of Police Work*. Boston: Northeastern University Press.

Björ, Jill, Johannes Knutsson, and Eckhart Kühlhorn. 1992. "The Celebration of Midsummer Eve in Sweden." *Security Journal* 3:169–74.

Bluestone, Daniel. 1991. "The Pushcart Evil." *Journal of Urban History* 18:68–92.

Braga, Anthony, and Brenda Bond. 2008. "Policing Crime and Disorder Hotspots." *Criminology* 46:577–607.

Braga, Anthony, David Weisburd, Elin Waring, Lorraine Green Mazerolle, William Spelman, and Francis Gajewski. 1999. "Problem-Oriented Policing in Violent Crime Places." *Criminology* 37:541–80.

Bratton, William. 1995. "New York City Police Department's Civil Enforcement of Quality-of-Life Crimes." *Journal of Law and Policy* 3:447–64.

Cartwright, Nancy. 1999. *The Dappled World*. New York: Cambridge University Press.

Cartwright, Nancy, and Pemberton, John. 2011. "Aristotelian Powers." In *Powers and Capacities in Philosophy*, edited by John Greco and Ruth Groff, 93–112. New York: Routledge.

Chauncey, George. 1995. *Gay New York*. New York: Basic Books.

Clarke, Ronald. 1997. *Situational Crime Prevention*. Albany: Harrow and Heston.

Douglas, William. 1960. "Vagrancy and Arrest on Suspicion." *Yale Law Journal* 70:1–14.

Dubber, Markus. 2001. "Policing Possession." *Journal of Criminal Law and Criminology* 91:829–996.

Duneier, Mitchell. 1999. *Sidewalk*. New York: Farrar, Straus, and Giroux.

Eck, John, and William Spelman. 1987. *Problem-Oriented Policing in Newport News*. Washington, DC: Police Executive Research Forum.

Ericson, Richard, and Kevin Haggerty. 1997. *Policing the Risk Society*. Toronto: University of Toronto Press.

Fagan, Jeffrey, and Garth Davies. 2000. "Street Stops and Broken Windows." *Fordham Urban Law Journal* 28:457–504.

Feinberg, Joel. 1984. *Harm to Others*. New York: Oxford University Press.

——. 1985. *Offense to Others*. New York: Oxford University Press.

Flaherty, David. 1972. *Privacy in Colonial New England*. Charlottesville: University of Virginia Press.

Fogelson, Robert. 1977. *Big-City Police*. Cambridge: Harvard University Press.

Foote, Caleb. 1956. "Vagrancy-Type Law and Its Administration." *University of Pennsylvania Law Review* 104:603–50.

Force, Robert. 1972. "Decriminalization of Breach of the Peace Statutes." *Tulane Law Review* 46:367–493.

Garnett, Nicole. 2010. *Ordering the City*. New Haven: Yale University Press.

Gau, Jacinta, and Robert Brunson. 2010. "Procedural Justice and Order Maintenance Policing." *Justice Quarterly* 27:255–79.

Glover, Jonathan. 1975. "It Makes No Difference Whether or Not I Do It." *Proceedings of the Aristotelian Society, Supplementary Volumes* 49:171–90.

Goffman, Erving. 1966. *Behavior in Public Places*. New York: Free Press.

Goldstein, Herman. 1977. *Policing a Free Society*. Cambridge: Ballinger.

——. 1990. *Problem-Oriented Policing*. New York: McGraw-Hill.

——. 1993. "Confronting the Complexity of the Policing Function." In *Discretion in Criminal Justice*, edited by Lloyd E. Ohlin and Frank J. Remington, 23–72. Albany: State University of New York Press.

Guerette, Robert. 2006. *Disorder at Day Laborer Sites.* Washington, DC: U.S. Department of Justice, Office of Community Oriented Policing Services.

Harcourt, Bernard. 2001. *Illusion of Order.* Cambridge: Harvard University Press.

Harring, Sidney. 1983. *Policing a Class Society.* New Brunswick: Rutgers University Press.

Heckman, James. 2005. "The Scientific Model of Causality." *Sociological Methods and Research* 35:1–97.

Ignatieff, Michael. 1979. "Police and People." *New Society* 30 (August): 443–45.

Jacobs, Jane. 1961. *The Death and Life of Great American Cities.* New York: Vintage.

Jencks, Christopher. 1992. *The Homeless.* New York: Basic Books.

Kagan, Shelley. 2011. "Do I Make a Difference?" *Philosophy and Public Affairs* 39:105–41.

Kaplan, Karen. 2008. "Wherefore, Litterbug?" *Los Angeles Times* (November 21).

Keizer, Kees, Siegwart Lindenberg, and Linda Steg. 2008. "The Spreading of Disorder." *Science* 322:1681–85.

Kelling, George. 1997. *"Broken Windows" and Police Discretion.* Washington, DC: National Institute of Justice.

Kelling, George, and Catherine Coles. 1996. *Fixing Broken Windows.* New York: Touchstone.

Kelling, George, Robert Wasserman, and Hubert Williams. 1988. "Police Accountability and Community Policing." Perspectives on Policing No. 7. Washington, DC: U.S. Department of Justice.

Kettles, Gregg. 2004. "Regulating Vending in the Sidewalk Commons." *Temple Law Review* 77:1–46.

Kleinig, John. 1996. *The Ethics of Policing.* New York: Cambridge University Press.

Kubrin, Charis E. 2008. "Making Order of Disorder: A Call for Conceptual Clarity." *Criminology and Public Policy* 7:203–14.

Kühlhorn, Eckhart. 1978. *Deprivation of Freedom and the Police.* Stockholm: The National Swedish Council for Crime Prevention.

Lane, Roger. 1967. *Policing the City.* Cambridge: Harvard University Press.

———. 1968. "Crime and Criminal Statistics in Nineteenth-Century Massachusetts." *Journal of Social History* 2:156–63.

Livingston, Debra. 1997. "Police Discretion and the Quality of Life in Public Places." *Columbia Law Review* 97:551–672.

Livingston, Debra. 1999. "Gang Loitering, The Court, and Some Realism about Police Patrol." *Supreme Court Review* 1999:141–202.

Lofland, Lynn. 1998. *The Public Realm.* New York: Adline de Gruyter.

Lynch, Kevin. 1990. "The Openness of Open Space." In *City Sense and City Design,* edited by Tridib Banerjee and Michael Southworth. Cambridge: MIT Press.

Manning, Peter. 1977. *Police Work.* Cambridge: MIT Press.

Mill, John Stuart. 1978 [1859]. *On Liberty.* Indianapolis: Hackett.

Miller, Wilbur. 1977. *Cops and Bobbies.* Chicago: University of Chicago Press.

Monkkonen, Eric. 1981a. "A Disorderly People?" *Journal of American History* 68:539–59.

———. 1981b. *Police in Urban America.* New York: Cambridge University Press.

Moore, Mark. 1995. *Creating Public Value.* Cambridge: Harvard University Press.

Moskos, Peter. 2008. *Cop in the Hood.* Princeton: Princeton University Press.

Oldenberg, Ray. 1999. *The Great Good Place.* New York: Marlowe and Company.

Parfit, Derek. 1984. *Reasons and Persons.* New York: Oxford University Press.

Philips, David. 1977. *Crime and Authority in Victorian England.* London: Croom Helm.

Rein, Martin, and Christopher Winship. 1999. "The Dangers of Strong Causal Reasoning." *Society* 36:38–46.

Reisig, Michael. 2010. "Community and Problem-Oriented Policing." *Crime and Justice* 39:2–53.

Reiss, Albert J., Jr. 1985. *Policing a City's Central District: The Oakland Story*. Washington, DC: U.S. Department of Justice, National Institute of Justice.

Richardson, James. 1970. *The New York Police: Colonial Times to 1901*. New York: Oxford University Press.

Roberts, Dorothy. 1999. "Race, Vagueness, and the Social Meaning of Order-Maintenance Policing." *Journal of Criminal Law and Criminology* 89:775–836.

Rosensweig, Roy, and Elizabeth Blackmar. 1992. *The Park and the People*. Ithaca, NY: Cornell University Press.

Sampson, Robert, and Stephen Raudenbush. 1999. "Systematic Social Observation of Public Spaces: A New Look at Disorder in Urban Neighborhoods." *American Journal of Sociology* 105:603–51.

——. 2004. "Seeing Disorder." *Social Psychology Quarterly* 67:319–42.

Schneider, John. 1978. "Public Order and the Geography of the City." *Journal of Urban History* 4:183–208.

——. 1980. *Detroit and the Problem of Order*. Lincoln: University of Nebraska Press.

Scott, Michael. 2001. *The Problem of Loud Car Stereos*. Washington, DC: Office of Community Oriented Policing Services.

——. 2004. *Disorderly Youth in Public Places*. Washington, DC: Office of Community Oriented Policing Services.

Sennett, Richard. 1970. *The Uses of Disorder*. New York: Knopf.

——. 1977. *The Fall of Public Man*. New York: Knopf.

Simester, A.P., and Andrew von Hirsch. 2002. "Rethinking the Offense Principle." *Legal Theory* 8:269–95.

Skogan, Wesley G. 2008. "Broken Windows: Why—and How—We Should Take Them Seriously." *Criminology and Public Policy* 7:195–202.

Sloan-Howitt, Maryalice, and George Kelling. 1990. "Subway Graffiti in New York City." *Security Journal* 1:131–36.

Smith, Joseph. 1961. *Colonial Justice in Western Massachusetts*. Cambridge: Harvard University Press.

Stinchcombe, Arthur. 1963. "Institutions of Privacy in the Determination of Police Administrative Practice." *American Journal of Sociology* 69:150–60.

Sykes, Gary. 1986. "Street Justice: A Moral Defense of Order Maintenance Policing." *Justice Quarterly* 3:497–512.

Teir, Robert. 1993. "Maintaining Safety and Civility in Public Spaces." *Louisiana Law Review* 54:285–338.

Thacher, David. 2001. "Policing is Not a Treatment: Alternatives to the Medical Model of Police Research." *Journal of Research in Crime and Delinquency* 38:387–415.

——. 2004. "Order Maintenance Reconsidered." *Journal of Criminal Law and Criminology* 94:381–414.

——. 2006. "The Normative Case Study." *American Journal of Sociology* 111:1631–76.

——. 2008. "Research for the Front Lines." *Policing and Society* 18:46–59.

——. 2009. "Community Policing Without the Police?" In *Community Policing and Peacekeeping*, edited by Peter Grabosky, 55–70. London: Taylor and Francis.

——. 2011. "Olmsted's Police." Unpublished Manuscript. Ann Arbor: University of Michigan.

——. Forthcoming. "Perils of Value Neutrality." *Research in the Sociology of Organizations*.

Tonry, Michael, and Harriet Bildsten. 2009. "Anti-Social Behavior." In *The Oxford Handbook of Crime and Public Policy*, edited by Michael Tonry, 578–598. New York: Oxford University Press.

Valentine, Gill. 2004. *Public Space and the Culture of Childhood*. London: Ashgate.

Vitale, Alex. 2008. *City of Disorder*. New York: New York University Press.

von Hirsch, Andrew. 1996. "'Remote' Harms and Fair Imputation." In *Harm and Culpability*, edited by Andrew Simester and Tony Smith, 259–276. Oxford: Clarendon.

von Hirsch, Andrew, and Clifford Shearing. 2000. "Exclusion from Public Space." In *Ethical and Social Issues in Situational Crime Prevention*, edited by Andrew von Hirsch, David Garland, and Allison Wakefield, 77–98. London: Hart.

von Hoffman, Alexander. 1992. "An Officer of the Neighborhood." *Journal of Social History* 26:309–30.

Waldron, Jeremy. 1991. "Homelessness and the Issue of Freedom." *UCLA Law Review* 39:295–324.

Walker, Samuel. 1977. *A Critical History of Police Reform*. Lexington, Mass.: DC Heath.

——. 1998. *Popular Justice*. New York: Oxford University Press.

Watts, Eugene. 1983. "Police Response to Crime and Disorder in Twentieth-Century St. Louis." *Journal of American History* 70:340–58.

Wertsch, Douglas. 1987. "The Evolution of the Des Moines Police Department." *Annals of Iowa* 48:435–49.

Whyte, William. 1988. *City*. New York: Anchor Books.

Wilson, James Q. 1968. *Varieties of Police Behavior*. Cambridge: Harvard University Press.

Wilson, James Q. 1969. "What Makes a Better Policeman." *Atlantic Monthly* (March):129–35.

Wilson, James Q., and George Kelling. 1982. "Broken Windows." *Atlantic Monthly* (March):29–38.

Winter, James. 1993. *London's Teeming Streets*. New York: Routledge.

Zeveloff, Naomi. 2008. "Denver Rids Parks of Homeless Meals." *Denver Post* (July 14).

Zimring, Franklin, and Gordon Hawkins. 1997. *Crime Is Not the Problem*. New York: Oxford University Press.

CHAPTER 7

....

COMMUNITY POLICING

....

GARY CORDNER

CASUAL observers might think that Bill Clinton invented community policing when he ran for president of the United States in 1991. His platform included a campaign promise to help local and state governments hire 100,000 additional police devoted to community policing, a promise he kept following his election. Or perhaps community policing was created by George Kelling and Mark Moore (1988) in their influential Executive Sessions paper, "The Evolving Strategy of Policing," published jointly by the National Institute of Justice and Harvard University. Or maybe the inventor of community policing was Chief Lee Brown, who began implementing it in Houston in 1983 (Pate et al. 1985), or Chief Ray Davis in Santa Ana, California in the late 1970s (Davis 1985). Perhaps the credit should go to San Diego's community profile initiative in the early 1970s (Boydstun and Sherry 1975), team policing in the late 1960s (Sherman, Milton, and Kelley 1973), Louis Radelet's police-community relations institutes started in the 1950s (Carter and Radelet 2002), or simply to Sir Robert Peel and his oft-cited principle that the police are the people, and the people are the police, laid down in 1829.

This uncertainty about the birth of community policing might exist because many people are largely unfamiliar with police history. But another important reason for historical confusion is that the term "community policing" means many things to many people. Community policing is really a metaphor or figure of speech. It is a "semantic sponge" (Manning 1997) that is loaded with ideological, political, philosophical, cultural, and occupational baggage. This makes it quite challenging to discuss in a sensible way, but ironically rather easy to do, since one can do almost anything and call it community policing.

This essay is presented in four main sections, plus a concluding section. Section 7.1 focuses on why community policing developed in the late twentieth century, emphasizing a confluence of many factors. Section 7.2 acknowledges that community policing is an elusive concept and therefore offers a broad description instead of a tight definition. Section 7.3 identifies challenges that have been encountered by agencies attempting to implement community policing, while Section 7.4 reviews what has been learned from evaluations of the effectiveness of community policing related to reducing crime, reducing fear, enhancing police legitimacy, and achieving other important policing outcomes. Section 7.5 briefly discusses the future prospects for community policing, including looming threats posed by the Great Recession of 2008, the rise of homeland security, and the inevitable influence of politics. A number of main points emerge from this essay:

- The vague nature of community policing has been both a blessing and a curse, creating a large tent for advocates and believers to gather within, but also making it a challenge to implement and evaluate.
- The implementation of community policing by thousands of independent law enforcement agencies in the United State has been difficult to measure, uneven, inconsistent, and, in many jurisdictions, halfhearted.
- Community policing arose primarily in response to concerns about deteriorated police-community relations, and the available evidence indicates that it has generally succeeded in improving the public's opinion of the police.
- Concurrent with the implementation of community policing in the United States, there has been a dramatic decrease in crime—however, there is no compelling evidence that community policing either caused this crime control effect or retarded it.
- There has been a strong impetus for twenty years to incorporate robust problem solving within community policing; while not completely successful, this strategic integration continues to represent the best opportunity for community policing to add crime-reduction effectiveness to its report card.
- Times change and many interests compete for police resources and attention— community policing continues to occupy contested ground with an uncertain future.

7.1 Why Community Policing?

Putting aside the genealogical quest for the origins of community policing DNA, there is little doubt that community policing achieved considerable popularity during the 1980s and then dominated the policing agenda throughout the 1990s, not only in the United States but around the world. One might wonder why this occurred, and why it occurred when it did, rather than in the 1930s, 1950s, or 1970s. There are several possible explanations.

7.1.1 Evolving Police Strategies

In the United States, community policing was preceded by the professional model of policing, which began replacing the political model in the early 1900s. The

professional model brought many improvements associated with training, specialization, and technology. By the 1960s and 1970s, however, it became clear that the
professional model was not the complete solution to all policing problems and issues
(Kelling and Moore 1988).

7.1.2 Police-Community Relations

The most glaring shortcoming of the professional model was police-community relations. Beginning as early as the 1950s, concerns arose about police being isolated and
distant from the public. The initial responses to this problem were public relations initiatives and then police-community relations programs. As these responses gradually
became more genuine and substantive, they evolved toward what is now called community policing (Strecher 1971; Roberg et al. 2012, 90–95).

7.1.3 Race Relations

A significant component of police-community relations in many jurisdictions was (and
is) intertwined with race relations (Williams and Murphy 1990). American police experienced this most dramatically during the civil rights era of the 1950s and 1960s, and
then again in the 1990s when racial profiling became such a difficult and controversial
professional, legal, and political issue (Fridell et al. 2001). As police have sought to shed
their image of an occupying army and narrow the gulf separating them from minority
groups and other vulnerable populations, community policing has seemed a logical and
natural choice.

7.1.4 Police Research

Before the 1970s, it was widely assumed that the strategies embedded within professional policing were effective (Kelling 1978). However, a decade of research showed that
motorized preventive patrol, rapid response, and follow-up criminal investigations were
far less effective than had been believed (Sparrow, Moore, and Kennedy 1992). This led to
an era of trial, error, and scientific experimentation in search of better police strategies.

7.1.5 Foot Patrol

One early product of police effectiveness research was the rediscovery of foot patrol.
Crucially, it was found that foot patrol made the public feel safer and improved the
public's attitudes toward the police (Police Foundation 1981; Trojanowicz 1982). At
a time when the police were anxious to improve their relations with the public, these

were important findings. Although widespread adoption of foot patrol was not viable for most police agencies, many jurisdictions implemented bicycle patrol, police sub-stations, and other techniques aimed at making police officers more accessible. It also became more common to instruct police officers to get out of their patrol cars as often as possible, in order to interact with the public on a more frequent basis.

7.1.6 Broken Windows

The "broken windows" thesis postulates that when police pay attention to minor crime and incivilities, neighborhood residents notice and are reassured about the safety of their neighborhoods and the dependability of their police. Significantly, Wilson and Kelling (1982) did not make up this theory out of thin air, but rather offered it as their explanation for why foot patrol made the public feel safer even if it did not necessarily lead to measurable reductions in serious crime. Broken windows became a very power-ful and influential metaphor both within policing and within popular discussions about crime and disorder, often presented as a key component or more muscular version of community policing.

7.1.7 Problem Solving

Sometime in the 1990s community policing might have hit an early plateau caused by its focus on improving police-community relations—an important objective of polic-ing, but only one objective. Had community policing stopped at the "Officer Friendly" stage it might have had limited impact, and it would also have been criticized as nothing more than the latest version of "the iron fist and the velvet glove" (Center for Research on Criminal Justice 1977). Thanks to the efforts of Herman Goldstein (1987, 1990), how-ever, problem solving got incorporated into community policing at just the right time, providing something substantive for Officer Friendly to do beyond just enforcing the law with a smile.

7.1.8 Police Organizational Development

Beginning in the 1960s, U.S. police departments started hiring more college-educated officers, women, and minorities. This diversified workforce often chafed against the traditional bureaucratic and paramilitary structures and practices found in police departments (Angell 1971; Cordner 1978). At the same time, the human relations approach to management was becoming more popular in private and public orga-nizations generally, including police departments (Cordner 2007). Inevitably, giv-ing higher priority to improved human relations *within* the police organization melded with putting more emphasis on improved relations *between* the police and the community (Wycoff and Skogan 1993). Reflecting this, "organizational transformation" is often cited today as an essential ingredient of community policing (COPS Office 2009).

7.1.9 Police Reform

Especially for those working from the outside of policing (civil rights groups, civil liberties groups, academics), community policing became a key feature of the progressive agenda for police reform. Those who were dissatisfied with police and wanted them to change often focused on reducing police abuses of authority and improving the quality of police-citizen encounters. With its emphasis on improving police-community relations, community policing fit this agenda nicely (Tyler 2003).

7.1.10 Politics

For most of the twentieth century, it was smart politics to emphasize tough-on-crime measures and stand firmly in favor of law and order. Somehow, in the 1990s, Bill Clinton managed to turn community policing into good politics, probably with his campaign pledge to hire 100,000 police. At the local level, since the mid-1980s, it has often been mayors (i.e., not necessarily police chiefs) who have decided that community policing should be the new policing strategy in their cities and towns.

7.1.11 Money

Among other things, the community policing experience in the United States shows that $8 billion is still a lot of money (or was in the 1990s, at least). Following Bill Clinton's election, the federal government did not have the capacity to mandate the adoption of community policing by 18,000 separate police departments, sheriff offices, and other law enforcement agencies, but it did offer a big carrot. As a result, by the year 2000, over 50 percent of U.S. police departments serving populations of 100,000+ had formal, written community policing plans, and over 90 percent of U.S. police officers worked for departments that had at least an informal community policing plan, if not a written one (Hickman and Reaves 2003, 14).

7.1.12 Democratization

The United States and the international community have been vigorously promoting democratization around the world since the 1980s. Especially for post-Soviet and post-conflict countries, the foreign policy establishment has discovered that police can play a significant role in creating conditions conducive to the development of civil society, free press, political parties, private companies, and other democratic institutions. Community policing is now widely recommended as the best model for curbing police abuses and restoring police-public relations in countries where, in the past, police were often the enemy of the people (Brogden and Nijhar 2005). Given this world-wide exporting effort, it would be rather hypocritical not to embrace community policing at home.

7.1.13 Crime

Despite the fact that community policing quickly became popular with the public and seems to make people feel safer, it has not been proven to reduce crime (more on this later). This might have been its Achilles heel and might have severely limited its adoption, except for three reasons: (1) during the heyday of the professional model of policing in the 1970s, crime went up substantially, costing that model its credibility as a crime fighting mega-strategy; (2) related to that, the crime-control effectiveness of the component strategies of the professional model (motorized patrol, rapid response, and follow-up investigations) was largely debunked by studies in the 1970s and 1980s (Moore, Trojanowicz, and Kelling 1988); and, (3) regardless of this evidence, though, community policing might still have had a very short run had its adoption been associated with crime increases. Instead, crime decreased in the United States throughout the 1990s and 2000s, with Part I crime rates 43 percent lower in 2010 than in 1991 (Federal Bureau of Investigation 2011, Table 1).

The relative significance of each of these factors in explaining why community policing became so popular in the 1980s and 1990s is certainly subject to debate, but collectively they gave the strategy a lot of momentum and cachet. The next section attempts to clarify just what community policing is, or is supposed to be.

7.2 WHAT IS COMMUNITY POLICING?

As noted, community policing means many things to many people. As it developed in the 1980s, community policing and its proponents were frequently criticized for failing to provide a clear definition, and it was often called "old wine in new bottles" (Bayley 1988). Defenders tended to emphasize that community policing was still evolving, that it was flexible, and that it was mainly a philosophy, not a set of concrete programs. Critics replied that if even its most ardent supporters could not define community policing, maybe there was nothing there. The definition of community policing promulgated by the COPS Office (2009, 3) is probably the best attempt so far:

> Community policing is a philosophy that promotes organizational strategies, which support the systematic use of partnerships and problem-solving techniques, to

proactively address the immediate conditions that give rise to public safety issues such as crime, social disorder, and fear of crime.

Describing what community policing is, or might be, may be more beneficial than trying to craft a concise definition that everyone can agree with. One framework that may be useful identifies four major dimensions of community policing, along with the most common elements associated with each dimension (Cordner 1995, 2010a).

7.2.1 The Philosophical Dimension

Many of its most thoughtful and forceful advocates emphasize that community policing is a new philosophy of policing, perhaps constituting even a paradigm shift away from professional-model policing, and not just a temporary program or specialized activity. The philosophical dimension includes the central ideas and beliefs underlying community policing. Three of the most important of these are citizen input, broad function, and personal service.

7.2.1.1 Citizen Input

Community policing incorporates a firm commitment to the value and necessity of citizen input to police policies and priorities. In a free and democratic society, citizens are supposed to have a say in how they are governed. Police departments, like other agencies of government, are supposed to be responsive and accountable. Also, from a more selfish standpoint, law enforcement agencies are most likely to obtain the citizen support and cooperation they need when they display interest in input from citizens. A few of the techniques utilized to enhance citizen input include advisory boards, community surveys, community meetings, and radio/television call-in shows. Today, agencies are increasingly using their web pages and social media as additional means of soliciting citizen input.

7.2.1.2 Broad Function

Community policing regards policing as a broad function, not a narrow law enforcement or crime fighting role. The job of police officers is seen as working with residents to enhance neighborhood safety. This includes resolving conflicts, helping victims, preventing accidents, solving problems, and fighting fear (Cordner 2010b) as well as reducing crime through apprehension and enforcement. Policing is inherently a multi-faceted government function—arbitrarily narrowing it to just call-handling and law enforcement reduces its effectiveness in accomplishing the multiple objectives that the public expects police to achieve. Some examples of the broad function of policing include traffic safety education, drug abuse prevention, search and rescue, and protecting "the lives of those who are most vulnerable—juveniles, the elderly, minorities, the poor, the disabled, the homeless" (Trojanowicz and Bucqueroux 1990, iv).

7.2.1.3 Personal Service

Community policing emphasizes personal service to the public, as contrasted with aloof or bureaucratic behavior. This is designed to overcome one of the most common complaints that the public has about government employees, including police officers—that they do not seem to care, and that they treat citizens as numbers, not real people. Of course, not every police-citizen encounter can be amicable and friendly. But whenever possible, officers should deal with citizens in a friendly, open, and personal manner designed to turn them into satisfied customers. This can best be accomplished by eliminating as many artificial bureaucratic barriers as possible, so that citizens can deal directly with "their" officer. A few of the methods that have been adopted in order to implement personalized service are customer relations training, officer business cards, and victim/complainant re-contact procedures. Modern technologies including cell phones, e-mail, and social media have opened up new methods by which police agencies can deliver services to people and by which community residents can contact "their" police officer directly.

7.2.2 The Strategic Dimension

The strategic dimension of community policing includes the key operational concepts that translate philosophy into action. These strategic concepts are the links between the broad ideas and beliefs that underlie community policing and the specific programs and practices by which it is implemented. They assure that agency policies, priorities, and resource allocation are consistent with the community policing philosophy. Three important strategic elements are re-oriented operations, prevention emphasis, and geographic focus.

7.2.2.1 Re-Oriented Operations

Community policing recommends re-oriented operations, with less reliance on the patrol car and more emphasis on face-to-face interactions. One objective is to replace ineffective or isolating operational practices (e.g., motorized patrol and rapid response to low priority calls) with more effective and more interactive practices. A related objective is to find ways of performing necessary traditional functions (e.g., handling emergency calls and conducting follow-up investigations) more efficiently, in order to save time and resources that can then be devoted to more community-oriented activities. Some illustrations of re-oriented operations include foot patrol, bicycle patrol, directed patrol, differential responses to calls for service, and case screening for more targeted investigations. Current initiatives associated with hot spots policing, intelligence-led policing, smart policing, and predictive policing also fit into this category (Ratcliffe 2008).

7.2.2.2 Prevention Emphasis

Community policing tries to implement a prevention emphasis, based on the common sense idea that although citizens appreciate and value rapid response, reactive investigations, and apprehension of wrongdoers, they would always prefer that their victimizations be prevented in the first place. Most modern police departments devote some resources to crime prevention, in the form of a specialist officer or unit. Community policing attempts to go farther by emphasizing that prevention is a big part of *every* officer's job. A few of the approaches to focusing on prevention that departments have adopted are situational crime prevention, crime prevention through environmental design (CPTED), youth-oriented prevention, and a variety of programs involving schools, communities, landlords, and businesses. In regard to homeland security, community policing emphasizes that police officers are not just first responders, but also first preventers (Kelling and Bratton 2006).

7.2.2.3 Geographic Focus

Community policing adopts a geographic focus to establish stronger bonds between officers and neighborhoods in order to increase mutual recognition, identification, responsibility, and accountability in furtherance of strengthening social organization and collective efficacy in neighborhoods (Reisig 2010). Although most police departments have long assigned patrol officers to beats, the officers' real accountability has usually been temporal (for their shift) rather than geographic. More specialized personnel within law enforcement agencies (such as detectives) have similarly been accountable for performing their functions, but not usually for any geographic areas. By its very name, however, *community* policing implies an emphasis on places more than times or functions. Some of the methods by which community policing attempts to emphasize geography are permanent beat assignments, lead officers, beat teams, mini-stations, and area commanders.

7.2.3 The Tactical Dimension

The tactical dimension of community policing ultimately translates ideas, philosophies, and strategies into concrete programs, tactics, and behaviors. Even those who insist that "community policing is a philosophy, not a program" must concede that unless community policing eventually leads to some action, some new or different behavior, it is all rhetoric and no reality. Indeed, many commentators have taken the view that community policing is little more than a new police marketing strategy that has left the core elements of the police role untouched (Klockars 1988; Manning 1988; Weatheritt 1988). Three of the most important tactical elements of community policing are positive interaction, partnerships, and problem solving.

7.2.3.1 Positive Interaction

Policing inevitably involves some negative contacts between officers and citizens—arrests, tickets, stops for suspicion, orders to desist, inability to make things much better for victims, et cetera. Community policing recognizes this fact and recommends that officers offset it as much as they can by engaging in positive interactions whenever possible. Positive interactions have several benefits, of course: they generally build familiarity, trust and confidence on both sides; they remind officers that most citizens respect and support them; they make the officer more knowledgeable about people and conditions in the beat; they provide specific information for criminal investigations and problem solving; and they break up the monotony of motorized patrol. Some methods for engaging in positive interaction include making an extra effort during call handling, attending community meetings, taking policing into schools, malls, and other settings where the public congregates, and simply shifting the emphasis of patrol from watching and waiting more toward interacting.

7.2.3.2 *Partnerships*

Community policing stresses the importance of active partnerships between police, other agencies, and citizens, in which all parties really work together to identify and solve problems. Citizens can take a greater role in public safety than has been typical over the past few decades, and other public and private agencies can leverage their own resources and authority toward the solution of public safety problems. Obviously, there are some legal and safety limitations on how extensive a role citizens can play in "co-producing" public safety. Just as obviously, it is a mistake for the police to try to assume the entire burden for controlling crime and disorder. Partnerships can take many forms including block watch groups, citizen police academies, police-school initiatives, landlord associations, code enforcement liaison, and even citizen patrols.

7.2.3.3 *Problem Solving*

Community policing urges the adoption of a problem-solving orientation toward policing, as opposed to the incident-oriented approach that has tended to prevail in conjunction with the professional model. Naturally, emergency calls must still be handled right away, and officers will still spend much of their time handling individual incidents. Whenever possible, however, officers should search for the underlying conditions that give rise to single and multiple incidents. When such conditions are identified, officers should try to affect them as a means of controlling and preventing future incidents. Basically, police officers should strive to have more substantive and meaningful impact than occurs from fifteen-minute treatments of individual calls for service. Typical ingredients of problem solving include the SARA process, the crime triangle, a commitment to carefully analyzing specific crime and disorder problems (Center for Problem-Oriented Policing 2012a), and a bias toward sharing the responsibility for problem solving with the community and with other public and private institutions (Scott and Goldstein 2005).

7.2.4 The Organizational Dimension

It is important to recognize an organizational dimension that surrounds community policing and greatly affects its implementation. In order to support and facilitate

community policing, police departments often consider a variety of changes in organization, administration, supervision, other internal systems, and the behavior of work
groups and individuals (Greene 2000). The elements of the organizational dimension
are not really part of community policing per se, but they are frequently crucial to its
successful implementation. Three important organizational elements of community
policing are structure, management, and information.

7.2.4.1 Structure

Community policing looks at various ways of restructuring police agencies in order to
facilitate and support implementation of the philosophical, strategic, and tactical elements described above. Any organization's structure should correspond with its mission and its technology (i.e., the nature of the work performed by its members and the
processes it uses to transform inputs into outputs and outcomes) (Greene 2000). Some
aspects of traditional police organization structure seem more suited to routine bureaucratic work than to the discretion and creativity required for community policing. The
types of restructuring associated with community policing include decentralization,
flattening of the hierarchy, de-specialization, teams, and civilianization.

7.2.4.2 Management

Community policing is often associated with styles of leadership, management, and
supervision that give more emphasis to organizational culture and values and less
emphasis to written rules and formal discipline. The general argument is that when
employees are guided by a set of officially sanctioned values they will usually make
good decisions and take appropriate actions. Although many formal rules will still be
necessary, managers might need to resort to them much less often in order to maintain control over subordinates. Management practices consistent with this emphasis
on organizational culture and values include mission and value statements, strategic
planning, mentoring and coaching, and positive discipline. More emphasis is put on
empowering officers and taking full advantage of their talents and creativity (Goldstein
1990), rather than on trying to tightly control them in order to avoid misbehavior.

7.2.4.3 Information

Doing community policing and managing it effectively require certain types of information that have not traditionally been available in all police departments. In the
never-ending quality versus quantity debate, for example, community policing tends to
emphasize quality. This emphasis on quality shows up in many areas: avoidance of traditional bean-counting (e.g., arrests, tickets) to measure success, more concern for how
well calls are handled versus merely how quickly they are handled, et cetera (Spelman
1988). Also, the geographic focus of community policing increases the need for detailed
information based on neighborhoods as the unit of analysis. The emphasis on problem
solving highlights the need for information systems that aid in identifying and analyzing
a variety of community-level problems (Boba 2003). There is a greater need for timely
crime analysis and problem analysis enhanced with geographic information systems

(GIS). Supervisors need additional information to do meaningful performance appraisals, and commanders need better information in order to function in a CompStat environment (Shane 2007). Executives need information from community surveys and
customer feedback surveys to augment their other sources of information about overall
agency performance.

7.3 IMPLEMENTING COMMUNITY POLICING

The evidence in regard to the actual implementation of community policing in the
United States is mixed and somewhat confusing (Morabito 2010), a situation that is
not surprising given its sponge-like nature and the extremely fragmented U.S. policing
system. For one thing, different law enforcement agencies have emphasized different
elements of community policing. Also, some agencies have implemented community
policing as a specialized activity performed by designated officers or assigned to a
stand-alone unit, while other agencies have taken the generalist approach and attempted
organization-wide implementation.

Much of the early discussion about the difficulty of implementing community policing
focused on organizational resistance. Entrenched bureaucratic interests were often cited
as key obstacles, such as middle managers who resist decentralization and empower-
ment of subordinates (Sherman 1975; Kelling and Bratton 1993), and a police culture that
resists engaging with the community and emphasizing prevention and positive interaction over traditional reactive policing (Kelling, Wasserman, and Williams 1988). Several
major efforts at community policing implementation were carefully studied in order to
identify lessons learned about managing organizational and cultural change (Wycoff
and Skogan 1993; Greene, Bergman, and McLaughlin 1994; Skogan and Hartnett 1997).

Studies have sought to measure the adoption of specific community policing programs across the United States, but for the most part have not been able to measure
the intensity of implementation (e.g., the proportion of all patrolling done on bicycles) or programmatic fidelity (e.g., whether mini-stations are part of a community
policing delivery system, or just window dressing) (Maguire and Mastrofski 2000).
Consequently, we can state that 50 percent of police agencies in 1997 sponsored land-
lord/property manager training programs (Fridell 2004, 51), and 16 percent of agencies
in 2007 reported administering citizen surveys (Reaves 2010, 27), but how often the
landlord training programs were conducted, or whether the results of the citizen surveys were actually taken seriously as input to police decision making, is unknown.

With these caveats in mind, it has to be recognized that a lot of community policing
has been implemented over the past 20 to 30 years. A 2002 survey found 16 different community policing activities that at least 75 percent of responding agencies reported having
implemented, including police-community meetings, neighborhood watch, citizen police
academies, and permanent beat assignments (Cordner 2004, 61). For 36 out of 56 total
activities covered by that survey, the proportion of agencies reporting implementation

was higher in 2002 than it had been in either 1992 or 1997, indicating an upward trajectory of implementation (Fridell 2004, fig. 4-4 to 4-7). As of 2007, over 50 percent of police agencies used regularly scheduled foot patrol, one-third used bicycle patrol, about 80 percent of new recruits received some community policing training, and about 47,000 local police officers were specifically assigned to community policing activities (Reaves 2010).

In contrast to this fairly positive picture, however, two major developments over the last decade may have slowed the expansion of community policing or even reversed it. One is police involvement in counter-terrorism and homeland security since 9/11, and the other is the Great Recession that began in 2008. While strategists and law enforcement executives have argued that community policing should be the foundation for the police role in homeland security (IACP 2002; Ramsey 2002; Burack 2003; Scheider and Chapman 2003; Newman and Clarke 2008), it is clear that the new homeland security mission has competed strongly with community policing for already-limited time, resources, and energy in many police departments (Foster and Cordner 2005; Lee 2010). On top of that, the 2008 recession led to budget reductions that caused many police agencies to cut back significantly on nearly everything other than emergency response and major crime investigation (COPS Office 2011; Melekian 2012).

Other information also suggests that, even before 9/11 and the great recession, community policing implementation was sometimes rather superficial. The 2002 survey found that less than 25 percent of agencies had adopted some of the more robust features of community policing, such as giving citizens a role in selecting and evaluating police officers and reviewing complaints against the police (Cordner 2004), indicating a reluctance to engage in real power sharing with the community (Brown 1985). Studies of the actual behavior of community policing officers found that they spent relatively little time interacting with citizens (Parks et al. 1999; Frank and Liederbach 2003). A study focused on problem solving by non-specialist patrol officers found a "glass half full" scenario—problem solving that was often more thoughtful, collaborative, and imaginative than traditional enforcement or call handling, but smaller in scope, less analytical, and less creative than the kinds of efforts usually held up as ideal examples of problem-oriented policing (Cordner and Biebel 2005). Another observation about community policing in practice is that it has usually been police-centered, with minimal success in truly engaging the community and little evidence of real police-citizen co-production of public safety (Kerley and Benson 2000). Moreover, when the community does become engaged, it is frequently not the entire community, but segments of it. Consequently, police working with engaged community members run the risk of helping them achieve their desired ends at the expense of other, less-engaged community members, or getting caught in the middle of competing community groups (Thacher 2001a, 2001b).

7.4 Evaluating Community Policing

At least five complicating factors, some of which have been discussed above, have made it extremely difficult to determine the effectiveness of community policing. One is programmatic complexity. Community policing is a flexible and loose concept. Police agencies have implemented a wide array of operational and organizational innovations under its banner. Because community policing is not one consistent "thing," it is difficult to say whether "it" works.

Another complication is that community policing in practice has varied widely in program scope. In different places, community policing has been implemented as a single-officer project, as a special-unit program, and as an organization-wide strategy. Some of the most positive results have come from projects that involved just a few specialist officers, a small special unit, and/or a narrowly defined target area. The generalizability of these results to full-scale department-wide and community-wide implementation is open to debate.

A third challenge for community policing evaluations is that the strategy has, or might have, multiple effects. The number of intended and unintended effects that might accrue to community policing is considerable. Community policing might affect crime, disorder, fear of crime, police-community relations, police officer attitudes, police use of force, or a host of other conditions that matter. This multiplicity of potential effects complicates any evaluation and reduces the likelihood of concluding with a simple yes or no answer to the bottom-line question, "Does community policing work?"

A fourth complication is that police executives and researchers have rarely been able to utilize experimental or strong quasi-experimental designs in their studies of community policing effectiveness. Rather, despite good intentions and significant effort, most community policing evaluations have employed case studies and similarly weak research designs. Limitations have included lack of control groups, lack of randomization, and a tendency to measure only short-term effects. Consequently, the findings of many community policing studies have not had as much scientific credibility as would be desired.

Finally, evaluations of community policing have not been able to control for other major concurrent changes going on within policing and the larger society. During the same time period over which community policing was implemented in many U.S. police agencies, several other big changes occurred, making it a challenge to tease out the specific effects of community policing. Within police departments, for example, additional officers were hired (including the 100,000 "Clinton cops"), technology exploded, CompStat was widely adopted, and the workforce became more diverse. In the larger criminal justice arena, incarceration rates increased substantially, and the crack cocaine epidemic came and went. From the mid-1990s onward, crime rates declined substantially, fueling a huge but unresolved debate over whether policing, incarceration, economics, demographics, or something else deserves the largest share of the crime control credit (Zhao, Scheider, and Thurman 2002; Ekstrand and Kingsbury 2003; Blumstein and Wallman 2005; Zimring 2006).

Most of the evaluations of community policing have been case studies, which sometimes have strong internal validity but rarely have much external validity. Following the early foot patrol studies in Newark and Flint (Police Foundation 1981; Trojanowicz 1982), community policing studies in Baltimore County, Madison, and Chicago, among other places, documented pretty clear-cut positive effects on fear of crime, public perceptions of crime, public attitudes toward the police, and even police officer attitudes (Cordner 1986; Wycoff and Skogan 1993; Lurigio and Rosenbaum 1994; Skogan and Hartnett 1997; Skogan 2006). However, case studies in Houston, Newark, New York, and other cities produced mixed results, as well as evidence of implementation challenges (Sadd and Grinc 1994; Skogan 1994). Case studies of hundreds of examples of problem-oriented policing (a key element of community policing) consistently cite positive impacts on crime, disorder, and other specific types of problems (Scott 2000; Center for Problem-Oriented Policing 2012b).

The scientific consensus on what this evidence adds up to is that community policing usually has positive effects on fear of crime as well as the public's perceptions of crime and policing, but unproven effects on the actual incidence of crime (Moore 1992; Skogan and Frydl 2004; Weisburd and Eck 2004). Meta-analyses have concluded that some specific components of community policing, such as neighborhood watch, problem-solving, and directed/hot spots patrolling do lead to crime reductions (Mazerolle, Soole, and Rombouts 2007; Holloway, Bennett, and Farrington 2008; Braga 2008; Weisburd et al. 2008; also see Reisig 2010). The prevailing interpretation is that targeted policing initiatives are more likely to cause crime and disorder reductions than broad, diffuse strategic interventions such as full-fledged community policing. This is reflected in the new Crime Solutions database (Office of Justice Programs 2012) that gives "effective" and "promising" ratings to quite a few specific crime prevention and law enforcement techniques but does not offer an overall assessment of community policing.

Table 7.1 summarizes the evidence on the effectiveness of community policing compared to reactive professional model policing. The criteria on which they are compared are the seven dimensions of the police performance "bottom line" suggested by Moore and Braga (2003). Community policing is given a "+" for three of the criteria: reducing fear, ensuring civility in public spaces, and satisfying the public. The generally positive

Table 7.1 Comparing the Effectiveness of Community Policing and Reactive Policing

	Community Policing	Reactive Policing
Reduce crime and victimization		
Call offenders to account		
Reduce fear and enhance personal security	+	
Ensure civility in public spaces (ordered liberty)	+	
Use force and authority fairly, efficiently, and effectively		
Use financial resources fairly, efficiently, and effectively		+
Quality services/customer satisfaction	+	

effects on fear of crime and public satisfaction were already discussed. The positive attribution for ensuring civility is based largely on broken windows policing, which emphasizes that police should pay close attention to minor crime and disorder (Kelling and Coles 1996). Studies of broken windows policing have generally shown that it can succeed in reducing incivilities and disorder, which in turn frequently results in improved public perceptions and reduced fear (Sousa and Kelling 2006). There has been a heated scientific debate over the effectiveness of broken windows policing, but it has not mainly focused on these outcomes. Rather, that debate centers on whether broken windows policing leads to reductions in more serious crime, and whether it results in fair and equitable policing (Tyler 2003; Taylor 2006).

Based on the meta-analyses mentioned earlier, an additional "+" mark for reducing serious crime could potentially be given to community policing if it incorporated a strong element of problem solving. Interestingly, a multi-site evaluation of reassurance policing (similar to community policing) in the United Kingdom concluded that it worked most effectively in those sites where problem solving was emphasized (Tuffin, Morris, and Poole 2006). As noted in the discussion of community policing implementation, however, problem solving in practice is often much less rigorous, analytical, collaborative, and creative than recommended by the advocates of problem-oriented policing.

Reactive policing is given a positive mark for using financial resources fairly, efficiently, and effectively primarily on the basis of efficiency, because it can serve as a leaner, back-to-basics approach, especially in times of financial constraint. Also, an argument can be made that a reactive strategy uses resources most fairly, as it allocates them upon request from citizens, including victims. Walker (1984) made the point that there is nothing quite so democratic and egalitarian as giving every citizen the opportunity to summon the awesome power of the state (the police) just by placing a free telephone call.

In addition to the reducing crime criterion, neither community policing nor reactive policing is given a positive advantage for calling offenders to account (crime solving) or using force and authority fairly, efficiently, and effectively. In regard to crime solving, there is evidence that when people view the law and law enforcement as fair, they are more likely to cooperate with investigations and prosecutions (Tyler 2003). With respect to police use of force, there is some reason to think that community policing could deserve a plus, since officers who are engaged with the community and knowledgeable about specific community residents might be expected to make better decisions and be more successful in gaining voluntary compliance from the public. However, it could also be true that an emphasis on reducing incivilities and disorder (i.e., broken windows policing) might lead to more confrontational encounters with the public and, overall, a more intrusive brand of policing. The evidence on whether community policing systematically leads to more positive or more negative outcomes related to the use of force and authority is inconclusive at this point.

Overall, one is tempted to conclude that police in the United States over the past twenty to thirty years have about half-implemented community policing, and it has about half-worked. In the annals of organizational change and government programs, that is pretty respectable. It is possible that, with more thorough and committed implementation, community policing would have even more beneficial outcomes. Alternatively, it is possible that community policing has "maxed out" in its potential to improve police performance.

Further practical experience and better evaluations should help sort these questions out in the years to come. A revitalized community policing research agenda could include several different components: (1) more careful analysis of contemporary police culture in multiple agencies to test the common assumption that police officers are inherently predisposed to resist doing community policing; (2) more careful measurement of actual community policing implementation at the individual, group, and organizational levels in order to provide a much firmer grasp on how much or how little community policing is really being done; (3) longer-term studies to help determine whether the benefits of community policing increase, stabilize, or decline over time; (4) outcome evaluations using more rigorous designs and more systematic criteria in order to build up the scientific evidence base regarding the effects of community policing; and (5) analysis of the impact of the newest modalities of community policing, such as social media. On this last point, one has to assume that as social relations and social networks change, what works for the police to engage the public, reassure them, and enhance police legitimacy is likely to change as well.

7.5 CONCLUSION

What does the future hold for community policing? If one takes the view that Bill Clinton invented it and made it happen with $8 billion in federal aid to local governments, then its days are probably numbered, if not over. On the other hand, if one takes the view that community policing is simply the latest reaffirmation of Peelian principles and democratic policing, then one hopes that it is here to stay.

From the perspective of evidence-based policing, community policing seems to have clear-cut advantages over competing police strategies when it comes to making the public feel safer and enhancing the public's satisfaction with the police. When community policing incorporates a strong broken windows orientation, then it also gets good marks for reducing disorder and incivilities, thus making public spaces safer and more orderly. However, as discussed, the challenge in this respect is to address minor crime and disorder without incurring negative consequences on using force and authority fairly, which in turn is liable to damage public satisfaction and police legitimacy. These negative consequences would not seem to be an inevitable result of broken windows policing, but they are frequently encountered, as recent news reports from New York and London demonstrate (Chang 2011; Dodd 2012).

Problem-oriented policing and problem solving would seem to represent the most effective methods by which community policing might overcome these side effects of broken windows policing, and also by which it might raise its grades on reducing serious crime. On the first issue, if police officers take a problem-solving approach to addressing disorder and incivilities, rather than a zero-tolerance enforcement approach, they are less likely to make as many unnecessary stops and as many arrests for minor offenses. The key, and this is entirely consistent with broken windows policing, is that officers must identify and take action against disorder and minor crime, including the immediate conditions that encourage them. But taking action need not be limited to enforcement—actions should be more preventive, substantive, collaborative, and creative whenever possible. The public should still see their police addressing disorder and incivilities, but police methods should go well beyond the easy, simplistic, and possibly counter-productive zero-tolerance enforcement campaigns that have sometimes been associated with broken windows policing in practice.

The same logic applies to serious crime reduction. Problem-oriented policing has attained a degree of scientific recognition for reducing crime that has so far eluded community policing. Problem solving is already a central component of full-fledged community policing. Logically, it would seem incumbent on the architects and implementers of community policing to pursue a stronger emphasis on that problem solving component, in order to improve community policing's standing in relation to the critical criterion of crime control. Of course, this is exactly what Goldstein (1987) proposed over twenty years ago. The continuing challenge is to move the actual practice of community policing from a minimalist adoption of problem solving toward a more complete implementation of problem-oriented policing. Efforts in this regard have been underway for many years now, with impressive resources available from the Center for Problem-Oriented Policing, but systematic in-depth implementation has been disappointing.

Three perhaps inter-related threats loom on the horizon. A big one is the economy. It takes time, and therefore resources, for police officers to actively engage the community, develop partnerships, deliver personal services, and carry out creative problem solving. In today's financial circumstances, it is common to label community policing the Cadillac (or Lexus) approach, and to conclude that we just cannot afford it anymore. The rebuttal is that, with whatever resources are available, generous or paltry, community policing is more effective than other options. But it is tempting to cut back on everything other than essential emergency services when finances are so tight.

A second threat is terrorism and homeland security. Despite strong feelings in some sectors of the police profession that community policing is the best foundation for the police role in counter-terrorism, the allure of intelligence-led policing, predictive policing, and modern technology are hard to resist. These twenty-first-century police strategies are sometimes also combined with a more militaristic approach to policing, and they tend to correlate with a stronger role (in the United States) for federal law enforcement versus local policing. The cumulative impact of all this might be to marginalize the ordinary patrol officer and minimize the importance of everyday community policing.

Finally, there is politics. The tendency of elected officials, and candidates for elected office, to emphasize tough-on-crime, law-and-order agendas runs deep. Law and order is currently not a particularly dominant issue in American politics, since crime has been on the decline for twenty years and other issues, like the economy, have taken precedence. Politics can change quickly, however. It would not be surprising in a few years to witness yet another war on crime, drugs, or terrorism. Whenever these wars are declared, it is usually a boon for hard-nosed enforcement-oriented policing, not community policing. Perhaps the pendulum swings a little less wildly each time, but it always swings.

REFERENCES

Angell, John E. 1971. "Toward an Alternative to the Classic Police Organizational Arrangements: A Democratic Model." *Criminology* 9:185–206.

Bayley, David. 1988. "Community Policing: A Report from the Devil's Advocate." In *Community Policing: Rhetoric or Reality,* edited by Jack R. Greene and Stephen D. Mastrofski, 225–238. New York: Praeger.

Blumstein, Alfred, and Joel Wallman, eds. 2005. *The Crime Drop in America.* New York: Cambridge University Press.

Boba, Rachel. 2003. *Problem Analysis in Policing.* Washington, DC: Police Foundation.

Boydstun, John E., and Michael E. Sherry. 1975. *San Diego Community Profile: Final Report.* Washington, DC: Police Foundation.

Braga, Anthony. 2008. *Police Enforcement Strategies to Prevent Crime in Hot Spot Areas: Crime Prevention Research Review No. 2.* Washington, DC: Office of Community Oriented Policing Services.

Brogden, Mike, and Preeti Nijhar. 2005. *Community Policing: International Models and Approaches.* Devon, UK: Willan.

Brown, Lee P. 1985. "Police Community Power Sharing." In *Police Leadership in America: Crisis and Opportunity,* edited by William A. Geller, 70–83. New York: Praeger.

Burack, James. 2003. "Community Policing in a Security-Conscious World: Working to Prevent Terrorism in Rural America." *Subject to Debate* 17(8): 1–7.

Carter, David L., and Louis A. Radelet. 2002. *Police and the Community,* 7th ed. Englewood Cliffs, NJ: Prentice Hall.

Center for Problem-Oriented Policing. 2012a. "The Key Elements of Problem-Oriented Policing." http://www.popcenter.org/about/?p=elements.

——. 2012b. "Case Studies and Databases." http://www.popcenter.org/casestudies/.

Center for Research on Criminal Justice. 1977. *The Iron fist and the Velvet Glove: An Analysis of the U.S. Police.* Ann Arbor: University of Michigan.

Chang, Ailsa. 2011. "Police Commissioner Calls on NYPD to Stop Improper Marijuana Arrests." *WNYC News* (September 23). http://www.wnyc.org/articles/wnyc-news/2011/sep/23/police-commissioner-calls-nypd-stop-improper-marijuana-arrests/.

COPS Office. 2009. *Community Policing Defined.* Washington, DC: Office of Community Oriented Policing Services. http://www.cops.usdoj.gov/files/RIC/Publications/e030917193-CP-Defined.pdf.

——. 2011. *The Impact of the Economic Downturn on American Police Agencies.* Washington, DC: Office of Community Oriented Policing Services. http://www.cops.usdoj.gov/files/RIC/Publications/e101113406_Economic%20Impact.pdf.

Cordner, Gary. 1978. "Open and Closed Models of Police Organizations: Traditions, Dilemmas, and Practical Considerations." *Journal of Police Science and Administration* 6(1): 22–34.

——. 1986. "Fear of Crime and the Police: An Evaluation of a Fear Reduction Strategy." *Journal of Police Science and Administration* 14(3): 223–33.

——. 1995. "Community Policing: Elements and Effects." *Police Forum* 5(3): 1–8.

——. 2004. "The Survey Data: What They Say and Don't Say." In *Community Policing: The Past, Present, and Future,* edited by Lorie Fridell and Mary Ann Wycoff, 59–69. Washington, DC: Police Executive Research Forum.

——. 2007. "Administration of Police Agencies, Theories of." In *The Encyclopedia of Police Science,* 3rd ed., edited by Jack R. Greene, 28–31. New York: Routledge/Taylor and Francis.

——. 2010a. "Community Policing: Elements and Effects." In *Critical Issues in Policing: Contemporary Readings,* 6th ed., edited by Roger G. Dunham and Geoffrey P. Alpert, 432–449. Long Grove, IL: Waveland.

——. 2010b. *Reducing Fear of Crime: Strategies for Police.* Washington, DC: Office of Community Oriented Policing Services. http://www.cops.usdoj.gov/files/RIC/Publications/e110913242-ReducingFear.pdf.

Cordner, Gary, and Elizabeth Perkins Biebel. 2005. "Problem-Oriented Policing in Practice." *Criminology and Public Policy* 4(2): 155–80.

Davis, Raymond C. 1985. "Organizing the Community for Improved Policing." In *Police Leadership in America: Crisis and Opportunity,* edited by William A. Geller, 84–95. New York: Praeger.

Dodd, Vikram. 2012. "Metropolitan Police to Scale Back Stop and Search Operation." *The Guardian* (January 12). http://www.guardian.co.uk/uk/2012/jan/12/met-police-stop-search-suspicion?.

Ekstrand, Laurie E., and Nancy Kingsbury. 2003. "Technical Assessment of Zhao and Thurman's 2001 Evaluation of the Effects of COPS Grants on Crime." GAO-03-867R. Washington, DC: Government Accounting Office. http://www.gao.gov/new.items/d03867r.pdf.

Federal Bureau of Investigation. 2011. *Crime in the United States: 2010.* Washington, DC: Federal Bureau of Investigation. http://www.fbi.gov/about-us/cjis/ucr/crime-in-the-u.s/2010/crime-in-the-u.s.-2010/tables/10tbl01.xls.

Foster, Chad, and Gary Cordner. 2005. *The Impact of Terrorism on State Law Enforcement: Adjusting to New Roles and Changing Conditions.* Lexington, KY: Council of State Governments.

Frank, James, and John Liederbach. 2003. "The Work Routines and Citizen Interactions of Small-Town and Rural Police Officers." In *Community Policing in a Rural Setting,* 2nd edition, edited by Quint C. Thurman and Edmund F. McGarrell, 49–60. Cincinnati, OH: Anderson. http://www.csg.org/knowledgecenter/docs/Misc0504Terrorism.pdf.

Fridell, Lorie. 2004. "The Results of Three National Surveys on Community Policing." In *Community Policing: The Past, Present, and Future,* edited by Lorie Fridell and Mary Ann Wycoff, 39–58. Washington, DC: Police Executive Research Forum.

Fridell, Lorie, Robert Lunney, Drew Diamond, and Bruce Kubu. 2001. *Racially Biased Policing: A Principled Response.* Washington, DC: Police Executive Research Forum.

Goldstein, Herman. 1987. "Toward Community-Oriented Policing: Potential, Basic Requirements and Threshold Questions." *Crime and Delinquency* 33:6–30.

——. 1990. *Problem-Oriented Policing.* New York: McGraw-Hill.

Greene, Jack R. 2000. "Community Policing in America: Changing the Nature, Structure, and Function of the Police." In *Criminal Justice 2000*, vol. 3, edited by Julie Horney, 299–370. Washington, DC: U.S. Department of Justice, National Institute of Justice

Greene, Jack R, William T. Bergman, and Edward J. McLaughlin. 1994. "Implementing Community Policing: Cultural and Structural Change in Police Organizations." In *The Challenge of Community Policing: Testing the Promises*, edited by Dennis P. Rosenbaum, 92–109. Thousand Oaks, CA: Sage.

Hickman, Matthew J., and Brian A. Reaves. 2003. *Local Police Departments 2000*. Washington, DC: Bureau of Justice Statistics. http://bjs.ojp.usdoj.gov/content/pub/pdf/lpd00.pdf.

Holloway, Katy, Trevor Bennett, and David P. Farrington. 2008. *Does Neighborhood Watch Reduce Crime? Crime Prevention Research Review No. 3*. Washington, DC: Office of Community Oriented Policing Services.

IACP. 2002. "Community Policing: A Valuable Tool in the Fight Against Terrorism." Resolution adopted by the general membership. Alexandria, VA: International Association of Chiefs of Police.

Kelling, George L. 1978. "Police Field Services and Crime: The Presumed Effects of a Capacity." *Crime and Delinquency* 24:173–84.

Kelling, George L., and William J. Bratton. 1993. "Implementing Community Policing: The Administrative Problem." Perspectives on Policing No. 17. Washington, DC: National Institute of Justice.

———. 2006. "Policing Terrorism." Civic Bulletin No. 43. New York: Manhattan Institute for Policy Research.

Kelling, George L., and Catherine M. Coles. 1996. *Fixing Broken Windows: Restoring Order and Reducing Crime in our Communities*. New York: Free Press.

Kelling, George L., and Mark H. Moore. 1988. "The Evolving Strategy of Policing." Perspectives on Policing No. 4. Washington, DC: National Institute of Justice.

Kelling, George L., Robert Wasserman, and Hubert Williams. 1988. "Police Accountability and Community Policing." Perspectives on Policing No. 7. Washington, DC: National Institute of Justice.

Kerley, Kent R., and Michael L. Benson. 2000. "Does Community-Oriented Policing Help Build Stronger Communities?" *Police Quarterly* 3(1): 46–69.

Klockars, Carl B. 1988. "The Rhetoric of Community Policing." In *Community Policing: Rhetoric or Reality*, edited by Jack R. Greene and Stephen D. Mastrofski, 239–258. New York: Praeger.

Lee, Jayson Vaughn. 2010. "Policing After 9/11: Community Policing in an ge of Homeland Security." *Police Quarterly* 13(4): 347–66.

Lurigio, Arthur J., and Dennis P. Rosenbaum. 1994. "The Impact of Community Policing on Police Personnel: A Review of the Literature." In *The Challenge of Community Policing: Testing the Promises*, edited by Dennis P. Rosenbaum, 147–163. Thousand Oaks, CA: Sage.

Maguire, Edward, and Stephen Mastrofski. 2000. "Patterns of Community Policing in the United States." *Police Quarterly* 3(1): 4–45.

Manning, Peter K. 1988. "Community Policing as a Drama of Control." In *Community Policing: Rhetoric or Reality*, edited by Jack R. Greene and Stephen D. Mastrofski, 27–45. New York: Praeger.

———. 1997. *Police Work: The Social Organization of Policing*, 2d ed. Prospect Heights, IL: Waveland.

Mazerolle, Lorraine, David W. Soole, and Sacha Rombouts. 2007. *Disrupting Street-Level Drug Markets: Crime Prevention Research Reviews No. 1*. Washington, DC: Office of Community Oriented Policing Services.

Melekian, Bernard K. 2012. "Policing in the New Economy: A New Report on the Emerging Trends from the Office of Community Oriented Policing Services." *The Police Chief* (January): 16–19.

Moore, Mark H. 1992. "Problem-Solving and Community Policing." In *Modern Policing*, edited by Michael Tonry and Nornal Morris, 99–158. Chicago: University of Chicago.

Moore, Mark H., and Anthony Braga. 2003. *The "Bottom Line" of Policing: What Citizens Should Value (and Measure) in Police Performance*. Washington, DC: Police Executive Research Forum.

Moore, Mark H., Robert C. Trojanowicz, and George L. Kelling. 1988. "Crime and Policing." Perspectives on Policing No. 2. Washington, DC: National Institute of Justice.

Morabito, Melissa Schaefer. 2010. "Understanding Community Policing as an Innovation: Patterns of Adoption." *Crime and Delinquency* 56(4): 564–87.

Newman, Graeme R., and Ronald V. Clarke. 2008. *Policing Terrorism: An Executive's Guide*. Washington, DC: Office of Community Oriented Policing Services.

Office of Justice Programs. 2012. "Crime Solutions." http://crimesolutions.gov/default.aspx.

Parks, Roger B., Stephen D. Mastrofski, Christina DeJong, and M. Kevin Gray. 1999. "How Officers Spend Their Time with the Community." *Justice Quarterly* 16(3): 483–518.

Pate, Anthony M., Wesley Skogan, Mary Ann Wycoff, and Lawrence W. Sherman. 1985. *Coordinated Community Policing: Executive Summary*. Washington, DC: Police Foundation.

Police Foundation. 1981. *The Newark Foot Patrol Experiment*. Washington, DC: Police Foundation.

Ramsey, Charles. 2002. "Community Policing: Now More Than Ever." *On the Beat* 19:6–7.

Ratcliffe, Jerry H. 2008. *Intelligence-Led Policing*. Devon, UK: Willan.

Reaves, Brian A. 2010. *Local Police Departments, 2007*. Washington, DC: Bureau of Justice Statistics.

Reisig, Michael D. 2010. "Community and Problem-Oriented Policing." *Crime and Justice: A Review of Research* 39:1–53.

Roberg, Roy, Kenneth Novak, Gary Cordner, and Brad Smith. 2012. *Police & Society,* 5th ed. New York: Oxford University Press.

Sadd, Susan, and Randolph Grinc. 1994. "Innovative Neighborhood Oriented Policing: An Evaluation of Community Policing Programs in Eight Cities." In *The Challenge of Community Policing: Testing the Promises,* edited by Dennis P. Rosenbaum, 27–52. Thousand Oaks, CA: Sage.

Scheider, Matthew and Rob Chapman. 2003. "Community Policing and Terrorism." *Journal of Homeland Security* (April). http://homelandsecurity.org/journal

Scott, Michael S. 2000. *Problem-Oriented Policing: Reflections on the First 20 Years*. Washington, DC: Office of Community Oriented Policing Services.

Scott, Michael S., and Herman Goldstein. 2005. *Shifting and Sharing Responsibility for Public Safety Problems*. Washington, DC: Office of Community Oriented Policing Services. http://www.popcenter.org/responses/responsibility/

Shane, Jon M. 2007. *What Every Chief Executive Should Know: Using Data to Measure Police Performance*. Flushing, NY: Looseleaf.

Sherman, Lawrence W. 1975. "Middle Management and Police Democratization: A Reply to John E. Angell." *Criminology* 12:363–78.

Sherman, Lawrence W., Catherine H. Milton, and Thomas V. Kelley. 1973. *Team Policing: Seven Case Studies*. Washington, DC: Police Foundation.

Skogan, Wesley G. 1994. "The Impact of Community Policing on Neighborhood Residents: A Cross-Site Analysis." In *The Challenge of Community Policing: Testing the Promises*, edited by Dennis P. Rosenbaum, 167–181. Thousand Oaks, CA: Sage.

——. 2006. *Police and Community in Chicago: A Tale of Three Cities*. New York: Oxford University Press.

Skogan, Wesley G., and Kathleen Frydl, eds. 2004. *Fairness and Effectiveness in Policing: The Evidence*. Washington, DC: National Research Council.

Skogan, Wesley G., and Susan M. Hartnett. 1997. *Community Policing, Chicago Style*. New York: Oxford University Press.

Sousa, William H., and George L. Kelling. 2006. "Of 'Broken Windows,' Criminology, and Criminal Justice." In *Police Innovations: Contrasting Perspectives*, edited by David Weisburd and Anthony A. 77–97. Braga. New York: Cambridge University Press.

Sparrow, Malcolm K., Mark H. Moore, and David M. Kennedy. 1992. *Beyond 911: A New Era for Policing*. New York: Basic Books.

Spelman, William. 1988. *Beyond Bean Counting: New Approaches for Managing Crime Data*. Washington, DC: Police Executive Research Forum.

Strecher, Victor G. 1971. *The Environment of Law Enforcement: A Community Relations Guide*. Englewood Cliffs, NJ: Prentice Hall.

Taylor, Ralph B. 2006. "Incivilities Reduction Policing, Zero Tolerance, and the Retreat from Coproduction: Weak Foundations and Strong Pressures." In *Police Innovations: Contrasting Perspectives*, edited by David Weisburd and Anthony A. Braga. New York: Cambridge University Press.

Thacher, David. 2001a. "Conflicting Values in Community Policing." *Law and Society Review* 35:765–98.

——. 2001b. "Equity and Community Policing: A New View of Community Partnerships." *Criminal Justice Ethics* 20:3–16.

Trojanowicz, Robert C. 1982. *An Evaluation of the Neighborhood Foot Patrol Program in Flint, Michigan*. East Lansing: Michigan State University.

Trojanowicz, Robert C., and Bonnie Bucqueroux. 1990. *Community Policing: A Contemporary Perspective*. Cincinnati, OH: Anderson.

Tuffin, Rachel, Julia Morris, and Alexis Poole. 2006. *An Evaluation of the Impact of the National Reassurance Policing Programme*. London: Home Office Research, Development and Statistics Directorate.

Tyler, Tom R. 2003. "Procedural Justice, Legitimacy, and the Effectiveness of Rule of Law." *Crime and Justice: A Review of Research* 30:283–357.

Walker, Samuel. 1984. "'Broken Windows' and Fractured History: The Use and Misuse of History in Recent Police Patrol Analysis." *Justice Quarterly* 1(1): 75–90.

Weatheritt, Molly. 1988. "Community Policing: Rhetoric or Reality?" In *Community Policing: Rhetoric or Reality*, edited by Jack R. Greene and Stephen D. Mastrofski, 153–177. New York: Praeger.

Weisburd, David, and John E. Eck. 2004. "What Can Police Do to Reduce Crime, Disorder, and Fear?" *Annals of the American Academy of Political and Social Science* 593:42–65.

Weisburd, David, Cody W. Telep, Joshua C. Hinkle, and John E. Eck. 2008. *The Effects of Problem-Oriented Policing on Crime and Disorder*. Campbell Systematic Reviews no. 2008-14. Oslo: The Campbell Collaboration.

Williams, Hubert, and Patrick V. Murphy. 1990. "The Evolving Strategy of Police: A Minority View." Perspectives on Policing No. 13. Washington, DC: National Institute of Justice.

Wilson, James Q., and George L. Kelling. 1982. "Broken Windows: The Police and Neighborhood Safety." *Atlantic Monthly* (March): 29–38.

Wycoff, Mary Ann, and Wesley Skogan. 1993. *Community Policing in Madison: Quality from the Inside Out*. Washington, DC: National Institute of Justice.

Zhao, Jihong, Matthew C. Scheider, and Quint Thurman. 2002. "Funding Community Policing to Reduce Crime: Have COPS Grants Made a Difference?" *Criminology and Public Policy* 2(1): 7–32.

Zimring, Franklin E. 2006. *The Great American Crime Decline*. New York: Oxford University Press.

CHAPTER 8

ZERO TOLERANCE AND POLICING

JACK R. GREENE

OVER the past four decades policing in the United States and elsewhere has sought to implement a clearer, more focused model and set of tactics concerning what the police should do where crime and social disorder are concerned. Most approaches to policing now eschew the generalized patrol approach of the past, and rather embrace a set of ideas that attempt to target discrete crime and disorder problems in high crime places with tailored police responses and community acceptance (Goldstein 1990; Greene 2000). Initial ideas about community and problem-oriented policing have evolved into several ways to think about the police, each with some overlapping intellectual and programmatic space, yet each with important distinctions. Perhaps like the "Old Testament" community and problem-oriented policing begot broken windows, zero-tolerance, "hot spots," intelligence-led and now predictive-policing models and their adherents.

The intellectual and programmatic overlap in these many approaches to policing can be confusing. Community policing focuses on community engagement, partnerships and solving discrete community problems to reduce fear and improve neighborhood safety and police and community relations (Greene 2000; Reisig 2010). Cordner (1998) correctly observed that problem-oriented policing calls for the creation of a wide array of police approaches conditioned, of course, by the specific problems to be addressed, while ideas associated with zero tolerance represent but one of the tools available to the police—that is aggressive police actions taken in confined high crime or disorder areas. Similarly, order-maintenance policing, "hot spots" and broken-windows policing can involve some zero-tolerance practices (e.g., aggressive enforcement practice) but can also use verbal and other less coercive approaches to address unruly places and situations (Thacher 2004; Braga and Bond 2008). Intelligence-led policing is similar to problem-oriented policing (Ratcliffe 2008) in that it seeks to identify, respond to, and assess crime and safety problems in advance of police interventions, while predictive policing (Uchida 2009) speaks more to the analytic capacities of the police to target places that have existing high crime rates, or are likely to have high crime rates in the near future, suggesting a forward-thinking crime prevention approach. Reisig (2010) noted that community and problem-oriented policing, as well as their progeny, employ differing theoretical models and tactics to address persistent crime and disorder problems, requiring clear specification of the underlying theories and approaches taken to properly sort out intervention effects. While a common ground among these approaches is now locating policing in particular places, these efforts suggest it is not where the police are but rather what they do that warrants clear specification and assessment.

Interestingly, while the police have become more analytic about what they do, the actual approaches to policing, that is, the tactics used, have often relied on quite historic approaches, those being people-based (known or suspected offenders) or place-based (locations) (Pate, Bowers, and Parks 1976). Place-based tactics have generally called for highly visible and aggressive police actions (Weisburd 2004) even for the most mundane of deviant social behaviors. Such interventions are thought to produce broader effects by increasing the deterrent effects of the police. Such tactics are now clearly associated with zero tolerance. This approach has captured the imagination of many in the police community, in part because it uses tactics quite familiar to the police, saturation patrol and aggressive order maintenance law enforcement, and, in part, because the targets of such interventions are high-crime or disorder locations, which are easily visible to the police. Additionally, these tactics are historically recognizable by the public, suggesting that the public generally understands such approaches.

Zero-tolerance policing focuses on police presence and aggressive order maintenance enforcement often for minor misdemeanor behaviors to create a deterrent effect and dissuade those disposed to crime from committing those crimes, at least in the target areas. Such efforts can result in some crime displacement, but often do not. At the same time this line of reasoning suggests that these efforts help assure the public that the police will strictly enforce social convention, thereby reducing public fear of deviance, crime, and victimization. The "zero-tolerance" mantra is also associated with affirming institutional values, demonstrating that the police take effective action against any and all law violators (Crank and Langworthy 1992), thereby reaffirming their public mandate.

The idea of zero tolerance suggests that no deviance and certainly no low-level crime or social disorder is tolerable. Shifting from the premise of the police as "philosopher, guide and friend" (Cumming, Cumming, and Edell 1965) which characterized much discussion on policing in the mid-twentieth century and where the focus was on balancing the social control and social facilitation roles of the police, zero tolerance is a rather blunt instrument, consistent with what Garland (2001) called the emerging punitive and control-centered criminal justice culture that emerged in the late twentieth century. Rousting low-level miscreants is assumed to create a police presence that further deters more serious crime. Adherents of the zero-tolerance idea suggest that such police interventions do indeed deter crime and in some cases without displacing it to other areas, while critics suggest that zero tolerance is oversold as a universalistic police tactic and has negative impacts on a range of things including public trust of the police.

The primary focus of this essay is to examine the rise of the zero-tolerance ideology and model, and its applications in policing, as well as what we presently know about the impact of such efforts on a range of police outcomes. Section 8.1 presents a discussion of deviance, crime, and social tolerance as a prelude to considering police notions of zero tolerance. Here the focus is with situating police interventions in the broader context of social deviance. Section 8.2 expands this set of ideas by considering the road to zero tolerance across several social concerns and institutions, including the police. The objective is to show that zero tolerance is not a new invention; rather such efforts have spanned much of American history with mixed results. Section 8.3 examines more closely policing and zero tolerance, that is, the practices the impacts of the zero-tolerance model. Section 8.4 concludes with a consideration of the consequences of this model for policing and for democratic governance, as well as some of the research issues that could improve our understanding of zero-tolerance policing.

A number of main points emerge from this discussion. They include:

- Zero-tolerance policies appear uninformed by broader theories of social deviance.
- Ideas associated with zero tolerance have been a persistent part of American social and institutional life and policing.
- There is a patchwork of overlapping police models that have some attachment to zero tolerance, but the linkages are complex and often confusing.
- Extant research on zero tolerance is mixed as to its actual effects; some studies find some impacts on crimes like robbery while others do not.
- In the main, current research on zero tolerance does not support the hypothesis that less serious crime leads to more serious crime.
- Zero-tolerance policing has become a significant form of police intervention across numerous models of policing, but the intervention mirrors historical police efforts (e.g., saturation patrol or aggressive order maintenance activity).
- The implementation of zero-tolerance policing has negative consequences as well, with some relating to the impact of these practices on police legitimacy and public relations, and others to wider issues of democratic policing.
- Research and policy development on zero tolerance needs to focus on the police processes used in zero-tolerance interventions as much as their outcomes.

8.1 DEVIANCE, CRIME, AND SOCIAL TOLERANCE

> The deviant and the conformist...are creatures of the same culture, inventions of the same imagination.
> —Kai Theodor Erikson

Deviance and crime have always been closely tied to notions of social tolerance. Simply put, the dividing line between lawful and deviant and lawless is the level of social tolerance for behaviors in any society or social grouping at any particular time. As Durkheim (1951) tells us, absent social tolerance, societies will devolve to classify even the most trivial behaviors as deviant and perhaps even criminal. Durkheim further explains that crime is intimately connected with the underlying conditions of all social life and the collective social tolerances of societies, that is, the general cultural, religious and social beliefs that condition how deviance and then crime are socially constructed and then addressed. As a matter of practice, over time societies develop levels of social tolerance for all social behaviors, including those considered criminal. There are of course many examples of periods and places in which a behavior is determined deviant or criminal, while in other times or places no such labels are applied to the same behavior. Moreover, deviance and crime are most often associated with what are perceived to be their genesis and level of harm produced.

This is perhaps most illustrated in legal notions of *malum in se*—evil or wrong in and of itself—and *malum prohibitum*—evil because it is prohibited. The former refers to what might be seen as universally wrongful behavior (e.g., murder, rape, and aggravated assault) and the latter refers to things considered wrong because of socially constructed prohibitions. While it is generally clear that most societies accepted the idea that murder is wrong, it is less clear what disturbing the peace and social disorder mean. Disturbing the peace is relative to its social context; Friday night on a college campus, may not look like Friday night in a suburban neighborhood. Similarly, use of public space (e.g., streets and the front steps of tenement houses) differ between the wealthy and the less wealthy (Banfield 1974), often making the policing of public space the policing of those less well off. Moreover, ambiguities in such things as white-collar or corporate crime versus street crime continue to strain social definitions and tolerances for crime. Consequently, behaviors considered legal, illegal, and deviant are certainly conditioned by their social context, and that conditioning changes over time and across geography.

So, it is perhaps the irony of the twentieth and twenty-first centuries that many western societies espouse social choice, individual liberty, community cohesion, and zero tolerance all at the same time (Foucault 1977). That is to say, in the late-modern world we appear to value broadening social and civil choice, while espousing individual freedoms and democratic values, but we often cling to notions of rather absolute interpretation of deviance and law breaking, most especially for crimes or behavior that can be best labeled as annoying and nuisances. As Garland (2001) has suggested in the United States, the United Kingdom, and much of the West, the ideologies and practices of the welfare-state model of the first half of the twentieth century yielded to late-modern notions of control and risk in the second half of the century and are continuing to the present. The lines dividing deviance from crime have shifted, and one approach for dealing with these shifts has been to increase policies aimed at punishment and deterrence. Such policies often emphasize zero tolerance.

8.2 Zero Tolerance and the American Experience

The rhetoric of zero-tolerance rhetoric creates the impression that something is out of control and needs direct and immediate action. As a strategy it is focused on deterrence not prevention. That is to say, zero tolerance seeks to identify and aggressively pursue individuals who violate social convention rather than identifying the underlying causes or conditions giving rise to such behavior. As a social statement it seeks to exert state dominance on aspects of social life thought connected to more serious crime.

In important ways zero-tolerance tactics are aimed at "symbolic assailants" (Skolnick 2011), those who are marginal to the mainstream and therefore threatening. They often target socially constructed "folk devils" (Cohn 2002), deviant types fueled by moral panics, or are directed toward deviant places (Stark 1987) where individual explanations of crime fail to account for ecological concentrations of crime and deviance. Such practices are also found in retail business settings where the privatization of public space continues to expand, effectively excluding those from the streets that pose uncertainly or risk (Kohn 2004). As a consequence, zero-tolerance policing targets less serious deviance and crime under the idea of "sending a message" to those in the public square that any and all forms of anti-social behavior will be met with aggressive police action, thereby deterring such behavior.

The idea of zero tolerance has historic roots. While there are any number of historical examples of zero tolerance in policing four come directly to mind: 1) "Blue Laws" that greatly shaped commerce pitting religious and social conventions; 2) Slave laws, maintaining control over those enslaved or indebted; 3) Prohibition, the "grand experiment" of the early twentieth century; and, 4) drug laws and their enforcement. More contemporary zero-tolerance initiatives are found in public housing, schools, and how the police deal with youth and popular culture. Each gives us some insight into how zero tolerance comes about, and its implications for public policing.

8.2.1 Zero Tolerance Blue Laws Against Commerce

It is interesting to travel around the United States and look at all of the laws and ordinances that attempt to regulate and control social behavior on the Sabbath, most particularly on Sunday, a largely Christian invention for worship. Moreover, how we regulate such things as retail alcohol sales, drinking ages, and other forms of social behavior is highly fragmented across the United States. The Puritans enacted many laws that regulated commercial activity and even recreation on Sunday, in observance of religious traditions. While many of these laws have since been repealed, many remain either as a convenience or in fidelity to the original purposes of the laws. In some states the sale of alcohol is banned on Sundays, except perhaps in restaurants. In other places there are "dry counties" where the sale of alcohol is banned entirely, often creating lucrative commercial opportunities in neighboring counties. In some other states it is the government that sells alcohol. Sunday sales of wine/spirits have been restricted in some states as well as sales on selected holidays. The patchwork quilt of laws pertaining to the sale of alcohol is a strong testament to shifting social tolerances. It also poses enforcement problems for the police in that public expectations may suggest a lessening of enforcement efforts, while the laws persist.

8.2.2   Zero-Tolerance Slave Laws

While the country was debating the secession of the South from the Union, the police at the time were in the business of enforcing slave laws. In the bigger picture, the country was debating slave versus free labor as well as the moral right to hold people as slaves, while at the "zero-tolerance" level, slaves were property to be recovered should they escape their slave owners, or from employers to whom they were indebted. Several federal Fugitive Slave Acts were enacted to enforce the rights of slave owners and to seek rendition of slaves fleeing the United States to Canada or Mexico (Andreas and Nadelman 2006). At the same time "slave patrols" emerged in the South as a means of ensuring the property rights of slave owners. Such patrols are the forerunners of early police agencies in the United States according to Samuel Walker, who reports that Charleston, South Carolina had slave patrols with over one hundred officers, much larger than emerging police agencies in the North (Walker 1993).

Following the Civil War, local police enforced segregation and other Jim Crow laws designed to keep blacks out of main stream social and economic life. It was not until 1954 with the decision of *Brown v. Board of Education* (347 U.S. 483) that a collective social tolerance was defined by the courts and imposed on states who would have otherwise continued to exclude blacks. But social tolerance being what it is, there remain many parts of the country that continue to exclude large groups of people (typically blacks) from basic rights like participating in elections. Under the guise of increased voter fraud (which has seldom been documented) numerous states have recently passed legislation regarding appropriate identification as a necessary condition for voting (Weiser and Norden 2011) resulting in increased difficulty in voting for an estimated five million voters. At the same time concerns with illegal immigration have also come to the forefront, particularly in border states, perhaps rekindling concerns with the management of "different people" by the police (Barry 2011).

8.2.3   Prohibition and Zero Tolerance

Prohibition is perhaps the most vivid example of the manufacture of social tolerance resulting in the creation of the Eighteenth Amendment to the U.S. Constitution. For those who would abolish alcohol, "demon rum" was the root of all social ills at the beginning of the twentieth century. Coalitions of abolitionists and those in the long-standing temperance movement, often with fundamental religious underpinnings, forced the country, even against President Wilson's veto of the legislation, to pass the National Prohibition Act of 1919 (P.L. 66-66, 41 Stat. 305), commonly referred to as the Volstead Act, prohibiting the manufacture, sale and transportation (but curiously not the drinking) of alcohol.

The passage of the Eighteenth Amendment ushered in a thirteen-year era of failed social tolerance and failed social policy. While the "constructed" social intolerance pushing for the passage of Prohibition won the legislative process, many American still drank regularly. The enforcement of the Volstead Act created an illegal marketplace for alcohol, filled by organized crime, pressed a rather rudimentary and locally-based criminal justice system into enforcement activities it was ill-suited to perform, vastly increased prison populations, and drew public ire and disregard for the law and for law making (Ruane and Cerulo 2008, 187). It is perhaps the best example to date of the legal system losing its legitimacy in the face of public behaviors concerning the use of alcohol. It is an epic failure in zero tolerance, having important and often negative consequences for policing.

8.2.4 Drug Laws and Zero-Tolerance Enforcement

In the nineteenth and early twentieth centuries drugs in the United States were much less attended to than they are today. The patent medicine industry's sale of all kinds of "Doctor Feel Good" remedies for nearly all physical and psychological ills was in full swing. The emerging Coca-Cola giant built its fortune on a drink containing cocaine and caffeine, claiming that together with carbonated water, this Coca-Cola was in part a health elixir (Pendergrast 2008). In major cities of the United States, most especially in California, opium dens flourished following the "gold rush era," and in the South and urban areas marijuana use was widespread. Social conventions toward these and other drug-based products were generally lax and uninformed. Moreover, there was little in the way of government apparatus—legal and administrative—to control the manufacture and distribution of such substances.

Beginning with the passage of the Harrison Narcotics Tax Act of 1914 (38 Stat. 785), aimed at regulating and taxing the production, sale, and distribution of opiates, the U.S. government began what has been a nearly hundred-year "war" on drugs. Subsequent legislation, the creation and expansion of drug enforcement apparatus first at the federal and then local levels of policing, the expenditure of billions of dollars, and the arrest of hundreds of thousands has not substantially changed drug use in America. In fact drug use has steadily increased over most of this period, especially since the 1960s and through the 1990s even in the face of considerable federal legislation and financing of enforcement activity. The consequences of this effort have been burgeoning prison populations, significant sentencing disparities, especially in the use of cocaine and crack cocaine, and collateral damages associated with the disenfranchisement of now millions of Americans, in the form of loss of voting rights as well as access to state benefits; the destabilization of what were already socially disadvantaged communities; and, the expenditure of vast sums of public monies for enforcement activities, with substantially less funding on matters of addiction and prevention.

8.2.5   Public Housing and Zero-Tolerance

Those living in public housing are ironically subjected to two sets of social tolerance issues. First, public housing was initially created because society collectively believed that everyone should have a place to live. Much of public housing in the United States came about through the New Deal and because of the return of large numbers of veterans from World War II. Creating clean, safe, and affordable housing for such veterans was seen as in the public domain and certainly a valued public good (Bloom 2009).

Unfortunately, over time public housing has become a warehouse for the poor, and particularly the urban poor. As the United States and other parts of the Western world have retreated from a social-welfare approach to providing public support, public housing today has become synonymous with concentrated misery and crime. Under these circumstances access to and continued use of public housing has come under public scrutiny, such that many cities and states have considered enacting or have enacted legislation subjecting those in public housing to drug testing as a condition of continued public housing access. Similarly, searches of those in and around public housing, as well as those visiting public housing communities has greatly increased, mostly under the guise of zero tolerance for crime, drugs, public drinking, and disorderly behaviors. In some respects America has become less tolerant of public housing and those using public housing (Mele and Miller 2005).

8.2.6   Zero Tolerance and Schools

Schools have become the new frontier for the enforcement of zero-tolerance policies. Beginning in the late 1980s and into the 1990s schools were viewed as places with considerable potential for violence and where drugs were widely available. The possession of drugs or weapons became a major focus of the zero-tolerance movement in schools. Much of crime prediction in the 1980s suggested that the United States was entering an era of "super predators" and that youth crime would increase exponentially (Bennett, DiIulio, and Walters 1996). Incidents like the Columbine School shootings in Littleton, Colorado, and more recently in Chardon, Ohio, heightened awareness and concern about school violence. While these incidents are relatively few in number, they nonetheless have dramatically influenced school safety, often with local police being assigned to schools for security and as a matter of building better police/youth relationships (Nolan 2011) with mixed results.

Zero-tolerance policies in schools have taken the form of no tolerance for any form of medication, including aspirin; the banning of anything that might be taken for a weapon; the use of random and unannounced locker searchers for contraband; and, now the focus on interpersonal relationships of students, most particularly those associated with bullying. There is considerable evidence that such school-based zero-tolerance policies result in many being sent home from school for non-violent behaviors, that schools may over-punish adolescent behavior especially among minority students, and that issues of privacy and constitutional protections are substantially diminished with such practices (see Ayers, Dohrn, and Ayers 2009).

8.2.7 Zero Tolerance and Popular Culture

Broadly speaking, popular culture seems inevitably juxtaposed to ideas of zero tolerance. In some important ways it is popular culture that simultaneously presses for a lessening of social convention, often producing more adamancy to control such expression at least initially (Cohn 2002). Modes of dress, popular music, social conventions, the relationships between men and women and the like are continually shaped by popular culture. Each shaping, of course, carries with it potential conflict between purveyors of popular culture and the police.

In the twentieth century, flappers, "reds," zoot suiters, hippies, mods and punk rockers, hip-hoppers and be-boppers, rap artists and "gangstas" have all represented cultural expressions that challenge social convention. Popular culture with its emphasis on youth and non-conventional behavior invariably challenges the status quo. Moreover, some of these movements have been associated with various forms of crime, most particularly drug use and some violence.

More recently America's youth have once again taken on the role of symbolic assailant in the forms of those who dress with low-hanging baggy pants, often belted tightly below the buttocks and revealing underwear or worse; skateboarders roving American's parking lots and malls; or any large grouping of youth in commercial space. In these cases these groups of youth symbolically represent the rejection of social convention, with their alternatively seeking an "outsider role." Perhaps this is the perennial definition of adolescence, but today being an outsider can result in some stern repurcussions, most particularly in what were heretofore thought as "public places." While hanging on the street corner was often adopted as the official role of youth, today those corners are seen less as public gathering places and more as places to be guarded and protected from youth. Here zero tolerance is more about youth than behavior. Large groups of youths in public malls raise anxiety for some, and often result in close surveillance and intervention of mall guards or local police. What were considered public places have increasingly been privatized and placed under the control of some policing function, typically with little tolerance for youth behavior (see Kohn 2004).

8.3 THE ROAD TO ZERO TOLERANCE AND POLICING

Over the past twenty-five years or so, policing in the United States and elsewhere has as a matter of philosophy and practicality shed its pretense of preventing crime and social disorder—in the sense of dealing with underlying conditions and motivations—moving instead to focus on increasing deterrence, in particular at locations and places (e.g., hot spots) as a central police practice. This has been generally facilitated through adoption of a range of zero-tolerance policies and a broader conceptual rationale of dealing with "broken windows," that is, aggressively addressing little things before they get bigger as a matter of crime control. Built on a rationale provided by James Q. Wilson and George Kelling (1982) and championed by the New York City Police Department through former Commissioner William Bratton (1998), this "new policing" embraced ideas about zero tolerance, cracking down on annoying behaviors (e.g., the squeegee guys) thought ultimately to lead to a spiral of community decline and crime (Skogan 1990). According to this view crime is the cumulative byproduct of social, legal, and physical decline, often beginning in small but persistent ways and culminating in increasingly more serious ways, especially in poor neighborhoods. The popularized argument is that crime is a "slippery slope," and that failure to address the onset of deviance and low-level crime will result in the increased occurrence of more serious anti-social and criminal behavior. "Spare the rod, spoil the child," as the widow told Samuel Butler's *Hudibras*, a character in a seventeenth-century poem. Absent swift, certain and severe action (the elements of deterrence), communities will slowly decay, we are told.

An underlying criminological rationale for such intervention comes from rational choice theory (Clarke and Cornish 1986) and situational crime prevention (Felson 2002), both of which emphasize offender choice in the commission of crimes (big and small). Such reasoned choices are capable of being influenced either though a vigilant presence of capable guardians, or through environmental design (Crowe 2000). In either case the offender is deterred from further action.

The elements of this new police orthodoxy have been encapsulated in what has come to be known as CompStat, which involves using computer assisted crime analysis, holding local commanders responsible for increases in crime in their districts, and aggressively policing locations for crime and disorder problems, all focused on creating a deterrent effect, that is, the swift apprehension of those who commit crime, no matter how serious or how trivial (Silverman 1999; Henry 2002). The spread of crime analysis, CompStat-like programs, and the focus on "hot spots" have converged in what has been called an important innovation in policing (see Weisburd and Braga 2006).

Adherents of zero-tolerance policies argue that these actions do indeed deter anti-social, potentially violent or just weird behaviors. They also suggest that such interventions do not "displace" these crimes, most particularly the low-level ones, elsewhere, and that there is a diffusion of benefits in the absence of displacement. Some further believe that aggressive pursuit of small problems creates a deterrent effect for larger ones (Kelling and Coles 1996; Kelling and Sousa 2001). While the adherents of zero tolerance are ardent defenders of this model, much of the literature on zero tolerance does not clearly reach such a conclusion. In fact there are those who see such efforts as misguided and illusionary (Harcourt 2001; Harcourt and Ludwig 2006; Taylor 2009), if not racially biased (Fagan 2004).

While ideas associated with zero tolerance have several intellectual and pragmatic roots, the concept of zero tolerance also taps into the emotions of many who see a decline in moral and social relations (Putnam 2000). Zero tolerance is at once a political, social, and deterrence-based concept. In its most extreme application it resembles Durkheim's perfect society focused on criminalizing the most trivial of behaviors. In its most general application it reminds us of the 1976 movie *Network*, where the main character Howard Beal, played by Peter Finch, is a beaten-down television news anchor in New York who exhorts his audience to go to their window, stick their heads out, and yell "I'm as mad as hell, and I'm not going to take it anymore." It is emotive, argues for clear rules and punishes transgressors, no matter the size of the transgression. The emotional anchor of zero tolerance should not be trivialized. Whether these emotions are triggered through "moral panics" (Cohn 2002) or through other institutional means, they remain central to ideas of zero tolerance.

Zero-tolerance policies of all types (e.g., community, domestic, school) carry with them the call to action as well as some assurance that the government is acting to protect communities, families, kids, and schools from a more generalized conception of the criminal, sometimes racially based, sometimes based on a sensational crime, or series of crimes (see Beckett 1997; Simon 2007).

Zero tolerance is connected to shifts in thinking about criminal motivation, from the offender as maladjusted, to the offender as rational actor (Clark and Cornish 1986; Felson 2002). Such views recalibrate criminal offending in ways that suggest that criminals make calculated decisions, and further that certainty of punishment will deter crime and that police and others can create such deterrence conditions.

The zero-tolerance movement is also associated with complex ideas about how crime evolves in communities, from small deviant behaviors to serious criminal violations. Proponents of this view suggest that taking care of the small things (e.g., broken windows) helps to avoid the larger and more serious ones (e.g., community decay and serious violent crime). But, a substantial literature on community decay, social and physical incivility, and their links to first social disorder and then crime are less supportive of the rather simple cause-and-effect relationships espoused by zero-tolerance advocates (see Taylor 2001, 2009).

Zero tolerance is also conditioned by newer modes of crime analysis and the management of crime, particularly in large urban settings, which has resulted in shifting consideration of who commits the crime to where it occurs—from people to places (Braga and Weisburd 2010). Here it is argued that while it may be difficult to identify the people most engaged in crime, crime-laden places are visible, and like criminal offenders, account for a large proportion of criminal victimization. By addressing the "hot spots" of crime, often using aggressive tactics, it is suggested that the police can deter crime at all levels.

Zero-tolerance policies are also connected to symbolic representations of doing something about deviance or crime. Such political connections often elevate discussions about zero tolerance, even in the face of evidence questioning the intended effects of such policies. Public preoccupation and fear of crime stem in part from the ubiquity of serious crime in the news, entertainment media, and popular culture, even when crime in the United States and Western world is on the decline. Such concerns evidence a public need for social assurance from government agencies, such as the police and other components of the criminal justice system, that are charged with protecting the public from real and imagined harm. From the perspective of institutional legitimacy, police reactions in quickly mounting such policies can be seen as an attempt to assure a wary public that police are aggressively addressing such concerns (Innis 2004).

Finally, zero tolerance comports with the "crime fighting" image of public policing, but interestingly it negates police discretion and variations in problem-solving: zero tolerance implies the police are compelled to act, no matter the context or circumstances, using one police tool—arrest or citation—as the means of enacting public safety. In many important ways, the idea of zero tolerance diminishes the professional judgment of the police to the extent that it calls for action at all times, in all circumstances, and with all perceived offenders.

The discretion of the police, once the hallmark of policing for the people (Mastrofski 1999), has yielded to the numeric actions of the police assigned to proscribed places with proscribed actions to be taken. In some ways the movement to zero tolerance helps to negate the idea of police professionalism and problem-oriented policing that is capable of discerning problems in people and places and calibrating actions to best deal with the situational conditions accounting for such problems. Zero tolerance levels the playing field for the police and for social deviants and criminals, but in doing so it also creates mechanical responses to shifting and often poorly defined social problems.

The old saying "the road to hell is paved with good intentions" may ultimately become the epitaph of zero tolerance. That is to say, many who advocate for zero-tolerance policies have worthy intentions to stop some perceived risk or harm and to see the abolition of the behavior and strict enforcement against it as the appropriate cause of action. Punishment is the underlying model and deterrence based on that punishment is supposed to produce the mechanism of zero tolerance. Why wouldn't we want our schools and workplaces safe; public parks free of social and sexual predators and drug free; and, business districts or malls free of unwanted homeless or gangs of youth? Such social benefits should cause us to understand that having no tolerance for a behavior should result in deterring the offending behavior, or so it would seem. At the same time, zero tolerance equates all criminal actions (even the smallest of transgressions) as having similar causes. It targets marginalized individuals, and it ignores the contextual elements or the situational nature of crime and deviance. It is the proverbial hammer in search of varying nails.

Zero tolerance introduces several complexities associated with the causal progression of crime, how crime evolves in social settings, what motivates crime, and how deterrent strategies actually work. Moreover, zero tolerance focuses only on the law enforcement role of the police, assuming that this role singularly shapes public attitudes, beliefs, and ultimately behavior. Each of these topics, of course, deserves a treatise in its own right, disentangling crime propensity, situational contexts, police interventions, and observed criminal behavior, while at the same time raising numerous questions about criminological theory and police interventions, among others.

There are several problems with the reasoning behind zero tolerance. First, while somewhat counterintuitive, social deviance, order-maintenance problems, and even marginal crime do not lead directly to larger crime. The causal connection between these differing behaviors is not particularly well developed and is certainly not exclusively place-bound. That is to say, how deviance, petty crime, and serious crime are developmentally linked is not particularly well known. All "deviants" do not become petty criminals; all petty criminals do not become serious criminals; and so forth. While there are those who end up pursuing criminal careers through their repeat actions, repeat offenders—mostly offenders associated with low-level disorder and crime—do not specialize and are thought to be less susceptible to deterrence strategies (Hirschi and Gottfredson 1994). And, while there are suggested gateways to criminality, the paths to and from crime vary considerably (Daly 1992; Laub and Sampson 2003). While there are certainly probabilities associated with an individual's onset into deviance and crime, there are other factors that shape desistance as well. Zero tolerance is not particularly informed by this literature; rather, it singularly focuses on the locations and proximate causes of publicly visible deviance and criminality.

In addition to the variability in pathways to and from crime and the sequencing of criminal behaviors from minor to major, or from less serious to more serious, how the justice system responds to criminality, real or imagined, is impacted by what has come to be known as institutional legitimacy, most especially through the idea of procedural justice (Tyler 2006)—that is people's feelings that the law or regulation is being enforced fairly. Simply put, people appear more sensitive to the ways in which laws are enforced, as opposed to legal outcomes; while most would not like to have an adverse legal outcome, if the law is perceived to be administered in an evenhanded way, even adverse legal outcomes can be accepted by the public. But if the law is perceived to be biased in its application, then the legitimacy of the legal outcome is called into question. Such a perspective is particularly relevant in communities that, through social, racial, or economic segregation, have come to be suspicious of the police and the invocation of the law.

As a practical matter zero tolerance is almost always criticized in its application, thereby having a substantial impact on the legitimacy the public accords to the police. Zero tolerance does not allow circumstance to intrude into the decision-making process, thereby violating in some ways considerations of fairness and justice. Moreover, it uses criminal law to address a wide range of social and cultural issues that, while bordering on legal violations, are always not completely illegal. Whereas in the past the police tended to ignore small-time deviant behaviors, the rush to enforce public order crimes such as panhandling, public drunkenness, and the like during the 1990s produced many arrests for these behaviors. But as we have come to learn, such behaviors are most associated with chronic addiction and mental health problems, likely minimizing the deterrence effects presumed to result from such efforts. The chronically addicted and mentally ill are not particularly likely to respond to zero tolerance to the extent that their behaviors are hardly rational choices. Similarly, other forms of acting out in public places are difficult to deter, given the underlying dynamics influencing these behaviors.

So, while the general idea of zero tolerance (e.g., dealing harshly with minor offenders lest they become more serious ones) may have some intuitive appeal, the theoretical and practical complexities of implementing such programs are more substantial than is perhaps realized. On some level, zero tolerance seems like an important political and social statement, but as a matter of enforcement it is much more problematic, potentially reducing public support for the police and for lawfulness.

8.4 THE PRACTICE OF ZERO TOLERNACE

8.4.1 Zero-Tolerance Policing in Concept

In their famous *Atlantic Monthly* article, Wilson and Kelling (1982) introduced the idea that serious crime is in part the result of not taking care of the little things—that is, repairing broken windows, the small and visible aspects of loss of neighborhood social control. The theory of broken windows suggests that left unattended, small violations of the social contract lead to increasingly large violations up to and including serious and predatory crime.

This new theory had a common-sense appeal to many. It harkened back to social homilies like Ben Franklin's "an once of prevention is worth a pound of cure," yet the mechanisms that connect little things with big things, especially in the crime arena, are not well known. Failure to take care of these smaller issues can afford crime to continue on a trajectory of less serious to more serious. Not attending to neighborhood youth problems may lead to public drinking and gambling, then on to prostitution and drug dealing, then to theft and assault. If people are arrested for minor infractions, broken window's advocates say, larger problems will not develop or, if they do, will not be as entrenched.

Today we see the fruits of this thinking with the widespread use of "stop and frisk" practices by the police in settings from targeted urban neighborhoods, transportation terminals, public housing, and central business districts. Such activities are thought to deter rational criminals from crime by increasing ownership or stewardship for places, consistent with ideas associated with situational crime prevention (Greene 2011).

The academic community has seriously questioned the efficacy of zero-tolerance policing and its "broken windows" rationale (see Eck and Maguire 2000, 224–28). Harcourt (2001) provides the most detailed critique of extant research on broken windows and its corresponding emphasis on aggressive police tactics. Harcourt (2001, 59–89) concludes that disorder is not statistically associated with more serious types of crime (e.g., homicide, burglary, assault, rape) and equally not well associated with lesser serious crimes (e.g., purse snatching and pocket-picking), as the broken windows metaphor suggests it is. Harcourt argues that research on proactive policing has "mixed" findings yielding inconclusive results in support of such tactics. As important, such zero-tolerance policies and practices can undermine support for the law and for policing (Greene 2011).

8.4.2 Zero-Tolerance Policing in Practice

Aggressive street tactics have increasing become an element of modern-day policing. More often than not, these tactics focus on particular behaviors (e.g., public drunkenness, panhandling, vagrancy), toward particular groups (e.g., youth, vagrants, and now immigrants or those suspected of being in the United States illegally), or in targeted places (e.g., typically high-crime neighborhoods), or in public settings where fear of crime persists, or where the focus is on reducing serious crime through attention to lesser serious crime.

Zero-tolerance tactics were championed in New York City by William Bratton and former Mayor Rudolph Giuliani and touted as largely responsible for the major crime drop witnessed in that city between 1993 and 1997. Much subsequent analysis exploring these drops has focused on New York. Praise for such tactics has been echoed by Kelling and Coles (1996); Kelling and Bratton (1998); and Kelling and Sousa (2001) among others. Bratton's approach was to emphasize "quality-of-life" policing, underscoring the tactic of taking care of the little things and the big things will follow—that is, fixing broken windows (Bratton 1998). Essentially such practices call for aggressive order-maintenance policing, and for swift, certain, and strict enforcement, what Cordner (1998) suggests has become a blanket approach to all problems, rather than one of many approaches to problem solving.

On a larger scale, beginning in the mid-1990s and continuing into the twenty-first century, crime in America has declined. Accounting for the decline in crime has occupied much criminological thought (see, e.g., Blumstein and Wallman 2000; Conklin 2003; Zimring 2007) including theories about how the police or their tactics may have contributed to this decline (Eck and Maguire 2000). Much of this discussion suggests that hiring more police officers or focusing them on zero-tolerance activities has had mixed if any effects on lowering crime rates.

While some continue to underscore the importance of zero-tolerance policing in New York City during the late 1990s, Zimring (2007) found that the crime declines witnessed in New York were also realized in Canada, without increases in police capacity or aggressive police tactics. More importantly, since the 1990s crime has declined in many parts of the world rather consistently, and under conditions of differing legal frameworks, social constructions, demographic shifts, and police tactics (Tseloni et al. 2010). Such a consistency in declining crime over many parts of the world calls into question the impacts of the police, and most especially in their use of zero-tolerance policies. While such tactics may be seen as working in selected settings and under selected circumstances, the wider drop in crime cannot be attributed to police interventions alone.

The mixed nature of research on zero-tolerance or aggressive policing raises questions about the efficacy of these tactics. In addition, such tactics are thought to produce collateral damage, ultimately affecting support for the police in profound ways.

In an early study of police proactive responses, Wilson and Boland (1978) found that police traffic enforcement, a proactive police enforcement practice, had an effect on crime by increasing arrest risk, through actually catching people, or by perceived risk, by communicating risk of detection and apprehension through a high police presence. Such practices were seen as reducing street-level crime such as robbery. Police presence, then, increased perceived risk, and negatively affected street crime, in this case robbery.

Research on proactive policing conducted by Sampson and Cohen (1988) found that proactive police responses to disorderly conduct and driving under the influence produced a deterrent effect for robbery and burglary in the 171 U.S. cities studied, but they could not conclude whether these effects were produced directly or indirectly, meaning that it was unknown whether such effects occur because the police actually catch more people, or whether the more general deterrent effects of police presence produce such results. Sampson and Raudenbush (1999), examining the consequences of public disorder policing in 196 Chicago neighborhoods, found that aggressive public-order policing had little relationship to crime, other than for robbery, suggesting that the causal connection between social disorder and crime is not well reflected in the zero-tolerance perspective. Weiss and Freels (1996), in a study examining increased traffic enforcement and reported crime in Dayton, Ohio using a controlled research design, found no difference between treatment and control areas.

By contrast MacDonald (2002) found deterrent results in a study of 164 American cities where he compared community policing versus proactive policing emphasizing arrest, finding that community policing produced little in the way of deterrent effects for violent crime, but proactive policing tactics were related to reductions in violent crime over time. Most recently Kubrin and her colleagues (2010), replicating the research of Sampson and Cohen (1988), found that proactive policing reduced robbery rates in a large sample of U.S. cities between 2000 and 2003.

Evidence in support of proactive policing tactics is offered by Kelling and Coles (1996), and more recently by Kelling and Sousa (2001). Kelling and Coles, after making the conceptual argument for "broken windows" and aggressive police tactics and the failure of "community" approaches, examine New York's campaign to "take back" everything—the streets, neighborhoods, business districts, and the subway, using similar tactics, that is, aggressively targeting these places, increasing police presence, and aggressively pursuing minor offenses—typically committed by the dispossessed, chronic alcoholics or those with mental health problems, and the "turnstyle jumpers," those who would beat the subway fare. Additionally, under the idea that broken windows also addresses physical incivility—tagging and other forms of graffiti—the authors trace developments in the New York subway system to rid of such incivility (Kelling and Coles 1996).

A study conducted by Kelling and Sousa (2001) involving precinct-level composite crime assessments (i.e., murder, rape, robbery, and felonious assault) in New York City, found that arrests for minor crimes impacted overall composite rates in the precincts observed. Their key independent variable was precinct-level arrests for misdemeanors, taken as a proxy for "broken windows policing." Overall, Kelling and Sousa conclude that the observed decline in violent crime was strongly associated with "broken windows" policing in that city. These findings have been challenged by Harcourt and Ludwig (2006) who in a re-analysis of the data find that declines in precincts with high violent crime are likely the result of reversion to the mean following high levels during earlier times. As such, tactics associated with zero-tolerance responses to misdemeanor behavior in these and other precincts appear to dissipate once the initial levels of these crimes are introduced into the models together with a wide range of demographic and police force-size variables.

Another study of declining crime rates in New York City police precincts conducted by Rosenfeld, Fornango, and Regifo (2007) indicated that while small-crime reductions could be detected in homicide and robbery rates as impacted by aggressive order enforcement, these findings are modest at best, a finding like others that does not conform to the idea that such efforts have immediate and significant impacts on serious crime.

In a critique of New York's crime drop, several researchers have found that while the New York decline was impressive it was not singular—a number of large American cities also experienced comparable declines without implementing zero-tolerance or aggressive police tactics. For example, in a review of the literature on declining crime relative to the New York experience, Harcourt (2001, 90–121) concludes that cities like Boston, San Francisco, San Diego, Los Angeles, Houston, Dallas, and San Antonio, among others, all posted significant declines of crime at the same time as New York, but without the corresponding zero-tolerance policies being used.

While much as been made about addressing minor offenses as a way of curbing major ones, extending the police "crime attack" model to public order crimes has not produced the results anticipated. In a thorough review of research on order maintenance policing, the National Research Council (2004) concluded that general police strategies, often aimed at order maintenance to deter serious crime, have not been supported. The report concludes, "There is a widespread perception among police policy makers and the public that enforcement strategies (primarily arrest) applied broadly against offenders committing minor offenses lead to reductions of serious crime. Research does not provide strong support for this proposition" (229). In its review of extant research the National Council suggests that the evidence is mixed, with some studies supporting modest crime reductions, while others find no such results.

The National Research Council's review supports much earlier research on Field Interrogations in San Diego, California (Boydstrum and Sherry 1975) that found a slight decline in crime following the implementation of this program but also showed that the decline was not substantial. More recent findings of Greene (1999) examining zero-tolerance practices in New York City and comparing them with problem-oriented policing practices in San Diego found that both cities witnessed declines in crime, but New York experienced significant increases in citizen complaints and law suits alleging police misconduct and abuse of force, much of which was associated with aggressive, zero-tolerance tactics of the New York Police Department.

8.5 THE CONSEQUENCES OF ZERO TOLERANCE

Sir Isaac Newton's Third Law of Motion indicates that forces occur in pairs such that for every action there is a corresponding and opposite reaction. This postulate is well established in classical mechanics and has a social analogue as well.

In the social world, ideas associated with zero tolerance can be seen as reactive to what is a perceived as laxity in the social contract. Those arguing for zero tolerance often point to a failure in society to control certain types of marginal and often offensive behaviors. Inevitably the voices supporting zero tolerance argue that more conservative and restrictive approaches to defining social behavior and then quickly acting on these definitions will lessen or deter what are portrayed as socially unacceptable behaviors. The opposite reaction to this, of course, is associated with the overreach of the law, or what has been associated with "net widening" (Brodgen 1982; Reed 1999) or the amplification of deviance (Cohn 2002).

Just as important, the actions of the police often produce reactions, some of which are opposite of the intended consequences. So, understanding the application of zero tolerance invovles more than observing the action and its effects, but also lies in examining the range of reactions that is produced. Here we consider two potential reactions: 1) under the norms of zero tolerance we may actually be increasing crime and criminals, particularly at the lower end of the behavioral spectrum; and, 2) such policies are often based on public fears and moral panics, such that they represent a peculiar form of governance, that is, governance through fear rather than through consensus.

8.5.1 Crime through Police Action

In a very ironic way, what the police do or fail to do can significantly shape the aggregate level of crime, especially officially documented crime. This has been known for any number of years, most particularly levels of crime associated with what is known as "vice" or inappropriate social behaviors.

Generally speaking, when crime occurs absent a police presence it is for the victim or observer of the crime to report to the police, and for the police to respond by apprehending the criminal, providing assistance to the victim, and in some way assuring the broader community that they will take actions against such offenders. But for many offenses and behaviors the crime occurs at the will or in the presence of the police alone. Under such circumstances it can be said that the police "make crime," that is, focus their attention on types of crime (often vice related) and thereby increase the level of crime detected, or through detective work that seeks to determine whether or not a particular crime occurred or not (Manning 1980; Ericson 1981). Such strategies are meant to help define the police to their many audiences, while at the same time emphasizing the types of crime or deviant behaviors on which the police are currently focused. As Manning (2003, 19) suggests:

> Control dramas well and truly display the dialectic between audiences and performers in that cycles of crackdowns and tolerance, traffic law enforcement "blitzes" and "turning a blind eye," zero-tolerance policies and chitchats with the homeless, reduce social distance, and then increase it for different groups.

Here it is also interesting to note that the National Advisory Commission on Civil Disorders (1968), known as the Warren Commission, suggested that most urban riots of the 1960s and 1970s occurred following a police action. Police actions then inflamed already existing community tensions, leading to massive rioting, the destruction of property and the loss of life, and of course further arrests. Similar reactions occurred following the Rodney King incident in Los Angeles.

Most drug crime, especially the crime of drug use, rises and falls in proportion to how much police attention is directed to such behavior. Police crackdowns for many public order crimes have the same implication; they create crime because of the police action. Those actions can focus on serious and less serious activities. They can also have a differential effect on sub-groups of the population, most notably persons of color and recent immigrants. Tonry (1995) observed that police targeted urban and predominantly black neighborhoods as part of the war on drugs, most particularly when it came to use of crack cocaine, whereas in areas where use of power cocaine was likely more prevalent enforcement did not proportionately increase.

At the lower end of the deviance spectrum aggressive police actions also amplify deviance, that is, they lower the boundaries of what is considered deviant and thus subject to police action, while at the same time increasing some social connection among those seen as deviant (Cohn 2002). As the police redefine deviance through zero tolerance, a larger number of offenders is actually created—offenders who may engage in secondary deviance stemming from the original labeling and social reactions to such labeling (Becker 1963).

8.5.2 Governance through Fear and Crime

Zero-tolerance policies have a rhetorical appeal and are useful in certain circumstances and with certain issues. Open-air drug markets, crime-riddled neighborhoods or "hot spots," may require concentrated and aggressive police action (see Weisburd and Braga 2006, 225–44). But they also have limitations. As Rosenbaum (2006245–63) indicates such limitations include their likely short-term impact, potential for police abuse and negative implications for police legitimacy.

At the level of governance zero tolerance is focused on mobilizing fear and government programs to address such fear (in urban areas, schools, and workplaces, and with respect to terrorism) (see Simon 2007). Experience with government policy and action based on fear in the United States and elsewhere has been troublesome and often socially destructive. While government is expected to reassure and reduce social fear and apprehension, it cannot be driven by it. Zero-tolerance policy is tautological in this regard; it may reinforce and act on public fear, rather than the underlying problems which produce those fears. In this sense the police help to create public perceptions about crime and social disorder and then act on those perceptions, in what Manning (1992, 26–30) referred to as reflexivity in knowledge—subjective interpretation and response.

So, do zero-tolerance actions of the police undermine public support for the police, especially in communities which are already distrustful of the police? Evidence from research on procedural justice suggests that how legal decisions are made and implemented is of concern to citizens (Tyler and Huo 2002). Moreover, how police are perceived in zero-tolerance situations, especially in minority communities, has import for public acceptance of police actions, recognizing that minority and majority communities often view the police differently (Engle 2005).

To partially examine these ideas Weisburd and his colleagues (2011) tested the impact of aggressive police practice using a randomized experimental design. Three hundred and seventy-one residents in fifty-five street segments with a corresponding set of controls were included in a panel study before and after the intervention. No differences were found on measures of fear of crime, police legitimacy, collective efficacy, or perceptions of crime and social disorder, suggesting that residents paid little attention to increased police patrolling. While this is an interesting finding, the treatment provided was a total of three hours of additional patrol time per week devoted to these "hot spot" areas, so it might be equally argued that a very small treatment went unnoticed, rather than drawing the conclusion that such efforts produce no negative effects. The authors conclude by indicating the need to replicate such a study to determine whether zero-tolerance or aggressive policing activity has negative community side effects.

An alternative viewpoint relative to police stopping and questioning people on the street in high-crime areas suggests that police may not act constitutionally (Skogan and Mears 2004; Gould and Mastrofski 2004) and often find themselves in communities of color where a sense of different treatment is pervasive (Weitzer 2000), and where procedural justice may become a greater civic question (Engle 2005). Such findings are yet to be fully tested relative to zero-tolerance police tactics, although Greene (1999) has highlighted some of the negative consequences of aggressive policing in New York City, and they have emerged in other areas including racial profiling.

8.5.3 Remaining Policy and Research Questions

Policy and research questions about zero tolerance are broad and complex. They ask about the underlying conditions that the zero-tolerance policy is meant to address, how such policies can be implemented, and the intended and unintended consequences of such policies. They also ask about what part of the intervention continuum the police are addressing and the consequences of such actions (see Greene 2010). Finally, they are concerned with the imposition of law on social behaviors, most especially those behaviors that might be called low-level or less serious when it comes to definitions of crime.

Addressing issues of crime and deviance requires some sense of what are the underlying factors giving rise to such behaviors. All too often the police deal with proximate causes of crime, that is, those things most closely associated with a particular crime or deviant act. Some might argue that public police cannot address root concerns about crime, but are rather resigned to dealing with the branches of crime when they appear (Wilson 1975).

A research concern of zero tolerance lies in understanding and detecting what the police are doing, when, with whom, and with what effects. Research has struggled with appropriate measures of preventive policing, as well as with understanding the appropriate lag between when such enforcement efforts are undertaken, the level of "dosage" (i.e., the level of effort applied), and any subsequent reductions of criminal and deviant behavior. These measurement questions also apply to zero-tolerance policing. Moreover, understanding the latent and negative consequences of zero tolerance, such as undermining the legitimacy of the police and the law, should be of great concern to policy makers. In democratic society effective and efficient policing is predicated on public acceptance of police interventions. Absent public legitimation the police cease to be an accepted part of social control; rather they become a force disconnected from civic consensus.

Today much is made of the use of experimental methods to better obtain "evidence" about the effectiveness of police interventions (Sherman 1998; Weisburd and Eck 2004). While such approaches have produced knowledge about some police efforts to reduce crime and disorder, they largely "black box" what the police do to achieve such results. That is to say, much of the effort to produce evidence of what works in policing, largely ignores the process by which such results are achieved; that is, what the police actually do to produce such results. Before and after measurement of crime and disorder in small places tells us little about how such change were achieved, whether by the police or other factors. Aligning qualitative, field-based research in these research efforts could vastly improve our understanding of how the police produce such results, as well as their community limits (Thacher 2001). Police interventions call for mixed research methods focused on process as well as outcome. In an age of concerns about police legitimacy, process concerns are accentuated. Moreover, as zero-tolerance policing is largely about process, that is, focusing police attention in problematic locations, linking effort to outcome is a major research task going forward.

REFERENCES

Andreas, Peter, and Ethan Nadelman. 2006. *Policing the Globe: Criminalization and Crime Control in International Relations*. Oxford: Oxford University Press.

Ayers, William, Bernadine Dohrn, and Rick Ayers, eds. 2009. *Zero Tolerance: Resisting the Drive for Punishment in our Schools: A Handbook for Parents, Students, Educators, and Citizens*. New York: New Press.

Banfield, Edward C. 1974. *The Unheavenly City Revisited*. Boston: Little. Brown and Co.

Barry, Tom. 2011. *Border Wars*. Cambridge, MA: MIT Press.

Becker, Howard. 1963. *The Outsiders: Studies in the Sociology of Deviance*. New York: Free Press.

Beckett, Katherine. 1997. *Making Crime Pay: Law and Order in Contemporary American Politics*. New York: Oxford University Press.

Bennett, William J., John J. DiIulio, and John P. Walters. 1996. *Body Count: Moral Poverty and How to Win America's War against Crime and Drugs*. New York: Simon and Schuster.

Bloom, Nicholas D. 2009. *Public Housing that Worked: New York in the Twentieth Century*. Philadelphia: University of Pennsylvania Press.

Blumstein, Alfred, and Joel Wallman, eds. 2000. *The Crime Drop in America*. New York: Cambridge University Press.

Boydstum, John E., and Michael E. Sherry. 1975. *San Diego Community Profile: Final report*. Washington, DC: Police Foundation.

Braga, Anthony A., and Brenda J. Bond. 2008. "Policing Crime and Disorder Hot Spots: A Randomized Controlled Trial." *Criminology* 46(3): 577–607.

Braga, Anthony A., and David Weisburd. 2010. *Policing Problem Places: Crime Hot Spots and Effective Prevention*. New York: Oxford University Press.

Bratton, William. 1998. *Turnaround: How America's Top Cop Reversed the Crime Epidemic*. New York: Random House.

Brogden, Michael. 1982. *The Police: Autonomy and Consent*. London: Academic Press.

Clarke, Ronald V., and Derrick Cornish. 1986. *The Reasoning Criminal*. New York: Springer-Verlag.

Cohn, Stanley. 2002. *Folk Devils and Moral Panics,* 3d ed. New York: Routledge.

Conklin, John. 2003. *Why Crime Rates Fell*. New York: Allyn and Bacon.

Cordner, Gary W. 1998. "Problem-Oriented Policing vs. Zero-Tolerance." In *Problem-Oriented Policing*, edited by Tara O'Connor Shelly and Anne C. Grant, 303–314. Washington, DC: Police Executive Research Forum.

Crank, John P., and Robert Langworthy. 1992. "An Institutional Perspective of Policing." *Journal of Criminal Law and Criminology* 83(2): 338–63.

Crowe, Timothy. 2000. *Crime Prevention through Environmental Design,* 2d ed. Louisville, KY: Crime Prevention Institute.

Cumming, Elaine, Ian Cumming, and Laura Edell. 1965. "Policeman as Philosopher, Guide and Friend." *Social Problems* 12(3): 276–86.

Daly, Kathleen. 1992. "Women's Pathways to Felony Court: Feminist Theories of Law-Breaking and Problems of Representation." *Southern California Review of Law and Women's Studies* 2:11–52.

Durkheim, Emile. 1951. *Suicide: A Study in Sociology*. New York: The Free Press.

Eck, John E., and Edward R. Maguire. 2000. "Have Changes in Policing Reduced Violent Crime? An Assessment of the Evidence." In *The Crime Drop in America*, edited by Alfred Blumstein and Joel Wallman, 207–265. Cambridge, UK: Cambridge University Press.

Engle, Robin S. 2005. "Citizen's Perceptions of Distributive and Procedural Justice during Traffic Stops with Police." *Journal of Research in Crime and Delinquency* 42(4): 445–81.

Ericson, Richard. 1981. *Making Crime: A Study of Detective Work.* Ontario: Butterworth.

Fagan, Jeffrey. 2004. "An Analysis of the NYPD's Stop-and-Frisk Policy in the Context of Claim of Racial Bias." *Columbia Public Law and Legal Theory Working Papers.* New York: Columbia Law School.

Felson, Marcus. 2002. *Crime in Everyday Life,* 3d ed. Thousand Oaks, CA: Sage.

Foucault, Michael. 1977. *Discipline and Punishment.* Translated by Alan Sheridan. New York: Vintage Books.

Garland, David 2001. *The Culture of Control.* Chicago: University of Chicago Press.

Goldstein, Herman. 1990. *Problem-Oriented Policing.* New York: McGraw-Hill.

Gould, Jon B., and Stephen D. Mastrofski. 2004. "Suspect Searches: Assessing Police Behavior under the U.S. Constitution." *Criminology and Public Policy* 3(3): 315–62.

Greene, Jack R. 2000. "Community Policing in America: Changing the Nature, Structure and Function of the Police." In *Criminal Justice 2000,* Vol. 3, *Policies, Processes and Decisions of the Criminal Justice System,* edited by Julie Horney, 299–370. Washington, DC: U.S. Department of Justice, National Institute of Justice.

———. 2010. *Policing Through Human Rights. Ideas in American Policing.* Washington, DC: Police Foundation.

———. 2011. "Police Field Stops: What Do We Know and What does it Mean?" Paper presented at the Urban Institute, Roundtable on Police Stops and Questioning Tactics, Washington, DC (September).

Greene, Judith. 1999. "Zero Tolerance: A Case Study of Police Policies and Practices in New York City." *Crime and Delinquency* 45(2):171–87.

Harcourt, Bernard E. 2001. *Illusion of Order: The False Promise of Broken Windows Policing.* Cambridge, MA: Harvard University Press.

Harcourt, Bernard E., and Jens Ludwig. 2006. "Broken Windows: New Evidence from New York City and a Five-City Social Experiment." *University of Chicago Law Review* 73: 271–320.

Henry, Vincent E. 2002. *The COMPSTAT Paradigm: Management Accountability in Policing, Business and the Public Sector.* New York: Looseleaf Law Publications.

Hirschi, Travis, and Michael R. Gottfiedson, eds. 1994. *The Generality of Deviance.* New Brunswick, NJ: Transaction.

Innes, Martin. 2004. "Reinventing Tradition? Reassurance, Neighbourhood Security and Policing." *Criminal Justice* 4(2): 151–71.

Kelling, George L., and William J. Bratton. 1998. "Declining Crime Rates: Insiders' Views of the New York City Story." *Journal of Criminal Law and Criminology* 88(4): 1217–32.

Kelling, George L., and Katherine M. Coles. 1996. *Fixing Broken Windows: Restoring Order and Reducing Crime in our Communities.* New York: Free Press.

Kelling, George L., and William H. Sousa, Jr. 2001. *Do Police Matter? An Analysis of the Impact of New York City's Police Reforms.* New York: Manhattan Institute Center for Civic Innovation.

Kohn, Margaret. 2004. *Brave New Neighborhoods: The Privatization of Public Space.* New York: Routledge.

Kubrin, Charis E., Stephen F. Messner, Glenn Derane, Kelly McGeever, and Thomas D. Stucky. 2010. "Proactive Policing and Robbery Rates across U.S. Cities." *Criminology* 48(1): 57–97.

Laub, John H., and Robert J. Sampson. 2003. *Shared Beginnings, Divergent Lives: Delinquent Boys to Age 70.* Cambridge: Harvard University Press.

MacDonald, John M. 2002. "The Effectiveness of Community Policing in Reducing Urban Violence." *Crime and Delinquency* 48:592–618.

Manning, Peter K. 1980. *Narc's Game,* 2nd ed. Prospect Heights, IL: Waveland Press.

———. 1992. *Organizational Communication.* New York: Walter de Gruyter.

———. 2003. *Policing Contingencies.* Chicago: University of Chicago Press.

Mastrofski, Stephen D. 1999. *Policing for People. Ideas in American Policing.* Washington, DC: Police Foundation.

Mele, Christopher, and Teresa A. Miller, eds. 2005. *Civil Penalties, Social Consequences.* New York: Routledge.

National Advisory Commission on Civil Disorders. 1968. *Report of the National Commission on Civil Disorders.* New York: Bantam Books.

National Research Council. 2004. *Fairness and Effectiveness in Policing: The Evidence.* Washington, DC: National Academies Press.

Nolan, Kathleen. 2011. *Police in the Hallways; Discipline in an Urban High School.* Minneapolis: University of Minnesota Press.

Pate, Tony, Robert A. Bowers, and Ron Parks. 1976. *Three Approaches to Criminal Apprehension in Kansas City: An Evaluation Report.* Washington, DC: Police Foundation.

Pendergrast, Mark. 2008. *For God, Country and Coca-Cola,* 2d ed. New York: Basic Books.

Putnam, Robert D. 2000. *Bowling Alone: The Collapse and Revival of American Community.* New York: Simon and Schuster.

Ratcliffe, Jerry H. 2008. *Intelligence-Led Policing.* Cullompton, UK: Willan.

Reed, Wilson E. 1999. *The Politics of Community Policing: The Case of Seattle.* New York: Garland.

Reisig, Michael D. 2010. "Community and Problem-Oriented Policing." *Crime and Justice: A Review of Research* 39:1–53.

Rosenbaum, Dennis P. 2006. "The Limits of Hot Spots Policing." In *Police Innovation: Contrasting Perspectives,* edited by David Weisburd and Anthony Braga, 245–263. New York: Cambridge University Press.

Rosenfeld, Richard, Robert Fornango, and Andres F. Rengifo. 2007. "The Impact of Order-Maintenance Policing on New York City Homicide and Robbery Rates: 1998-2001." *Criminology* 45:355–84.

Ruane, Janet, and Karen Cerulo. 2008. *Second Thoughts: Seeing Conventional Wisdom through the Sociological Eye,* 4th ed. Thousand Oaks, CA: Pine Forge Press.

Sampson, Robert J., and Jacqueline Cohen. 1988. "Deterrent Effects of the Police on Crime: A Replication and Theoretical Extension." *Law and Society Review* 22:163–89.

Sampson, Robert J., and Stephen W. Raudenbush. 1999. "Systematic Social Observation of Public Spaces: A New Look at Disorder in Urban Neighborhoods." *American Journal of Sociology* 105:603–51.

Sherman, Lawrence W. 1998. "American Policing." In *The Handbook of Crime and Punishment,* edited by Michael Tonry, 429–456. New York: Oxford University Press.

Silverman, Eli B. 1999. *NYPD Battles Crime: Innovative Strategies in Policing.* Boston: Northeastern University Press.

Simon, Jonathan. 2007. *Governing Through Crime.* New York: Oxford University Press

Skolnick, Jerome. 2011. *Justice without Trial: Law Enforcement in Democratic Society,* 4th ed. New Orleans: Quid Pro, LLC.

Skogan, Wesley G. 1990. *Disorder and Decline: Crime and the Spiral of Decline in American Neighborhoods.* New York: Free Press.

Skogan, Wesley G., and Tracy L. Meares. 2004. "Lawful Policing." *Annals of the American Academy of Political and Social Sciences* 593:66–83.

Stark, Rodney. 1987. "Deviant Places: A Theory of the Ecology of Crime." *Criminology* 25(4): 893–910.

Taylor, Ralph B. 2001. *Breaking Away from Broken Windows: Baltimore Neighborhoods and the Nationwide Fight against Crime, Grime, Fear and Decline.* Boulder, CO: Westview Press.

———. 2009. "Hot Spots do not Exist, and other Fundamental Concerns about Hot Spots Policing." In *Contemporary Issues in Criminal Justice Policy: Policy Proposals from the American Society of Criminology Conference,* edited by Natasha Frost, Joshua Freilich, and Todd Clear, 271–278. Belmont, CA: Cengage/Wadsworth.

Thacher, David. 2001. "Policing is not a Treatment: Alternatives to the Medical Model of Police Research." *Journal of Research in Crime and Delinquency* 38(4): 387–415.

———. 2004. "Order Maintenance Reconsidered: Moving Beyond Strong Casual Reasoning." *Journal of Criminal Law and Criminology* 94(2): 381–414.

Tonry, Michael. H. 1995. *Malign Neglect: Race, Crime, and Punishment in America.* New York: Oxford University Press.

Tseloni, Andromachi, Jen Mailley, Graham Farrell, and Nick Tilley. 2010. "Exploring the International Decline in Crime Rates." *European Journal of Criminology* 7(5): 375–94.

Tyler, Tom R. 2006. *Why People Obey the Law.* Princeton, NJ: Princeton University Press.

Tyler, Tom R., and Yuen J. Huo. 2002. *Trust in the Law: Encouraging Public Cooperation with the Police and Courts.* New York: Russell Sage.

Uchida, Craig D. 2009. *A National Discussion on Predictive Policing: Defining our Terms and Mapping Successful Implementation Strategies.* Washington, DC: National Institute of Justice.

Walker, Samuel. 1993. *Taming the System: The Control of Discretion in Criminal Justice, 1950–1990.* New York: Oxford University Press.

Weisburd, David. 2004. "The Emergence of Crime Places in Crime Prevention." In *Developments in Criminological and Criminal Justice Research,* edited by Gerben E. B. Bruinsma, Henk Elffers, and Jan de Keijser, 155–168. Cullompton, UK: Willan.

Weisburd, David, and Anthony Braga. 2006. "Hot Spots Policing as a Model for Police Innovation." In *Police Innovation: Contrasting Perspectives,* edited by David Weisburd and Anthony Braga, 225–244. New York: Cambridge University Press.

Weisburd, David, and John Eck. 2004. "What Can Police Do to Reduce Crime, Disorder and Fear?" *The Annals of the American Academy of Political and Social Science* 593:42–65.

Weisburd, David, Josh Hinkle, Christine Famega, and Justin Ready. 2011. "The Possible 'Backfire' Effects of Hot Spots Policing: An Experimental Assessment of Impacts on Legitimacy, Fear and Collective Efficacy." *Journal of Experimental Criminology* 7:297–320.

Weiser, Wendy R., and Lawrence Norden. 2011. *Voting Law Changes in 2012.* New York: New York University School of Law, Brennan Center for Justice.

Weiss, Alexander, and Sally Freels. 1996. "Effects of Aggressive Policing: The Dayton Traffic Enforcement Experiment." *American Journal of Police* 15(3): 45–64.

Weitzer, Ronald. 2000. "Radicalized Policing: Residents' Perceptions in Three Neighborhoods." *Law and Society Review* 34:129–55.

Wilson, James Q. 1975. *Thinking About Crime.* New York: Vintage.

Wilson, James Q., and Barbara Boland. 1978. "The Effect of the Police on Crime." *Law and Society Review* 12:367–90.

Wilson, James Q., and George L. Kelling. 1982. "Broken Windows: The Police and Neighborhood Safety." *Atlantic Monthly* 249:29–38.

Zimring, Franklin E. 2007. *The Great American Crime Decline.* New York: Oxford University Press.

CHAPTER 9

···

POLICING VULNERABLE
POPULATIONS

···

MELISSA SCHAEFER MORABITO

VULNERABILITY can be the result of individual characteristics such as age, gender, race, or relationship status, or of geographic limitations such as access to resources like education, employment, or housing (Aday 2001). Mechanic and Tanner (2007) note that vulnerability has multiple dimensions: individual capacities, the availability or lack of social support, and access to neighborhood or community resources. Poverty is largely determinative of individual capacity and is linked with a variety of negative outcomes (Mechanic and Tanner 2007) such as poor prenatal care and early nutrition (Barker et al. 2001) which can subsequently affect future health outcomes that cause more permanent vulnerability. Without social support, individuals can become socially isolated as a result of illness or family disruptions such as divorce or death (Mechanic and Tanner 2007). This isolation can affect all people from the very young to the very old and can be particularly challenging during temporary disasters such as hurricanes or heat waves. Finally, the lack of community resources can be characteristic of vulnerability. Physical location of housing can limit individual access to transportation and health care as well as employment and educational opportunities (Mechanic and Tanner 2007). These deprivations can further isolate the most vulnerable individuals in the community. While the variation in these characteristics can help us better understand sources of vulnerability and inform public policy decisions, we must remember that police are called upon to respond to vulnerable citizens, regardless of the source of that vulnerability.

The essay is organized into five sections. Section 9.1 discusses the types of vulnerable populations who typically have contact with the police, ultimately homing in on persons with mental illnesses. Section 9.2 expands that discussion by describing in detail the history of police contacts with persons with mental illness, identifying the nature of so-called mercy bookings, as well as the myth of criminalization. This section also highlights the historical contexts of deinstitutionalization, which has led to large increases in the number of homeless persons with mental illness. Section 9.3 argues that largely as a function of deinstitutionalization, the number of homeless persons with mental illness has increased in communities not structurally equipped to support them. Indeed, this section uses social disorganization theory to explain why persons with mental illness often have a disproportionately high rate of contact with the police. Often, these contacts can be traced to a scarcity (or absence) of social support resources, many opportunities to engage in substance abuse behaviors, and in some cases, the inability to self-advocate when contacted by the police. Section 9.4 describes the collective historical police response to vulnerable populations, using persons with mental illness as a primary example. This section also identifies some emerging strategies—such as Crisis Intervention Teams—to increase officer safety and reduce bookings of persons with mental illness. Finally, Section 9.5 offers several policy recommendations related to how the police should respond to vulnerable populations, emphasizing the importance of strategies designed to increase procedural justice.

This essay draws a number of conclusions:

- Vulnerability as a social construct is often hard to define, which means that at any given time a large portion of the population may be considered "vulnerable."
- Contrary, perhaps, to commonly held beliefs, arrest is not the most common police response to vulnerable populations.
- Members of vulnerable populations are often victims—rather than offenders—of crime, particularly when they reside in communities characterized by social disorganization.
- Police response to vulnerable populations is often mitigated by poverty and drug use.
- Crisis Intervention Teams are the most popular police response to people with mental illnesses but evidence of the effectiveness of the approach is limited.
- Police should consider a focus on procedural justice in responding to vulnerable citizens.

9.1 DEFINING VULNERABLE POPULAIONS

Police work necessitates contact with citizens that possess all characteristics of vulnerability—ranging from individual to neighborhood-based characteristics as well as those that are temporary and permanent. For example, after a natural disaster such as Hurricane Katrina, police are tasked with aiding individuals who are unable to evacuate. These stressful events require the police to engage with individuals who are made both temporarily vulnerable by the disaster and those whose more permanent vulnerabilities are made more evident by the stressful event. More typically, the vulnerable citizens that police encounter are homeless or juvenile or are people with mental illnesses and/or substance abuse problems. These vulnerabilities can certainly be attenuated by stressful events but are challenging on a more regular basis and can come to the attention of the police in the absence of extenuating circumstances.

The homeless population is one that police must address and presents a difficult job considering the diversity of needs among this population. The majority of homeless are "sheltered" (Chamard 2010). These are individuals who reside in motels, emergency shelters, transitional housing or other programs. They compare to the "unsheltered" homeless population that reside in parks, sidewalks, abandoned buildings, and other places that are considered to be uninhabitable (Chamard 2010). Police are more likely to encounter the chronic homeless and particularly those who are "unsheltered" because they sleep out in the open and engage in other activities that are troublesome. For example, homeless or transient individuals can engage in panhandling (Scott 2002) which can be distressing behavior for business owners who want the police to respond. Some communities have responded by passing anti-panhandling ordinances but these statutes are difficult for the police to enforce both practically and legally (Scott 2002) and are problematic on other levels as well. Lee and Farrell (2003) find that homeless individuals who engage in panhandling tend to have more personal problems than their peers. These citizens are more likely to be struggling with alcohol or drug addiction as well as mental illness and to have been previously incarcerated and victimized. This is the population that is marginalized even among those that are considered vulnerable.

The lack of a secure place to sleep as well as engagement in dangerous or aggressive activities can place individuals who are homeless at risk for physical and verbal assault (Goldstein 1993). Yet, their experiences are not completely separate from their homeless peers. Overall, homeless people are at greater risk for victimization—a direct result of their vulnerability—lacking social support, grappling with problems of mental illness and addiction—as well as being situated in geographically isolated areas (Lee and Schreck 2005).

Other vulnerable populations such as the elderly, juveniles, and individuals with chronic health conditions can face similar challenges of victimization, isolation, and instability. In an examination of vulnerable populations, it is clear that an overlap exists among these characteristics of vulnerability. For example, people who are homeless may also have chronic health conditions, have low socioeconomic status and be socially isolated. One characteristic that affects all of these groups is mental illness (Fyfe 2000). It is estimated that approximately 10 to 17 percent of police contacts are with people with mental illnesses (Cordner 2006). People with mental illnesses can possess any number of other vulnerabilities including homelessness and drug addiction, thus presenting a complex population to whom police must respond. The sections that follow will focus on police response to one vulnerable population—people with mental illnesses.

9.2 MENTAL ILLNESS

Given gaps in available services to vulnerable populations, police officers have become de facto service providers (Menzies 1987; Fry, O'Riordan, and Geanellos 2002), often acting as "street corner psychiatrists" (Teplin and Pruett 1992). Due to the sheer number of interactions, attention has been focused on the nature and effects of police response to people with mental illnesses. The police have been criticized for ignoring or criminalizing acute symptoms that can be associated with illness and therefore serving as the gateway for unnecessary involvement of people with mental illnesses in the criminal justice system (Abramson 1972; Teplin 1984). What these criticisms ignore is that these encounters can be equally onerous for the police (Lurigio and Watson 2010), and consume large amounts of time (Bittner 1967a) and police resources (Cordner 2006). More importantly, criminal justice involvement of people with mental illness is not necessarily solely the result of police response.

The next section includes a discussion of how people with mental illness first became involved in the criminal justice system with an emphasis on resource allocation and social context.

9.2.1   A Brief History of People with Mental Illness in the Community

In order to explain how police became responsible for serving people with mental illnesses, this discussion begins with World War II. Difficulties with military recruitment made policy makers and practitioners aware of the extent and depth of the mental health problem in the United States. With the introduction of widespread mental health screening, more than one million men were rejected from military service because of mental and neurological disorders (Starr 1982). At the time, psychiatrists used these statistics to make the case for an unmet need for mental health care. As a result of this "newfound" mental health crisis, the censuses at psychiatric facilities swelled with groups of people who had never before been committed to these asylums. Eight hundred and fifty thousand soldiers were hospitalized, as well as conscientious objectors (Starr 1982). Institutionalization was at its peak in 1954 with over 600,000 patients reported in the National Census of Psychiatric Institutions (Starr 1982). This number of patients was costly to maintain (Richter 2007), and the quality of care in psychiatric institutions quickly declined—providing little treatment and often shockingly poor conditions. The mental health system was at a crossroads because it could not afford to continue to provide services to such a large population.

In the late 1950s and early 1960s the decline of the state hospital became imminent due to these increased costs (Richter 2007). At this time, advances emerged in the treatment of mental illness. Medications, like Thorazine, advanced care meaning that more patients could be treated on an outpatient basis (Starr 1982). In *Wyatt v. Stickney* (325 F. Supp. 781 [M.D. Ala. (1971)]), a federal court ruled that patients in the Alabama state psychiatric hospital were entitled to treatment if the state kept them confined—a direct response to the warehouse culture of these facilities. This ruling further increased the already expensive venture of housing people with mental illness. At the same time, commitment criteria were tightened and the federal government offered medical assistance funding, making it possible for the elderly to collect federal support if they resided in a nursing home or other residence—but not a psychiatric facility. As such, because states were eager to shift the financial burden of care for the elderly to the federal government, psychiatric institutions moved the elderly.

As hospitals emptied, many people with mental illnesses returned to their communities but a full commitment was never made to fund the community mental health providers that were meant to replace inpatient care (Starr 1982). Weak funding was followed by a block grant allocation structure which meant that not enough money was ever made available to provide effective community mental health services. Because allocations were no longer tied to the extent of the affected populations, it allowed for easier reductions in funding by the federal government in spending. Uneven funding translated into uneven care. Community mental health care in practice was very different than the care originally intended by reformers. This left people with mental illness in the community without access to regular mental health care. While state psychiatric facilities continued to exist, they no longer provided primary care to people with mental illness—instead hospitalization still today remains used only in the most extreme circumstances.

With deinstitutionalization, increasing numbers of people with mental illnesses returned to the community. Without access to adequate care or basic resources, they ended up on the streets engaged in troublesome activities and many entered the criminal justice system, causing concern for their welfare (Teplin 1983). These contacts were new and little understood because people with mental illness had been institutionalized and lacked opportunity to interact with the police until then. This also meant that police simultaneously lacked information about the symptoms associated with mental illness and related problems such as co-occurring disorders and poor physical health.

9.2.2 Understanding the Role of the Police: Mercy Bookings and the Myth of Criminalization

Current research makes it difficult to determine the extent to which people with mental illnesses are involved in the criminal justice system. There is agreement however, that overrepresentation is a problem. The causes for this disproportionate involvement are still undetermined. Researchers and advocates have argued that "criminalization" of this population is the fault of the police—due to ignorance and discrimination against people with mental illnesses, or alternatively, "mercy booking," the use of arrest to provide for the safety and shelter of persons with mental illnesses. This is a narrow view of the experiences of all vulnerable populations and particularly for those citizens with mental illnesses.

This is not to suggest that there is not disproportionate inclusion of vulnerable populations—particularly people with mental illnesses in the criminal justice—or that individual police officer discretion is unrelated to this outcome. When police respond to any of these calls for service, they have several options. Officers can dispose of the situation informally. This may involve bringing a person in crisis home or making a linkage to a provider that the individual already has ties to. Alternatively, if a person is in crisis but no crime has been committed, police may take a person to the hospital to address any medical or behavioral health emergencies. Finally, a police officer can decide to make an arrest if a crime has been committed. Police officers can be guilty of ignorance and discrimination and overuse arrest or conversely they may arrest people with mental illness as a protective measure rather than a punitive one. Mercy bookings deserve additional attention, as it costs more money to incarcerate someone than to provide services or food and shelter (Lee and Farrell 2003). It is unlikely however, that individual officer behavior is the sole cause of this overrepresentation since as suggested by Engel and Silver (2001) the majority of contacts between police and people with mental illnesses are disposed of informally, meaning that there is no arrest and therefore no entrance into the criminal justice system.

Instead, I propose that there is an alternative explanation for the increased involvement of people with mental illnesses and other vulnerable populations in the criminal justice system. Systemic factors rather than individual officer or even agency characteristics may provide a better explanation for the disproportionate involvement of people with mental illnesses in the criminal justice system. Instead of fully placing the responsibility on police for this problem, attention should be placed on the context within which police respond to the community (c.f. Draine 2002; Fisher, Silver, and Wolff 2006) as well as the discretion that they exercise to maintain order (Bittner 1967a; Morabito 2007; White 2011). Specifically, when the issue is framed as an individual officer problem, a number of systemic factors are ignored—factors that will be discussed in the section that follows.

First, people with mental illnesses do not typically commit the crimes of violence reported by the media (Steadman et al. 1998) but rather those of poverty, meaning crimes of survival that are similar to the crimes committed by others of the same socio-economic status in the same neighborhoods (Draine et al. 2002). Fisher et al. (2007) find evidence to suggest that people with mental illnesses commit crimes that are not significantly different than their peers without mental illnesses. Steadman and associates (1998) found that people with mental illnesses discharged from psychiatric hospitals are no more likely to be involved in violent activity than people living in the same neighborhoods. Peterson et al. (2010) also offer evidence to support this finding, suggesting that most offenders with mental illnesses commit crimes due to hostility, disinhibition, and emotional reactivity—the same criminogenic factors that relate to the commission of crimes by all offenders regardless of mental health status. It is likely that police respond the same to people in these same disadvantaged communities regardless of their mental health status.

Next, the prevalence of drug use and abuse in criminal outcomes (White, Goldkamp, and Campbell 2006; Fisher et al. 2007; Swartz and Lurigio 2007) is also commonly ignored. In a sample of parolees with and without mental illnesses, Peterson et al. (2010) found that much of the criminal activity was driven by substance abuse and particularly so in the group diagnosed with a mental illness, with more than half of the offenders in that sub-sample diagnosed with a co-occurring disorder. Mental illness and substance abuse are commonly co-occurring disorders (Abram 1990). Much of the criminal justice involvement of people with mental illnesses is based on the relationship between drug use and arrest (Draine 2002; Swartz and Lurigio 2007), and increased arrest of this population may be a consequence of heightened criminal justice attention to the problem of drug abuse. Police may have considerable discretion in their response to people with mental illnesses but much less so in encounters involving drugs. It is not surprising that Swartz and Lurigio (2007) find substance abuse to be a mediating factor—increasing likelihood of arrest for people with all types of serious mental illnesses. Furthermore, there is some evidence to suggest that people with mental illnesses are arrested for drug crimes at rates similar to the general population (Fisher et al. 2007), and as Harcourt (2006) notes, enhanced focus on drug users has increased the numbers of all offenders in the criminal justice system due to harsher sentences for drug offenders. People with mental illnesses may have just been caught up in this mass incarceration rather than targeted for the behaviors associated with illness.

9.3 THE ROLE OF SOCIAL DISORGANIZATION

As deinstitutionalization progressed, the police took over increasing responsibility and ultimately became the default provider when other services were not available and/or accessible. This is particularly an issue in communities that lack access to other service providers. It has been well established that the police role expands beyond the traditional crime fighter orientation to include social service responsibilities (Walker 1977). In his essay on managing skid-row populations, White (2010) articulates the diverse skill set necessary to effectively police vulnerable populations as first articulated by Bittner (1967b). Effectively policing vulnerable populations, and in particular those who reside on skid row, involves the use of three techniques: the *particularization of knowledge*, or getting to know the terrain and population; the restricted *relevance of culpability*, or the use of alternatives to arrest; and the *background of* ad hoc *decision making*, or making decisions that will benefit the community as a whole (Bittner 1967b; White 2010). These techniques all call for the thoughtful use of police discretion, a conversation that has been part of the police literature since the 1960s beginning with some of the earliest sociological examinations of the police. Based alone on the longevity of this dialogue, it is clear that effectively responding to vulnerable populations is at minimum a consideration in police operations.

Responding to calls involving vulnerable populations—particularly those citizens with mental illnesses—has been a difficult responsibility for police but it is far from new and certainly is familiar to police (Bitter 1967b; Morabito 2007). Officers have historically noted that they lack the necessary tools, training, and access to resources to conduct this work (Bittner 1967a) and that they are interested in learning more about more effective responses (Vermette, Pinels, and Appelbaum 2005). Empirical evidence suggests, however, in fact that individual police officers do use their knowledge of communities and individuals to put these three techniques in practice to provide service to vulnerable populations whenever possible (Engel and Silver 2011; Watson et al. 2011; Morabito et al. 2012).

To look beyond the behavior of individual officers, social disorganization theory may help to better explain the criminal justice involvement of people with mental illnesses. People with mental illnesses have lower employment rates than people with other disabilities (Draine et al. 2002; Fisher, Silver, and Wolff 2006). This means that they live in less affluent areas and are more likely to be idle and in public during the day in communities where the antecedents of social disorganization are more likely to be present. Subsequently, this may expose them to more encounters with the police.

Given the types of crimes that people with mental illnesses commit and the communities where these crimes are committed, social disorganization theory provides a framework for understanding the police response. Social disorganization theory is based upon the premise that the residents of a community are assumed to share a common goal of living in a crime free area (Bursik and Grasmick 1993). Problems of crime and disorder are thought to violate these shared beliefs. Populations of stable areas are able to develop initiatives and take action to combat problems of crime and deviance (Skogan 1990), but other localities lack the internal mechanisms or are too "disorganized" to control these violations without formal intervention (Bursik and Grasmick 1993). As jurisdictions become increasingly disorganized, opportunities for crime increase and residents are unable control this behavior on their own. To understand how a locality becomes "disorganized," it's necessary to explore the conditions and factors that are antecedents to disorganization: residential mobility, structural disadvantage, and ethnic heterogeneity (Shaw and McKay 1942; Bursik and Grasmick 1993). The combination of these conditions explains why some communities flourish and others decline or become disorganized. In their seminal work, Bursik and Grasmick (1993) expanded the original social disorganization framework by suggesting that social disorganization may not just cause variation in crime and disorder but also result in other outcomes including fear of crime and violence.

Evidence suggests that these same disorganized communities with absent social and fiscal capital are also lacking in available social services and mental health infrastructure (Watson et al. 2011). The disorganization extends beyond informal social control to include the services necessary for vulnerable populations to be successful. As a result of little social capital and lack of available services, police become the primary service providers for a variety of different non-crime problems by default. This is not a surprising development. Beginning with deinstitutionalization, limited investment was made into community mental health services. The availability of these services does matter, as evidence suggests that when mental health services are available, police may be less likely to be called to address problems with people with mental illnesses (Watson et al. 2011). Given the prevalence of co-occurring disorders (Abram 1990) and unemployment (Fisher et al. 2006) among this population, people with mental illnesses are likely to be living in communities that are marked by poverty as well as few mental health resources.

These disorganized communities might also be more at risk for problems such as police misconduct (Kane 2002), decreased legitimacy (Kane 2005; Kubrin and Weitzer 2003), and police-citizen conflict (Jacobs and O'Brien 1998). The combination of these factors presents a different problem in the policing of vulnerable populations. The police in these neighborhoods, however, lack legitimacy among all citizens and not just the vulnerable. It is possible that police begin their encounters with all citizens in these communities at a disadvantage as a result of decreased respect there. The role of police may be problematic in disorganized communities but the combination of poverty and lack of accessible services suggests that police may not be targeting vulnerable populations and specifically people with mental illnesses. Rather, police response to vulnerable populations is instead largely shaped by the way that police agencies respond to disorganized neighborhoods generally without specifically targeting the vulnerable. Disadvantaged neighborhoods receive a greater amount of police services than more advantaged communities and may get subjected to more aggressive police tactics. Disadvantaged communities have disproportionate crime (Sampson and Radenbush 1999), and they also receive a disproportionate dosage of formal social control that can further exacerbate the disorganization (Rose and Clear 1998).

In short, police practices are different in various communities (Smith 1986). This means that while members of vulnerable populations may be more likely to be arrested in these communities, *so is everyone else*. This is particularly important when considering drug crime and its related behavior (Harcourt 2006). More research is needed to understand the general role of these varying doses of formal social control across communities (Kubrin and Weitzer 2003) and specifically how these responses affect vulnerable populations and in particular, people with mental illnesses. In short, it would appear that people with mental illnesses live in communities that are subject to greater police intervention and therefore are more likely than their peers without mental illnesses to become involved in the criminal justice system.

9.4 Current Models Of Police Response To Vulnerable Populations: The Example Of People With Mental Illness

Police encounter members of vulnerable populations in a number of different situations including those with which we are most familiar: as the subjects of nuisance calls, as a danger to themselves or others, and as possible offenders (Reuland 2007). There are other circumstances, however, where police may interact with members of vulnerable populations including as witnesses and victims of crime. Officers have long complained that they lack the training to adequately deal with situations involving vulnerable populations, particularly people with mental illnesses (Bittner 1967a). These feelings of ill preparation can result from officers' misunderstanding the behavior of some people with mental illnesses. Although people with mental illnesses are usually not dangerous, they can behave bizarrely and may not respond to police officer cues in a predictable manner based on the behavior of others (Cordner 2006; Reuland, Schwarzfeld, and Draper 2009).

9.4.1 Crisis Intervention Teams (CIT)

The current preferred police response to address these problems of ill preparation is the Crisis Intervention Team (CIT) model. CIT was designed to address these problems and create a new model for collaborative problem solving. The Crisis Intervention Team (CIT) model was first developed in Memphis, Tennessee to address the challenges that police face during these encounters (Council of State Governments 2002). CIT can best be described as a police-based pre-booking approach with specially trained officers that provide first-line response to calls involving people with mental illnesses and who act as liaisons to the mental health system (Borum et al. 1998). This approach involves three elements (Watson et al. 2008). First, officers self-select to participate. The Memphis model calls for 10 percent of officers within an agency to be CIT-trained. There are several other models of police response to mental illness, including having mental health professionals co-respond with police, comprehensive advance response, and mobile crisis teams that co-respond (Reuland 2007). These responses involve different levels of training and involvement of mental health professionals and police. For example, some agencies may require that all officers are trained in crisis intervention to better serve persons with mental illnesses while other agencies may rely more heavily on mental health professionals to provide the response. The Memphis model, however, is the most widely embraced model of police response.

In this model, once volunteer officers are approved, they receive 40 hours of specialized training regarding mental illness. The knowledge and skills necessary for making linkages to available community resources is an important part of CIT training (Borum et al. 1998). As officers learn to recognize signs and symptoms of mental illnesses and become aware of mental health treatment resources, they are able to make referrals and link people in need to services. This can include transporting the person to the hospital for an emergency psychiatric evaluation (voluntarily or involuntarily), linking the person to community mental health services, and/or helping the person contact his or her current service provider. The final element of a CIT intervention is a system-level approach to addressing the needs of people with mental illnesses (Watson et al. 2008). This system-level approach involves the development of drop-off procedures at designated locations (Borum et al. 1998). The CIT partnership is designed to reduce the bureaucracy associated with admission to care and allows officers to more quickly and easily direct people in need to services. By creating partnerships with local advocacy groups and providers, people with mental illnesses get access to services more quickly and officers are able to return to their jobs.

Since the emergence of the Memphis model, best practice elements have been developed and work has been conducted to develop a CIT model (Council of State

Governments 2002; Thompson, Reuland, and Souweine 2003; Reuland, Schwarzfeld, and Draper 2009). There is some evidence to suggest that CIT may be working (Compton et al. 2006; Bahora et al. 2008; Watson et al. 2009; Canada, Angell, and Watson 2010). Growing funding and research on CIT exists, but the program has not been completely evaluated.

To date, empirical evidence does support the positive benefits of CIT for police officers (Compton et al. 2008). Research suggests that CIT training can result in greater knowledge about mental illness and community resources (Compton et al. 2006). There is some evidence to suggest that after CIT training, officers demonstrate enhanced self-efficacy for interacting with individuals with a variety of mental health and substance abuse issues (Bahora et al. 2008). Another study conducted by Canada and associates (2010) provides supporting evidence that CIT training makes officers feel more competent in their interactions with people with mental illnesses. CIT officers also report feeling more efficacious in their dealings with the families of people with mental illnesses and mental health providers (Canada, Angell, and Watson 2010).

There are other concrete outcomes associated with CIT. Evidence suggests that CIT can increase the identification of calls for service involving people with mental illnesses, ensuring that responding officers are more likely to make connections to available resources (Teller et al. 2006). Specifically, evidence also suggests that CIT can increase referrals and transports to emergency services (Watson et al. 2011). Despite these findings, the efficacy of CIT remains unclear. Specifically because CIT also requires a significant commitment of resources, it may not be the best response for every police department. For communities where these resources are not available, there are other steps agencies can take to better serve this population.

9.5 Other Police Responses to Vulnerable Populations

Programs like CIT may improve outcomes for both the police and people with mental illnesses, but they can be resource intensive. There are, however, other steps that can be taken to improve police response to people with mental illnesses that can have positive effects. The procedural justice literature can be applied to police encounters with people with mental illnesses. Procedural justice as it relates to the police entails fair treatment which is perceived as legitimate by citizens. As Sunshine and Tyler (2003) note, this perception of legitimacy is based not only on their ability to catch rule-breakers and their performance in fighting crime but also on the fairness of their distribution of outcomes. These determinations are based upon personal experiences. Procedural justice is important because when present, it could also increase cooperation of vulnerable populations and the police and potentially therefore decrease formal contacts (Watson et al. 2008).

Watson et al. (2008) note that in particular people with mental illnesses are fearful of encounters with the police—regardless of the nature of the encounter—and that the behavior of the police shapes their expectations and responses to future encounters. The literature informs us that people with mental illnesses walk into encounters with the police expecting to be mistreated with negative outcomes (Watson et al. 2008). This is not surprising given that there is much stigma (Corrigan et al. 2005) surrounding mental illness that prevents people with mental illnesses from fully engaging in public life. This population comes to expect differential treatment not just in encounters with police but in all interactions—particularly those involving agents of social control. People with mental illnesses expect to be treated poorly in their encounters with the police and are pleasantly surprised when this is not the case (Watson et al. 2008). People with mental illnesses who are also living in disadvantaged communities have low expectations of how they will be treated in encounters with police.

By emphasizing procedural justice, police can reduce the stigma associated with mental illness and other characteristics of vulnerability. When police treat these citizens with respect and dignity, those encounters are perceived differently. To achieve this officers can make efforts to narrow the social distance between themselves and members of vulnerable populations (Watson et al. 2008), thus affirming their value in the larger society (Lind and Tyler 1992). Training officers to treat people with mental illnesses in this manner may offer a good use of police resources as it could also have a positive impact on police relations with all citizens. White (2011) refers to this as the *particularization of knowledge*—by giving citizens with mental illness a feeling of equality, managing this vulnerable population becomes easier, which suggests that legitimacy can bolster the core functioning of police and highlight the importance of policing as craft as well as the importance of procedural justice.

9.6 Conclusion and Public Policy Implications

Researchers need to begin to rethink the way that we discuss police response to vulnerable populations and in particular people with mental illnesses. While arrest and the use of force are not in fact common outcomes, they are still the basis for most of the research on vulnerable populations. We still do not know a lot about interactions where these formal responses are used. Much of the criminal justice research does not take into account important contextual information. There are few areas that must be considered in any future research.

First, it is a common misconception that people with mental illnesses or members of other vulnerable populations are always easily identifiable. This is untrue. For example, people with mental illnesses are not constantly in active states of psychosis. Mental health practitioners and researchers often repeat that mental illnesses is a "state and not a trait." The discussion about vulnerable populations and in particular people with mental illnesses is almost always focused on offenders in an active state of psychosis. People with mental illnesses are still a vulnerable population *even* if they are not exhibiting signs of mental illness. Researchers must consider more nuanced measures of mental state and overall vulnerability.

Next, the multiple roles of members of vulnerable populations including people with mental illnesses must be considered. Researchers and practitioners may not think of people with vulnerabilities such as mental illnesses as victims but rather as perpetrators of violence. Evidence suggests, however, that people with serious mental illnesses are more likely to be victimized than members of the general population (Teplin et al. 2005). This finding indicates that police should not primarily think of vulnerable populations as perpetrators of crimes but instead as victims and witnesses. Much of the existing criminal justice literature ignores the victimization of this population.

The literature must also include recognition that there are times when arrest is in fact warranted and the police should not ignore illegal behavior. Police discretion has its limits and arrest is an appropriate response to illegal behavior (Morabito 2007). People with vulnerabilities should not be infantilized when crimes are committed. The need for formal response comes with some caveats. We know that mass incarceration has disproportionately affected people of color and those in disadvantaged communities (Harcourt 2006). Draine (2002, 16) notes that "[police] may use arrest to respond to acute illness, but the extent to which this response represents a 'criminalization' of mental illness is yet unclear, and needs further empirical development." There is some evidence to suggest that the life circumstances of vulnerable populations including people with mental illnesses cause them to be exposed to increased formal social control (Fisher, Silver, and Wolff 2006). This means that they are subjected to an elevated level of scrutiny and visibility by social control agents that can affect the likelihood of involvement or re-involvement with the criminal justice system. This can result in increased violation of parolees and probationers with mental illnesses than their peers which may not be indicative of more criminality but rather greater attention from probation and parole" (Fisher et al. 2006).

Most importantly, the criminal justice involvement of vulnerable populations is not completely a police problem. We must also not lose sight of the context in which the police operate and people with vulnerabilities and in particular mental illnesses live. Police have long lamented the difficulty that people with mental illnesses have in accessing services (Bittner 1967a; Dupont and Cochran 2000). Until the mental health system and other social service providers increase the availability of services beyond normal business hours, this will be something the police have to address. We can train the police to be medical practitioners, but if there are no available services after initial contact, there is little that the police can do. In fact, evidence suggests that police are already good at identifying when individuals do have mental illnesses (Strauss et al. 2005) but without available resources and assistance, this is not enough. All community stakeholders must sit down at the table to develop a strategy to address this problem. Keeping vulnerable populations and specifically people with mental illnesses out of the criminal justice system requires that behavioral health service providers—including mental health and substance abuse—work with the police.

REFERENCES

Abram, Karen M. 1990. "The Problem of Co-occurring Disorders among Jail Detainees: Anti-social Disorder, Alcoholism, Drug Abuse and Depression." *Law and Human Behavior* 14:333–45.

Abramson, Marc F. 1972. "The Criminalization of Mentally Disordered Behavior: Possible Side Effects of a New Mental Health Law." *Hospital and Community Psychiatry* 23:101–07.

Aday, LuAnn. 2001. *At Risk in America: The Health and Health Care Needs of Vulnerable Populations in the United States*, 2d ed. San Francisco: Jossey-Bass.

Bahora, Masuma, Sonya Hanafi, Victoria Chien, and Michael Compton. 2008. "Preliminary Evidence of Effects of Crisis Intervention Team Training on Self Efficacy and Social Distance." *Adminstration and Policy Mental Health and Mental Health Services Research* 35:159–67.

Barker, David J., Tom Forsen, Clive Osmond, and Johan Eriksson. 2001. "Size at Birth and Resilience to Effects of Poor Living Conditions in Adult Life: Longitudinal Study." *British Medical Journal* 323:1273–1278..

Bittner, Egon. 1967a. "Police Discretion in the Emergency Apprehension of Mentally Ill Persons." *Social Problems* 14(3): 278–92.

——. 1967b. "The Police on Skid Row: A Study of Peace Keeping." *American Sociological Review* 32:699–715.

Borum, Randy, Martha Deane, Henry Steadman, and Joseph Morrissey. 1998. "Police Perspectives on Responding to Mentally Ill People in Crisis: Perceptions of Program Effectiveness." *Behavioral Sciences and the Law* 16:393–405.

Bursik, Robert J., Jr., and Harold G. Grasmick. 1993. *Neighborhoods and Crime: The Dimensions of Effective Community Control.* Lanham, MD: Lexington.

Canada, Kelli, Beth Angell, and Amy Watson. 2010. "Crisis Intervention Teams in Chicago: Successes on the Ground." *Journal of Police Crisis Negotiations* 10:86–100.

Chamard, Sharon. 2010. "The Problem of Homeless Encampments." In *Problem Oriented Policing Guide.* Washington, DC: Office of Community Oriented Policing Services.

Compton, Michael, Masuma Bahora, Amy Watson, and Janet Oliva. 2008. "A Comprehensive Review of Extant Research on Crisis Intervention Team (CIT) Programs." *Journal of the American Academy of Psychiatry and the Law* 36:47–55.

Compton, Michael, Michelle Esterberg, Robin McGee, Raymond Kotwicki, and Janet Oliva. 2006. "Crisis Intervention Team Training: Changes in Knowledge, Attitudes, and Stigma Related to Schizophrenia." *Psychiatric Services* 57(8): 1199–202.

Cordner, Gary. 2006. *People with Mental Illness.* Washington, DC: Office of Community Oriented Policing Services.

Corrigan, Patrick, Amy Watson, Peter Byrne, and Kristin Davis. 2005. "Mental Illness Stigma: Problem of Public Health or Social Justice." *Social Work* 50(4): 363–68.

Council of State Governments. 2002. *Criminal Justice/Mental Health Consensus Project.* New York: Council of State Governments.

Draine, Jeffrey. 2002. "Where is the 'Illness' in the Criminalization of Mental Illness?" *Community-Based Interventions for Criminal Offenders with Severe Mental Illness* 12:9–21.

Draine, Jeffrey, Mark Salzer, Dennis Culhane, and Trevor Hadley. 2002. "The Role of Social Disadvantage in Crime, Joblessness and Homelessness among Persons with Serious Mental Illness." *Psychiatric Services* 53(5): 565–73.

Dupont, Randy, and Sam Cochran. 2000. "Police Response to Mental Health Emergencies: Barriers to Change." *Journal of the American Academy of Psychiatry and the Law* 28(3): 338–44.

Engel, Robin, and Eric Silver. 2001. "Policing Mentally Disordered Suspects: A Re-examination of the Criminalization Hypothesis." *Criminology* 39(2): 225–52.

Fisher, William, Eric Silver, and Nancy Wolff. 2006. "Beyond Criminalization: Toward a Criminologically Informed Framework for Mental Health Policy and Services Research." *Adminstration and Policy Mental Health and Mental Health Services Research* 33:544–57.

Fisher, William, Nancy Wolff, Albert Grudzinskas Jr., Kristen Roy-Bujnowski, Steven Banks, and Jonathan Clayfield. 2007. "Drug Related Arrests in a Cohort of Public Mental Health Service Recipients." *Psychiatric Services* 58(11): 1448–553.

Fry, Anne J., Declan O'Riordan, and Rene Geanellos. 2002. "Social Control Agents or Front-Line Carers for People with Mental Health Problems: Police and Mental Health Services in Sydney, Australia." *Health and Social Care in the Community* 10(4): 277–86.

Fyfe, James J. 2000. "Policing the Emotionally Disturbed." *Journal of the American Academy of Psychiatry and the Law* 28(3): 345–47.

Goldstein, Brandt J. 1993. "Panhandlers at Yale: A Case Study in the Limits of Law." *Indiana Law Review* 27(2): 295–359.

Harcourt, Bernard. 2006. "From the Asylum to the Prison: Rethinking the Incarceration Revolution." *Texas Law Review* 84:1751–86.

Jacobs, David, and Robert O'Brien. 1998. "The Determinants of Deadly Force: A Structural Analysis of Police Violence." *American Journal of Sociology* 103:837–62.

Kane, Robert J. 2002. "The Social Ecology of Police Misconduct." *Criminology* 40(4): 867–96.

——. 2005. "Compromised Police Legitimacy as a Predictor of Violent Crime in Structurally Disadvantaged Communities." *Criminology* 43(2): 469–98.

Kubrin, Charis E., and Ronald Weitzer. 2003. "New Directions in Social Disorganization Theory." *Journal of Research in Crime and Delinquency* 40:374–402.

Lee, Barrett, and Chad Farrell. 2003. "Buddy, Can You Spare A Dime?: Homelessness, Panhandling, and the Public." *Urban Affairs Review* 38:299–321.

Lee, Barrett, and Christopher Schreck. 2005. "Danger on the Streets: Marginality and Victimization among Homeless People." *American Behavioral Scientist* 48(8): 1055–81.

Lind, E. Allen, and Tom Tyler. 1992. *Procedural Justice in Organizations. The Social Psychology of Procedural Justice.* New York: Plenum.

Lurigio, Arthur, and Amy Watson. 2010. "The Police and People with Mental Illness: New Approaches to a Longstanding Problem." *Journal of Police Crisis Negotiations* 10:3–14.

Mechanic, David, and Jennifer Tanner. 2007. "Vulnerable People, Groups, and Populations: Societal View." *Health Affairs* 26(5): 1220–30.

Menzies, Robert. 1987. "Psychiatrists in Blue: Police Apprehension of Mental Disorder and Dangerousness." *Criminology* 25(3): 429–53.

Morabito, Melissa S. 2007. "Horizons of Context: Understanding the Police Decision to Arrest People with Mental Illness." *Psychiatric Services* 58:1582–87.

Morabito, Melissa S., Amy Kerr, Amy Watson, Jeffrey Draine, Victor Ottati, and Beth Angell. 2012. "The Police and People with Mental Illness: Exploring the Factors that Influence the Use of Force." *Crime and Delinquency* 58(1): 57–77.

Peterson, Jillian, Jennifer Skeem, Eliza Hart, and Sarah Vidal. 2010. "Analyzing Offense Patterns as a Function of Mental Illness to Test the Criminalization Hypothesis." *Psychiatric Services* 61:1217–22.

Reuland, Melissa. 2007. "Law Enforcement Policy Recommendations." In *Improving Police Response to Persons with Mental Illness*, edited by Thomas Jurkanin, Larry Hoover, and Vladimir Sergevnin, 61–74. Springfield, IL: Charles C. Thomas.

Reuland, Melissa, Matthew Schwarzfeld, and Laura Draper. 2009. *Law Enforcement Responses to People with Mental Illnesses: A Guide to Research Informed Policy and Practice.* New York: Council of State Governments Justice Center.

Richter, Michelle. 2007. "Community Treatment and The Police." In *Improving Police Response to Persons with Mental Illness*, edited by Thomas Jurkanin, Larry Hoover, and Vladimir Sergevnin, 24–38. Springfield, IL: Charles C. Thomas.

Rose, Dina R., and Todd R. Clear. 1998. "Incarceration, Social Capital, and Crime: Implications for Social Disorganization Theory." *Criminology* 36:441–80.

Sampson, Robert J., and Stephen W. Raudenbush. 1999. "Systematic Social Observation of Public Spaces: A New Look at Disorder in Urban Neighborhoods." *American Journal of Sociology* 105:603–51.

Scott, Michael. 2002. "The Problem of Panhandling." In *Problem Oriented Policing Guide.* Washington, DC: Office of Community Oriented Policing Services.

Shaw, Clifford R., and Henry D. McKay. 1942. *Juvenile Delinquency and Urban Crime.* Chicago: University of Chicago Press.

Skogan, Wesley G. 1990. *Disorder and Decline: Crime and the Spiral Decay in American Neighborhoods.* Berkeley: University of California Press.

Smith, Douglas A. 1986. "The Neighborhood Context of Police Behavior." In *Crime and Justice: A Review of Research*, vol. 8, edited by Albert J. Reiss, Jr. and Michael Tonry, 313–342. Chicago: University of Chicago Press.

Starr, Paul. 1982. *The Social Transformation of American Medicine.* New York: Basic Books.

Steadman, Henry. J., Edward Mulvey, John Monahan, Pamela Robbins, Paul Appelbaum, Thomas Grisso, and Eric Silver. 1998. "Violence by People Discharged from Acute Psychiatric Inpatient Facilities and by Others in the Same Neighborhoods." *Archives of General Psychiatry* 55(5): 393–401.

Strauss, Gordon, Mark Glenn, Padma Reddi, Irfan Afaq, Anna Podolskaya, Tatuana Rybakova, Osman Saeed, Vital Shah, Baljit Singh, Andrew Skinner, and Rif S. El-Mallakh. 2005. "Psychiatric Disposition of Patients brought in by Crisis Intervention Team Police Officers." *Community Mental Health Journal* 41:223–28.

Sunshine, Jason, and Tom R. Tyler. 2003. "The Role of Procedural Justice and Legitimacy in Shaping Public Support for the Police." *Law and Society Review* 37:513–48.

Swartz, James, and Arthur Lurigio. 2007. "Serious Mental Illness and Arrest: The Generalized Mediating Effect of Substance Use." *Crime and Delinquency* 53(4): 581–604.

Teller, Jennifer, Mark Munetz, Karen Gil, and Christian Ritter. 2006. "Crisis Intervention Team Training for Police Officers Responding to Mental Disturbance Calls." *Psychiatric Services* 57:232–37.

Teplin, Linda. 1983. "The Criminalization of the Mentally Ill: Speculation in Search of Data." *Psychological Bulletin* 94:54–67.

——. 1984. "Criminalizing Mental Disorder: The Comparative Arrest Rates of the Mentally Ill." *American Psychologist* 29:794–803.

Teplin, Linda, Gary McClelland, Karen Abram, and Dana Weiner. 2005. "Crime Victimization in Adults with Severe Mental Illness: Comparison with the National Crime Victimization Survey." *Archives of General Psychiatry* 62(8): 911–21.

Teplin, Linda, and Nancy S. Pruett. 1992. "Police as Streetcorner Psychiatrists: Managing the Mentally Ill." *International Journal of Law and Psychiatry* 142:593–99.

Thompson, Michael, Melissa Reuland, and Daniel Souweine. 2003. "Criminal Justice/Mental Health Consensus: Improving Responses to People with Mental Illness." *Crime and Delinquency* 49(1): 30–51.

Vermette, Heidi S., Pinals, Debra A., and Paul S. Appelbaum. 2005. "Mental Health Training for Law Enforcement Professionals." *Journal of the American Academy of Psychiatry and Law* 33:42–46.

Walker, Samuel. 1977. *A Critical History of Police Reform: The Emergence of Professionalism.* Lexington, MA: Lexington Books.

Watson, Amy, Beth Angell, Melissa S. Morabito, and Noel Robinson. 2008. "Defying Negative Expectations: Dimensions of Fair and Respectful Treatment by Police Officers as Perceived by People with Mental Illness." *Administration and Policy in Mental Health and Mental Health Services Research* 35(6): 449–57.

Watson, Amy, Victor Ottati, Melissa S. Morabito, Jeffrey Draine, Amy Kerr, and Beth Angell. 2009. "Outcomes of Police Contacts with Persons with Mental Illness: The impact of CIT." *Administration and Policy in Mental Health and Mental Health Services Research* 35:449–57.

Watson, Amy, Victor Ottati, Jeffrey Draine, and Melissa S. Morabito. 2011. "CIT in Context: The Impact of Mental Health Resource Availability on Call Outcomes." *International Journal of Law and Psychiatry* 34:287–94.

White, Michael. 2010. "Jim Longstreet, Mike Marshal, and the Lost Art of Policing Skid Row." *Criminology and Public Policy* 9(4): 883–96.

White, Michael, John Goldkamp, and Suzanne Campbell. 2006. "Co-Occurring Mental Illness and Substance Abuse in the Criminal Justice System." *Prison Journal* 86(3): 301–26.

PART III

POLICE AUTHORITY

CHAPTER **10**

··

POLICE AUTHORITY IN LIBERAL-CONSENT DEMOCRACIES: A CASE FOR ANTI-AUTHORITARIAN COPS

··

WILLEM DE LINT

A phalanx of police officers in body armour with shields and expandable riot batons extended are poised to advance on a group of demonstrators who have mobilized a sit-in in a public square to express grievances against an American government that they say is "owned" by the top 1 percent of American society. Behind the demonstrators is the First Amendment, "the right of the people peaceably to assemble, and to petition the Government for a redress of grievances." Behind the officers, inched out in increments of police action, lies the destiny of American liberal democracy.

The grounding of police authority is a matter of longstanding development. Emerging after the French and American Revolutions and the development of liberal theories that alternately proposed that authorities should be animated by positive and negative rights, modern police systems have shifted between intrusive and cautious practices of social and political control. It is via the executive branch that police in liberal democracies enforce both negative (protective) and positive prescriptive rights. Police may deploy due process protections for crime control (McBarnett 1979). In a "policing by exception," and more prosaic forms, they may also deploy a prescriptive or preemptive capacity to co-produce the serious crime problem or existential risk that they are normally vigilant to oppose. This shiftiness or accommodation to expectations in changing political and socio-cultural contexts is no accident, as police have been adapted to absorb or rebuff emergent movements in a long view of legitimacy. Rights are crucial restrictions on executive and police authority, but they are also enablers of police warrant or mandate. In this dual function and double potential they offer police actors and actions exceptional sovereign decision-making capacity that is at the same time grounded in liberal limits.

In this essay, we will explore the traditional liberal doctrine—particularly the principle that policing authority must be grounded on earned consent—as a tenet that must not be vacated. At the same time, we will also push the idea that a police authority that is too rigid and resistant to considerable take-up of democratizing political and cultural forces is on the cusp of police authoritarianism. If policing is informed by political philosophy, including social contract liberalism and natural or positive rights, a requirement of a consent authority is that it must be continuously refreshed from below.

Section 10.1 of this essay reviews police authority in liberal democracies as a balance of negative and positive rights. Section 10.2 examines the new geography of authority post-9/11 with particular emphasis placed on the fusions or plural authorities as well as the mediated formats that drive police applications. In Section 10.3 the essay argues the importance of police discretion (institutional authority) as an open-ended check on political and other authorities, which is noted and further developed in Section 10.4, where the argument that policing as a dialogical enterprise also implicates it in anti-authoritarian movements or forces like Occupy Wall Street.

The points raised in this essay may be summarized:

- Law enforcement is understood traditionally in terms of a balance of negative and positive rights.
- Added to these authorities is the mediated environment of police work that requires that justice and security is what is seen to be done.
- The fusion of law enforcement and security intelligence in preventive or precautionary forms of intervention threaten this classical balance.
- This and other developments would appear to take the authority of police steps closer to authoritarianism.
- However, the argument presented is that police legitimacy will continue to require police discretion in a context of plural authorities.
- Institutionalized through plural authorities, police in liberal democracies are existentially an anti-authoritarian agency.
- At this historical moment, police must be credited when they are active in deploying the legacy of those institutional authorities and capacities to resist the authoritarian impulse.

10.1 POLICE AUTHORITY IN LIBERAL DEMOCRACIES

The authority asserted by public police is a determinant of both the liberalism and democracy in liberal democracies. From the Anglo-American viewpoint, we contrast types of government with reference to the relationship between partisan politics, republican values, and police capacities or powers. If we are citizens or denizens in liberal democracies, we expect policing to be reflective of practices and values that make this more than wishful thinking, and we contrast our policing with that of the police state, a synonym for authoritarianism.

That being said, few of us really view public police as being quite as fluid as the politics and values that they are authorized to uphold. To some extent we push a self-fulfilling prophecy that assumes that police reflect not authority but authoritarianism and then wonder why it is that this is what we (expect to) find. To correct this it is necessary to remind ourselves that police authority is both a normative idea and an empirical fact: it is an idea about how to arrive at a condition of proper order; it is an observation about the real workings or experience of the world as it is. We will begin with the normative idea. This requires a brief sojourn into how we have institutionalized police authority, including how liberal authority is structured by negative and positive rights.

Weber argued famously that there are three types of authority: traditional, legal-rational, and charismatic. Much traditional analysis of policing concentrates, to a large extent rightly, on police authority as stemming from the "foundational" or "original" prerogatives of the state's negative power and on police as exercising legal-rational authority in the necessary capacity to monopolize violence.[1] In constituting authority, the first consideration, following Giddens (1985) and Tilly (1985) among others, is to ensure both the capacity and reach of sovereign occupation. It is not just the ability to "take" a site from others but the ability to hold captured ground that is important. As Westley (1970) and Bittner (1970) make plain, public police officers bring to the interstices or quotidian of society a coercive capacity backed by the state. They literally carry the flag of state will and capacity where they tread. To keep that power requires some quotient of legitimacy. Put another way, the preferred view of liberal democrats is that states are more robust where the practice of power retention (holding ground) is consistent with a liberalized rule of law, or where, through law's reference to universality, the pastoral claim to order, included among people is continuous with the sovereign claim to demarcate frontiers and keep outsiders without law or legal protections.

This view has found support in the study of so-called failed states (O'Donnell 1999; Rodgers 2006).[2] It also accords with comparative studies of police work within liberal democracies (Bayley 1985; Weitzer 1995). It is consistent with Wilson's *Varieties of Police Work* (1968), where sovereignty is more definitive or less widely contested where police authority may upgrade from defensive deterrence to a compliance or service approach that is calibrated more precisely to population or popular needs.

10.1.1 Negative Rights

Influenced by natural rights theory, a tradition of negative rights runs through liberalism and impacts police authority. Accordingly, the relationship between government authority and the individual citizen was conceived in terms of rights and duties, the idea being to conserve for the individual citizen the maximum "original authority" of self-government possible. Social contract theorists[3] attempted to give individuals adequate tools to battle government action on an equal footing.[4]

Political and human rights were devised to negate excessive governmental power and inveigh against unbridled authority by institutionalizing a counterforce in the consent of the governed. According to legal principles developed from this thinking, individuals are invested with rights of privacy and may engage in corporate enterprises covered by freedoms of association, while the administration of government, and particularly justice, is expected to be public, visible, contestable and offered through representative decision-making bodies (Lustgarten and Leigh 1996). And while individual citizens enjoy a wall of privacy, public authority is to be open to citizenry scrutiny. Parliament as "government by discussion" (Laski 1921) forces authorities to declare positions openly. Similarly, actionable information is to be vetted in the quintessentially public forum of the adversarial court. These challenge the natural tendency toward power maximization in the executive. This basis of limited self-government and its reference to public debate and discussion in checks and balances is evident in liberal democracies everywhere and reflected in the American Constitution.

To generalize much distinct literature that has criticized this liberal legacy (in answering problems of government generally and of authority in policing specifically), the institutionalization of liberal values offers a normative discourse but does not resolve the basic challenge of the power relationship between governments and individuals. With respect to self-government in politics, liberalism and specifically parliamentary democracy received one of its sharpest criticisms from Carl Schmitt, who saw a "modern political machine" in the Reichstag or German parliament of the early 1920s that was not characterized by openness and discussion but by "small and exclusive committees" who would make decisions "behind closed doors" (Schmitt 1988, 49–50).[5] This criticism that the most deliberately liberal institutions cannot function in the manner hypothesized has only become more robust. In the United States, C. Wright Mills coined the term "the power elite" in recording the circulation of people between the top echelon of government, military, and private industry. The Supreme Court's *Citizens United* decision[6] is one of countless recent examples of the interpretive subordination of common negative rights to corporate interests.

In sum, far from providing adequate institutional means for self-government or government by consent in a powerful deterrent to authoritarianism, the development of modern political institutions has been attended by a persistent systemic disenfranchisement and discrimination against an underclass of persons who are challenged continuously on their "citizen" bona fides. Majorities are denied access to goods and services and cannot acquire the necessary means to present a robust adversary to state authority. Put another way, instead of celebrating liberalism as a means of fostering social equality, critics have pointed out that even democratic liberal institutions have been adept at maintaining and even exacerbating structural inequalities and have done so by indoctrinating authorities into stratifying practices.

10.1.2 What's in the Balance?

In classic liberal thought much is achieved by distinguishing and separating government into relatively equal and separate branches, as per Montesquieu's famous influence
on the drafting of the American Constitution. This produces the necessity, among other
positive outcomes, that policy and action by one branch must be explained as a matter
of constitutional jurisdiction, consistency, and intention. Following the logic of the division of institutional interests in liberal government—or in the idea, also advanced by
Locke, among others, that liberty depends on a separation of powers so that each institution may prevent the other from acting tyrannically—Herbert Packer (1968) argued
in *The Limits of the Criminal Sanction* that police as well are bifurcated between institutional forces: the necessities of sovereign efficiency and constitutional legality. Packer
compared the tension between the urge to control crime and the need to uphold legality
and due process by reference to the metaphor of the assembly line versus the obstacle
course. With the former, there is urgency to clear up criminal cases quickly and efficiently; with the latter, there is a deliberation and parsing of each stage of the process
through contest: to provide teeth to "reasonable doubt," to sort out false positives, to
provide for alternative resolutions, et cetera.

Following up on Packer several studies in the post-civil rights era of the 1970s and
1980s were attracted to the intriguing question of how practitioners actually negotiate
the subsystems of the criminal process (e.g., Reiss 1971). Drawing on practitioner observation to clarify the interaction of due process and crime control, studies found practices that fall afoul of the public profile of law, going so far as to find that due process
may be for crime control, thus turning Packer on his head (McBarnett 1979; Ericson
1981, 1982). As learned from these and recent studies, everyday practical considerations
may overcome inter-agency and inter-institutional checks and balances (Stuntz 2006).
In short, one can make too much of the negative role in practice and of legality as a limitation on "crime control" or law enforcement.[7]

10.1.3 Positive Rights

A contrasting response to the problem of the grounding of authority tracks legitimacy
in the development of second- and third-generation rights (from negative to positive;
from group and sovereignty), some of which respond to the interplay of domestic and
international orders. Accordingly, there is a positive duty for the maintenance of wellbe-
ing (health, security) that allows for the decolonization of the oppressed from tyranny
(something Locke had also offered). For instance, a justification for intrusive action
beyond self defense is found in the harm principle of John Stuart Mill (1859, 21–22): "the
only purpose for which power can be rightfully exercised over any member of a civilized
community, against his will, is to prevent harm to others. His own good, either physical
or moral, is not sufficient warrant."

The right or duty to prevent harm to others is a powerful invitation to those in authority to make a prediction about the relative harm that may be prevented with this or that course of action. Consequently, intimately connected to the idea of positive rights is the other strand of Locke's classical liberal thought, the idea of governmental prerogative. This forms the basis of a positive duty to security as a "common good" and, the life and vitality of the sovereign capacity, without which government itself has no legitimate basis. By the concept of prerogative, Locke understands a "[p]ower to act according to discretion, for the public good, without prescription of the law, and sometimes even against it." Prerogative power by the sovereign authority is permitted "where the law is silent" and also where law is insufficient (Locke, Two Treatises II, Sections 159, 160, 164, in Hay 1823).

So here we have both an affirmative and proscriptive capacity that is resident in both negative and positive rights. The sovereign must be vital and strong enough to preserve the peace, and it must take prerogative action to project, and perhaps even to maintain, that vital power. Also of key importance, that prerogative action is carried out not by a hypothetical heuristic invention, but by flesh and blood people making decisions. As we shall see, it is the police who often act as the sovereign authority and sometimes assert the exception.

10.2 THE NEW GEOGRAPHY OF AUTHORITY: WHO'S WHO IN POLICING?[8]

Post-9/11 there has been enormous pressure on domestic law enforcement to find a new metaphor, to move away from the constraining imagery of due process and crime control as outlined by Packer (McBarnett 1979; Ericson 1981). We are now situating police authority against the positive and social rights that have emerged in the past half-century and collapsing the distinction between frontier and external and domestic or internal orders. In current configurations of justice and security, liberal democracies are increasingly permissive of authoritarian state practices.[9] In the "fusing" of criminal justice and (national) security actions, we are witnessing a reversal of the separation between domestic law enforcement and security intelligence or political policing (Brodeur 1983). The preemptive, preventative, and precautionary mode (de Lint et al. 2007; Monaghan and Walby 2011) is entrenching itself well beyond the traditional reserves for such exceptional measures. In the wake of the expanding "security" practices, many analysts are expressing concern over the emergence of a state of "exception," "surveillance," or "control" (Agemben 1998; Garland 2000; Lyon 2007).

To understand this transition, it is important to recognize the distinction between the optics and practices of government. Governmental authority is seen to be carried out in liberal democracies with the consent of the governed through information sufficient for informed decision making that may buttress effective policies, and by individuals with rights, particularly privacy rights, that stem from the protection of private property. Ideally, this gives citizens the ability to provide or deny consent, which is required because de facto authority, or authority by raw force, is anathema to the liberal doctrine, with the restriction on public police representing that limitation in negative liberal government.

However, as Holquist (1997) and others have argued, the emergence of modern nation-states in France, Germany, the Soviet Union, and Great Britain featured the growth of propaganda and governmental public relations for the manipulation of consent: population information, the liquid of government (Holquist 1997), is collected, interpreted, and acted on by governmental authorities to demonstrate the relationship between the so-called necessities of executive action and requirements of liberal legitimacy. Modern states now conduct pre-democracy exercises in opinion polling and propaganda. In the meantime, and quite contrary to the ideal of openness that is expected of liberal democracies, a "wider security agenda" will continue to be ordered via the economic values of capitalism and neoliberalism (Buzan 2000, 17), making the idea of pre-crime increasingly reasonable. Official secrecy buttressing a wider security agenda (Neocleous 2008; de Lint and Bahdi 2012) in a national security infrastructure that has been spreading within and between states ensures that information necessary to provide informed consent is possessed by those few people who also "need to know."

Foucault deepens this observation by contending that neoliberalism turns the principle of self-limitation against government itself: "It is a sort of permanent economic tribunal confronting government" (Foucault 2007, 247). What this means, as also argued by his student, Donzelot (2008, 131), is that under neoliberal practices, regulatory interventions can only be justified where they can serve competition (as opposed to reducing inequalities), a point in accord with current interventionism. Following Foucault (1977, 1988), O'Malley (1999), Garland (2000, 2002), and Rose (2000) have argued that the stratifying practices of liberalism maintain what has been referred to as the "powers of freedom" (Rose 1999) or liberal "intelligence" (Donzelot 2008).[10] Policing and security are deployed to uphold the vitality of enterprise (Donzelot 2008) because under neoliberal and neoconservative government policy it is the "resilient entrepreneurial subject" (O'Malley 2011), and not the rights-bearing citizen,[11] that is the well-spring of liberal power.[12] That police act with the consent of the governed, then, is not an empirical fact, but a belief or affirmation stemming from a particular way of universalizing the individual and world, a way of talking up a very rare person, perhaps even just 1 percent, the resilient neoliberal entrepreneur. From this interpretation liberalism is simply a style of power relations that continuously support ongoing ideological or discursive subordinations (Foucault 1980).[13]

10.2.1 Brokering Access

While neoliberal doctrine has supported the protection of a sphere of economic vitality, neoconservative doctrine has tempered this protection with prudential authoritarianism

(O'Malley 2011). Locke was concerned to couple liberty with market vitality or free enterprise, but he was also keen to preserve the vitality of the state by reference to the prerogative (Arnold 2007; Neocleous 2008). In Arnold's view, the War on Drugs and the War on Terror are explained as consistent with Locke's thinking that prerogative power may be exercised through bureaucracy, allowing the rule of law to lead directly to the suspension of law (see also Ericson 2007). Neoconservatives have been keen to pursue a wide-ranging deterrence strategy against drugs and terrorism inasmuch as this is targeted at non-vital "overflow" populations both within and without the borders of the nation-state. Stimulated by anxiety over rising crime and disorder and penal populism (Pratt 2007), prudential authoritarianism finds expression in order maintenance policing and "zero-tolerance" campaigns that target overflow, or non-vital, population groups.[14]

The neoconservative position overlaps with thinking on objectivity and power associated with the left that discredits with equal fervor the ideal of a restrictive (negative rights) or affirmative (positive rights) policy agenda. According to post-critical accounts of the social world, it is no longer reasonable to assume an objective unitary observer to a power relation (Digeser 1992)—one who may claim to know the relative disadvantages of two parties conflicted over a clearly observable interest or objective.[15] On the contrary, there are multiple canvasses upon which an inscription of the dynamic interaction may be written. The role of the audience—and of several audiences—is now part of the reflexive concatenation of power flows.[16] As a consequence, critics on the left are faced with a choice: to "do nothing" for fear of doing harm that cannot be predicted (once described as "impossibilism" (McMahon 1990)) or to persist to presume to know better (in a form of neo-colonial/expert interventionism). Consequently, the position to the left of center has been to act with little confidence in the legitimacy of the action. A reluctant attitude towards certainty in matters of security is also the pedigree of the classic conservatism, but neoconservatives do not shirk the necessity to choose, and to choose boldly.

Less radical opinion also rallied against adversarial or oppositional constructions of crime and crime policy. Moderates questioned the efficiency and effectiveness of public policing and wondered if progress could be made following the recipe of an accord between crime control and due process. There was widespread concern that rising crime rates could not be countered by rising public expenditures on security and social services (despite evidence collected subsequently that showed they could (Levitt 2004)). Consequently, under the new public management in the 1990s, public police were to account more exactingly for public expenditures and choose to conserve only those core functions that could not be offloaded (Posen 1994). By applying the new business models, reformers also sought to disrupt moribund (unionised) rank and file solidarities (cf. Brogden and Shearing 1993; Bayley and Shearing 2001; Deukmedjian and de Lint 2007).

10.2.2 Plural Policing and Fusions

Neoliberal policy options were reflected in steps to open up the "public monopoly" of policing. It would be commodified (Loader 2000), and providers and citizens divided into "responsibilized partners," "third parties," "active clients," or consumers of policing service products. In lobbying for privatization and civilianization, reformers supported policing as a plurality of auspices, governing authorities, or corporate entities (Johnston 1992; Bayley and Shearing 1996), a view that fits nicely with Third Way politics (Giddens 1998).

At the same time that the Reagan-Thatcher years normalized neoliberal doctrine and "a more radically laissez faire 'social' entrepreneurialism," so did it produce a "defensive neoconservatism" that "valorised social and prudential authoritarianism" (O'Malley 2011, 9). Re-alignments across institutional authorities are seen dramatically in the configuration of the Department of Homeland Security, in more than one hundred Joint Terrorism Task Forces (JTTFs), and in fusion centers and other multi-agency linkages generically. These intelligence hubs or nodes were established to overcome traditional silos. They are sites of vital liberal intelligence (Donzelot 2008) that produce unstable and fluid decision-making authorities. And they are dramatically altering the pointy end of police work by inserting military conventions and protocols into the nodes, particularly in the control of information and in the perception and mitigation of risk.

For example, at 55 Broadway in Manhattan, New York, there is a surveillance center, the Lower Manhattan Security Coordination Center, operating and analyzing video from two thousand private surveillance cameras in the financial district and about one thousand from the NYPD. One hundred and fifty million dollars of public money, from municipal and federal sources, is funding this operation. The Center's technology is used to track people in the financial district and beyond that are "suspicious" or may pose a threat or disrupt the business of the Wall Street firms. It is jointly staffed by the NYPD and the Wall Street firms. Ironically, the analysts in this public/private partnership collect information on Occupy Wall Street protesters who gather to demand that the Wall Street 1 percent is held to account for the economic disenfranchisement of the 99 percent (Martens 2012).

In its interpretation of its community protection mandate and with its intelligence unit, the NYPD has also made the boldest fusion of law enforcement and security intelligence authorities. Its counterintelligence and counterterrorism activities are carried out by over one thousand officers, many of them stationed overseas.[17] The NYPD has used former CIA officers, trained its own officers at the Farm (the CIA training academy), and spent more than $1.6 billion in funding from the federal government in aggressive monitoring, data collection, and active surveillance. Much like Military Operations in Urban Terrain (MOUT), counter-insurgency (COIN) actions overseas, and the FBI's infamous Counterintelligence Operations (COINTELPRO), the NYPD has been acting preemptively and preventively (as per the post-9/11 discourse) against a threat to New York that it perceives will derive largely from radicalized Muslims.

This is doing much to shift the institutional position of policing under the division of powers. In legislation extending from petty drug offenses right up to anti-terrorism the criminal process is "bent" away from modern rule of law idealism toward a post-Wilsonian international relations realism (Chesney and Goldsmith 2008; Weisselberg 2008). Disciplining of police authority by the lower judiciary is compromised by a culture of post-legality, as illustrated in recent work by a variety of policing scholars (Ericson 2007; Zedner 2009; Monaghan and Walby 2011) that is targeted differentially at subordinate populations. Its transparency and dialogical character is strained by adaptations to a culture of control, intelligence, and ubiquitous surveillance (Garland 2000; Kane 2007; Lyon 2007; Ratcliffe 2010). The privacy wall is differentially viable so that immunity from a more imposing prudential authoritarianism is a function of economic means or relative economic power (cf. Herbert 1997). In line with post-9/11 standards of efficacy against asymmetric threats, domestic policing is more impervious, duplicitous, and unpredictable.[18] In accord with existential prerogatives of the executive there is a substitution of public accountability in checks and balances for an intelligence doctrine that gives primary value to information control. Police as "the new centurions" (Wambaugh 1970) indeed!

It is arguable that the limited view of state authority (and policing practices) is bifurcated. Limit and caution (in the protection of economic vitality) does apply to interference in the market and in much commercial or corporate transaction, where the interpretation of a near certainty of preventable harm is needed before intrusions may be made. The more proactive and authoritarian view is applied to public and common places and against those parties without sufficient means or community support to erect a sufficient property wall against government intrusions. New York's "stop and frisk" search policy is exemplary. In the context of flat or declining crime rates, it is protection of community and vigilance against terror risks that permits New York police to increase stop-and-frisk searches of mostly black and Latino youth, with numbers reaching 601,055 in 2010 and 2.4 million between 2009 and 2012 (NYCLU 2011).

Under the post-9/11 geography, police actors draw from a plurality of authorities in neoliberal and neoconservative politics, redraw the balance of consent to stipulate the in its place the greater good of prerogative necessity, and insert the means and methods of security intelligence deep into the body politic. Altogether, this view of police authority strains and stretches the meaning of public law and the traditional liberal doctrine's basis in visibility, contestability, public ownership, and accountability.[19] In this context, is it really imaginable that police might deploy their discretionary power for the common well-spring of authorities and against anti-authoritarian practices? Via a discussion of plural authorities and policing as a dialogical enterprise, it is to this question we now turn.

10.3 POLICE DISCRETION AND PLURAL AUTHORITY

An adequate account of the development of police authority must take on board both ends of the classic liberal dilemma of negative and positive governance. Slogans, such as that "police are the public and the public are the police" serve a discursive value: that, for example, police are evenly distributed according to public need or perceived risk of depredations to property. But a counter-narrative or genealogy of policing will take adequate stock of this other side of liberal-consent in which liberal political theory and a good section of popular opinion support the subservience of individual rights to collective or social rights. Since it is police "who temporarily act as sovereign" (Agemben 1998, 3) where decisions must be carried out with celerity by actors on the ground, it is police who experience strong pressures to intrude beyond their negative capacity to do proactive and prophylactic harm reduction and to offer a definitive expression of the limit of sovereign authority.

It is much appreciated that police work draws from a variety of authorities to be both productive and conservative. For example, police deploy charismatic and de facto authority more than is sometimes considered polite to admit. The "discovery" of police discretion—by Goldstien (1960), La Fave (1962) and others in the early 1960s—referred to this latent or "original" capacity of the public police. It is now well-recognized that the work of the sovereign requires a certain presence and projection of de facto authority (or decision); otherwise police appear too much as poor actors, not sufficiently convincing. Following suit, the earliest ethnographies of police work corrected the false impression left by top-down, "institutional" texts on policing (Fosdick 1920; Wilson 1950; Smith 1960) that overlooked that police authority was also an accomplishment of "method actors" (Manning 1977) who take "a line of action." As many policing ethnographers make plain, a connection to state capacity requires further work at the occupational cultural level (Banton 1964; Rubinstien 1973; Manning 1977). This is because, as Herbert (1996, 800) summarizes, the legal order of the state requires a moral justification in order to avoid looking "nakedly coercive and illegitimate."

Consequently, police are—and must be—invested and invest themselves with many kinds of authority consistent with the requirements of changes to the political environment in which they are situated.[20] Work by Herbert (1997), Shearing and Ericson (1991), and de Lint (1999) situate police actors in a multiplicity of authority relations. Decisions are made not only to (not) invoke the law, but also to (not) liaison with other service providers, to (not) provide a lesson on morality, to (not) lend a hand to restore a particular order, to (not) input data about an individual into a computer-assisted dispatch (CAD) system. Police powers are an expedient of liberal democracies that allow situated actors to gain access to places and people in a manner consistent with the preservation of privacy and liberal freedoms. However, it is now more readily accepted that the public and highly visible authority of the police officer is situated in a policing or security assemblage that involves multi-agency linkages (Monaghan and Walby 2011) and derives from a variety of institutional and mediated sources (Herbst 2003). The craft of policing is therefore found in leveraging access to troublesome people or places in such a way as to coexist with sovereign, common, and political expediencies—and not merely law enforcement efficiencies (de Lint 2003). As pivotal actors in governance, public police are placed to absorb and cast off the full range of these authorities, and a complete evaluation of police authority must reference each of them.

The situational platform of this one actor is pivotal to shaping normative relations throughout what is often called a security or policing assemblage (Haggerty and Ericson 2000).[21] Yes, uniformed public police officers practice and project the character of what passes for legal authority in many of the mundane or quotidian surfaces of social interaction. Public police officers act though warrant of legal instruments, but they also deploy violence and surveillance or information systems to push through the privacy wall of the putatively sovereign individual. They deploy these tools while walking a fine line between legitimate and illegitimate expression of the authorities that pass through them. The line is fine because the appearance (at least) of legitimate and consensual relations depends upon embedding police authority deep into a polity, through institutions that gain legitimacy by reference to common origins in common values. The result is that each actor is Janus-like, switched on to orders and transactions, trust building and information collection, needs and risks, and capable of turning on a dime, if necessary: acting for the will of the executive or, in a manner, to negate that will by referencing quasi-institutional independence or a nullifying public pressure.

10.4 POLICING AS A DIALOGICAL ENTERPRISE AND ANTI-AUTHORITARIAN FORCE

As we know, sovereign instability or insecurity is related to police function and the legitimacy of police authority is vulnerable to the sedimentation of various transgressing forces. In the analogy of public protest, the thin blue police line may become an impenetrable barrier or disintegrate altogether. This is in the very design of the agent of authority or "he who decides the exception." It is evident as police everywhere adopt a line of law enforcement in the context of many competing institutional, practical, and ideological considerations. For those committed to the idea of a highly iterative policing—a policing by consent that builds up the negating power of the individual and recognizes the need to redress positive harms and risks that may be sourced without and within government—this idea need not be too radical. In line with the anti-authoritarian strategy of liberal democratic precautionary government structure, police are indeed positioned between the institutions of government. The institution of public police is constituted to allow for considerable discretionary uptake of information and coercion into authoritative action. It is an error to anticipate that the exercise of this authority will routinely track toward authoritarianism. On the contrary, a common prerogative or rule nullifying authority is consistent with liberal democracy's negative capacity, as per Locke's argument, and belongs as much with public police action as anywhere.

To revitalize this anti-authoritarian latency in policing it is necessary that public police take a more nuanced and wider view of disorder and use their capacities according to an appreciation of those various authorities that push them to action. First, take discretion. Police discretion is understood as the decision not to enforce the law where it might be justifiably applied (Goldstein 1960; La Fave 1962). It is an institutional stopper and buffer that places liberal police actors in situ between various authorities and as choosers who initiate a line of action. This capacity is a requirement of legitimate authority. The power to work the thin blue line against tyranny need refer only to the capacity of police to use discretion. Police choose a remedy from a variety of choices in a troublesome situation. They may use their tools to interpret lawful coercion consistent with the letter of the law or the principles of legality. Consistent with the definition of sovereignty, police discretion is the choice (not) to act and decide exceptions to norms or law. It is also stipulated by the optics of executive necessity (action) where certain distinctions are disallowed as offensive to cultural aspirations (as prejudice) or economic vitalities. Discretion in the craft of policing is therefore choosing the sovereign or political expediencies that inform how or when to leverage access to troublesome people or places.

This takes from our discussion of plural authority. Police authority is the complement of discretion. If one accepts that the police role encompasses legal, coercive, and informational powers, to meet needs and risks, the navigation of authority within a privacy labyrinth is sufficiently wide. The metaphor "thin blue line" evokes the idea that the barrier between police authority and a citizenry is not meant to be too sharp and bold. This is well-represented in the earliest discourses about the New Police, particularly in famous phrase "the police are the public and the public are the police." Indeed, policing *is* a dialogical enterprise. Public order policing is defined as "the use of police authority and capacity to establish a legitimate equilibrium between governmental and societal, collective and individual, rights and interests" (de Lint 2005). In each interaction between police and citizen cohorts or denizens, the currency of authority passes back and forth across "the thin blue line." The legal basis for action is often an open question as a narrative or line of action is chosen or trialed and then pursued by actors. De facto or natural authority is challengeable and tested. Good dialogue depends on reference to the good, or something of value, and a good faith effort to attach a line of action to this value. These are ethical questions at the heart of "good policing" (Brodeur 2010) and must be asked. But there is no necessary constancy in either party to the dialogue. Both are shifting and adaptive. Police are actors who take a line noting the review of performance, who search for a proper footing in various kinds of authority, and who play to the most appreciative pockets of the audience; imperatively, to the heart of liberal doctrine in the protection of a sphere of liberty.

Lastly and in sum, may we situate police discretionary authority in minor rather than major politics (Mouffe 2005)? As a dialogical enterprise reflective of the polity policing is required to be absorptive of the common and popular. Too many think that taking popular direction is always a short step toward authoritarian policing, as evidenced in the penal populism literature. However, to take direction from popular movements is not to abandon the requirement to modify or modulate this impulse with principles of legality. The interaction between various politics and policing does directly influence police mandates and authority, but the direction of that influence is not predetermined, nor should it be thought to be a matter of inevitability. It is incumbent upon public police to ensure more than adequate uptake of minor politics and political movements, given that in our most established liberal democracies political power has been unseated from polities and functions poorly, if at all, to match societal preferences with official policy.

As this is being written, the Occupy Wall Street rebellion is building into a popular social movement, the first from the left in the United States since the 1930s, according to Dorian Warren (2011). Solidarity in the movement is achieved by reference to the slogan "We are the 99 percent," referring to the economic, political, and social disparity between the vast majority of Americans and the 1 percent that comprise the elites that have gained from the policies of the past thirty years. The NYPD is caught directly between these so-called 1 percent and 99 percent forces. Protesters are calling for the NYPD to allow the occupation, with one protester saying, "They're our NYPD" (*Democracy Now* 2011), while JPMorgan Chase—which paid out $156 million to settle a fraud case in which it was accused of deceiving clients into buying risky mortgage-backed securities (a precipitator of the 2008 crash that led to the Occupy movement)—donated $4.6 million to the New York Police Association on the eve of the protests.

How will police deal with this protest movement, particularly if it continues to grow? Police are not only to be judged against liberal institutions, and liberal democratic institutions are not necessarily averse to more blunted police instrumentation. Many scholars have pointed out that police respond to emergent social, political, and cultural conditions. Governments adapt to conditions of so-called emergency conditions by relaxing restrictions on arrest and detention, search and seizure, and monitoring or snooping. Although this provides police with extra leverage in accessing potentially troublesome people, it also narrows the options and cuts off the dialogue with minority politics (Mouffe 2005). Political authorities can lead police away from constructive negotiations about political grievances. Likewise, police may insist that avoidance of serious disorder requires that political authorities negotiate with minority politics spokespersons in occupied space to push a democratizing cause. Like the protestors, many recent commentators do not despair of this requirement and also seek to finesse the position of policing in the reinvigoration of liberal democratic practices (Loader and Walker 2001; Shearing and Wood 2003). This is in evidence in plural policing, nodal governance, capacity building, and in many other works of policing scholarship and policy innovation, measures that have a strong pedigree in grounded realist genealogies and practice.

10.5   A Scorecard for Anti-Authoritarian Policing

The right mix of authorities has thus far secured a strong role for public police in domestic governance and ordering (cf. Garland 2001). Police authority in liberal democracies is connected to diverse institutional supports (cf. Turk 1982). In situ, the legality of police authority is a matter of the exchange rates that public police barter between various government actors and a view of order. Actors reach out with (often) less visible capacities and instruments so that, as Brodeur (2010, 68) expressed it, the synoptic form of surveillance is augmented by the panoptic form. Viewed bureaucratically under conditions of resource competition, it is also guided by risk-aversion.

As constituted, public police possess a tremendous capacity to restore the footing of liberal democratic policing. They may act thus without adding a whit to the authority or formidable independence that they already possess. Who better than they to utilize professional expertise and craft to ensure survival of the institutions that in turn support them? Police are still very much visible and responsive to the policed community, and they elicit its trust by engaging in partnership dialogue.

That said, liberal democratic policing—or the actors that carry out public policing in liberal democracies—faces a stark choice right now. Foundational features of liberal democracies are in peril. Processes of appointments to legislative, executive, and judicial bodies and of the chief executive (the president) are now more than ever dominated by big money and machine politics. Popular disconnection from the traditional political process is at an all-time high. This democratic deficit can hardly be made up singlehandedly by public police as the "thin blue line." Yet, as in decision making in public order policing, whose accommodation of minor politics may avert wider societal and political disorder, it is public police who will be at the vanguard one way or another. It may be a time to read the tarot cards or tea leaves and avoid the more dangerous result: the wholesale abandonment of the institutional foundation of liberal consent, a consequence of which will be visible in the destruction of our modern police. One starting point for encouraging best practice is a scorecard for anti-authoritarian practice. Such a scorecard would itemize practice against the common good. Luckily, it would not take much work to find the basis for such a device. There are over two hundred years of trial and error to draw from.

NOTES

1. Lord Denning, in *R. v. Metropolitan Police Commissioner, ex parte Blackburn* [1968]. All E.R. 763 (English Court of Appeal), at p. 769.
2. O'Donnell (1999) found that many Latin American states enjoy the capacity only partially, so that only in "blue zones" is there an effective bureaucracy, a functioning legal system, and clear monopoly over legitimate violence. In "brown zones," there are strong "systems of local power" and the state is negligibly present. In colonial and frontier policing (Weitzer 1995; Hills 2009), the assertion of a state's claim of jurisdiction is more tentative and manifest in a patchwork or tapestry in which the "rule of law" and "rule of men" are mixed and matched.
3. Including John Locke, Jean-Jacques Rousseau, Edmund Burke, John Stuart Mill, Jeremy Bentham, and other founders of liberal doctrine.
4. The crafters of limited government argued in favor of the principle of a freedom that belongs with all citizens (by which was meant people who were freeholders of property and male).

5. Other criticism abounds. Utilitarians discredited negative rights and ridiculed social contract theorists for their fanciful heuristic device and the idea that social reality was a product of prescriptive invention. Jeremy Bentham called the idea "nonsense on stilts." Early social philosophers, including Emile Durkheim and Karl Marx, saw in liberal rights not so much a universal edifice as social conventions, relations, or norms set in contingency, historical specificity, and materiality. The social reality predicate and reality principal is now fully developed. Corrigan and Sayer (1985) argue that state institutions are formed through cultural revolutions. Tilly (1985) makes a strong case that states emerge as a normalization of organized criminal activities. Realist and critical legal scholars and a host of others criticized the non-materiality of the liberal subject, who is so often structurally prevented from achieving advantage from the rights she is told she is privileged to possess.

6. Citizens United v. Federal Election Commission, 558 U.S. 310 (2010).

7. Doreen McBarnett (1979) and others (Ericson 1981; Skolnick 1966; Manning 1977) have argued that the distinction between due process is overwrought when it comes to what police do at much of the low-level criminal intake where it would offer sovereign authority a good contest. McBarnett (1979) found that "due process is for crime control." Ericson (1981) found that accused persons were dependents in the criminal process, a process that was not so much a contest or conflict between relatively equal parties as the bureaucratization or administering of accused. The high use of the plea bargain is also an unintended consequence, as it is an avoidance of the ambiguity of the process by both parties.

8. I am borrowing this phrase from Wilson (2000, 111), who used the term to refer to "beat" and "community" as a site "on which neoconservatives would later build."

9. The United States is a so-called stronghold of liberal freedoms, but with less than 5 percent of the world's population it accounts for 25 percent of the world's incarcerated population, incarcerating more people for drug offences than Western Europe incarcerates for all its offences combined (Andreas and Nadelmann 2005, 251–52).

10. For instance, community policing was a response to the trust-gap between minority inner city residents and municipal, state, and police authority that resulted in an information gap that threatened police credibility (Silver 1967). Reassurance policing is another such innovation that is doubly-edged to gain both trust and information (Heatherington and Millie 2006).

11. Marx argued that to be governed through the ideal of liberties is not the same as being liberated or free, or it is a certain kind of liberation: liberation from an alternative, a connectedness to the material needs of others.

12. An illustration of the latter is Monsanto's employment of Pinkerton's as "the gene police." Hired by the agribusiness giant, "the eye that never sleeps" gives Monsanto loss protection by developing informants, providing monitoring and surveillance of farmers, and "comb[ing] the countryside" for gene "seed pirates" (Robin 2011, 206, 207).

13. Many police analysts draw a version of police institutional purity from the historical interaction between an idealized police mission and the minor politics of a bygone day. This is partly because Anglo-American policing references back to Peel's sensitization to fears and anxieties present at the formative moment of police modernization, a consequence of which is well-versed in various "Whig histories": the diminution of the less visible, less dialogical "high policing" authority. Many analysts make rather less of the idea that liberalism in policing is currently connected to neoliberal ideals and practices. Today, fear of merchant class civilities may still discipline police authority, but the direction of the modulating impact is in favor of a so-called "zero tolerance" or public activities that deviate from the "look" of legitimate commercial transactions.

14. This challenges traditional limits on the sovereign's right to act unilaterally across the divide of domestic and foreign affairs, a right that flows from the "lean, mean state" (Hall 1988), one that acts against the resuscitated classical idea of a free-choosing criminal who may be countered by rational deterrence.

15. Following Lukes (1976), consent is a "discursive production": what is meant by "consent" or "self-government" is a strategy of power or the manipulation of meanings and appearances (Lukes 1976). Following both Lukes (1976) and Foucault (1977) power and authority is now understood as dynamic and contingent, incorporating not one but many audiences.

16. Many students of authority now acknowledge that it is not only de facto or natural, charismatic, and legal-rational (or de jure), but also the epistemic, moral, and media-derived (Herbst 2003).

17. The idea both of precaution and targeted policing is also reflected in other innovations of similar consequence. Under the Crime and Disorder Act, police in England and Wales have asserted themselves more deliberately across service providers from health to corrections, in a ubiquitous social control of offenders deemed prolific and priority. Multi-agency partnerships are "force multipliers," seeing more by sharing information, and acting more singularly for "community protection."

18. New York is also known for its "police surge" demonstrations, in which police unexpectedly converge in a variety of deployments (helicopter, car, motorcycle, mounted) in order to demonstrate an unpredictable counter-force that keeps the issues of terrorism and its antithesis in the public eye and consciousness (de Lint et al. 2007).

19. At the high end, University of Texas law professor Robert M. Chesney is just one legal scholar to contend the legality of extra-judicial executions like that of al-Alwaki (Chesney 2007; Shane 2011).

20. There are dissenting views on this purported relationship between sovereignty, democracy, and police power. For instance, many analysts take the view that it is precisely the openness of liberal democracy that leaves it more vulnerable than a totalitarian state to destabilizing forces from within and without. When dissent against a government policy builds or when a strong constituency is angered and wants to use alternative political vehicles to shift government policy or change government itself, there is a challenge to the social and political order and to the relationship between a particular political party and sovereign authority. This can produce a crisis of legitimacy, place public police in the difficult position of choosing sides, and leave liberal democracies appearing weak and vulnerable.

   A deeper criticism is that political sovereignty in modern liberal democracies is more powerful because it has much more subtle capacities to collect, absorb, and co-opt dissenting voices—the function of much of the police assemblage. In this line of thought, civil institutions including a free press can still reproduce an ideological or even hegemonic view much more effectively than a totalitarian regime, even with its state propaganda apparatus and openly authoritarian practices (Holquist 1997).

   At the highest levels, police also serve at the discretion of political authorities. This may be less problematic where politicians do not meet great resistance in instituting the real or perceived law enforcement, crime prevention, or order maintenance mandate on which they succeeded to win elected office. However, political authority is a matter of contention and is supported or undermined by other sources of power or authority within and without politics proper, including the charismatic or personal reputations of individual actors, the influence of pressure or lobby and demand groups, etc. In addition, there is, as is well documented, the sediment of bureaucratic forces and, in public policing, the significant capacity of the union-buttressed rank-and-file to resist ill-favored political direction.

21. The development of a "policing web" in the United States and other countries underscores this idea that policing is comprised of a multiplicity of actors carrying out a common purpose across a plurality of spaces, domains, sectors, spheres, and institutions (Brodeur 2010).

REFERENCES

Andreas, Peter, and Ethan Nadelmann. 2006. *Policing the Globe: Criminalization and Crime Control*. Oxford: Oxford University Press.

Agamben, Giorgio. 1998. *Homo Sacer: Sovereign Power and Bare Life*. Stanford, CA: Stanford University Press.

Arnold, Kathleen. 2007. "Domestic War: Locke's Concept of Prerogative and Implications for U.S. 'Wars' Today." *Polity* 39(1): 1–28.

Banton, Micheal. 1964. *Policeman in the Community*. New York: Basic Books.

Bayley, David. 1985. *Patterns of Policing: A Comparative International Analysis*. New Brunswick, NJ: Rutgers University Press.

———. 1996. *Policing for the Future*. Oxford: Oxford University Press.

Bayley, David, and Clifford D. Shearing. 1996. "The Future of Policing." *Law and Society Review* 30(3): 585–606.

———. 2001. *The New Structure of Policing: Description, Conceptualization, and Research Agenda*. Washington, DC: U.S. Department of Justice, National Institute of Justice.

Bittner, Egon. 1970. *The Functions of the Police in Modern Society*. Chevy Chase, MD: National Institute of Mental Health.

Brodeur, Jean-Paul. 1983. "High Policing and Low Policing: Remarks about the Policing of Political Activities." *Social Powers* 30(5): 507–20.

———. 1998. *How to Recognize Good Policing*. London: Sage.

———. 2010. *The Policing Web*. Oxford: Oxford University Press.

Brogden, Michael, and Clifford D. Shearing. 1993. *Policing for a New South Africa*. London: Routledge.

Buzan, Barry. 2000. "Change and Insecurity Reconsidered." In *Critical Reflections on Security and Change*, edited by Stuart Croft and Terriff Terriff, 1–17. London: Frank Cass.

Chesney, Robert M. 2007. "Beyond Conspiracy? Anticipatory Prosecution and the Challenge of Unaffiliated Terrorism." *Southern California Law Review* 80:425–502.

Chesney, Robert M., and Jack Goldsmith. 2008. "Terrorism and the Convergence of Criminal and Military Detention Models." *Stanford Law Review* 60(4): 1079–133.

Corrigan, Peter, and Derek Sayer. 1985. *The Great Arch: English State Formation as Cultural Revolution*. Oxford: Blackwell.

de Lint, Willem. 1999. "A Post-Modern Turn in Policing: Policing as Pastiche?" *International Journal of the Sociology of Law* 27(2): 127–52.

———. 2003. "Keeping Open Windows: Police as Access Brokers." *British Journal of Criminology* 43(2): 379–97.

———. 2005. "Public Order Policing: A Tough Act to Follow?" *International Journal of the Sociology of Law* 33(4): 179–99.

de Lint, Willem, and Reem Bahdi. 2012. "Access to Information in an Age of Intelligencized Governmentality." In *Brokering Access: Politics, Power and Freedom of Information in Canada*, edited by Mike Larsen and Kevin Walby, 114–141. Vancouver, BC: UBC Press.

de Lint, Willem, Sirpa Virta, and John Deukmedjian. 2007. "The Simulation of Crime Control: A Shift in Policing?" *American Behavioral Scientist* 50(12): 1631–47.

Deukmedjian, John, and Willem de Lint (2007). "Community into Intelligence: Resolving Information Uptake in the RCMP." *Policing and Society* 17(4): 239–56.

Digeser, Peter. 1992. "The Fourth Face of Power." *Journal of Politics* 54(4): 977–1007.

Donzelot, Jacques. 2008. "Michel Foucault and Liberal Intelligence." *Economy and Society* 37(1): 115–34.

Ericson, Richard V. 1981. *Making Crime: A Study of Detective Work*. Toronto: Buttersworth.

——. 1982. *The Ordering of Justice*. Toronto: University of Toronto Press.

——. 2007. *Crime in an Insecure World*. Cambridge, UK: Polity Press.

Fosdick, Robert. 1920. *American Police Systems*. New York: Century.

Foucault, Michel. 1977. *Discipline and Punish*. New York: Vintage.

——. 1980. "On Popular Justice: A Conversation with Maoists." In *Power/Knowledge: Selected Interviews and other Writings 1972-1977*, edited by Colin Gordon, 1–36. New York: Pantheon.

——. 1988. "The Political Technology of Individuals." In *Techologies of the Self: A Seminar with Michel Foucault*, edited by Luther Martin, Huck Gutman, and Patrick H. Hutton, 145–162. Amherst: University of Massachusetts Press.

——. 2007. *Security, Territory, Population: Lectures at College de France 1977–78*, edited by M. Smellart and translated by C. Burtchell. London: Palgrave Macmillan.

Garland, David. 2000. "The Culture of High Crime Societies: Some Predictions of Recent 'Law and Order' Policies." *British Journal of Criminology* 40:347–75.

——. 2001. *The Culture of Control: Crime and Social Order in Contemporary Society*. Chicago: University of Chicago Press.

——. 2002. "The Cultural Uses of Capital Punishment." *Punishment and Society* 4(4): 459–87.

Gearty, Conor. 2006. *Human Rights in an Age of Counter-Terrorism*. Oxford Amnesty Lecture (February 26) http://www2.lse.ac.uk/humanRights/articlesAndTranscripts/Oxford_Amnesty_Lecture.pdf.

Giddens, Anthony. 1985. *Nation-State and Violence: A Contemporary Critique of Historical Materialism*. Cambridge, UK: Polity Press.

——. 1998. *The Third Way: The Renewal of Social Democracy*. Cambridge, UK: Polity Press.

Goldstein, Jerome. 1960. "Police Discretion Not to Invoke the Criminal Process: Low-Visibility Decisions in the Administration of Justice." *Yale Law Journal* 69:542–94.

Haggerty, Kevin, and Richard V. Ericson. 2000. "The Surveillant Assemblage." *British Journal of Criminology* 51(4): 605–22.

Hall, Stuart. 1988. "The Toad in the Garden: Thatcherism among the Theorists." In *Marxism and the Interpretation of Culture*, edited by Cary Nelson and Lawrence Grossberg, 35–57. Urbana: University of Illinois Press.

Hay, Rod. 1823. *Two Treatises of Government: From the Works of John Locke*. London: McMaster University Archive.

Heatherington, Victoria, and Andrew Millie. 2006. "Reassurance Policing: Is it Business as Usual?" *Policing and Society* 16(2): 146–63.

Herbert, Steve. 1996. "Morality and Law Enforcement: Chasing Bad Guys with the Los Angeles Police Department." *Law and Society Review* 30(4): 799–818.

——. 1997. *Territoriality and the Los Angeles Police Department*. Minneapolis: University of Minnesota Press.

Herbst, Susan. 2003. "Political Authority in a Mediated Age." *Theory and Society* 32(4): 481–503.

Hills, Alice. 2009. "Security as a Selective Project." *Studies in Social Justice* 3(1): 79–97.

Holquist, Peter. 1997. "Information is the Alpha and Omega of our work: Bolshevik Surveillance in its Pan-European Context." *Journal of Modern History* 69(3): 415–50.

Johnston, Les. 1992. *The Rebirth of Private Policing*. New York: Routledge.

Kane, Robert J. 2007. "Collect and Release Data on Coercive Police Actions." *Criminology and Public Policy* 10(4): 774–80.

La Fave, William. 1962. "The Police and the Non-Enforcement of the Law." *Wisconsin Law Review* 1:104–37.

Laski, Harold. 1921. *The Foundations of Sovereignty*. New York: Harcourt Brace.

Levitt, Steven. 2004. "Understanding Why Crime Fell in the 1990s: Four Factors that Explain the Fall and Six that Do Not." *Journal of Economic Perspectives* 18(1): 163–90.

Loader, Ian 1999. "Consumer Culture and the Commodification of Policing and Security." *Sociology* 33(2): 373–92.

——. 2000. "Plural Policing and Democratic Governance." *Social and Legal Studies* 9(3): 323–45.

Loader, Ian, and Neil Walker. 2001. "Policing as Public Good: Reconstituting the Connection Between Policing and the State." *Theoretical Criminology* 5(1): 9–35.

Lukes, Steven. 1976. *Power: A Radical View*. London: Macmillan.

Lustgarten, Laurence, and Ian Leigh. 1996. *In from the Cold: National Security and Parliamentary Democracy*. New York: Oxford University Press.

Lyon, David. 2007. *Surveillance Studies: An Overview*. Cambridge, UK: Polity Press.

McBarnett, Doreen. 1979. "Arrest: the Legal Context of Policing." In *The British Police*, edited by Simon Holdaway, 24–40. London: Edward Arnold.

McMahon, Maeve. 1990. "Net-widening: Vagaries in the Use of a Concept." *British Journal of Criminology* 30(2): 121–49.

Manning, Peter. 1977. *Police Work*. Cambridge, MA: MIT Press.

Martens, Pam. 2012. "Wall Street's Secret Spy Centre, Run for 1%, by the NYPD." CounterPunch (February 6). http://www.counterpunch.org/2012/02/06/wall-streets-secret-spy-center-run-for-the-1-by-nypd.

Mill, John S. 1859. *On Liberty*. Oxford: Oxford University Press.

Monaghan, John, and Kevin Walby. 2011. "Making up 'Terror Identities': Security Intelligence and Canada's Integrated Threat Assessment Centre." *Policing and Society* 22(2): 133–51.

Mouffe, Chantal. 2005. *The Political*. London: Versa.

Neocleous, Mark. 2008. *Critique of Security*. Edinburgh, UK: Edinburgh University Press.

New York Civil Liberties Union. 2011. *Stop and Frisk Practices: NYCLU*. http://www.nyclu.org/files/publications/NYCLU_2011_Stop-and-Frisk_Report.pdf.

O'Donell, Graham. 1999. *Counterpoints: Selected Essays on Authoritarianism and Democratization*. South Bend, IN: University of Notre Dame Press.

O'Malley, Pat. 1999. "Volatile and Contradictory Punishments." *Theoretical Criminology* 3(2): 175–96.

Packer, Herbert. 1968. *The Limits of the Criminal Sanction*. Stanford, CA: Stanford University Press.

Posen, Ian. 1994. *Review of Police Core and Ancillary Tasks*. London: Home Office.

Pratt, John. 2007. *Penal Populism*. New York: Taylor and Francis.

Ratcliffe, Jerry, and Kyle Walden. 2010. "State Police and the Fusion Centre: A Study of Intelligence Flow to and from the Street." *IELEIA Journal* 19(1): 1–19.

Reiss, Albert, Jr. 1971. *The Police and the Public*. New Haven, CT: Yale University Press.

Robin, Marie-Monique. 2011. *The World According to Monsanto: Pollution, Politics and Power*. New York: Spinifex.

Rodgers, Dennis. 2006. "The State as a Gang: Conceptualizing the Governmentality of Violence in Contemporary Nicaragua." *Critique of Anthropology* 26(3): 315–30.

Rose, Nikolas. 1999. *Powers of Freedom: Reframing Political Thought*. Cambridge, UK: Cambridge University Press.

——. 2000. "Government and Control." *British Journal of Criminology* 40:321–39.

Rubinstein, Jonathan. 1973. *City Police*. New York: Farrar, Strauss and Giroux.

Schmitt, Carl. 1988. *Political Theology: Four Chapters on the Concept of Sovereignty*. Chicago: University of Chicago Press.

Shane, Scott 2011. "Judging a Long, Deadly Reach." New York Times (September 30). http://www.nytimes.com/2011/10/01/world/american-strike-on-american-target-revives-contentious-constitutional-issue.html.

Shearing, Clifford D., and Richard V. Ericson. 1991. "Culture as Figurative Action." *British Journal of Sociology* 42(4): 481–506.

Shearing, Clifford D., and Jennifer Wood. 2003. "Nodal Governance, Democracy, and the New 'Denizens.'" *Journal of the Law and Society* 30(3): 400–19.

Silver, Allan. 1967. "The Demand for Order in Civil Society: A Review of Some Themes in the History of Urban Crime, Police and Riot." In *The Police: Six Sociological Essays*, edited by David Bordua, 1–24. New York: Wiley.

Skolnick, Jerome. 1966. *Justice Without Trial*. New York: Wiley.

Smith, Bruce, 1960. *Police Systems in the United States*. New York: Harper.

Stuntz, William. 2006. "The Political Constitution of Criminal Justice." *Harvard Law Review* 119(3): 780–851.

Tilly, Charles. 1985. "War Making and State Making as Organized Crime." In *Bringing the State Back*, edited by Peter Evans, Dietrich Rueschemeyer, and Theda Skocpol, 169–186. Cambridge, UK: Cambridge University Press.

Turk, Austin. 1982. *Political Criminality: The Defiance and Defense of Authority*. Beverley Hills: Sage.

Wambaugh, Joseph. 1970. *The New Centurions*. Boston: Little, Brown and Company.

Warren, Dorian. Interviewed by Amy Goodman. *Democracy Now* (October 11). http://www.democracynow.org/appearances/dorian_warren.

Weisselberg, Charles. 2008. "Terror in the Courts: Beginning to Assess the Impact of Terrorism-Related Prosecutions on Domestic Criminal Law and Procedure in the USA." *Crime, Law, and Social Change* 50:25–46.

Weitzer, Ronald. 1995. *Policing Divided Societies: Ethnic Conflict and Police-Community Relations in Northern Ireland*. Albany: State University of New York Press.

Westley, William. 1970. *Violence and the Police: A Sociological Study of Law, Custom, and Morality*. Cambridge, MA: MIT Press.

Wilson, Christopher D. 2000. *Police Power and Cultural Narrative in Twentieth-Century America: Cop Knowledge*. Chicago: University of Chicago Press.

Wilson, James Q. 1968. *Varieties of Police Behavior: The Management of Law and Order in Eight Communities*. Cambridge, MA: Harvard University Press.

Wilson, Orlando Winfield. 1950. *Police Administration*. New York: McGraw Hill.

Zedner, Lucia. 2009. *Security*. London: Routledge.

CHAPTER 11

POLICE LEGITIMACY

JUSTICE TANKEBE

WHY do people obey the law? The question that relates to a central issue of social theory, namely the "problem of order." Indeed for scholars, it is "*the* fundamental question of all social science," a claim which "abounds in implications" (Rule 1988, 224). Arguably within criminology the claim rings even truer; whether concerned with the *causes* of crime or with social reactions to criminal behavior and the workings of criminal justice systems, criminologists are students of the "problem-of-order problematic" par excellence. The problem of order, as Dennis Wrong (1994, 36) argued, is "rooted in inescapable conflict between the interests and desires of individuals and the requirements of society; to wit, the pacification of violent strife among [humans] and the secure establishment of cooperative social relations making possible the pursuit of collective goals."

Wherever we find them, police forces have sought to reproduce order largely through the prism of deterrence. The deterrence model, articulated eminently in the work of Cesare Beccaria, operates on the idea that people are rational, calculative beings whose decisions to avoid criminal action is grounded in fear of detection and punishment from the criminal justice system. However, deterrence has not lived up to its promises; the evidence, especially for the *severity* of sanctions, is weak (Pratt et al. 2006 Nagin 2013). Perhaps more crucially, deterrence strategies neglect the longstanding recognition that human beings are "norm-users, whose interactions with each other depend on mutually recognizable patterns that can be articulated in terms of right versus wrong conduct, or of what one ought to do in a certain setting" (MacCormick 2007, 20). This observation has decisive consequences for police organizations because it suggests that while direct orders from the officers will likely be obeyed due to fear of punishment, information—part of the life-blood of effective policing—will be much more readily offered to police organizations whose authority has the moral assent of citizens (Bottoms and Tankebe 2012).

A major development in police research in the last two decades is the "discovery" of legitimacy after years of neglect. The volume of research on the subject since Tyler's seminal publication in 1990 has been enormous; undoubtedly, we are witnessing a *legitimacy turn* in criminology (Tankebe 2013). Although there is a rich body of studies from other criminal justice contexts such as prisons (Sparks, Bottoms, and Hay 1996; Liebling 2004; Reisig and Meško 2009), my primary focus in the present essay is on "police legitimacy." However, whether regarding prisons or policing, it is undoubtedly Tom Tyler's work that opened the way for the present stature of legitimacy within criminology. This essay probes key theoretical and empirical issues on police legitimacy. In his important work on the subject (see further below), Beetham (1991, 7) notes that "social scientists have in fact been thoroughly confused about legitimacy, and their confusion has its starting point in their failure to conceptualize it adequately, or to offer a coherent account of what makes power legitimate in particular societies." As the present essay will show, hardly any of us studying legitimacy can hope to defend ourselves against this charge with much success. Indeed, a key argument in this essay is that police researchers have so far not developed an adequate theoretical analysis of legitimacy, and have tended to conflate the concept with cognate concepts such as trust and obligation. I will therefore offer suggestions to correct measurement errors present in current studies of legitimacy in the hope that researchers will chart a different course devoid of those past errors.

The essay is structured into three main sections. Section 11.1 offers a conceptual analysis of police legitimacy. I will draw upon the work of political scientists and legal theorists such as David Beetham, Jean-Marc Coicaud, and David Dyzenhaus. The analysis draws attention to a distinction between two conceptions of legitimacy that are often easily confused, namely, *empirical* legitimacy (this is the social-scientific approach, concerned with analysis of legitimacy as constructed in each society) and *normative* legitimacy (this is the preoccupation of the moral philosopher, focused upon developing "objective" indicators against which legitimacy in different societies can be assessed). The work of David Beetham and Jean-Marc Coicaud is drawn upon to outline a view of police legitimacy focused upon legality and shared values. Section 11.2 reviews some of the current evidence on police legitimacy; I discuss in particular the way legitimacy is currently operationalized, and the determinants and consequences of legitimacy. Finally, in Section 11.3, I identify three areas for future research: scale development; measurement of legitimacy; and legitimacy as perceived by power-holders themselves—a dimension of legitimacy that remains undeveloped.

A number of main points emerge:

- Police legitimacy is multi-dimensional in character, comprising judgments about actual or perceived police procedural justice, distributive justice, legality, and effectiveness.
- Empirical studies of police legitimacy have operationalized the concept mainly with survey items that measure people's *feelings of obligation to obey the law or police directives*. This approach is problematic because while legitimacy and obligation are closely related, it can be argued that they are conceptually distinct. The latter is a much wider concept, to be explained, in part, by perceived police legitimacy.

- Police legitimacy (measured mainly as perceived obligation-to-obey) is shaped predominantly by assessments of procedural justice in police-public encounters. Legitimacy, in turn, has been consistently found to influence people's willingness to cooperate with the police, and to comply with the law.
- Public perceptions constitute only one dimension of legitimacy; equally important is what Bottoms and Tankebe (2012) call "power-holder legitimacy." This refers to the recognition on the part of power-holders (e.g., police officers) that they have a moral right to exercise power. Taking this aspect of legitimacy seriously necessarily means adopting a *dialogic* approach to approach to legitimacy, by which I mean a view of legitimacy as a continuous claim-response dialogue between power-holders and their audience(s).

11.1 The Concept of Legitimacy

There is a surfeit of definitions of legitimacy. The definition I find instructive contends that an institution is legitimate "if and only if it is morally justified in wielding political power, where to wield political power is to attempt to exercise a monopoly, within a jurisdiction, in the making, application, and enforcement of law" (Buchanan 2002, 689–90). It is instructive because when it is juxtaposed with Edwin Sutherland's (1939, 1) well-known definition of criminology as the study of *the process of law-making, law-breaking, and of reacting to the breaking of laws,* it would seem that the subject of legitimacy should constitute one of the central issues of criminology. Regrettably, this has not been the case; a cursory search of the website of *Criminology*—the discipline's leading and most prestigious journal—reveals that it was not until 2004 that one could find a paper with an explicit reference to police legitimacy. However, even that paper by Tyler and Wakslak did not engage conceptually with legitimacy. There have been subsequent publications in the journal with varying degrees of conceptual engagement with the subject (see Kane 2005; Tankebe 2009; Kirk and Matsuda 2011; Ariel 2012). Thus adequate theorization appears to have so far lagged behind empirical analysis. My aim in the present essay is to try to correct this lacuna, drawing on the rich literature in political science and political sociology.

It is appropriate at the outset to distinguish between two easily confused conceptions of legitimacy: "empirical" and "normative" (Hinsch 2010). The former concerns a judgment that as a matter of empirical fact, most citizens recognize a claim to legitimacy as valid within the society in question. A normative conception, on the other hand, relates to whether by some objective standards of ethical evaluation, a claim to legitimacy can be recognized as valid. This distinction corresponds respectively to the approaches of social scientists and moral philosophers to the subject of legitimacy. Unlike the moral philosopher, the concern of the social scientist has to do with legitimacy in particular historical societies rather than universally. Social scientists are fully aware that what makes power legitimate in one society may differ from, or be repudiated by, another (Beetham 1991). The empirical understanding does not require an external observer to make

any judgment about the appropriateness or otherwise of the social order she investigates (Hinsch 2010). A clear implication of this line of thought is that it is possible for
a researcher to conclude that a police organization is legitimate in the empirical sense
(i.e., it finds wide moral acceptance among citizens) and yet for that researcher to believe
that that organization is deeply unjust or even "evil" (Smith 2007; but see Bottoms and
Tankebe 2012). For my present purposes, I shall focus on the empirical conception.

Max Weber's (1978 [1922]) work on legitimacy continues to frame social-scientific
conception of legitimacy. As it is well known, Max Weber identified three pure types
of authority according to the principles on which claims to legitimacy are made. First
is *charismatic authority*, which rests on the exceptional or exemplary character of an
individual who makes claims to legitimate rule. The second is *traditional authority*,
which depends on the sanctity of customs and traditions for validation. Here, power
is legitimate if it can be demonstrated that it is acquired and exercised in a manner that
is consistent with longstanding customs and traditions of the society. Finally, there is
legal-rational authority, which is grounded in "a belief in the legality of the enacted rules
and the right of those elevated to authority under such rules to issue commands" (Weber
1978 [1922], 215). Weber asserts that in the modern State, legality is the dominant ground
for claims to legitimacy, an assertion that has led some to argue that Weber equates
legitimacy with "legality, with the proviso that the laws must in fact usually be obeyed"
(Lassman 2000, 88).

Criticisms of Weber's analysis are well-known (see Bensman 1979; Matheson 1987;
Coicaud 2002). For scholars who approach the question from the normative perspective
(see above), Max Weber's theory is "amoral" (Barker 1990, 25). Robert Grafstein (1981)
has summarized that critique of Weber's analysis thus:

> The most common complaint is that in his effort to construct a useful concept for
> empirical research, Weber distorts the essential meaning of legitimacy. The concept
> should properly signify a normative evaluation of a political regime: the correct-
> ness of its procedures, the justification for its decisions, and the fairness with which
> it treats its subjects. In Weber's hands, however, legitimacy no longer represents an
> evaluation of a regime; indeed, it no longer refers directly to the regime itself. Rather,
> it is defined as the *belief* of citizens that the regime is, to speak in circles, legitimate.
> Legitimacy becomes, for Weber, simply a matter of fact, the fact that citizens hold a
> certain belief. (456)

Social scientists who criticize Max Weber have focused on the conceptual adequacy
of his analysis of legitimacy. One of such criticisms comes from David Beetham.
I cited earlier Beetham's strong charge of confusion in the understanding of legitimacy among social scientists. For Beetham the source of that confusion is the dominance of Weber's analysis in social science: this, he maintains, is most evident in
Weber's definition of legitimacy as "the *belief in legitimacy* on the part of the relevant
social agents; and power relations as legitimate where those involved in them, subordinate as well as dominant, believe them to be so" (Beetham 1991, 6). Beetham argues

Table 11.1 Beetham's Three Dimensions of Legitimacy

Criteria of legitimacy	Corresponding form of non-legitimate power
Conformity to rules (legal validity)	Illegitimacy (breach of rules)
Justifiability of rules in terms of shared beliefs	Legitimacy deficit (discrepancy between rules and supporting shared beliefs, absence of shared beliefs)
Legitimation through expressed consent	Delegitimation (withdrawal of consent)

Source: Beetham 1991, 20.

that such an approach does not provide an accurate representation of the relationship between beliefs and legitimacy; far from a concern with delivering a score-card on the contours of people's beliefs, an enquiry into legitimacy is an attempt to establish the degree of congruity between a given system of power and the values that are the foundation of its justification (11).

Beetham advances a different conceptual scheme for the analysis of legitimacy, which he describes as "legitimacy-in-context"; it captures "an underlying structure of legitimacy common to all societies, however much its content will vary from one to the other" (Beetham 1991, 22). According to this scheme, power is legitimate if it meets three conditions: it must have *legality, shared values,* and *consent.* For Beetham, this scheme is not merely one among several possible types but rather the most fundamental to understanding legitimacy across all societies. In other words, and despite their obvious social-structural and cultural differences, societies as different from one another as Saudi Arabia, the United States, and Ghana nonetheless share the same underlying structure of legitimacy (Bottoms and Tankebe 2012). As shown in Table 11.1, each of these criteria has its corresponding negative conditions. For the purposes of this essay, I want to focus on the legality and shared-values dimensions, because they are the "two fundamental concepts [which] figure prominently and persistently in the history of the problem of political legitimacy" (Claude 1966, 368; see also Buchanan [2002] for the case against the inclusion of consent as a condition for legitimacy).

11.1.1 Legality

Beetham (1991, 16) describes legality as "the first and most basic level of legitimacy." It is concerned with the question of whether or not power has been acquired and exercised in accordance with established rules in a given society. These rules may be unwritten or they may take the form of formalized legal codes. In liberal democracies, discussions of legality's legitimating role relates particularly to the notion of the "rule of law," described by Tamanaha (2001, 98) as "the dominant legitimating slogan of law at the close of the twentieth century" (see also Dyzenhaus 2007). At the heart of the rule of law are principles of due process and equality, with equality being secured through the generality of the law (Allan 2001; Tamanaha 2004). The law must also be applied pro-spectively, thereby allowing those subject to power to know in advance when they will be subject to coercion and thus avoiding needless interference in their lives (Tamanaha 2004; Bingham 2010). Beetham's legality condition therefore implies that powers which permit police officers to stop and search citizens, to intercept conversations, to shoot-to-kill suspects under specified circumstances, or to interrogate suspects in the absence of defense lawyers are powers that should be consistent with pre-existing law.

The same is true of *how* those powers are exercised. In contemporary liberal democ-racies, the powers of police officers, for example, are to be exercised in a manner that is "unbiased, free of passion, prejudice, and arbitrariness, loyal to the law alone" (Tamanaha 2004, 123). Officers are expected to follow due process by respecting the legal rights of citizens, which include treating all parties in a case fairly and providing them with opportunities to make a representation of their own side of the case before decisions are made (Allan 1998; Tamanaha 2004; Bingham 2010). Thus, some aspects of Tyler's procedural fairness model appear to be embraced within this condition of Beetham's argument; I am referring, in particular, to Tyler's concept of "quality of decision-making" which emphasizes the importance of impartiality, participation, and consistency in people's assessments of procedural justice in democratic societies (see further below). Although the evidence from police studies shows that there is often, for reasons that are beyond the scope of this essay, a gap between the requirements of official law and police behavior on the beat (see Crank 1998; Herbert 1998, 2006), the implica-tions of Beetham's analysis is that citizens' perceptions of police *legality* are an important component of their judgments about the legitimacy of the police. However, law always operates in a social context, so it must always be considered in relation to community values—a subject which brings me to the other condition of legitimate power, namely, the need to justify the law within a society's shared values and beliefs.

11.1.2 Shared Values

In Weber's analysis of legitimacy in the modern State, decisions made in conformity with pre-existing legal procedure suffice to establish legitimacy, without there being a need to base these decisions on particular substantive values (Kronman 1983; Coicaud 2002). But, as Beetham points out, rules cannot justify themselves simply by being rules; they have to be justified in terms of the prevailing beliefs and values in the society in question. When such a common framework of belief is lacking, as in the case of colonial rule (see Tankebe 2008), "the powerful can enjoy no moral authority for the exercise of their power, whatever its legal validity; and their requirements cannot be normatively binding, though they may be successfully enforced" (Beetham 1991, 69). By Beetham's analysis, shared values perform various functions in the legitimation process. For example, they can be a reference point for interpreting existing law and for assessing the validity of that law (see also Honoré 2002; Cane 2012). More fundamentally, shared beliefs and values specify and institutionalize the rightful source of power and define the qualities appropriate to the assumption and exercise of that power. A defining feature of shared values is that they express the identity of society, and part of the condition of legitimate power is that those who lay claim to it act in ways that protect and promote that identity (Coicaud 2002). Understood in this way, conformity with the law bestows legitimacy only to the extent that the law is an expression of recognized and accepted values—recognized and accepted both by those in power and those subject to it (Beetham 1991; Coicaud 2002).

One of the "extraordinary" developments in the moral history of humankind is what James Q. Wilson calls the "rise of universalism"; that is, the idea that all human beings are of equal worth and therefore entitled to equal respect and treatment (Wilson 1993). For the greater part of human history, there was "no suggestion that the rights or condition of the weak should be equal or comparable to that of others of greater status in their society" (Johnston 2011, 17). Just how the transformation developed is beyond the scope of this essay. The point I want to make here is that modern democratic societies are characterized by this universalistic ideology of human equality (Fukuyama 1992; Dunn 2005; Wolterstorff 2008). In these societies, each citizen is deemed to have the same equal dignity and should therefore not be the subject of discrimination on account of social class, gender, race, or sexual orientation. This, of course, is not to say that all citizens receive the same recognition in their everyday encounters with criminal justice institutions. There is evidence to suggest, for instance, racial discrimination by criminal justice agencies against racial minorities and the poor (Bowling 2000; Unnever and Gabbidon 2011).

Three main aspects of shared values can be extrapolated from Beetham's analysis (Bottoms and Tankebe 2012). First is *distributive justice*, which relates to how a police organization allocates its resources among groups or individuals with competing claims or needs (Roemer 1996). Lerner and Clayton (2011) have differentiated between two types of resources: *concrete* and *symbolic* resources. Concrete resources are easily observable and quantifiable, while symbolic resources are not. In the context of criminal justice, concrete resources may include court fines, tickets for traffic offenses, and police personnel, while symbolic resources include respect, courtesy, and dignity. Lerner and Clayton argue that distributive justice involves the acquisition and distribution of both sets of resources (2011, 98). Thus, an investigation into police distributive justice seeks to understand how fairly police allocate these resources across different social groups (as between rich/poor, different ethnic groups, or male/female). Take, for example, the distribution of police personnel to patrol and enforce the law. There is evidence to show that, for reasons beyond this essay, the allocation of police officers to patrol duties and to investigate reported victimization is often skewed to the disadvantage of ethnic minorities and vulnerable groups (Anderson 1999; Bowling 2000). Natapoff (2006, 1746) as "underenforcement" which, as she argues, can take the form not only of "overt intentional hostility" and "indifference." Such an uneven distribution of police resources, whether real or perceived, can be injurious to the universalistic values that are supposed to be the foundation of policing in a liberal democracy.

The second aspect of shared values is *procedural justice*, which focuses on symbolic resources (Lerner and Clayton 2011). Procedural justice is perhaps the most researched topic in the literature on police legitimacy. Using data from a panel study of citizens in Chicago, Tyler (1990) found that people are often more concerned about such symbolic resources as respect, dignity, and recognition during their everyday encounters with the police and the courts. In later work, Tyler and Blader (2000) identified two main dimensions of procedural justice: "quality of decision-making" (which relates to judgments of about police honesty, provision of opportunities for representation, opportunities for error correction, and whether or not legal authorities have behaved impartially); and "quality of decision-making" (which concerns whether or not police have treated people with respect, dignity, and courtesy). Tyler argues that although these issues may seem superficial and inconsequential, they communicate to citizens information about their standing and membership in society. In short, ordinary everyday encounters between police and citizens (or even sighting of the police by citizens) can be read as a "socializing experience" or "teachable moment," which may build or undermine people's views about the legitimacy of the police (Tyler 2011, 257).

The third aspect of shared values Bottoms and Tankebe (2012) discuss is *performance or effectiveness*. It is not enough to act in accordance with the law and to ensure distributive and procedural justice during encounters with citizens; police organizations have to demonstrate, in addition, a capacity to obtain effective results. On first blush it may seem hard to discuss effectiveness within this context since—in contradistinction to legitimacy—it is often argued that effectiveness is an entirely utilitarian consideration. This approach is common in the current literature on police legitimacy, which tends to examine empirically the relative influence of legitimacy and effectiveness upon compliance and cooperation (e.g., Sunshine and Tyler 2003; Tankebe 2009). However, there is a crucial difference between, on the one hand, the use of incentives to encourage cooperation and obedience and, on the other hand, the claim that part of what it means for legal authorities to establish power that is both normatively justified and justifiable is for them to be seen to serve the best interests of society. The first consideration is purely instrumental but the second one entails the recognition that citizens have interests which merit consideration, so effective performance satisfies a normative criterion (Beetham 1991). Understood in this way, when citizens demand that the police demonstrate effectiveness in tackling crime and disorder in their local areas, it means that they are not simply making crude instrumental demands; on the contrary, they are entreating the police to fulfill a normative condition for their legitimacy. (Bottoms and Tankebe 2012).

11.1.3 Conclusion

This brief theoretical analysis shows that two key questions are at the heart of any analysis of whether power is more or less legitimate: *Is power valid in terms of the law? Is the law justifiable in terms of the beliefs and values established in the society?* The first question is not unknown in the police literature; there is a strong body of work on legality or lawfulness in police work, which sees "the legitimacy of police activity [as] closely tied to police compliance with legal standards" (Skogan and Frydl 2003, 253).

However, substantial evidence from work on police subculture has shown that law alone is inadequate to establish police legitimacy. The reason is that there is often a gap between the dictates of official law and what officers actually do on the beat (Skolnick 1966; Dixon 1997; Herbert 1998). Even if such a gap does not exist, "it is very much an open question how much of the official law is any part of the working consciousness of laypersons... [and] to what extent their sense of what is right and proper depends on, and how far it diverges from, what the official law enjoins either in the sense of abstract texts or in the mediated form filtered through professional and official practice" (MacCormick 2007, 71).

Thus, discussions of police legitimacy have to move beyond—but emphatically not jettison—lawfulness. Additionally, the laws to which police conformity is required must themselves be grounded in the prevailing common beliefs and values in society. According to this view, public assessments of police legitimacy hinge on the perception that police work on activities are lawful and that the law governing police work is itself in accord with recognized values in the society. As I have noted, shared values in liberal democratic societies entail, upon closer examination, distributive justice, procedural justice, and effectiveness in the maintenance of social order. Thus, the logical conclusion from the analysis presented here is that police legitimacy is a multi-dimensional concept constituted by police procedural fairness, distributive fairness, effectiveness, and lawfulness. This conclusion has important implications for the way police legitimacy is operationalized in the extant literature. As discussed in Section 11.2 below, the main feature of measurement of police legitimacy in that literature is *feelings of obligation to obey the law or police directives*. Yet legitimacy and obligation are conceptually distinct, and therefore to conflate them is to obstruct the quest to understand both concepts (Bottoms and Tankebe 2012).

11.2 THE RESULTS OF POLICE LEGITIMACY RESEARCH

During that period, a fairly strong body of evidence has accrued based particularly, but not exclusively, on survey data. This section of the essay will seek to summarize the results from that general body of evidence, focusing in particular on three issues: the first concerns how legitimacy is operationalized in empirical analyses. Second, what kinds of considerations underpin people's judgments about police legitimacy? Third, what are the consequences of legitimacy judgments for people's behavior? It is important to note that what I attempt here is a brief narrative review of some of the key studies rather than a comprehensive systematic review of all the evidence. For such a grander objective, a meta-analysis will be required (see, e. g., Mazerolle et al 2013).

11.2.1 Measuring Police Legitimacy

It was Gouldner (1964, 17) who observed that "measurement, it would seem, first requires some degree of clarity about what is to be measured." The importance of conceptual clarity lies in its capacity to help recognize and avoid problems of measurement validity. Measurement validity is concerned with whether a construct "meaningfully [captures] the ideas contained in the corresponding concept" (Adcock and Collier 2001, 530). When one examines the way legitimacy is operationalized in light of the meaning of the concept as outlined above, it becomes evident that there are important questions about the measurement validity. I will examine the issue briefly here.

In Tyler's original work, two principal subscales were employed to measure legitimacy, namely: *perceived obligation to obey the law* and *expressed allegiance or support for legal authorities* (Tyler 1990, 45). Three subsequent pieces of analysis followed this approach to legitimacy. First, Tyler and Huo (2002, xiv) saw legitimacy as "the belief that legal authorities are entitled to be obeyed and that the individual ought to defer to their judgments." Secondly, in their New York study, Sunshine and Tyler (2003, 524) saw legitimacy as "connected with people's internal sense of obligation to authority." Finally, in a conceptual overview, Tyler (2006, 390) argued that legitimacy is a "perceived obligation to societal authorities or to existing social arrangements." Thus, feelings of obligation feature prominently in the literature on police legitimacy. Indeed, for Tyler (2003, 310), obligation is "the most direct extension of the concept of legitimacy." It is consequently the main feature of measurement of police legitimacy (e.g., Tyler and Huo 2002, 109; Sunshine and Tyler 2003, 539–40; Reisig, Bratton, and Gertz 2007, 1014; Tyler, Schulhofer, and Huq 2010, 389; Reisig and Lloyd 2009, 51).

However, expressions of obligation to obey the directives of legal authorities cannot necessarily be equated with legitimacy. Theoretically, obligation is a much wider concept than legitimacy. Tankebe (2013) contends that the simplest way to convey the distinction between the two concepts is to ask what answers we might obtain to a question such as, "Why should you obey the directives of the police?" Some respondents will certainly reply that they consider the police to be legitimate; that is, they recognize as valid the police claim to exercise power. But others might say they are afraid of the costs of non-obedience, feel powerless, or consider it to be in their self-interest to obey the police. From this, obligation can be seen as a "dependent variable," sometimes explained by perceived legitimacy, rather than as a component of legitimacy (Tankebe 2013). "If something is a precondition for another thing, both things cannot be the same" (Kaina 2008, 515). To affirm the contrary is to confuse the effect with the cause.

One of the earliest criticisms against the use of obligation as a measure of legitimacy was that one could not tell whether the obligation so expressed was normative or the result of powerlessness (Tankebe 2009). Some researchers have recognized this difficulty and sought to overcome it by emphasizing the idea of "duty." Thus Jackson and his colleagues, in their innovative attempt to develop indicators of legitimacy across selected European countries, asked respondents whether they thought they had a "duty to do what the police tell [them] to do, even if [they] don't like how they treat [them]" (Jackson et al. 2010). As Bottoms and Tankebe (2012) argue, however, inability of Jackson and his colleagues to elaborate on the term "duty" means that respondents could reasonably regard "duty" as a legal duty, or a moral duty, or a mixture of the two; yet still, some might treat it as being neither. Thus it remains for legitimacy researchers to seek to disentangle the varied motives that might underpin people's feelings of obligation to obey criminal justice agencies. However, even when it is established that such feelings of obligation are normative, it still cannot be equated with legitimacy for the reasons advanced above.

11.2.2 Determinants of Police Legitimacy

The starting point for this brief review of the evidence on the determinants of legitimacy is undoubtedly Tyler's (1990) *Why People Obey the Law*. The study, conducted in Chicago, sought to uncover people's views of the police and courts, and to explore their levels of compliance with law. The data came from two waves of telephone interviews. The first wave of data was based on interviews with 1,575 people, of whom 652 reported prior experiences with the police or courts. The second data came from interviews with 804 respondents randomly sampled from the first wave. The second wave was particularly important because it allowed Tyler to control for prior experiences and evaluations of the police. Perceived legitimacy was measured in two ways: 1) "perceived obligation to obey the law" (e.g., "a person should obey the law even if it goes against what they think is right"), and 2) "support for legal authorities" ("I have a great deal of respect for the Chicago police") (Tyler 1990, 45–48).

The results from Tyler's analysis showed that evaluations of legitimacy of police officers and judges were contingent on contact or experience with those legal authorities. Further analysis showed that it was the fairness of the procedures employed to deal with citizens' problems that underpinned the effects of experience on legitimacy. The main elements constituting the basis of procedural justice assessments included: "the authorities' motivation, honesty, bias, and ethicality; their opportunity for representation; the quality of decisions; and the opportunity for correcting errors" (Tyler 1990, 137; see also Paternoster et al. 1997). Tyler argued that the ability of procedural justice to mediate the relationship between experience and legitimacy means that "fairness can act as a cushion of support when authorities are delivering unfavorable outcomes. If unfavorable outcomes are delivered through procedures viewed as fair, the unfavorable outcomes do not harm the legitimacy of legal authorities" (Tyler 1990, 107).

Why People Obey the Law was the dawn of an explosion in police legitimacy research in a variety of contexts. For example, about a decade later Tyler and his colleague Jason Sunshine collected survey data from a random sample of registered voters to examine the determinants of public perceptions of police legitimacy before and after the terrorist attacks on the World Trade Center in 2001 (Sunshine and Tyler 2003). The authors found that judgments of police legitimacy were contingent principally on perceived procedural justice, and to a lesser extent on distributive justice and police perfor-mance. Further, they found that legitimacy influenced people's compliance with the law as well as their willingness to cooperate with the police. Procedural justice had an indirect impact on cooperation and compliance, while perceived police performance directly shaped cooperation but not compliance. Sunshine and Tyler's second study was conducted during the summer of 2002 and therefore very much within the context of heightened security. In spite of the security concerns, procedural justice emerged as the most powerful predictor of legitimacy; distributive justice and police performance also shaped legitimacy judgments but to a lesser extent. A recent quasi-experimental study in Israel confirms Sunshine and Tyler's post-9/11 findings. Jonathan-Zamir and Weisburd (2013) investigated the relative effects of police performance and procedural justice in people's assessments of police legitimacy under situations of "acute security threats" and of "no threat." The authors found that although emphasis on police perfor-mance naturally increased in the area suffering security threats, procedural justice was the primary determinant of police legitimacy.

Michael Reisig and his colleagues conducted one of the most methodologically sophisticated tests of the process-based model (Reisig, Bratton, and Gertz 2007). Using data from a nationwide telephone survey of 432 adult residents in the United States, the authors examined the construct validity of the key substantive variables employed in legitimacy research, namely, "legitimacy," "procedural justice," and "distributive justice." Here, the authors found that as much as 30 percent of the items routinely used to con-struct those scales "failed to load on the hypothesized latent construct" (1023), leading them to revise the original scales. Their second aim was then turned to the more tradi-tional focus of examining the key determinants of legitimacy. Many interesting findings emerged here. For instance, the authors found that both procedural justice and distribu-tive justice were key drivers of perceived police legitimacy, regardless of whether one used the original or revised scales; consistent with Sunshine and Tyler's findings, proce-dural justice emerged as the more powerful driver of legitimacy. What they also found, however, was that the effects of procedural justice on legitimacy were larger with the revised scales.

In his preface to Tom Tyler's (2007) edited volume on *Legitimacy and Criminal Justice*, Tonry (2007) argued that scholarly work on procedural justice and legitimacy had thus far been "distinctively American," a situation he attributed to "the United States' distinc-tive constitutional scheme premised on notions of limited powers of government and entrenched rights of citizens" (Tonry 2007, 3–4). He further contended that "it would be an exaggeration to refer even to nascent literature in other English-speaking countries" (4). It is however no exaggeration because there was indeed such research already under-way in Australia, where Hinds and Murphy (2007) attempted to test the Tylerian model. Measuring legitimacy with a mixture of items on "confidence" and "obligation to obey the police," the authors employed survey data from a sample of 2,611 residents to test the procedural justice arguments in Australia. Consistent with the American studies, they found that procedural justice was the main determinant of perceived police legitimacy; distributive justice and performance also exhibited statistically significant influence on legitimacy, with the latter showing a larger impact than the former. Subsequent studies in Australia have replicated those findings. For example, using survey data from 1,204 respondents, Murphy and Cherney (2011) found that procedural justice was more important than effectiveness in shaping judgments of legitimacy. Distributive justice was, however, found to be unrelated to police legitimacy. In Jamaica, Reisig and Lloyd (2009) found that procedural justice predicted legitimacy among students, but distributive justice did not. In Slovenia, Reisig, Tankebe, and Meško (2012) report that procedural justice and effectiveness shaped judgments about police legitimacy.

Race or ethnicity is one of the most researched topics in studies of general public assessments of criminal justice systems (Hagan and Albonetti 1982; Brown and Benedict 2002; Weitzer and Tuch 2006; Bradford 2011; Kautt and Tankebe 2011). Tonry (2007, 6) argues that if it is indeed "true" that "even-handedness, impartiality, respectfulness, and a chance to say one's piece are predicates of greater legitimacy [then] it would be astonishing if perceptions of police legitimacy held by some minority groups were not lower than those of majority populations." What does the evidence tell us about the relative perceptions of minority and majority ethnic groups? In her study of ethnic differences in drivers' experiences of procedural and distributive justice during traffic stops, Engel (2005, 470) found that in comparison with white citizens, African Americans were on average twice more inclined to view police stops as illegitimate and that the "police acted improperly" during those stops. In New York, Sunshine and Tyler (2003) found that white respondents evaluated police legitimacy more positively than African Americans did; however, there was no discernible difference between whites and Hispanics. Other studies have reported no differences in perceptions of legitimacy by different ethnic groups (Reisig, Bratton, Gertz 2007; Murphy and Cherney 2011). Murphy and Cherney's (2012, 10) recent results from Australia affirm those findings. They report mean scores of 3.21 for minorities and 3.26 for non-minorities. Indeed, given that items measuring procedural justice were on a scale of one to five, the results would seem to suggest both groups were rather ambivalent about police procedural justice.

11.2.3 Consequences of Legitimacy

Legitimacy, as Beetham (1991) argues, provides moral grounds for cooperation and compliance on the part of those subject to power. In this section, I want to do two things: first, examine the evidence on the effects, on public behavior, of the dimensions of legitimacy that emerged from the theoretical analysis presented in Section 11.1. Second, I review the influence of legitimacy as measured by obligation and/or trust.

On the first objective, a number of previous studies have examined in one form or another the influence of procedural justice, distributive justice, effectiveness, and lawfulness on public behavior. Tyler, Schulhofer, and Huq (2010) found in their study among Muslims in New York that assessments of procedural fairness determined the willingness to cooperate with the police by alerting them about terrorism activities in local areas. Using survey data from the United States, Reisig and his colleagues (2007) found that distributive justice was correlated with cooperation with the police. In Tyler's (1990) original study, distributive justice was found to be directly related to compliance with the law, a finding Tyler described as "most striking" but did not discuss it. In all, many studies tend to either not to examine the influence of distributive fairness upon cooperation or, when they do, find it to be unrelated to cooperation (e.g., Sunshine and Tyler 2003; Reisig and Lloyd 2009; Tankebe 2009; Murphy and Cherney 2011). A similar sporadic treatment of effectiveness is found in the literature. But in Ghana, Tankebe (2009) found that perceived police effectiveness was the main factor that determined cooperation. In a recent analysis of data from a survey of young people in London, Bradford (2012) found that effectiveness and procedural fairness were both correlates of cooperation with the police. In their New York study, Sunshine and Tyler (2003) found that effectiveness was associated with cooperation in the first wave of data collected before the September 11 terror attacks; however, the second wave of data did not replicate that finding. Another study in the same city found results similar to Sunshine and Tyler's post-9/11 findings (Tyler and Fagan 2008). Analyzing survey data from Australia, Murphy and Cherney (2012) found that perceived "legitimacy of law" (i.e., police lawfulness) shaped people's willingness to cooperate with the police.

The preceding studies have all been correlational, and therefore do not deal with causation. To tackle the question of causation will require data from experimental studies. This is what Paternoster and his colleagues allow us to do (Paternoster et al. 1997). The authors re-analyzed data from the Minneapolis Domestic Violence Experiments to test the effects of procedural justice. What they did was to compare the rates of recidivism among people who had been arrested for spousal assault and those who received warnings from the police. The results showed that an arrest increases significantly the risk of recidivism. However, when arrestees rated the way they had been treated to be procedurally just, their rates of recidivism returned to the levels of the "warned-only group." Within the arrest group, the authors found substantial difference between those who reported high perceived procedural justice and those who reported low procedural justice. A further interesting finding from the analysis was that "the suppression effect observed for perceived procedural justice decayed for individuals who were detained for longer periods [on average 11 hours]" (Paternoster et al. 1997, 187). The authors offer two possible explanations for this finding on procedural justice decay. First, the procedurally just treatment the suspects received at the point of arrest might not have been maintained throughout subsequent stages of their interactions with the authorities. Secondly, procedural justice effects might be more pronounced among people who receive more favorable outcomes. Müller and Kals's (2007) study of the interaction effects of procedural justice and outcome favorability on conflict resolution would seem to confirm the second line of reasoning. They discovered that even when people knew that their outcomes would be favorable, they were still extremely "sensitive to procedural fairness information" (Müller and Kals 2007, 136). Müller and Kals found that the establishment of procedural justice reduced entrenched positions in conflict resolution when people expected unfavorable outcomes.

The second set of evidence I want to examine is on the association between legitimacy (measured variously as obligation, obligation and trust, or trust and confidence), and compliance and cooperation. One of the widely-cited studies here is Sunshine and Tyler's (2003) study in New York. The results from the pre-9/11 data showed that legitimacy was the most powerful predictor of compliance with the law and citizens' willingness to cooperate with the police to fight crime in their communities. Perceived police performance predicted cooperation but not compliance, while perceived risk of sanctions (proxy of deterrence effects) influenced compliance but not cooperation. The legitimacy effects remained unchanged in the second wave of data collected in the post-9/11 survey. However the influence of performance and deterrence diminished. A decade later, Tyler, Schulhofer, and Huq (2010) returned to New York and found that among American Muslims, legitimacy was associated with general cooperation with the police and willingness to alert police about terrorist activities in local communities.

In their study in the United States, Reisig, Bratton, and Gertz (2007) disaggregated the two common subscales of legitimacy—*trust* and *obligation*—and examined their relative impact on public behavior. They found that the former predicted both compliance with the law and cooperation with the police, but "obligation to obey had no meaningful influence" (1024). The authors concluded with the suggestion, quite rightly, for researchers to report the effects not of an overall legitimacy index but also of subscales in order to reduce the risk of erroneously inferring that the "subscales featured in the legitimacy index (e.g., obligation to obey) behave as expected" (1024). Ultimately, this study marked a huge advancement on the methodological front. Reisig, Tankebe, and Meško (2012) followed this methodological lead in their study in Slovenia. The results from their analysis were consistent with those reported by Reisig, Bratton, and Gertz (2007); trust predicted cooperation with police, but obligation did not. The Slovenian study measured cooperation using five items: willingness to *report stolen wallet, volunteer information about stolen wallet, report bribery of a government official, report house or car break-in*, and *volunteer as a witness in criminal court case*. The authors examined the impact of legitimacy on each these components of cooperation and found that legitimacy explained only the willingness to volunteer information about the stolen wallet and to report house or car break-ins. These results are interesting in the sense that they imply caution against the commonplace conclusion that legitimacy procures cooperation, without differentiating between cooperative behaviors. The Slovenian data suggest that where the concern of a police organization is to encourage people to assist with information in tackling corruption, legitimacy might not be such an effective tool.

The Slovenian study is the latest in a burgeoning corpus of studies that explores the consequences of legitimacy in post-colonial settings. In their study in Australia, Murphy and Cherney (2012) found that police legitimacy (measured with a combination of items on trust and confidence) predicted cooperation with police (see also Murphy and Cherney 2011). This was found to be invariant across different ethnic groups. Operationalizing police legitimacy as felt obligation to obey the police, Reisig and Lloyd (2009) examined the legitimacy-cooperation nexus using data from students in Jamaica. The authors reported a widespread perception of police legitimacy among the students (mean score of 4.23 on a scale of 1 to 5). However, when legitimacy was regressed on cooperation, they found no support for the legitimacy–cooperation association. This is consistent with what Tankebe (2009) found in his city-wide survey in Ghana. He found that legitimacy (measured as felt obligation to obey the police) did not explain cooperation with the police; what appeared important in Ghana was perceived police effectiveness in fighting crime.

11.3 AREAS FOR FUTURE RESEARCH

Since Tyler published Why People Obey the Law, research on police legitimacy has grown exponentially. The weight of the evidence from the brief review undertaken in this essay suggests that procedural justice is central to people's constructions of police legitimacy. It further demonstrates that overall compliance with the law as well as the willingness to cooperate with the police depend largely on legitimacy. Thus cooperative behavior "cannot be sufficiently created by incentives and sanctions on their own; it depends on the normative status of the power holder, and on normative considerations that engage us as moral agents" (Beetham 1991, 38). Yet, there are many areas that await carefully empirical analysis. I want to focus on three key areas that future empirical studies should prioritize, and which I believe will move the field forward.

The first relates to how police legitimacy is operationalized. As I noted earlier, to date, studies of police legitimacy tended to equate legitimacy with perceived obligation to obey the law or police directives. Police effectiveness, procedural justice, distributive justice, and lawfulness are then employed to explain legitimacy. This approach, I have argued, is problematic because obligation and legitimacy are distinct, and that what has hitherto been considered predictors of legitimacy are, upon careful theoretical consideration, components of legitimacy. In other words, legitimacy does not exist apart from effectiveness, procedural justice, distributive justice, and lawfulness. Yet, the findings suggest that questions about legitimacy's influence on public behavior should therefore focus on the following: which of the components or dimensions of legitimacy are more or less important in explaining cooperation and compliance? What effects (if any) do these dimensions have on different areas of public regulations across different social groups? Are some dimensions more influential in certain settings among certain social groups than others, and why? In *Causes of Delinquency*, Hirschi (1969, 26) argued that people differed in their propensity to offend because "there is *variation* in the extent to which people believe they should obey the rules of society, and, furthermore, that the less a person believes he should obey the rules, the more likely he is to violate them." Given my argument in this essay that felt obligation to obey the law is a dependent variable to be explained, in part, by legitimacy, there is the question of whether or not the association between the components of legitimacy and behavior is direct, or mediated by differential feelings of obligation. How do each of these elements of legitimacy (or composite measure of legitimacy) compare with other grounds for compliance, for example, habit, deterrence, and powerlessness? These are just a few questions that await empirical analysis.

The second area in need of careful investigation has to do with scale development. I started my theoretical analysis with a distinction between *empirical* and *normative* legitimacy, both of which imply different research strategies. The normative approach to legitimacy sets itself the task of discovering the "objective" conditions against which the legitimacy of criminal justice practices across different societies can be assessed. The implication for scale development is that the researcher can determine a priori what legitimacy means to citizens; she then proceeds to formulate a set of items that she thinks reflects the concept, and then goes to the field to administer questionnaires to a random sample of citizens who are encouraged to express agreement or disagreement with those items. The responses are then analyzed to establish, through a series of statistical tests, whether indeed those items measure police legitimacy so "normatively" defined. In other words, I am describing the present approach to scale construction in legitimacy research. Because this approach is more consistent with the normative approach to legitimacy, it is very much an open question what congruence there is between the researchers and her respondents in their understanding of legitimacy.

I think a way out of this situation for the police researcher is a more social-scientific approach, involving two stages. The first is to conduct focus group discussions and in-depth interviews to try to discover what constitutes legitimacy to the people in the particular society under investigation. What does legitimacy mean to them? What to them makes police power morally valid? What sort of issues come to their minds when they think about whether or not the police have the right to exercise power? What can a police organization do to improve its moral standing among them? Answers to these questions are interesting for their own sake, and can illuminate our understanding of legitimacy in different socio-cultural contexts. Yet, they can also form the basis for the second stage of scale development: that is, to develop scale items from the data collected, which can then be tested among a larger sample. This grounded approach to legitimacy has already been used by some prison researchers (see Liebling 2004) and has produced fascinating results. It would be a challenging method, but fresh experimentation might lead to huge advances in how police legitimacy is understood and researched in different contexts.

Finally, police researchers have so far tended to focus almost exclusively on what Bottoms and Tankebe (2012) call "audience legitimacy," that is, the recognition by citizens of police right to exercise power. This emphasis is undoubtedly of momentous importance since, as Jürgen Habermas argues, "the efficacy of law is contingent upon the support of the populace, and any form of legitimation must appeal to 'a posttraditional moral consciousness of citizens who are no longer disposed to follow commands, except for good reasons'" (cited in Tamanaha 1999, 1002). Yet, such emphasis overlooks the police's own need to believe that their individual positions as officers are morally justified. Bottoms and Tankebe (2012) describe this aspect of legitimacy as "power-holder legitimacy." It is important to note that Tyler and Blader (2000) and

Tyler and his colleagues (Tyler, Callahan, and Frost 2007) have studied judgments that employees (e.g., law enforcement officers) make about the legitimacy of their organizations. Tyler, Callahan, and Frost (2007), for instance, found that perceptions of organizational legitimacy influence rule adherence among military and law enforcement personnel. Neither of these studies, however, covers the key issue in power-holder legitimacy, namely the degree of self-belief that those employees have in the moral rightness of their own individual claims to exercise power (Bottom and Tankebe 2013). In other words, power-holder legitimacy is concerned with officers' perceptions of their own individual legitimacy, and not that of the organization although both may be related.

Empirically, very little is known about perceptions of their own legitimacy by low-level power-holders in criminal justice agencies. Tankebe's (2007) study of 181 officers in Ghana is an exception. The study used survey data from frontline officers in Accra to examine the conditions that shape the officers' confidence in their own legitimacy. The evidence from this study showed that the nature of social relations among officers at the same rank, as well as between those at different ranks, was related to the officers' levels of confidence in their own legitimacy. For example, those with the least belief in their own legitimacy were officers with longer service who reported strained relationships with colleagues, and who perceived themselves to have been treated unfairly by senior officers.

There is a clear need for more studies to try to understand this dimension of legitimacy. A number of questions await empirical scrutiny: to what extent are officers with differential levels of confidence in their own legitimacy able to nourish or undermine a department's audience legitimacy? As Boulding (1967, 299) has argued, "a person who has confidence in himself tends to create confidence in others. Self-hatred, on the other hand, tends to produce hatred on the part of others." What is the relationship (if any) between power-holder legitimacy and organizational legitimacy? Do officers who view their organizations as more legitimate more likely to view their own positions as legitimate, or vice versa? There is already evidence to show that power-holder legitimacy is associated with greater organizational commitment among frontline officers (Tankebe 2010). Might power-holder legitimacy help to explain differences among officers in the quality of the interactions they have with citizens? Margaret Archer (2003, 139) has argued that "people with different identities will evaluate the same situations quite differently and their responses will vary accordingly." If that is correct, it would seem to suggest that a study of the magnitude of power-holder legitimacy can help to account for differences in the quality of encounters that they have with citizens. Indeed we should expect differences in power-holder legitimacy to shape how officers perceive, evaluate, and respond to situations, such as a decision to use (lethal) force or not. Thus, Bottoms and Tankebe (2012, 163) argue that "properly developed, power-holder legitimacy should result in a *critical self-awareness* by the police of the importance of the ways in which they view themselves, and use power." Investigating this empirically would require data from systematic social observations (Mastrofski et al. 1998) and interviews of the kind Rydberg and Terrill (2010) employed in their study of the effects of educational attainment on police behavior.

REFERENCES

Adcock, Robert, and David Collier. 2001. "Measurement Validity: A Shared Standard for Qualitative and Quantitative Research." *American Political Science Review* 95(3): 529–46.

Allan, Trevor. 1998. "Procedural Fairness and the Duty of Respect." *Oxford Journal of Legal Studies* 18:497–515.

———. 2001. *Constitutional Justice: A Liberal Theory of the Rule of Law*. Oxford: Oxford University Press.

Anderson, Elijah. 1999. *Code of the Street: Decency, Violence, and the Moral Life of the Inner City*. New York: William W. Norton.

Archer, Margaret. 2003. *Structure, Agency and Internal Conversation*. Cambridge: Cambridge University Press.

Ariel, Barak. 2012. "Deterrence and Moral Persuasion Effects on Corporate Tax Compliance: Findings from a Randomized Trail." *Criminology* 50(1): 27–69.

Barker, Rodney. 1990. *Political Legitimacy and the State*. Oxford: Clarendon Press.

Beetham, David. 1991. *The Legitimation of Power*. London: Macmillan.

Bensman, Joseph. 1979. "Max Weber's Concept of Legitimacy: An Evaluation." In *Conflict and Control: Challenge to Legitimacy of Modern Governments*, edited by Arthur. J. Vidich and Ronald. M. Glassman, 17–48. Beverly Hills, CA: Sage.

Bingham, Tom. 2010. *The Rule of Law*. London: Allen Lane.

Bottoms, Anthony E., and Justice Tankebe. 2012. "Beyond Procedural Justice: A Dialogic Approach to Legitimacy in Criminal Justice." *Journal of Criminal Law and Criminology* 102(1): 119–70.

Bottoms, Anthony E., and Justice Tankebe. 2013. "Voice Within: Power-Holders' Perspectives on Authority and Legitimacy. In Legitimacy and Criminal Justice: An International Exploration, edited by Justice Tankebe and Alison Liebling, 60–82. Oxford: Oxford University Press.

Boulding, Kenneth. 1967. "The Legitimacy of Economics." *Western Economic Journal* 5(4): 299–307.

Bowling, Ben. 2000. *Violent Racism: Victimization, Policing and Social Context*. Oxford: Oxford University Press.

Bradford, Ben. 2011. "Convergence, Not Divergence? Trends and Trajectories in Public Contact and Confidence." *British Journal of Criminology* 51:179–200.

———. 2012. "Policing and Social Identity: Procedural Justice, Inclusion, and Cooperation between Police and Public." Oxford Legal Studies Research Paper No. 06/2012. Available at SSRN: http://ssrn.com/abstract=1994350.

Brown, Ben, and William R. Benedict. 2002. "Perceptions of the Police: Past Findings, Methodological Issues, Conceptual Issues and Policy Implications." *Policing: An International Journal of Police Strategies and Management* 25(3): 543–80.

Buchanan, Allan. 2002 "Political Legitimacy and Democracy." *Ethics* 112:689–719.

Cane, Peter. 2012. "Morality, Law And Conflicting Reasons For Action." *Cambridge Law Journal* 71:59–85.

Claude, Inis. 1966. "Collective Legitimization as a Political Function of the United Nations." *International Organization* 20:367–79.

Coicaud, Jean-Marc. 2002. *Legitimacy and Politics: A Contribution to the Study of Political Right and Political Responsibility*. Cambridge: Cambridge University Press.

Crank, John. 1998. *Understanding Police Culture*. Cincinnati: Anderson.

Dixon, David. 1997. *Law in Policing: Legal Regulation and Police Practices*. Oxford: Clarendon Press.

Dunn, John. 2005. *Setting the People Free*. London: Atlantic Books

Dyzenhaus, David. 2007. "The Rule of Law as the Rule of Liberal Principle." In *Ronald Dworkin*, edited by Arthur Ripstein, 56–81. Cambridge: Cambridge University Press.

Engel, Robin. 2005. "Citizens' Perceptions of Distributive and Procedural Injustice during Traffic Stops with Police." *Journal of Research in Crime and Delinquency* 42:445–81.

Fukuyama, Francis. 1992. *The End of History and the Last Man*. New York: Avon Books.

Gouldner, Alvin. 1964. *Patterns of Industrial Bureaucracy*. New York: Free Press.

Grafstein, Robert. 1981. "The Failure of Weber's Conception of Legitimacy: Its Causes and Implications." *Journal of Politics* 43:456–72.

Hagan, John, and Celesta Albonetti. 1982. "Race, Class and the Perception of Criminal Injustice in America." *American Journal of Sociology* 88:329–55.

Herbert, Steve. 1998. "Police Subculture Reconsidered." *Criminology* 36:343–70.

——. 2006. "Tangled Up in Blue: Conflicting Paths to Police Legitimacy." *Theoretical Criminology* 10:481–504.

Hinds, Lynn, and Katrina Murphy. 2007. "Public Satisfaction with Police: Using Procedural Justice to Improve Police Legitimacy." *Australian and New Zealand Journal of Criminology* 40(1): 27–43.

Hinsch, Wilfried. 2010. "Justice, Legitimacy, and Constitutional Rights." *Critical Review of International Social and Political Philosophy* 13(1): 39–54.

Hirschi, Travis. 1969. *Causes of Delinquency*. Berkeley: University of California Press.

Honoré, Tony. 2002. "The Necessary Connection between Law and Morality." *Oxford Journal of Legal Studies* 22(3): 489–95.

Jackson, Jon, Ben Bradford, Mike Hough, Jouni Kuha, Sally Stares, Sally Widdop, Rory Fitzgerald, Maria Yordanova, and Todor Galev. 2010. "Trust in Justice: Notes on the Development of European Social Indicators." Available at SSRN: http://ssrn.com/abstract=1717924.

Johnston, David. 2011. *A Brief History of Justice*. Oxford: Wiley-Blackwell.

Jonathan-Zamir, Tal, and David Weisburd. 2013. "The Effects of Security Threats on Antecedents of Police Legitimacy: Findings from a Quasi-Experiment in Israel." *Journal of Research in Crime and Delinquency* 50(1):5–32.

Kaina, Viktoria. 2008. "Legitimacy, Trust and Procedural Fairness: Remarks on Marcia Grimes' Study." *European Journal of Political Research* 45:510–21.

Kane, Robert J. 2005. "Compromised Police Legitimacy as a Predictor of Violent Crime in Structurally Disadvantaged Communities." *Criminology* 43:469–98.

Kautt, Paula, and Justice Tankebe. 2011. "Confidence in the Criminal Justice System in England and Wales: A Test of Ethic Effects." *International Criminal Justice Review* 21:93–117.

Kirk, David S., and Mauri Matsuda. 2011. "Legal Cynicism, Collective Efficacy, and the Ecology of Arrest." *Criminology* 49:443–72.

Kronman, Anthony. 1983. *Max Weber*. London: Edward Arnold Publishers.

Lassman, Peter. 2000. "The Rule of Man over Man: Politics, Power and Legitimation." In *Cambridge Companion to Weber*, edited by Stephen Turner, 81–98. Cambridge: Cambridge University Press.

Lerner, Melvin J., and Susan Clayton. 2011. *Justice and Self-Interest*. Cambridge: Cambridge University Press.

Liebling, Alison. 2004. *Prisons and Their Moral Performance: A Study of Values, Quality, and Prison Life*. Oxford: Oxford University Press.

MacCormick, Neil. 2007. *Institutions of Law*. Oxford: Oxford University Press.

Mastrofski, Stephen. D., Roger B. Parks., Albert J. Reiss Jr., Robert E. Worden., Christina DeJong., Jeffrey B. Snipes., and William Terrill. 1998. *Systematic Observation of Public Police: Applying Field Research Methods to Policy Issues*. Washington, DC: National Institute of Justice.

Matheson, Craig. 1987. "Weber and the Classification of Forms of Legitimacy." *British Journal of Sociology* 38:199–215.

Mazerolk, Lorraine, Sarah Bennett, Jacqueline Davis, Elise Sargeant, and Matthew Manning. 2013. "Procedural Justice and Policy Legitimacy: A Systematic Review of Research." *Journal of Experimental Criminology* 9(3):245–274.

Müller, Markus M., and Elisabeth Kals. 2007. "Interactions between Procedural Fairness and Outcome Favorability in Conflict Situations." In *Distributive and Procedural Justice*, edited by Kjell Törnblom and Riel Vermunt, 125–140. Aldershot: Ashgate.

Murphy, Katrina, and Adrian Cherney. 2011. "Fostering Cooperation with the Police: How do Ethnic Minorities in Australia Respond to Procedural Justice-based Policing?" *Australian and New Zealand Journal of Criminology* 44:235–57.

——. 2012. "Understanding Cooperation with Police in a Diverse Society." *British Journal of Criminology* 52:181–201.

Nagin, Daniel S. 2013. "Deterrence in the 21st Century: A Review of Evidence," In Crime and Justice: An Annual Review of Research, edited by Michael Tonry. Chicago: University of Chicago Press.

Natapoff, Alexandra. 2006. "Underenforcement." *Fordham Law Review* 75:1715–76.

Paternoster, Raymond, Robert Brame, Ronet Bachman, and Lawrence Sherman. 1997. "Do Fair Procedures Matter? The Effects of Procedural Justice on Spousal Assault." *Law and Society Review* 31:163–204.

Pratt, Travis C., Francis T. Cullen, Kristie Blevins, Leah Daigle, and Tamara Madensen. 2006. "The Empirical Status of Deterrence Theory: A Meta-Analysis." In *Taking Stock: The Empirical Status of Criminological Theory—Advances in Criminological Theory*. Vol. 15, 367–395. New Brunswick, NJ: Transaction.

Reisig, Michael D., Jason Bratton, and Marc Gertz. 2007. "The Construct Validity and Refinement of Process-based Policing Measure." *Criminal Justice and Behavior* 34:1005–27.

Reisig, Michael D., and Camille Lloyd. 2009. "Procedural Justice, Police Legitimacy, and Helping the Police Fight Crime: Results from a Survey of Jamaican Adolescents." *Police Quarterly* 12:42–62.

Reisig, Michael D., and Gorazd Meško. 2009. "Procedural Justice, Legitimacy and Prisoner Misconduct." *Psychology, Crime and Law* 15(1): 41–59.

Reisig, Michael D., Justice Tankebe, and Gorazd Meško. 2012. "Procedural Justice, Police Legitimacy, and Public Cooperation with the Police among Young Slovene Adults." *Journal of Criminology and Security* 14(2): 147–169.

Roemer, John. E. 1996. *Theories of Distributive Justice*. Cambridge, MA: Harvard University Press.

Rule, James. 1988. *Theories of Civil Violence*. Berkeley: University of California Press.

Rydberg, Jason, and William Terrill. 2010. "The Effect of Higher Education on Police Behavior." *Police Quarterly* 13(1): 92–120.

Skogan, Wesley G., and Kathleen Frydl. 2003. *Fairness and Effectiveness in Policing: The Evidence*. Washington, DC: National Academy Press.

Skolnick, Jerome H. 1966. *Justice Without Trial: Law Enforcement in a Democratic Society*. New York: John Wiley.

Smith, David. 2007. "The Foundations of Legitimacy." In *Legitimacy and Criminal Justice*, edited by Tom Tyler, 30–58. New York: Russell Sage Foundation.

Sparks, Richard, Anthony E. Bottoms, and Will Hay. 1996. *Prisons and the Problem of Order*. Oxford: Clarendon Press.

Sunshine, Jason, and Tom R. Tyler. 2003. "The Role of Procedural Justice and Legitimacy in Shaping Public Support for Policing." *Law and Society Review* 37(3): 513–548.

Sutherland, Edwin. 1939. *Principles of Criminology*. Philadelphia: J.B. Lippincott.

Tamanaha, Brian Z. 1999. "The View of Habermas From Below: Doubts about the Centrality of Law and the Legitimation of Enterprise." *Denver University Law Review* 76:989–1008.

——. 2001. *A General Jurisprudence of Law and Society*. Oxford: Oxford University Press.

——. 2004. *On the Rule of Law*. Cambridge: Cambridge University Press.

Tankebe, Justice. 2007. "Policing and Legitimacy in a Post-Colonial Democracy: A Theoretical and Empirical Study of Ghana." PhD dissertation, University of Cambridge.

——. 2008. "Police Effectiveness and Police Trustworthiness in Ghana: An Empirical Appraisal." *Criminology and Criminal Justice* 8:185–202.

——. 2009. "Public Cooperation with the Police in Ghana: Does Procedural Fairness Matter?" *Criminology* 47(4): 701–30.

——. 2010. "Identifying the Correlates of Police Organizational Commitment in Ghana." *Police Quarterly* 13:73–91.

——. 2013. "Viewing things Differently: Examining the Dimensions of Public Perceptions of Legitimacy." *Criminology* 51(1): 103–135.

Tonry, Michael. 2007. "Preface: Legitimacy and Criminal Justice." In *Legitimacy and Criminal Justice*, edited by Tom Tyler, 3–8. New York: Russell Sage Foundation.

Tyler, Tom R. 1990. *Why People Obey the Law*. New Haven, CT: Yale University Press.

——. 2003. "Procedural Justice, Legitimacy, and the Effective Rule of Law." In *Crime and Justice: Review of Research*, edited by Michael Tonry, 283–357. Chicago: University of Chicago Press.

——. 2006. "Psychological Perspectives on Legitimacy and Legitimation." *Annual Review of Psychology* 57:375–400.

——. 2011. "Trust and Legitimacy: Policing in the USA and Europe." *European Journal of Criminology* 8:254–66.

Tyler, Tom R., and Steven L. Blader. 2000. *Co-operation in Groups: Procedural Justice, Social Identity, and Behavioral Engagement*. Philadelphia: Psychology Press.

Tyler, Tom R., Patrick. E. Callahan, and Jeffrey Frost. 2007. "Armed, and Dangerous(?): Can Self-Regulatory Approaches Shape Rule Adherence among Agents of Social Control." *Law and Society Review* 41(2): 457–92.

Tyler, Tom R., and Jeffrey Fagan. 2008. "Legitimacy and Cooperation: Why Do People Help the Police Fight Crime in their Communities?" *Ohio State Journal of Criminology* 6:231–75.

Tyler, Tom R., and Yuen J. Huo. 2002. *Trust in the Law*. New York: Russell Sage Foundation.

Tyler, Tom R., Stephen Schulhofer, Aziz Z. Huq. 2010. "Legitimacy and Deterrence Effects in Counterterrorism Policing: A Study of Muslim Americans." *Law and Society Review* 44(2): 365–402.

Tyler, Tom R., and Cheryl Wakslak. 2004. "Profiling and Police Legitimacy: Procedural Justice, Attributions of Motive, and Acceptance of Police Authority." *Criminology* 42:253–81.

Unnever, James D., and Shaun L. Gabbidon. 2011. *A Theory of African American Offending: Race, Racism, and Crime*. London: Routledge.

Weber, Max. 1978 [1922]. *Economy and Society: An Outline of Interpretive Sociology*, edited by Guenther Roth and Claus Wittich. Berkeley: University of California Press.

Weitzer, Ronald, and Steven Tuch. 2006. *Race and Policing in America: Conflict and Reform*. Cambridge: Cambridge University Press.

Wilson, James Q. 1993. *The Moral Sense*. New York: Free Press.

Wolterstorff, Nicholas. 2008. *Justice: Rights and Wrongs*. Princeton, NJ: Princeton University Press.

Wrong, Dennis. H. 1994. *The Problem of Order: What Unites and Divides Society*. New York: Free Press.

CHAPTER **12**

··

POLICE COERCION

··

WILLIAM TERRILL

IT is an almost inevitable chain of events in the life of a policing scholar. A young researcher writes and submits an article for publication review and then patiently (or not so patiently) waits for the editor's decision along with feedback from reviewers. Found within the reviews will be at least one comment referring to a "lack of theory." One such review pulled from the author's own archive simply states, "I think the most important limitation of this piece of research is its failure to integrate and/or utilize theory." To an inexperienced scholar, such a critique may set in motion what will ultimately become a frustrating search that will eventually lead to more questions than answers. What are the "theories" of police behavior? Surely these theories must exist since reviewers keep referring to them (although at the same time curiously failing to identify any by name). Adding to the angst is the fact that most police scholars are at least marginally acquainted with criminological theories and the relative ease of identifying them. But what about theories of policing? Perhaps they can be discovered in the works that focus more on criminal justice as opposed to criminology, but this search also proves futile. Eventually, the question becomes not *what are* the theories of police behavior, but rather *are there* theories of police behavior. In a word, no!

This is not to say that all readers may agree with such a dismissive statement. Perhaps many at this point are already thinking about scholarly legends such as Bittner (1974, 1991), Black (1976), Brown (1981), Manning (1977) Muir (1977), Skolnick (1966), Van Maanen (1974), Westley (1970), and Wilson (1968), among others, and their conceptual contributions to thinking about, and understanding, how police officers think and act. However, the key word here is conceptual. Clearly there have been any number of scholars who have provided conceptual guidance in the form of a theoretical "framework" or "perspective" (a cop out to say the least—pun intended), but are any of these really full-scale theories per se? No. At least not in a more traditionally defined manner if we borrow from our criminological brethren. For instance, a number of years ago Don Gottfredson (1989) wrote an intriguing piece titled "Criminological Theories: The Truth as Told by Mark Twain." In his offhanded manner he explicitly noted the characteristics of an adequate theory (14–15):

1. The basic metasystem, including the theory of knowledge adopted by the theorist, should be clear. This portion of theory construction should include explicit statements of the postulates that form the starting point for the development of the theory.
2. The type of theoretical constructs to be included in the theory should be explained and justified in relation to their empirical meanings.
3. The derivation of hypotheses from the assumptions should be demonstrated to have been done according to accepted rules of logic.
4. Operational definitions of terms used in the hypotheses should be provided, the construct validity of resulting variables should be justified, and evidence of reliabilities should be offered.
5. The empirical evidence bearing on the hypotheses should be presented. Limits to generalizability, both on the basis of definitional concepts of measured variables and on the basis of such considerations as samples observed should be explained.
6. The theory should be reexamined in light of the evidence and revised if necessary.

If we look closely at the policing literature as a collective whole we would be hard pressed to uncover many, if any, theories meeting these parameters.[1] What we do find are a hodgepodge of descriptions, observations, postulates, hypotheses, constructs, and varying pieces of empirical evidence that at times suggest a semblance of a theory but rarely, if ever, specify an adequate theory. What has emerged is a framework from which police scholars generally draw on for theoretical guidance. This framework has a very distinct template and primarily cuts across several levels of analysis, where varying correlates of police behavior are subsumed within legal, sociological, psychological, organizational, and community based explanations. This fact was first highlighted by Sherman (1980), and later by Riksheim and Chermak (1993, 377), who after reviewing previous studies on police behavior regarding the decision to use force, arrest, detect criminal activities, and engage in service behaviors, concluded, "[c]learly, theoretical development [of police behavior] is lagging far behind the quantitative attempts to estimate the relationships between variables."

So where does this leave us if we restrict our attention to one type of police behavior—the use of coercion? The simple answer is pretty much the same. All too often the fall-back position is to rely on one or more of the legal, sociological, psychological, organizational, or community based explanations—what Worden (1995, 32) cleverly called "explanatory rubrics."[2] Yet, as succinctly stated by Sherman (1980, 70) more than thirty years ago, and still true today, "[n]one of these approaches constitutes a substantive theory of police behavior." Imagine a criminological researcher who has no theoretical guidance beyond broad levels of abstraction. For instance, no social disorganization, no strain, no differential association, nor life course theories from which to draw. For the most part, such is the state for a police use of force researcher unless s/he is willing to make a series of conceptual leaps, or rely on partially defined and loosely linked posited relationships interspersed with scattered pieces of empirical outcomes. At best, scholars (as the author himself has done, see Terrill 2005) attempt to fit their data to a specific theory out of desperation.

This essay examines police use of force issues across a variety of contexts, from definitional issues, to frequency of use, to why officers use coercive tactics, to the impact of force usage on society. Section 12.1 explores the numerous ways police coercion has been conceptualized and defined. While defining lethal force has been a relatively straightforward endeavor, there is less clarity when it comes to defining different types of less lethal force and attaching meaning to varying forms of inappropriate force. The most contemporary debate revolves around defining and understanding everyday types of force ranging from nonphysical actions such as commands and threats, to physical hands on and weapons use. Section 12.2 then considers what we know about the frequency with which police officers use different forms of force. A multitude of methodological approaches combined with the varying types of force identified in Section 12.1 demonstrate how widely force rates vary.

Sections 12.3 and 12.4 serve as the central focus of the essay and assess the varying reasons officers use coercion, but in a manner that neither adheres to the traditional rubrics nor one that pretends there are neatly packaged theories within which to place such behavior. While the works of many influential scholars are discussed (e.g., Bittner, Muir, Van Maanen, Skolnick) in terms of why the police use coercion, their contributions are organized in a format ranging from the legitimate to the not so legitimate, from the perspective of internal influences to that of external influences, and from the easily understandable to the more convoluted. Along the way, the goal is to illuminate the complexity of force decision making and come out the other side with a greater appreciation for why adequate theories of police behavior in general, and coercion in particular, are so elusive. Finally, Section 12.5 concludes with a brief summary regarding the impact that force has on both the public and the police.

Some key points identified throughout the essay:

- Understanding the application of police use force is anything but a parsimonious process, one that involves a mixture of complex factors.
- While police researchers and practitioners have struggled to universally define police coercion, there is growing consensus that forceful acts include not only physical behavior, but also verbal threats and warnings.
- The conventional wisdom that police officers rarely use force is challenged, and must be placed within the context of how force is defined and measured.
- Historical attempts to foster theoretical development of police coercion are primarily rooted in loosely-coupled posited relationships with great intuitive appeal, but minimal systematic empirical support.

- Contemporary scholars interested in theory building and testing should account for prior work, but not to the detriment of failing to think beyond such conceptualizations.
- Future theoretical contributions should consider an underlying feature of nearly all coercive tactics in nearly any form—the element of control, which may manifest in a variety of formats ranging from legally based legitimate reasons to unlawfully based illegitimate reasons, with an enormous and often confounding gray area in between.

12.1 DEFINING COERCION (OR IS IT FORCE?)

As astute students of policing already know, one definitional struggle at the outset involves the potential interchangeability of the terms coercion and force. Is coercion the same as force? While one could make a plausible argument for distinguishing these terms, most scholars treat them as similar. With this in hand, an entire chapter on the varying ways in which coercion has been described by various researchers over the years could be written. Interestingly, more often than not researchers have failed to offer an explicit definition when studying force decision making. Rather, they simply identify types of acts or behaviors considered force. For example, in one study Alpert and Dunham (2004, 45) state, "[f]orce was defined as the use of physical force, chemical agent, or a weapon to control a suspect." Similarly, some researchers (Garner, Maxwell, and Heraux 2002; MacDonald et al. 2003; Alpert, Dunham, and MacDonald 2004; Kaminski, Digiovanni, and Downs 2004; Bazley, Lersch, and Mieczkowski 2007) simply provide a list of force types or tactics as part of an implicit definition (e.g., handcuffs, firm grips, pressure point controls, weapons, etc.). Nonetheless, there is a body of research where coercion is defined more explicitly:

"a means of controlling the conduct of others through threats to harm" (Muir 1977, 37).
"acts that threaten or inflict physical harm on citizens, including forms of both verbal and physical force" (Terrill 2005, 115).
"any act or behavior that compelled a person into submission" (Williams and Westall 2003, 471).
"the application of physical strength for coercive purposes" (Klockars 1995, 12).

As these conceptualizations illustrate, there is no one central or universal definition of force.[3] Much of the disagreement that emerges involves whether nonphysical acts, such as verbal commands and threats, are deemed coercive.[4] Muir (1977), Terrill (2005), and Williams and Westall (2003) all clearly advocate in this direction, while Klockars (1995) does not. Klockars (1995, 12) goes so far as to argue that force "does *not* include verbal or non verbal threats, pleadings, warnings, or commands, all of which are a wholly different order of sociological means of domination and control" (italic emphasis original).

Herein contains one of the key difficulties surrounding a conceptual definition, not to mention an operational one. Researchers have tended to blur various acts with various reasons for engaging in such acts, whether it is to control, to harm, to maintain safety, or any other number of reasons. This issue will be further explored in Section 12.3, so suffice it to note at this stage that a broader more inclusive definition of coercion is becoming more widely accepted. As properly stated by Garner and colleagues (1995, 152), "threats, attempts, and actual physical force, does a good job of capturing what the research literature on police use of force typically means by force."[5]

This then takes us to the issue of distinguishing among different forms of force. One of the primary distinctions made is between lethal and less lethal force. According to Model Penal Code § 3.11(2), deadly force is "force which the actor uses with the purpose of causing or which he knows to create a substantial risk of causing death or serious bodily harm" (Black 1979, 580). Skolnick and Fyfe (1993, 40) simply define lethal force as "force capable of killing or likely to kill." This primarily includes the use of firearms but can also include police vehicles, some neck control holds (e.g., carotid control hold and bar arm control hold), as well as some weapons designed to be less lethal. Conversely, nondeadly force is any type of force that is not designed to cause, or likely to result in, death. Such force would include varying types of hands-on tactics (e.g., firm grips, pressure point techniques, takedown maneuvers, empty hand strikes), as well as numerous weapon-based tactics (e.g., Oleoresin Capsicum spray, baton, beanbag, conducted energy devices) (Terrill 2001).

Another distinction centers on what constitutes appropriate versus inappropriate force, whether in the form of lethal or less lethal force. As argued elsewhere (see Terrill and Mastrofski 2002), inappropriate force has taken on a number of labels such as: excessive use of force, use of excessive force, brutality, unauthorized force, wrongful force, unjustified force, misuse of force, and unnecessary force. While these phrases are interchangeable to some, others note fine distinctions. For example, use of excessive force can be defined as more force than needed to gain compliance in any given incident, while excessive use of force may be defined as using force in too many incidents (Adams 1995). Fyfe (1997) makes the distinction between brutality (a willful and knowingly wrongful use of force) and unnecessary force (force used by well-meaning officers who are ill-equipped to handle various incidents). Worden (1995) also distinguishes between different types of force. He defines excessive force as that which is more than required to subdue a citizen, and unnecessary force as that which precedes a citizen's resistance or continues after citizen resistance has ceased.

Yet Klockars (1995) believes emphasizing inappropriate force in any of these ways is simply an inadequate approach to the issue in general. He argues that most police agencies gauge officer use of force using minimum standards. That is, the criterion for the legitimate use of force is that which is not a criminal violation, prevents any civil liability, and is of a nature that will not bring embarrassment to the department. These standards are necessary, but are they sufficient? He states, "[we] would not find the behavior of a physician, lawyer, engineer, teacher, or any other professional acceptable merely because it was not criminal, civilly liable, or scandalous and it is preposterous that we continue to do so for police" and calls for broadening the focus of excessive force to include "the use of any more force than a highly skilled police officer would find necessary to use in [a] particular situation" (17–18).

Even dating back to Bittner (1991), there has been an awareness that the skill of policing lies in ways to avoid using force. This seems to be the most popular perspective. In fact, it is a virtually uncontested theoretical perspective toward the application of coercion. The notion is that the best officers are those who use less, not more force (i.e., a good officer is one who can handle a situation by not having to rely on force—a necessary evil, but one that should be avoided if at all possible). However, is less force always the most desirable choice? What if the police did not show up to a dispute between two parties and order them to separate for the night? Would such an incident eventually be resolved with more or less force? An argument can be made that by investing the police with the authority to apply force, and to go and issue such a command as in this example, despite the use of some coercion being applied, the ultimate outcome may actually be less, rather than more force. In this case, the officer only issues a verbal command or threat. It may be that failure for the police to show up at all, or to use no form of coercion, may have led to the two citizens resolving the conflict on their own. If that were the case, what is the probability that it could have been resolved verbally as opposed to physically? Would a verbal command or threat from one of the disputing parties carry the same weight as the officer's command? Or, would it have come down to a physical altercation? Thus, while on the face of it, less force on the part of the police is generally perceived to be the most desirable, this may result in more violence on the part of private citizens.

12.2   HOW OFTEN DO THE POLICE USE FORCE?

The police rarely rely on forceful tactics. This seems to be the conventional wisdom by many of those who study police use of force (Reiss 1971; Croft 1985; Adams 1995; Worden 1995; Langan et al. 2001; Terrill 2003). In fact, a report issued by the National Institute of Justice (1999, vii) went so far as to state what is "[k]nown with substantial confidence is that police use force infrequently." But a closer look shows a much more muddied picture. First, the definitional issues discussed in Section 12.1 play a large role in determining the frequency in which the police use force. Second, the data collection strategy employed (e.g., observational, use of force reports, surveys) can have a substantial impact. These two issues intertwined result in substantial variation in force usage, and not all pointing in the direction of force being an "infrequent" event in all instances or across all contexts.[6]

Studies relying on official data, such as arrest reports or use of force reports, most frequently apply a more exclusive definition, to only include physical forms of force *beyond* simple restraint (e.g., excluding firm grips and handcuffing). For example, Croft and Austin's (1987) analysis of two years of arrest data from Rochester and Syracuse showed that such force was used in 5 percent of arrests in Rochester and 4 percent of arrests in Syracuse. Around this same time, using force reports from custody arrests over a 12-month period in St. Paul, Lundstrom and Mullan (1987) found that force was used in 14 percent of the cases. A few years later, McLaughlin (1992) looked at use of force reports filed by Savannah police officers, finding that physical force, beyond handcuffing, was used only 1 percent of the time in arrest cases. Garner and colleagues (1995, 2002) examined force using official data in two different studies. They first looked at arrests over a two-week period in Phoenix and found that officers used some form of physical force in 22 percent of the cases (Garner et al. 1995). A more recent study examined use of force behavior across six jurisdictions (Charlotte, Colorado Springs, Dallas, St. Petersburg, San Diego city, San Diego sheriff) and showed that officers used physical force in 17 percent of the arrests (Garner, Maxwell, and Heraux 2002).

The most comprehensive look at police use of force to date (e.g., reporting mechanisms, officer perceptions of force, degree of force usage, injuries, complaints, lawsuits) using official records comes from the recently completed *Assessing Police Use of Force Policy and Outcomes* project conducted in eight cities (Albuquerque, Charlotte-Mecklenburg, Colorado Springs, Columbus, Fort Wayne, Knoxville, Portland, and St. Petersburg). Terrill, Paoline, and Ingram (2012) examined not only how often force was used in relation to arrest, but also two additional workload factors: calls for service and reported crimes. What they found was enormous variation in force usage from one city to another and from one workload comparison to another. For example, Columbus officers used force (above simple restraint) over five times more frequently than Colorado Springs officers when making arrests (one of every 2.3 arrests compared to one of every 12.0 arrests); Portland officers used force seven times more frequently than Colorado Springs officers when responding to calls for service (one of every 102 calls for service compared to one of every 729 calls for service); and, Fort Wayne officers used force over seven times more frequently than Charlotte-Mecklenburg officers when considering Part I Index crimes (one of every 12 Part I Index crimes compared to one of every 87 Part I Index crimes).

Unlike studies based on official data, observational studies have generally examined force usage compared to all observed police suspect encounters. Within this context, data gathered in the 1960s (Crime and Law Enforcement Study) and 1970s (Police Services Study) showed that officers resorted to some type of physical force (beyond handcuffing) in roughly 3 percent (Friedrich 1980) and 2 percent (Worden 1995) of the observed police suspect encounters, respectively. The former study involved the Boston, Chicago, and Washington, DC police departments, while the latter consisted of 24 departments in three surrounding metropolitan areas (Rochester, St. Louis, and Tampa). In the 1980s, data collected by Bayley and Garofalo (1989) in New York City showed that officers used some form of physical force in about 8 percent of their encounters with suspects, a slight increase in force behavior. A decade later, Klinger's (1995) analysis of data collected from the Miami-Dade study (1995) showed an even higher percentage of physical force (17 percent). However, when verbal commands were included, the percentage increased to 39 percent.

Using Project on Policing Neighborhoods (POPN) data, Terrill (2003) went on to further highlight how force usage can vary based on definitional changes. Using the most inclusive definition of force (verbal and physical), he found that officers relied on force in over half the observed police-suspect encounters (i.e., 58 percent). When commands and threats were excluded, the percentage dropped to 21 percent. When commands and threats, as well as handcuffing, were excluded the percentage dropped to 15 percent. When commands and threats, handcuffing, and pat downs were excluded (similar to a measure used in many of the studies relying on official records), the figure dropped to 4.7 percent.

Of course, the rates of force identified above do not take into consideration citizen views regarding how often the police use force, as few studies rely on such a methodology. However, Eith and Durose (2011), drawing on data gathered as part of the Police-Public Contact Survey (PPCS) conducted by the Bureau of Justice Statistics (BJS), found that 1.9 percent of persons who had contact with the police in the previous 12 months reported that they had been subjected to force or the threat of force. Such a percentage would seem to validate the opening statement made in this section—that the police rarely rely on forceful tactics. However, to confound the issue yet again, Eith and Durose (2011) extrapolate this percentage to include the raw number of persons affected by the 1.9 percent, which accounts for roughly 776,000 persons who have experienced force or the threat of force within a single year.

12.3 CAUSES OF COERCION: WHY DO THE POLICE USE FORCE?

In asking why the police use force, it is tempting to simply state: because they can. Unlike the common citizenry, the police posses a legal mandate to use coercive tactics. The primary legal stipulation attached to this right is that force must be administered in an "objectively reasonable" manner (*Graham v. Connor*, 490 U.S. 386 [1989]). However, applying this standard still requires some degree of subjective interpretation. Hence, those charged with determining whether force was properly applied in any given incident (i.e., officers themselves, police supervisors, judges, community, juries) must at some point interject a measure of subjectivity. Someone ultimately must apply the "facts and circumstances," and removing subjective decision making from the process is a near impossible task. Relatedly, given that the legal standard calls for officers to use nothing other than reasonable force, any requirement that the *least* amount of force be used is essentially removed. In this respect, appropriateness from a lawful perspective (i.e., within the realm of being objectively reasonable), and the use of "good force" do not always equate. There are certainly uses of force that are essentially "lawfully awful." Thus, the police are given wide latitude in their application of force, which ultimately makes the task of answering "why do the police use force" a difficult proposition.

To help guide the discussion, it is helpful to consider an underlying feature of nearly all coercive tactics in nearly any form (physical and nonphysical, serious and nonserious, good and bad, right and wrong, etc.): the element of control. The police ultimately use coercion as a means of controlling someone. I would further posit that the reasons for such control (i.e., the why) may be loosely arranged along a three-tiered continuum, with legally legitimate reasons at one end, unlawful illegitimate reasons at the other end, and then a rather enormous and often confounding gray area in between.

12.3.1 The Legitimate

It is almost impossible to discuss police use of force and not mention Egon Bittner's influential writings on the topic. One of his most famous quotes, "something-that-ought-not-to-be-happening-and-about-which-someone-had-better-do-something-now" (1974, 30), identifies why the public calls on the police. Of course, the obvious implication is that the police have the power to legally use coercive means to do something if so needed. A second, and perhaps even more famous statement is that "the role of the police is best understood as a mechanism for the distribution of non-negotiable coercive force employed in accordance with the dictates of an intuitive grasp of situational exigencies" (1991, 48). The implication here is that officers on the street decide whether force is needed, and how much of it, depending on given circumstances.[7] There is a substantial amount of research that supports the notion that force usage is situationally determined, and most studies illustrate that such variables (e.g., suspect demeanor, antagonistic or aggressive behavior, intoxication, etc.) are the strongest predictors of forceful action, while other factors (e.g., organizational, individual officer-based, etc.) have traditionally explained less variance (see Terrill 2001 for a review).

Bittner (1991, 43) goes on to note that "the frequently heard talk about the lawful use of force by the police is practically meaningless and, because no one knows what is meant by it, so is the talk about the use of minimum force." While it may be sacrilegious for a fellow force scholar to argue against Bittner, I could not disagree more. Discussing lawful use of force could not be any more *meaningful*, even if it is difficult to define as previously illustrated. This is not to say that Bittner's point is not well taken (i.e., the police most assuredly determine how force is characterized as being necessary in most situational contexts), but a failure to explicitly recognize that a portion (a good portion) of the coercive tactics used by the police is wholly necessary and legal does a disservice to the occupation as a whole. For example, the most consistent predictor of force is citizen compliance. Citizens who comply are less likely to experience a forceful outcome; citizens who resist are more likely to experience a forceful outcome (Terrill 2001). However, admittedly not all situational factors are legally relevant factors. While citizen compliance is, citizen demeanor is not. Hence, officers are legally permitted to use coercion when citizens are resisting their attempts at control, but not when simply being disrespectful. Taking this view, force used on "assholes," as characterized by Van Maanen

(1978), would be illegitimate force (although not to those subscribing to the police fraternity and need to re-establish or address an affront to police authority).

Returning to the question at hand, if we ask why do the police use force there are a host of legitimate reasons in a broader sense. Officers use force to maintain order, enforce the law, and to ensure safety. Hence, officers can order a suspect to "stay in the car" during a traffic stop, use handcuffs on a suspect during an arrest, use mace when faced with an attacking suspect, and even frisk a citizen on the street suspected of carrying a weapon. Officers are paid to stop a suspicious motorist, determine if something is amiss, order the suspect out of the car, and if need be, use physical force. They are paid to wade into a street fight and break it up. They are paid to shoot a suspect posing an imminent deadly threat. The use of such tactics, however, is restricted to lawful purposes, and naturally this is where the danger zone comes into play, as it is not always clear the extent to which the police must rely on coercion (and Bittner argues it is determined almost solely by the police themselves, rendering a term such as lawful meaningless). Trying to resolve this dilemma is a difficult task as lawful force often depends on the lens one looks through (see Terrill 2009; Terrill and Paoline 2010). So within the context that it is mainly an officer-based determination, I agree, but it certainly does not mean attempts to determine lawful police coercion are meaningless. Moreover, using force for a legitimate reason (such as safety) does not preclude how officers come to view such threats as illustrated by Skolnick's (1966) "symbolic assailant," which can incorporate illegitimate factors.

Yet several scholars have observed that legitimate use of force behavior moves beyond a legal determination. For instance, Klockars (1995) attempts to lay out a "theory of excessive force" within the confines of how highly skilled officers would act when deciding to use or not use force, which is perhaps an unrealistic guide post. Nonetheless, it suggests that legitimate force may sometimes require a broadening of one's consideration of how we as a society measure proper police behavior in terms of force. Muir (1977) would appear to mix nicely in this regard when discussing what he refers to as the "professional" police officer. A good police officer according to Muir (1977) is someone who espouses and puts to use two key virtues: passion and perspective. In short, good police officers (ones who are professional and apply coercion in the most proper form) are those who understand and grasp the nature of human suffering (i.e., incorporate empathy), while also coming to grips with the reality that the use of coercive means is a necessary feature of police work. In other words, the best police work is generally accomplished when carried out as judiciously as possible. Forceful tactics are not to be avoided, but properly cast and measured.

12.3.2 The Illegitimate

History has proven that when the power to coerce is placed within the hands of those entrusted to distribute force for lawful purposes, such behavior sometimes runs amuck (Terrill 2001). Force that "crosses the line" or is deemed inappropriate, however, is not always entirely clear in terms of meaning or purpose. While inappropriate force takes on a number of labels (e.g., excessive use of force, use of excessive force, brutality, unauthorized force, wrongful force, unjustified force, misuse of force, unnecessary force), when pondering why officers use force for illegitimate means, the term police brutality certainly seems to fit (i.e., using force that is willful and knowingly wrong). I would posit that for many observers, the force used on Rodney King represents a classic example of officers playing out their own personal biases. That is, they used force because they were essentially "pissed off" at the audacity of King to flee and then continue to resist the authority of the law as represented by these particular officers. Interestingly, however, even in such an egregious case, not everyone may see it this way, least of which the officers themselves given their ill-equipped and lack of training defense. Assuming, however, that the force was willful and knowingly wrong, the reason for the force used in such a case can still vary. Was it because King was viewed as an asshole à la Van Maanen (1978), where the primary reason becomes one stemming from the need to restore order and address the affront? Was it because King was a black man and the officers took great delight in the opportunity to manifest racial prejudice?[8] Was it because of broader organizational influences? Or alternatively, was it a combination of some or all of these?

Additionally, officers may use force simply to harass. For instance, officers may frisk citizens on the street not because they suspect them of carrying weapons (portraying a legitimate safety reason), but rather to harass, which may result in some sort of intrinsic benefit (e.g., enhancing a power trip, showing them who is boss, keeping the underclass down, etc.). At times, prejudice and harassment are interwoven (Brunson 2007). Moreover, some research has shown that the police are more likely to rely on forceful tactics when encountering criminal suspects in high-crime areas and neighborhoods with high levels of concentrated socioeconomic disadvantage independent of suspect behavior and other statistical controls (Terrill and Reisig 2003). Thus, the police sometimes act more coercively toward suspects because of where they are located as opposed to how they are explicitly behaving.

In addition, officers can use force as a mechanism of corruption. Whether one considers the corruption scandal resulting in the formation of the Knapp Commission in New York City in the 1970s, the Miami River Cops scandal in the 1980s, or the Los Angeles Rampart Scandal in the 1990s, officers wrongly used force as part of their corrupt activity. In the Rampart case, officers went so far as to engage in beatings and shootings for the purposes of economic gain (Chemerinsky 2001). Another form of corruption, noble cause, often entails the use of force as well (Caldero and Crank 2004). When this is done, officers engage in force that goes beyond legal parameters because they essentially want to "catch the bad guy" and the law is in the way. Look no further than the once popular network television series *NYPD Blue* featuring Andy Sipowicz, who portrayed the hero by "tuning up" bad guys all over the city to get at the "truth." It is the classic ends over means phenomenon. In short, the use of force for illegitimate reasons does not always look so ugly or deviant to some. In fact, I would guess that if readers were honest with themselves, they sometimes (if not often) found themselves pulling for Sipowicz because they too wanted the bad guy off the street.

12.3.3 The Legitimate/Illegitimate

It is not a very controversial stance to state that much of the public would like a safe and orderly society. This message is transferred to police agencies with top management acutely aware of the public's desire. When crime increases there is often a very predictable flow of events. The public starts to become alarmed, the media begins to sensationalize crime, the public becomes increasingly anxious, and the message is communicated to police brass to "do something." This pressure is then pushed down to street officers who are charged with actually doing something (Lipsky 1980). This creates a potentially powerful mix of influences where the public, and subsequently police agencies, begin to encourage and possibly tolerate forceful tactics at the street level.

The "go to" reference on attempting to link broader sociopolitical influences with organizational behavior is undoubtedly Wilson's (1968) classic organizational thesis. In this part-organizational analysis and part-theoretical framework, he sought to glean an understanding of the posited interspersion of local political culture and police behavior in terms of varying operational styles. Despite the legendary status given this book, there have actually been few empirical studies confirming the posited relationship (see Liederbach and Travis 2008). Nonetheless, Wilson's depiction of organizational behavior and the broader political environment leads nicely to an awareness of the pushing and pulling that can occur within the occupation (see also Skolnick and Fyfe 1993). When this is mixed with more individualistic ethnographic examinations highlighting the police socialization process and resultant cultural dynamics (Skolnick 1966; Westley 1970; Van Maanen 1974; Brown 1981; Crank 1994; Paoline 2001), the fact that some officers are simply less skilled or trained than others (Klockars 1995), varying personal motivations and comfort zones that exist (Muir 1977), varying opportunities to engage in force through different types of assignments (Terrill 2001), and the protection of police unions (Kelling and Kliesmet 1995), what are we left with? A convoluted, difficult to untangle mix of factors influencing the extent to which police officers rely on coercive means. This is where the simplicity of the traditional explanatory rubric breaks down (i.e., legal, community, organizational, sociological, psychological explanations). The reasons officers use force are often a combination of some or all these varying influences. The resultant force used then is sometimes difficult to characterize as being proper or improper.

Let us string together varying influencing factors of force that cut across different levels of analysis using the "police culture" as an anchor. The police culture is often viewed as the culprit for why officers use force (which is often viewed in a negative light). Besides a poor, or at best loose, understanding as to what police culture is or is not, "the traditional view of police culture is said to consist of a set of attitudes and values that are shared by officers who collectively cope with the strains of their work environment" (Terrill, Paoline, and Manning 2003, 1006; see also Paoline 2001). Westley's (1970) characterization of culture stressed the secrecy and loyalty aspects among officers working in a dangerous and hostile work environment. Skolnick's (1966) depiction of culture described a "police personality" that, similar to Westley's characterization, was a function of the dangers of policing. The cultural prescriptions of suspiciousness and maintaining the edge over citizens in creating, displaying, and maintaining their authority (Manning 1995) divides police and their clientele. Officers who are socially isolated from citizens, and who rely on one another for mutual support from a dangerous and hostile work environment, are then said to develop a "we versus they" attitude toward citizens and strong norms of loyalty to fellow officers (e.g., blue wall of silence, thin blue line).

The collectiveness of culture among officers, and the mechanisms used to cope with the strains of the occupation, are related to the use of coercion over citizens. That is, officers, as culture carriers, are expected to "show balls" (Reuss-Ianni 1983, 14) on the street during encounters with citizens. Despite the inherent link between culture and coercion, findings from some studies suggest that not all officers equally share the attitudes, values, and norms of the traditional police culture (White 1972; Broderick 1977; Muir 1977; Brown 1981; Paoline 2001). Moreover, Terrill and colleagues (2003) went on to demonstrate that those officers more apt to subscribe to the traditional tenets of the police culture are more likely to use higher levels of force. While they did not further investigate *why* this occurs, it is certainly plausible that officers buying into the culture may also feel that the use of more coercion is not only appropriate, but will be protected by other officers if they should stray over the line.

Now enter the fact that some officers are simply less skilled than others. Klockars (1995) talks a great deal about the importance of drawing on highly skilled officers to improve the police profession, as do Bayley and Bittner (1997) when discussing the "craft" of policing. There are roughly 700,000 sworn officers in the United States working in over 15,000 distinct police agencies (Reaves 2010), so it is unrealistic (although worthy of continual pursuit) to believe that all of these officers are high performers and have a good feel as to when and how much force to use in any given instance. Add to the equation the standard organizational practice of assigning the least skilled and most inexperienced officers to the time and areas that often pose the greatest challenges (e.g., the night shift in high-crime beats), and one can reasonably expect that not all officers will be up to the task at hand. For example, Officer Jones may have been best in his academy class and had the best field training officer, and so when faced with an unarmed suspect who is verbally threatening him, he is able to resolve it using verbal commands, or at most no more than low-level, hands-on force. Conversely, Officer Smith is faced with the same scenario but was last in his academy class and had an apathetic, if not old-school crime fighter (Paoline 2003) type field training officer, and so he ends up using heavy handed tactics or his baton.

Of the two scenarios offered above, is one approach more legitimate than the other? Of course, most lay persons would probably opt for the former, but perhaps "the culture" would not only encourage the latter but would protect it, drawing on the "blue wall of silence" should an internal affairs investigation occur. The police union would more than likely add another element of protection, as might the officers' supervisors who understand the "thin blue line" (and feel pressure from the community and higher level management to curb crime). But perhaps Officer Smith's behavior was simply an instance not of deviance or deliberate illicit force, but "unnecessary force" (i.e., force used by well-meaning officers ill-equipped to handle various incidents) as classified by Fyfe (1997). What if Officer Smith continues to struggle in other encounters with when and how to use force and ends up coming to realize that using force is simply the easy or most direct way to resolve conflict—so he begins to use it regularly in what Adams (1995) referred to as "excessive use of force" (i.e., using force in too many incidents) rather than "excessive force" (i.e., more force than needed to gain compliance in any given incident).

12.4 THE ELUSIVENESS OF FORCE THEORY

So where does this leave us? At the outset I noted one of the primary goals of the essay was to illuminate the complexity of force decision making and come out the other side with a greater appreciation for why adequate theories of coercion are so elusive. Thus, if we collectively consider the multitude of reasons officers resort to forceful means (as illustrated throughout Section 12.3), it is no wonder why it is difficult to characterize the reasons why officers use force, and hence develop theory, let alone label the types of force used as legitimate or illegitimate, proper or improper, right or wrong. Nonetheless, to some extent, it is still at least a little surprising that there has not been more theoretical development. While it is true that police officers use force for many different reasons, and the appropriateness of such force also varies, the same can be said for criminal offending for which there is not a lack of theory. That is, offenders offend for many different reasons, and they do so with varying degrees of severity. There are perhaps a few plausible reasons for this state of affairs (i.e., the apparent disconnect of theory development between the two).

First, I would argue, with nothing more than speculation combined with personal experience (which means I have no "evidence" per se), that there is just not the same level of zeal for theoretical development within policing circles as there is in criminological circles. Perhaps this is due to the pragmatic nature of those interested in studying the police, who for the most part are not overly interested in theory themselves. Scholars interested in criminal justice and policing, as opposed to those with an interest in criminology and offending, seem to almost be theory averse more often than not. In this sense, it is as if some policing scholars, I would argue most at this stage, buy into the oft heard lament of police practitioners—theory sucks! Phrased more appropriately, it is seen as not very beneficial for front-line officers actually doing street-level work. The result is that there is little interest in spending time theorizing policing. Interesting, however, this was not the case with the early scholars (Skolnick 1966; Westley 1970; Bittner 1974; Van Maanen 1974; Black 1976; Manning 1977; Muir 1977), who mainly had traditional sociological backgrounds.

Second, many of the early police scholars provided a sound basis for why police officers act the way they act, including why they resort to force. Skolnick's (1966) "working personality" thesis, Van Maanen's (1978) "asshole" depiction, and Muir's (1977) officer typologies, to name just a few, have been intuitively appealing to several generations of police scholars. Although such "theorizing" may not meet the strict metrics of adequate "theory making" as depicted by Gottfredson (1989), the postulates laid out, the rich descriptive variable relationships offered, and the empirical pieces of evidence that have emerged come together in helping to explain and predict patterns of police coercion. As a result, such work should not be dismissed, and there should be continued refining and testing, although I would caution not to the detriment of failing to think beyond such conceptualizations.

Third, there is a key difference when attempting to theorize criminal offending compared to theorizing police use of force. For offending, a key element is why someone chooses to engage in law breaking. The presumption is that some people choose to break the law and some people choose not to break the law. The same type of parallel does not exist when it comes to police use of force. It is not a question of if the police will use force; it is a question of when and how often the police will use force. The police are the coercive arm of the law, so not using force is off the table. Of course it is more complicated and involved than this simple depiction, but the default position is sufficiently different, which makes developing theory surrounding why officers use force perhaps more challenging than developing theory for criminal offending. This takes us back to the primary underlying feature for why officers use force—in one capacity or another—and that is to control. Thus, perhaps a key foundational element at this stage would be for scholars to develop theoretical direction as to why officers choose to manifest their coercive power in varying ways that are rooted in the legitimate to illegitimate parallels outlined earlier in this section. To do so, I would hope that there would be a recognition of the contributions of the earlier scholarly pioneers, but not an over-reliance on them (as a crutch, or what appears to my naked eye to be more of a romanticized infatuation), which may delay progress in this endeavor. While I wish I had the will and skill to begin doing so, unfortunately I posses neither of these elements. For those that do, however, there is an entire frontier for which to make one's way.

12.5 THE IMPACT OF FORCE

Given the coercive authority granted to the police, it is no surprise that this topic generates a great deal of interest from any number of stakeholders (i.e., the public, legal scholars, researchers, police administrators, patrol officers, etc.). Yet the application of force continues to be anything but a parsimonious process. As noted throughout this essay, 1) defining force can be somewhat varied; 2) determining how often police officers resort to forceful tactics can be difficult to generalize; and 3) classifying the reasons why officers use force, and how much of it, involves a mixture of complex factors.

First, from a definitional standpoint, some scholars argue for a more narrow approach (i.e., the use of physical and weapons-based force), while others take a more inclusive viewpoint (i.e., verbal commands and threats along with the use of physical and weapons-based force). Relatedly, there are a multitude of ways to characterize improper uses of force (i.e., excessive use of force, use of excessive force, brutality, unauthorized force, wrongful force, unjustified force, misuse of force, unnecessary force). Second, because of the varying ways to define force in general, as well as the number of different types of improper force, determining how often officers use force varies widely, despite claims to the contrary that indicate force is used "infrequently" (since such a claim is based solely on the broader definitional view of force). Third, in large part, the decision to use force has a great deal to do with the interplay between suspect and officer. However, to say that force occurs simply as a result of what goes on during the process of citizens and officers interacting, at least within the context of the immediate situation, is naive. There are many factors that come into play, including who the citizen is, who the officer is, where the encounter takes place, and the broader organizational and sociopolitical environment.

When the police act as a mechanism to distribute coercion for illicit reasons (e.g., to punish suspects, to play out individual prejudice, to harass, etc.) their legitimacy is undermined. When police coercion is applied legally to those who break the law or otherwise threaten safety and good order, police legitimacy is substantially enhanced. As Tyler (1990, 2004) theorizes, when citizens perceive legal authorities as legitimate, they are generally more likely to obey the law, comply during police encounters, and cooperate as victims and witnesses in helping to control crime. As such, it is in the best interest of the police to preserve this public image, since compromised legitimacy could result in citizens deciding not to follow societal rules, resisting and fighting with police during encounters, and not assisting police when asked about crime. Moreover, legitimacy is manifested not only by first-hand experiences that citizens have with the police, but vicariously through others as well (i.e., relatives, friends, and the media) (Brunson 2007; Gau and Brunson 2010). In this sense, establishing, maintaining, and diminishing legitimacy in the eyes of the public during use-of-force situations is based on both direct and indirect sources. This does not mean that police cannot (or should not) use force on citizens. Procedurally, the public may understand that coercion is a necessary part of the police response, but if citizens perceive it as improper in some manner, it can certainly work to erode public trust. In essence, there is a balancing act between the utilization of coercion in performing the duties of a police officer and maintaining public trust as legitimate criminal justice agents. To suggest that such a balancing act is always easy, however, would be a mistake. One only has to witness the ongoing debate surrounding Conducted Energy Devices (CEDs, e.g., TASER) (see Paoline, Terrill, and Ingram 2012, as well as Terrill and Paoline 2012) to glean a glimpse of a contemporary issue that illustrates this very dilemma, but there will surely be new issues in the future that will continue to emerge.

Notes

1. See Snipes and Maquire (2007) for a broader discussion of criminal justice theory.
2. I do not intend to throw stones in the proverbial glass house with this assessment, as I am as guilty as others in playing this hand.

3. Alpert and Dunham (2004, 20) explicitly state that "[the] consensus among law enforcement officials and researchers is that force can be defined as physical action taken to control the movement or freedom of an individual." Perhaps the crux of this strong statement centers on the phrase "can be defined" rather than "is defined," because there is certainly no consensus among either practitioners or researchers that force must be solely physical in nature.

4. To be fair, most researchers usually adapt their definition of force to the type of data source they possess (i.e., a broader definition when relying on observational data, which contain verbal forms of force, and a narrower definition when relying on official data, which often do not contain verbal forms of force).

5. They draw on the National Academy of Sciences (NAS) definition of violence.

6. For detailed discussion on measuring inappropriate force, and related challenges, see Adams (1995) and Brown and Langan (2001).

7. Bittner (1991, 37) further notes that "police work can, with very few exceptions, accomplish something *for* somebody only by proceeding *against* someone else" (emphasis original).

8. Of course race is not the only sociodemographic indicator police officers may use (e.g., nationality, class, gender, sexual orientation, etc.).

References

Adams, Kenneth. 1995. "Measuring the Prevalence of Police Abuse of Force." In *And Justice for All: Understanding and Controlling Police Abuse of Force*, edited by William A. Geller and Hans Toch, 61–98. Washington, DC: Police Executive Research Forum.

Alpert, Geoffrey P., and Roger G. Dunham. 2004. *Understanding Police Use of Force: Officers, Suspects, and Reciprocity*. Cambridge, UK: Cambridge University Press.

Alpert, Geoffrey P., Roger G. Dunham, and John M. MacDonald. 2004. "Interactive Police-Citizen Encounters that Result in Force." *Police Quarterly* 7:475–88.

Bayley, David H., and Egon Bittner. 1997. "Learning the Skills of Policing." In *Critical Issues in Policing: Contemporary Readings*, edited by Roger. G. Dunham and Geoffrey Alpert, 114–138. 3d ed. Prospect Heights, IL: Waveland.

Bayley, David H., and James Garofalo. 1989. "The Management of Violence by Police Patrol Officers." *Criminology* 27:1–27.

Bazley, Thomas D., Kim M. Lersch, and Thomas Mieczkowski. 2007. "Officer Force Versus Suspect Resistance: A Gendered Analysis of Patrol Officers in an Urban Police Department." *Journal of Criminal Justice* 35:183–92.

Bittner, Egon. 1974. "Florence Nightingale in Pursuit of Willie Sutton: A Theory of the Police." In *The Potential for Reform of Criminal Justice*, edited by Herbert Jacob, 17–44. London: Sage.

———. 1991. "The Functions of the Police in Modern Society." In *Thinking About Police: Contemporary Readings*, edited by Carl B. Klockars and Stephen D. Mastrofski, 35–51. 2d ed. New York: McGraw-Hill.

Black, Donald. 1976. *The Behavior of Law*. New York: Academic Press.

Black, Henry Campbell. 1979. *Black's Law Dictionary*. St. Paul, MN: West Publishing.

Broderick, John J. 1977. *Police in a Time of Change*. Morristown, NJ: General Learning Press.

Brown, Jodi M., and Patrick A. Langan. 2001. *Policing and Homicide, 1976–98: Justifiable Homicide by Police, Police Officers Murdered by Felons*. Washington, DC: Bureau of Justice Statistics.

Brown, Michael K. 1981. *Working the Street: Police Discretion and the Dilemmas of Reform.* New York: Russell Sage Foundation.

Brunson, Rodney K. 2007. "Police Don't like Black People: African-American Young Men's Accumulated Police Experiences." *Criminology and Public Policy* 6:71–101.

Caldero, Michael, and John P. Crank. 2004. *Police Ethics: The Corruption of Noble Cause.* Cincinnati, OH: Anderson.

Chemerinsky, Erwin. 2001. "Independent Analysis of the Los Angeles Police Department's Board of Inquiry Report on the Rampart Scandal." *Loyola of Los Angeles Law Review* 34:545–656.

Crank, John P. 1994. *Understanding Police Culture.* Cincinnati, OH: Anderson.

Croft, Elizabeth Benz. 1985. "Police Use of Force: An Empirical Analysis." PhD dissertation, University of Michigan.

Croft, Elizabeth Benz, and Bruce A. Austin. 1987. "Police Use of Force in Rochester and Syracuse, New York 1984 and 1985." In *Report to the New York State Commission on Criminal Justice and the Use of Force,* 1–128. Albany, NY: New York State Commission on Criminal Justice and the Use of Force.

Eith, Christine, and Matthew R. Durose. 2011. *Contacts between Police and the Public, 2008.* Washington, DC: U.S. Department of Justice, Bureau of Justice Statistics.

Friedrich, Robert J. 1980. "Police Use of Force: Individuals, Situations, and Organizations." *The ANNALS of the American Academy of Political and Social Science* 452:82–97.

Fyfe, James J. 1997. "The Split-Second Syndrome and Other Determinants of Police Violence." In *Critical Issues in Policing: Contemporary Readings,* edited Roger G. Dunham and Geoffrey P. Alpert, 531–546. 3d ed. Prospect Heights, IL: Waveland Press.

Garner, Joel H., Christopher Maxwell, and Cedric G. Heraux. 2002. "Characteristics Associated with the Prevalence and Severity of Force Used by the Police." *Justice Quarterly* 19:705–46.

Garner, Joel H., Thomas Schade, John Hepburn, and John Buchanan. 1995. "Measuring the Continuum of Force Used By and Against the Police." *Criminal Justice Review* 20:146–68.

Gau, Jacinta M., and Rodney K. Brunson. 2010. "Procedural Justice and Order Maintenance Policing: A Study of Inner-city Young Men's Perceptions of Police Legitimacy." *Justice Quarterly* 27:255–79.

Gottfredson, Don M. 1989. "Criminological Theories: The Truth as Told by Mark Twain." In *Advances in Criminological Theory,* edited by William S. Laufer and Freda Adler, 1–16. New Brunswick, NJ: Transaction.

Kaminski, Robert J., Clete Digiovanni, and Raymond Downs. 2004. "The Use of Force Between the Police and Persons with Impaired Judgment." *Police Quarterly* 7:311–38.

Kelling, George, and Robert B. Kliesmet. 1995. "Police Unions, Police Culture, and Police Use of Force." In *And Justice for All: Understanding and Controlling Police Abuse of Force,* edited by William A. Geller and Hans Toch, 187–204. Washington, DC: Police Executive Research Forum.

Klinger, David A. 1995. "The Micro-Structure of Nonlethal Force: Baseline Data from and Observational Study." *Criminal Justice Review* 20:169–86.

Klockars, Carl B. 1995. "A Theory of Excessive force and Its Control." In *And Justice for All: Understanding and Controlling Police Abuse of Force,* edited by William A. Geller and Hans Toch, 11–30. Washington, DC: Police Executive Research Forum.

Langan, Patrick A., Lawrence A. Greenfeld, Steven K. Smith, Matthew R. Durose, and David J. Levin. 2001. *Police and the Public: Findings from the 1999 National Survey.* Washington, DC: U.S. Department of Justice, Bureau of Justice Statistics.

Liederbach, John, and Lawrence F. Travis, III. 2008. "Wilson Redux: Another Look at Varieties of Police Behavior." *Police Quarterly* 11:447–67.

Lipsky, Michael. 1980. *Street Level Bureaucracy: Dilemmas of the Individual in Public Services.* New York: Russel Sage Foundation.

Lundstrom, Ross, and Cynthia Mullan. 1987. "The Use of Force: One Department's Experience." *FBI Law Enforcement Bulletin* 57: 6–9.

MacDonald, John M., Patrick W. Manz, Geoffrey P. Alpert, and Roger G. Dunham. 2003. "Use of Force: Examining the Relationship between Calls for Service and the Balance of Police Force and Suspect Resistance." *Journal of Criminal Justice* 31:119–27.

Manning, Peter K. 1977. *Police Work: The Social Organization of Policing.* Cambridge, MA: MIT Press.

——. 1995. "The Police Occupational Culture in Anglo-American Societies." In *The Encyclopedia of Police Science*, edited by William G. Bailey, 472–475. New York: Garland Publishing.

McLaughlin, Vance. 1992. *Police and the Use of Force: The Savannah Study.* Westport, CT: Praeger.

Muir, William Ker, Jr. 1977. *Police: Streetcorner Politicians.* Chicago: University of Chicago Press.

National Institute of Justice Research Report October, 1999. *Use of Force by Police: Overview of National and Local Data.* Washington, DC: U.S. Department of Justice, Office of Justice Programs.

Paoline, Eugene A., III. 2001. *Rethinking Police Culture: Officers' Occupational Attitudes.* New York: LFB Scholarly Publishing.

——. 2003. "Taking Stock: Toward a Richer Understanding of Police Culture." *Journal of Criminal Justice* 31:199–214.

Paoline, Eugene A., III., William Terrill, and Jason Ingram. 2012. "Police Use of Force and Officer Injuries: Comparing Conducted Energy Devices (CEDs) to Hands and Weapon Based Tactics." *Police Quarterly*, forthcoming.

Reaves, Brian A. 2010. *Local Police Departments, 2007.* Washington, DC: U.S. Department of Justice, Bureau of Justice Statistics.

Reiss, Albert J., Jr. 1971. *The Police and the Public.* New Haven, CT: Yale University Press.

Riksheim, Eric C. and Steven M. Chermak. 1993. "Causes of Police Behavior Revisited." *Journal of Criminal Justice* 21:353–82.

Reuss-Ianni, Elizabeth. 1983. *Two Cultures of Policing.* New Brunswick, NJ: Transaction.

Sherman, Lawrence W. 1980. "Causes of Police Behavior: The Current State of Quantitative Research." *Journal of Research in Crime and Delinquency* 17:69–100.

Skolnick, Jerome. 1966. *Justice Without Trial: Law Enforcement in Democratic Society.* New York: Wiley.

Skolnick, Jerome, and James J. Fyfe. 1993. *Above the Law: Police and the Excessive Use of Force.* New York: The Free Press.

Snipes, Jeffrey B., and Edward R. Maguire. 2007. Foundations of Criminal Justice Theory. In *Criminal Justice Theory: Explaining the Nature and Behavior of Criminal Justice*, edited by David E. Duffee and Edward R. Maquire, 27–50. New York: Taylor and Francis.

Terrill, William. 2001. *Police Coercion: Application of the Force Continuum.* New York: LFB Scholarly Publishing.

——. 2003. "Police Use of Force and Suspect Resistance: The Micro-process of the Police-Suspect Encounter." *Police Quarterly* 6:51–83.

——. 2005. "Police Use of Force: A Transactional Approach." *Justice Quarterly* 22:107–38.

——. 2009. "The Elusive Nature of Reasonableness." *Criminology and Public Policy* 8:163–72.

Terrill, William, and Stephen D. Mastrofski. 2002. "Situational and Officer Based Determinants of Police Coercion." *Justice Quarterly* 19:215–48.

Terrill, William, and Eugene A. Paoline, III. 2010. "Non-Lethal Force by Police: The Various Lenses through which Appropriateness is Examined." In *Police Use of Force: A Global Perspective*, edited by Johannes Knutsson and Joseph Kuhns, 6–13. Santa Barbara, CA: Praeger.

Terrill, William, and Eugene A. Paoline, III. 2012. "Conducted Energy Devices (CEDs) and Citizen Injuries: The Shocking Empirical Reality." *Justice Quarterly* 29:153–82.

Terrill, William, Eugene A. Paoline III., and Jason Ingram. 2012. *Assessing Police Use of Force Policy and Outcomes*. Final Report to the National Institute of Justice. Washington, DC: U.S. Department of Justice, National Institute of Justice.

Terrill, William, Eugene A. Paoline III., and Peter K. Manning. 2003. "Police Culture and Coercion." *Criminology* 41:1003–34.

Terrill, William, and Michael D. Reisig. 2003. "Neighborhood Context and Police Use of Force." *Journal of Research in Crime and Delinquency* 40:291–321.

Tyler, Tom T. 1990. *Why People Obey the Law*. New Haven, CT: Yale University Press.

——. 2004. "Enhancing Police Legitimacy." *The ANNALS of the American Academy of Political and Social Science* 593:84–99.

Van Maanen, John. 1974. "Working the Street: A Developmental View of Police Behavior." In *The Potential for Reform of Criminal Justice*, edited by Herbert Jacob, 81–130. Beverly Hills, CA: Sage.

——. 1978. "The Asshole." In *Policing: A View from the Street*, edited by Peter K. Manning and John Van Maanen, 221–238. Santa Monica, CA: Goodyear Publishing.

Westley, William. 1970. *Violence and the Police: A Sociological Study of Law, Custom, and Morality*. Cambridge, MA: MIT Press.

White, Susan O. 1972. "A Perspective on Police Professionalization." *Law and Society Review* 7:61–85.

Williams, Jimmy J, and David Westall. 2003. "SWAT and Non-SWAT Police Officers and the Use of Force." *Journal of Criminal Justice* 31:469–74.

Wilson, James Q. 1968. *Varieties of Police Behavior: The Management of Law and Order in Eight Communities*. Cambridge, MA: Harvard University Press.

Worden, Robert E. 1995. "The 'Causes' of Police Brutality: Theory and Evidence on Police Use of Force." In *And Justice for All: Understanding and Controlling Police Abuse of Force*, edited by William A. Geller and Hans Toch, 31–60. Washington, DC: Police Executive Research Forum.

···

CHAPTER 13

RESTRAINT AND TECHNOLOGY: EXPLORING POLICE USE OF THE TASER THROUGH THE DIFFUSION OF INNOVATION FRAMEWORK

···

MICHAEL D. WHITE

Whatever the substance of the task at hand... police intervention means above all else making use of the capacity and authority to overpower resistance.

(Bittner 1970, 40)

Any experienced police officer knows the potentially devastating effects of even justified shootings by police—loss of life and bereavement, risks to an officer's career, the government's liability to civil suits, strained police-community relations, rioting and all the economic and social crises that attend major civil disturbances.

(Geller and Scott 1992, 1)

The videotape Holliday shot showed a large black man down on hands and knees, struggling on the ground, twice impaled with wires from an electronic TASER gun, rising and falling while being repeatedly beaten, blow after blow after blow—dozens of blows, fifty-six in all...

(Skolnick and Fyfe 1993, 8)

THE oft-cited quote from Bittner above highlights the use of force as a defining feature of the police role. The potential for injury and death to citizens as a result of police use of force is highly controversial and can have devastating, long-term effects for the police, the community and the relationship between them (see also the National

Advisory Commission on Civil Disorders 1968). As the Geller and Scott quote indicates, these effects have in some instances included civil disorder and riots; most notably in the 1960s, but also more recently in Miami (1980), Los Angeles (1992), St. Petersburg (1996), and Cincinnati (2001). As a result, for more than forty years there has been a concerted effort to develop viable and practical technologies that give police less-lethal alternatives to the firearm and reduce the likelihood of injury or death (and their consequences) among both police and those who they are attempting to control (Klinger 2007; Summers and Kuhns 2010; White and Ready 2010).[1] Examples of less-lethal weapons include early forms of impact munitions, tear gas, and mace (developed in the 1960s and 1970s), and more recently, oleoresin capsicum (OC) spray (developed in the 1990s).

Over the past decade, Conducted Electrical Weapons (CEWs, most commonly the TASER) have emerged as a popular less-lethal alternative among American police.[2] In fact, since TASER International introduced its M26 and X26 TASER models in 1999 and 2003, respectively, the diffusion of the weapon in American law enforcement has been quite remarkable. For example, by January 2012 more than 12,000 police departments in the United States (two-thirds of all departments) have purchased the device, including departments in 29 of the 33 largest cities (National Institute of Justice [NIJ] 2011). Moreover, TASER International estimates that there have been more than 1.99 million deployments of the TASER in the field by police officers (as of October 1, 2013). The introduction of the TASER in American policing has occurred with a fair amount of controversy, however. Activist and civil rights groups have scrutinized police use of the TASER on several fronts, including tactical aspects of deployment (e.g., multiple activations, use in the drive-stun mode) and its use against vulnerable populations (e.g., children and the mentally ill; White and Ready 2007). Moreover, allegations that the device poses an increased risk of death have also surfaced (see *Amnesty International* 2004, 2008). Recent research by White et al. (2013), for example, documented nearly 400 cases where suspects have died following exposure to a TASER device.

The rapid and widespread diffusion of the TASER, particularly in the face of this public scrutiny, raises interesting questions about the processes by which police departments adopt new technologies, the manner in which initial concerns or questions over that technology are overcome, and the progression that occurs over time to normalize use of that technology. In the case of the TASER, specific questions center on why the diffusion of this technology has been so rapid, as well as how police departments have resolved ongoing questions about the device with their constituents. There are a variety of sociological theories that can offer insights into these processes, but perhaps none more so that the Diffusion of Innovation framework.

Diffusion of Innovation refers to the spread of an idea, information, tool, or practice from a source to a larger group (Rogers 1995). The spread of the innovation involves the movement from the original source outward. Sociologists have long been interested in how and why things move within and across groups, countries, and societies (Wejnert 2002). Whether an innovation spreads, as well as the rate of diffusion, is affected by a number of things. For example, the influence and connectivity of the source is likely to affect rates of diffusion. Logically, the adoption rate would be slower when the source has little influence, or is not well-connected to other potential adopters (Rogers 1995). But there are clearly other things at play that might affect whether an innovation spreads. Does the innovation have some perceived utility? Does it also have risks or consequences? Are those risks the same for every group of potential adopters? Clearly, there is great value in understanding the diffusion of innovations as it enhances our knowledge of the core processes that explain the exchange of ideas, practices, and technology across people, groups, and cultures. Wejnert (2002, 297) noted that this enhanced understanding also facilitates the modeling of diffusion processes, allowing for predictions of which innovations will spread and how quickly that movement will occur.

Though the Diffusion paradigm can be traced back to Ryan and Gross's 1943 study of hybrid seed corn and has been used in nearly 4,000 studies since then, Klinger (2003) notes that its use in criminology and criminal justice has been scant at best.[3] Notably, Wejnert (2002) recently extended the Diffusion of Innovation theory by creating a single conceptual framework that includes three different sets of factors that can influence Diffusion—characteristics of the innovation (public and private consequences; costs and benefits), the innovators (nature of the entity; status and personal characteristics) and the environment (geographic and political conditions; societal culture)—and by highlighting the interplay that can occur across these factors.

This essay views the emergence of the TASER as a popular restraint technology through Wejnert's (2002) Diffusion of Innovation framework. The author applies this framework by first examining aspects of the innovation itself (the TASER) that have influenced diffusion, including the public and private consequences of the technology, and the costs and benefits of adoption. The next section explores characteristics of the innovators (police) that have influenced diffusion through increased familiarity with the technology, including informal social networks, status and personal characteristics of early adopters, guidance leadership organizations, and use of the media, as well as the role of the manufacturer (TASER International). The third section examines characteristics of the external environment including geographic settings and cultural (and political) factors. From this perspective, the widespread and rapid diffusion of the TASER will be seen as a natural, rational development in policing. The essay concludes with a discussion of how this case-study approach with the TASER will lay a foundation for future work by highlighting the value of the Diffusion of Innovation framework for criminal justice policy makers who are seeking to implement new technologies, and for criminologists who are seeking to understand the nature and impact of those technologies on crime and crime-control efforts.

A number of conclusions can be drawn:

- The emergence of the TASER can be understood in the larger context of police departments' efforts to provide viable less-lethal alternatives to their officers that overcome suspect resistance, reduce injuries, and reduce the potential for encounters to end in lethal force.

- Social and medical research has significantly quelled many of the concerns raised over the TASER and paved the way for continued diffusion.
- The innovators themselves (police) have facilitated diffusion of the technology through informal networks, guidance from leadership organizations, and use of the media.
- Environmental context also plays a key role in diffusion, demonstrated through the success of small and mid-sized departments as early adopters, as well as reluctance by the state of New Jersey to approve TASER use by police.
- Application of the Diffusion of Innovation framework to police use of the TASER highlights the value of the framework for understanding more generally the role of technology in policing, for explaining why some innovations fail to diffuse, and for anticipating which technologies will successfully diffuse in the future.

13.1 CHARACTERISTICS OF INNOVATION

13.1.1 Introduction

During the 1960s, John H. Cover, a NASA aerospace physicist, began experimenting with technology to develop a weapon that emulated the "electric rifle" in the fictional story, *Tom Swift and His Electric Rifle* (Appleton 1911; Stratbucker 2009). Although originally designed to subdue "skyjackers," Cover's device was adopted by a handful of police departments throughout the 1980s and early 1990s, including the Los Angeles Police Department (LAPD) which used the device more than six hundred times in 1986 (Meyer 2009). However, in the late 1980s the manufacturer of the TASER device reduced the power output, which resulted in the device being less effective at stopping suspect resistance.[4] The Rodney King incident in 1991 is perhaps the most famous failure of this early version of the TASER (see the quote by Skolnick and Fyfe at the beginning of the essay).

In response to these effectiveness concerns, TASER International introduced its M26 model in 1999, with an increased power output. The X26 model, introduced in 2003, had a lower, more efficient power output as well as a sleeker design (Meyer 2009). These two models represent the vast majority of TASER devices in use by law enforcement today. Both the M26 and X26 TASER devices fire two small probes at a rate of 180 feet per second and, upon striking the subject, deliver a 50,000 volt shock over a five-second cycle. Vilke and Chan (2007, 349) describe how the device functions:

> CEDs work by incapacitating volitional control of the body. These weapons create intense involuntary contractions of skeletal muscle, causing subjects to lose the ability to directly control the actions of their voluntary muscles. CEDs directly stimulate motor nerve and muscle tissue, overriding the central nervous system control and causing incapacitation regardless of the subject's mental focus, training, size, or

drug intoxication state... This effect terminates as soon as the electrical discharge is halted. Immediately after the TASER shock, subjects are usually able to perform at their physical baseline.

In plain terms, the device is intended to overcome suspect resistance, allowing police officers to control and restrain suspects with minimal physical confrontation. The innovation has a number consequences, risks, and benefits, however, and these are described below through the Diffusion of Innovation framework.

13.1.2 Public and Private Consequences

The consequences of an innovation both for the entities who adopt it (private entities, such as the police) and for others who might be affected by it (public entities, or the community) are key aspects that will strongly influence a technology's diffusion pattern.[5] The consequences of TASER use for police (the innovators) are widespread, ranging from direct financial costs of purchasing the technology and training officers in its use, to the implications of use of the device by police against citizens (see below). These consequences, of course, are tied to the more general goal of less-lethal alternatives, which is to give officers more options to overcome suspect resistance, and importantly, to do so with a reduced likelihood of injuries to both officers and suspects. The TASER also has consequences that extend beyond the innovators to the general public. Though data from the Police-Public Contact Survey (PPCS) consistently shows that police use of force (or threatened use) is rare, occurring in less than 2 percent of encounters, the sheer volume of police-citizen contacts in a given year (approximately 40 million; BJS 2011) translates to nearly 2,000 use-of-force incidents per day in the United States. Given the number of police officers who carry the TASER (estimated at 370,000), the potential for TASER use during a police-citizen encounter is real. Indeed, TASER International estimates that there have been more than 1.99 million uses of its device since 1999 (i.e., 132,000 uses per year; White et al. 2013). In sum, the TASER device has consequences for both the actors who adopt the innovation (the police), as well as the larger society that interacts with those adopters. Those consequences, both positive and negative, are explored in greater detail in the next section.

13.1.3 Costs and Benefits

The analysis of costs and benefits of the innovation involves a more detailed discussion of the consequences that are alluded to above. Wejnert (2002, 301) states that "cost variables relate to monetary and nonmonetary direct and indirect costs, or risks associated with the adoption of the innovation." Clearly, innovations that bring with them more risks than rewards will not diffuse rapidly (or at all), compared to innovations with greater upsides (Klinger 2003). A full discussion of the risks and rewards of the TASER highlights this point. In terms of rewards, the TASER offers a number of advantages over other less-lethal alternatives including its relatively short duration of recovery time among those who are exposed, its reliability from a distance (up to 35 feet depending on the model), its compact size and utility, and its perceived effectiveness (White and Ready 2010). For example, the effects of OC spray are often felt for several hours, and its range of effectiveness is much shorter (just a few feet). Also, one of the biggest complaints regarding OC spray is the potential for fellow officers to be exposed during a physical altercation with a suspect. Moreover, impact munitions such as bean bag guns and similar technologies often require a specialized firearm or shotgun which tends to be larger and more cumbersome than a TASER.

With regard to perceived effectiveness, research has consistently confirmed the efficacy of the device in terms of overcoming suspect resistance and reducing injuries. For example, field data analyzed by TASER International (2006), internal evaluations by police agencies (Seattle Police Department 2002, 2004), and studies by police researchers (e.g., White and Ready 2007) consistently place the effectiveness rate of the TASER somewhere between 80 to 94 percent—suggesting that the technology is quite efficient in overcoming suspect resistance.[6] Second, several police agencies have reported reductions in officer and suspect injuries after issuing the TASER to their line personnel (Jenkinson et al. 2006; Smith et al. 2007; PERF 2009). Alpert et al. (2011) examined nearly 25,000 use-of-force incidents across 12 departments and found that CEW use decreased the odds of suspect injury by 70 percent (see also MacDonald et al. 2009; Smith et al. 2009). The National Institute of Justice (2011, 31) recently concluded that "CED use is associated with a significantly lower risk of injury than physical force, so it should be considered as an alternative in situations that would otherwise result in the application of physical force."[7]

There are a number of costs or risks associated with the TASER, however. Like any technology, the TASER has direct costs for those considering its adoption. For example, the price of a new X26 TASER device is currently $779.95, with each cartridge costing about $25.[8] Also, the devices do have a shelf life. For example, in November 2011, the Chandler (AZ) City Council approved spending $471,028 to buy 340 new TASERs. Chandler PD was one of the earliest adopters of the TASER, and many of their devices were well past the projected five-year life span of the device (Jensen 2011). Also, a police department's decision to adopt the TASER will likely have other indirect financial costs, such as expenses associated with training, supervision, and changes in policies and procedures.

More generally, prior research on police use of the TASER has identified several areas of concern, or risks associated with the device. One area of controversy has centered on general policy-related questions governing the terms of use of the device by police (e.g., when, against whom, and under what conditions the device should be used). The most controversial aspects of police use of the device have included its use against passive resisters (e.g., citizens not following verbal commands) and vulnerable persons (e.g., children, elderly, pregnant women), repeated activations against a single person, and use of the device in the direct contact ("drive stun") mode (*Amnesty*

International 2007; NIJ 2011). Despite guidelines from national police leadership organizations such as the Police Executive Research Forum (PERF 2005) and International Association of Chiefs of Police (IACP 2005), recent studies suggest that there is still substantial variation in departmental policies and practices with regard to the TASER. Alpert and Dunham (2010) found that 27 percent of departments classified the CEW as a low-level force option (appropriate for passive resisters), 62 percent classified it as a medium–force option, and 11 percent classified it as a high-force option (e.g., violent and life-threatening encounters only).[9] Clearly, the lack of consensus on these key policy issues presents risks for potential adopters of the device, but those risks can be minimized by adhering to standards promulgated by leadership organizations such as PERF and IACP.

Another area of concern for adopters involves the physiological effects of the TASER, most notably whether it poses an increased risk of death for those who are exposed to the device. For example, White et al. (2013) used a unique data triangulation method that combined media reports and medical examiner reports, and they identified 392 cases in which an individual died following exposure to a TASER. Importantly, a large body of research has examined various aspects of the physiological risks associated with CEWs. First, several studies have examined arrest-related deaths (ARDs) more generally to determine the percentage of death cases that have involved a CEW. Ho et al. (2009) identified 162 ARDs from May 2004 to April 2005, and approximately one-third involved CEWs (see also Ross 1998; Stratton et al. 2001). The Bureau of Justice Statistics (BJS) published a special report in 2007 on ARDs, which described more than 2,000 deaths from 2003 to 2005 (Mumola 2007). However, the report identified only 36 cases where a TASER device (or another CEW) was used (Mumola 2007).

Second, there have been a handful of studies that have examined TASER exposures in the field. Bozeman et al. (2009) conducted physician reviews of 1,000 real-world CEW incidents, and found that 99.75 percent of suspects had minor or no injuries (see also Strote et al. 2010).[10] Eastman et al. (2008) examined 426 TASER device activations in Dallas and reported similar findings. Importantly, the authors also concluded that in 5.4 percent of the incidents, the TASER device "prevented the use of lethal force by the arresting officer(s)" (Eastman et al. 2008, 1570). Third, there have also been a few studies that have sought to assess the impact of CEW adoption by a police department on injury and death rates over time. PERF (2009) compared nine different safety outcomes among seven law enforcement agencies that deploy the TASER device and a matched sample of six agencies that do not. It found that CEW sites, post-TASER adoption, had improved safety outcomes across six of the nine measures, though sites did not differ on the number of ARDs (PERF 2009).

Fourth, a few studies have sought to examine the incident-level characteristics of ARDs where a TASER was deployed. White et al. (2013) examined 392 TASER-proximate ARDs and found that the incidents were complex, dynamic encounters between persistently aggressive suspects and officers who were drawing deeply into their arsenal of force options in an attempt to control and arrest them. In fact, police used the TASER by itself (no other force required), with one standard activation, in only a handful of cases

(55 cases, 14 percent; White et al. 2013). Last, the National Institute of Justice convened a steering group of experts that included representatives from the College of American Pathologists, the Centers for Disease Control and Prevention, and the National Association of Medical Examiners. The group conducted mortality reviews of nearly 300 death cases and concluded:

> There is no conclusive medical evidence in the current body of research literature that indicates a high risk of serious injury or death to humans from the direct or indirect cardiovascular or metabolic effects of short-term CED exposure in healthy, normal, nonstressed, nonintoxicated persons. Field experience with CED use indicates that short-term exposure is safe in the vast majority of cases. The risk of death in a CED-related use-of-force incident is less than 0.25 percent, and it is reasonable to conclude that CEDs do not cause or contribute to death in the large majority of those cases. (NIJ 2011, viii)

In sum, there are aspects of the innovation that pose risks for potential adopters, but the current research suggests that those risks are outweighed by the benefits of the TASER device.

13.2 CHARACTERISTICS OF INNOVATORS

Wejnert (2002) argues that characteristics of the innovation itself are not sufficient to explain diffusion patterns. There are also numerous aspects of the innovators or adopters themselves, in this case police departments, that influence the rate of diffusion. This section highlights some of these key innovator features, and demonstrates how they might help explain diffusion patterns of the TASER.

13.2.1 Societal Entity of Innovators and their Social Networks

The societal entity of innovators refers to the size of adopters, whether they be individual actors, small collective groups (e.g., group of friends), or a large collective group. In this case, the societal entity of innovators is quite large and is made up of nearly 18,000 local and state law enforcement agencies in the United States that employ approximately 800,000 sworn officers (BJS 2011). Wejnert (2002) notes that actors or innovators maintain relationships with one another through a variety of social networks. Importantly, these social networks, which can include face-to-face interactions as well as both formal and informal organizational networks, are the primary means by which actors communicate information regarding an innovation. The large collective of U.S. police departments communicate through a variety of networks, including informal relationships with nearby agencies and partners (e.g., by word of mouth); through attendance at regional trainings, meetings, and conferences; and through national-level meetings, such as the annual conferences of the International Association of Chiefs of Police, and the Center for Problem Oriented Policing. Several aspects of these networks warrant further discussion.

The President's Commission on Law Enforcement and the Administration of Justice (1967) recommended that all states establish a Peace Officer Standards and Training Commission (or POST) to develop statewide standards for training and certification of police officers; and to offer that training on a regular basis. Nearly all states have followed this recommendation. Importantly, the POST can serve as a clearinghouse for information on a wide range of law enforcement topics, including new technologies. As an illustration, one section of the California POST's website is called "Case Law Today," which reviews timely issues related to police practice and civil liability. The June 2010 edition of "Case Law Today" included an interview with a deputy district attorney from Alameda County regarding court rulings involving the use of the TASER, and more specifically, when courts have found TASER use to be excessive.

Also, there are several leadership organizations in law enforcement in the United States, including the IACP and PERF, and these organizations have offered important information and guidance to local law enforcement on emerging TASER technology. Both IACP and PERF offered public support for police use of the TASER early on, and in 2005, both published model policies to offer guidance to agencies in their deployment of CEWs. The IACP also publishes *Police Chief*, a monthly magazine that is widely read among law enforcement professionals in the United States. A brief review of past issues indicates that this has often been an outlet for distributing information on the TASER and other less-lethal weapons. For example, the magazine has a section titled "Advances and Applications" which reviews departments' experiences with the latest in technology. In June 2004, this section described the purchase of TASER X26 devices by three different police departments, with an interview of an officer from one of the departments: "We would like one TASER X26 for each patrol car in hopes of giving us one more tool in the use-of-force continuum before deadly force," said Fort Worth Police Lieutenant Abdul Pridgen. "From everything we have read, the Taser system reduces injuries to officer and suspects," Pridgen added (*Police Chief* 2004). The February 2005 issue included an article that reviewed liability concerns associated with CEWs, as well as some early recommendations on use of these devices (Means and Edwards 2005).

Lastly, in 1979 four organizations (the IACP, PERF, the National Organization of Black Law Enforcement Executives [NOBLE], and the National Sheriff's Association [NSA]) came together to create the Commission on Accreditation for Law Enforcement Agencies (CALEA). CALEA offers a process for accrediting law enforcement agencies that centers on the promulgation of administrative policies on a wide range of organizational issues. In 2005 CALEA partnered with the U.S. Department of Justice to create a website to "assist local, state and federal law enforcement agencies in developing, implementing and enhancing policies governing the use of less lethal technologies." A wealth of relevant information on the TASER can be found on this website,[11] including specific agency policies, training (and training locations), model policies, updates on legislation and litigation, and promising practices.

13.2.2 Familiarity with the Innovation

Wejnert (2002, 303) states that the "familiarity associated with an innovation relates to how radical it is." In simple terms, innovations that are radical and novel tend to diffuse slowly, and as the novelty of an innovation decreases, its rate of diffusion will tend to increase. There are a variety of things that can increase familiarity and diffusion. With regard to the TASER, the social networks described above offer important avenues of communication that have distributed information and increased familiarity with the innovation. There are also a variety of other law enforcement advocacy groups that share information on new technologies including the TASER, such as the Law Enforcement Executive Forum and the Police Policy Studies Council. There are two additional information sources that have served to increase familiarity with the TASER, and both warrant further discussion. The first is the media. White and Ready have published a series of papers on police use of the TASER using media data. For example, Ready et al. (2008) documented a more than 700 percent increase in the number of news reports about the TASER from 2002 to 2004 (see also White and Ready 2009). Ready et al. (2008) found that news reports on police use of the TASER disproportionately focus on high-profile incidents, such as the 2007 incident in which a University of Florida student famously said "don't taze me, bro," or those resulting in citizen death. For example, more than one-third of the articles identified by Ready et al. (2008) described arrest-related deaths involving the TASER, though available research suggests that such cases are rare (Bozeman et al. 2009; NIJ 2011).[12]

TASER International, the manufacturer of the most popular CEWs (M26 and X26), is also an important source of information on the innovation. TASER International is very proactive in terms of marketing and advertising, and it has no doubt played a role in increasing the familiarity of its device. Company representatives attend local and national conferences, including the annual IACP Conference and the NIJ Research and Evaluation conference. The company also supports local, state, and regional law enforcement leadership organizations. For example, TASER International is a gold-level sponsor of the Arizona Association of Chiefs of Police (AACOP). In addition, TASER International routinely issues press releases regarding equipment purchases, uses of its device in the field, lawsuit outcomes, and research studies. Also, the TASER International website is designed to provide detailed information on the technology (and increase familiarity). In addition, the company posts media stories regarding use of the device in the field by police, and it maintains a field deployment database composed of incident-level data submitted voluntarily from agencies around the world (see Jenkinson et al. 2006 for an example of a research study using the database).[13] TASER International has also compiled the *TASER Research Compendium* (now in its

5th edition), a collection of articles, letters, and documents presenting TASER-related research. The *Compendium*, more than 2,000 pages in length, is available in hard copy and on CD.

TASER International is also heavily involved in training. The company operates its own training academy based in its Scottsdale, AZ headquarters. It offers training certification in the use of its devices, as well as instructor certification courses. The company also offers a one-day seminar for law enforcement executives and legal counsel on risk management, legal, and policy issues, and the latest in medical research. TASER International also organizes and schedules training across the country, allowing interested parties to search on its website for training opportunities by state and region. In sum, TASER International has played an important role in both increasing familiarity with its technology, and facilitating diffusion of the technology to law enforcement agencies across the United States and internationally.

13.2.3 Status, Personal, and Socioeconomic Characteristics of the Innovator

Wejnert (2002) notes that there are aspects of individual innovators or adopters that can also influence diffusion patterns. *Status characteristics* of the adopter refers to the prominence of a given actor in the network of actors (Wejnert 2002). Arguably, actors with high social status tend to adopt innovations first, and then actors with lower social status follow suit. In the social network of police departments, there is a general correlation between department size and department status (e.g., New York Police Department, Los Angeles Police Department). However, this is not always the case. Some police departments have long traditions of being on the cutting edge and are always searching for the newest developments and technologies—regardless of their size (i.e., *personal characteristics* that favor innovation). Moreover, there may be regional cultural differences that come into play. For example, the west and southwest tend to be more progressive in terms of city and political governance, compared to the more traditional northeastern and southern regions of the country. Wejnert (2002) also highlights the role of *socioeconomic characteristics* of the adopter. That is, the likelihood of diffusion of an innovation is often strongly influenced by the "objective feasibilities" of the innovation itself, such as the financial costs of the innovation (Wejnert 2002, 305).

In the case of the TASER, many of these issues have come into play and influenced the diffusion of the technology.[14] For example, early on TASER International experienced the greatest success with sales in Arizona, Colorado, California, and Washington—all states in the more progressive western and southwestern regions of the country. With the exception of the LAPD (see discussion at the beginning of the essay), the vast majority of earlier adopters of the TASER were small and medium-sized agencies (Tuttle 2011). The early diffusion of the technology in smaller departments was tied to the "objective feasibilities" of the innovation (Wejnert 2002, 305), most notably the cost and nature of bureaucratic decision making in larger departments (Tuttle 2011). With regard to cost, chiefs in larger departments were burdened with the choice of purchasing hundreds or even thousands of TASER devices, rather than five or ten (or fifty). Smaller departments tended to be able to absorb the cost of a smaller number of device purchases, and they also had more flexibility in their decision making. That is, those agencies were less likely to be in the spotlight or to be targeted by special interest groups, and they typically did not have to secure approval from politicized city councils.

Moreover, there were several cases where smaller or medium-sized agencies purchased TASERs, which then led to adoption by larger nearby agencies (Tuttle 2011). For example, the Chandler and Glendale Police Departments in Arizona were early TASER adopters, and there were several cases in which Phoenix officers called upon their counterparts in Chandler and Glendale to assist during potentially violent encounters (e.g., to deploy the TASER). A short time later, the Phoenix Police Department became the first large city department to deploy the TASER to all sworn officers (Tuttle 2011). A similar experience occurred in the Denver area with the Denver Police Department and smaller surrounding agencies such as Longmont and Westminster Police (Tuttle 2011). Lastly, when big-city police departments began adopting the TASER, the majority of those departments were in the west and southwest (Seattle, Phoenix, Albuquerque and Sacramento), again suggesting the role of regional cultural issues (e.g., less conservative philosophy in the western region of the United States) in determining diffusion patterns.

13.3 CHARACTERISTICS OF THE ENVIRONMENT

Wejnert (2002, 310) states that, "A fundamental element in adoption theory is recognition that innovations are not independent of their environmental context but that they rather evolve in a specific ecological and cultural context and their successful transfer depends on their suitability to the new environments they enter during diffusion." In other words, environment matters.

13.3.1 Geographic Settings and Political Conditions

Wejnert (2002) noted that geography and political considerations often play an influential role in diffusion. Both of these aspects of the environment have affected the diffusion of the TASER in policing. With regard to geography, there are clear examples of police departments adopting the TASER after witnessing nearby counterparts adopt and deploy the device (see examples above with Phoenix and Denver). Moreover, when TASER International sought to expand into the larger metropolitan areas in California, the company specifically targeted smaller suburban agencies outside of those major cities first. As many of the smaller agencies adopted the TASER and experienced success, larger agencies like the Los Angeles County Sheriff's Department and the Oakland Police Department followed suit (Tuttle 2011).

There are also several recent experiences that highlight how political considerations can influence innovation adoption. For example, in March 2010 the San Francisco Police Commission initially rejected a proposal by then-Police Chief George Gascon to adopt the TASER and conduct a study of its use by police (Flagler 2011). Nearly a year later and after three commissioners had been replaced, the Police Commission approved the TASER pilot study proposal. However, although the political barriers had been overcome, by January 2012 the San Francisco Police Department still had not purchased TASER devices because of budgetary concerns, which highlights the objective feasibilities that confront large police departments. The state of New Jersey represents another good example of how political conditions can influence diffusion of an innovation. Until October 2011, New Jersey was the last state in the country to prohibit use of CEWs by law enforcement officers. However, the New Jersey Office of Attorney General issued a press release on October 14, 2011 allowing the use of certain CEWs (TASER International's X26 and X2) by law enforcement.

13.3.2 Societal Culture

Societal culture often can play an influential role in diffusion of an innovation. Such things as laws, values, norms, ideologies, and belief systems can either facilitate or hinder the adoption patterns of an innovation (Wejnert 2002). There are two aspects of culture that are especially relevant for examination of technology in policing, especially technology that involves police use of force. The first is the court system. The courts play a critical role through examination of use of force incidents on a case-by-case basis to assess reasonableness (i.e., *Graham v. Connor* 490 U.S. 386 [1989]). Smith et al. (2007, 399) conducted an important analysis of court rulings involving police use of the TASER, using the ALLSTATES and ALLFEDS databases through *Westlaw*, and they reported that "courts routinely approve of the use of the TASER against assaultive and physically resistant suspects."[15] In simple terms, courts have recognized and accepted the TASER as a viable and useful less-lethal alternative for police.

The second aspect of culture that is relevant for the TASER discussion is the police culture. Wejnert (2002, 314) states that "a high degree of cultural traditionalism is often associated with social inertia in adopting new practices and ideas, adversely affecting a country's [or police department's] adoption of technological developments." There is a substantial literature establishing that police departments are complex bureaucracies defined by rigidity, inflexibility, and resistance to change (Perrow 1972; Wilson 1989). Guyot (1979) coined the term "bending granite" to describe police resistance to change, and this organizational inflexibility is coupled with a strong subculture governed by elaborate rules and customs that favor the status quo (Westley 1956; Skolnick 1966; Reuss-Ianni 1983; Kappeler, Sluder, and Alpert 1998). Whether it is related to the bureaucratic nature of a police agency or the subcultural norms that govern a department, diffusion of an innovation can be slowed by this organizational inertia.[16] For the most part, however, the traditional inflexibility that defines police departments has not been a strong influence on diffusion of the TASER. This acceptance of the TASER among the organizational culture is likely tied to convergence among courts' acceptance of the device, police departments' goals (overcoming resistance while minimizing injuries and deaths), and the effectiveness of the TASER in terms of achieving those goals.[17]

13.4 CONCLUSION

13.4.1 Summary

This essay sought to explain the rapid diffusion of the TASER across the American policing landscape, from just a handful of departments at the turn of the twenty-first century to nearly three-quarters of all departments (more than 12,000) by the end of 2011. This diffusion continued even as serious questions emerged regarding police use of the technology, its effectiveness, and its potential physiological risks. In order to understand these trends the author employed the Diffusion of Innovation framework. Klinger (2003, 461) notes:

> The study of diffusion of innovations has a longstanding history in the social sciences—shedding considerable light on just how and why a wide range of ideas, technologies, social arrangements, and other aspects of collective life emerge, gain a foothold, and spread—but criminologists have largely ignored the topic. And we are a poorer discipline as a consequence.

Through this lens, the diffusion of the TASER can be understood more clearly as the rational consequence of an interplay between key features of the innovation itself, those who adopt it (the innovators), and the environmental context. With regard to characteristics of the innovation, this technology can be understood in the larger context of police departments' long-term efforts to provide viable less-lethal alternatives to their officers that can effectively overcome suspect resistance, reduce injuries to both officers and suspects, and more specifically, reduce the potential for police-citizen encounters to escalate to the use of lethal force. Though potential risks associated with the device have been raised, social and medical research has significantly quelled many of these concerns and paved the way for continued diffusion.

Aspects of the innovators and the environment have been equally important for diffusion of the TASER. The innovators include a large collective of more than 18,000 law enforcement agencies who communicate through a variety of means, from informal meetings and conferences, to leadership organizations and the media. These networks, along with the manufacturer of the technology, have significantly increased the familiarity of the device and reduced concerns over perceived risks. Last, the importance of environmental context was also demonstrated through the success of small and mid-sized departments as early adopters, as well as more recently by the experiences in San Francisco and the state of New Jersey.

13.4.2   Using the Framework to Understand Unsuccessful Innovation

Application of the Diffusion of Innovation theory to police use of the TASER highlights the value of the framework for understanding more generally the role of technology in policing, including when innovations fail to diffuse across the profession. Impact munitions are one example of technology that has not experienced widespread adoption, and the Diffusion of Innovation framework can provide a lens for examining this phenomenon. Klinger (2007) notes that various forms of impact munitions (rubber bullets, bean bags, etc.) were developed in the 1960s and 1970s as a form of crowd control and to disperse rioters. However, LEMAS data from 2003 (Hickman and Reaves 2006) indicate that just 36 percent of police departments in the United States have authorized the use of soft and rubber munitions. Given that this technology has been around for more than 40 years, arguably 30 years longer than current models of the TASER, why have impact munitions not diffused more widely?[18]

There are a number of features of the innovation itself that may explain why impact munitions have not been more widely adopted. Downs (2007, 360) states that impact munitions are propelled by gunpowder or compressed air and produce "blunt trauma as the debilitating or partially immobilizing effect." These soft projectiles are typically fired from either a 12-gauge shotgun or 37- to 40-mm launcher, and as a result, distance between the officer and suspect is typically 10 to 40 feet or more (Downs 2007). The nature of this less-lethal weapon makes it ill-suited for police-citizen interactions that occur in close quarters, such as when police are attempting to control or arrest a suspect (e.g., objective feasibilities are limited). Klinger (2007) notes that impact munitions became a popular alternative for SWAT teams, especially when dealing with mentally disturbed individuals and barricaded suspects. With regard to their effectiveness, Downs (2007, 362) concludes:

> They are fairly crude weapons and with few exceptions are not very accurate. Their biggest challenge is to deliver a projectile with enough energy to be effective at long standoff distances (a maximum of about 130 feet for thrown rocks) yet not be deadly at short distances. Blunt trauma weapons can be deadly if the impact force is too great or if there is significant penetration of the skin. Effectiveness and particularly safety degrade rapidly with loss of accuracy down range.

The potential for serious injury and death presents real concerns for potential adopters. For example, Hubbs and Klinger (2004) examined 316 cases where impact munitions were fired, and among the 969 rounds fired in those incidents, 772 struck a suspect (for an 80-percent hit rate). But those 772 hits produced 721 injuries, for an injury rate of 93 percent. And six suspects died after being struck by the impact round (6 deaths in 316 cases, for a fatality rate of about 2 percent). Compared to the TASER, these injury and fatality rates are exceptionally high.

There are aspects of the innovators (e.g., police) which may also help to explain the slow diffusion rate of impact munitions. For example, Klinger (2007) notes that the innovation has experienced greater diffusion among large departments. By 2000, 69 percent of agencies serving populations of 1,000,000 or more had authorized the use of soft projectiles, compared to just 13 percent of agencies serving populations of 25,000 or less. It is unclear why smaller agencies have not embraced impact munitions as a less-lethal alternative, though it may be related to their more limited applicability (typically SWAT units and barricaded persons), their reliance on bulkier shotguns and launchers, and their potential to cause injury. Moreover, there is much less familiarity with these types of weapons. For example, searches of "impact munitions" on the PERF and IACP websites produced six and four hits, respectively (with zero hits dealing specifically with impact munitions). Searches of "TASER" on the PERF and IACP websites produced 50 and 112 hits, respectively. A query on one of the major academic search engines produced 133 hits for "TASER." A search of "impact munitions" on the same engine produced three hits. Moreover, though Defense Technology is the largest manufacturer of impact munitions in the United States (Klinger 2007), the company has not achieved the level of marketing, advertising and advocacy of its counterpart CEW-manufacturer (TASER International).

Last, there are environmental factors that have likely limited the diffusion of impact munitions. The elevated injury and death rates come with significant political ramifications for cities, law enforcement agencies, and their constituents. There are, of course, financial consequences as well resulting from civil litigation. There is also the perception issue. These types of less-lethal alternatives involve firing a shotgun or other type of "rocket launcher" at citizens. While these weapons may be deemed by many as an acceptable use of force in mass crowd demonstrations, civil disorder, and dangerous barricaded person encounters, their use in more "routine" encounters where officers are trying to control or arrest aggressive suspects may be viewed as something altogether different.

13.4.3 Using the Framework to Anticipate Future Innovation

The Diffusion of Innovation framework can also be used to anticipate whether new technologies will become widely adopted. As an illustration, TASER International has developed a wearable camera system (called AXON) that has the capability to record police-citizen encounters on video and provide real-time evidence. This technology has the potential to alter the very nature of police interactions with citizens, especially the small but critically important number of encounters where force is required. However, the probability of wearable camera systems diffusing rapidly will be determined by key features of the innovation, innovators, and environments as described in this essay. For example, diffusion of the AXON system may be inhibited by its financial cost and practicality. The AXON system includes a data management system that stores the video recording, which adds substantially to the cost. Moreover, the camera attaches to glasses which must be worn by the officer indoors and outdoors, day and night. These objective feasibilities of the innovation may affect its rate of diffusion. However, the benefits of recording police-citizen contacts—providing real-time evidence and the potential positive impact on police legitimacy—may ultimately outweigh those limitations. Also, characteristics of the innovators may come into play. There may be reluctance among some police unions to allow officer-worn cameras, arising from concerns that the technology will be used as an internal affairs tool against officers. And concerns over privacy among members of the community may also have an impact on diffusion of this technology (e.g., an environmental factor).

Another example is the Long Range Acoustic Device (LRAD, and other forms of "acoustic bullets") which emits sound levels that cause pain and incapacitate suspects (Summers and Kuhns 2010). The NYPD recently deployed the LRAD during an "Occupy Wall Street" protest, though it was used as a megaphone rather than a "sound cannon" (Parascandola and Connor 2011). The potential spread of the LRAD technology can also be considered through the Diffusion of Innovation framework. For example, can the LRAD be utilized in general use of force situations (and not just crowd control)? Is it effective at overcoming suspect resistance? Can police departments afford the technology? Will police officers accept this form of technology as a viable less-lethal alternative? These are core questions that will define police use of this technology in the future.

13.4.4 When Innovation Becomes Standard Practice

The Diffusion of Innovation framework provides a valuable lens from which to examine these emerging technologies, and it offers important insights about which innovations will fall by the wayside and which will diffuse throughout law enforcement and shape large numbers of police-citizen encounters in the future. The framework also represents a starting point for understanding how tools, policies, and practices become "normalized" in the police profession. That is, at some point during the diffusion process a tipping point is achieved where an innovation is no longer an innovation; rather, it has become a professional norm, custom, or practice. When this tipping point is reached, agencies no longer have to rationalize why they want to adopt the innovation. It is simply perceived to be the professional and responsible thing to do, and agencies instead have to explain why they have *failed to adopt* the technology. When an innovation achieves this level of integration in the societal entity of adopters, the Diffusion of Innovation theory is no longer a necessary explanatory framework, and other perspectives such as isomorphism can take over to explain continued long-term use of the tool or practice. Examples of technology that have reached this level of acceptance in the police profession include the firearm, the patrol car, and more recently, the dashboard computer. With regard to the TASER, the diffusion patterns over the next five to ten years will likely determine whether the device reaches a level of integration where it is viewed as a professional norm and no longer an innovation.

NOTES

1. These efforts can be traced back to recommendations from the President's Commission on Law Enforcement and the Administration of Justice (1967).
2. Though the TASER device is one brand of CEW, it is by far the most commonly used device in the United States. Also, the terms "CEW" and "CED" (conducted electrical or electronic device) are used interchangeably.
3. Klinger (2003) uses the Framework to consider the diffusion of both CompStat and SWAT teams in American policing.
4. The original model of the TASER was 7 watts. Meyer (2009, 4) notes that the power was increased to 11 watts when the device proved ineffective in the field, but then in the late 1980s, it was brought back down to 7 watts "to match the power output of the rest of the company's law enforcement distribution."
5. Wejnert (2002, 301) notes that innovations tend to have consequences that are either public or private, but in some cases, the consequences "are not so dichotomous" and may have significance among both private and public entities. The TASER falls into this latter category.
6. In a follow-up study, White and Ready (2010) found that the impact of the device on suspect resistance was mitigated by several factors including suspect weight, intoxication, and the distance between the suspect and officer.
7. But see also Lin and Jones (2010) and Terrill and Paoline (2012), which documented increased suspect injury rates following TASER adoption.
8. This is the model (and price) available to law enforcement agencies in October 2011. The X26(c) model, which is available to the general public, sells for just under $1,000.
9. Moreover, only 16 percent of departments restrict the activation length of the TASER, and just 5 percent limit the actual number of activations of the device against a single suspect (Alpert and Dunham 2010).
10. There were two cases in which suspects died, but neither was attributed to the TASER.
11. www.less-lethal.org
12. With the exception of an over-emphasis on death cases, White and Ready have found consistency across media and official reports and concluded that media coverage of TASER incidents is a viable source of information on police use of the device.
13. Access to the database is granted to any agency that is licensed for TASER use.
14. The information in this section describing the diffusion patterns by region and department size was obtained by the author through personal communication with Steve Tuttle, vice president of communications, at TASER International on November 1, 2011.
15. Noting that courts differed in their assessments of use of the device against passive resisting suspects, Smith et al. (2007) highlighted the need for departments to review their policies and training, and to look to national-level standards for guidance (e.g., IACP and PERF).
16. For example, Schroeder and White (2009) offered these aspects of police culture as a potential explanation for the NYPD's limited use of DNA evidence in homicide investigations.
17. Wejnert's (2002) framework also includes an environmental feature called "global uniformity," which addresses the diffusion of an innovation worldwide. This feature was set aside, given the focus of the essay on the diffusion of the technology in American law enforcement. However, the TASER has become a popular less-lethal device for law enforcement and military outside of the United States. According to TASER International, as of October 2013, TASERs have been purchased by 17,000 agencies in 107 different countries worldwide.

18. Though early versions of the CEW can also be traced back to the 1960s, the technology experienced major developments in 1999 (and in 2003), with TASER International's M26 and X26 models. The author believes that this is a more appropriate time frame for comparison.

References

Alpert, Geoffrey, and Roger Dunham. 2010. "Policy and Training Recommendations Related to Police Use of CEDs: Overview of Findings from a Comprehensive National Study." *Police Quarterly* 13(3): 235–59.

Alpert, Geoffrey, Michael R. Smith, Robert Kaminski, Lori Fridell, Jon MacDonald, and Bruce Kubu. 2011. *Police Use of Force, TASERs and Other Less-Lethal Weapons.* Washington, DC: National Institute of Justice.

Amnesty International. 2004. *United States of America. Excessive and Lethal Force? Amnesty International's Concerns about Deaths and Ill Treatment Involving Police Use of Tasers.* London: Amnesty International.

Amnesty International. 2007. *Amnesty International's Concerns about TASER Use: Statement to the U.S. Justice Department Inquiry into Deaths in Custody.* London: Amnesty International.

Amnesty International. 2008. *"Less than Lethal"? The Use of Stun Weapons in US Law Enforcement.* London, UK: Amnesty International.

Appleton, Victor. 1911. *Tom Swift and his Electric Rifle.* www.Gutenberg.org/etext/3777.

Bittner, Egon. 1970. *The Functions of Police in Modern Society.* Chevy Chase, MD: National Institute of Mental Health.

Bozeman, William. P., William E. Hauda, Joseph J. Heck, Derrel D. Graham, Brian P. Martin, and James E. Winslow. 2009. "Safety and Injury Profile of Conducted Electrical Weapons Used by Law Enforcement Officers against Criminal Suspects." *Annals of Emergency Medicine* 53:480–89.

Bureau of Justice Statistics. 2011. *Contacts between Police and the Public, 2008.* Washington, DC: U.S. Department of Justice.

Downs, Raymond L. 2007. "Less Lethal Weapons: A Technologist's Perspective." *Policing: An International Journal of police Strategies and Management* 30(3): 358–84.

Eastman, Alexander L., Jeffery Metzger, Paul Pepe, Fernando Benitez, James Decker, Kathy Rinnert, Craig Field, and Randall S. Friese. 2008. "Conductive Electrical Devices: A Prospective, Population-based Study of the Medical Safety of Law Enforcement Use." *Journal of Trauma, Injury, Infection, and Critical Care* 64(6): 1567–72.

Flager, Chris. 2011. "SFPD Not Likely to Embrace the TASER Anytime Soon." October 18. www.thesfnews.com/artman2/publish/local/SFPD_Not_Likely_To_Embrace_The_Taser_Anytime_Soon.shtml.

Geller, William, and Michael S. Scott. 1992. *Deadly Force: What We Know.* Washington, DC: Police Executive Research Forum.

Guyot, Dorothy. 1979. "Bending Granite: Attempts to Change the Rank Structure of American Police Departments." *Journal of Police Science and Administration* 7:253–84.

Hickman, Matthew, and Brian Reaves. 2006. *Local Police Departments, 2003.* Washington, DC: U.S. Department of Justice.

Ho, Jeffrey D., William G. Heegaard, Donald M. Dawes, Sridhar Natarajan, Robert F. Reardon and, James R. Miner. 2009. "Unexpected Arrest-Related Deaths in America: 12 months of Open Source Surveillance." *Western Journal of Emergency Medicine* 2:68–73.

Hubbs, Ken, and David Klinger. 2004. *Impact Munitions Use: Types, Targets, Effects.* Washington, DC: National Institute of Justice.

International Association of Chiefs of Police. 2005. *Electro-Muscular Disruption Technology (EMDT): A Nine-Step Strategy for Effective Deployment.* Alexandria, VA: IACP.

Jenkinson, Emma, Clara Neeson, and Anthony Bleetman. 2006. "The Relative Risk of Police Use-of-Force Options: Evaluating the Potential for Deployment of Electronic Weaponry." *Journal of Clinical Forensic Medicine* 13:229–41.

Jensen, Edythe. 2011. "Chandler to Replace Police Tasers." *AZ Central.* http://www.azcentral.com/community/chandler/articles/2011/11/14/20111114chandler-replace-police-tasers.html.

Kappeler, Victor E., Richard D. Sluder, and Geoffrey P. Alpert. 1998. *Forces of Deviance: Understanding the Dark Side of Policing.* Prospect Heights, IL: Waveland Press.

Klinger, David A. 2003. "Spreading Diffusion in Criminology." *Criminology and Public Policy* 2:461–68.

Klinger, David A. 2007. "Impact Munitions: A Discussion of Key Information." *Policing: An International Journal of Police Strategies and Management* 30(3): 385–97.

Lin, Yu-Sheng, and Tonisha R. Jones. 2010. "Electronic Control Devices and Use of Force Outcomes: Incidence and Severity of Use of Force and Frequency of Injuries to Arrestees and Police Officers." *Policing: An International Journal of Police Strategies and Management* 33:152–78.

Means, Randy, and Eric Edwards. 2005. "Electronic Control Weapons: Liability Issues." *Police Chief* 72(2): 1–2.

Meyer, Greg. 2009. "Conducted Electrical Weapons: A User's Perspective." In *TASER Conducted Electrical Weapons: Physiology, Pathology, and Law*, edited by Mark W. Kroll and Jeffrey D. Ho, 1–9. New York: Springer.

MacDonald, John, Robert J. Kaminski, and Michael R. Smith. 2009. "The Effect of Less-Lethal Weapons on Injuries in Police Use-of-Force Events." *American Journal of Public Health* 99:2268–74.

Mumola, Christopher. 2007. *Arrest-Related Deaths in the United States, 2003–2005.* Washington, DC: Bureau of Justice Statistics.

National Advisory Commission on Civil Disorder (Kerner Commission). 1968. *Report of the National Advisory Commission on Civil Disorder.* Washington, DC: U.S. Government Printing Office.

National Institute of Justice. 2011. *Study of Deaths Following Electro Muscular Disruption.* Washington, DC: National Institute of Justice.

Parascandola, Rocco, and Tracy Connor. 2011. "Police Use Military Megaphone for OWS." New York Daily News. http://www.nydailynews.com/new-york/occupy-wall-street-police-military-megaphone-amplify-point-protesters-article-1.979585.

Perrow, Charles. 1972. *Complex Organizations: A Critical Essay.* Glenview, IL: Scott Foresman.

Police Executive Research Forum. 2009. *Comparing Safety Outcomes in Police Use-of-Force Cases for Law Enforcement Agencies that Have Deployed Conducted Energy Devices and a Matched Comparison Group That Have Not: A Quasi-experimental Evaluation.* Washington, DC: PERF.

Police Executive Research Forum. 2005. *PERF Conducted Energy Device Policy and Training Guidelines for Consideration.* Washington, DC: PERF Center on Force and Accountability.

President's Commission on Law Enforcement and Administration of Justice. 1967. *Task Force Report: The Police.* Rockville, MD: National Institute of Justice.

Ready, Justin, Michael D. White, and Christopher F. Fisher. 2008. "Shock Value: A Comparative Analysis of News Reports and Official Police Records on TASER Deployments." *Policing: An International Journal of Police Strategies and Management* 31:148–70.

Rogers, Everett M. 1995. *Diffusion of Innovations.* 4th ed. New York: Free Press.

Ross, Darrell L. 1998. "Factors Associated with Excited Delirium Deaths in Police Custody." *Modern Pathology* 11(1): 1127–37.

Reuss-Ianni, Elizabeth. 1983. *Two Cultures of Policing.* New Brunswick, NJ: Transaction.

Schroeder, David A., and Michael D. White. 2009. "Exploring the Use of DNA Evidence in Homicide Investigations: Implications for Detective Work and Case Clearance." *Police Quarterly* 12(3): 319–42.

Seattle Police Department. 2002. *The M26 Taser: Year One Implementation.* Seattle, WA: Seattle Police Department.

Seattle Police Department. 2004. *Seattle Police Department TASER Use and Deployment Fact Sheet.* Seattle, WA: Seattle Police Department.

Skolnick, Jerome H. 1966. *Justice without Trial: Law Enforcement in a Democratic Society.* New York: John Wiley.

Skolnick, Jerome H., and James J. Fyfe. 1993. *Above the Law: Police and the Excessive Use of Force.* New York: Free Press.

Stratbucker, Robert A. 2009. "The Scientific History." In *TASER Conducted Electrical Weapons: Physiology, Pathology, and Law,* edited by Mark W. Kroll and Jeffrey D. Ho, 11–21. New York: Springer.

Stratton, Samuel J., Christopher Rogers, Karen Brickett, and Ginger Gruzinski. 2001. "Factors Associated with Sudden Death of Individuals Requiring Restraint for Excited Delirium." *American Journal of Emergency Medicine* 19(3): 187–91.

Smith, Michael R., Robert J. Kaminski, Jeffrey Rojek, Geoffrey P. Alpert, and Jason Mathis. 2007. "The Impact of Conducted Energy Devices and Other Types of Force and Resistance on Officer and Suspect Injuries." *Policing: An International Journal of Police Strategies and Management* 30:423–46.

Smith, Michael R., Robert J. Kaminski, Geoffrey P. Alpert, Lorie A. Fridell, John MacDonald, and Bruce Kubu. 2009. *A Multi-method Evaluation of Police Use of Force Outcomes.* Washington, DC: National Institute of Justice.

Smith, Michael R., Matthew Petrocelli, and Charlie Scheer. 2007. "Excessive Force, Civil Liability, and the TASER in the Nation's Courts." *Policing: An International Journal of Police Strategies and Management* 30:398–422.

Strote, Jared, Mimi Walsh, Matthew Angelidis, Amaya Basta, and H. Range Hutson. 2010. "Conducted Electrical Weapon Use by Law Enforcement: An Evaluation of Safety and Injury." *Journal of Trauma Injury, Infection, and Critical Care* 68(5): 1239–46.

Summers, Diana L., and Joseph B. Kuhns. 2010. "Currently Available Less-than-Lethal Alternatives and Emerging Technologies for the Future." In *Police Use of Force: A Global Perspective,* edited by Joseph B. Kuhns and Johannes Knutsson, 188–198. Santa Barbara, CA: Praeger.

TASER International. 2006. *TASER Research Compendium.* Scottsdale, AZ: TASER International.

Terrill, William, and Eugene Paoline. 2012. "Conducted Energy Devices (CEDs) and Citizen Injuries: The Shocking Empirical Reality." *Justice Quarterly* 29(2): 153–82.

Tuttle, Steve. 2011. Personal communication with author, November 1.

Vilke, Gary M., and Theodore C. Chan. 2007. "Less Lethal Technology: Medical Issues." *Policing: An International Journal of Police Strategies and Management* 30:341–57.

Westley, William A. 1956. "Secrecy and the Police." *Social Forces* 34:254–57.

Wejnert, Barbara. 2002. "Integrating Models of Diffusion of Innovations: A Conceptual Framework." *Annual Review of Sociology* 28:297–326.

White, Michael D., and Justin Ready. 2010. "The Impact of the TASER on Suspect Resistance: Identifying Predictors of Effectiveness." *Crime and Delinquency* 56(1): 70–102.

White, Michael D., and Justin Ready. 2009. "Examining Fatal and Nonfatal Incidents Involving the TASER: Identifying Predictors of Suspect Death Reported in the Media." *Criminology and Public Policy* 8(4): 865–91.

White, Michael D., and Justin Ready. 2007. "The TASER as a Less-Lethal Force Alternative: Findings on Use and Effectiveness in a Large Metropolitan Police Agency." *Police Quarterly* 10:170–91.

White, Michael D., Justin Ready, Courtney Riggs, Donald M. Dawes, Andrew Hinz, and Jeffrey D. Ho. 2013. "An Incident-Level Profile of TASER Device Deployments in Arrest-Related Deaths." *Police Quarterly* 16(1):85–112.

Wilson, James Q. 1989. *Bureaucracy.* New York: Basic Books.

CHAPTER 14

··

POLICE MISCONDUCT

··

SANJA KUTNJAK IVKOVIĆ

STORIES of police officer misconduct are cover-page news; they sell the newspapers, increase the viewership of the evening news, and prompt people to search the Internet for the latest update. Conversations about police misconduct typically revolve around high-profile incidents. Over the years, several well-publicized incidents have shaped public view of the police and lead toward dramatic changes in the way policing is done:

- The Rodney King incident, captured by a citizen's video camera on March 3, 1991 and broadcast overnight across the world, shows an African American motorist stopped for speeding and beaten by four Los Angeles Police Department officers. The events that took place in the aftermath of the incident—the scandal, the establishment of the Christopher Commission (1991), the state criminal trial, the riots, the federal criminal trial, and the civil trial—captured media and public attention for years.
- The story of Michael Dowd and his "crew," arrested on May 6, 1992 and charged with extremely serious violations of criminal law, drew public attention not only of fellow New Yorkers, but also of people across the country. As the events unfolded, the scandal emerged, and the Mollen Commission (1994) was established, Dowd and his fellow police officers were put on trial and convicted, and the New York Police Department went through a thorough investigation and extensive reform.
- In 1997, Abner Louima, a Haitian immigrant, was arrested by the NYPD officers and then beaten up and sodomized with a toilet plunger inside the 70th Precinct station. The torture of Louima resulted in outrage in New York's minority community, a political scandal, criminal trials of the officers involved, a 30-year sentence for former police officer Justin Volpe, and a civil lawsuit with the largest police brutality settlement in the history of New York, $8.75 million.
- On February 4, 1999, four plainclothes NYPD officers shot 41 times and killed Amadou Diallo, an unarmed 23-year-old immigrant from Guinea. Although all four police officers were acquitted in the resulting trial and their conduct declared to be in accordance with NYPD policy, outrage in New York and across the country

resulted in numerous demonstrations against police brutality and racial profiling, the disbandment of the Street Crime Unit, and the settlement of $3 million with his family.

These incidents shaped people's confidence in the police and their understanding of what police misconduct is. However, compared to the overall number of contacts between the citizens and police every day, they represent extremely rare and highly atypical events. In the aftermath of the Michael Dowd arrest, the Mollen Commission (1994, 4) investigated the nature and extent of police corruption in the NYPD and concluded that the vast majority of police officers in the NYPD were "honest and hard-working."

These infamous cases are just the tip of the iceberg; the overwhelming majority of cases of police misconduct likely do not even come close to these levels of severity. The challenge for scholars and practitioners is to develop appropriate tools that help to draw the line between police misconduct—behavior that is prohibited—and proper police conduct, in an effort to better understand the nature and extent of police (mis)conduct. This essay explores these issues while focusing on police corruption and use of excessive force. It also analyzes mechanisms used to control police misconduct and their potential in providing long-term and continuous control.

The essay is organized in five sections. Section 14.1 defines police misconduct, noting the heterogeneous nature of the construct. Section 14.2 focuses on police corruption, namely its causes and known prevalence. Section 14.3 discusses the excessive use of force, making etiological distinctions between it and profit-motivated corruption. This section also examines the extent of excessive use of force. Section 14.4 examines various forms of internal and external mechanisms of police accountability, such as internal review, police department policies, and the U.S. Supreme Court. This section also identifies several "mixed" mechanisms of accountability, such as citizen oversight and accreditation. Section 14.5 offers concluding remarks on the nature and future of police misconduct and its control.

This essay draws several conclusions:

- Police corruption and police excessive use of force are distinct from one another and frequently result from different etiological processes.
- The traditional internal mechanisms designed to control police misconduct generally are internal affairs units, police chiefs and their policies, and supervisors—all of which are critical to protecting against misconduct.
- External mechanisms of police misconduct include the U.S. Supreme Court and citizen oversight.
- Although accreditation through CALEA may emerge as a promising method of helping control police misconduct by encouraging sound policy and organizational integrity, currently such organizations have no enforcement authority over police departments.
- In order for the mechanisms of police accountability to work effectively, they must move from reacting to misconduct (such as establishing independent commissions) to proactively developing strategies to protect against misconduct.

14.1 POLICE MISCONDUCT

Police misconduct is a police act or omission that violates legal rules. Its definition contains three critical elements. The first element is the subject of the definition. It can be an individual police officer, as is typically the case in the literature. However, it is possible to envision that the nature of police misconduct is so complex as to involve many individuals, sometimes almost everybody in the whole police agency (e.g., the widespread corruption in the NYPD in the 1960s and 1970s, according to the Knapp Commission [1972]). Thus, there is a need to go beyond individual misconduct and regard the behavior as organizational misconduct involving groups of officers, units, or maybe even whole police agencies.

The second aspect of the definition involves legal rules. The applicable legal rules include both the federal and state constitutions and federal and state criminal and civil statutes (e.g., U.S. Code, Title 18, Chap. 11, Sec. 201 [1999]; U.S. Code, Title 18, Sec. 872 [1999]; U.S. Code, Title 18, Sec. 242 [1999]). In addition, police agencies have their own internal official rules and regulations that regulate conduct expected of police officers and that prohibit police misconduct. In the 2000s, more than 95 percent of local police agencies have written policies covering codes of conduct and appearance, use of lethal force, and use of non-lethal force (Reaves 2010). Lastly, codes of ethics contain professional standards of appropriate conduct.

The third aspect of the definition focuses on an action or omission. Police officers could engage in misconduct by doing something they are not supposed to do, such as releasing information about an upcoming drug house raid to the drug dealer, shooting at an unarmed person who is following their verbal commands, planting evidence on a person, or giving a false testimony. Police officers could also engage in misconduct by failing to do something they are supposed to do, such as by accepting a bribe in exchange for not issuing a speeding ticket to a person caught running a red light, or by not executing an arrest warrant on a known drug dealer.

14.1.1 Forms of Police Misconduct

Police misconduct encapsulates a heterogeneous group of activities. A police officer could perjure himself on the stand; beat up a suspect, take his drugs and money, and sell the drugs; engage in a high-speed pursuit against the rules of his police agency; sleep on duty and miss the dispatcher's call; email his fellow police officers sexist jokes from a police agency-issued laptop; verbally abuse a citizen; stop a citizen for speeding because of the citizen's race; pose naked for a magazine with the police agency's handcuffs, revolver, and hat; or be constantly late for his shift.

Although this list is long and complex, the activities can be classified into several categories: police corruption, use of excessive force, and other forms of misconduct.

Typically, police corruption and use of excessive force (brutality) are viewed as two distinct categories. Police corruption refers to cases involving some material gain obtained as a result of police-citizen exchange, while use of excessive force focuses on the police officer's inappropriate use of force, regardless of the motivation. Independent commission reports (e.g., Knapp Commission 1972; Pennsylvania Crime Commission 1974; Mollen Commission 1994) and descriptions of court cases (e.g., Buder 1982; Neuffer and Freedenthal 1989; Miller 1999) suggest that use of excessive force and corruption are not distinct in all cases and, in fact, may well overlap. Use of excessive force could be the modus operandi for corruption. On the other hand, use of excessive force can serve as a rite of passage or the beginning of the slippery slope toward corruption (Mollen Commission 1994). The Mollen Commission noted that there was an overlap of the cases of police corruption and use of excessive force in the same low-income, minority, drug-infested neighborhoods. The Mollen Commission compared records of police officers who had extensive corruption complaints with the records of a random sample of police officers, and it concluded that "the corruption-prone officers were more than five times as likely to have five or more unnecessary force allegations filed against them then the officers from the random sample group" (Mollen Commission 1994, 46).

The third category—"other" forms of police misconduct—also contains diverse forms of police misconduct, such as police sexual violence (e.g., Sapp 1994; Kraska and Kappeler 1995; McGurrin and Kappeler 2002; Maher, 2003), police perjury (e.g., Barker and Carter 1994), racial profiling (e.g., Cordner, Williams, Velasco 2002; Engel and Calnon 2004; Engel 2005; Engel and Johnson 2006; Northeastern University Data Collection Resource Center 2010; Weitzer and Tuch 1999, 2002, 2006), Fourth Amendment violations (e.g., Leo 1998; Gould and Mastrofski 2004), and drug-related misconduct (e.g., Carter and Stephens 1994; Mieczkowski and Lersch 2002; Lersch and Mieczkowski 2005).

14.2 POLICE CORRUPTION

Police corruption is a form of police misconduct. It can be distinguished easily from other forms of police misconduct by its motivation: corruption is motivated primarily by the achievement of personal gain for the police officer (e.g., Sherman 1974, 1978; Goldstein 1975; Klockars et al. 2000; Kutnjak Ivković 2005). In addition to its focus on gain, police corruption can be defined as a violation of penal codes, administrative agency rules, or the codes of ethics. For example, federal codes prohibit bribery of public officials and witnesses (U.S. Code, Title 18, Chapter 11, Sec. 201 [1999]), extortion by public officials (U.S. Code, Title 18, Sec. 872 [1999]), as well as deprivation of civil rights (U.S. Code, Title 18, Sec. 242, [1999]). Large municipal and state agencies use their official rules to regulate police officer conduct and prohibit inappropriate conduct such as the acceptance of bribes, gifts, gratuities, rewards (see, e.g., National Research Council 2004; Walker and Katz 2008). The International Association of the Chiefs of Police developed the code of ethics. When police officers take their oath, they explicitly state that they will not engage in acts of corruption or bribery (Barker 2002). Finally, corruption can include an act or an omission. An example of an act is an instance in which a police officer extorts money from a known drug dealer. An example of an omission is an instance in which a police officer accepts a bribe in exchange for not ticketing a speeding motorist.

The literature discusses the nature of the gain itself. The gain does not need to be only monetary; it can be non-monetary as well (see Kutnjak Ivković 2005). The gain can be obtained on a one-time basis, as is the case with "scores," or on a regular basis, as is the case with "pads" (see Knapp Commission 1972). It is typically understood that the beneficiary of the gain is the individual police officer, although some authors argue that the beneficiary of the gain could be the organization as well (e.g., Carter 1990; Bracey 1995). Based on the nature of the gain itself, "traditional corruption"—corruption for personal gain—can be differentiated from "noble-cause corruption"—corruption "in the name of the moral rightness of good ends" (Caldero and Crank 2000).

The size of the gain itself is also discussed in the literature, and there is disagreement over whether there is a minimum value of the gain that would make its acceptance a rule-violating behavior (Barker and Wells 1982; Kania 1988, 2004; Kleinig 1996). Arguments against the tolerance of the acceptance of gratuities and other gifts of small value typically emphasize that the division between tolerated gratuities and other unacceptable gifts is artificial and that the value may be small in individual cases but substantial across the whole police agency (e.g., Pennsylvania Crime Commission 1974; Ruiz and Bono 2004); that the purpose might be to entice biased policing (Knapp Commission 1972; Pennsylvania Crime Commission 1974; Mollen Commission 1994); or that this symbolizes the beginning of the slippery slope of corruption (Mollen Commission 1994; Kleinig 1996). On the other hand, arguments for the tolerance of gratuities and other small gifts typically emphasize that these gifts are offered as kind gestures with no ulterior motives, that they serve to develop a friendly relationship between community members and individual police officers, and that they are part of society's customs (e.g, Kania 1988, 2004).

Corruption is a set of heterogeneous behaviors, as the typology developed by Barker and Roebuck (1973; Roebuck and Barker 1974) demonstrates. The authors classified corrupt activities using acts and actors involved, nature of the norms violated by the act, the extent of support by the peer group, the extent of organization required, and the potential police agency's reaction. According to them, police corruption can be classified into eight categories: corruption of authority, kickbacks, opportunistic thefts, shakedowns, protection of illegal activity, the fix, illegal criminal activity, and internal payoffs. Punch (1985, 2003) expanded the classification by adding flaking or padding of evidence as the ninth category.

Klockars and colleagues (2000) used Barker and Roebuck's typology to develop 11 hypothetical scenarios that describe a range of police corruption. They surveyed more than 3,000 police officers in 30 U.S. police agencies. The results of their study show that acceptance of gratuities was evaluated as the least serious form of corruption and shakedowns, and opportunistic thefts as the most serious ones (Klockars, et al. 2000). Internal corruption and kickbacks are classified somewhere between these two extremes. This hierarchy of seriousness has also been confirmed in a number of other countries surveyed using the same questionnaire (see Klockars, Kutnjak Ivković, and Haberfeld 2004).

14.2.1 Causes of Police Corruption

Many theoretical explanations have been proposed to explain why police officers engage in corruption, but, as the National Research Council (2004, 271) summarized, "[t]he research literature [on causes of police corruption] is long on theory and short on evidence about what causes police corruption."

Individualistic theories emphasize individual police officers' characteristics (e.g., low moral values) and their influence on police misconduct (e.g., Muir 1977). They explain police corruption through the failures of individual police officers ("rotten apples"; Knapp Commission 1972). Although the literature does not clearly describe what these characteristics are, they are typically understood to include prior criminal record, low moral values, drug use, and other potential deviant behavior. As a way to filter out those with low moral values, psychology tests have been used. However, these tests—screening for particular personality traits—did not turn out to be accurate predictors of actual behavior (e.g., Malouff and Schutte 1986; Talley and Hinz 1990).

Occupational theories or functional theories emphasize characteristics of policing as an occupation and the opportunities available. Policing is an occupation with a substantial degree of discretion, performed outside of the supervisors' sight, and before witnesses who often lack credibility as witnesses; as such, it provides many opportunities for corruption (e.g., Caldero and Crank 2000; Klockars et al. 2000). These opportunities are not evenly distributed across ranks, assignments, and service areas. Detectives, especially if assigned to vice or narcotics units, are in an especially privileged position (General Accounting Office 1998).

Organizational theories emphasize the role of police agencies themselves in tolerating and/or controlling police corruption. Instead of "rotten apples," the focus is on "rotten barrels" (Punch 2003); police agencies are entrusted to deal with corruption in the agency. They establish official rules, enforce them, detect and investigate corrupt behavior, discipline corrupt police officers, and control the code of silence (e.g., Sherman 1974, 1978; Klockars et al. 2000; Kutnjak Ivković 2005). These heterogeneous functions are performed by a multitude of actors, from the police chief to individual police officers. Although the police chief and his top administrators perform some of the key roles (e.g., Knapp Commission 1972; Pennsylvania Crime Commission 1974; Goldstein 1975; Weisburd and Greenspan 2000; Kutnjak Ivković 2005), roles performed by first-line supervisors (e.g., Knapp Commission 1972; Burns and Sechrest 1992; Mollen Commission 1994; Weisburd and Greenspan

2000) and peers (e.g., Stoddard 1974; Klitgaard 1988; Sparrow, Moore, and Kennedy 1990; Weisburd and Greenspan, 2000; Kutnjak Ivković 2005) should be relevant as well. By failing to engage in control efforts, be it completely or partly, agencies create conditions that foster corruption.

Sociological theories emphasize the role of the society at large within which the police agency operates. A police agency is just one part of the municipal, state, or federal government and, as such, is influenced by the legal norms, events, and attitudes that dominate in the society at large. Police agencies are influenced by the legal environment (e.g., Knapp Commission 1972; Walker 1999) and by public expectations of the appropriate conduct (e.g., Goldstein 1975; Sherman 1977; Klockars 2003). Communities that expect their public servants to perform their roles with integrity should have police agencies with higher levels of police integrity as well. A comparative study by Kutnjak Ivković (2003) explored the relation between perceptions of overall corruption in society and the prevalence with which citizens were asked by the police to pay a bribe. Kutnjak Ivković found that countries perceived to be more corrupt also have higher percentages of surveyed citizens reporting that the police officers had demanded bribes from them.

14.2.2   Extent of Police Corruption

Although different sources paint a fragmented picture about the extent of police corruption, there are no data available that can show the extent of police corruption in different police agencies across the country. There are several reasons for this state of affairs. To begin with, there are serious issues related to the definition of the phenomenon under observation. Using criminal codes or agency's official rules as a yardstick to define corrupt behavior leads to the problem that the legal rules rarely use the word "corruption" and typically prohibit corrupt behavior using different terminology (e.g., bribery, extortion, theft). Furthermore, even when the rules—be they legal norms or official rules—prohibit corrupt behavior, the specifics vary substantially across time and space.

Arrest, prosecution, and conviction rates could be used as measures of the rate with which police officers have been officially processed for violations of criminal laws. On the other hand, complaint and disciplinary rates could be used as measures of the rate with which police officers have been officially processed for violations of agencies' official rules. Between 1993 and 1997, there were 80 to 150 cases of conviction for federal police corruption annually (General Accounting Office 1998). In a country with more than 600,000 active sworn officers (Bureau of Justice Statistics 2007b), 80 to 150 cases of federal police corruption annually does not indicate that police corruption is out of control.

However, there are additional serious shortcomings of these official data. Citizens and police officers alike may have good reasons not to want to initiate official proceedings, be it by submitting complaints or starting investigations (e.g., Mollen Commission 1994;

Royal Commission 1997; Kutnjak Ivković 2003); they may be partners in illegal transactions, be afraid of reprisal, share the belief that the behavior is acceptable, be willing to tolerate misconduct of other police officers, or be too overburdened with their jobs to notice corrupt behavior (see, e.g., Kutnjak Ivković 2005). Consequently, the official data at best are biased estimates of the actual extent of police corruption. The NYPD in the 1960s and 1970s is an illustrative example. At the time the Knapp Commission investigation (1972) found police corruption to be widespread in the NYPD across precincts and ranks, prosecutors filed charges in about 30 cases of corruption annually (Kutnjak Ivković 2003) and the internal complaint rates suggested that there was less than 1 complaint per 100 officers (Cohen 1972).

Another way of trying to assess the extent of police corruption is through citizen and police officer surveys. Estimates of how widespread police corruption is vary substantially across the surveys. In a 1960s survey, fewer than 2 percent of Caucasian respondents perceived corruption to be widespread (President's Commission on Law Enforcement and Administration of Justice 1967b). On the other hand, an overwhelming majority of the surveyed New Yorkers in the 1990s perceived corruption to be widespread (Kraus 1994). The findings of the International Crime Victimization Survey suggested than less than 1 percent of respondents in the United States and other surveyed Western democracies reported being asked to pay a bribe to the police, while about 10 to 20 percent of surveyed respondents from East European, Asian, and Latin American countries reported the same (Kutnjak Ivković 2003).

When citizens and police officers are asked whether they participate in corruption themselves or whether they have observed others participating in corruption, they may be reluctant to say anything about it (see, e.g., Kutnjak Ivković 2003; National Research Council 2004). They may be partners in this illegal/criminal activity and, if anything, exposure to potential prosecution gives them a reason not to report it (e.g., Stoddard 1974; Klockars 1999; Klockars et al. 2000; Kutnjak Ivković 2003, 2005).

When the Knapp Commission (1972) and the Pennsylvania Crime Commission (1974) investigated police corruption in the 1970s, they found it to be widespread and highly organized in New York City and Philadelphia, respectively. Two decades after the Knapp Commission (1972), the Mollen Commission (1994) investigated police corruption in New York City. The Mollen Commission reported a completely different nature of corruption in the same city. The corruption was concentrated in several precincts, with the majority of police officers being honest. According to the Mollen Commission, the corruption it uncovered seemed to be more aggressive and drug-related.

Despite the potential to provide the most accurate data on the extent of police corruption, independent commissions are not without flaws. They are established to investigate a specific form of police misconduct in a specific city at a specific time period, limiting the generalizability of their findings; they are not permanent, but temporary institutions; they depend on the city management for their resources and legal powers. The Knapp Commission (1972) and the Pennsylvania Crime Commission (1974) reported serious challenges to their successful operation.

14.3   USE OF EXCESSIVE FORCE

As Bittner (1970) and Klockars (1985) emphasize, the right to use force is the key defining feature of the police; "[p]olice are institutions or individuals given the general right
to use coercive force by the state within the state's domestic territory" (Klockars 1985,
12). Police across the world and throughout history have been relying on this right to use
coercive force to compel people to comply with their orders (Klockars 1985). As a crucial
and defining feature, police use of force has been studied extensively since the 1960s.

Conceptually, the definition of the police rests on the idea that they have the right to
use coercive force. The problem appears when there is a need to distinguish between
legitimate and illegitimate use of force, or use of force and use of excessive force.
Deciding whether a police officer used appropriate force typically starts with a comparison of the events in question with the use of force continuum (see e.g., Desmedt and
Marsh 1990) that the agency has. However, the choice and the order of the items on the
continuum differ across agencies (e.g., National Institute of Justice 1999). For example,
some police departments recognize police presence and verbal commands as part of the
continuum, while others do not.

Use of excessive force is even more difficult to define. The Rodney King case is a
prominent example, with two criminal cases and one civil case coming up with different decisions about whether police officers used excessive force. Klockars (1995) wrote
about ways to define excessive force and to separate the legitimate force from excessive
force. He discusses several different standards that could be used to determine what
level of force crosses the boundary. He argues that three standards of defining excessive
force—force that creates criminal responsibility; force that results in civil liability; and
force that results in a scandal—set the bar too low and proposes that the appropriate
standard should be the standard of the skilled police officer. According to this standard,
excessive force should be defined as force beyond the force that a skilled police officer
would use. The problem with this standard, though, is that skilled police officers from
different police agencies could have heterogeneous views about what level of force they
need to use in a particular situation, which in turn depends on many factors, including
their training, the use of force matrix used in their agency, the agency's record of discipline for excessive force, and so on.

The U.S. Supreme Court established the legal standard to be used to evaluate excessive force cases in *Graham v. Connor* (490 U.S. 386 [1989]). There the Court rejected the
notion that all excessive force lawsuits should be judged by the same standard; instead,
the Court pointed to the specific constitutional right that was allegedly violated with the
use of excessive force and said that decisions about whether police officers used excessive force should be based on the standard for the specific right. The issue for arrest, stop,
and seizure should be judged by the Fourth Amendment standard. Thus, as the Fourth
Amendment provides citizens with the guarantee to be protected against "unreasonable seizures," the use of excessive force cases involving arrest, stop, and search should

be judged by the "reasonableness" standard—a perspective of a reasonable officer at the scene. This objective standard does not take into account motivation or intent of the police officer in question.

The Supreme Court also established the legal standard to be used to evaluate deadly force cases. The Court held in *Tennessee v. Garner* (471 U.S. 1 [1985]) that the fleeing-felon rule, which authorized police officers to use "all the means necessary to effect an arrest," including deadly force, was unconstitutional. The Court imposed a new, more limiting standard. According to this new standard, police officers are authorized to use deadly force only in cases in which the police officer has probable cause to believe that a fleeing suspect presents clear and present danger to himself or others ("deadly force... may not be used unless necessary to prevent the escape and the officer has probable cause to believe that the suspect poses a significant threat of death or serious physical injury to the officer or others"). Use of deadly force that does not meet this standard constitutes excessive force.

14.3.1 Causes of Use of Excessive Force

Unlike police corruption, which is characterized by different theoretical arguments but little empirical support, study of the use of excessive force has mostly suffered from a lack of strong theories, with a presence of extensive empirical research. Although use of force and use of excessive force may not always be labeled as a separate part of policing literature and can be found under the subject of police discretion and police behavior, there is a growing body of literature exploring police officers' use of force and use of excessive force (e.g., Riksheim and Chermak 1993; Terrill 2001; Klahm and Tillyer 2010). Based on the topics explored, empirical research on use of force and use of excessive force can be classified into several distinct categories.

The individualistic approach focuses on police officers' individual characteristics (e.g., Muir 1977). This strand of research seeks out characteristics that make police officers more likely to use force and to use excessive force. Research in the 1960s and 1970s attempted to unearth features of the authoritarian personality (e.g., Balch 1972). Decades later, research has not been able to determine these characteristics with certainty; for example, Scrivner (1994) found evidence of some of these features in the group of police officers prone toward use of excessive force. Even if the scope is broadened to include different personality traits that lead police officers to be more likely to use excessive force, the results of empirical research are not promising. In particular, research found very limited support for individual characteristics as key explanations for police officers' use of excessive force (e.g., Worden 1995; Terrill and Mastrofski 2002). For example, Terrill (2003) reported that police officers who had more negative views of the public, laws, and supervisors on the one hand and more favorable opinions of aggressive police tactics and the war on crime philosophy on the other hand, tended to be more likely to use force. Furthermore, Worden (1995) found that the police officers' views about citizens, rather than their views about the police role, are related to the use of excessive force. The search for these personality traits is burdened with their low predictive power. That is, even if police officers exhibit these characteristics, they need not behave in accordance with them. In fact, contextual or organizational factors may play a stronger role in officers' lives and decision making.

The situational approach focuses on the dynamics of police-citizen encounters as the key explanation for the use of excessive force. Based on Donald Black's (1976) theory of law, policing research developed predictions using the situational approach. The expectations were that the police would be more likely to use force and to use excessive force in contacts with citizens characterized by low socioeconomic status, namely minorities and the poor. Existing research has typically found supporting evidence for the situational approach, and it seems to be more relevant than the individualistic approach (see, e.g., Riksheim and Chermak 1993; Klahm and Tillyer 2010 for reviews). Empirical research established that police officers are more likely to use force and, if included in the study, use excessive force as well, in situations involving citizens who are defiant and antagonistic toward the police (although recent evidence seems to be somewhat less supportive (Engel, Sabol and Worden 2000; Garner, Maxwell and Heraux 2002; Terrill and Mastrofski 2002), lower-class (e.g., Terrill and Mastrofski 2002; McCluskey, Terrill and Paoline 2005), intoxicated (e.g., Engel, Sabol, and Worden 2000; Terrill 2001), male (e.g., Mastrofski, Worden, and Snipes 1995; Worden 1995; Terrill 2001; Terrill and Mastrofski 2002), and black/nonwhite (recent evidence is more mixed; e.g., Fyfe 1982; Alpert 1989; Worden 1995; Garner, Maxwell, and Heraux 2002; Terrill and Mastrofski 2002; Terrill and Reisig 2003).

The organizational approach focuses on the police agency itself, its hierarchical organization, and the formal contributions it is making to channel and control police use of force and police use of excessive force, as well as the informal contributions it is making by allowing police culture to flourish. Every police agency is a hierarchy, characterized in many instances by a complex set of official rules governing the work of the police, including use of force and use of excessive force. In addition to establishing rules regulating use of force and proscribing use of excessive force, a critical step is their enforcement as well. Fyfe's (1982) study on shooting rates illustrates this point. Having established that shooting rates in the Memphis and New York police departments differed, Fyfe argued that the discrepancy is a reflection of differences in both the content of official rules and their enforcement. In another study, Fyfe (1979) analyzed the effect that more restrictive official rules have on actual shooting rates, concluding that the introduction of a more restrictive official rule on the use of firearms in the NYPD in 1972 resulted in a decline in the rate of firearm discharges of about 30 percent. In a more recent study, Alpert and MacDonald (2001) explored the relation between police officer use of force and police agency characteristics and found that agencies that required supervisors to fill out use of force reports had lower levels of use of force, while agency accreditation and unionization turned out not to be related to use of force rates.

The second part of the organizational approach emphasizes the informal police culture and its relation to use of force and use of excessive force. Police culture is viewed as a shared set of values centered around issues of danger. The inherent danger officers face can result in social isolation, solidarity, and group loyalty (see, e.g., Bittner 1970; Stoddard 1974; Reuss-Ianni 1983). The shared assumption is that police culture includes a preset collection of values that change relatively slowly (see, e.g., National Research Council 2004); more recent studies typically try to assess whether the introduction of more women and minorities into policing, as well as the concept of community policing, influence the rates with which police officers use force and use excessive force. In his study of use of force, Worden (1995) found that the degree of bureaucratization affects use of force, but police culture and community-policing values do not.

The sociological approach focuses on society at large, its socioeconomic characteristics, and their influence on use of force and use of excessive force. The argument is that the police would be more likely to use force and use excessive force in socially disadvantaged neighborhoods. Liska, Chamlin, and Reed (1985) used the "racial threat" hypothesis to argue that, as minorities in a certain population reach a certain threshold, they become perceived as a social threat and may face more severe treatment by the police, including more frequent use of force and excessive force. Studies provide support for this hypothesis. At the neighborhood level, empirical studies found that the police were more likely to use force in disadvantaged neighborhoods (e.g., Terrill and Reisig 2003). At the state level, Jacobs and Britt (1979) reported that higher rates of police use of deadly force were found in states with higher income inequality.

14.3.2   Extent of the Use of Excessive Force

One of the key obstacles to measurement of police corruption is its precise definition. The situation with the measurement of use of force and use of excessive force is analogous. Despite the fact that the U.S. Supreme Court established the objective legal standard of a reasonable police officer at the scene for civil cases, there is still heterogeneity of interpretations—as the Rodney King case illustrated—of whether the force used by officers in a specific case is within the legal boundaries of acceptable force. Consequently, there is no nationwide data source that provides information about use of force and use of excessive force:

> The incidence of wrongful use of force by police is unknown. Research is critically needed to determine reliably, validly, and precisely how often transgressions of use-of-force powers occur. We do not know how often police use force in ways that can be adjudged as wrongful. For example, we do not know the incidence of excessive force, even though this is a very serious violation of public trust. We could pull together data on excessive force using police disciplinary records and court documents, for example, but the picture would be sketchy, piecemeal, and potentially deceiving. When it comes to less grave or less precise transgressions, such as "improper," "abusive," "illegitimate," and "unnecessary" use of force, the state of knowledge is even more precarious. (Adams 1999, 10)

Empirical research tells us that, compared to the overall number of police-citizen contacts, police officers use force rarely (e.g., McLaughlin 1992; Klinger 1995; Garner et al. 1996). Early studies conducted in the 1960s and 1970s (e.g., Reiss 1967; Friedrich 1977) reported that police officers used force very infrequently, in fewer than 5 percent of police-citizen encounters. More recent nationwide surveys provide strong support to these early studies. In the 1999 Bureau of Justice Police-Public Contact Survey (Bureau of Justice Statistics 2001), nationwide results show that police officers used force or threatened to use force in fewer than 1 percent of contacts with the citizens. The findings of the 2005 survey are very similar; they show that about 1.6 percent of citizens experienced a police officer using force or threatening to use force (Bureau of Justice Statistics 2007a). In the IACP database containing police agency information about calls for service, police used force in 0.042 percent of the calls to which they responded (Adam 1999).

However, although it seems that police officers tend to use force in a small percentage of everyday encounters with citizens, citizens have characterized a relatively large proportion of these instances as use of excessive force. In particular, more than three-quarters of citizens who said that the police had used force characterized it as excessive in both the 1999 survey and the 2005 survey (75 percent in 1999, and 83 percent in 2005; Bureau of Justice Statistics 2007a). These evaluations, though, are based on citizens' perceptions of the incidents and may be subjective interpretations of those events.

When police officers do use force, they seem to use it on the lower end of the continuum, such as the use of verbal commands or grabbing the citizen (e.g., Klinger 1995; Garner and Maxwell 1999; Terrill 2001). In the Police-Public Contact Survey, in more than 7,500 adult arrests, in about 80 percent of the arrests in which police officers had used force, the level of force used did not involve use of weapons; it was mostly grabbing (Adams 1999). Pate and Fridell's survey of more than 1,000 police agencies (1993) also showed that police officers from all surveyed agencies used force on the lower end of the continuum more frequently. In particular, police officers from the surveyed city agencies used handcuffs at the rate of 490 per 1,000 and bodily force at the rate of 272 per 1,000, while, at the same time, they shot at civilians at the rate of less than 5 per 1,000, used electrical devices at the rate of 5 per 1,000, and used neck restraints at the rate of 1 per 1,000 sworn officers (Pate and Fridell 1993).

While citizen surveys may suffer from "Type I errors" (or "false positives"), police agencies' review of citizen complaints may also suffer from "Type II errors" (or "false negatives"). Compared to some objective measure of use of excessive force, citizens may perceive too many cases involving use of excessive force, while the police agencies may tend to downplay the number of cases featuring use of excessive force. Pate and Fridell's study (1993) of more than 1,000 police agencies, including sheriff's departments, country police departments, city police departments, and state agencies, found that fewer than 15 percent of use of force complaints have been sustained. The authors also found substantial heterogeneity in complaint rates, from 16 per 1,000 sworn officers for the state agencies to 48 per 1,000 officers for the city agencies (Pate and Fridell 1993).

14.4 CONTROL OF POLICE MISCONDUCT

Any society interested in control of police misconduct—be the interest rhetorical or real—develops a system of institutions and entrusts them with responsibility for controlling police misconduct. Systems may vary in complexity from simple ones, in which the primary reliance is on the police to police themselves, to complex and heterogeneous ones, encompassing a multitude of players and a diversity of tasks. Traditionally, the control system is organized in the first instance around institutions of control (e.g., courts, police agency), and in the second instance around specific tasks (e.g., investigate cases of police corruption; try police officers accused of extortion). The mechanisms of control may be internal (housed within the police agency itself), external (housed outside of the police agency), or mixed (housed outside of the police agency, but having police officers as members).

14.4.1 Internal Mechanisms of Control

Although control of police misconduct involves a series of tasks that transcend the boundaries of a police agency, nevertheless, police agencies should carry a substantial part in overall control efforts. From the way in which official rules are made by administrators and understood by police officers, to reactive internal investigations that the agency conducts, the agency should have a crucial influence on the level of police misconduct within it. Reports by independent commissions, established at the peaks of scandals, contain descriptions of how police agencies troubled by serious misconduct failed to engage internal control mechanisms effectively (see, e.g., Knapp Commission 1972; Christopher Commission 1991; Mollen Commission 1994; Pennsylvania Crime Commission 1974).

14.4.1.1 Official Rules and Policies

The purpose of administrative rules and policies, typically established by the police chief, is to determine appropriate conduct or behavior (e.g., on-time arrival on the job), prohibit inappropriate behavior (e.g., acceptance of a bribe, illegal use of deadly force), channel police officers' use of discretion in critical incidents (e.g., use of force, arrest, high-speed pursuits), guide officers in how to complete written reports (e.g., the use of force form), and establish supervisory oversight (e.g., National Research Council 2004; Walker and Katz 2008). As Bittner (1970) argued, these rules try to overemphasize less serious segments of police officers' job.

The content of these rules and their extent vary across police agencies; some agencies barely have written rules, while others have standard operating procedure manuals several hundred pages long (e.g., Barker and Wells 1982). In the 1980s, a survey found that about one-quarter of police agencies, mostly smaller ones, did not have written official rules at all (Barker and Wells 1982). The situation has improved greatly over the last three decades; the most recent survey by the Bureau of Justice Statistics (Reaves 2010) revealed that the overwhelming majority of police agencies—more than 95 percent of local police agencies—had written policies in place and that these rules covered code of conduct and appearance, use of lethal force, and use of non-lethal force (Reaves 2010).

Administrative rules have been used successfully to control several different aspects of police work: use of deadly force, high-speed pursuits, and domestic violence. Several empirical studies (e.g., Fyfe 1979; Geller and Scott 1992) found that the number of the use of deadly force incidents decreased after a new official policy, more restrictive in nature, had been enacted. Similarly, empirical research (e.g., Alpert 1997) has demonstrated that the introduction of more restrictive high-speed pursuit policies in the Miami-Dade Police Department substantially decreased the number of instances of high-speed pursuits and that the introduction of the more relaxed high-speed pursuit policies in the Omaha Police Department resulted in a substantially increased number of instances of high-speed pursuits (e.g., Alpert 1997). Empirical research did not report such positive and strong effects of administrative rules on other forms of police work/police misconduct (e.g., use of force in general, domestic violence; National Research Council 2004).

The presence of official rules does not guarantee that police misconduct will end. Official rules could prohibit only the most flagrant, serious, and outrageous forms of police misconduct. Police officers may not know what behavior is prohibited or may find the rules unclear. Fishman's study (1978) found that police officers from agencies characterized by widespread corruption tended to emphasize that the rules are not clear more often than police officers from less corrupt police agencies did. In addition, police chiefs and other administrators may create conflicting unofficial rules that can easily trump the official ones (e.g., Kutnjak Ivković 2005). Reports by independent commissions (e.g., Knapp Commission 1972; Pennsylvania Crime Commission 1974; Mollen Commission 1994) contain descriptions of numerous instances in which police chiefs in New York and Philadelphia allowed the existence of unofficial rules that were in conflict with official rules. Finally, if police administrators keep the official rules on the books but never enforce them, they create a police culture in which official rules do not have any weight.

14.4.1.2 Police Chief/Administration

Police chiefs and police administrators are at the top of the police agency's hierarchy; what they do and how they do it resonates throughout the police agency. A police chief's own unethical behavior or double standards have a direct influence on how subordinates in the agency behave (see, e.g., Knapp Commission 1972).

Terrill's study (2001) on the use of force showed that the police chief's and administrator's stance on the "style of policing practiced" influenced how police officers used force; when the police chief and his administration in Indianapolis adhered to the "get tough" approach, police officers in this agency used a higher level of force than police officers in St. Petersburg, where the police chief and his administration emphasized the problem-solving model. The effects of the police chief's views could be a powerful force within the police agency indeed; the majority of police officers participating in a 2000 nationwide survey (Weisburd and Greenspan 2000, 6) supported the idea that "a chief's strong position against the abuse of authority can make a big difference in deterring officers from abusing authority."

The police chief's role transcends his own behavior and the stance on a particular issue; police chiefs perform traditional managerial tasks, including planning, organizing, coordinating, and controlling (e.g., Moore and Stephens 1991). Although the exercise of their managerial functions is limited by the existing laws and court precedents (as well as by the mayor, politicians, public, media, civil service, and police unions), their lack of determination or a complete failure in any of the managerial functions could substantially affect the extent of police misconduct in a police agency. Within the legal boundaries, police chiefs have control over a number of issues, including official rules, recruitment standards, nature and extent of police officer training in ethics, supervisory accountability, internal control, and disciplining of officers who engage in police misconduct. Reports by independent commissions investigating allegations of widespread police corruption in police agencies (e.g., Knapp Commission 1972; Pennsylvania Crime Commission 1974) provide numerous examples of how the police chief's failures to carry out certain managerial tasks, such as refusal to address subordinate's misconduct, failure to enforce the official rules, or adherence to the "rotten apple approach," contributed toward continuation of a police culture widely tolerant of police misconduct.

14.4.1.3 *Supervisors*

In a hierarchical organization such as a police agency, supervisors represent another layer of misconduct control (see, e.g., Kutnjak Ivković 2005). Although they are not at the very top of the hierarchy, their role nonetheless is perceived as crucial, as reported by an overwhelming majority of police officers participating in the 2000 nationwide survey (Weisburd and Greenspan 2000). Supervisors' duties are primarily to oversee their subordinates, which can include tasks such as reviewing their reports and forms (e.g., the use of force reports), monitoring their conduct, writing reports about those suspected of police misconduct, opening investigations in cases of police misconduct, disciplining officers who engage in misconduct, and advising them when their conduct is rule-violating (see, e.g., Walker and Katz 2008).

Supervisors could fail to perform their role by participating in misconduct themselves (and along with their subordinates), as the Knapp Commission (1972) and the Pennsylvania Crime Commission (1974) documented was the case in the New York Police Department and the Philadelphia Police Department in the 1960s and 1970s, or could fail to take a firm stance on misconduct or enforce the official rules, as the Christopher Commission (1991) and the Mollen Commission (1994) documented was the case in the Los Angeles and New York Police Departments in the 1990s. The Christopher Commission (1991) wrote in its report that supervisors in the LAPD failed to monitor racist and sexist language that their subordinates used in communications on the LAPD system.

The Mollen Commission (1994) documented instances of supervisors' complete failure to oversee reports submitted by their subordinates or to challenge search and arrest, and overtime payment forms filed by their subordinates. The LAPD Board of Inquiry (Los Angeles Police Department 2000) noticed similar issues with the supervisors' failure to review the reports submitted by their subordinates in the Rampart area. In fact, the LAPD Board of Inquiry (Los Angeles Police Department 2000) documented cases in which subordinates, working in areas characterized by corruption and use of excessive force, simply singed their supervisors' names on booking approvals and arrest reports.

Not only were supervisors in the agencies characterized with widespread misconduct not rewarded for reporting, but they were also informally punished if they tried to report misconduct (e.g., Mollen Commission 1994). Supervisors in agencies riddled with misconduct are typically not held accountable for the performance of their supervisory role (e.g., Knapp Commission 1972; Christopher Commission 1991; Mollen Commission 1994; Los Angeles Police Department 2000). The Christopher Commission (1991, ix), investigating the allegations of racism, sexism, and use of excessive force, heard testimony from Assistant Chief Dotson, who stated that "we [the top administration] have failed miserably" to hold supervisors accountable for excessive force by officers under their command.

A new attempt to hold supervisors accountable—CompStat—was introduced in the New York Police Department in 1994 by William Bratton and his administrators (e.g., McDonald, Greenberg, and Bratton 2001). The idea behind CompStat is that regularly scheduled meetings will force supervisors to discuss crime problems before other peers and their own supervisors and hold them accountable for success or failure in dealing with crime problems in their area. By 1999, about one-quarter of police agencies with one hundred or more employees participating in the study had already introduced CompStat in their agencies, and about one-third planned to do so in the future (Weisburd et al. 2003). Finally, it has also been noted that CompStat, developed to deal with crime control and establish accountability of middle and top administrators (e.g., Silverman 1999), could not work well as a way of establishing accountability of first-line supervisors who don't take part in the regular CompStat meetings (National Research Council 2004).

14.4.1.4 Internal Control

Internal control of police misconduct consists primarily of receipt of complaints, their investigation, and referral of completed case files to decision makers (e.g., chain of command, police chief). Thus, the internal affairs office performs a fact-finding role (e.g., Carter 1994) and another part of the police agency, perhaps immediate supervisors, the chain of command, or the police chief, makes decisions in such cases.

In terms of its organization, internal control can range from this task being entrusted to an individual police officer assigned on a case-by-case basis by the police chief, to an elaborate system of internal control offices consisting of both the main office in the headquarters and field offices. The complexity of the organization typically depends on the police agency size, available resources, the number of complaints received annually, and the overall public service demands (e.g., Carter 1994). According to the 2000 LEMAS (Reaves and Hickman 2004), the presence of a permanent internal affairs office has become a norm; more than three-quarters of both state police agencies (84 percent) and local police agencies (79 percent) now have permanent internal affairs offices (Reaves and Hickman 2004). However, regardless of its organization, a common feature of the internal affairs office is that its police officers are directly responsible to the chief of police.

Although the work performed by internal affairs offices could be proactive (e.g., integrity testing; Baueris 1977; Giuliani and Bratton 1995), it is mostly reactive in nature; proactive investigations are more an exception than the rule (e.g., Kutnjak Ivković 2005). Internal affairs investigations are governed by rules that differ from those that prevail in criminal investigations; as a consequence of the U.S. Supreme Court ruling in *Garrity v. New Jersey* (385 U.S. 483 [1967]), police agencies separate the investigation of cases involving police misconduct into an administrative investigation (run by the internal affairs office) and, if the police misconduct could be serious enough to constitute a crime, a criminal investigation (run by detectives in the detective unit). Whereas the full set of constitutional rights applies in the criminal investigation, the accused police officer is not allowed to claim Fifth Amendment privileges and has to answer the questions truthfully in administrative investigations.

A typical reactive investigation starts with a complaint filed by a citizen or a police officer, or with a report filed by an immediate supervisor. Prior research has documented many reasons why citizens and police officers may be reluctant to file a complaint, ranging from unfamiliarity with the system and its elaborate requirements imposed before the complaint is officially submitted, to distrust in police and fear of retaliation (see, e.g., President's Commission on Law Enforcement and Administration of Justice 1967a; Russell 1978; Walker and Bumphus 1992; Pate and Fridell 1993; Guerrero-Daley 2000). It comes as no surprise that existing research reports that complaint rates exhibit great variation across police agencies. In a 1991 survey of the six largest police agencies, Pate and Hamilton (1991) reported that the rates varied from as low as 5.5 per 100 sworn officers in Philadelphia to as high as 36.9 per 100 sworn officers in Houston. Pate and Fridell (1993) also found a substantial variation in the use of force complaint rates per 1,000 police officers, from 15.7 for state agencies, 20.7 for sheriff's departments, 33.8 for county agencies, to 47.5 for municipal agencies. A more recent (2002) survey of large local and state police agencies (Hickman 2006) uncovered variations in the use of force complaint rates as well; the rates varied from 1.3 for state agencies to 9.5 for municipal agencies.

During an investigation, police investigators collect and examine physical evidence, interview witnesses, analyze records, and interview the accused police officer (Carter 1994). Once the evidence has been collected, an internal affairs investigator completes the case file and forwards it to the unit or person in charge of making a decision concerning the disposition of the case. The disposition in the case is made either through the chain of command review or through a disciplinary hearing by an administrative board (Carter 1994). If the decision is made through a hearing, the hearing itself can vary from a very formal one, resembling a trial, to a more relaxed one, resembling a meeting (Carter 1994).

When the complaint is sustained—the decision maker finds that there is substantial evidence to prove that the police officer in question engaged in the rule-violating behavior—official discipline will be meted out. Its severity will be related to the severity of the rule-violating behavior, aggravating and mitigating circumstances, and the police officer's prior disciplinary history. Police agencies do not sustain a large proportion of the complaints; on average, they sustain between 0 and 25 percent of all complaints (Dugan and Breda 1991; Pate and Fridell 1993; Perez 1994; Hickman 2006), with 8 to 10 percent being typical (e.g., Wagner 1980; Pate and Fridell 1993; Hickman 2006). However, just like the complaint rates are affected by a host of reasons unrelated to the level of police misconduct itself, rates of sustained complaints could also vary across the agencies for reasons directly unrelated to the level of police misconduct in police agencies (see, e.g., West 1988; Pate and Hamilton 1991; Perez 1994; Adams 1999; Walker 2001; Hickman 2006; Klockars, Kutnjak Ivković, and Haberfeld 2006). In fact, Pate and Hamilton (1991) caution that, because of the differences in methods of filing and investigating complaints across the agencies, complaint rates are really not comparable across agencies.

Although the idea of police policing themselves sounds promising, prior research (e.g., Sherman 1978) and in-depth investigations and reports by independent commissions (e.g., Knapp Commission 1972; Pennsylvania Crime Commission 1974; Christopher Commission 1991; Mollen Commission 1994) demonstrate that, in reality, such internal systems of control exhibit serious problems precisely in the agencies that need them the most—agencies characterized by widespread corruption, racism, sexism, and use of excessive force. Although the specific issues documented in these reports can vary from not establishing written guidelines and providing resources and manpower to internal affairs units, to failing to investigate complaints, ignoring information, and openly hiding complaints (see, e.g., Knapp Commission 1972; Pennsylvania Crime Commission 1974; Christopher Commission 1991; Mollen Commission 1994), they all suggest numerous failures of internal systems of control.

14.4.1.5 *Early Warning Systems*

Although early warning systems were recommended by the U.S. Commission on Civil Rights (1981) in 1981, they did not become widely popular until the 1990s. In 2001, the U.S. Department of Justice listed early warning systems as one of the best practices in its "Principles for Promoting Police Integrity" (U.S. Department of Justice 2001). A 1998 nationwide survey of municipal police agencies found that about one-third of police agencies have already established an early warning system in their agencies or are in the process of developing one (Walker, Alpert, and Kenney 2000). Decrees between the U.S. Department of Justice and several police agencies have lead to the establishment of several additional early warning systems (Walker and Katz 2008).

Typically, early warning systems are housed within the internal affairs offices and, unlike most of the internal affairs work, have a primarily proactive purpose. The idea is to identify potential problem officers—those who generate an unusually large number of complaints—and try to intervene before they indeed become problem officers. Warning systems collect information about each police officer (e.g., complaints, financial records, use of force reports, accident reports), analyze the information, and, if something unusual is spotted (e.g., a police officer has a disproportionately large number of use of force reports), a red flag is raised (see, e.g., Walker, Alpert, and Kenney 2000; Walker and Katz 2008). The process that will be initiated differs from the typical internal affairs investigation. During the intervention stage, typically there will be an informal counseling by the supervisor or retraining. During the post-intervention stage, a police officer's performance will be monitored for a certain period of time (see, e.g., Walker, Alpert, and Kenney 2000).

Despite the promising concept—early intervention before the problem becomes too serious—empirical research on the topic is limited; nevertheless, it consistently shows some reduction in the number of citizen complaints and use of force reports by police officers subject to early warning system intervention (e.g., Walker, Alpert, and Kenney 2000; Vera Institute of Justice 1999).

14.4.2 External Mechanisms of Control

Control of police misconduct should go beyond a police agency's own control efforts. Many organizations and institutions participate in control efforts, albeit mostly on a reactive basis. Very few, such as independent review boards and potentially the U.S. Supreme Court, play preventive roles.

14.4.2.1 *The U.S. Supreme Court*

As the court at the very top of the hierarchical organization of U.S. federal courts, the Supreme Court's decisions have the power to influence all future decisions by the Court itself and by all lower courts. However, the chances of having a case heard by the Supreme Court are very slim; the Court grants certiorari in fewer than 5 percent of the cases filed (Supreme Court 2011). The Justices carefully select the cases to be argued before the Court because of the potential widespread influence of these decisions. Although the initial way in which the Supreme Court gets involved is predominantly reactive, because of the widespread and long-term influence of its decisions on the numerous subsequent lower court decisions, the Court's true role in controlling police conduct/misconduct is primarily preventive.

Since the 1960s, the U.S. Supreme Court has expanded the application of many federally established standards to state and local police. The Court's precedents regulate proper police conduct, such as the establishment of the requirement of giving Fifth Amendment warnings to arrestees (*Miranda v. Arizona,* 372 U.S. 436 [1966]). It also decided cases drawing the line between appropriate and inappropriate police conduct, such as the ruling determining that illegally obtained evidence cannot be used in court proceedings (*Mapp v. Ohio,* 367 U.S. 643 [1961]). The nature of the Court's decisions has encapsulated aspects of substantive criminal/constitutional law, as was the case in sentencing for the violation of Rodney King's constitutional rights under color of law (*Koon v. United States*, 518 U.S. 81 [1996]), or aspects of procedural criminal/constitutional law, as was the case in the prohibition of the denial of Fifth Amendment rights to police officers under criminal investigation (*Garrity v. New Jersey*, 385 U.S. 483 [1967]).

The influence of Supreme Court decisions can be measured not only through the effect they have on the lower courts and their future decisions, but also through the changes of behavior of police officers. Two Supreme Court decisions have received extensive empirical treatment. In *Mapp*, the Court confirmed the inclusion of the exclusionary rule in court proceedings, prohibiting the use of illegally obtained evidence. Empirical studies conducted shortly after the decision showed mixed results (e.g., Skolnick 1966; Oaks 1970; Canon 1974), but more recent studies (e.g., Orfield 1987; Canon 1991) suggested stronger effects on police officer conduct.

The Supreme Court held in *Miranda* that a suspect's confession obtained during custodial police interrogation constitutes a violation of the Fifth Amendment right against self-incrimination unless the police provide specific warnings that the suspect has the right to remain silent, that anything he or she says could be used against him or her, and that he or she has the right to counsel. The research ongoing at the time the Supreme Court issued the ruling (Black and Reiss 1967) showed that police officers rarely gave Miranda warnings. Studies from the 1970s, conducted a decade after the ruling, showed that police officers did issue the warning routinely, but they also noted that the routine warning could be superficial. More recent studies (Leo 1998; Leo and Thomas 1998) report that police officers issued the warning in the overwhelming majority of the cases under study (96 percent) and thus offer evidence supporting the Supreme Court's long-term effect on police behavior.

14.4.2.2 *Criminal Proceedings*

Criminal proceedings play a dual role in the control of police misconduct. First, as citizens of a particular state, police officers could be prosecuted, tried, and convicted for numerous crimes such as murder, theft, or assault. Second, because of their public service employment, police officers could be prosecuted, tried, and convicted for crimes requiring that the perpetrator be a public employee (e.g., extortion and criminal liability for deprivation of civil rights).

Nationwide statistics on the overall number of criminal cases of police misconduct are non-existent. Even when broken down into types of police misconduct (e.g., corruption, use of excessive force), the problem of accurate definitions makes the counting extremely complicated (e.g., what behavior should be counted as use of excessive force). Taking these caveats into account, prosecutions and convictions for the use of excessive force cases at both the federal and state levels are rare (e.g., Adams 1999; Cheh 1995; Human Rights Watch 1998). The U.S. Department of Justice receives about 8,000 complaints of police misconduct per year (Cheh 1995). Out of these 8,000 complaints, the Department of Justice investigates about 3,000 (about one-third). However, only about 50 cases, or less than 1 percent of the submitted complaints, are presented to a grand jury

(Cheh 1995). Because of the low arrest and conviction rates, criminal proceedings in use of excessive force cases cannot be an effective deterrent (e.g., Skolnick and Fyfe 1993).

The situation with corruption is by no means more positive. Kutnjak Ivković (2005) reported fewer than 50 convictions annually for federal law enforcement corruption. Similarly, state prosecutions and trials for corruption are infrequent. The findings reported by the Knapp Commission (1972) and the Pennsylvania Crime Commission (1974) are indicative of the problem. In the 1970s, at the time the Knapp Commission (1972) found corruption to be widespread in the NYPD, the prosecutors in New York City initiated only about 30 cases of police corruption annually (Knapp Commission 1972). In addition, chances of convictions and severe punishment were low; fewer than one out of five police officers indicted for corruption were prosecuted, tried, and convicted to a prison sentence of one year or longer (Knapp Commission 1972). About the same time, the Pennsylvania Crime Commission (1974) found that the Philadelphia Police Department was plagued by corruption, but only about seven police officers were arrested for corruption and criminal cases initiated against them annually (Pennsylvania Crime Commission 1974).

14.4.2.3   Civil Proceedings

Civil proceedings allow citizens to hold police officers and municipal police agencies civilly liable for police misconduct that violates citizens' civil rights guaranteed by federal and state laws. Thus, not all forms of police misconduct or all types within the same form of police misconduct qualify for this type of control. For example, in a typical case of quid-pro-quo bribery, the citizen participating in the bribery has no basis in civil law for a lawsuit against the police officer or the police department. On the other hand, a citizen who sustains severe injuries as a consequence of a police officer's use of excessive force might be a potential plaintiff for such a lawsuit.

The legal basis for civil lawsuits exists at both federal and state levels. The federal code in Section 1983 (U.S. Code, Title 42) establishes the key tool for civil proceedings. Two U.S. Supreme Court decisions expanded the application of Section 1983 to police misconduct. Specifically, in *Monroe v. Pape* (365 U.S. 167 [1961]) the Supreme Court determined that police officers could be held liable for deprivation of Fourth Amendments rights under the civil rights statute. In *Monell v. Department of Social Services* (436 U.S. 658 [1978]) the Supreme Court established that municipalities could be held liable for police misconduct if it was carried out pursuant to the agency's policy or custom. Thus, through these two rulings, the Supreme Court opened the door for citizens to sue both individual police officers and police departments. Since the first decision in the 1960s, the number of Section 1983 lawsuits has increased (Cheh 1996, 250). Amounts paid to successful plaintiffs in these types of lawsuits vary across the country, from an average of $1.6 million annually in Cincinnati to an average of $35.8 million annually in Los Angeles (Kappeler 2006).

The power and effect of Section 1983 lawsuits is limited by the U.S. Supreme Court's ruling in *City of Los Angeles v. Lyons* (461 U.S. 95 [1983]), in which it effectively eliminated the possibility of injunctive relief for individual citizens. Thus, plaintiffs in Section 1983 lawsuits are limited to the compensatory and punitive damages against police departments and individual police officers (Cheh 1995). However, the reality is that the potential effect on individual police officers and police agencies is ameliorated by the fact that compensatory damages and sometimes punitive damages are paid by the city government, not by individual police officers and/or the police agency. In fact, police officers in some jurisdictions are protected by law from paying legal fees and damages, and city attorneys represent the officers in the lawsuits (e.g., Patton 1993). Thus, the reality is that police officers face no financial incentives to change their behavior as a consequence of these lawsuits. Furthermore, even when police officers are found liable, their careers as police officers are not affected; their chances of being disciplined by their police agencies are slim (see, e.g., Chevigny 1995). Despite this, empirical studies suggest that police officers are bothered by the idea that they could be sued (e.g., Kappeler 1997).

The effect of these lawsuits on police agencies is not very powerful either. In fact, a number of studies (e.g., *Yale Law Journal* 1979; Littlejohn 1981) report that these lawsuits have very limited effect on police agencies. Neither New York nor Los Angeles implemented any resulting changes (see Chevigny 1995). One police agency, concerned with the rising costs of lawsuits (e.g., Los Angeles County Sheriff's Department), took proactive steps to address the issue of civil lawsuits. In 1993, the Office of the Special Counsel was established to investigate problems, recommend reforms, and reduce the costs of litigation. The reports issued by the Special Counsel (a form of citizen review) suggested positive changes (Special Counsel to the Los Angeles County Sheriff's Department 1999, 2002).

In 1994, the US government passed the Violent Crime Control Act (42 U.S.C. 14141). The Act expanded the list of potential plaintiffs, adding the U.S. Department of Justice to the list. The Department of Justice was thus authorized to act as a plaintiff in cases against police agency when there is "a pattern or practice of conduct by law enforcement officers... that deprives persons of rights, privileges, or immunities secured or protected by the Constitution." According to the latest available count (U.S. Department of Justice 2010), an investigation of 14 police agencies is ongoing and 10 lawsuits have ended either with consent decrees or out-of-court settlements. These lawsuits resulted in court-imposed systematic and widespread reforms of police agencies, including revisions of the use of force reporting system, establishments of early warning systems, revisions of complaint procedures, and improvements in police training (Walker and Katz 2008). To ensure that the required reforms are performed, courts typically appoint an outside monitor. The limited empirical evidence is mixed; while reports by the Vera Institute (serving as the monitor for the Pittsburgh Police Department) suggest that Pittsburgh is on track with the changes (Vera Institute of Justice 2002), reports from Los Angeles and Washington, D.C. are less positive (Walker and Katz 2008).

14.4.2.4 Independent Commissions

Independent commissions are not a permanent part of the control system; rather, they are established on a temporary basis, typically almost overnight, as a way to address blossoming political scandals that result from critical police-citizen incidents. For example, the Mollen Commission was established after the arrest of NYPD police officer Michael Dowd and five other police officers became front-page news. The video recording of the beating of Rodney King by LAPD officers was televised across the globe, compelling the Los Angeles government to establish the Christopher Commission.

These independent commissions (President's Commission on Law Enforcement and Administration of Justice 1967a, 1967b; Kerner Commission 1968; Knapp Commission 1972; Pennsylvania Crime Commission 1974; Mollen Commission 1994) are typically composed of prominent community members and experts on policing. Their primary tasks are to investigate the extent and nature of misconduct and propose changes to the existing system of control. Because of their "big-picture" approach, these commissions have a chance to provide recommendations that could lead toward long-term solutions, not only for specific police agencies, but, because of publicity, to policing in general. In fact, these independent commissions are in a position to set standards that could be used by police agencies across the country (see, e.g., National Research Council 2004; Walker and Katz 2008).

However, potential success of these independent commissions is limited by their temporary nature and the lack of authority to enforce their recommendations (e.g., National Research Council 2004; Kutnjak Ivković 2005; Walker and Katz 2008), as well as inadequate resources (e.g., Pennsylvania Crime Commission 1974), lack of political independence (e.g., Pennsylvania Crime Commission 1974), and insufficient legal authority (e.g., Knapp Commission 1972). Lack of authority to enforce their recommendations is critical in terms of the effect they might have on the long-term changes in police agencies. At the end of its investigation into accusations of police officer use of excessive force, racism, and sexism, the Christopher Commission (1991) strongly recommended that the Office of Inspector General be established to audit, investigate, and oversee the LAPD's own efforts to handle complaints and that an early warning system be established. In the early 2000s, the LAPD still did not have the early warning system (Walker 2005). It took several years to establish the Office of Inspector General. In 1995, the office was finally established, but the inspector general resigned in 1998—less than three years after taking office—citing strong resistance from the police administration and the police commission as the primary reason for his resignation (Walker 2001).

14.4.3 Mixed Mechanisms of Control

The mechanisms of control classified in this category share some characteristics of external mechanisms (e.g., they are housed outside of the police agency itself) and some characteristics of internal mechanisms (e.g., they have police officers as members).

14.4.3.1 Citizen Reviews

The idea behind citizen reviews, developed in the 1960s, has been to provide an independent and external review of citizen complaints against the police. However, as research demonstrates, about one-quarter of citizen reviews have police officers as members (Walker and Kreisel 2001), which positions citizen reviews in the mixed mechanism of control. While the concept of independent citizen reviews did not get country-wide acceptance in the 1960s, the number of citizen reviews increased dramatically in the last two decades (e.g., Walker 2005). Estimates suggest that almost all large municipal police agencies had established citizen review by the 2000s (Walker 2005); by 2000, "[o]ver 100 different agencies exist, covering law enforcement agencies that serve nearly one-third of the American population, and they are found in about 80 percent of the big cities of this country" (Walker 2001, 6).

Walker and Kreisel (2001) surveyed existing citizen reviews. Their classification of citizen reviews, based on the functions they perform, consists of four categories. Type I citizen reviews ("citizen review")—about 34 percent—provide an initial fact-finding completely independently from the police agency (Walker 2001). Type II citizen reviews ("citizen input")—about 46 percent—provide input in the investigation conducted by the police agency (Walker 2001; Walker and Kreisel 2001). Type III citizen reviews ("citizen monitors")—about 17 percent—serve as the appellate review after the police investigation has been completed (Walker 2001; Walker and Kreisel 2001). Lastly, Type IV citizen reviews ("citizen auditors")—about 3 percent—"review, monitor, or audit the police department's complaint process" (Walker 2001, 62).

Unless they are authorized to perform policy review as well, the majority of citizen reviews—Type I to Type III—focus on individual cases; their work is limited to the case at hand and does not have the potential of going beyond the individual case. Even if they are authorized to review policy, their review is limited to the issues raised in the complaint. On the other hand, Type IV citizen reviews, such as the San Jose Police Auditor and the Special Counsel to the Los Angeles County Sheriff's Department (Walker 2005), are much better suited to provide a thorough review of the complaint system and the operation of the police agency. For example, the San Jose Independent Police Auditor started from individual complaints as a means to detect potential problem areas, and then expanded its inquiries into other areas. In the period from 1993 to 2005, the auditor made more than 95 policy recommendations, the overwhelming majority of which (93 percent) have been accepted by the San Jose Police Department (Walker 2005). However, merely establishing an auditor does not guarantee success. Research suggests that the San Jose Independent Police Auditor and the Special Counsel to the Los Angeles County Sheriff's Department have been evaluated as successful, but the Seattle Police Auditor and the Albuquerque Independent Counsel have not (Walker 2005). Typical problems included lack of leadership, vision, direction, and cooperation (Walker 2005).

Empirical research on the effectiveness of citizen review suffers from inherent problems: even if the citizen review group and the police agency are both in charge of investigating citizen complaints, they rarely handle the same types of cases, thus making direct comparison very difficult. Hudson's (1972) study of citizen reviews uncovered that the Philadelphia Police Department sustained a larger percentage of complaints than the citizen review ("Police Advisory Board") did. This unexpected result could be explained by the different nature of cases handled by each agency.

14.4.3.2 *Accreditation*

The Commission on Accreditation for Law Enforcement Agencies (CALEA) was established in 1979. However, although CALEA is an independent agency, housed outside of any police agency, it still has police officers as members next to community members. Because of this combination (housed outside of a police agency, but having police officers as members), accreditation is classified as a mixed mechanism of control.

CALEA publishes model official rules and standards. By 2009, CALEA had provided 463 standards (CALEA 2010). The idea is that these standards and model rules should be used by police officers across the country. The introduction of an early warning system—a promising and proactive control tool—is a required standard for accreditation. Police agencies that seek CALEA accreditation should adopt the CALEA rules and design their own rules based on the model rules and standards. By 2008, about 500 police agencies were accredited by CALEA (Walker and Katz 2008) and thus have incorporated the CALEA standards into their official agency rules.

However, CALEA does not have the power to force police agencies to incorporate its standards into their official agency rules. In other words, police agencies' participation in the CALEA program and the adaptation of these CALEA standards into police agencies' official rules is strictly voluntary. The obvious problem is that police agencies characterized by serious and/or widespread misconduct, be it corruption, use of excessive force, racial profiling, or planting of evidence, are the least likely to volunteer and change their official rules in accordance with CALEA standards. In addition, the CALEA standards are not ideal or optimal standards, but are merely basic or minimum standards (Walker and Katz 2008).

Existing empirical research on the effectiveness of CALEA accreditation on the nature and extent of police misconduct is scarce. Walker and Katz (2008) list examples of police agencies in which, as a consequence of accreditation, the agency was able to reduce insurance costs, improve the use of force reporting, and refine the procedures used in juvenile cases.

14.5 CONCLUDING THOUGHTS

Police misconduct is a complex set of heterogeneous behaviors, encompassing activities such as sleeping on duty, accepting a bribe, stealing money from a drug dealer, beating a suspect to obtain a confession, extorting sexual favors, and lying on the stand. These behaviors differ along many dimensions such as seriousness of the acts, legal norms they violate, levels of support they might generate among police officers, severity of the discipline, and motivation for the acts. Despite all these differences, they have a common theme: to engage in these behaviors, police officers abuse their office.

Different forms of police misconduct share another feature: it is difficult to define them. There is substantial disagreement among scholars over definitions of even basic forms of police misconduct such as police corruption, use of excessive force, or racial profiling. Lack of commonly embraced definitions yields limited ability to assess the nature and the extent of the problem at hand. Most of the information about the prevalence and characteristics of different forms of police misconduct is limited to bits and pieces of information obtained sporadically and cannot be readily generalized at the nationwide level. Accordingly, there is a pressing need to provide reliable, nationwide, and systematic estimates or measures of the prevalence and features of police misconduct (e.g., Adams 1999; Kutnjak Ivković 2005). Scholars and police chiefs alike would benefit from knowing whether the level of police corruption in an agency has changed over the years, or from developing a deeper understanding of the relation between use of force and police officer race or education. Engaging in agency-wide reforms cannot yield satisfactory results if good measures of the levels of misconduct before and after the reform are lacking. The demand is clearly there, and projects such as the Bureau of Justice Statistics' police-citizen survey are prime examples of promising ways of collecting data.

However, because of the nature of the beast, collecting data in a direct way could be troublesome; police officers and citizens may be reluctant to discuss their experiences and engagement in police misconduct, even when researchers promise them confidentially and/or anonymity. Police chiefs may be reluctant to open their doors to researchers because of their fear that the results will create serious problems for them. Despite all the problems, we do need the information and future projects should seek to address them. To avoid the pitfalls encountered by traditional research that asked direct questions regarding police officer engagement in police misconduct, Klockars and Kutnjak Ivković (2003) developed a novel approach that relies on questions of fact and opinion. They have inverted the problem by measuring the extent of police integrity instead of measuring the extent of police misconduct. A study of thirty police agencies (Klockars et al. 2000) and extensive international applications (Klockars, Kutnjak Ivković, and Haberfeld 2004) show that it is possible to use this approach to survey the police successfully. They also revealed that police agencies varied considerably in the contours of their police integrity. The research also provides useful feedback to police administrators about police officers' knowledge of agency rules, views about seriousness of police misconduct, perceptions of disciplinary fairness, and the extent of the code of silence.

Control of police misconduct is challenging and, as the findings of independent commissions (e.g., Knapp Commission 1972; Christopher Commission 1991; Mollen Commission 1994) show, it is most troublesome in the agencies facing serious integrity challenges. Agencies that need effective control seem to be least likely to maintain an effective control system. Thus, the external layer of control is critical; police cannot always be trusted to police themselves effectively. Although a number of these external control mechanisms are necessary because they fulfill different aspects of the control process (e.g., the U.S. Supreme Court establishes legal standards, courts try and convict officers charged with bribery or use of excessive force), very few of them provide a general oversight of the police agency and its control. For the overall control system to be effective, these parts of the control system providing attention to specific functions and the general overview mechanisms both should be in place, able and willing to provide continuous input.

One of the key problems with both internal and external control mechanisms is that, with few notable exceptions (e.g., early warning systems, police auditors), the mechanisms of control are reactive by design; they do not operate proactively by trying to prevent misconduct, but, rather, are reactive, trying to address misconduct once it happens and the incident becomes public knowledge. These mechanisms are set and left to react if and when new cases occur. These mechanisms do not provide continuous, but sporadic attention to police misconduct. Even superbly designed mechanisms deteriorate over time if they are not controlled and adjusted regularly; it is not unusual for a police agency gradually to fail to enforce the rules, relax supervision and accountability, omit to engage in detection and investigation of misconduct, and allow the development of a police culture tolerant of police misconduct. Similarly, it is not difficult to imagine that, over time, the public, politicians, and legislature lose interest in police misconduct in the agency and neglect to perform functions of police misconduct control (see, e.g., Kutnjak Ivković 2005).

Police auditors are the only institutions in the control system whose task is to provide continuous and permanent oversight over the police agency's control system. Some of the existing auditors seem to be more effective than others (e.g., Walker 2005); current research on the effectiveness of police auditors (and other forms of citizen reviews) is quite limited. Future research should explore not only what makes some auditors a success and others a failure, but also what makes some police agencies' internal system more effective than others. Research should also explore the most promising aspects of the agency's internal control mechanisms (e.g., early warning systems, CompStat). Clearly, police misconduct is an everyday part of policing, and high-quality research can help develop effective practices of preventing it and addressing it once it happens.

REFERENCES

Adams, Keith. 1999. "What We Know About Police Use of Force." In *Use of Force by Police: Overview of National and Local Data*. Washington, DC: Office of Justice Programs.

Alpert, Geoffrey P. 1989. "Police Use of Deadly Force: The Miami Experience." In *Critical Issues in Policing: Contemporary Readings*, edited by Robert Dunham and Geoffrey P. Alpert, 480–496. Prospect Heights, IL: Waveland Press.

——. 1997. *Pursuit Policies and Training*. Washington, DC: Government Printing Office.

Alpert, Geoffrey P., and John MacDonald. 2001. "Police Use of Force: An Analysis of Organizational Characteristics." *Justice Quarterly* 18:393–409.

Anonymous. 1979. "Project: Suing the Police in Federal Court." *Yale Law Journal* 88:781–824.

Balch, Robert W. 1972. "Police Personality: Fact or Fiction?" *Journal of Criminal Law, Criminology and Police Science* 63:106–19.

Barker, Thomas. 2002. "Ethnical Police Behavior." In *Police Misconduct*, edited by Kim Lersch, 1–25. Upper Saddle River, NJ: Prentice Hall.

Barker, Thomas, and David L. Carter. 1994. "A Typology of Police Deviance." In *Police Deviance*, 3d ed., edited by Thomas Barker and David L. Carter, 3–12. Cincinnati, OH: Anderson.

Barker, Thomas, and Julian Roebuck. 1973. *An Empirical Typology of Police Corruption*. Springfield, IL: Charles C. Thomas.

Barker, Thomas, and Robert O. Wells 1982. "Police Administrator's Attitudes Toward Definition and Control of Police Deviance." *FBI Law Enforcement Bulletin* 51:8–16.

Baueris, Vic. 1977. *New York Police Department: Preventing Crime and Corruption*. http://www.icac.nsw.gov.au

Bittner, Egon. 1970. *Functions of the Police in Modern Society*. Washington, DC: National Institute of Mental Health, Center for Studies of Crime and Delinquency.

Black, Donald. 1976. *The Behavior of Law*. New York: Academic Press.

Black, Donald, and Albert J. Reiss. 1967. "Patterns of Behavior in Citizen and Police Transactions." In *Studies of Crime and Law Enforcement in Major Metropolitan Areas*, Field Surveys III, vol. 2, 1–139. President's Commission on Law Enforcement and the Administration of Justice. Washington, DC: U.S. Government Printing Office.

Bracey, Dorothy H. 1995. "Police Corruption." In *The Encyclopedia of Police Science*, 2d ed., edited by William G. Bailey, 545–549. New York and London: Garland.

Buder, Leonard. 1982. "7 Officers Indicted for Corruption." New York Times, July 21.

Bureau of Justice Statistics. 2001. *Contacts between Police and the Public: Findings from the 1999 National Survey*. Washington, DC: U.S. Department of Justice.

——. 2007a. *Contacts between Police and the Public, 2005*. Washington, DC: U.S. Department of Justice.

——. 2007b. *Census of State and Local Law Enforcement Agencies, 2004*. Washington, DC: U.S. Department of Justice.

Burns, Pamela, and Dale K. Sechrest. 1992. "Police Corruption: The Miami Case." *Criminal Justice and Behavior* 19:294–313.

Caldero, Michael A., and John P. Crank. 2000. *Police Ethics: The Corruption of Noble Cause*. Cincinnati, OH: Anderson.

Canon, Bradley C. 1974. "Is the Exclusionary Rule in Failing Health? Some New Data and a Plea against a Precipitous Conclusion." *Kentucky Law Journal* 62:681–730.

——. 1991. "Courts and Policy: Compliance, Implementation, and Impact." In *American Courts: A Critical Assessment*, edited by John B. Gates and Charles A. Johnson, 435–466. Washington, DC: Congressional Quarterly Press.

Carter, David L. 1990. "Drug-related Corruption of Police Officers: A Contemporary Typology." *Journal of Criminal Justice* 18:85–98.

——. 1994. "Police Disciplinary Procedures: A Review of Selected Police Departments." In *Police Deviance*, edited by Thomas Barker and David L. Carter, 355–376. Cincinnati, OH: Anderson.

Carter, David, and D. W. Stephens. 1994. "Overview of Issues Concerning Police Officers Drug Use." In *Police Deviance*, edited by Thomas Barker and David L Carter, 101-122. Cincinnati, OH: Anderson.

Cheh, Mary M. 1995. "Are Law Suits an Answer to Police Brutality?" In *And Justice for All*, edited by William A. Geller and Hans Toch, 233–260. Washington, DC: Police Executive Research Forum.

Chevigny, Paul. 1995. *Edge of the Knife: Police Violence in the Americas*. New York: The New Press.

Christopher Commission. 1991. *Report of the Independent Commission on the Los Angeles Police Department*. Los Angeles: Author.

Cohen, Bernard. 1972. "The Police Internal System of Justice in New York City." *Journal of Criminal Law, Criminology, and Police Science* 63:54–67.

Commission on Accreditation of Law Enforcement Agencies. 2010. *Law Enforcement Accreditation*. http://www.calea.org/content/law-enforcement-program-benefits

Cordner, Gary, Brian Williams, and Alfredo Velasco. 2002. *Vehicle Stops in San Diego, 2001.* Report to the San Diego Police Department.

Desmedt, John C., and James F. Marsh. 1990. *The Use of Force Paradigm for Law Enforcement and Corrections*. http://www.pss.cc/uofm.htm

Dugan, John R., and Daniel R. Breda. 1991. "Complaints about Police Officers: A Comparison among Types and Agencies." *Journal of Criminal Justice* 19:165–72.

Engel, Robin S. 2005. "Citizens' Perceptions of Procedural and Distributive Injustice During Traffic Stops with Police." *Journal of Research in Crime and Delinquency* 42:445–81.

Engel, Robin, and Jennifer Calnon. 2004. "Comparing Benchmark Methodologies for Police-Citizen Contacts: Traffic Stop Data Collection for the Pennsylvania State Police." *Police Quarterly* 7:97–125.

Engel, Robin, and Richard Johnson. 2006. "Toward a Better Understanding of Racial and Ethnic Disparities in Search and Seizure Rates for State Police Agencies." *Journal of Criminal Justice* 34:605–17.

Engel, Robin, James Sobol, and Robert E. Worden. 2000. "Further Exploration of the Demeanor Hypothesis: The Interaction Effects of Suspects' Characteristics and Demeanor on Police Behavior." *Justice Quarterly* 17:235–58.

Fishman, Janet E. 1978. *Measuring Police Corruption*. New York: John Jay College of Criminal Justice.

Friedrich, Robert J. 1977. "The Impact of Organizational, Individual, and Situational Factors on Police Behavior." PhD dissertation, University of Michigan.

Fyfe, James J. 1979. "Administrative Interventions on Police Shooting Discretion: An Empirical Examination." *Journal of Criminal Justice* 7:303–23.

——. 1982. "Blind Justice: Police Shootings in Memphis." *Journal of Criminal Law and Criminology* 73:707–22.

Garner, Joel H., John Buchanan, Tom Schade, and John Hepburn. 1996. *Understanding the Use of Force By and Against the Police*. Washington, DC: National Institute of Justice.

Garner, Joel H., and Christopher D. Maxwell. 1999. "Measuring the Amount of Force Used By and Against the Police in Six Jurisdictions." In *Use of Force by Police: Overview of National and Local Data*. Washington, DC: National Institute of Justice.

Garner, Joel H., Christopher D. Maxwell, and Cedric G. Heraux. 2002. "Characteristics Associated with the Prevalence and Severity of Force Used by the Police." *Justice Quarterly* 19:705–46.

Garner, Joel H., Thomas Schade, John Hepburn, and John Buchanan. 1995. "Measuring the Continuum of Force Used By and Against the Police." *Criminal Justice Review* 20:146–69.

General Accounting Office. 1998. *Law Enforcement: Information on Drug-Related Police Corruption*. Washington, DC: General Accounting Office.

Geller, William A., and Michael S. Scott. 1992. *Deadly Force: What We Know: A Practitioner's Desk Reference on Police-Involved Shootings*. Washington, DC: Police Executive Research Forum.

Giuliani, Rudolph W., and William J. Bratton. 1995. *Police Strategy No. 7: Rooting Out Corruption. Building Organizational Integrity in the New York Police Department*. New York: New York Police Department.

Goldstein, Herman. 1975. *Police Corruption: A Perspective on Its Nature and Control*. Washington, DC: The Police Foundation.

Gould, Jon B., and Stephen Mastrofski. 2004. "Suspect Searches: Assessing Police Behavior under the US Constitution." *Criminology and Public Policy* 3:901–48.

Guerrero-Daley, Teresa. 2000. *Office of the Independent Police Auditor: 1999 Year End Report.* San Jose, CA: Office of the Independent Police Auditor.

Hickman, Matthew. 2006. *Citizen Complaints about Police Use of Force.* Washington, DC: Bureau of Justice Statistics.

Hudson, James R. 1972. "Organizational Aspects of Internal and External Review of the Police." *Journal of Criminal Law, Criminology, and Police Science* 63:427–32.

Human Rights Watch. 1998. *Shielded from Justice: Police Brutality and Accountability in the United States.* New York: Human Rights Watch.

Jacobs, David, and David Britt. 1979. "Inequality and Police Use of Deadly Force: An Empirical Assessment of a Conflict Hypothesis." *Social Problems* 26:404–12.

Kania, Richard E. 1988. "Should We Tell the Police to Say 'Yes' to Gratuities?" *Criminal Justice Ethics* 7:37–49.

———. 2004. "The Ethical Acceptability of Gratuities: Still Saying 'Yes' After All these Years." *Criminal Justice Ethics* 23:54–63.

Kappeler, Victor E. 1997. *Critical Issues in Police Civil Liability.* 2d ed. Prospect Heights, IL: Waveland Press.

———. 2006. *Police Civil Liability.* 2d ed. Long Grove, IL: Waveland Press.

Kerner Commission. National Advisory Commission on Civil Disorders. 1968. Report. Washington, DC: Government Printing Office.

Klahm, Charles F., and Rob Tillyer. 2010. "Understanding Police Use of Force: A Review of Evidence." *Southwest Journal of Criminal Justice* 72:214–39.

Kleinig, J. 1996. *The Ethics of Policing.* Cambridge: Cambridge University Press.

Klinger, David A. 1995. "Policing Spousal Assault." *Journal of Research on Crime and Delinquency* 32:308–24.

Klitgaard, Robert. 1988. *Controlling Corruption.* Berkeley: University of California Press.

Klockars, Carl B. 1985. *The Idea of Police.* Newbury Park, CA: Sage.

———. 1995. "A Theory of Excessive Force and Its Control." In *And Justice for All: Understanding and Controlling Police Abuse of Force*, edited William A. Geller and Hans Toch, 11–30. Washington, DC: Police Executive Research Forum.

———. 1999. "Some Really Cheap Ways of Measuring What Really Matters." In *Measuring What Matters: Proceedings from the Policing Institute Research Meetings*, edited by Robert H. Langworthy, 195–214. Washington, DC: National Institute of Justice.

———. 2003. "The Virtues of Integrity." In *Police Corruption: Paradigms, Models and Concepts—Challenges for Developing Countries*, edited by Stanley Einstein and Menachem Amir, 75–89. Huntsville, TX: Office of International Criminal Justice.

Klockars, Carl B., and Sanja Kutnjak Ivković. 2003. "Measuring Police Integrity." In *Police Integrity and Ethics*, edited by Matthew J. Hickman, Alex R. Piquero, and Jack R. Greene, 1.3–1.20. Belmont, CA: Wadsworth.

Klockars, Carl B., Sanja Kutnjak Ivković, and Maria R. Haberfeld. 2006. *Enhancing Police Integrity.* Dordrecht, The Netherlands: Springer.

Klockars, Carl. B., Sanja Kutnjak Ivković, and Maria R. Haberfeld, eds. 2004. *The Contours of Police Integrity.* Newbury Park, CA: Sage.

Klockars, Carl B., Sanja Kutnjak Ivković, S., William E. Harver, and Maria R. Haberfeld. 2000. *The Measurement of Police Integrity.* Research in Brief. Washington, DC: Government Printing Office.

Knapp Commission. Commission to Investigate Allegations of Police Corruption and the City's Anti-Corruption Procedures. 1972. *Report on Police Corruption.* New York: G. Braziller.

Kraska Peter B., and Victor E. Kappeler. 1995. "To Serve and Pursue: Exploring Police Sexual Violence Against Women." *Justice Quarterly* 12:85–111.

Krauss, Clifford. 1994. "Poll Finds a Lack of Faith in the Police." *New York Times,* June 19.

Kutnjak Ivković, Sanja. 2003. "To Serve and Collect: Measuring Police Corruption." *Journal of Criminal Law and Criminology* 93:593–649.

———. 2005. *Fallen Blue Knights: Controlling Police Corruption.* New York: Oxford University Press.

Leo, Richard A. 1998. "The Impact of Miranda Revisited." In *The Miranda Debate: Law, Justice, and Policing,* edited by Richard A. Leo and George C. Thomas, 208–221. Boston: Northeastern University Press.

Leo, Richard A., and George C. Thomas. 1998. *The Miranda Debate: Law, Justice, and Policing.* Boston: Northeastern University Press.

Lersch, Kim M., and Tom M. Mieczkowski. 2005. "Drug Testing Sworn Law Enforcement Officers: One Agency's Experience." *Journal of Criminal Justice* 33:289–97.

Liska, Allen E., Mitchell B. Chamlin, and Mark D. Reed. 1985. "Testing the Economic Production and Conflict Models of Crime Control." *Social Forces* 64:119–38.

Littlejohn, Edward J. 1981. "Civil Liability and the Police Officer: The Need for New Deterrents of Police Misconduct." *University of Detroit Journal of Urban Law* 58:365–431.

Los Angeles Police Department. 2000. *Board of Inquiry into the Rampart Area Corruption Incident: Executive Summary.* http://www.lapdonline.org.

Maher, Timothy M. 2003. "Police Sexual Misconduct: Officers' Perceptions of its Extent and Causality." *Criminal Justice Review* 28:355–81.

Malouff, John M., and Nicole S. Schutte. 1986. "Using Biographical Information to Hire the Best New Police Officers: Research Findings." *Journal of Police Science and Administration* 14:175–77.

Mastrofski, Stephen D., Robert Worden, and Jeffrey B. Snipes. 1995. "Law Enforcement in a Time of Community Policing." *Criminology* 33:539–63.

McCluskey, John, and William Terrill. 2005. "Departmental and Citizen Complaints as Predictor of Police Coercion." *Policing: An International Journal of Police Strategies and Management* 28:513–29.

McCluskey, John, William Terrill, and Eugene Pauline III. 2005. "Peer Group Aggressiveness and the Use of Coercion in Police-Suspect Encounters." *Police Practice and Research: An International Journal* 6:19–37.

McDonald, Phyllis Parshall, Sheldon Greenberg, and William J. Bratton. 2001. *Managing Police Operations: Implementing the NYPD Crime Control Model Using COMPSTAT.* Belmont, CA: Wadsworth.

McGurrin, Danielle, and Victor E. Kappeler. 2002. "Media Accounts of Police Sexual Violence: Rotten Apples or State Supported Violence?" In *Policing and Misconduct,* edited by Kim Michelle Lersch, 121–142. Upper Saddle River, NJ: Prentice Hall.

McLaughlin, Vance. 1992. *Police and the Use of Force: The Savannah Study.* Westport, CT: Praeger.

Mieczkowski, Tom, and Kim M. Lersch. 2002. "Drug Testing Police Officers and Police Recruits: The Outcome of Urine Analysis and Hair Analysis Compared." *Policing: An International Journal of Police Strategies and Management* 25:581–601.

Miller, Bill. 1999. "Shakedown Gets Ex-Officer 15 Months: Former District Detective Credited With Prompting Investigation of FBI Agents." *Washington Post,* April 27.

Mollen Commission. New York City Commission to Investigate Allegations of Police Corruption and the Anti-Corruption Procedures of the Police Department. 1994. *Commission Report.* New York: Author.

Moore, Michael H., and Daniel W. Stephens. 1991. "Organization and Management." In *Local Government Police Management,* edited by William A. Geller, 22–55. Washington, DC: International City Management Association.

Muir, William K. 1977. *Police: Street Corner Politicians.* Chicago: University of Chicago Press.

National Institute of Justice. 1999. *Use of Force by Police.* Washington, DC: U.S. Government Printing Office.

National Research Council. 2004. *Fairness and Effectiveness in Policing: The Evidence. Committee to Review Research on Police Policy and Practices,* edited by Wesley Skogan and Kathleen Frydl. Washington, DC: The National Academies Press.

Neuffer, Elizabeth, and Stacey Freedenthal. 1989. "Jury Convicts Former Boston Detective of Extortion." *Boston Globe,* July 27.

Northeastern University Data Collection Resource Center. 2010. *Racial Profiling Data Collection Resource Collection.* http://www.racialprofilinganalysis.neu.edu.

Oaks, Dallin H. 1970. "Studying the Exclusionary Rule in Search and Seizure." *University of Chicago School Law Review* 37:655–757.

Orfield, Myron W., Jr. 1987. "The Exclusionary Rule and Deterrence: An Empirical Study of Chicago Narcotics Officers." *University of Chicago Law School Review* 54:1016–69.

Pate, Anthony, and Lorie Fridell. 1993. *Police Use of Force: Official Reports, Citizen Complaints, and Legal Consequences.* Washington, DC: Police Foundation.

Pate, Anthony, and Edwin E. Hamilton. 1991. *The Big Six: Policing America's Largest Cities.* Washington, DC: Police Foundation.

Patton, Alison L. 1993. "The Endless Cycle of Abuse: Why 42 U.S.C. §1983 is Ineffective in Deterring Police Brutality." *Hastings Law Journal* 44:753–808.

Pennsylvania Crime Commission. 1974. *Report on Police Corruption and the Quality of Law Enforcement in Philadelphia.* Saint Davids, PA: Author.

Perez, Douglas W. 1994. *Common Sense about Police Review.* Philadelphia, PA: Temple University Press.

President's Commission on Law Enforcement and Administration of Justice. 1967a. *A National Survey of Police-Community Relations: Field Surveys V.* Washington, DC: U.S. Government Printing Office.

——. 1967b. *Task Force Report: The Police.* Washington, DC: U.S. Government Printing Office.

Punch, Maurice. 1985. *Conduct Unbecoming.* London: Tavistock.

——. 2003. "From 'Rotten Apple' to 'Rotten Orchards.'" In *Police Corruption,* edited by Menachem Amir and Shlomo Einstein, 305–333. Huntsville, TX: OICJ.

Reaves, Brian. 2010. *Local Police Departments.* Washington, DC: U.S. Government Printing Office.

Reaves, Brian, and Matthew Hickman 2004. *Law Enforcement Management and Administrative Statistics, 2000: Data for Individual State and Local Agencies with 100 or More Officers.* Washington, DC: U.S. Government Printing Office.

Reiss, Albert J., Jr. 1967. *Studies in Crime and Law Enforcement in Major Metropolitan Areas.* Washington, DC: U.S. Government Printing Office.

Reuss-Ianni, Elizabeth. 1983. *Two Cultures of Policing: Street Cops and Management.* New Brunswick, NJ: Transaction.

Riksheim, Eric C., and Steven M. Chermak. 1993. "Causes of Police Behavior Revisited." *Journal of Criminal Justice* 21:353–82.

Roebuck, Julian B., and Thomas Barker. 1974. "A Typology of Police Corruption." *Social Problems* 21:423–37.

Royal Commission into the New South Wales Police Service. 1997. *Final Report*. Sydney, Australia: NSW Police Integrity Commission.

Russell, Kenneth. 1978. "Complaints Against the Police: An International Perspective." *Police Journal* 51:34–44.

Ruiz, Jim, and Christine Bono. 2004. "At What Price a 'Freebie'? The Real Cost of Police Gratuities." *Criminal Justice Ethics* 23:44–54.

Sapp, A. 1994. "Sexual Misconduct by Police Officers." In *Police Deviance*, edited by Thomas Barker and David Carter, 187–200. Cincinnati, OH: Anderson.

Scrivner, Ellen M. 1994. *Controlling Police Use of Excessive Force: The Role of the Police Psychologist*. Washington, DC: National Institute of Justice.

Sherman, Lawrence L. 1974. "Becoming Bent: Moral Careers of Corrupt Policemen." In *Police Corruption*, edited by Lawrence Sherman, 191–208. Garden City, NY: Anchor Press.

——. 1977. "Police Corruption Control." In *Police and Society*, edited by David Bayley, 143–155. Thousand Oaks, CA: Sage.

——. 1978. *Scandal and Reform*. Berkeley: University of California Press.

Silverman, Eli B. 1999. *NYPD Battles Crime: Innovative Strategies in Policing*. Boston: Northeastern University Press.

Skolnick, Jerome H. 1966. *Justice without Trial*. New York: John Wiley and Sons.

Skolnick, Jerome H., and James J. Fyfe. 1993. *Above the Law: Police and the Excessive Use of Force*. New York: Free Press.

Sparrow, Malcom K., Mark H. Moore, and David M. Kennedy. 1990. *Beyond 911: A New Era for Policing*. New York: Basic Books.

Special Counsel to the Los Angeles County Sheriff's Department. 1999. *11th Semiannual Report*. Los Angeles: Los Angeles County.

——. 2002. *15th Semiannual Report*. Los Angeles: Los Angeles County.

Stoddard, Edwin R. 1974. "A Group Approach to Blue-Coat Crime." In *Police Corruption*, edited by Lawrence W. Sherman, 277–304. Garden City, NY: Anchor Press.

Talley, Joseph E., and Lisa D. Hinz. 1990. *Performance Prediction of Public Safety and Law Enforcement Personnel: A Study in Race and Gender Differences and MMPI Subscales*. Springfield, IL: C.C. Thomas.

Terrill, William. 2001. *Police Coercion: Application of the Force Continuum*. New York: LFB Scholarly Publishing.

——. 2003. "Police Use of Force and Suspect Resistance: The Micro-Process of the Police-Suspect Encounter." *Police Quarterly* 6:51–83.

Terrill, William, and Stephen Mastrofski. 2002. "Reassessing Situational and Office Based Determination of Police Coercion." *Justice Quarterly* 19:215–48.

Terrill, William, and Michael D. Reisig. 2003. "Neighborhood Context and Police Use of Force." *Journal of Research in Crime and Delinquency* 40:291–321.

U.S. Commission on Civil Rights. 1981. *Who is Guarding the Guardians?* Washington, DC: U.S. Government Printing Office.

U.S. Department of Justice. 2001. *Principles for Promoting Police Integrity*. Available at https://www.ncjrs.gov/pdffiles1/ojp/186189.pdf.

U.S. Department of Justice. 2010. *FAQ*. http://www.justice.gov/crt/split/faq.php#primsource.

U.S. Supreme Court. 2011. *The Justices' Caseload*. Available at http://www.supremecourt.gov/about/justicecaseload.aspx.

Vera Institute of Justice. 1999. *Respectful and Effective Policing: Two Examples in the South Bronx*. New York: Author.

———. 2002. "Turning Necessity into Virtue: Pittsburgh's Experience with a Federal Consent Decree.

http://www.vera.org/sites/default/files/resources/downloads/Pittsburgh_consent_decree.pdf

Wagner, Allen E. 1980. "Citizen Complaints against the Police: The Complainant." *Journal of Police Science and Administration* 8:373–77.

Walker, Samuel. 1999. *The Police in America: An Introduction*. 3d ed. Boston: McGraw-Hill.

———. 2001. *Police Accountability: The Role of Citizen Oversight*. Belmont, CA: Wadsworth.

———. 2005. *The New World of Police Accountability*. Newbury Park: Sage Publications.

Walker, Samuel, Geoffrey Alpert, and Dennis Kenney. 2000. *Responding to the Problem Officer: A National Evaluation of Early Warning Systems*. Washington, DC: U.S. Government Printing Office.

Walker, Samuel, and Vic W. Bumphus. 1992. "The Effectiveness of Civilian Review: Observations on Recent Trends and New Issues Regarding the Civilian Review of Police." *American Journal of Police* 11:1–26.

Walker, Samuel, and Charles M. Katz. 2008. *The Police in America: An Introduction*. 6th ed. Boston: McGraw-Hill.

Walker, Samuel, and Betsy Wright Kreisel. 2001. "Varieties of Citizen Review." In *Critical Issues in Policing*, edited by Roger G. Dunham and Geoffrey Alpert, 338–355. Prospect Heights, IL: Waveland Press.

Weisburd, David, and Rosann Greenspan, with Edwin E. Hamilton, Hubert Williams, and Kellie A. Bryant. 2000. *Police Attitudes toward Abuse of Authority: Findings from a National Survey*. Washington, DC: U.S. Government Printing Office.

Weisburd, David, Stephen D. Mastrofski, Ann Marie McNally, Rosann Greenspan, and James J. Willis. 2003. "Reforming to Preserve: Compstat and Strategic Problem-Solving in American Policing." *Criminology and Public Policy* 2:421–56.

Weitzer, Ronald, and Steven A. Tuch. 1999. "Race, Class, and Perceptions of Discrimination by the Police." *Crime and Delinquency* 45:494–507.

———. 2002. "Perceptions of Racial Profiling: Race, Class, and Personal Experience." *Criminology* 40:435–56.

———. 2006. *Race and Policing in America: Conflict and Reform*. Cambridge: Cambridge University Press.

West, Paul. 1988. "Investigation of Complaints against the Police: Summary Report of a National Survey." *American Journal of Police* 7:101–21.

Worden, Robert E. 1995. "The Causes of Police Brutality: Theory and Evidence on Police Use of Force." In *And Justice for All: Understanding and Controlling Police Abuse of Force*, edited William A. Geller and Hans Toch, 31–60. Washington, DC: Police Executive Research Forum.

PART IV

RACE/ETHNICITY AND
POLICING

CHAPTER 15

....

POLICE RACE RELATIONS

....

RONALD WEITZER

RACE and ethnicity condition policing in societies throughout the world. Insofar as minority racial/ethnic background is fused with low socioeconomic status, it is almost everywhere the case that such populations are treated worse by the police, who view them more critically than their counterparts in the higher-class racial majority. This pattern applies to societies with severe economic inequality and ethnic polarization as well as to societies where economic and ethnic divisions are less severe.

Some societies are characterized by *extreme discord* between the police and minority groups: the police lack any semblance of legitimacy among the subordinate groups, who are estranged from all state institutions, and the social control apparatus is essentially an instrument of the dominant ethnic group. In these deeply divided societies, citizens' orientations toward the police are very heavily shaped by their *loyalty to or estrangement from the state*. Insofar as minorities view the state and the police as illegitimate and diametrically opposed to their interests, a substantial share of police resources will be devoted to preempting or repressing minority resistance. Examples include contemporary Iraq and Afghanistan, Israel, Chechnya, Northern Ireland, and white-ruled South Africa, Rhodesia, and Namibia (Weitzer 1995; Milton-Edwards 1997; Ellison and Smyth 2000). These cases demonstrate just how dire police-citizen relations can be—marked by a deep, unbridgeable gulf between the authorities and the subordinate ethnic population. But the more general point is that what the police represent politically as well as citizen orientations to other state institutions are important determinants of public opinion of the police. A unique study of twenty-eight countries found that, net of country-level factors, public approval of the police was linked to citizens' views of other state institutions, such as the legislature, legal system, and military (Ivković 2008).

Citizens' orientations to the state are also crucial, albeit usually overlooked by researchers, in democratic nations where racial and ethnic conflict is more muted. In these more integrated societies the state enjoys diffuse legitimacy and is not itself an object of fundamental contention. Diffuse popular support for the political system appears to have a beneficial spillover effect on citizens' views of the police, with subordinate racial groups having a less contentions relationship with agents of control than in ethnically polarized societies (Marenin 1985).

The police-race relations nexus is complicated in nations where there are *several subordinate* racial/ethnic groups. In these contexts, the latter may share relatively similar dispositions toward the police or may differ significantly on this score. In apartheid South Africa, for instance, Indians and mixed-race people had generally more positive views of the police than black people, just as Druze Arabs have better relations with the Israeli police than Muslim Arabs (Hasisi and Weitzer 2007). How can we explain these differences? Surprisingly, this question has rarely been addressed by scholars, because most of the (especially Anglo-American) literature has centered on black-white differences and neglects other minority groups. In the American context, it is increasingly important to include Hispanics and Asians as well, as their proportion of the population has steadily increased in the past two decades. This essay will do so to the extent that the extant research literature allows.

The following points are made in the essay:

- More research has been conducted on certain topics and some groups than on others.
- Knowledge of the ways in which racial and ethnic minority groups understand and experience the police is limited by this lopsided body of research.
- Less is known about patterns in *police* treatment of citizens and in contextual patterns of police practices than about *citizen* perceptions and reported experiences with the police.
- Theoretical perspectives that have been applied to blacks and whites may need to be adjusted when analyzing other populations.

After briefly sketching in Section 15.1 some historical background, Section 15.2 presents several ways in which theoretical models can shed light on different aspects of race and policing. Section 15.3 discusses several under-researched topics and populations with the purpose of stimulating future exploration of these issues.

15.1 Some Historical Patterns

One way of theorizing on this topic is to identify a particular racial or ethnic group's *mode of incorporation* into a society (Alexander 2001; Weitzer 2010). Minorities differ considerably in the degree to which they are integrated into any given society and in their historical treatment by major institutions. The mode-of-incorporation lens highlights key differences in group stratification:

> Among racial minority groups, the level of alienation [from social institutions] would vary based on differences in the persistence, pervasiveness across domains of

life, and extremity of inequality of life chances. This argument implies that members of more recent and voluntarily incorporated minority groups will feel less alienation than members of long-term and involuntarily incorporated minority groups. (Bobo 1999, 461)

Regarding criminal justice institutions, "Latinos occupy a disadvantaged middle ground where they are a less comprehensive and intensive focus of criminalization efforts than African Americans, but more at risk than whites" (Hagan, Shedd, and Payne 2005, 384). Asian Americans appear to have a less contentious relationship with the police than the other minority groups, which is largely consistent with their mode of incorporation into Ameican society. But this conclusion must be regarded as tentative because so few studies focus on Asians.

The mode of ethnic incorporation is important in other societies as well. Middle Eastern and African immigrants residing in Western nations typically experience greater structural and cultural marginality (rooted in both institutionalized discrimination and immigrant estrangement from the predominant value system) and more tenuous relations with the police than either the dominant group or other minority ethnic groups. These patterns have been documented in research on Moroccans, Turks, Algerians, Pakistanis, Roma, and other immigrant groups in Western Europe (Junger 1990; Vrij and Winkel 1991; Hebberecht 1997; Hutterman 2003; Zauberman and Lévy 2003). Roma minorities in Bulgaria, Hungary, and Spain, for instance, have experienced widespread ethnic profiling; they are stopped by the police more often than members of the dominant ethnic populations and report more negative treatment during stops (Miller 2007). And an observational study of five locations in Paris found that blacks and Arabs were far more likely than whites to be stopped by the police (Goris, Jobard, and Lévy 2009). Observers recorded benchmark data on the numbers of each racial group present in the five locations and then compared the benchmark to the number of persons who were stopped (N = 525 distinct stops). Blacks were six times more likely than whites to be stopped, and Arabs were nearly eight times more likely to be stopped—and this was especially the case for young males. The researchers attempted a post-stop interview with everyone who was not arrested. Four-fifths of the 173 individuals interviewed stated that this was not their first time stopped by police officers; about half stated that they were annoyed or upset about being stopped; and more than 60 percent stated that the police gave no reason for the stop. It is well known that blacks, Arabs, Pakistanis, Turks, and other ethnic minorities are not well integrated into French society.

15.2 THEORETICAL FRAMEWORKS

The mode-of-incorporation thesis is situated at the macro-historial level of analysis and, as such, is not intended as a complete explanation of police-minority relations.

But it offers considerable insight into group-level patterns and is a useful counterbalance to individual-level and situational explanations. At the same time, the historical stratification of racial and ethnic groups can significantly color contemporary interactions between citizens and police officers. Engel suggests that the greater the stratification gap between a citizen and an officer, the higher the odds of disrespectful behavior toward the other party. For example, "it is possible that particular types of citizens (e.g., young minority males) may act in disrespectful or otherwise resistant ways to symbolize their perceptions of injustice" (Engel 2003, 477). Researchers who analyzed 313 video recordings of police interactions with drivers in Cincinnati found that, compared to white drivers, black drivers were less courteous, less apologetic, less respectful, and more belligerent toward officers (Dixon et al. 2008). The chances of this happening are increased when minority citizens interact with white cops, because the citizen may interpret police behavior as a result of "the officer's own ethnic group's superordination" (Sykes and Clark 1975, 590). Indeed, the Cincinnati study found that when white officers were interacting with black citizens the officers displayed "more indifference to comments of the driver, were less approachable, were more dismissive of driver comments, showed a pronounced appearance of superiority, gave less respect, and did less listening," and the same pattern was observed between black police officers and white drivers (Dixon et al. 2008, 541). It is not surprising that in the former situation blacks would define white officers as a "visible sign of majority domination" (Bayley and Mendelsohn 1969, 195). This dynamic can be linked to the *group-position thesis*, insofar as individual actions and perceptions are rooted in larger patterns of intergroup relations and different groups' overarching orientations toward the police (Weitzer and Tuch 2006, 8–16). Some minority individuals interpret their encounters with police in terms of their *group's societal position* rather than, or in addition to, the immediate circumstances of a contact with the police. By contrast, whites who feel that, as a group, they are allies with the police may be influenced by this affinity even in involuntary stops by police officers. Although we do not know how frequently citizens construe encounters as sites of racial oppression, it remains clear that structural inequality can influence how disadvantaged individuals respond to officers in personal encounters as well as their general perceptions of the police (Weitzer and Tuch 2006).

The mode-of-incorporation thesis and the group-position thesis are two sides of the same structural paradigm centered on aggregate group-level patterns in police-minority relations. But several other theories—at the micro and meso levels—are also pertinent in understanding race and policing. I sketch these below.

Social-psychological models are one type of micro-level explanation. Here, racial prejudice among police officers is seen as a cause of disparate treatment of different ethnic groups. Jefferson (1988, 522) argues, "All the major British and North American studies, from the early post-war period on, agree that negative, stereotypical, prejudiced, and hostile attitudes to blacks are rife amongst police officers." Even if this claim is somewhat exaggerated, there is no doubt that racial prejudice can influence police behavior. As members of a society in which racism persists, it is not surprising that at least some police officers stereotype racial minorities and that prejudice motivates some of these officers to discriminate against members of these groups either occasionally or frequently. Such prejudice may be reinforced among officers assigned to work in high-crime, predominantly black or Hispanic neighborhoods insofar as they come to see all residents through the same lens—as crime prone or tolerant of neighborhood deviance and disorder. Racial prejudice may be so ingrained in cognition and perception that the person is unaware of it. Some fascinating research demonstrates how threat perceptions may be influenced by split-second racial associations when subjects are asked in a video-game experiment to shoot at images of individuals holding guns and not shoot individuals holding other objects, images that alternated black and white targets. Some twenty laboratory experiments of this kind "consistently show racial bias in both the speed and accuracy with which such decisions can be made." Subjects were "more accurate when responding 'don't shoot' to an unarmed white man than an unarmed black man" (Correll et al. 2007, 1007). Most of these studies relied on college student participants; one that included police officers found that they were less inclined than the students to exhibit racial bias, perhaps because of their training, but also that certain kinds of racial bias were detected for the police participants as well (Correll et al. 2007). This and other research (Plant and Peruche 2005) shows how racial factors can subtly influence the cognitive and behavioral reactions of at least some police officers.

A second micro-level explanation is *social interactionism*, centering on the dynamics of face-to-face encounters between officers and minority citizens. Many studies have documented the ways in which the situational contingencies of such encounters and the demeanor of both parties affect outcomes (e.g., arrest, use of force) (Black 1971; Wiley and Hudik 1974; Sykes and Clark 1975; Mastrofski, Reisig, and McCluskey 2002; Reisig et al. 2004). Research also shows that these interactions shape citizens' attitudes toward the police long after the encounter: Irrespective of race, citizens have the same kinds of expectations for proper treatment by officers, and police behavior has similar effects on individuals' larger opinions of the police; negatively evaluated encounters have lasting, adverse effects on one's opinions of the police regardless of the citizen's racial background (Tyler and Huo 2002). However, African Americans and Latinos are much more likely than whites to report that they have been personally mistreated in their encounters with the police (Tyler and Huo 2002; Weitzer and Tuch 2006).

Not only do one's personal contacts with police officers matter; their "vicarious experiences" are important as well. *Social learning theory* illuminates the process whereby individuals experience the police indirectly, through the prism of others. This has been documented at two levels: a person's social networks (Edwin Sutherland's differential association theory) and exposure to media portrayals of the police (Daniel Glaser's differential identification theory). A growing body of research indicates that one's social networks play an important role, and that this is especially important for African Americans. In other words, quite apart from one's personal experiences with police officers, one can "vicariously experience" the police through the reported encounters of friends, family members, and neighbors, and these indirect experiences have a significant impact on how one sees the police. Research shows that bad experiences conveyed by significant others are often internalized and negatively influence a person's general views of the police—an outcome shared among whites, blacks, and Hispanics alike (Rosenbaum et al. 2005; Weitzer and Tuch 2006). The picture is more mixed for the impact of *good experiences* with police officers translating into favorable views of the police, with some research reporting this finding (Rosenbaum et al. 2005) other studies finding that good experiences during encounters (both vicarious and personal) do not enhance overall satisfaction with the police (Reisig and Parks 2000; Shafer, Huebner, and Bynum 2003; Skogan 2006b). For African Americans especially, personal experiences and opinions are often transmitted both within peer groups and from one generation to the next with the express purpose of shielding young blacks from having adverse interactions with police officers. Recent research documents this dynamic within black youth peer groups (Weitzer and Brunson 2009) and on the part of their parents and other elders who attempt to inculcate conduct norms in the youths to reduce the chances that they will have clashes with the police (Brunson and Weitzer 2011). There is no research investigating whether Hispanics, Asians, or whites instruct their peers or children similarly.

Individuals also learn from persons who are featured in the mass media. One can "learn" about the police—in however distorted a manner—when individual officers are publicly accused of misconduct in the media, such as the officers involved in the beating of Rodney King or Abner Louima or the killing of Malice Green or Amadou Diallo. Media coverage of controversial police actions and scandals often minimizes the problems (Lawrence 2000), but there are clearly exceptions to this pattern. Several studies document significant decreases in public approval of the police after major publicized incidents of misconduct, also finding that minority confidence was more deeply affected than for whites (Sigelman et al. 1997; Kaminski and Jefferis 1998). Weitzer (2002) found that public attitudes typically returned to their pre-incident level after a period of time, yet this recovery was more delayed for blacks and Hispanics than for white residents of the study sites: Los Angeles and New York. In a nationwide survey, Weitzer and Tuch (2006) assessed the impact of longer-term exposure to media coverage of police misconduct. As exposure to such reports increases, people are more likely to believe that police officers are prejudiced, discriminate against minorities, and engage in misconduct, and more likely to support a host of reforms in the police department—and this applies to white, black, and Hispanic citizens alike. In an Indianapolis study, residents who reported high news consumption during the course of a trial of officers accused of beating two citizens were more likely to believe the officers were guilty, net of other factors (Chermak, McGarrell, and Gruenewald 2006). Learning may also take place when people are exposed to positive portrayals of the police. For instance, whites who frequently watch the television shows *Cops* and *America's Most Wanted*, which portray the police favorably, held more positive views of the police than other whites, but this was not true for blacks (Eschholz et al. 2002).

Another theoretical lens can be called *compositional*—a meso-level explanation. Here, the emphasis is on (1) the racial and ethnic composition of police departments, or (2) the racial and class makeup of residential neighborhoods or the entire city. An age-old question is whether the racial complexion of a police department makes a difference in public attitudes toward the police and, likewise, whether the race of individual officers affects their interactions with members of the public. Many governments around the world assume that diversity in police organizations is important and have encouraged diversification of racially homogeneous departments (Zauberman and Lévy 2003). The question of whether the race of officer affects behavior toward citizens has been answered with somewhat mixed results (see Sklansky 2006). Some research finds that when the dyad is interracial (white officer-black citizen, and vice versa) the officer is less courteous and respectful and more authoritarian than when the race of officer and citizen is matched (Dixon et al. 2008). Another study (Sun and Payne 2004) found that black officers were more inclined than white officers to engage in supportive activities in black neighborhoods (e.g., offering information, providing assistance, making referrals to other agencies, and comforting residents). Interestingly, this study also found that black officers were more likely to use physical force against citizens in conflict situations.

These findings are important, but the general consensus is that white, black, and Hispanic officers vary little in carrying out their jobs (Walker, Spohn, and DeLone 2000, 111). Members of the public, however, differ in whether they accept the "no differences" position or think that officers' race indeed makes a difference on the ground. In a 1981 Milwaukee study, 32 percent of the city's black residents agreed while 38 percent disagreed with the idea that black officers treat black citizens more fairly than do white officers (Dresner et al. 1981), and a more recent study, of Washington, DC found black residents to be similarly split on this question, with about one-third believing that there were no differences by race of officer (Weitzer 2000b; cf. Weitzer, Tuch, and Skogan 2008). Similarly divergent views were reported in a national survey of whites, blacks, and Hispanics, where a sizeable number of respondents subscribed to the "blue cops" position—that the color of the uniform was the only color that mattered. This race-neutral view was held by a majority of whites and Hispanics and a third of blacks when asked whether there are differences in the way white and black officers treat citizens, and a majority of all three groups when the comparison was between white and Hispanic officers (Weitzer and Tuch 2006, 97). At the same time, the majority of all three groups felt that an ethnically diverse police department was important for *symbolic* reasons (i.e., in positively reflecting the diversity of the nation).

Neighborhood racial and class composition is another compositional factor. Studies that include this variable in analyses of police behavior patterns have found that officers were more likely to use coercion toward residents of nonwhite or racially mixed neighborhoods than in white areas (Smith 1986), more likely to engage in "stop and frisk" practices in communities with a large concentration of poor African American and Latino residents (Fagan et al. 2010), and more likely to engage in misconduct (e.g., unjustified stops, bribery, verbal abuse, excessive force) in disadvantaged, nonwhite neighborhoods (Kane 2002; Mastrofski, Reisig, and McCluskey 2002; Terrill and Reisig 2003; Weitzer 1999, 2000a). Such studies demonstrate that policing is typically more aggressive in neighborhoods that lie at the intersection of class (economically disadvantaged) and race (subordinate minority).

If police practices vary across different types of communities (and more research is needed to further corroborate this), it is reasonable to expect residents' views of the police to reflect this. Comparisons of white, black, and Hispanic neighborhoods show this to be the case, though data are lacking on other types of neighborhoods. Community-level orientations toward the police are generally more tepid or negative in predominantly black or Hispanic neighborhoods than in white neighborhoods. A large number of residents of minority, disadvantaged neighborhoods feel that their communities receive insufficient police protection, for example (Velez 2001; Weitzer and Tuch 2006). It is important, however, to factor in other neighborhood characteristics in addition to racial composition, such as neighborhood class profile, crime rates, social ties, and other ecological factors.

This is where *social disorganization theory* is salient. Classic Chicago School studies of urban problems in the 1920s and 1930s accounted for the spatial distribution of street crime, vice, and various social problems by the presence of a set of ecological conditions (e.g., poverty, ethnic heterogeneity, family instability, transience, physical deterioration) and the absence of social control over deviant actors. Virtually all social disorganization researchers, however, focus on *informal* social control and neglect the possible role of *formal* control or its absence (i.e., the practices of the authorities to maintain order and enforce legal and regulatory codes). Informal control is viewed as more likely to curb crime than is formal control by the authorities, which usually takes place after the fact (Bursik 1988; Kubrin and Weitzer 2003). Yet, the amount and quality of police activity in a neighborhood is also crucial. Disadvantaged communities are typically the least able to secure needed police protection and services. In Chicago, for instance, residents of poor areas were significantly more likely than residents of other areas to criticize officers' performance in preventing crime and maintaining order on the streets, and the police were also accused of poor treatment of crime victims (Sampson and Bartusch 1998). And in a study of Rochester, St. Louis, and Tampa, an average difference of 18 percentage points separated the low- and extremely-disadvantaged areas in residents' satisfaction with the quality of police services to their neighborhoods; likewise, a 14-percentage-point difference between the neighborhood types was reported regarding the question of whether police provide the kind of services community members desire (Velez 2001).

In addition, residents of disadvantaged, minority neighborhoods typically lack the capacity to hold officers accountable for their behavior. Extending social disorganization theory, it can be argued that the same conditions that foster crime in a neighborhood can also loosen some of the restraints on police conduct. Residents' weak social ties or lack of participation in local organizations may be associated not only with residents' incapacity to mobilize against crime and disorder—as social disorganization theory holds—but also with their powerlessness in the face of abusive police practices. And even if they were able to organize collectively to challenge police abuses of power, residents of such neighborhoods have little confidence that their complaints will be taken seriously (Kane 2002; Weitzer 1999). By contrast, residents of more affluent communities typically have connections to local elites who can be called upon to hold officers accountable for their practices (Weitzer 1999).

Some studies find that, net of other factors, racial composition is a predictor of ecological patterns of police behavior and/or residents' views of the police, but other research suggests that racial composition recedes in significance once other ecological variables are included (Sampson and Bartusch 1998; Reisig and Parks 2000; Velez 2001; Kubrin and Weitzer 2003; MacDonald et al. 2007; Schafer, Huebner, and Bynum 2007). A comparison of a disadvantaged black neighborhood and an upper middle-class black neighborhood in Washington, DC found that social class made a huge difference, with residents of the middle-class neighborhood holding much more favorable views of the city's police than residents of the lower-class community (Weitzer 1999, 2000a). These results are consistent with those of a study of 343 Chicago neighborhoods. After controlling for neighborhood racial composition and violent crime, residents of impoverished areas were significantly more likely than residents of other areas to report that officers performed poorly in preventing crime and maintaining order on the streets, responded poorly to crime victims, and were not responsive to local issues (Sampson and Bartusch 1998). In another Chicago study, middle-class blacks and Hispanics who resided in disadvantaged neighborhoods held more negative views of the police than their counterparts living in middle-class communities (Schuck, Rosenbaum, and Hawkins 2008). In El Paso, Texas, both Hispanics and whites residing in poor neighborhoods were more likely than people living in middle-class neighborhoods to report having observed a range of police abuses (Holmes 1998). And in Lexington and Louisville, Kentucky, whites and blacks living in disadvantaged neighborhoods expressed similar levels of dissatisfaction with the police, whereas in economically advantaged areas, blacks were less likely than whites to hold favorable attitudes toward the police (Wu, Sun, and Triplett 2009). In these studies, neighborhood class profile trumps neighborhood racial composition for at least one of the racial or ethnic groups studied.

Another ecological context in which race and ethnicity can influence citizens' experiences and opinions of the police is what happens when individuals travel outside their residential neighborhoods, where they may be viewed by officers as out of place and perceived more suspiciously than in their own residential areas. A few studies document how African Americans, of any social class, attract special attention when they are deemed out of place by police officers. Meehan and Ponder (2002) reported increased stops of blacks when they were encountered in white and affluent neighborhoods, and Stults, Parker, and Lane (2010) found that police stops of black motorists in Miami were most prevalent in areas with large white populations, whereas the stop rates of whites and Hispanics decreased in whiter areas. The authors suggest that this may be due to the greater "racial threat" presented by blacks in predominantly white communities, resulting in enhanced social control manifested by police stops. One interesting finding is that Hispanics were less likely to be stopped in predominantly white areas than in areas where the proportion of Hispanics was greater. This may suggest that police officers are not inclined to see Hispanics as out-of-place in white neighborhoods (Stults, Parker, and Lane 2010). We can also compare reported personal experiences inside and outside a person's residential neighborhood. When residents of a black middle-class community in Washington, DC traveled outside their neighborhood, they were 3.4 times more likely to be stopped, whereas the difference was much narrower for middle-class whites and for lower-class blacks in the study (Weitzer 1999). Race trumped their (invisible) class status when they were stopped outside their community, whereas their middle-class status was a buffer mitigating police suspicion inside their neighborhood. Moreover, when they encountered police outside their community they reported much more negative treatment from officers than what they received inside their neighborhood.

Conflict theory overlaps to some extent with social disorganization theory in the sense that both perspectives highlight social inequality and structural conditions as key to understanding patterns of social control. The simplest version of conflict theory holds that class and racial inequality is associated with enhanced social control over subordinate populations. Regarding social class, it has been argued that the "more economically stratified a society becomes, the more it becomes necessary for dominant groups in society to enforce through coercion the norms of conduct which guarantee their supremacy" (Chambliss and Seidman 1971, 33). This argument can be applied to race and ethnicity as well. Enter the "minority threat" version of conflict theory. According to this thesis, the amount of formal control on the part of the criminal justice system in a city is related to the real or perceived threat that minority groups present to the dominant group. In other words, a large minority population increases whites' fear of crime, which then catalyzes more intensive control over the minority. Although some studies report that black population size is not a predictor of formal control (Parker, Stults, and Rice 2005), support for the threat thesis is found in several other studies. The larger the proportion of African Americans in a city, the higher the per capita expenditure and size of the police force, arrest rates, and frequency of police killings of blacks (Liska, Lawrence, and Benson 1981; Liska, Chamlin, and Reed 1985; Liska and Yu 1992; Jacobs and O'Brien 1998; Smith 2005). These outcomes have been interpreted as indicators of amplified control over the black population. Similarly, a large or growing Hispanic population in a city might be viewed as a threat by the dominant, white population. One study advanced this Hispanic-threat explanation for the correlation between police misconduct incidents in neighborhoods with large numbers of Hispanics, and this relationship may obtain at the broader city level as well (Kane 2002).

Some intriguing questions can be asked about the logic of the minority threat thesis. First, in cities where the vast majority of the population is African American or Latino and where this translates into political power, in what sense can the minority white population be considered "dominant" (i.e., having its interests reflected in public policy and law enforcement)? Does the minority-threat thesis apply only to cities where blacks and Hispanics remain numerical minorities and politically marginalized, or does it apply to other types of cities as well? This question has not been addressed in the extant literature. Second, even in those cities where whites remain the politically dominant group, the minority-threat literature assumes that demands for law and order emanate from the white majority alone. An alternative and quite plausible explanation, not tested in these studies, is that the minority population itself may be in the forefront in demanding more crime control. A substantial majority of blacks and Hispanics desire robust law enforcement, so this interest is hardly unique to whites (Weitzer and Tuch 2006). At police-community meetings African Americans have been vocal in demanding more police patrols and proactive measures to fight crime (Skogan 2006a). Minority populations are not always powerless and may have at least some political clout, resulting in additional police resources or interventions in high-crime neighborhoods (Kane 2002). This minority-demand explanation and the minority-threat thesis are not mutually exclusive: both the white majority and nonwhite minority may perceive a sizeable minority population as a threat, with both populations calling for intensified policing.

To complicate matters, the effect of a city's racial composition and residents' threat assessments may be affected by patterns of racial segregation. In other words, the key variable may be not size of the minority population but instead its spatial proximity to or isolation from the white population. The segregation of minorities into urban ghettos reduces their mobility and may function as an informal mechanism of control, insulating whites from black crime, which, in turn, "should alleviate white pressure on political authorities to do something about crimes committed by blacks" (Kent and Jacobs 2005, 736). Relatively low racial segregation, by contrast, may present a stronger perceived threat to whites, thus generating more expansive crime control. Empirical support for this argument is reported in studies finding an association, independent of crime rates, between higher levels of racial segregation and smaller per capita police force size (Liska, Lawrence, and Benson 1981; Kent and Jacobs 2005) and lower arrest rates of blacks (Liska and Chamlin 1984; Liska, Chamlin, and Reed 1985; Stolzenberg, D'Allesio, and Eitle 2004). Some studies, however, find no such segregation effect (see, e.g., Parker, Stults, and Rice 2005; Stults and Baumer 2007).

Racial segregation also may influence citizen perceptions of the police. Insofar as the police are blamed for insufficiently controlling crime and insofar as residential segregation has a containment effect on minority crime, whites' approval of the police may be inflated in cities with higher racial segregation. Segregation's effect on blacks' and Hispanics' satisfaction with the police may be more complex, however. If police are less likely to intervene in residentially isolated ghetto neighborhoods because crimes committed in such neighborhoods are less threatening to those living elsewhere in the city, as the studies cited above suggest, we might expect this depolicing to have either a positive or negative effect on the residents of isolated, poor minority neighborhoods: For those who desire more robust crime control, the relaxed law enforcement associated with high segregation should generate disapproval of the police. But for those who already have a negative impression of the local police or feel that police mistreat neighborhood residents, a reduced police presence in their community may be greeted with relief. For these residents, the relaxed law enforcement associated with high segregation should temper their disapproval of the police. Research indicates that *both* of these orientations are present among residents of disadvantaged black neighborhoods (Block 1970; Weitzer and Tuch 2006, 14). In the context of these dual perspectives, segregation (and its corollary, depolicing) may not have a uniform effect on residents' views of the police. Instead, residents' mixed orientations may cancel out and preclude any aggregate effect of high segregation on minority approval of the police. Researchers have yet to explore this question.

15.3 HISPANICS: WHAT WE KNOW AND
NEED TO KNOW

The lion's share of research on race and policing in America has centered on blacks and whites. As the fastest growing population in the United States and one that has achieved majority status in several major cities, more research on Hispanics is desperately needed. What do we know, so far, about Hispanics' orientations to the police? Studies that include Hispanics show that, overall, they tend to take an intermediate position between whites and blacks, being more critical of the police than whites but less critical than blacks. This pattern has been described as a "racial hierarchy"—white/Hispanic/African American—in contrast to a more cohesive black/Hispanic "minority-group orientation" (Weitzer and Tuch 2006). At the same time, although racial hierarchy is evident on many specific policing issues, there are some areas where the two minority groups are largely in agreement, such as the kinds of reforms they want to see in policing (Weitzer and Tuch 2006).

A racial-hierarchy pattern is evident in contacts with police officers as well. The Bureau of Justice Statistics (BJS) Police-Public Contact Survey reports that blacks, whites, and Hispanics were about equally likely to be stopped by the police in 2008 (8.8, 8.4, and 9.1 percent, respectively) but were searched at different rates: black drivers were three times more likely than whites (12.3 and 3.9 percent, respectively) and twice as likely as Hispanics (5.8 percent) to be searched during a traffic stop (BJS 2011). Of those who experienced a face-to-face contact with the police in 2008, blacks were more likely than Hispanics or whites to be the recipients of force or threatened force (3.4, 1.6, and 1.2 percent, respectively [BJS 2011]). The type of force involved ranged from officer shouting to hitting or pointing a gun at the citizen. Racial background may also shape other differences in what happens during a stop. A survey of 1,375 Hispanics conducted by the Pew Hispanic Center reported that 5 percent had been stopped by police in the past year and asked about their immigration status (Lopez, Morin, and Taylor 2010). Although the survey did not include other groups, it is likely that police ask few whites and African Americans about their immigration status. Four-fifths of Hispanics disapprove of the Arizona law that instructs police to check the legal status of persons they stop if they suspect that the person is in the country illegally (Lopez, Morin, and Taylor 2010). And a study of 732 Hispanic and African American high-school students in Chicago found that, while the two groups were about equally likely to report being stopped by the police (60 and 55 percent, respectively), black students were more likely than Hispanics to say they were treated disrespectfully during the encounter (62 and 45 percent, respectively). Moreover, being stopped and disrespected lowered overall respect for the police among blacks but not Hispanics (Lurigio, Greenleaf, and Flexon 2009).

One problem with the "Hispanic" or "Latino" category is that it masks internal differences along the axes of nativity and ancestry. Immigrants may differ significantly from native-born citizens. First, the frame of reference for the former may be radically different from that of the latter: For recent immigrants, the reputation of the police in their home countries (e.g., fair, corrupt, paramilitary, violent) may continue to be salient in the new country, in contrast to more indigenous influences among the native-born population. Aversion to the police back home can translate into deep suspicion and hence avoidance of the police in the new country or, by contrast, may be conducive to more positive views of police in the new country if they are seen as superior to their counterparts back home (Correia 2010). Second, a person's legal status makes a difference, with recent immigrants more inclined than the native born to avoid the police. Yet the immigrant-native variable has almost never been examined. A recent survey of 2,015 Hispanics in the United States reported that foreign-born Latinos are less favorably disposed toward the police than native-born Latinos: 40 percent and 51 percent, respectively, expressed confidence that the police in their community "will treat Hispanics fairly," and 42 percent and 50 percent believed that the police in their community will not use excessive force on suspects (Lopez and Livingston 2009). And, consistent with black-white differences, a study comparing black Hispanics with nonblack Hispanics found that the former were more likely to see racial profiling as unjustified, to believe that it is widespread in America, and to say they had personally experienced such profiling (Rice, Reitzel, and Piquero 2005).

The effects of police involvement in the immigration arena are documented in a longitudinal study conducted before and after a city's criminal justice system began to report individuals to immigration authorities (Vidales, Day, and Powe 2009). In the "before" survey in 2001, Latinos living in Costa Mesa, California, generally had positive views of the local police. But in the period after a 2005 policy change that involved reporting detained individuals to the immigration service—a policy that was widely publicized and prompted street demonstrations and a boycott of local businesses—confidence in the local police dropped considerably. In the 2007 survey, Latino's opinions of the police were significantly lower on almost all of the 15 policing questions. Moreover, whereas 13 percent of Latinos reported being stopped by the police while driving in the previous year in 2001, the proportion tripled in 2007 (39 percent), at the same time as stops of non-Hispanics dropped (from 20 to 8 percent, respectively).

Similarly neglected is the impact of national origin or ancestry. A couple of surveys report that Puerto Ricans stand out: they are significantly more dissatisfied with the police in their community than other Latinos (Kaiser Foundation 2000) and more likely to believe that the police often abuse people verbally and physically, engage in unjustified stops on the street, and are corrupt (Weitzer and Tuch 2006, 52). These critical views may be traceable to Puerto Ricans' socioeconomic status, which is lower than that of other Hispanics (except Dominicans) and is consistent with conflict theory's prediction that deprivation breeds dissatisfaction with state authorities. There are also reasons to expect Cuban Americans to have a very different relationship with the police—due to their privileged legal status—than Hispanics whose status is more open to question (e.g., those with Mexican or Central American backgrounds), as a Phoenix study suggested (Menjivar and Bejarano 2004). And Alpert and Dunham (1988) found that Cubans who arrived in Miami in the 1960s were much more supportive of the police than those who arrived in the 1980s, suggesting that residential longevity may be a predictor in addition to national origin. But, aside from these tidbits of information, little is known about the impact of ancestry on Hispanic subgroups' orientations toward the police.

Skogan (2006a) reported differences in Chicago between English- and Spanish-speaking Hispanics. Spanish-speaking Hispanics were more likely than both their English-speaking counterparts and African Americans to believe that excessive force was a big problem in their neighborhood, and twice as likely to think that police officers were corrupt. This may be due to Spanish-speaking immigrants' greater suspicion of police in their home country (mostly Mexico, among Chicago Hispanics) which is grafted on to their views of American police.

Similarly, a study of San Antonio found that Spanish-speaking and foreign-born Hispanics were less satisfied with the police who work in their neighborhoods than Hispanics who were more acculturated (McCluskey, McCluskey, and Enriquez 2008). A striking finding was that, overall, Hispanics were slightly more satisfied with the city's police than white residents. The researchers suggest that this may be due to the fact that San Antonio is a majority-Hispanic city and that Hispanic officers comprise about half of a police department whose chief was Hispanic as well. In another majority-Hispanic city with a majority of Hispanic officers, El Paso, neighborhood context was incorporated into the analysis. Holmes (1998) reported that Hispanics living in a middle-class community were more likely than similarly situated whites, but about as likely as poor Hispanics, to believe that the police engaged in misconduct toward city residents (e.g., abusive language, excessive force, warrantless searches), while whites living in a poor neighborhood were more likely than middle-class whites to perceive police misconduct, lending credence to the views of their Hispanic counterparts in the poor area.

15.4 NEW DIRECTIONS

In the remainder of the essay I discuss some deficiencies in the existing literature that need to be rectified with the help of new research. From the above discussion it should be obvious that much more research has been done on citizens' perceptions of the police than on police perceptions and treatment of citizens. Why? It is generally more difficult to study the latter than the former—because researchers usually have difficulty gaining access to officers and to relevant police records and because of the high cost of conducting systematic observational research on police-citizen interactions while on patrol. Other gaps in knowledge are outlined below.

15.4.1 Examine Under-Researched Populations

Much more research is needed not only on Hispanics but also on Asians, Arabs, and Muslims in the United States and on other ethnic minorities elsewhere in the world.

And it is crucial that pan-ethnic groups be disaggregated along lines of national origin, nativity, and immigration status.

It is remarkable how few studies have been done on Asian Americans and the police. The few national surveys that contain a sufficiently large number of Asian respondents typically report that their attitudes differ little from those of white Americans, but these surveys have not disaggregated the Asian category by they key variables of ancestry and national origin. We do have a few city-level studies that focus on one population: Chinese Americans. A survey of 198 Chinese immigrants in San Francisco found that seven out of ten said they had experienced a communication barrier with the city's police; almost all favored hiring more officers who could speak Chinese as a way to improve relations with Chinese residents; just over a third (36 percent) said they were satisfied with the city's police, while a majority (51 percent) took a neutral view, being neither satisfied nor dissatisfied; respondents who had a positive view of police in China were more likely to perceive the San Francisco police positively; and as respondents' length of time in the United States increased, their overall ratings of the police decreased, perhaps, the authors suggest, because immigrants may hold high expectations of institutions in this country, which are only tarnished as they become more familiar with them (Chu and Hung 2010). A Toronto study echoed some of these findings: Chinese immigrants cited poor communication between police and the Chinese community as a serious problem; many felt there were not enough bilingual officers in Toronto; and one-fifth said police prejudice against Asians was a serious problem, with longer residence in Canada correlating with lower perceived prejudice (Chu and Song 2008). Comparing opinions of Toronto police with their counterparts in New York City, a follow-up study found that Chinese immigrants in New York (N = 151) were more likely than those in Toronto (N = 293) to see the city's police as prejudiced against the Chinese and less likely to express respect for the police (Chu and Song 2011). The authors suggest that the differences may be attributable to different policing styles in the two cities: with the New York Police Department taking a more aggressive approach and the Toronto police better known for their multi-culturalism and community policing orientation.

Missing from the policing literature are comparable studies of other Asian populations. Such studies would be especially valuable in cities with sizeable Asian immigrant populations of Koreans, Vietnamese, Chinese, or Filipinos (e.g., Los Angeles, New York, and San Francisco).

Relations between the police and Arab and Muslim Americans have become especially important since September 11, 2001. It should be noted that the majority of Arab Americans are not Muslim (two-thirds being Christian) and many Muslim Americans do not have Arab ancestry; it is thus important that researchers not conflate Muslims and Arabs. Moreover, the pan-ethnic Arab category includes several different ancestries, including the three most populous in the United States: Lebanese, Syrian, and Egyptian.

One survey found that the percentage of Muslim Americans who say that they have been "singled out by" police (i.e., profiled) in the past year rose from 9 percent in 2007 to 13 percent in 2011 (Pew Research Center 2011). A nationwide poll found that 38 percent of Americans agreed that "U.S. Muslims are unfairly singled out for scrutiny by law enforcement officials" (*Newsweek* 2007). Interestingly, two-thirds say that Muslim Americans are cooperating as much as they should with law enforcement agencies that investigate extremism in their community; only 14 percent said the Muslim community was not cooperating enough and 18 percent selected the "don't know" option (Pew Research Center 2011). (This poll question is somewhat problematic in the meaning of the term "should" cooperate and in its assumptions that the public has even a rough idea of how much cooperation is taking place.)

Interviews with Arab American community leaders in 16 cities asked them to identify the kind of barriers that prevent Arab citizens from working with law enforcement on public safety issues. The top five barriers cited by the community leaders were—in order of importance—distrust, lack of cultural awareness among the police, reluctance or fear of having contact with law enforcement authorities, language difficulties, and immigration status (Henderson et al. 2006, 94). Interviews with local police and FBI personnel similarly found distrust to be the most significant barrier mentioned, followed by Arab reluctance to have contact with law enforcement. Not surprisingly, the community leaders expressed greater trust in their local, city police than in the FBI, a finding replicated in Thatcher's (2005) in-depth study of Dearborn, Michigan (where Arabs comprise one-third of the population). Local Dearborn authorities sought, both before and after September 11, 2001, to build positive relations with the local Arab population. After 9/11, the police enhanced patrols in Arab communities in order to thwart retaliatory hate crimes, while being pressured by federal law enforcement to engage in greater surveillance and intelligence gathering. Local police agreed to facilitate interviews between the FBI and selected Arab residents but declined to conduct the interviews themselves for fear of jeopardizing their relationship with the Arab community (Thatcher 2005). In 2008, Dearborn appointed its first Arab American police chief.

A 2003 survey of Arab Americans living in the Detroit metropolitan area found that 23 percent supported giving the police the power to stop and search anyone at random while only 7 percent endorsed this practice against persons who appeared to be Arab or Muslim; 15 percent supported increased government surveillance of Arab Americans; and 12 percent agreed with the idea that police could detain "suspicious" Muslims or Arabs even in the absence of evidence sufficient to prosecute them (Sun, Wu, and Poteyeva 2011). Muslims were less likely to support these measures than non-Muslim Arabs or the general public, and Arab Americans who had less confidence in the U.S. government were less likely to favor these measures. The reported differences, as well as the general lack of support for such measures in Detroit's Arab population, are perhaps not surprising in a survey conducted two years after 9/11, but the more recent nationwide data (mentioned above) suggest that such views may have remained relatively stable since that time.

Aside from scattered evidence such as this, very little is known about Arab and Muslim Americans' experiences and perceptions of law enforcement as well as possible internal differences along lines of nativity and national origin. Research in Britain suggests that the Muslim population there may have significantly worse relations with the police than in the United States. One study concluded that Muslims and non-Muslims who live in the same geographical areas live "parallel lives": the police practice of using counterterrorism powers to stop and search people is one reason that many Muslims feel that "they are being treated as a 'suspect community' and targeted by the authorities simply because of their religion," with the net effect being one a "climate of fear and suspicion" and strong perceptions of discrimination by the police (Choudhury and Fenwick 2011, v). From 2001 to 2009, the police conducted 542,400 stops and searches of individuals in England and Wales under the Terrorism Act, resulting in 283 arrests and no convictions; one-fifth of those stopped were British Asian (e.g., Pakistanis and Indians) (Choudhury and Fenwick 2011, 31).

Returning to the theoretical frameworks discussed earlier, many seem applicable to racial and ethnic groups other than African Americans. But we need to ask whether any of these perspectives would lack salience or need modification when applied to other groups. For instance, does the minority-threat model apply to Asian Americans in America? I know of no work that makes that argument. By contrast, both the group-position and minority-threat theses would seem to be especially relevant to Muslim and Arab minorities, insofar at they are regarded as a physical threat to the entire population (and not just the dominant racial group) in the aftermath of the 9/11 attacks. Broad popular support for racial profiling of these populations in the United States and in Europe seems to confirm this pattern. More examination of under-researched populations will help to locate them on the hierarchy of ethnic group orientations to the police, and help to identify what, if anything, is uniquely problematic in their relations with law enforcement.

15.4.2 Conduct More Qualitative Studies

Most of the literature on race and policing has been quantitative, usually consisting of surveys of citizens' attitudes and experiences with the police. While these studies are quite valuable for identifying frequencies and predictors of citizens' relations with the police, other types of studies are needed as well. We know much more about the demographic and ecological *factors* that have been identified as predictors of citizens' attitudes than about the deeper *meanings* citizens attach to policing or the *substantive* nature of police-citizen interactions. Much more qualitative research—in the form of in-depth interviews, focus groups, and systematic observations—is needed to document:

- How police treat people during contacts;
- Productive and counterproductive communication patterns between police officers and the individuals they approach;
- The various ways in which people perceive the police and the main sources of these perceptions; and
- The kinds of policing practices, or reforms, residents want to see in their neighborhood and city.

Research shows that young minority males are uniquely susceptible to being stopped by the police because of the "triple jeopardy" of being young, minority, and male (Weitzer and Tuch 2006; cf. Goris, Jobard, and Lévy 2009). In one study, fully 73 percent of black males 18 to 34 years old reported that they had been stopped by the police solely because of their race, compared to 11 percent of same-age white males, 38 percent of same-age black females, and 40 percent of black males aged 50 and older (Weitzer and Tuch 2002). We have some interview data bearing on *how it feels* to be repeatedly stopped and questioned by the authorities, to be frisked in public, and to be treated with a presumption of criminality, as well as the cumulative impact of such experiences. Not surprisingly, the dominant outcome is that of feeling demeaned and dehumanized (Williams 1997; Weitzer 1999, 2000a; Brunson 2007; Carr, Napolitano and, Keating 2007; Sharp and Atherton 2007; Brunson and Weitzer 2009; Weitzer and Brunson 2009). But much more research is needed to document what individuals take away from encounters with the police, and the dimensions along which these experiences vary between racial and ethnic groups. Do some individuals or neighborhoods come to expect poor treatment from the police as a result of their cumulative experiences? And do they feel that, because they lack political clout in the city, their calls for police accountability fall on deaf ears? Some research suggests that neighborhoods do differ significantly—along racial and class lines—in whether residents feel empowered to hold police accountable (Weitzer 1999). Qualitative studies are also well-suited to identifying multiplier effects associated with vicarious experiences, network communication, and the intergenerational transmission of conduct norms to youth.

The frequencies reported in survey research can sometimes mask important underlying meanings. For instance, in a Washington, DC study, I found that a large percentage of whites agreed that whites and blacks are often treated differently by the police—giving the appearance that both groups were aware of racial discrimination by officers. Yet, when asked why they thought this disparity existed, many whites thought that it reflected blacks' greater involvement in crime. Hence, more stops of blacks was considered not racial animus but "rational discrimination" on the part of the police (Weitzer 2000a). What this shows is that responses to fixed-choice questions should not necessarily be accepted at face value and may require further qualitative probing.

15.4.3   Research Media and Social Network Effects

The media can play a major role in shaping public perceptions of the police. Highly publicized controversies involving the police have documented effects on citizen attitudes and it appears that long-term exposure to media depictions may influence public perceptions as well. Yet a media-exposure variable has been absent from the research designs of most studies in the area of race and policing. This factor should be included not only in studies of the obvious cases of cities where there have been recent well-publicized incidents involving the police (e.g., New Orleans post-Katrina) but also where ongoing news coverage of local law enforcement may be salient. Research on the impact of urban contextual conditions is deficient if focused exclusively on socioeconomic and demographic variables without also incorporating measures related to police practices that attract media coverage and may affect popular confidence in the authorities and demands for reforms.

15.5 CONCLUSION

Scholarly attention to the under-researched populations and factors described above will help to enrich our understanding of police-minority relations in both the United States and other multi-ethnic societies. The greater use of qualitative research methods, perhaps in conjunction with quantitative approaches, will yield major dividends as well. But we also need well designed research. Some quantitative studies can be faulted for problematic research designs that include variables that lack theoretical grounding, and some qualitative studies are deficient due to their small samples and/or lack of sufficient rigor. And some research methods have been under-utilized. Systematic observational research of police patrols seems to be a method relegated to the past; focus groups dealing with race and policing have rarely been done but could produce insights that go beyond the findings of interview-based studies; and we need much more comparative contextual research on different kinds of neighborhoods and different kinds of cities.

REFERENCES

Alexander, Jeffrey. 2001. "Theorizing the Modes of Incorporation." *Sociological Theory* 19:237–49.

Alpert, Geoffrey, and Roger Dunham. 1988. *Policing Multi-Ethnic Neighborhoods.* New York: Greenwood.

Black, Donald. 1971. "The Social Organization of Arrest." *Stanford Law Review* 23:1087–111.

Block, Richard. 1970. "Support for Civil Liberties and Support for the Police." *American Behavioral Scientist* 13:781–96.

Bobo, Lawrence. 1999. "Prejudice as Group Position." *Journal of Social Issues* 55:445–72.

Brunson, Rod. 2007. "'Police Don't Like Black People': African American Young Men's Accumulated Police Experiences." *Criminology and Public Policy* 6:71–102

Brunson, Rod, and Ronald Weitzer. 2009. "Police Relations with Black and White Youths in Different Urban Neighborhoods." *Urban Affairs Review* 44:858–85.

——. 2011. "Negotiating Unwelcome Police Encounters: The Intergenerational Transmission of Conduct Norms." *Journal of Contemporary Ethnography* 40:425–56.

Bureau of Justice Statistics. 2011. *Contacts between Police and the Public, 2008.* Washington, DC: U.S. Department of Justice.

Bursik, Robert. 1988. "Social Disorganization and Theories of Crime and Delinquency." *Criminology* 26:519–51.

Carr, Patrick, Laura Napolitano, and Jessica Keating. 2007. "'We Never Call the Cops and Here's Why': A Qualitative Examination of Legal Cynicism in Three Philadelphia Neighborhoods." *Criminology* 45:445–80.

Chambliss, William, and Robert Seidman. 1971. *Law, Order, and Power.* Reading, PA: Addison-Wesley.

Chermak, Steven, Edmund McGarrell, and Jeff Gruenewald. 2006. "Media Coverage of Police Misconduct and Attitudes toward Police." *Policing: An International Journal of Police Strategies and Management* 29: 261–81.

Choudhury, Tufyal, and Helen Fenwick. 2011. *The Impact of Counter-Terrorism Measures on Muslim Communities.* Manchester, UK: Equality and Human Rights Commission.

Chu, Doris, and Linda Hung. 2010. "Chinese Immigrants' Attitudes toward the Police in San Francisco." *Policing: An International Journal of Police Strategies and Management* 33:621–43.

Chu, Doris, and John Song. 2008. "Chinese Immigrants' Perceptions of the Police in Toronto, Canada." *Policing: An International Journal of Police Strategies and Management* 31:610–30.

——. 2011. "A Comparison of Chinese Immigrants' Perceptions of the Police in New York and Toronto." *Crime and Delinquency* doi:10.1177/0011128711405008

Correll, Joshua, Bernadette Park, Charles Judd, Bernd Wittenbrink, Melody Sadler, and Tracie Keesee. 2007. "Across the Thin Blue Line: Police Officers and Racial Bias in the Decision to Shoot." *Journal of Personality and Social Psychology* 92:1006–23.

Dixon, Travis, Terry Schell, Howard Giles, and Kristin Drogos. 2008. "The Influence of Race in Police-Citizen Interactions." *Journal of Communication* 58:530–49.

Dresner, Morris, Tortorello, and Sykes Research. 1981. *The State of Police-Community Relations: A Report to the Milwaukee Fire and Police Commission.* Milwaukee, WI: Dresner, Morris, Tortorello, and Sykes Research.

Ellison, Graham, and Jim Smyth. 2000. *The Crowned Harp: Policing Northern Ireland.* London: Pluto.

Engel, Robin. 2003. "Explaining Suspects' Resistance and Disrespect toward Police." *Journal of Criminal Justice* 31:475–92.

Eschholz, Sarah, Brenda Blackwell, Marc Gertz, and Ted Chiricos. 2002. "Race and Attitudes toward the Police: Assessing the Effects of Watching 'Reality' Police Programs." *Journal of Criminal Justice* 30:327–41.

Fagan, Jeffrey, Amanda Geller, Garth Davies, and Valerie West. 2010. "Street Stops and Broken Windows Revisited." In *Race, Ethnicity, and Policing: New and Essential Readings*, edited by Stephen Rice and Michael White, 309–348. New York: NYU Press.

Goris, Indira, Fabien Jobard, and Rene Lévy. 2009. *Profiling Minorities: A Study of Stop-and-Search Practices in Paris.* New York: Open Society Institute.

Hagan, John, Carla Shedd, and Monique Payne. 2005. "Race, Ethnicity, and Youth Perceptions of Criminal Injustice." *American Sociological Review* 70:381–407.

Hasisi, Badi, and Ronald Weitzer. 2007. "Police Relations with Arabs and Jews in Israel." *British Journal of Criminology* 47:728–45.

Hebberecht, Patrick. 1997. "Minorities, Crime, and Criminal Justice in Belgium." In *Minorities, Migrants, and Crime: Diversity and Similarity across Europe and the United States*, edited by Ineke H. Marshall, 151–174. London: Sage.

Henderson, Nicole, Christopher Ortiz, Naomi Sugie, and Joel Miller. 2006. *Law Enforcement and Arab American Community Relations after September 11, 2001.* New York: Vera Institute of Justice.

Holmes, Malcolm. 1998. "Perceptions of Abusive Police Practices in a U.S.-Mexican Border Community." *Social Science Journal* 35:107–18.

Hutterman, Jorg. 2003. "Policing an Ethnically Divided Neighborhood in Germany." *Policing and Society* 13:381–97.

Ivković, Sanja Kutnjak. 2008. "A Comparative Study of Public Support for the Police." *International Criminal Justice Review* 18:406–34.

Jacobs, David, and Robert O'Brien. 1998. "The Determinants of Deadly Force: A Structural Analysis of Police Violence." *American Journal of Sociology* 103:837–62.

Jefferson, Tony. 1988. "Race, Crime, and Policing: Empirical, Theoretical, and Methodological Issues." *International Journal of the Sociology of Law* 16:521–39.

Junger, Marianne. 1990. "Studying Ethnic Minorities in Relation to Crime and Police Discrimination." *British Journal of Criminology* 30:493–502.

Kaiser Foundation. 2000. Kaiser Foundation/*Washington Post*/Harvard University poll (May).

Kaminski, Robert, and Eric Jefferis. 1998. "The Effect of a Violent Televised Arrest on Public Perceptions of the Police." *Policing: An International Journal of Police Strategies and Management* 21:683–706.

Kane, Robert. 2002. "The Social Ecology of Police Misconduct." *Criminology* 40:867–96.

Kubrin, Charis, and Ronald Weitzer. 2003. "New Directions in Social Disorganization Theory." *Journal of Research in Crime and Delinquency* 40:374–402.

Lawrence, Regina. 2000. *The Politics of Force: Media and the Construction of Police Brutality*. Berkeley: University of California Press.

Liska, Allen, Mitchell Chamlin, and Mark Reed. 1985. "Testing the Economic Production and Conflict Models of Crime Control." *Social Forces* 64:119–38.

Liska, Allen, and Jiang Yu. 1992. "Specifying and Testing the Threat Hypothesis: Police Use of Deadly Force." In *Social Threat and Social Control*, edited by A. Liska, 53–68. Albany: State University of New York Press.

Liska, Allen, Joseph Lawrence, and Michael Benson. 1981. "Perspectives on the Legal Order: The Capacity for Social Control." *American Journal of Sociology* 87:412–26.

MacDonald, John, Robert Stokes, Greg Ridgeway, and K. Jack Riley. 2007. "Race, Neighborhood Context, and Perceptions of Injustice by the Police in Cincinnati." *Urban Studies* 13:2567–85.

Marenin, Otwin. 1985. "Police Performance and State Rule." *Comparative Politics* 18:101–22.

Mastrofski, Stephen, Michael D. Reisig, and John McCluskey. 2002. "Police Disrespect toward the Public." *Criminology* 40:519–51.

McCluskey, John, Cynthia McCluskey, and Roger Enriquez. 2008. "A Comparison of Latino and White Citizen Satisfaction with Police." *Journal of Criminal Justice* 36:471–77.

Meehan, Albert, and Michael Ponder. 2002. "Race and Place: The Ecology of Racial Profiling African American Motorists." *Justice Quarterly* 19:399–429.

Menjivar, Cecilia, and Cynthia Bejarano. 2004. "Latino Immigrants' Perceptions of Crime and Police Authorities in Phoenix." *Ethnic and Racial Studies* 27:120–48.

Miller, Joel. 2007. *"I Can Stop and Search Whoever I Want": Police Stops of Ethnic Minorities in Bulgaria, Hungary, and Spain*. New York: Open Society Institute.

Milton-Edwards, Beverly. 1997. "Policing Palestinian Society." *Policing and Society* 7:19–44.

Newsweek. 2007. Poll, Princeton Survey Research Associates, cited in Angus Reid Public Opinion. http://www.angus-reid.com/polls/1018/americans_ponder_police_actions_on_muslims/.

Parker, Karen, Brian Stults, and Stephen Rice. 2005. "Racial Threat, Concentrated Disadvantage, and Social Control." *Criminology* 43:1111–34.

Pew Research Center. 2011. *Muslim Americans: No Signs of Growth in Alienation or Support for Extremism*. Washington, DC: Pew Research Center.

Plant, E. Ashby, and B. Michelle Peruche. 2005. "The Consequences of Race for Police Officers' Responses to Criminal Suspects." *Psychological Science* 16:180–83.

Reisig, Michael D., John McCluskey, Stephen Mastrofski, and William Terrill. 2004. "Suspect Disrespect toward the Police." *Justice Quarterly* 21:241–68.

Reisig, Michael D., and Roger Parks. 2000. "Experience, Quality of Life, and Neighborhood Context." *Justice Quarterly* 17:607–29.

Rosenbaum, Dennis, Amie Schuck, Sandra Costello, Darnell Hawkins, and Marianne King. 2005. "Attitudes toward the Police: The Effects of Direct and Vicarious Experience." *Police Quarterly* 8:343–65.

Sampson, Robert, and Dawn Bartusch. 1998. "Legal Cynicism and (Subcultural?) Tolerance of Deviance." *Law and Society Review* 32:777–804.

Schafer, Joseph, Beth Huebner, and Timothy Bynum. 2003. "Citizen Perceptions of Police Services: Race, Neighborhood Context, and Community Policing." *Police Quarterly* 6:440–68.

Schuck, Amie, Dennis Rosenbaum, and Darnell Hawkins. 2008. "The Influence of Race/ Ethnicity, Social Class, and Neighborhood Context on Residents' Attitudes toward the Police." *Police Quarterly* 11:496–519.

Sharp, Douglas, and Susie Atherton. 2007. "To Serve and Protect? The Experiences of Policing in the Community of Young People from Black and other Ethnic Minority Groups." *British Journal of Criminology* 47:746–63.

Sigelman, Lee, Susan Welch, Timothy Bledsoe, and Michael Combs. 1997. "Police Brutality and Public Perceptions of Racial Discrimination." *Political Research Quarterly* 50: 777–91.

Sklansky, David. 2006. "Not Your Father's Police Department: Making Sense of the New Demographics of Law Enforcement." *Journal of Criminal Law and Criminology* 96:1209–43.

Skogan, Wesley. 2006a. *Police and Community in Chicago: A Tale of Three Cities*. New York: Oxford University Press.

———. 2006b. "Asymmetry in the Impact of Encounters with the Police." *Policing and Society* 16:99–126.

Smith, Brad. 2005. "The Impact of Police Officer Diversity on Police-Caused Homicides." *Policy Studies Journal* 31:147–62.

Smith, Douglas. 1986. "The Neighborhood Context of Police Behavior." In *Crime and Justice*, vol. 8, edited by A. Reiss and M. Tonry, 313–341. Chicago: University of Chicago Press.

Stults, Brian, Karen Parker, and Erin Lane. 2010. "Space, Place, and Immigration: New Directions for Research on Police Stops." In *Race, Ethnicity, and Policing: New and Essential Readings*, edited by Stephen Rice and Michael White, 411–434. New York: New York University Press.

Sun, Ivan, Yuning Wu, and Margarita Poteyeva. 2011. "Arab Americans' Opinion on Counterterrorism Measures." *Studies in Conflict and Terrorism* 34:540–55.

Sykes, Richard, and John Clark. 1975. "A Theory of Deference Exchange in Police-Civilian Encounters." *American Journal of Sociology* 81:584–600.

Terrill, William, and Michael D. Reisig. 2003. "Neighborhood Context and Police Use of Force." *Journal of Research in Crime and Delinquency* 40:291–321.

Thatcher, David. 2005. "The Local Role in Homeland Security." *Law and Society Review* 39:635–76.

Tyler, Tom R., and Yuen J. Huo. 2002. *Trust in the Law*. New York: Russell Sage Foundation.

Velez, Maria. 2001. "The Role of Public Social Control in Urban Neighborhoods." *Criminology* 39:837–63.

Vrij, Albert, and Frans Winkel. 1991. "Encounters between Dutch Police and Minorities." *Police Studies* 14:17–23.

Walker, Samuel, Cassia Spohn, and Miriam DeLone. 2000. *The Color of Justice*. Belmont, CA: Wadsworth.

Weitzer, Ronald. 1995. *Policing under Fire: Ethnic Conflict and Police-Community Relations in Northern Ireland*. Albany: State University of New York Press.

——. 1999. "Citizens' Perceptions of Police Misconduct: Race and Neighborhood Context." *Justice Quarterly* 16:819–46.

——. 2000a. "Racialized Policing: Residents' Perceptions in Three Neighborhoods." *Law and Society Review* 34:129–55.

——. 2000b. "White, Black, or Blue Cops? Race and Citizen Assessments of Police Officers." *Journal of Criminal Justice* 28:313–24.

——. 2002. "Incidents of Police Misconduct and Public Opinion." *Journal of Criminal Justice* 30:397–408.

——. 2010. "Race and Policing in Different Ecological Contexts." In *Race, Ethnicity, and Policing: New and Essential Readings*, edited by Stephen Rice and Michael White, 118–139. New York: New York University Press.

Weitzer, Ronald, and Rod Brunson. 2009. "Strategic Responses to the Police among Inner-city Youth." *Sociological Quarterly* 50:235–56.

Weitzer, Ronald, and Steven Tuch. 2002. "Perceptions of Racial Profiling: Race, Class, and Personal Experience." *Criminology* 40:435–56.

——. 2006. *Race and Policing in America: Conflict and Reform*. New York: Cambridge University Press.

Weitzer, Ronald, Steven Tuch, and Wesley Skogan. 2008. "Police-Community Relations in a Majority-Black City." *Journal of Research in Crime and Delinquency* 45:398–428.

Wiley, Mary, and Terry Hudik. 1974. "Police-Citizen Encounters: A Field Test of Exchange Theory." *Social Problems* 22:119–27.

Williams, Brian. 1997. *Citizen Perspectives on Community Policing*. Albany: State University of New York Press.

Wu, Yuning, Ivan Sun, and Ruth Triplett. 2009. "Race, Class or Neighborhood Context: Which Matters More in Measuring Satisfaction with Police?" *Justice Quarterly* 26:125–56.

Zauberman, Renee, and Rene Lévy. 2003. "Police, Minorities, and the French Republican Ideal." *Criminology* 41:1065–100.

....

CHAPTER 16

RACE, PLACE, AND POLICING THE INNER-CITY

....

ROD K. BRUNSON AND JACINTA M. GAU

> We was playin' basketball and [my friend] put a wristband in his gym
> bag.... The police thought it was some crack so they stopped him and
> was harassing him, like, "where its at?" He was like, "I ain't got nothin."
> After they checked him, they checked all of us. Only thing they found was
> wristbands, white wristbands.... [The police officers] took all six of us in
> [to the station] and was checkin' our mouth[s] and [other body parts]...
> to see if we have drugs and they found out [that] we didn't.

THE involuntary and extremely intrusive police encounter presented above was reported
to us by Martez, a teenage study participant (Gau and Brunson 2010, 268). Regrettably,
similar scenarios unfold daily on inner-city streets throughout the United States (e.g.,
Gould and Mastrofski 2004). Thus, Martez and his friends' unpleasant police experience is easily confirmed by countless urban residents' parallel accounts of routinely
attracting police attention in situations where they believed there was clearly no basis
for suspecting them of criminal involvement. A substantial body of scholarship has
sought to cast light on this phenomenon. For example, roughly two decades ago, sociologist Elijah Anderson devoted a chapter of his award-winning book, *Streetwise: Race,
Class, and Change in an Urban Community*, to pinpointing the wellspring of tensions
between police and urban black males. He explains that the process police officers use to
distinguish between law-abiding and law-violating individuals is imperfect, and is further complicated by the perceptual frameworks officers bring to their interactions with
residents of perceived "high-crime" places (see also Terrill and Reisig 2003). Anderson
(1990, 190) notes:

> On the streets, color-coding often works to confuse race, age, class, gender, incivility,
> and criminality, and it expresses itself most concretely in the person of the anony-
> mous black male. In doing their job, the police often become willing parties to this

general color-coding of the public environment, and related distinctions, particularly those of skin color and gender, come to convey definite meanings. Although such coding may make the work of police more manageable, it may also fit well with their own presuppositions regarding race and class relations, thus shaping officers' perceptions of crime "in the city."

Anderson makes clear how officers' preconceived notions about race and place inevitably converge, affirming their views of urban young black men as symbolic assailants (see Skolnick 1994). Since Anderson, a number of scholars have likewise considered the complex nature of race and place concerning inner-city, young black men's unwelcome police experiences (Harris 1994; Skolnick 1994; Kennedy 1997; Bridges and Steen 1998; Quillian and Pager 2001). Some have expressed concern about the fact that courts rarely require police to produce data supporting the veracity of an assertion that a certain area is justly classified as "high crime" (Ferguson and Bernache 2008). Much of this work corroborates that "black young men view their treatment by the police as multi-faceted, intimately tied to their status as young men in disadvantaged communities, but nonetheless ultimately, inescapably, about race" (Brunson and Miller 2006a, 634).

Blacks in the United States have had a long and tumultuous history of being unjustly targeted, stopped, questioned, and searched by the police (Bass 2001; Websdale 2001). Disproportionate police attention has proven especially harmful to scores of urban black males, who consider themselves officers' primary targets, and who frequently describe their communities as having been besieged by police. Ironically, public debate surrounding discriminatory policing tactics flares when the media discovers that a prominent, respected black person (e.g., Henry Louis Gates, Jr.) alleges maltreatment (Meeks 2000; Harris 2002), while it typically requires an especially horrific incident involving poorer blacks and the police to generate comparable levels of public outrage (e.g., Abner Louima, Amadou Diallo, Sean Bell, Oscar Grant).

A great deal of research reveals that African Americans report less favorable views of the police when compared to members of other racial groups, especially whites (e.g., Skogan 2005; Tyler 2005). Prior research has also demonstrated that youths' views of police are more negative than are those of their adult counterparts (Taylor et al. 2001), and there is some evidence that this is related to the frequency of adolescents' involuntary police contacts (Lieber, Nalla, and Farnworth 1998). It is surprising, then, that most of the research on the matter has focused on adults rather than juveniles and is largely based on survey research or official data on citizen complaints.

A growing number of studies on the topic, however, have benefitted enormously from insights gained by speaking directly with urban residents—particularly juveniles and young adults—about their perceptions of and experiences with the police. These qualitative approaches supply considerable information concerning not just the context and circumstances of events, but also their meanings for those involved (Anderson 1990; Weitzer 1999, 2000). It is therefore critically important that scholars continue to move beyond simply documenting *how often* the police do certain things (e.g., stop, frisk, arrest), and move toward a more comprehensive understanding of how citizens make sense of *why* they do them. Such efforts might go a long way toward understanding how "perceptions of unfair and disrespectful treatment, coupled with high rates of being targeted by the police, likely have a cumulative effect on urban black young men's perceptions of police" (Brunson 2007, 76).

While it is well documented that inner-city, minority males bear the brunt of frequent, unwelcome police contacts—including disproportionate stops, frisks, and arrests (Fagan and Davies 2000)—there is considerable debate about the role of social class in shaping these disparate outcomes (Weitzer and Tuch 2002). For example, some scholars suggest that race has been confounded with neighborhood context in studies of urban black men's negative police encounters, such that attributions of racial bias are actually the result of police perceptions of ecologically "contaminated" places (Werthman and Piliavin 1967; Terrill and Reisig 2003). Few studies have been able to disentangle the impact of race from that of disadvantaged community context in explaining inner-city police practices (for exceptions, see Ridgeway 2006; Brunson and Weitzer 2009; Stewart et al. 2009), because the urban disadvantage found in poorer African American neighborhoods is ecologically unmatched (Sampson and Wilson 1995; Sampson and Bartusch 1998; Weitzer 1999).

It is likely that the effects of race and class are interactive rather than additive (Weitzer and Tuch 2002). Further, because of systemic racial residential segregation, it is really an interaction between race, class, and place that is operative in structuring the unique brand of crime control that inner-city residents consistently report experiencing. For instance, our prior work involving Martez (and forty-four other adolescent males residing in inner-city neighborhoods) reveals that "an over-reliance on stop-and-frisks to carry out order maintenance policing can have implications for police legitimacy because it can damage citizens' perceptions of the fairness with which police utilize their law enforcement authority" (Gau and Brunson 2010, 261). Moreover, a considerable body of knowledge painstakingly confirms the deleterious impacts of the heavy-handed policing strategies currently underway in many disadvantaged minority neighborhoods.

It is our contention here that efforts to improve police-minority relations must be set in motion by inner-city police executives and related policy makers because they are the ones with the capacity to make meaningful organizational changes (see Chevigny 1995; Mastrofski, Reisig, and McCluskey 2002). As we highlight in the following sections, these reforms should focus on improving satisfaction with and confidence in the police among disadvantaged people of color. We suggest that these reforms be delivered via high-quality interpersonal interactions with civilians and through the use of effective departmental discipline of misbehaving officers.

In the following sections, we review the evidence supporting the procedural justice model of police legitimacy and highlight some of the "urban warfare" tactics that pose considerable threats to the institutional legitimacy of policing. Section 16.1 describes the evolution of academic interest in police legitimacy, appealing largely to the classic sociologist/political scientist Max Weber for theoretical grounding. This section also identifies both the importance of maintaining legitimacy when policing the inner-city, and the consequences of aggressive policing, such as tactics associated with the "war" on drugs, on legitimacy in (primarily) communities of color. Section 16.2 makes several policy recommendations that we hope would increase police legitimacy in inner-city communities. Some recommendations include requiring police departments to develop collective cultures of procedural justice; identifying and disciplining officers who engage in misconduct; and appealing to a model of procedural justice that engages the community as partners in the co-production of police accountability and community safety. Section 16.3 draws several conclusions regarding the importance of police legitimacy in inner-city areas, reiterating the role of procedural justice as a cornerstone philosophy of fair and effective policing, particularly in communities of color. Several main points unfold throughout the essay:

- It is a fundamental precept of policing that police officers and agencies must have the support of the community in order to be effective at law-enforcement and order-maintenance activities.
- Approaches conceived under the rhetoric of "urban warfare" emphasize aggressive, intrusive policing that can violate urban dwellers' rights and undermine their trust in police; this alienation of the community impedes police effectiveness.
- The urban warfare model should be replaced with an alternative one stressing the importance of good police-community relations; specifically, urban police should adopt the premise of the procedural justice model of police legitimacy by recognizing that their interpersonal interactions with local residents shape the landscape of urban crime fighting and peacekeeping in a fundamental way.
- Full implementation of the procedural justice model requires commitment from police executives, managers, and other agency leaders. Three policy recommendations are made: internal policy should make it clear that fair, respectful treatment is expected of all officers in all encounters; chronically misbehaving officers must be identified and dealt with effectively; and urban police should engage with the community for the mobilization of coproduction.

16.1 POLICE LEGITIMACY: EARNING AND MAINTAINING THE RESPECT OF THE URBAN POPULACE

There is growing recognition among academics and police leaders that the urban warfare model of crime control has failed. In particular, the "fight fire with fire" and "under siege" rationales advanced to justify guerilla-like law enforcement tactics are increasingly viewed as specious among many policing experts, even if these aggressive mentalities continue to excite the public and provide fodder for box-office hits and cable network programming. In the sense that war involves long-standing, mutual hostilities with occasional casualties on both sides, then indeed, there is a war underway; however, unless and until police executives reconsider their current strategies and tactics, the conflict will be perpetual and both sides will continue to lose. Simply put, it is time to stop viewing the ineffectiveness of current policing methods as a testament to the incorrigibility of inner-city "troublemakers" and to start seeing it, instead, as clear and compelling evidence of the need to change the way that inner-city streets are policed.

Fortunately, the twenty-first century represents an era of numerous innovations in policing (Reisig 2010). New models are being proposed, and experimentation is increasingly encouraged by various key constituencies, such as local elected officials, community leaders, and federal funding agencies. A crux of this move toward progressive policing is the enduring belief that police activity can be both fair and highly successful (Skogan and Frydl 2004). One of the groundbreaking models that has been advanced, the theory of procedural justice and police legitimacy, extends this logic a step further to argue that police actually *must* be fair in order to be effective (e.g., Tyler 2006). The procedural justice model of policing is grounded in classic philosophies pertaining to the ways in which any government attempting to exert control over its masses must legitimate itself in the eyes of the people (see Chambliss and Seidman 1982).

A government cannot survive unless it promulgates a theory that adequately explains why it is more powerful than its subjects are and, moreover, why it has the right to compel the masses within its borders to obey its edicts. As Max Weber (1978, 953) phrased it, any system wherein one power is dominant over another possesses a "generally observable need…to justify itself." Weber offered a tripartite classification of the types of legitimacy upon which a government might rely to justify its coercive authority: traditional, charismatic, and rational/legal. Traditional legitimacy makes a plea to history. It explains the current governmental structure in terms of precedent. Monarchies are an example of traditional governments. This type of government survives only as long as the subordinate classes are content to be lorded over, such as when they believe that social positions are ordained by God and therefore inherently righteous (953). The second type, charismatic legitimacy, is premised upon the face value of a certain leader who proves especially dynamic and appealing. This is a fragile form of legitimacy, as it renders the uncritical masses vulnerable to beguiling swindlers and, from the perspective of the ruler, depends upon a public that is often fickle and temperamental (242).

Weber's third type of legitimacy, rational/legal, embodies the notion of participative liberty wherein the legal code is the product of a transparent legislative process and applies with equal force to both the rulers and the ruled (1978, 217). Integral to the rationality of laws is that people trust them to guarantee or, at least, substantially increase the probability of certain outcomes. If a law prohibits a certain action, for instance, then the government must consistently intervene on behalf of any citizen who is injured by the actions of another citizen who violated that law. Similarly, rationality requires that people can trust that if they are not engaged in proscribed behavior, the government will not intervene against them (667). Obedience to the law and government flows naturally from the stake that each individual has as a member of a participatory community where laws help preserve order and civility.

Rational legitimacy is the groundwork from which the procedural justice model of policing arises. As summarized above, Weber argued that the public needs to see empirical proof that the government possesses the moral authority to generate and enforce laws. Likened to a Weberian framework, procedural justice functions as tangible evidence of a government's legitimacy. It is a method by which a government proves to its people that it is rational, consensus-based, and deserving of deference. This testament is central to the success of a government's monopolization of control (see Weber 1978, 314; Chambliss and Seidman 1982).

Procedural justice was originally framed in terms of outcome satisfaction; most notably, Thibaut and Walker (1975) articulated a theory of process control whereby parties to a dispute must feel they have input into, and some measure of directive authority over, the means by which a resolution is achieved in order to be satisfied with that solution. Tyler and colleagues (e.g., Tyler 2006; Tyler and Huo 2002) later modified this theory so that it is the process itself, rather than the outcome, that is the focus of justice-based judgments. This represented a subtle but important shift in this line of reasoning. An outcome is an end unto itself; a person may be either satisfied or dissatisfied, and the inquiry basically ceases at that point. The process, though, represents Weberian empiricism—the procedures that an authority figure employs during the course of decision making offers a window into the true nature of the government or governmental entity that is the source of that decision maker's power. Procedural justice during police-civilian encounters represents a barometer that civilians use to gauge just how legitimate the police, as an institution, actually are.

The procedural justice model of police legitimacy emphasizes the importance of professional, respectful, and equitable treatment of all citizens during every police-public contact. It rejects an "us versus them" mindset and instead focuses on the social-psychological impacts that encounters with police exert upon citizens. Perhaps most critical to the matter of policing disadvantaged, predominantly-minority urban areas, the procedural justice model highlights the importance of individuals' perceptions of themselves as valued members of society as conveyed through the way in which they are treated by officers. Rational legitimacy depends upon consensus; people must feel that they are part of the system, that irrespective of their race, gender, age, or socioeconomic status, they are a member of the "majority" in a societal sense. For this reason, police officers serve not only a practical function but a symbolic one.

The theory of procedural justice in policing posits that police institutional legitimacy exists when the public views officers as possessing the moral authority to enforce the law and to otherwise influence public behavior. Traditional definitions of police revolve around their state-granted authority to use coercive force (Bittner 1970). State-sanctioned authority is, though, a necessary but insufficient condition for policing in a democracy, as it contains none of the elements required for rational legitimacy. Indeed, the history of policing in the United States evinces clearly the deep-rooted distrust that members of a free society harbor toward armed agents of domestic social control. Police institutional legitimacy rests upon mutual cooperation, whereby citizens allow themselves to be policed in exchange for knowing that they can trust officers to act with restraint, competency, and in good faith. Possessing moral authority also benefits officers: with it, they can issue requests that will be met with compliance; without it, they have no leverage beyond their power to forcibly induce obedience.

Procedurally-just policing is theorized to comprise two subcomponents: officers' ability to make impartial decisions based on existing facts and applicable laws; and the way officers treat citizens, including extending them courtesy and allowing them to present their side of the story (Tyler 2006; Reisig, Bratton, and Gertz 2007). Empirical tests have consistently demonstrated a strong link between procedural justice and police legitimacy (Sunshine and Tyler 2003; Tyler 2006; Murphy, Hinds, and Fleming 2008; Reisig and Lloyd 2009; Tyler, Schulhofer, and Huq 2010). Procedural justice also positively impacts people's overall satisfaction with police and their general views of them as authority figures (Tyler 1987; Tyler and Huo 2002). The relationship is robust against methodological changes and holds when items from each scale are altered (Gau 2011; Reisig, Bratton, and Gertz 2007).

The outcomes of police legitimacy are generally conceived of as compliance with the criminal law and cooperation with the police. Empirical studies have lent credence to the hypothesis that there is a positive relationship between people's perceptions of police as (il)legitimate and their self-reported adherence to the law (Sunshine and Tyler 2003; Tyler 2006; Reisig, Bratton, and Gertz 2007; Gau 2011). Legitimacy also tends to increase people's expressed willingness to cooperate with police by reporting crimes and providing valuable information about known and suspected offenders (Sunshine and Tyler 2003; Tyler 2006; Reisig, Bratton, and Gertz 2007; Murphy, Hinds, and Fleming 2008; Tyler and Fagan 2008; Gau 2011; Kochel, Parks, and Mastrofski, forthcoming; but see Reisig and Lloyd 2009, Tankebe 2009 pointing out contextual limitations in developing nations). Similarly, legitimacy seems to prompt individuals to become more actively involved in police-community partnerships (Reisig 2007; Tyler and Fagan 2008).

16.1.1 The Benefits of Procedural Justice and Police Legitimacy for Inner-City Policing

The procedural justice model is not a generic call for police to simply be nice to people. It is, to the contrary, a targeted and calculated approach that should be tailored to the specifics of a given police-citizen interaction. Steadily amassing evidence shows that the impact of procedural justice may vary according to the given dynamics of a particular police-citizen encounter. Worthy of note in this regard is the special significance that procedural justice has for the subjects of involuntary, police-initiated contacts (Murphy 2009a), including those who have been arrested (Paternoster et al. 1997; Bouffard and Piquero 2010; Myrstol and Hawk-Tourtelot 2011; see also Sherman 1993). The prevalence of unwelcome police contacts in the urban environment (Brunson and Miller, 2006a, 2006b; Carr, Napolitano, and Keating 2007; Gau and Brunson 2010) makes it an ideal setting for the widespread distribution of fair and respectful treatment. The other side of the coin is that procedural injustice in the form of serious police misconduct is especially devastating to police legitimacy in urban, disadvantaged areas (Kane 2005). This latter finding also underscores the urgency of the need for procedural justice in severely-distressed neighborhoods and communities.

There is also some preliminary evidence of a possible interaction effect between procedural justice and people's perceptions of the legitimacy of the criminal law. Those whose existing attitudes are the most cynical may be the very ones upon whom procedurally-just treatment can leave the most profound impressions (Murphy, Tyler, and Curtis 2009). This has general implications for urban policing, as residents of distressed inner-city areas express high levels of legal cynicism (Sampson and Bartusch 1998), dissatisfaction with local police (Reisig and Parks 2000), and high rates of perceived race-based maltreatment (Stewart et al. 2009).

Speaking to the issue of police-minority relations, the interaction effect described above could hold specific promise for improving officer interactions with citizens of color. Blacks and Latinos report significantly higher levels of mistrust in the institution of policing and in the motives of individual officers relative to Whites (Tyler 2005). Drawing from the theory of expectancy disconfirmation (see Chandek 1998; Reisig and Chandek 2001), the procedural justice model seems particularly well-suited for policing inner-city streets, where residents of color have come to expect negligent, rude, or even hostile treatment (Carr, Napolitano, and Keating 2007; Stewart et al. 2009; Brunson and Weitzer 2011; Brunson and Gau, forthcoming). Unexpectedly attentive and respectful treatment could make a lasting impression simply because it takes people by surprise. Research also confirms that procedural justice during face-to-face encounters can reduce the likelihood that minority citizens who have had police contact will feel that officers profiled them on the basis of their race (Tyler and Wakslak 2004). This has important implications, as the belief that one has been profiled significantly damages overall satisfaction with police (Weitzer and Tuch 2002).

In sum, the empirical literature offers compelling support for the procedural justice model and underscores the need for a justice-oriented mandate in urban areas. It is an attractive alternative to the professional model, the latter of which encourages the continued use of strategies that do not maximize police effectiveness (e.g., random motorized patrol) or that may have short-term benefits but that harm police-community relations and, ultimately, help perpetuate inner-city crime and disorder (Schulhofer, Tyler, and Huq 2011; Tyler 2011). Unfortunately, aggressive approaches are common features of urban policing (Fagan and Davies 2000). In the following section, we discuss some ways in which heavy-handedness can seriously damage police legitimacy.

16.1.2 Aggressive Urban Policing and the Erosion of Police Legitimacy

The confluence of racial marginalization, poverty, racial residential segregation, and crime makes urban policing uniquely challenging. Gang and drug violence is a prolific threat in many inner-city neighborhoods, and the fear of retaliation serves to silence victims, witnesses, and others in possession of information that would be valuable to police. In these locales, the code of the street (Anderson 1999) runs strong, and male youth—either voluntarily or due to pressure from others—come to accept the instrumentality of violence (Brunson and Stewart 2006; Stewart and Simons 2006, 2010). Retaliatory violence claims the lives of civilians and police alike (Kubrin and Weitzer 2003). As one teen resident of a high-crime, gang-plagued city put it, "It's getting crazy out there" (Maxson, Hennigan, and Sloane 2005).

The police response in high-crime areas most often takes the form of intensive suppression efforts. One tactic is the widespread use of stop-and-frisks where people whom police view as suspicious or dangerous are detained and possibly patted down. Such efforts are commonplace in the context of "wars" on drugs and gangs. Evidence suggests that in agencies utilizing them as a primary enforcement tool, stop-and-frisks have a discriminatory impact on racial minorities (Fagan and Davies 2000), are often unconstitutional (Gould and Mastrofski 2004), and gravely erode police legitimacy (Gau and Brunson 2010).

Also common among suppression approaches is the formation of specialized units and task forces. The guiding philosophy of these squads is revealed in their telling acronyms, such as the Los Angeles Police Department's former CRASH unit, nearby San Bernardino County's ongoing S.M.A.S.H. unit, and the Chicago Police Department's Mobile Strike Force. These teams tend to be more tactical than strategic. They generally emphasize intelligence gathering and deemphasize community partnerships, crime prevention, and geographic accountability (see Decker 2007 for a review). Informal evidence noted by community activists suggests that although crashing, smashing, and striking may occasionally yield successful arrests of dangerous offenders, the collateral consequences for police legitimacy are widespread and devastating (Boyle 1999; Siska 2008). The disbanding of Los Angeles' CRASH unit and Chicago's disgraced SOS gang unit under embarrassing allegations that officers routinely beat suspects, planted evidence, and stole drugs highlights the limitations inherent in such approaches. Further, a "good arrest" resulting from the deployment of tactical teams is an isolated incident that is likely the product of work done primarily or solely by the police as opposed to community-wide efforts.

Inner-city police also must be mindful of the negative impact of repeated, unwelcome police-initiated contacts. In highly-distressed neighborhoods, greater concentrations of officers are associated with elevated violent crime rates over time; this relationship is not evident in more affluent neighborhoods (Kane 2005). This finding makes sense given that police-initiated events such as stop-and-frisks are more common in impoverished neighborhoods than in less-disadvantaged ones (Fagan and Davies 2000). Over time, the impact of these unpleasant encounters accumulates (Brunson 2007) and, ultimately, translates into pervasive distrust and dislike of police. Direct interactions with officers are a major driving force behind people's evaluations of police, even after controlling for demographic factors such as race (Scaglion and Condon 1980).

There is a feedback loop between people's specific assessments of firsthand encounters with police and their global opinion of the policing institution. The procedural justice literature summarized above demonstrates the specific-to-global portion of this iterative cycle, but what police also must be cognizant of is that preexisting attitudes can influence people's perceptions of the fairness and quality of police actions during future encounters (Brandl et al. 1994; Tyler and Huo 2002; Rosenbaum et al. 2005; Tyler 2006; Gau 2010). An officer who abuses a citizen—even if that citizen is engaged in wrong-doing—jeopardizes the civility and safety of that person's next encounter with police. When abuses are not infrequent, the lawless and the law-abiding alike may come to fear, dislike, and avoid the police. An account relayed by Mike, a black teen residing in a distressed city neighborhood, illustrates how arbitrary, harsh enforcement of the law fosters a sense among the populace that officers are volatile, unpredictable, and, therefore, dangerous:

> People I know, every time they see [the police], they just run. I be runnin' sometimes because I don't know what kinda day the police is having. They have pissed off days where they just come through [the neighborhood]... tryin' to lock everybody up... People [are] scared to come out in the neighborhood. They think they gonna get locked up. (Weitzer and Brunson 2009, 241)

Police department disciplinary practices are heavily implicated in the opinions that the public forms about officers and about the institution. Ongoing misconduct implies either tacit approval or incompetence on the part of police administrators (see Brunson and Gau, forthcoming). Set against this backdrop, the procedurally-just actions of a handful of well-intentioned officers will fail to alter the prevalent conclusion that corruption and aggression are endemic to the institution. The change must be systemic if it is to be change at all.

The following set of policy recommendations implicate police executives as the ones who must lead the establishment of a procedural justice mandate to make fair, high-quality, respectful treatment a foundational aspect of inner-city policing. Some of the recommendations are substantial in scope and scale. This is deliberate. The current hierarchical, bureaucratic structure of police organization and administration (Maguire 1997) was developed during the reform era of policing (see Kelling and Moore 1988) and was designed to execute random motorized patrol, rapid response to calls for service, and the detached, neutral, legalistic manner that characterized the professional model. If policing is to shift its emphasis and embrace contemporary, progressive philosophies, the organization and administration of police agencies must be restructured to facilitate the implementation and delivery of these new models (Maguire 1997). Anything short of substantive renovation will leave the status quo intact.

16.2 Policy Recommendations

The following set of policy recommendations proceeds from the premise that policing is symbolic and not merely instrumental. In practice, this means that every action taken in the name of crime control or public order is inevitably imbued with a meaning that extends beyond the facts of any given situation. The role of police as agents of social control makes the creation of obedience a central function of the job, yet it is insufficient to merely note that obedience has occurred and to conclude from there that the police have succeeded. It is, in fact, the *motives* for compliance that determine the legitimacy of the law and its agents (Weber 1978, 314). It is one thing to cooperate with the police out of genuine respect for their authority, and another entirely to submit to them out of fear of what noxious consequences they may mete out if displeased. Officers can encourage widespread, voluntary compliance by acting in ways that demonstrate the rationality of the legal order, or they can secure incident-based, temporary obedience by leveraging their authority severely and showing the public that the law, far from being rational, is whimsical, arbitrary, and violent.

16.2.1 Make Procedural Justice an Administrative Mandate

Executives (e.g., chiefs, captains) and mid-level managers (e.g., sergeants) are instrumental in the creation of the occupational culture (Paoline 2003, 2004) that dictates how police should view citizens and, in particular, how they ought to behave toward minority residents of inner-city areas. The importance of the role that executives and managers play in creating the culture that guides officers' street-level conduct is perhaps nowhere more apparent than in the report issued by the Christopher Commission in the wake of the Rodney King incident in Los Angeles. The Commission lambasted managers and top administrators for participating in racist, derogatory discourse, and for failing to effectively discipline officers who used excessive force (Christopher Commission 1991).

Procedural justice must be a blanket mandate required of all personnel in all situations. The model will not succeed if its implementation depends on the sporadic efforts of a handful of officers. What is needed is a top-down approach in which every level of the organization explicitly endorses fair, respectful treatment of civilians. This is no easy task, however, as initiatives spearheaded from the top can face opposition from the rank-and-file if the directives are inconsistent with officers' existing beliefs and attitudes (Gau and Gaines 2012). Procedural justice may well encounter opposition by those who embrace law-and-order-style policing and have come to see inner-city residents as undeserving of any help at all (Klinger 1997), much less of assistance delivered with diligence and respect. Nevertheless, procedural justice as a top-down approach can work if correctly implemented.

To enforce a procedural justice mandate, executives will need to hold officers responsible for putting the model into practice on the streets. Line officers' adherence to the tenets of procedural justice must be part of their performance evaluations both in the course of their regular employment and in bids for promotion. Executives' and managers' verbal support for procedural justice alone is insufficient—their words must be backed by tangible rewards and consequences in order for the model to gain traction.

Further, executives should hold mid-level supervisors accountable for the actions of the officers under their command (Christopher Commission 1991). Patrol supervisors should be required to demonstrate that their officers are actively engaged in fair, high-quality, respectful treatment of civilians. This sort of "trickle-down" accountability system is already advocated under the CompStat generation of strategies designed to reduce crime by holding district managers responsible for the crime rates in their geographic areas (e.g., Bratton 1999). There would be nothing revolutionary, then, in utilizing this model to effect agency-wide implementation of a procedural justice mandate. For their part, executives are responsible for ensuring small officer-to-supervisor ratios—supervisors cannot be justly expected to monitor their subordinates closely if the span of control is unreasonably large.

16.2.2 Effectively Identify and Discipline Officers Who Mistreat Citizens, and Let the Community Know about It

> [The police] took [my cousin's] money 'cuz he had like a large amount of money on him, but he didn't sell no drugs or nothing. They couldn't find no drugs or nothing like that either but he just had large amounts of money and they took his money and they left him somewhere. He had to walk from, I think the West side. (Brunson 2007, 86)

The above quote from William, a black youth from an urban neighborhood, illustrates the visibility of police misconduct in some inner-city areas. Witnesses see it firsthand, and friends and relatives later hear it recounted (Rosenbaum et al. 2005; Brunson 2007). Simply put, when officers engage in misconduct, citizens will likely know about it. Police executives' failure to discipline offending officers deals a crushing blow to police legitimacy; the agency becomes complicit in the abuse.

An even greater insult to the community is that the majority of all serious malfeasance is concentrated among a minority of repeat offenders who could be identified and penalized or removed. Unconstitutional searches (Gould and Mastrofski 2004), excessive uses of force (Christopher Commission 1991), and career-ending misconduct (Kane and White 2009) are disproportionately perpetrated by relatively small numbers of officers. While it is tempting to quickly dismiss this as an issue of "bad apples" and to seek solace in the more optimistic perspective that the majority of officers commit very little or no misconduct, such reasoning turns a willfully blind eye to the fact that problem officers could be identified and disciplined if police leaders wished to do so. Bad apples can continue to operate only when higher-ups ignore emerging patterns in complaints, lawsuits, arrestee injuries, media accounts, suppressed evidence, and other signs that trouble is afoot. Despite the importance of early detection of problem officers, most police agencies do not systematically collect and analyze officer-level data that would allow proactive identification (Kane 2007). The result is the perception among inner-city residents that police malfeasance is the norm rather than the exception, as exemplified by remarks made by Lamont:

> [The police] they crooked. I mean they try to do anything [to you]. I ain't tryin' to be prejudice[d] but I think the police don't like black people. You know like all the crooked cops always be in the ghettos, where all the black people at and they try to get as many black people off the street as they can. (Brunson 2007, 85)

While perhaps the most difficult form of police wrongdoing for supervisors to monitor, widespread use of discourteous, dehumanizing language by officers has grave consequences for police legitimacy. Bob seemed to think that police had negative attitudes, in general, when he remarked, "[Police] like to curse at people for no apparent reason. They shout bitches, hoes, niggers" (Gau and Brunson 2010, 270). Martez, likewise, attributed officers' frequent use of offensive language toward himself and his friends to blatant racism. He surmised, "I think cops [are] racists. That's what I think because they call us niggas" (Gau and Brunson 2010, 270). In addition to being highly offensive, police officers' frequent use of antagonistic language, including name-calling and racial slurs, have implications for both citizens' and officers' safety (see Weitzer and Brunson 2009). Thus, front-line supervisors must be vigilant in ensuring that their subordinates' behavior reflects the organization's core mission.

Prior research has revealed that citizens' demeanor is often prejudiced by police officers' behavior toward them (Wiley and Hudik 1974); thus, heavy-handed or unsettling police actions have the potential to needlessly inflame otherwise routine situations, causing citizens to challenge police authority. The end result is that civilians and officers are both exposed to greater risk of serious physical injury. Martez described how he challenged officers' rough treatment of his 13-year-old brother, receiving his own physical punishment in response. He explained:

> Me and my brothers was sitting out one summer just chillin.' The police came up outta nowhere and just slammed my brother['s] face in the dirt.... I'm like, "Dang, what's the problem?" And [another officer] pulled out a nightstick and hit me four times in the chest. (Brunson and Weitzer 2009, 871)

Recent technological advances offer various ways in which supervisors can monitor officers' language and behavior on a routine basis. For instance, dashboard-mounted cameras can capture video and audio recordings. Listening devices installed in patrol cars (with officers' knowledge) record everything said by an officer or pair of officers during a shift. Further, two-way radios now have the capacity to be switched on remotely, allowing a listener in one location to hear what is happening in the vicinity of the radio. Supervisors could use this capability to "drop in" on officers randomly or during high-intensity encounters with civilians. The use of technology in this way would serve two purposes. The first is deterrence—officers who know that their words and actions are, or could be, monitored would likely be more alert to avoiding impropriety. The second use is that of effective identification and punishment of offending officers. This point is particularly important to the issue of police legitimacy and merits further discussion.

To convince the public that the police are legitimate and deserve respect, executives must demonstrate that they are as intolerant of antisocial behavior within their own ranks as they are of such behaviors among the general public. Publicizing incidents of police misconduct is of course a sensitive matter—it does not look good when officers break the very laws they swore to uphold. What is perhaps most important, though, is for the public to see that an agency swiftly delivers an appropriately-severe penalty to an offending officer rather than citing "personnel matters" and opting for nondisclosure. Public outrage is incited by officer misconduct itself, but even more so when alleged wrongdoing goes unpunished, thus conveying the impression that police act with impunity (Brunson and Gau, forthcoming). Police organizations should therefore begin to collect and analyze "self-auditing" data (Kane 2007, 775). The institutional legitimacy of police rests, in part, on agencies proactively identifying problem officers, meting out discipline that is commensurate with an offense and to an officer's history of misconduct, and making disciplinary processes visible. This would allow communities to take comfort in knowing that officers are bound to a standard of conduct and will face serious consequences if they violate the rules. It is only through transparency that agencies can demonstrate to the public that they are worthy of the community's respect (Kane 2007).

16.2.3 Use Procedural Justice and Police Legitimacy to Mobilize the Community

A community-wide effort is necessary if things are to change, and the police can spearhead the effort by adhering to the tenets of procedural justice as a means of enhancing their own institutional legitimacy. Many people residing in distressed urban areas currently do not call the police to ask for help or offer information about known crimes (Carr, Napolitano, and Keating 2007). A primary contributor to residents' reluctance to call is cynicism (Sampson and Bartusch 1998). Many urban dwellers feel that officers will either not respond at all, or that their response will be slow and lackluster (Brunson and Gau, forthcoming). Under these circumstances, it is difficult or impossible to enlist the community's support in effective crime-control efforts.

The procedural justice model offers a promising solution to the problem. Empirical evidence indicates that people who view the police as legitimate are more willing to actively participate in community policing strategies (Reisig 2007), to offer information about crimes and offenders (Tyler and Fagan 2008), and to report their own victimizations to police (Kochel, Parks, and Mastrofski 2013). All of these cornerstones of community mobilization must be present for genuine crime reduction to occur. Police must actively combat cynicism by responding to calls in a timely manner, listening closely to citizen concerns, being diligent in the course of action they take toward problem solving, and by following up with callers, referring them to victim services, and providing other assistance as needed.

An important characteristic of inner-city areas is the highly-interconnected nature of familial and friendship networks—information travels fast and bad news even faster. This is not a good thing when the police treat people in a way that makes them feel dehumanized (Brunson and Miller 2006a, 2006b), as reports of these actions spread and provide fodder for existing animosities and fertile ground for the beginnings of new ones (Brunson 2007). Police could, though, capitalize upon these dense networks by using them as a vehicle for changing their image within the community. For a person holding negative attitudes toward police, a single positive encounter may not be sufficient to shake those preexisting views (Brandl et al. 1994; Rosenbaum et al. 2005), but a policy of consistent, sustained positive interactions could begin to slowly chip away at them. When enough urban dwellers start having positive police experiences, then their networks of friends, family, and local institutions (Wood and Brunson 2011) that currently serve as media for the spread of accounts of acrimonious interactions will become channels for the dissemination of stories about amicable ones. By utilizing these networks, police can foster a sense of legitimacy even among individuals who have no direct interactions with officers but who are swayed by favorable contacts they have heard about from friends and family members (Brunson and Weitzer 2011).

To mobilize the community, police will also have to address the fear of retaliation that leads many people to avoid reporting information to the police. Even individuals who see police as legitimate may be unwilling to cooperate with them if they live in areas controlled by gangs or other criminal groups (Reisig and Lloyd 2009). The threat of retaliatory violence is very real (Kubrin and Weitzer 2003). A potential first step is to maximize the use of technology to facilitate anonymous tip reporting. There are a number of ways for people to contact the police without revealing their identities (e.g., telephones, email, and social networking sites). Directed community policing efforts could help link those who do not have phone or Internet access, or who remain fearful despite promises of anonymity, to local leaders such as clergy and community activists who would be willing to serve as liaisons. Creative ways to encourage anonymous or confidential reporting could help undermine serious offenders' ability to enforce silence through the use of intimidation.

16.3 CONCLUSION

The continuation of violence, drug activity, and disorder in inner-city areas demonstrates the ineffectiveness of traditional policing styles and strategies. Calls to "get tough" or "crack down" are, in essence, requests for more of the same. It makes little sense to call for a ramping-up of efforts that are not working. It is time to revisit the fundamental assumptions and philosophies upon which current police practices are premised and to craft new approaches to inner-city policing.

The procedural justice model of police legitimacy is a promising approach that, in conjunction with community and problem-oriented policing tactics, could create genuine change in inner-city communities. Grounded in classic theories of governments premised upon rational legitimacy (Weber 1978), procedural justice is an effort to promote the belief that the policing institution possesses moral authority and is worthy of respect. Procedural justice is a person-based approach in the sense that it emphasizes the importance of what transpires between an officer and a citizen during a face-to-face encounter, but even more than that, it is a community-based model because the ultimate goal is to make entire segments of society (see, e.g., Tyler et al. 2010) see the police as benevolent and trustworthy.

Substantial empirical evidence demonstrates that procedural justice enhances people's beliefs that the police are legitimate (Tyler 1987, 2006; Tyler and Huo 2002; Sunshine and Tyler 2003; Tyler and Wakslak 2004; Reisig, Bratton, and Gertz 2007; Murphy et al. 2008; Murphy 2009; Reisig and Lloyd 2009; Tyler et al. 2010; Gau 2011; Kochel, Parks, and Mastrofski, forthcoming). Legitimacy, in turn, has a range of beneficial outcomes. It can make people more likely to take an active role in the citizen side of community policing (Reisig 2007; Tyler and Fagan 2008), to call the police when they are personally victimized (Kochel, Parks, and Mastrofski, forthcoming), and to offer the police information about crimes and offenders (Tyler and Fagan 2008; Tyler et al. 2010). The procedural justice model is not more of the same—it is an innovative, empirically-grounded approach that can work.

REFERENCES

Anderson, Elijah. 1990. *Streetwise: Race, Class, and Change in an Urban Community.* Chicago: University of Chicago Press.

——. 1999. *Code of the Street: Decency, Violence and the Moral Life of the Inner City.* New York: W.W. Norton and Company.

Bass, Sandra. 2001. "Policing Space, Policing Race: Social Control Imperatives and Polic Discretionary Decisions." *Social Justice* 28:156–76.

Bittner, Egon. 1970. *The Functions of Police in Modern Society.* Rockville, MD: National Institute of Mental Health.

Bouffard, Leana A., and Nicole Leeper Piquero. 2010. "Defiance Theory and Life Course Explanations of Persistent Offending." *Crime and Delinquency* 56(2):227–52.

Boyle, Gregory J. 1999. "LAPD must Drop CRASH in order to Regain Public's Trust." *Los Angeles Times*, September 27.

Brandl, Steven, James Frank, Robert Worden, and Timothy Bynum. 1994. "Global and Specific Attitudes toward the Police." *Justice Quarterly* 11:119–34.

Bratton, William J. 1999. "Great Expectations: How Higher Expectations for Police Departments Can Lead to a Decrease in Crime." In *Measuring what Matters: Proceedings from the Policing Research Institute Meetings*, edited by Robert H. Langworthy, 11–26. Washington, DC: National Institute of Justice.

Bridges, George S., and Sara Steen. 1998. "Racial Disparities in Official Assessments of Juvenile Offenders: Attributional Stereotypes as Mediating Mechanisms." *American Sociological Review* 63:554–70.

Brunson, Rod K. 2007. "'Police Don't Like Black People': African-American Young Men's Accumulated Police Experiences." *Criminology and Public Policy* 6(1): 71–102.

Brunson, Rod K., and Jacinta M. Gau. Forthcoming. "Officer Race vs. Macrolevel Context: A Test of Competing Hypotheses about Black Citizens' Experiences with and Perceptions of Black Police Officers." *Crime and Delinquency* DOI 10.1177/0011128711398027.

Brunson, Rod K., and Jody Miller. 2006a. "Young Black Men and Urban Policing in the United States." *British Journal of Criminology* 46:613–40.

——. 2006b. "Gender, Race, and Urban Policing: The Experience of African American Youths." *Gender and Society* 20(4):531–52.

Brunson, Rod K., and Eric A. Stewart. 2006. "Young African American Women, the Street Code, and Violence: An Exploratory Analysis." *Journal of Crime and Justice* 29:1–19.

Brunson, Rod K., and Ronald Weitzer. 2009. "Police Relations with Black and White Youths in Different Urban Neighborhoods." *Urban Affairs Review* 44:858–85.

——. 2011. "Negotiating Unwelcome Police Encounters: The Intergenerational Transmission of Conduct Norms." *Journal of Contemporary Ethnography* 40:425–56.

Carr, Patrick J., Laura Napolitano, and Jessica Keating. 2007. "We Never Call the Cops and Here Is Why: A Qualitative Examination of Legal Cynicism in Three Philadelphia Neighborhoods." *Criminology* 45(2):445–80.

Chambliss, William, and Robert Seidman. 1982. *Law, Order, and Power*, 2d ed. Reading, MA: Addison-Wesley.

Chandek, Meghan Stroshine. 1998. "Race, expectations and evaluations of police performance: An Empirical Assessment." *Policing: An International Journal of Police Strategies and Management* 22(4):675–95.

Chevigny, Paul. 1995. *Edge of the Knife: Police Violence in the Americas*. New York: New Press.

Christopher Commission. 1991. *Report of the Independent Commission on the Los Angeles Police Department*. Los Angeles: Independent Commission on the Los Angeles Police Department.

Decker, Scott H. 2007. "Expand the use of Police Gang Units." *Criminology and Public Policy* 6(4):729–34.

Fagan, Jeffrey, and Garth Davies. 2000. "Street Stops and Broken Windows: Terry, Race and Disorder in New York City." *Fordham Urban Law Journal* 28:457–504.

Ferguson, Andrew Guthrie, and Damien Bernache. 2008. "The 'High-Crime Area' Question: Requiring Verifiable and Quantifiable Evidence for Fourth Amendment Reasonable Suspicion Analysis." *American University Law Review* 57:1587–644.

Gau, Jacinta M. 2010. "A Longitudinal Analysis of Citizens' Attitudes about Police." *Policing: An International Journal of Police Strategies and Management* 33(2): 236–52.

——. 2011. "The Convergent and Discriminant Validity of Procedural Justice and Police Legitimacy: An Empirical Test of Core Theoretical Propositions." *Journal of Criminal Justice* 39:489–98.

Gau, Jacinta M., and Rod K. Brunson. 2010. "Procedural Justice and Order Maintenance Policing: A Study of Inner-City Young Men's Perceptions of Police Legitimacy." *Justice Quarterly* 27(2):255–79.

Gau, Jacinta M., and D. Cody Gaines. 2012. "Top-Down Management and Patrol Officers' Attitudes about the Importance of Public Order Maintenance: A Research Note." *Police Quarterly* 15(1):45–61.

Gould, Jon B, and Stephen D. Mastrofski. 2004. "Suspect Searches: Assessing Police Behavior under the U.S. Constitution." *Criminology and Public Policy* 3(3):315–62.

Harris, David A. 1994. "Factors for Reasonable Suspicion: When Black and Poor Means Stopped and Frisked." *Indiana Law Journal* 69:659–87.

——. 2002. *Profiles in Injustice*. New York: The New Press.

Kane, Robert J. 2005. "Compromised Police Legitimacy as a Predictor of Violent Crime in Structurally Disadvantaged Communities." *Criminology* 43(2):469–98.

——. 2007. "Collect and Release Data on Coercive Police Actions." *Criminology and Public Policy* 6(4):773–80.

Kane, Robert J., and Michael D. White. 2009. "Bad Cops: A Study of Career-Ending Misconduct among New York City Police Officers." *Criminology and Public Policy* 8(4):737–69.

Kelling, George L., and Mark H. Moore. 1988. "The Evolving Strategy of Policing." In *Perspectives on Policing*. Washington, DC: National Institute of Justice.

Kennedy, Randall. 1997. *Race, Crime and the Law*. New York: Vintage.

Klinger, David A. 1997. "Negotiating Order in Patrol Work: An Ecological Theory of Police Response to Deviance." *Criminology* 35:277–306.

Kochel, Tammy Rinehart, Roger Parks, and Stephen D. Mastrofski. 2013. "Examining Police Effectiveness as a Precursor to Legitimacy and Cooperation with Police." *Justice Quarterly* 30(5):895–925.

Kubrin, Charis, and Ronald Weitzer. 2003. "Retaliatory Homicide: Concentrated Disadvantage and Neighborhood Culture." *Social Problems* 50:157–80.

Leiber, Michael J., Mahesh K. Nalla, and Margaret Farnworth. 1998. "Explaining Juveniles' Attitudes toward the Police." *Justice Quarterly* 15(1):151–74.

Maguire, Edward R. 1997. "Structural Change in Large Municipal Police Organizations during the Community Policing Era." *Justice Quarterly* 14(3):547–76.

Mastrofski, Stephen D., Michael D. Reisig, John D. McCluskey. 2002. "Police Disrespect toward the Public: An Encounter-Based Analysis." *Criminology* 40:515–51.

Maxson, Cheryl L., Karen M. Hennigan, and David C. Sloane. 2005. "'It's Getting Crazy Out There': Can a Civil Gang Injunction Change a Community?" *Criminology and Public Policy* 4(3):577–606.

Meeks, Kenneth. 2000. *Driving while Black: Highways, Shopping Malls, Taxi Cabs, Sidewalks: How to Fight Back If You Are a Victim of Racial Profiling*. New York: Broadway Books.

Murphy, Kristina. 2009a. "Public Satisfaction with Police: The Importance of Procedural Justice and Police Performance in Police-Citizen Encounters." *Australian and New Zealand Journal of Criminology* 42(2):159–78.

——. 2009b. "Procedural Justice and Affect Intensity: Understanding Reactions to Regulatory Authorities." *Social Justice Research* 22:1–30.

Murphy, Kristina, Lyn Hinds, and Jenny Fleming. 2008. "Encouraging Public Cooperation and Support for Police." *Policing and Society* 18(2):136–55.

Murphy, Kristina, Tom R. Tyler, and Amy Curtis. 2009. "Nurturing Regulatory Compliance: Is Procedural Justice Effective When People Question the Legitimacy of the Law?" *Regulation and Governance* 3:1–26.

Myrstol, Brad A., and Shila René Hawk-Tourtelot. 2011. "In Search of Respect: Examining Arrestee Satisfaction." *American Journal of Criminal Justice* 36:371–91.

Paoline, Eugene A. III. 2003. "Taking Stock: Toward a Richer Understanding of Police Culture." *Journal of Criminal Justice* 31:199–214.

———. 2004. "Shedding Light on Police Culture: An Examination of Police Officers' Occupational Attitudes." *Police Quarterly* 7(2):205–36.

Paternoster, Raymond, Robert Brame, Ronet Bachman, and Lawrence W. Sherman. 1997. "Do Fair Procedures Matter? The Effect of Procedural Justice on Spouse Assault." *Law and Society Review* 31(1):163–204.

Quillian, Lincoln, and Devah Pager. 2001. "Black Neighbors, Higher Crime? The Role of Racial Stereotypes in Evaluations of Neighborhood Crime." *American Journal of Sociology* 107(3):717–67.

Reisig, Michael D. 2007. "Procedural Justice and Community Policing—What Shapes Residents' Willingness to Participate in Crime Prevention Programs?" *Policing: A Journal of Policy and Practice* 1(3):356–69.

———. 2010. "Community and Problem-Oriented Policing." In *Crime and Justice: A Review of Research*, vol. 39, edited by Michael Tonry, 1–53. Chicago: University of Chicago Press.

Reisig, Michael D., Jason Bratton, and Marc G. Gertz. 2007. "The Construct Validity and Refinement of Process-Based Policing Measures." *Criminal Justice and Behavior* 34(8):1005–28.

Reisig, Michael D., and Meghan Stroshine Chandek. 2001. "The Effects of Expectancy Disconfirmation on Outcome Satisfaction in Police-Citizen Encounters." *Policing: An International Journal of Police Strategies and Management* 24(1): 88–99.

Reisig, Michael D., and Camille Lloyd. 2009. "Procedural Justice, Police Legitimacy, and Helping the Police Fight Crime." *Police Quarterly* 12(1):42–62.

Reisig, Michael D., and Roger B. Parks. 2000. "Experience, Quality of Life, and Neighborhood Context: A Hierarchical Analysis of Satisfaction with Police." *Justice Quarterly* 17(3):607–30.

Rosenbaum, Dennis P., Amie M. Schuck, Sandra K. Costello, Darnell F. Hawkins, and Marianne K. Ring. 2005. "Attitudes toward the Police: The Effects of Direct and Vicarious Experience." *Police Quarterly* 8:343–65.

Sampson, Robert J., and Dawn Jeglum Bartusch. 1998. "Legal Cynicism and (Subcultural?) Tolerance of Deviance: The Neighborhood Context of Racial Differences." *Law and Society Review* 32(4):777–804.

Sampson, Robert J., and William Julius Wilson. 1995. "Toward a Theory of Race, Crime and Urban Inequality." In *Crime and Inequality*, edited by John Hagan and Ruth D. Peterson, 37–54. Stanford, CA: Stanford University Press.

Scaglion, Richard, and Richard G. Condon. 1980. "Determinants of Attitudes toward City Policing." *Criminology* 17(4):485–94.

Schulhofer, Stephen J., Tom R. Tyler, and Aziz Z. Huq. 2011. "American Policing at a Crossroads: Unsustainable Policies and the Procedural Justice Alternative." *Journal of Criminal Law and Criminology* 101(2):335–74.

Sherman, Lawrence W. 1993. "Defiance, Deterrence, and Irrelevance: A Theory of the Criminal Sanction." *Journal of Research in Crime and Delinquency* 30:445–73.

Siska, Tracy. 2008. "Chicago Police Mobile Strike Force A.K.A. SOS 2: Someone call Patrick Fitzgerald!" *The Huffington Post*, October 31.

Skogan, Wesley G. 2005. "Citizen Satisfaction with Police Encounters." *Police Quarterly* 8(3):298–321.

Skogan, Wesley, and Kathleen Frydl. 2004. *Fairness and Effectiveness in Policing: The Evidence.* Washington, DC: The National Academies Press.

Skolnick, Jerome H. 1994. *Justice without Trial: Law Enforcement in Democratic Societies*, 3rd ed. New York: MacMillan.

Stewart, Eric A., Eric Baumer, Rod K. Brunson, and Ronald L. Simons. 2009. "Neighborhood Racial Context and Perceptions of Police-based Racial Discrimination among Black Youth." *Criminology* 47:847–87.

Stewart, Eric, and Ronald L. Simons. 2006. "Structure and Culture in African-American Adolescent Violence: A Partial Test of the Code of the Street Thesis." *Justice Quarterly* 23(1):1–33.

Stewart, Eric A., and Ronald L. Simons. 2010. "Race, Code of the Street, and Violent Delinquency: A Multilevel Investigation of Neighborhood Street Culture and Individual Norms of Violence." *Criminology* 48(2):569–605.

Sunshine, Jason, and Tom R. Tyler. 2003. "The role of Procedural Justice and Legitimacy in Shaping Public Support for Policing." *Law and Society Review* 37(3):513–47.

Tankebe, Justice. 2009. "Public Cooperation with the Police in Ghana: Does Procedural Fairness Matter?" *Criminology* 47(4):1265–93.

Taylor, Terrance J., K.B. Turner, Finn-Aage Esbensen, and Thomas L. Winfree, Jr. 2001. "Coppin' an Attitude: Attitudinal Differences among Juveniles toward the Police." *Journal of Criminal Justice* 29:295–305.

Terrill, William, and Michael D. Reisig. 2003. "Neighborhood Context and Police Use of Force." *Journal of Research in Crime and Delinquency* 40(3):291–321.

Thibaut, John W., and Laurens Walker. 1975. *Procedural Justice: A Psychological Analysis.* New York: L. Erlbaum Associates.

Tyler, Tom R. 1987. "Procedural Justice Research." *Social Justice Research* 1(1): 41–65.

———. 2005. "Policing in Black and White: Ethnic Group Differences in Trust and Confidence in the Police." *Police Quarterly* 8(3):322–42.

———. 2006. *Why People Obey the Law*. Princeton, NJ: Princeton University Press.

———. 2011. "Trust and Legitimacy: Policing in the USA and Europe." *European Journal of Criminology* 8(4):254–66.

Tyler, Tom R., and Jeffrey Fagan. 2008. "Legitimacy and Cooperation: Why Do People Help the Police Fight Crime in Their Communities?" *Ohio State Journal of Criminal Law* 6:231–75.

Tyler, Tom R., and Yuen J. Huo. 2002. *Trust in the Law*. New York: Russell Sage Foundation.

Tyler, Tom R., Stephen Schulhofer, and Aziz Z. Huq. 2010. "Legitimacy and Deterrence Effects in Counterterrorism Policing: A Study of Muslim Americans." *Law and Society Review* 44(2):365–402.

Tyler, Tom R., and Cheryl J. Wakslak. 2004. "Profiling and Police Legitimacy: Procedural Justice, Attributions of Motive, and Acceptance of Police Authority." *Criminology* 42(2):253–81.

Weber, Max. 1978. *Economy and Society*. Berkeley: University of California Press.

Websdale, Neil. 2001. *Policing the Poor: From Slave Plantation to Public Housing*. Boston: Northeastern University Press.

Weitzer, Ronald. 1999. "Citizen Perceptions of Police Misconduct: Race and Neighborhood Context." *Justice Quarterly* 16:819–46.

———. 2000. "Racializing Policing: Residents' Perceptions in Three Neighborhoods." *Law and Society Review* 34:129–55.

Weitzer, Ronald, and Rod K. Brunson. 2009. "Strategic Responses to the Police Among Inner-City Youth." *Sociological Quarterly* 50:235–56.

Weitzer, Ronald, and Steven A. Tuch. 2002. "Perceptions of Racial Profiling: Race, Class, and Personal Experience." *Criminology* 40:435–56.

Werthman, Carl, and Irving Piliavin. 1967. "Gang Members and the Police." In *The Police: Six Sociological Essays*, edited by David J. Bordua, 56–98. New York: John Wiley and Sons.

Wiley, Mary, and Terry Hudik. 1974. "Police-Citizen Encounters: A Field Test of Exchange Theory." *Social Problems* 22:119–27.

Wood, Tricia, and Rod K. Brunson. 2011. "Geographies of Resilient Social Networks: The Role of African American Barbershops." *Urban Geography* 31:228–43.

CHAPTER 17

....

RACIAL PROFILING

....

ROBIN S. ENGEL AND DEREK M. COHEN

THE history of race and policing in the United States is long and troubled. For centuries, the police in America were used as instruments of the state to enforce discriminatory laws and uphold the status quo of the time (Richardson 1974; Monkonen 1981). The discriminatory treatment by police of minorities—and blacks in particular—was reflective of a socially unjust and biased society (Kerner Commission 1968). While the systematic targeting and biased treatment endured by minorities at the hands of American police has been well documented (Williams and Murphy 1990), significant progress has been made in the last several decades toward equity and legitimacy in American policing (Walker 2003; Warren and Tomaskovic-Devey 2009; Bayley and Nixon 2010). Nevertheless, the legacy that this troubled past brings to modern policing bears repeating. A current concern in American society remains the use of race or ethnicity by police as reason for some form of coercive action. This police practice—often referred to as racial profiling—is widely recognized by politicians, the public, and even the police themselves as inherently problematic. Yet reducing this problem to a single term—racial profiling—simultaneously reduces the nuances surrounding the multifaceted and complicated issues regarding police, race, and crime in America.

In this essay, we first begin with a brief historical overview of the ground previously traveled as it relates to policing, race, and research. In our discussion, we note the historical application of racially-biased police practices as a result of policies arising from the "War on Drugs" in the 1980s. Thereafter we describe the use and definition of the term "racial profiling" and trace the resulting changes in policies, legislation, litigation, and data collection across the country. The changes in data collection in particular resulted in the development of a body of research designed specifically to determine racial/ethnic disparities in police treatment during pedestrian and traffic stops. We summarize this body of research, including a focus on stops and stop outcomes (e.g., citations, arrests, searches, and seizures), and offer a critique of the research methods and statistical analyses often used by researchers. Finally, we issue a new call to action for future research in the area of racial profiling. Rather than seeking incremental improvements in data collection and methodology, we argue for a fundamental reconceptualization of research on race and policing. While we note that this essay is predominately focused on the experiences and research surrounding one racial group (blacks) within one country (United States), it is widely applicable to other minority groups within the United States, as well as minority groups within other countries. Indeed, it seems that the core components of the American story of racial bias, policing, and research is widely generalizable across cultures.

This essay represents a broad examination of racial profiling in the United States, both from historical and contemporary perspectives. Section 17.1 of the essay describes the history of racial profiling, as it was originally developed as a tactic to detect and apprehend drug couriers along the I-95 corridor of the Eastern Seaboard. Section 17.1 also describes the initial efforts to collect data on racial profiling, as well as identifying the evolving definition of the term. Section 17.2 reviews the literature on racially-biased policing starting with the classic ethnographic work that first identified issues related to race and policing; it then examines the more recent empirical evidence on the extent to which racial and ethnic disparities have appeared evident during vehicle and pedestrian stops, citation outcomes, and searches and seizure. Section 17.3 offers a new collective research agenda to help us begin to determine if the observed racial disparities in stops, citations, and searches and seizures amounts to racial/ethnic bias and discrimination. That section also draws some conclusions as to the state of the science on racially-biased policing.

A number of conclusions can be drawn:

- Despite large-scale data collection efforts, the extent of racially-biased policing in the United States remains largely unknown
- Despite calls from researchers to reform institutional practices, increase accountability and supervision, and engage in better data collection, the evidence regarding the actual impact of such recommendations on racially-biased policing is nearly non-existent.
- While many agencies can readily identify racial/ethnic disparities, they often cannot detect bias, and further cannot determine why these disparities exist or how to effectively reduce them.
- As police agencies continue to promote and advance practices that have demonstrated effectiveness (e.g., hot spots and other types of focused policing strategies), it is likely that racial/ethnic disparities in stops and stop outcomes will continue or perhaps even increase based on differential offending patterns and saturation patrols in predominately minority areas.
- More, and better, research is necessary if we are serious about both the role of science in policing and the need to reduce racial/ethnic bias in policing.

17.1 HISTORY OF RACIAL PROFILING

While the troubled history of race and policing in the United States is lengthy and complex, a more recent focus on racial profiling emerged in the last two decades. The use of the term "racial profiling" gained popularity in the mid-1990s and originally referred to the use of race as an explicit criterion in "profiles" of offenders that some police organizations issued to guide police officer decision-making (Engel, Calnon, and Bernard 2001; Harris 2006). These profiles were used as part of a larger strategy for the "War on Drugs" from the 1980s and 1990s that led to dramatic changes in criminal justice strategies nationally, including the aggressive targeting of drug offenders at the street level and increased rates of incarceration and sentence length (Scalia 2001; Harris 2006; Tonry 2011). Racial profiling specifically referred to criminal interdiction practices based on drug-courier profiles that were identified and provided to law enforcement officers through federal, state, and local law enforcement training. As part of police efforts to interdict drug trafficking on the nation's highways, police agencies developed guidelines or "profiles" to help officers identify characteristics of drug couriers that could be used to target drivers and vehicles. This training sometimes identified subjects' race and ethnicity as part of a larger "profile" of drug courier activity. The focus of this training was on Interstate highways on the East Coast, particularly around the I-95 corridor that linked Miami, Florida with cities and drug distribution points in the major mid-Atlantic and Northeastern cities (Harris 1999; Engel, Calnon, and Bernard 2002). Based on this profile, police would make pretextual stops (*Whren v. U.S.*, 517 U.S. 806 [1996]) and attempt to establish a legal basis to search for contraband.

   Another police tactic resulting from the "War on Drugs" was the increased use of pedestrian stops, along with stop and frisk tactics (*Terry v. Ohio*, 392 U.S. 1 [1968]) to maximize the number of police-citizen encounters with individuals believed to be involved in criminal behavior. These targeted enforcement strategies were especially felt by young minority males, who were disproportionately subject to police surveillance and imprisonment for drug offenses (Kennedy 1997; Walker 2001; Harris 2002; Tonry 2011). The controversy surrounding the aggressive use of traffic and pedestrian stops by police still exists today (Fagan 2004; Gelman, Fagan, and Kiss 2007; Ridgeway and MacDonald 2009).

17.1.1 The Rise of Data Collection

High-profile litigation efforts in the states of New Jersey (*New Jersey v. Soto*, 734 A.2d 350 [1996]) and Maryland (*Wilkins v. Maryland State Police*, MJG 93-468 [1993]) alleging racial profiling by law enforcement agencies brought a discussion of these practices to the forefront of American public debate (GAO 2000; Buerger and Farrell 2002; Harris 2002). Based on the notoriety and successful litigation involving these claims of racial profiling, the public, media, and politicians began to exert pressure on law enforcement to address perceived racial/ethnic bias, particularly as related to traffic stops (Walker 2001; Barlow and Barlow 2002; Novak 2004). As a result of this pressure, law enforcement agencies and politicians across the country began erecting policies and legislation designed to "eliminate" racial profiling practices by local, state, and federal law enforcement agencies (Harris 2002, 2006; Tillyer, Engel, and Wooldredge 2008). These policies were often focused on traffic stops and included mandates to collect data regarding driver and passenger demographics from every traffic stop (regardless of disposition). The data collection efforts originally designed to uncover racial/ethnic disparities in vehicle stops were initiated by litigation, legislative mandate, and proactive action by law enforcement agencies to address community concerns (Ramirez, McDevitt, and Farrell 2000; Davis 2001; Davis, Gillis, and Foster 2001; Tillyer, Engel, and Cherkauskas 2010). As noted by Tillyer et al. (2010), by 2009, thirty-nine states had passed some form of legislation regarding racial profiling. Specifically, eleven states enacted legislation that prohibited racial profiling, five states mandated traffic-stop data collection, and twelve states both prohibited racial profiling and mandated data collection, while eight states had bills under consideration and three states had other forms of racial profiling policies.

The heavy focus on data collection during traffic stops was based in part on the original definition of racial profiling, but also because of the recognition that traffic stops are the most frequently occurring type of police-citizen interaction and can be initiated for a wide variety of reasons including legal violations, departmental policy requirements, and officer discretion (Skolnick 1966; Walker 2001; Meehan and Ponder 2002; Alpert, MacDonald, and Dunham 2005). Analyses of the Police Public Contact Survey demonstrate that of the 19 percent of citizens surveyed who reported having some form of contact with police, the majority of these citizens (56 percent) indicated that contact occurred as the result of a traffic stop (Durose, Schmitt, and Langan 2007). In addition, police officers have wide and often unfettered discretion when determining when to initiate traffic stops and the outcomes that motorists receive as a result of those stops (Wilson 1968; Ramirez, McDevitt, and Farrell 2000; Lundman and Kaufmann 2003; Engel and Calnon 2004b; Novak 2004; Engel 2005).

When initial claims of racial profiling during traffic stops were leveled against police, it was clear that law enforcement agencies across the country were poorly prepared to demonstrate, document, or defend their current practices. Quite simply, most law enforcement agencies did not routinely collect information about all motorists who were stopped by police, nor did they collect basic demographic information about those who were stopped (including race/ethnicity) (Ramirez, McDevitt, and Farrell 2000). While many agencies did routinely collect information about citations and arrests, this information could not be compared to the population of all motorists stopped by police that did not result in further official action. Likewise, the population of drivers "eligible" to be stopped for traffic violations was also unknown. Described as the "benchmark" problem, the need to compare traffic stops to those eligible to be stopped created a new stream of research across the country (Walker 2001; Engel and Calnon 2004b). Unfortunately, as noted in more detail below, over two decades of subsequent research produced very little, as the benchmark problem has never been adequately addressed by the research community.

17.1.2 Defining Racial Profiling

The initial narrow focus on "racial profiling" did not adequately address a much larger issue in American police-community relations. Specifically, claims of inappropriate police targeting of minorities for purposes of enhanced criminal apprehension and punishment have been recognized throughout American history. While the term "racial profiling" referred directly to the specific policies and practices in the 1990s of targeting minorities traveling on interstates for increased scrutiny to obtain drug seizures, concerns of racial bias and illegitimate practices by police have existed for many decades. Therefore, researchers recognized the need to broaden the conversation by calling for examinations of all forms of police bias. A more comprehensive definition allowed policy makers, practitioners, and academics to better focus on issues of racial bias beyond drug profiles during traffic stops.

As noted by Fridell and Scott (2005) the term racial profiling has evolved over time. Despite the rather narrow definition of profiling that began with policing drug trafficking, the growing public consensus became that any and all decisions made by officers based solely or partially on the race of the suspect were considered racial profiling. It was this change from a narrowly defined term of profiling to an all-encompassing term that led Fridell et al. (2001) to first introduce the new term. They argued that some past definitions of profiling may have been too restrictive, focusing exclusively on "sole" reliance on race. They noted that police decision making is rarely based on any *sole* factor, including race. Furthermore, in focus groups with citizens and police officers, Fridell et al. (2001) noted that citizens defined profiling as encompassing any and all demonstrations of racial bias in policing and viewed it as widespread. On the other hand, for police officers "profiling" connoted only the narrow definition of sole reliance on race; therefore, they viewed it as a much rarer occurrence. The differing definitions of profiling led to defensiveness and frustration as the two groups talked past each other, thus the development of the new term, *racially biased policing*, which Fridell and her colleagues defined as follows: "Racially biased policing occurs when law enforcement inappropriately considers race or ethnicity in deciding with whom and how to intervene in an enforcement capacity."

As noted by Engel (2008), economists and other academics have identified two different types of police racial/ethnic bias: 1) "taste discrimination" or "disparate treatment" and 2) "statistical discrimination" or "disparate impact" (Becker 1957; Arrow 1973). The difference between these two concepts is based on the individual intentions of police officers—in the former, racial/ethnic discrimination is the direct result of intentional police bias, while in the later, racial/ethnic discrimination is the result of factors other than individual police bias (i.e., deployment patterns, differences based on deployment patterns, offending behavior, etc.) (Knowles, Persico, and Todd 2001; Ayres 2002, 2005; Persico and Castleman 2005). Accurately measuring and classifying these two general types of police bias, however, have proved difficult for researchers. A summary of the evidence regarding racially biased policing is reviewed below.

17.2 THE EVIDENCE

Initial systematic research of the police began in the 1950s when a few ethnographic studies reported the realities of policing and the use of discretion. These studies described police agencies and culture (e.g., Wilson 1968; Van Maanen 1974; Reiss 1983; Manning 1997); police-citizen encounters (e.g., Skolnick 1966; Reiss 1971; Muir 1977); and the use of coercive power during interactions, particularly with minorities (e.g., Westley 1953, 1970; Skolnick 1966; Bayley and Mendelsohn 1969; Bittner 1970). From this beginning, a body of research emerged that exposed issues surrounding racial bias, abuse of force, corruption, and poor police-community relations (Bernard and Engel 2001). Much of this work was informed by an implicit assumptions that police decision making was inherently biased and exposure of these practices was necessary for reform. Given the tenor of the times, these assumptions are hardly surprising. More importantly, these assumptions created a lasting legacy that is seldom directly challenged in current studies of police decision making.

Over time, a more quantitative body of research developed that examined coercive outcomes of police-citizen encounters (i.e., citations, arrests, use of force) and whether citizens' characteristics influenced these outcomes. This research evolved from simple bivariate comparisons of police decisions and citizen characteristics (e.g., Pivilian and Briar 1964; Black and Reiss 1970; Black 1971), to the use of multivariate statistical techniques designed to explore the effects of extra-legal factors on police decision making, after controlling for legal factors (e.g., Smith and Visher 1981; Smith, Visher, and Davidson 1984; Worden 1989; Klinger 1994; Mastrofski et al. 2000). The body of research that emerged compared the impact of legal to extra-legal factors, including the effect of race on police decision making (Sherman 1980; Riksheim and Chermak 1993; National Research Council 2004).

Although researchers made significant methodological and statistical advances from the 1970s through the 1990s, the actual research questions being asked remained relatively constant. With only a handful of exceptions, this work focused on police decisions to use specific coercive sanctions, including citations, arrests, and use of force. The focus of this research was to determine whether police used their considerable discretion in a morally defensible manner. Summary reviews of this body of research generally indicate that despite differences in measures and methods, a majority of the studies demonstrate legal factors have the largest impact over police behavior (Gottfredson and Gottfredson 1988; Riksheim and Chermak 1993; Klinger 1994; National Research Council 2004). Research has also demonstrated that to a lesser extent, some extra-legal factors impact officer decision making even when legal factors are controlled for; in particular, citizen demographics (including race/ethnicity) have been identified as correlated with some coercive outcomes (Riksheim and Chermak 1993; National Research Council 2004).

Based on this larger literature examining police behavior, a growing area of more narrowly focused research has emerged in the last two decades to inform our understanding of "racial profiling" during traffic stops in particular. This research considers stop and search practices (e.g., Fagan and Davies 2000; Gould and Mastrofski 2004; Alpert, MacDonald, and Dunham 2005; Warren and Tomaskovic-Devey 2009), and more nuanced decision making points, including the development and interpretation of cues of suspicion (Alpert, MacDonald, and Dunham 2005), and decisions to patrol certain areas (Tomaskovic-Devey, Mason, and Zingraff 2004).

Traffic stop research generally examines two types of police decision making situations: 1) the decision to initiate a traffic stop, and 2) the resolution/disposition of that traffic stop (Ramirez, McDevitt, and Farrell 2000; Smith and Alpert 2002). However, given the inherent methodological limitations of examining racial disparities in stop decisions, recent research has focused nearly exclusively on identifying and explaining racial/ethnic disparities in traffic stop outcomes (Tillyer, Engel, and Wooldredge 2008; Tillyer and Engel 2012). The findings and limitations of research on stops and post-stop outcomes are reviewed in greater detail below.

17.2.1 Traffic and Pedestrian Stops

Initial research examining racial profiling relied on the use of traffic stop studies to determine racial/ethnic disparities in officers' decisions to stop motorists. These initial studies reported differences in aggregate rates of stops across racial groups and often interpreted these disparities as evidence of racial discrimination (e.g., Lamberth 1994, 1997). After these initial studies, dozens of published studies and agency reports followed that reported the degree to which police agencies over-stop minority drivers, relative to white drivers (Fridell 2004; Tillyer, Engel, and Wooldredge 2008). Over time, however, researchers were more careful to note that while these studies demonstrated racial/ethnic disparities in traffic stops, it could not be determined if these disparities actually represented racial bias by police. Researchers lacked the ability to determine *why* disparities existed. Rather, researchers focused on establishing a standard basis for determining that particular demographic groups were overrepresented in police stops, by comparing the percentage of drivers of a particular racial/ethnic group to the percentage that are *expected* to be stopped assuming no bias (i.e., a benchmark) (Zingraff et al. 2000; Engel, Calnon, and Bernard 2002; McMahon et al. 2002; Smith and Alpert 2002; Fridell 2004; Rojek, Rosenfeld, and Decker 2004; Schafer, Carter, and Katz-Bannister 2004; Gaines 2006; Tillyer, Engel, and Wooldredge 2008).

Benchmark comparisons represent researchers' attempts to isolate race as an explanatory factor for disparity in traffic stops from the driving quality explanation and other possible alternative factors, including driving quantity, driving location, time of travel, etc. (Engel, Calnon, and Bernard 2002). However, this approach has considerable limitations, the most important of which is the inability to identify and measure a scientifically valid benchmark for comparison purpose (Walker 2001; Engel and Calnon 2004a; Fridell 2004; Tillyer, Engel, and Wooldredge 2008; Ridgeway and MacDonald 2009). In this effort to rule out factors other than racial discrimination in traffic stop research, social scientists utilized several different data sources to measure comparison groups, some of which were readily available and others that involved initiating new data collection. The most common types of benchmark data include: Residential Census populations, "adjusted" Census populations, official accident data, DMV records of licensed drivers, citizen surveys, internal departmental comparisons, observations of roadway usage, and assessments of traffic violating behavior (for review, see Fridell et al. 2001;

Walker 2001; Engel and Calnon 2004a; Fridell 2004). Each type of data has strengths and limitations as a representative measure of motorists at risk of being stopped by police. Importantly, no benchmark data has demonstrated the ability to adequately measure all the risk factors associated with the likelihood of being stopped and no consensus exists regarding which benchmarks are the most accurate (Engel and Calnon 2004b).

Early studies into disparate stop practices often used census data and other official records as the relevant denominator. For example, Verniero and Zoubek (1999) sought to uncover racial bias in the state of New Jersey by comparing the percentage of minority motorists stopped compared to their percentage in the residential population or eligible driving population. Similar analyses were conducted using data from Cincinnati, Ohio (Browning et al. 1994). Both studies reported that minority drivers constituted a greater proportion of stops compared to their representation in the residential population. Later studies marginally improved on this method by using the driving-eligible portion of the population. For example, in an analysis of traffic stops in Richmond, Virginia, Smith and Petrocelli (2001) found that when compared to the driving-eligible population minority motorists were overrepresented in the stop data, concluding that minority motorists were 46 percent more likely to be stopped than nonminority motorists. This finding was echoed by Meehan and Ponder (2002); using the alternative measure of observed roadway composition in a mostly-white suburban community, the authors found that the minority drivers were three times more likely to be stopped by the police. Disparities between driving population and stoppage rates were also observed when using spatially-weighted benchmark to account for confounding issues presented by cross-jurisdictional commuters (Rojek, Rosenfeld, and Decker 2004). In an analysis of the greater St. Louis, Missouri area, the authors found concentrated areas of small instances of disparate stop practices, with blacks being more likely to be stopped, searched, and arrested than white and Hispanic motorists in the areas in which a relationship was found.

Disparity via a disproportionate share of stops has been observed in studies of the San Jose and Sacramento Police Departments' traffic practices as well. During the period of study from July to September 1999, Hispanics represented 43 percent of motorists stopped by police while accounting for just 31 percent of San Jose's population (Withrow 2004). Similarly, using Census data as a benchmark Greenwald (2001) it was shown that during a one-year period black motorists were stopped by the Sacramento police at greater frequency than justified by their percentage in the general population.

Census data, however, are limited in their ability to measure alternative explanations of racial disparities including factors influencing drivers' risk of being stopped (e.g., where and when they drive, frequency of driving, what and how they drive) (Engel and Calnon 2004a; Gaines 2006). The Census' lack of measures of alternative explanatory factors, however, did not prevent some of the initial studies of traffic stops from prematurely interpreting disparity as discrimination and attributing racial disparities in stops and/or stop outcomes to unmeasured officers' racial prejudice (Engel, Calnon, and Bernard 2002). Most researchers in the field began to realize, however, that the hypothesis that police are racially biased in their stopping decisions is just one of numerous possible hypotheses or explanations for disparity in stops. Without measuring alternative explanatory factors, researchers cannot determine whether differences in traffic stops and stop outcomes reflect disparity or discrimination (Engel, Calnon, and Bernard 2002).

One suggested reason for these reported racial disparities among stopped motorists is the use of traffic stops as a pretext for criminal or drug interdiction purposes. Some support has been found for this hypothesis in studies of suburban communities (Meehan and Ponder 2002; Novak 2004), highlighting that while the correlation of race and the decision to stop is weak, minorities are more likely to be stopped at night and to reside in areas outside where the stop has taken place. This has given rise to a conflict theory-oriented explanation of police behavior (i.e., that police officers disproportionately target minorities when found outside of the areas where they typically reside or travel). Likewise, Petrocelli, Piquero, and Smith (2003) demonstrated that contextual variables, such as a neighborhood's percentage of black and UCR Part I crime rate, influence the number of stops performed in the area. Subsequently, searches of black suspects in these high-search areas resulted in fewer arrests or summons being issued. This general trend has been shown in self-reported data sources as well. A telephone survey of licensed drivers in North Carolina illustrated differential practices between the local police departments and the North Carolina State Highway Patrol (NCSHP). The decision of local police officers to issue tickets is related to driver age, race, and traffic history, while NCSHP ticketing decisions were driven both by legal factors (i.e., speeding) as well as quasi-legal factors (i.e., driver age and home-ownership status) (Warren et al. 2006; Miller 2008). Similar (though insignificant) disparities were found by Gaines (2006) in Riverside, California. Reviewing all traffic stops made in 2003, the author established that stops made by traffic units showed no evidence of racial bias, while stops made by patrol and investigative units exhibited slight, statistically insignificant bias. Further, Gaines found that that the stop data correlated strongly with race variables found in neighborhood crime data and received police reports.

Similar findings have been observed in studies of pedestrian stops as well. Using internal benchmarking (i.e., comparing the decisions of one officer to others similarly assigned; Walker 2001), Ridgeway and MacDonald (2009) developed a statistical method for identifying potentially problematic officers. These officers were more likely to stop black and Hispanic pedestrians, net of situational characteristics, compared to officers in similar assignments. Of the 2,756 officers whose approximately 500,000 cumulative stops were analyzed, the authors identified only 15 officers (0.54 percent) as significantly more likely to stop minority pedestrians. A multilevel analysis of pedestrian stops in New York City revealed similar patterns. Fagan (2004) found that after controlling arrest rates by race, black and Hispanic pedestrians were stopped more often than white pedestrians. This may be attributable to zero-tolerance policing strategies, the application of which was found to be driven more by neighborhood characteristics including poverty rate, racial makeup, and social disorganization (Fagan and Davies 2000).

Rojek, Rosenfeld, and Decker (2004) sought to correct the problems using Census data as a benchmark by spatially weighting motorists by their residential proximity to the various municipalities under analysis. This was believed to account for the fact that motorists spend more time driving in and around their own neighborhoods, and that race effects could be seen as spurious if observed in a majority-white neighborhood where a disproportionate number of minorities are stopped should that neighborhood abut majority-nonwhite neighborhoods.

Researchers have also developed benchmarks through the use of self-reported citizen surveys. General and purposive surveys have been used in both creating a more accurate composite of individuals' driving practices as well as recording the nuances of their interaction with the police (e.g., Lundman and Kaufman 2003; Miller 2008). Citizen surveys offer researchers the benefit of circumnavigating official data collection protocols and observational reports that may fail to capture key variables (such as perceived cause for the stop or officer demeanor) or erroneously categorize the demographic information of the stopped motorist. However, survey response data is prone to errors in recollection, desirability bias, and false reporting (Engel and Calnon 2004a).

A shared problem of these various benchmarks, however, is that they do not account for possible racial variations in driving behavior. For example, the differential offending hypothesis holds that certain racial groups may drive more frequently, more aggressively, or in locations with more police presence, and are therefore more likely to attract the attention of law enforcement. The literature offers measured support for this hypothesis; several studies have shown that certain minority subgroups are likely to engage in aggressive driving behaviors at a higher rate and to greater severity than white drivers (Lange, Blackman, and Johnson 2001; Lange, Johnson, and Voas 2005; Tillyer and Engel 2012).

In summary, the available analyses of traffic stop data have rather consistently demonstrated racial disparities in stopping patterns (Engel and Johnson 2006; Warren et al. 2006; Tillyer, Engel, and Wooldredge 2008). However, the methodological and analytical problems associated with this body of research are now widely recognized, including the inherent limitations associated with using benchmarks to determine racial disparities in vehicle stops (Walker 2001; Engel, Calnon, and Bernard 2002; Engel and Calnon 2004a; Fridell 2004; Tillyer, Engel, and Wooldredge 2008; Ridgeway and MacDonald 2009). As a result, research emphasis shifted away from examining officers' initial decisions to stop motorists and more toward officers' decisions during the stop (e.g., issuing citations, making arrests, and conducting searches). The study of traffic stop outcomes allowed for the use of more robust analytical techniques including multivariate analysis (Tillyer, Engel, and Wooldredge 2008).

17.2.2 Traffic and Pedestrian Stop Outcomes

Many researchers examining racial bias by police have reinvigorated the study of post-stop outcomes, including citations, arrests, and searches. This shift in focus may be due in part to the inherent methodological and statistical problems associated with examining racial disparities in traffic and pedestrian stops. Additionally, some have argued that racial/ethnic bias may be more likely to manifest itself after an initial stop is made and officers interact with citizens (Ramirez, McDevitt, and Farrell 2000; Alpert et al. 2006). As noted previously, research examining arrests dominated the policing literature in the 1970s and 1980s. Academics interested in examining racial profiling simply applied the widely used statistical techniques of multivariate regression modeling used in previous examinations of systematic social observation data to current studies using traffic and pedestrian stop data.

17.2.2.1 *Citations and Arrests*

Rather than focusing on stop or search decisions, the earliest exploration of racially-biased police practices examined the effect of race in the issuance of formal sanctions, such as citations and arrests. The evidence generated regarding the impact of drivers' race over the likelihood of citations has been mixed. While most studies have reported that drivers' race has a significant impact over citations, the direction of these reported findings have been both positive and negative (Tillyer and Engel 2012). While some studies have demonstrated that minority drivers were *more* likely to be cited compared to whites (Smith et al. 2003; Engel, Cherkauskas, and Tillyer 2007; Ingram 2007), other research suggests that black drivers were *less* likely to be cited (Alpert Group 2004; Engel et al. 2007; Lovrich, et al. 2007; Tillyer and Engel 2012). These results also varied across racial groups. For example, Alpert et al. (2006) reported that Hispanics, Asian, and Native American drivers were more likely to be cited, while black drivers were less likely to be cited, compared to whites. As a result, there appears to be little consistency regarding the reported influence of race/ethnicity over the likelihood of being issued citations during traffic stops. As concerned in the context of possible police bias, this mixed evidence correlates with differing hypotheses regarding the likely direction of the effect (Tillyer and Engel 2012). Some have suggested that minorities are more likely to be cited once stopped as a form of enhanced punishment. Others have suggested that minorities may be more likely than whites to be stopped as a pretext for criminal interdiction purposes, and then are released with a warning.

Studies examining the impact of race on arrests during traffic and pedestrian stops have been slightly more consistent. Tillyer and Engel (2012) reported that most traffic stop studies found that minority drivers were between 1.5 and 2.6 times *more* likely to be arrested compared to similarly situated white drivers (Smith and Petrocelli 2001; Withrow 2004; Alpert et al., 2006). A few studies, however, have reported no racial disparities in arrest (e.g., Alpert Group 2004; Engel et al. 2006; Tillyer and Engel 2012). Other studies suggest that arrest decisions are impacted by both citizen and officer race. For example, Brown and Frank's (2006) analysis of police-citizen encounters in Cincinnati, Ohio found that after controlling for characteristics of the officer and citizen along with contextual effects, black officers were more likely to arrest black citizens, while white officers are equally likely to arrest both black and white citizens.

394 ROBIN S. ENGEL AND DEREK M. COHEN

In sum, the body of science surrounding racially-biased policing is generally seen as inconclusive (National Research Council 2004). Most recently however, in a meta-analysis of 40 arrest studies using 23 different datasets, Kochel, Wilson, and Mastrofski (2011) systematically computed an effect size for the effect of race in arrest decisions net of offense severity, demeanor, intoxication, and other factors. The researchers reported "with confidence that the results are not mixed. Race matters." This declaration was based on observed effect sizes ranging from 1.32 to 1.52 (498). The study concluded that blacks were 30 percent more likely be arrested compared to whites, even after controlling for other factors. The authors noted that although previous policing experts have described the collective research findings as "mixed" regarding the effects of race (e.g., Riksheim and Chermak 1993; National Research Council 2004; Rosich 2007), their comprehensive review of the available research, however, is necessarily limited by the quality of the individual studies reviewed. Due to the nature of meta-analysis as a technique, the quality of the meta-analytic results is based on the quality of the individual studies included in the meta-analysis (Gendreau and Smith 2007). Further, their analyses cannot systematically explain why, how, and when race matters in arrest decisions, only that it does.

Specific to traffic and pedestrian stops, the research available generally shows an inconsistent impact of race over the likelihood of issued citations. In contrast, the impact of race over the likelihood of arrest during traffic and pedestrian stops appears to be more consistent, demonstrating racial disparities in arrest decisions. Further, the bulk of the available research demonstrates that minorities (and especially blacks) continue to be arrested at much higher rates than their representation in the general population (Engel and Swartz, forthcoming). Whether this disparity is the result of police bias, however, remains a point of contention throughout the research community.

17.2.2.2 Searches and Seizures

Beyond the decision to stop a minority motorist, racial profiling could potentially manifest itself in officers' decisions to search. While extant Fourth Amendment precedent limits the utility of contraband discovered outside of reasonable or warranted searches, officers may seek consent to search an individual's person, effects, or automobile. The relationship between race and search likelihood has been observed across a multitude of jurisdictions, using qualitative and quantitative analyses on both official and unofficial data sources. The bulk of scholarship examining traffic searches suggests that minority motorists are more likely to be searched compared with other racial groups (Rojek, Rosenfeld, and Decker 2004; Withrow 2004; Engel and Johnson 2006; Roh and Robinson 2009; cf. Smith and Petrocelli 2001; Paoline and Terrill 2005; Schafer et al. 2006).

Engel and Johnson's (2006) review of agency reports from twelve different state highway police/patrol agencies demonstrated consistently higher rates of minority searches compared to white drivers stopped for traffic offenses. For example, using data from the Washington State Patrol, Pickerell, Mosher, and Pratt (2009) found that black and Hispanic drivers were more likely to be searched compared to white drivers, regardless of the reason for the search. Close and Mason's (2007) examination of traffic stop data from the Florida Highway Patrol also showed that black and Hispanic drivers were more likely to be searched compared to white drivers, irrespective of the search type.

Examining interaction effects using college campus data, Moon and Corley (2007) found that black male students were more likely to be searched compared to their white counterparts. Based on results from propensity score matching, Ridgeway (2006) reported that black motorists were twice as likely as whites to be searched based on probable cause in Oakland, California. And most recently, Rojek, Rosenfeld, and Decker (2012) reported that young, black males were more likely to be searched compared to young white males during traffic stops in St. Louis, Missouri and Cincinnati, Ohio. Likewise, analyses of survey data from the Police Public Contact Survey indicated that younger drivers, male drivers, and minority drivers all reported higher rates of search compared with other drivers (Engel and Calnon 2004a). Similar racial disparities in search rates have been reported in survey and qualitative research (Brunson 2007; Brunson and Weitzer 2009).

Despite these consistent findings, Tillyer, Klahm, and Engel (2012) identified several limitations of the analyses examining racial disparities in search rates. First, many studies did not separate mandatory from discretionary searches. Mandatory searches (e.g., searches incident to arrest, inventory searches, etc.) are required by departmental policy and should not be included in analyses designed to examine officer discretion. Second, as with other post-stop analyses, the statistical analyses of searches often are misspecified due to the omitted variable problem (cf. Mustard 2003; Gelman, Fagan, and Kiss 2007). Third, examinations of officer search behavior is often based on pooled variance models (Lundman 2003; Alpert, Dunham, and Smith 2007; Moon and Corley 2007), without taking into account the nested nature of traffic stop data that requires the use of hierarchical models. Finally, as with studies of citations and arrests, research examining searches is often not guided by a theoretical framework necessary to understand the reasons for racial disparities in search rates (Engel, Calnon, and Bernard 2002; Tomaskovic-Devey, Mason, and Zingraff 2004; Engel and Johnson 2006).

The current discussion regarding racial profiling has also shifted from examinations of stops, benchmarks, and search rates, to examinations of contraband seizures during searches. A "hit rate" commonly refers to the percentage of searches conducted by police that result in discoveries of contraband (Engel 2008). In addition to criminologists and legal scholars, economists have entered the racial profiling debate by publishing articles using police vehicle and pedestrian stop, search and seizure data in an effort to determine racial and ethnic discrimination at the hands of the police. Specifically, economists have argued that a statistical comparison of search success rates can be used to distinguish between statistical discrimination and officer bias (Knowles, Persico, and Todd 2001; Ayres 2002; Persico and Castleman 2005; Persico and Todd 2006). The economic perspective explicitly suggests that if one racial/ethnic group is found to be more involved in criminal activity, members of that racial/ethnic group should be subjected to increased police scrutiny in an effort to maximize police resources and increase the rates of discovering contraband. Therefore, under these economic principles, a difference in search rates across racial/ethnic groups is tolerable if the rates of recovering contraband across racial groups are statistically equivalent (Knowles, Persico, and Todd 2001; Anwar and Fang 2006).

To identify racial/ethnic discrimination, the analytical strategy utilized is a statistical comparison of search outcomes across racial/ethnic groups, commonly referred to as the "outcome test" (Ayres 2002). If the hit rates are different across racial/ethnic groups, economists argued this is evidence of discrimination (Knowles, Persico and Todd 2001; Ayres 2002; Hernandez-Murillo and Knowles 2004; Persico and Castleman 2005; Anwar and Fang 2006; Persico and Todd 2006). Using the outcome test method, most studies have reported that first, minorities are more likely to be searched, and second, when searched, minorities are less likely to be found with contraband compared to whites. However, the use of the outcome test as a tool to determine police discrimination has been met with sharp criticism. As noted by criminologists and economists, many of the underlying assumptions required by the statistical model do not coincide with what is known about decision-making during police-citizen encounters, and further the underlying conditions necessary to support the outcome test cannot be met (Anwar and Fang 2004; Dharmapala and Ross 2004; Hernandez-Murillo and Knowles 2004; Engel 2008; Engel and Tillyer 2008; Antonovics and Knight 2009).

Nevertheless, the accumulating evidence that minorities are more likely to be searched, but less likely to be discovered with contraband begs the question *why*? Why are minority citizens searched more frequently for discretionary reasons, but less frequently found to be carrying contraband? The outcome test assumes the response is officer bias, but there are many other potential contributing factors (Engel 2008). Questioning why racial disparities exist demonstrates the severe limitation of this body of research—a nearly exclusive focus on *outcome*, rather than *process*. Studying the *process* of officer decision making is crucial to fully developing an understanding of the relationship between citizen race/ethnicity and police behavior. Unpacking and understanding the process of officer decision making is the next great challenge in understanding police discretion and is rooted in the existence of officer suspicion (e.g., Alpert Group 2004; Alpert, MacDonald, and Dunham 2005).

17.3 THE FUTURE

As noted above, the empirical body of evidence available has clearly demonstrated the routine existence of racial and ethnic disparities in stops, citations, arrests, and searches in police agencies across the country. What remains in debate, however, is whether these racial/ethnic disparities are indicative of officer bias. Unfortunately, our research methods and statistical analyses thus far cannot determine officers' motivation and intent, and therefore cannot determine racial bias and discrimination. While researchers can identify patterns and trends of disparities, we cannot readily determine the causes of these disparities. This is, of course, a critical limitation of social scientific research in this area. And, as a result, our current research cannot readily assist police agencies with the difficult task of developing policies and procedures designed to reduce racial disparities.

In the majority of studies examining bias-based policing, academics typically acknowledge these limitations of their research designs and statistical techniques, while simultaneously noting the importance of their work as adding to the accumulating body of research. Academics then often advocate for more of the same types of research to continue this incremental advancement in knowledge. In contrast to these recommendations, we believe a significant departure from the existing line of research in this area is necessary to advance the field. It appears to us that the current research has exhausted its value, particularly to practitioners struggling to reduce racial/ethnic disparities in police outcomes. Incremental increases in knowledge based on analyses of new data from traffic stop studies, or slight changes in the measurement of variables in yet one more multivariate statistical equation used to model stops, citations, arrests, and searches will not address the overarching methodological limitations that plague this line of research. We agree with Piquero (2009, 376) that "there should be a high priority of focused theoretical and research efforts that use multiple methods to generate a careful description and understanding of police-citizen encounters, as well as the myriad of factors that influence both police and citizen decisions." We further note that repeated application of the statistical technique *du jour* (e.g., outcome tests, propensity score matching, hierarchical linear modeling, etc.) also will not solve the underlying benchmark problem, nor will it address why racial/ethnic disparities persist despite multiple forms of police intervention. After over two decades of focused research on racial profiling, the research community is no closer to assisting practitioners in the reduction of racial/ethnic disparities than we were in the early 1990s.

While patterns of racial/ethnic disparities have been routinely identified and confirmed, research dedicated to understanding *why* these patterns exist has been limited. Despite the abundance of academic study devoted to this topic, researchers have limited theories to explain the mounting evidence of racial/ethnic disparities. Although some researchers developed partial theories to explain these disparities post hoc (e.g., Parker et al. 2004; Tomaskovic-Devey, Mason, and Zingraff 2004; Warren et al. 2006; Smith and Alpert 2007), these theories have not been adequately tested (Tillyer and Engel 2012). As a result, researchers continue to struggle with determining *why* disparities exist in coercive outcomes during police-citizen encounters (Engel and Swartz, forthcoming).

Importantly, there is also little evidence available to suggest that the frequency of racial disparities have been reduced as a result of research efforts, or based on changes in police policies, procedures, and training. National estimates of the rates of police-citizen contacts with minorities have remained relatively stable over time (Langan et al. 2001; Durose, Scmitt, and Langan 2005, 2007), suggesting there have not been significant reductions in racial disparities despite years of attention by legislatures, police administrators, academics, and the public. The only other study attempting to examine this issue suffers from severe methodological constraints. Although

Warren and Tomaskovic-Devey (2009) reported that racial disparities in hit rates decreased as a result of media attention and changes in legislation in North Carolina, they did not control for any other rival explanations—including changes in specific training, supervisory oversight, departmental policies, among many others—and further were unable to properly establish time ordering to demonstrate cause and effect (Piquero 2009). Therefore, despite this important first step forward taken by Warren and Tomaskovic-Devery (2009) in an attempt to address these issues, the impact of specific attempts to reduce officer bias remains untested.

Further, we believe that even using new statistical techniques in racial profiling research that are promising (e.g., Ridgeway and MacDonald 2010) will not result in significant progress until theories of police discretion grounded in the daily work of police officers are developed and applied to this research (Engel and Swartz, forthcoming). As clearly articulated by Piquero (2009, 372),

> the science of racial profiling research rests on a weak data and knowledge base, and although there has been some important methodological/statistical progress, we are likely not yet in a position to reach definitively any strong set of conclusions concerning whether racial profiling exists (even if we can arrive at some working definition and operationalization of it) and most certainly which set of policies can diminish and/or eliminate the explicit/sole use of race/ethnicity in police decision making.

Therefore, the challenges that remain for both research and practice are considerable.

17.3.1   A New Research Agenda

It is based on this review of the state of research in bias-based policing that we call for new approaches and changes in our current research agenda. In short, we argue that it is time to advance research that will better aid practitioners interested in reducing racial/ethnic disparities. A similar argument was made fifteen years ago by Sherman (1998) when he advocated for the use of science to help the police find humane crime fighting practices rather than simply look for failures in policing. That Sherman felt compelled to justify the moral soundness of police crime reduction research illustrates how radical this idea was at the time. This also led to the changing of the core research questions that were being asked by prominent researchers in the field and promoted the evidence-based movement in policing (Weisburd and Neyroud 2011). In the same vein, we argue that rather than continually documenting racial/ethnic disparities in police stops and stop outcomes (e.g., citations, arrests, searches), academics should pursue and advance research specifically designed to *reduce* racial/ethnic disparities in police decision making and then test the results. How do we know, for example, that the changes in police policies, procedures, and training recommended by researchers have any impact on police behavior? Police agencies across the country spent millions of dollars on changes to policies and training designed to eliminate racial profiling—has it had an impact? The research community has been silent on these critical issues. Many academics, private companies, former practitioners, etc. provide training for police agencies to reduce racial profiling; yet are these trainings effective?

The research questions that must be addressed are: (1) *why* racial disparities persist in the outcomes of police-citizen encounters, and (2) what works to reduce these disparities. To address these questions, we propose the advancement of a research agenda that includes the implementation of stronger research designs, greater use of mixed methods and qualitative research, and increased use of panel-wave and longitudinal data.

First, the selection of strong research designs is critical, though the selection of the appropriate design should be guided by the questions asked rather than simply relying on external standards. The considerable advances in police effectiveness research, compared to racial profiling research, is due in part to the use of strong quasi-experimental designs, and when appropriate, randomized controlled trials. There is no reason these designs cannot be applied to study the impact of policies, procedures, and training on racial bias. The type of research proposed might include pre- or post-tests of the impact of different policies, procedures, and training implemented by police agencies, or even quasi-experimental designs where some officers, units, etc. are provided specialized training and others are not. Changes in officers' attitudes, levels of racial disparities in stops, post-stop outcome measures, and citizens' perceptions could all be measured outcomes. This is not to suggest that other research designs have no value. To the contrary, many important topics cannot be examined with randomized controlled trials or even strong quasi-experiments. But to say that there is a place for all systematic methods is not to say that *any* method can be fruitfully applied to *any* question, or that all research methods are created equal. Concerns over police discrimination against minorities can be, and must be, translated into falsifiable and therefore testable hypotheses.

Moreover, research has demonstrated that citizens' experiences during police-citizen encounters significantly influence their attitudes toward law enforcement (Brandl, Frank, Worden, and Bynum 1994; Weitzer and Tuch 2004, 2005; Engel 2005). Given that citizens' contact with police is most likely to occur as the result of a traffic stop (Durose, Schmitt, and Langan 2007), coupled with the impact that these contacts have on the formation of citizen attitudes, perceptions of racial/ethnic disparities within this context could seriously undermine police legitimacy (Tillyer and Engel 2012). Therefore, researchers might also focus on testing the impact of particular focused policing strategies on citizens' perceptions of racial bias and police legitimacy. Additionally, police research that examines effectiveness (often measured as reductions in crime) might also include measures of changes in disparate outcomes as an indicator of success. In short, we argue that our collective research agenda should be expanded to focus on research that will assist in the reduction of racial/ethnic disparities, and increases in legitimacy and transparency in policing (e.g., Weitzer and Tuch 2004, 2005; Tyler 2006) rather than simply continuing to document racial/ethnic disparities in stops and stop outcomes.

Second, prior to the development of testable interventions, studies of police bias will inevitably rely on non-experimental approaches. But to better understand racial bias, we clearly need to better use mixed method and qualitative examinations of police decision making. In this regard, direct observation of the police, their decision making, and their interactions with the public is critical. Some promising research in this area includes rich qualitative work (e.g., Kennedy 1997; Brunson and Miller 2006; Brunson and Stewart 2006; Engel et al. 2007) that helps provide context and may stimulate further theoretical development. This work successfully expands the initial research questions asked in the biased-based policing literature to incorporate police legitimacy research.

It should now be clear to the research community that black box evaluations and secondary data analyses without detailed descriptions of the original data collection effort are seldom helpful. It is essential to capture information about the *process* so that practitioners can implement and researchers can replicate. For example, a recent study showed that police removal of homeless encampments may have lowered crime (Berk and MacDonald 2010), but the results are unlikely to help policy makers because of inadequate descriptions of the intervention, outcomes, setting, and mechanisms (Eck 2010). Further, this study led to uninformed speculations on the nature of the intervention (White 2010), which in turn led police administrators to question "who will police the criminologists" (Beck, Bratton, and Kelling 2011). Though this example comes from the police effectiveness literature, the same sort of problems exist in racial profiling research when secondary data sets are used and the researchers neither directly observed the police nor understand the details of how the data were collected, and consequently cannot sufficiently describe or understand police decision making.

Longitudinal studies, such as those using panel or time-series designs, show promise in addressing many of the methodological shortcomings found in the current body of research. Unfortunately, these types of data are very limited and attempts to compile an applicable dataset would introduce a host of measurement issues, as independent data sources vary widely. One promising research endeavor is the National Institute of Justice's recently funded National Police Research Platform (Rosenbaum, Schuck, and Cordner 2011). Providing researchers with longitudinal data on police practice will allow analyses to model the effects of changes in training protocol, workforce changes, and officer perception over time (National Research Council 2004).

17.3.2 Conclusion

Fridell and Scott (2005) have suggested that police administrators need to be concerned about three ways that issues of police racial bias might manifest themselves: "Bad apple" officers, well-intentioned officers in need of guidance, and institutional practices or policies that might inadvertently contribute to the problem. Each involves different types of agency responses to identify and correct the problems. Fridell and Scott identified seven areas that police agencies can consider for responses to racially biased policing: (1) institutional practices and priorities; (2) accountability and supervision; (3) recruitment and hiring; (4) education and training; (5) minority community outreach; (6) policies prohibiting racially biased policing; and (7) data collection. Within each of these categories are a set of reasonable recommendations that, on their face, are believed to reduce police bias. Yet the evidence regarding the actual impact of these recommendations is nearly non-existent. A closer look at the available research surrounding these recommendations demonstrates that we are often operating in the dark. For example, only a handful of studies have considered the impact of recruitment, training, and education, on police behavior generally, and even fewer have focused specifically on reducing biased policing (e.g., Worden 1990; Sun 2002; Engel and Worden 2003). The same critique regarding the lack of evidence can be applied to each of the categories noted by Fridell and Scott (2005).

Fridell and Scott concluded their article by arguing that "law enforcement has never been better situated to address these issues" (2005, 359) and that "the police are more capable than ever of effectively detecting and addressing police racial bias" (2005, 343). However, based on the lack of available evidence to guide practitioners, we are less optimistic at this stage. While many agencies can readily identify racial/ethnic disparities, they often cannot detect bias, and they further cannot determine why these disparities exist or how to effectively reduce them. Further, as police agencies continue to promote and advance practices that have demonstrated effectiveness (e.g., hot spots and other types of focused policing strategies), it is likely that racial/ethnic disparities in stops and stop outcomes will continue or perhaps even increase based on differential offending patterns and saturation patrols in predominately minority areas (Engel, Smith, and Cullen 2012). This is not to suggest that Fridell and Scott's identified categories to reduce police bias are inaccurate; we agree that these areas are ripe for reform and that changes in these areas have the potential to reduce racial bias in policing. Rather we argue that specific guidance based on social scientific evidence regarding the types of training, practices, recruitment, policies, supervision, education, etc. to reduce police bias currently does not exist. This is where, we believe, our research community should focus if we are serious about both the role of science in policing and the need to reduce racial/ethnic bias in policing.

REFERENCES

Alpert, Geoffrey, Elizabeth Becker, Mark Gustafson, Alan Meister, Michael Smith, and Bruce Strombom. 2006. *Pedestrian and Motor Vehicle Post-stop Data Analysis Report.* Los Angeles: Analysis Group.

Alpert, Geoffrey, Roger Dunham, and Michael Smith. 2007. "Investigating Racial Profiling by the Miami-Dade Police Department: A Multimethod Approach." *Criminology and Public Policy* 6:25–56.

Alpert, Geoffrey, John MacDonald, and Roger Dunham. 2005. "Police Suspicion and Discretionary Decision Making During Citizen Stops." *Criminology* 43:407–34.

Alpert Group. 2004. "Miami-Dade Police Department Racial Profiling Study." Retrieved from http://www.policeforum.org/library/racially-biased-policing/supplemental-resources/Alpert_MDPDRacialProfilingStudy[1].pdf, November 5, 2012.

Antonovics, Kate, and Brian Knight. 2009. "A New Look at Racial Profiling: Evidence from the Boston Police Department." *The Review of Economics and Statistics* 91:163–77.

Anwar, Shamena, and Hanming Fang. 2006. "An Alternative Test of Racial Prejudice in Motor Vehicle Searches: Theory and Evidence." *The American Economic Review* 96:127–51.

Arrow, Kenneth. 1973. "The Theory of Discrimination." In *Discrimination in Labor Markets*, edited by O. Ashenfelter and A. Rees, 1–33. Princeton, NJ: Princeton University Press.

Ayres, Ian. 2002. *Pervasive Prejudice? Unconventional Evidence of Racial and Gender Discrimination*. Chicago: University of Chicago Press.

——. 2005. "Three Tests for Measuring Unjustified Disparate Impacts in Organ Donation: The Problem of 'Included Variable' Bias." *Perspectives in Biology and Medicine* 48:S68–S87.

Barlow, David, and Melissa Barlow. 2002. "Racial Profiling: A Survey of African American Police Officers." *Police Quarterly* 5:334–58.

Bayley, David, and Harold Mendelsohn. 1969. *Minorities and the Police*. New York: Free Press.

Bayley, David, and Christine Nixon. 2010. *The Changing Environment for Policing: 1985–2008*. Washington, DC: Office of Justice Programs, National Institute of Justice.

Beck, Charlie, William Bratton, and George Kelling. 2011. "Who Will Police the Criminologists?" *City Journal* 21.2. Retrieved from: http://www.city-journal.org/2011/21_2_snd-criminology.html, November 5, 2012.

Becker, Gary. 1957. *The Economics of Discrimination*. Chicago: University of Chicago Press.

Berk, Richard, and John MacDonald. 2010. "Policing the Homeless: An Evaluation of Efforts to Reduce Homeless-related Crime." *Criminology and Public Policy* 9:813–40.

Bernard, Tom, and Robin Engel. 2001. "Conceptualizing Criminal Justice Theory." *Justice Quarterly* 18:1–30.

Bittner, Egon. 1970. *The Functions of Police in Modern Society*. Washington, DC: U.S. Government Printing Office.

Black, Donald. 1971. "The Boundaries of Legal Sociology." *Yale Law Journal* 81:1086–100.

Black, Donald, and Albert Reiss. 1970. "Police Control of Juveniles." *American Sociological Review* 35:63–77.

Brandl, Steven, James Frank, Robert Worden, and Timothy Bynum. 1994. "Global and Specific Attitudes Toward the Police: Disentangling the Relationship." *Justice Quarterly* 11:119–34.

Brown, Robert, and James Frank. 2006. "Race and Officer Decision Making: Examining Differences in Arrest Outcomes Between Black and White Officers." *Justice Quarterly* 23:96–126.

Browning, Sandra, Francis Cullen, Liquan Cao, Renee Kopache, and Thomas Stevenson. 1994. "Race and Getting Hassled by the Police: A Research Note." *Police Studies* 17:1–11.

Brunson, Rod. 2007. "'Police Don't Like Black People': African-American Young Men's Accumulated Police Experiences." *Criminology and Public Policy* 6:71–102.

Brunson, Rod, and Jody Miller. 2006. "Gender, Race, and Urban Policing: The Experience of African American Youths." *Gender and Society* 20:531–52.

Brunson, Rod, and Eric Stewart. 2006. "Young African American Women, the Street Code, and Violence: An Exploratory Analysis." *Journal of Crime and Justice* 29:1–19.

Brunson, Rod, and Ronald Weitzer. 2009. "Police Relations with Black and White Youth in Different Urban Neighborhoods." *Urban Affairs Review* 44:858–85.

Buerger, Michael, and Michael Farrell. 2002. "The Evidence of Racial Profiling: Interpreting Documented and Unofficial Sources." *Police Quarterly* 5:272–305.

Close, Billy, and Patrick Mason. 2007. "Searching for Efficient Enforcement: Officer Characteristics and Racially Biased Policing." *Review of Law and Economics* 3:263–321.

Davis, Ronald. 2001. *What Does the Data Mean?* Alexandria, VA: National Organization of Black Law Enforcement Executives.

Davis, Ronald, Ida Gillis, and Maurice Foster. 2001. *A NOBLE Perspective: Racial Profiling—A Symptom of Bias-based Policing*. Alexandria, VA: National Organization of Black Law Enforcement Executives.

Dharmapala, Dhammika, and Stephen Ross. 2004. "Racial Bias in Motor Vehicle Searches: Additional Theory and Evidence." *Contributions to Economic Analysis and Policy* 3:1–23.

Durose, Matthew, Erica Schmitt, and Patrick Langan. 2005. *Contacts between Police and the Public: Findings from the 2002 National Survey*. Washington, DC: U.S. Department of Justice.

——. 2007. *Contact Between Police and the Public, 2005*. Washington, DC: Bureau of Justice Statistics.

Eck, John. 2010. "Policy Is in the Details: Using External Validity to Help Policy Makers." *Criminology and Public Policy* 9:859–66.

Engel, Robin. 2005. "Citizens' Perceptions of Procedural and Distributive Injustice During Traffic Stops with Police." *Journal of Research in Crime and Delinquency* 42:445–81.

——. 2008. "A Critique of the Outcome Test in Racial Profiling Research." *Justice Quarterly* 25:1–36.

Engel, Robin, and Jennifer Calnon. 2004a. "Examining the Influences of Drivers' Characteristics During Traffic Stops with Police: Results from a National Survey." *Justice Quartly* 21:49–90.

——. 2004b. "Comparing Benchmark Methodologies for Police-citizen Contacts: Traffic Stop Data Collection for the Pennsylvania State Police." *Police Quarterly* 7:97–125.

Engel, Robin, Jennifer Calnon, and Thomas Bernard. 2002. "Theory and Racial Profiling: Shortcomings and Future Directions in Research." *Justice Quarterly* 19:249–73.

Engel, Robin, Jennifer Cherkauskas, and Rob Tillyer. 2007. *Traffic Stop Data Analysis Study Final Report: Literature Review and Review of Other Jurisdictions*. Phoenix, AZ: Submitted to the Arizona Department of Public Safety.

Engel, Robin, James Frank, Rob Tillyer, and Charles Klahm. 2006. *Cleveland Division of Police Traffic Stop Data Study: Final Report*. Cleveland, OH: Submitted to the City of Cleveland, Division of Police, Office of the Chief.

Engel, Robin, and Richard Johnson. 2006. "Toward a Better Understanding of Racial and Ethnic Disparities in Search and Seizure Rates." *Journal of Criminal Justice* 34:605–17.

Engel, Robin, Michael Smith, and Francis Cullen. 2012. "Race, Place, and Drug Enforcement: Reconsidering the Impact of Citizen Complaints and Crime Rates on Drug Arrests." *Criminology and Public Policy* 11:603–35.

Engel, Robin, and Kristin Swartz. Forthcoming. "Race, Crime, and Policing." In *Oxford Handbook on Ethnicity, Crime, and Immigration*, edited by S. Bucerius and Michael Tonry. New York: Oxford University Press.

Engel, Robin, Rob Tillyer, Jennifer Cherkauskas, and James Frank. 2007. *Traffic Stop Data Analysis Study: Year 1 Final Report*. Submitted to the Arizona Department of Public Safety, Phoenix, AZ: University of Cincinnati.

Engel, Robin, and Robert Worden. 2003. "Police Officers' Attitudes, Behavior, and Supervisory Influences: An Analysis of Problem Solving." *Criminology* 41:131–66.

Fagan, Jeffrey. 2004. "An Analysis of the NYPD's Stop-and-frisk Policy in the Context of Claims of Racial Bias." *Columbia Public Law and Legal Theory Working Papers*, no. 0959:1–22.

Fagan, Jeffrey, and Garth Davies. 2000. "Street Stops and Broken Windows: Terry, Race, and Disorder in New York City." *Fordham Urban Law Journal* 28:457–504.

Fridell, Lorie. 2004. *By the Numbers: A Guide for Analyzing Race Data from Vehicle Stops*. Washington, DC: Police Executive Research Forum.

Fridell, Lorie, Bob Lunney, Drew Diamond, Bruce Kubu, Michael Scott, and Colleen Laing. 2001. *Racially Biased Policing: A Principled Response*. Washington, DC: The Police Executive Research Forum.

Fridell, Lorie, and Mike Scott. 2005. "Law Enforcement Agency Responses to Racially Biased Police and the Perceptions of Its Practice." In *Critical Issues in Policing*, edited by Roger Dunham and Geoffrey Alpert, 304–321. Prospect Heights, IL: Waveland Press.

Gaines, Larry. 2006. "An Analysis of Traffic Stop Data in Riverside, California." *Police Quarterly* 9:210–33.

Gelman, Andrew, Jeffrey Fagan, and Alex Kiss. 2007. "An Analysis of the New York City Police Department's 'Stop-and-frisk' Policy in the Context of Claims of Racial Bias." *Journal of the American Statistical Association* 102:813–23.

Gendreau, Paul, and Paula Smith. 2007. "Influencing the 'People Who Count': Some Perspectives on the Reporting of Meta-analytic Results for Prediction and Treatment Outcomes with Offenders." *Criminal Justice and Behavior* 34:1536–59.

General Accounting Office [GAO]. 2000. *Racial Profiling: Limited Data Available on Motorist Stops*. Washington DC: General Accounting Office.

Gottfredson, Michael, and Don Gottfredson. 1988. *Decision Making in Criminal Justice: Toward the Rational Exercise of Discretion*. New York: Plenum Press.

Gould, Jon, and Stephen Mastrofski. 2004. "Suspect Searches: Assessing Police Behavior Under the U.S. Constitution." *Criminology and Public Policy* 3:315–62.

Greenwald, Howard. 2001. *Final Report: Police Vehicle Stops in Sacramento, California*. Los Angeles: University of Sourthern California, School of Policy, Planning, and Development.

Harris, David. 1999. "The Stories, the Statistics, and the Law: Why 'Driving While Black' Matters." *Minnesota Law Review* 54:265–326.

——. 2002. *Profiles in Injustice: Why Racial Profiling Cannot Work*. New York: New Press.

——. 2006. "U.S. Experiences with Racial and Ethnic Profiling: History, Current Issues, and the Future." *Critical Criminology* 14:213–39.

Hernandez-Murillo, Ruben, and John Knowles. 2004. "Racial Profiling or Racist Policing? Bounds Tests in Aggregate Data." *International Economic Review* 45:959–89.

Ingram, Jason. 2007. "The Effect of Neighborhood Characteristics on Traffic Citation Practices of the Police." *Police Quarterly* 10:371–93.

Kennedy, Randall. 1997. *Race, Crime, and the Law*. New York: Vintage Books.

Kerner Commission. 1968. *Report of the National Advisory Commission on Civil Disorders*. New York: Bantam Books.

Klinger, David. 1994. "Demeanor or Crime? Why 'Hostile' Citizens Are More Likely to Be Arrested." *Criminology* 32:475–93.

Knowles, John, Nicola Persico, and Petra Todd. 2001. "Racial Bias in Motor Vehicle Searches: Theory and Evidence." *Journal of Political Economy* 109:203–29.

Kochel, Tammy, David Wilson, and Stephen Mastrofski. 2011. "Effect of Suspect Race on Officers' Arrest Decisions." *Criminology* 49:473–512.

Lamberth, John. 1994. *Revised Statistical Analysis of the Incidence of Police Stops and Arrests of Black Drivers/Travelers on the New Jersey Turnpike Between Exits or Interchanges 1 and 3 from the Years 1998 through 1991*. New York: American Civil Liberties Union.

——. 1997. *Report of John Lamberth*. New York: American Civil Liberties Union.

Langan, Patrick, Lawrence Greenfeld, Steven Smith, Matthew Durose, and David Levin. 2001. *Contacts between Police and the Public: Findings from the 1999 National Survey.* Washington, DC: U.S. Department of Justice, Bureau of Justice Statistics.

Lange, James, Kenneth Blackman, and Mark Johnson. 2001. *Speed Violation Survey of the New Jersey Turnpike: Final Report.* Trenton, NJ: Office of the Attorney General.

Lange, James, Mark Johnson, and Robert Voas. 2005. "Testing the Racial Profiling Hypothesis for Seemingly Disparate Traffic Stops on the New Jersey Turnpike." *Justice Quarterly* 22:193–223.

Lovrich, Nicholas, Michael Gaffney, Clayton Mosher, Travis Pratt, and J. M. Pickerill. 2007. *Results of the Monitorting of WSP Traffic Stops for Biased Policing: Analysis of WSP Stop, Citation, Search and Use of Force Data and Preliminary Results of the Use of Observational Studies for Denominator Assessment.* Olympia, WA: Report to the Washington State Patrol.

Lundman, Richard. 2003. "Driver Race, Ethnicity, and Gender and Citizen Reports of Vehicle Searches by Police and Vehicle Search Hits: Toward a Triangulated Scholarly Understanding." *Journal of Criminal Law and Criminology* 94:309–49.

Lundman, Richard, and Robert Kaufman. 2003. "Driving While Black: Effects of Race, Ethnicity, and Gender on Citizen Self-reports of Traffic Stops and Police Actions." *Criminology* 41:195–220.

Manning, Peter. 1997. *Police Work: The Social Organization of Policing.* Cambridge, MA: MIT Press.

Mastrofski, Stephen, Jeffrey Snipes, Roger Parks, and Christopher Maxwell. 2000. "The Helping Hand of the Law: Police Control of Citizens on Request." *Criminology* 38:307–42.

McMahon, Joyce, Joel Garner, Ronald Davis, and Amanda Kraus. 2002. *How to Correctly Collect and Analyze Racial Profiling Data: Your Reputation Depends on It!* Washington, DC: Office of Community Oreinted Policing Services.

Meehan, Albert, and Michael Ponder. 2002. "How Roadway Composition Matters in Analyzing Police Data on Racial Profiling." *Police Quarterly* 5:306–33.

Miller, Kirk. 2008. "Police Stops, Pretext, and Racial Profiling: Explaining Warning and Ticket Stops Using Citizen Self-reports." *Journal of Ethnicity in Criminal Justice* 6:123–49.

Monkkonen, Eric. 1981. *Police in Urban America, 1860–1920.* Cambridge: Cambridge University Press.

Moon, Byongook, and Charles Corley. 2007. "Driving Across Campus: Assessing the Impact of Drivers' Race and Gender on Police Traffic Enforcement Actions." *Journal of Criminal Justice* 35:29–37.

Muir, William. 1977. *Police: Streetcorner Politicians.* Chicago: University of Chicago Press.

Mustard, David. 2003. "Reexamining Criminal Behavior: The Importance of Omitted Variable Bias." *The Review of Economics and Statistics* 85:205–11.

National Research Council. 2004. *Fairness and Effectiveness in Policing: The Evidence.* Washington, DC: Committee on Law and Justice.

Novak, Kenneth. 2004. "Disparity and Racial Profiling in Traffic Enforcement." *Police Quarterly* 7: 65–96.

Paoline, Eugene, and William Terrill. 2005. "The Impact of Police Culture on Traffic Stop Searches: An Analysis of Attitudes and Behavior." *Policing: An Inernational Journal of Police Strategies and Management* 28:455–72.

Parker, Karen, John MacDonald, Geoffrey Alpert, Michael Smith, and Alex Piquero. 2004. "A Contextual Study of Racial Profiling: Assessing the Theoretical Rationale for the Study of Racial Profiling at the Local Level." *American Behavioral Scientist* 47:943–62.

Perisco, Nicola, and David Castleman. 2005. "Detecting Bias: Using Statistical Evidence to Establish Intentional Discrimination in Racial Profiling Cases." *University of Chicago Legal Forum* 2005(1):217–35.

Perisco, Nicola, and Petra Todd. 2006. "Generalising the Hit Rates Test for Racial Bias in Law Enforcement, With an Application to Vehicle Searches in Wichita." *The Economic Journal* 116:F351–67.

Petrocelli, Matthew, Alex Piquero, and Michael Smith. 2003. "Conflict Theory and Racial Profiling: An Empirical Analysis of Police Traffic Stop Data." *Journal of Criminal Justice* 31:1–11.

Pickerell, J. Mitchell, Clayton Mosher, and Travis Pratt. 2009. "Search and Seizure, Racial Profiling, and Traffic Stops: A Disparate Impact Framework." *Law and Policy* 31:1–30.

Pivilian, Irving, and Scott Briar. 1964. "Police Encounters with Juveniles." *American Journal of Sociology* 70:206–14.

Ramirez, Deborah, Jack McDevitt, and Amy Farrell. 2000. *Resource Guide on Racial Profiling Data Collection Systems: Promising Practices and Lessons Learned.* Washington, DC: U.S. Department of Justice.

Reiss, Albert. 1971. *Police and the Public.* New Haven, CT: Yale University Press.

——. 1983. "The Policing of Organizational Life." In *Control in the Police Organization*, edited by Maurice Punch, 78–97. Cambridge, MA: MIT Press.

Richardson, James. 1974. *Urban Police in the United States.* New York: Oxford University Press.

Ridgeway, Greg. 2006. "Assessing the Effect of Race Bias in Post-traffic Stop Outcomes Using Propensity Scores." *Journal of Quantitative Criminology* 22:1–29.

Ridgeway, Greg, and John MacDonald. 2009. "Doubly Robust Internal Benchmarking and False Discovery Rates for Detecting Racial Bias in Police Stops." *Journal of the American Statistical Association* 104:661–68.

——. 2010. "Methods for Assessing Racially Biased Policing." In *Race, Ethnicity, and Policing*, edited by Stephen K. Rice and Michael D. White, 180–204. New York: New York University Press.

Riksheim, Eric, and Steven Chermak. 1993. "Causes of Police Behavior." *Journal of Criminal Justice* 21:353–82.

Roh, Sunghoon, and Matthew Robinson. 2009. "A Geographic Approach to Racial Profiling." *Police Quarterly* 12:137–69.

Rojek, Jeff, Richard Rosenfeld, and Scott Decker. 2004. "The Influence of Driver's Race on Traffic Stops in Missouri." *Police Quarterly* 7:126–47.

——. 2012. "Policing Race: The Racial Stratification of Searches in Police Traffic Stops." *Criminology* 50:993–1024.

Rosenbaum, Dennis, Amie Schuck, and Gary Cordner. 2011. *The National Police Research Platform: The Life Course of New Officers.* Washington, DC: National Institute of Justice.

Rosich, Katherine. 2007. *Race, Ethnicity, and the Criminal Justice System.* Washington, DC: American Sociological Association.

Scalia, John. 2001. "The Impact of Changes in Federal Law and Policy on the Sentencing of and Time Served in Prison by Drug Defendents Convicted in U.S. District Courts." *Federal Sentencing Reporter* 14:152–58.

Schafer, Joseph, David Carter, and Andra Katz-Bannister. 2004. "Studying Traffic Stop Encounters." *Journal of Criminal Justice* 32:159–70.

Schafer, Joseph, David Carter, Andra Katz-Bannister, and William Wells. 2006. "Decision Making in Traffic Stop Encounters: A Multivariate Analysis of Police Behavior." *Police Quarterly* 9:184–209.

Sherman, Lawrence. 1980. "Causes of Police Behavior: The Current State of Quantitative Research." *Journal of Research in Crime and Delinquency* 17:69–100.

———. 1998. *Evidence-based Policing: Ideas in American Policing.* Washington, DC: Police Foundation.

Skolnick, Jerome. 1966. *Justice Without Trial.* Hoboken, NJ: John Wiley and Sons.

Smith, Douglas, and Christy Visher. 1981. "Street-level Justice: Situational Determinants of Police Arrest Decisions." *Social Problems* 29:167–77.

Smith, Douglas, Christy Visher, and Laura Davidson. 1984. "Equity and Discretionary Justice: The Influence of Race on Police Arrest Decisions." *Journal of Criminal Law and Criminology* 75:234–49.

Smith, Michael, and Geoffrey Alpert. 2002. "Searching for Discretion: Courts, Social Science, and the Adjudication of Racial Profiling Claims." *Justice Quarterly* 19:673–703.

———. 2007. "Explaining Police Bias: A Theory of Social Conditioning and Illusory Correlation." *Criminal Justice and Behavior* 34:1262–83.

Smith, Michael, and Matthew Petrocelli. 2001. "Racial Profiling? A Multivariate Analysis of Police Ttraffic Stop Data." *Police Quarterly* 4:4–27.

Smith, William, Donald Tomaskovic-Devey, Matthew Zingraff, Marcinda Mason, Patricia Warren, and Cynthia Wright. 2003. *The North Carolina Highway Traffic Study: Final Report to the National Institute of Justice.* Washington, DC: U.S. Department of Justice.

Sun, Ivan. 2002. "Police Officer Attitudes Toward Peers, Supervisors, and Citizens: A Comparison between Field Training Officers and Regular Officers." *American Journal of Criminal Justice* 27:69–83.

Tillyer, Rob, and Robin Engel. 2010. "The Impact of Drivers' Race, Gender, and Age During Traffic Stops: Assessing Interaction Terms and the Social Conditioning Model." *Crime and Delinquency* 20:1–27.

———. 2012. "Racial Differences in Speeding Patterns: Exploring the Differential Offending Hypothesis." *Journal of Criminal Justice* 40:285–95.

Tillyer, Rob, Robin Engel, and Jennifer Cherkauskas. 2010. "Best Practices in Vehicle Stop Data Collection and Analysis." *Policing: An International Journal of Police Strategies and Management* 33:69–92.

Tillyer, Rob, Robin Engel, and John Wooldredge. 2008. "The Intersection of Racial Profiling Research and the Law." *Journal of Criminal Justice* 36:138–53.

Tillyer, Rob, Charles Klahm, and Robin Engel. 2012. "The Discretion to Search: A Multi-level Examination of Driver Demographics and Officer Characteristics." *Journal of Contemporary Criminal Justice* 28:184–205.

Tomaskovic-Devey, Donald, Marcinda Mason, and Matthew Zingraff. 2004. "Looking for the Driving while Black Phenomena: Conceptualizing Racial Bias Processes and Their Associated Distributions." *Police Quarterly* 7:3–29.

Tonry, Michael. 2011. *Punishing Race: A Continuing Dilemma.* New York: Oxford University Press.

Tyler, Tom. 2006. *Why People Obey the Law.* Princeton, NJ: Princeton University Press.

Van Maanen, John. 1974. "Working the Street: A Developmental View of Police Behavior." In *The Potential for Reform of Criminal Justice*, edited by Herbert Jacob, 83–130. Beverly Hills, CA: Sage.

Verniero, Peter, and Paul Zoubek. 1999. *Interim Report of the State Police Review Team Regarding Allegations of Racial Profiling.* Trenton, NJ: Office of the Attorney General.

Walker, Samuel. 2001. "Searching for the Denominator: Problems with Police Traffic Stop Data and an Early Warning System Solution." *Justice Research and Policy* 3:63–95.

——. 2003. "The New Paradigm of Police Accountability: The U.S. Justice Department 'Pattern or Practice' Suits in Context." *St. Louis University Public Law Review* 22:3–52.

Warren, Patricia, and Donald Tomaskovic-Devey. 2009. "Racial Profiling and Searches: Did the Politics of Racial Profiling Change Police Behavior?" *Criminology and Public Policy* 8:343–69.

Warren, Patricia, Donald Tomaskovic-Devey, William Smith, Matthew Zingraff, and Marcinda Mason. 2006. "Driving While Black: Biased Processes and Racial Disparity in Police Stops." *Criminology* 44:709–38.

Weisburd, David, and Peter Neyroud. 2011. *Police Science: Toward a New Paradigm.* Cambridge, MA: Harvard Kennedy School Program in Criminal Justice Policy and Management.

Weitzer, Ronald, and Steven Tuch. 2004. "Race and Perceptions of Police Misconduct." *Social Problems* 51:305–25.

——. 2005. "Determinants of Public Satisfaction with the Police." *Police Quarterly* 8:279–97.

Westley, William. 1953. "Violence and the Police." *American Journal of Sociology* 59:34–41.

——. 1970. *Violence and the Police.* Cambridge, MA: MIT Press.

White, Michael. 2010. "Jim Longstreet, Mike Marshall, and the Lost Art of Policing Skid Row." *Criminology and Public Policy* 9:883–96.

Williams, Hubert, and Patrick Murphy. 1990. *The Evolving Strategy of Police: A Minority View.* Cambridge, MA: Kennedy School of Government, Program in Criminal Justice Policy and Management.

Wilson, James Q. 1968. *Varieties of Police Behavior: The Management of Law and Order in Eight Communities.* Cambridge, MA: Harvard University Press.

Withrow, Brian. 2004. "A Comparative Analysis of Commonly Used Benchmarks in Racial Profiling: A Research Note." *Justice Research and Policy* 6:71–92.

Worden, Robert. 1990. "A Badge and a Baccalaureate: Policies, Hypotheses, and Further Evidence." *Justice Quarterly* 7:565–92.

——. 1989. "Situational and Attitudinal Explanations of Police Behavior: A Theoretical Reappraisal and Empirical Assessment." *Law and Society Review* 23:667–711.

Zingraff, Matthew T., H. Marcinda Mason, William R. Smith, Donald Tomaskovic-Devey, Patricia Warren, Harvey L. McMurray, and C. Robert Fenlon. 2000. *Evaluating North Carolina Highway Patrol Data: Citations, Warnings, and Searches in 1998.* Raleigh, NC: Report submitted to North Carolina Department of Crime Control and Public Safety and North Carolina Highway Patrol.

CHAPTER 18

···

ILLEGAL IMMIGRATION AND LOCAL POLICING

···

MELANIE A. TAYLOR, SCOTT H. DECKER,
DORIS M. PROVINE, PAUL G. LEWIS, AND
MONICA W. VARSANYI

HISTORICALLY the role of immigration enforcement has been the responsibility of the federal government. The enforcement powers of states were eliminated in 1875 when the U.S. Supreme Court ruled that "the passage of laws which concern the admission of citizens and subjects of foreign nations to our shores belongs to Congress, and not to the states" (*Chy Lung v. Freeman*, 92 U.S. 275 [1875]). Responsibility for immigration enforcement has been in the hands of the federal government ever since then and is currently conducted by the Immigration and Customs Enforcement (ICE) branch of the Department of Homeland Security (DHS).[1] However, changes in legislation have increasingly delegated the responsibility of enforcement from the federal government to local law enforcement agencies. This devolution of enforcement authority has gained momentum in recent years, yet has serious repercussions for local law enforcement officers who have become increasingly focused on building strong ties in immigrant communities.

Political and social pressures over the past twenty years to become more punitive toward undocumented immigrants have resulted in shifts in how local police respond to immigration status. In addition to new laws allowing local law enforcement to partner with federal immigration authorities, policies have also limited the housing options for undocumented immigrants and forced businesses to check the immigration statuses of employees. Changing policies were spurred in part by unprecedented growth and shifting settlement patterns of immigrants from Mexico and Central and South America; false perceptions that immigration led to increased crime rates; the terrorist attacks on September 11, 2001; and beliefs that economy and government budgets were harmed because undocumented immigrants were using social programs while not paying taxes. Subsequent responses to undocumented immigrants by local police have been inconsistent both between and within departments, contributing to local law enforcement agencies having a difficulty in balancing traditional policing roles with newly adopted roles, a problem faced not only in the United States, but in Europe as well (Decker, Van Gemert, and Pyrooz 2009).

Partnerships between local and federal law enforcement in responding to immigration issues have led to conflicting responsibilities for local law enforcement agencies. While once tasked with maintaining strong community relations to ensure public safety (Greene 2000; Reisig 2010), departments taking on the role of federal law enforcement run the risk of damaging relationships that are critical to their success in providing public safety. On the other hand, local law enforcement now has the opportunity to remove undocumented immigrants, especially those who have committed serious and violent crimes, leaving departments with a difficult decision about how to balance their roles.

The enforcement of local and federal immigration policies are complicated by the varying responsibilities of sheriffs and neighboring city police who may partner with federal authorities. Further complicating an already complex situation, local governments are increasingly making policies regarding undocumented immigration, with some openly accepting undocumented immigrants, others actively creating policies to deter their presence, and still others lacking a policy altogether. Varsanyi and colleagues (2012) have termed the outcome of immigration federalism as being a multilayered jurisdictional patchwork, where there is substantial variation in local responses to immigration enforcement. This patchwork is seen nationwide, leading to confusion for both residents and law enforcement.

The devolution of immigration enforcement authority has not only strained local police who are faced with dual roles; it has also impacted undocumented immigrants negatively in their communities. Social costs resulting from the increased enforcement of undocumented immigrants by local police include racial profiling, reluctance to report crime, increased vulnerabilities to crime, and negative social consequences of deportation. Such issues affect not only the safety of undocumented immigrants, but of all residents who are impacted by the changing roles of police.

This essay explores the variation of local police responses to undocumented immigrants. Section 18.1 begins with a brief overview of the history of immigration and law enforcement responses as a background for understanding recent changes in policing. Section 18.2 outlines public policies that have shaped current relationships between local and federal law enforcement departments. The pressures that communities place on local law enforcement to deal with undocumented immigrants are then considered. Section 18.3 explores how policies have led to conflicting roles for local law enforcement, where police are expected to both maintain strong relationships with communities and carry out immigration enforcement. The transference of responsibility from the federal government to local police then contributes to inconsistent immigration enforcement across municipalities. Finally, Section 18.4 reviews the social consequences of increased immigration enforcement, which has been a factor in increased racial profiling of undocumented immigrants and decreased participation of undocumented immigrants with the police, and has contributed to declining social conditions in immigrant communities. Conclusions are then made about the future of undocumented immigration and local policing.

The main points addressed in this essay are:

- Changing social and political conditions have contributed to the partnership between local, state, and federal law enforcement agencies in responding to immigration status; shifting responsibility from the federal government to local police.
- Local police departments do not always have clear policies and/or training regarding undocumented immigrants, leaving officers with little guidance when confronting these issues.
- Increased partnerships between local law enforcement and the federal government in the enforcement of immigration offenses have left police with the impossible task of keeping strong relationships with immigrant communities while also fulfilling departmental policies.
- Hispanics and undocumented immigrants in enforcement oriented communities may be less cooperative with police investigations.
- Risks associated with the transference of responsibility from the federal to local level include the potential for racial profiling of undocumented immigrants and other residents, weakened ties between local police and immigrant communities, and communities compromised by deportation.
- Not all localities support the shift in responsibility, with some cities adopting a policy of "don't ask, don't tell."

18.1 Historical Nature of Undocumented Immigration and Local Policing

Global demands for inexpensive labor have contributed to nearly 40 million people living without authorization in foreign countries. In the United States alone there are over 39 million foreign-born immigrants (i.e., all persons born outside of the United States who reside in the United States), with about 11 million of the foreign-born population being undocumented immigrants (i.e., persons residing in the United States who do not have legal authorization to be in the country) (U.S. Census Bureau 2010). Significant demographic shifts in the percentage of minorities and foreign-born persons in the United States have been predicted for the next forty years, with the largest growth expected in the Latino population (Passel and Cohn 2008).[2] The share of immigrants in the U.S. population is also expected to increase from 12 percent in 2005 to 19 percent in 2050. In 2010, Mexicans comprised the largest group of immigrants in the United States, with 30 percent emigrating both legally and illegally from Mexico, followed by 5 percent from China (U.S. Census Bureau 2010).

In the early 1990s, immigration policy was a salient topic in areas with high immigration rates (e.g., California and Florida) and had yet to capture the national spotlight. This changed with California's Proposition 187 (Burns and Gimpel 2000). The bill was one of the first attempts by a state to address concerns of the economic burden of undocumented immigration by making them ineligible for social services, health care, and public school. Although ultimately ruled unconstitutional, the bill highlighted the growing concerns of the public over the social costs of illegal immigration.

In response to the growing number of undocumented immigrants in the United States, a number of local law enforcement agencies began pushing back against their presence by partnering with federal authorities. Immigration enforcement has historically been the responsibility of the federal government, but legislation began to shift this responsibility to local police (Kanstroom 2007). In 1996 the Anti-terrorism and Effective Death Penalty Act (AEDPA) and the Illegal Immigration Reform and Immigrant Responsibility Act (IIRIRA) allowed local law enforcement to participate in immigration enforcement. While the AEDPA allowed local police to deport undocumented felons, the IIRIRA allowed for the enforcement of federal immigration laws by local police. Currently 69 local law enforcement agencies have partnered with the federal government in 24 states, including city police, sheriff's departments, and jails (U.S. Immigration and Customs Enforcement 2011a). Such policy responses are due in part to negative perceptions about illegal immigrants in the United States; however these perceptions are typically inconsistent with actual offending rates.

18.1.1   Immigration-Crime Nexus and the Latino Paradox

Historical reports of multi-national immigration have long claimed that immigration contributes to crime increases, especially in socially disorganized neighborhoods (Bingham 1908; Shaw and McKay 1942). During the late 1800s and early 1900s, concerns over an immigrant-crime link were primarily limited to the migration of Europeans to America. Recently, these same claims have falsely been placed upon newly arriving immigrants, including Latinos and Afro-Carribeans (Hagan and Paloni 1998; Martinez and Lee 2000). Whereas crime rates did actually increase with the growing presence of immigrants in the early twentieth century, this has not been the case for the most recent immigrants to the United States (Sampson and Bean 2006).

Extensive research has shown that the presence of immigrants, whether documented or undocumented, over the past two decades has had negative effects on crime rates (Stowell et al. 2009; Martinez 2010; Martinez, Stowell, and Lee 2010). This unique relationship between crime and immigration has been termed the "Latino Paradox" (Sampson and Bean 2006; Hagan, Levi, and Dinovitzer 2008). For many immigrants who commonly establish themselves in disorganized neighborhoods, it would be expected based on previous community trends that they would experience high crime rates (Sampson 2008). However, this does not appear to be the case in communities where documented and undocumented immigrants reside, as immigrants have strong incentives to work and avoid deportation.

A high concentration of immigrants is also associated with lower crime rates (Sampson, Morenoff, and Raudenbush 2005). In response to the concurrence of the crime drop and the increased percentage of immigrants during the 1990s and 2000s, Sampson (2008) argued that while these two events cannot be seen as having a direct correlation, they at least refute critics who claim that more immigration causes crime.

The Latino Paradox does not necessarily extend to all offense types or persist across generations. Research examining the offending practices of noncitizens (i.e., documented and undocumented immigrants) and citizens (i.e., U.S.-born and naturalized citizens) reveals that noncitizens were arrested less frequently than citizens for homicides, robberies, and aggravated assaults (Olson et al. 2009). The paradox did not extend to sexual assault offenses, with noncitizens committing the greatest number of sexual assaults. The Latino Paradox also appears to not always impact more general neighborhood problems. Skogan's (2006) examination of a police program designed to improve neighborhood decay showed that while African Americans and whites observed improved conditions, neighborhoods with large numbers of immigrants actually became more disorganized. Also, it is clear that the Latino Paradox begins to wane across generations (Hagan, Levi, and Dinovitzer 2008). However, at no time does it appear that immigrants or later generations offend at a greater rate than native-born citizens.

To add further complexity to analyses of the Latino Paradox, official data can be misleading for crimes committed by both documented and undocumented immigrants. On the one hand, immigrants may be underrepresented in crime reports. For example, Skogan's (2006) analysis of crime reporting in Chicago demonstrated that, consistent with national trends, official police reports showed crimes by Latinos declining over the past two decades. In contrast, self-reports in the Latino community revealed that crime rates were actually increasing. Skogan argues that this misconception is the result of Latino immigrants purposely avoiding the police when they are victimized. On the other hand, data have presented immigrants as being increasingly involved with the criminal justice system. For example, federal incarceration rates of undocumented immigrants have increased over the past two decades. However, 75 percent of those arrested were charged with crimes related only to an immigration offense, suggesting that allegations of immigration being tied to serious and violent crimes are simply untrue (Lopez and Light 2009).

More aggressive immigration enforcement practices based on skewed perceptions of immigrant offending patterns may harm communities where immigrants reside. The specific harms to immigrant communities will be discussed in depth below, but it should be noted that the presence of immigrants can serve as a protective factor against crime for both foreign- and native-born residents (Sampson 2006). It has been speculated that the unique conditions of neighborhoods with high concentrations of immigrants creates a protective factor against crime, where crime rates are low when there is either a high concentration of immigrants or presence of first-generation immigrants

(Sampson, Morenoff, and Raudenbush 2005). As a result of aggressive policing in these communities, the potential exists that the factors contributing to these low rates of crime and the protective nature of the presence of immigrants could be compromised.

The inconsistent criminal justice responses to the crime rates of undocumented immigrants have implications for future public policies, police resources, and community safety. Research has demonstrated the lower rate of offending by both documented and undocumented immigrants to the United States, yet public policy and policing responses have grown increasingly punitive. The basis for the perceived harm caused by increased immigration appears to still be linked to the criminality of immigrants in the 1800s and 1900s, resulting in recent immigrants becoming "convenient scapegoats" for current national crime rates (Martinez and Valenzuela 2006). Hagan and Phillips (2008, 84) argue that "enforcement as a means of controlling immigration has less to do with deterring illegal crossing and removing suspect immigrants than with symbolically reasserting national and territorial sovereignty." As a result, local police could potentially be diverting valuable resources from issues that residents feel are more pressing and instead use them for the identification, arrest, and housing of undocumented immigrants. An accusation of resource misuse and diversion recently led one state senator in Arizona to become the first sitting Arizona lawmaker to be recalled after he was accused of devoting too much attention to the policing of illegal immigration rather than other community needs (Caesar 2011).[3] The following section will discuss how policy responses over the past twenty-five years have resulted in the devolution of authority of enforcement from the federal government to local law enforcement agencies.

18.2 CHANGING POLICIES, LEGISLATION AND ROLES OF LOCAL LAW ENFORCEMENT

Changes in immigration enforcement have been shaped by economic, crime, terrorism, and border concerns. One of these responses has been deemed "immigration federalism" (Spiro 1997). Immigration federalism, or the devolution of responsibility for immigration enforcement from the federal government to local authorities, has been institutionalized by federal and state policies over the past twenty years. While initial reforms passively enforced immigration by targeting the hiring practices of employers, subsequent alterations in policies have focused on increasing national security by actively policing in immigrant communities.

Beginning in 1986, the Immigration Reform and Control Act (IRCA) made it illegal for employers to hire undocumented immigrants and required them to verify eligibility for individuals to work in the United States (Brownell 2005). This required employers to obtain identity and employment documents of all potential employees (e.g., U.S. passport, resident alien card, social security card, driver's license) (INA 274A [8 U.S.C. 1324a] [1986]). Employers who violated these laws could be fined anywhere from $250 to $10,000. The purpose of requiring employers to verify the right to work in the United States was to deter undocumented immigration by eliminating the incentive of employment for those without legal authorization to be in the country.

Post-IRCA hiring practices have been of particular concern to both anti- and pro-immigration groups. As immigrant supporters worry about the tensions and fears that such practices bring about in the immigrant community, those who advocate for stricter enforcement of prohibitions against illegal immigration claim that employment checks are not being conducted consistently enough to be effective. The maintenance of a policy targeting employers who hire undocumented immigrants that is not enforced results in "tacit amnesty" for employers (Hagan and Phillips 2008, 92).

Devolution of authority from the federal government to local law enforcement was institutionalized in 1996 through Section 287g of the IIRIRA, which allowed local and state police to enforce federal immigration laws. Federal authorities would then train local police in the checking of immigration status, questioning of suspected undocumented immigrants, and initiating deportations (U.S. Immigration and Customs Enforcement 2011a). Touted as a way for local law enforcement to identify and remove undocumented immigrants who have committed serious and violent offenses, concerns have been raised that this newfound authority is being used to target lower-level offenders.

The disjuncture between the stated goal of removing violent offenders and the actual practice of arresting and deporting minor offenders was raised in a report for the U.S. Government Accountability Office (Stana 2009). One of the key issues was that officers who were unclear about their roles and responsibilities would improperly arrest low-level offenders. Stana's (2009) evaluation of the Section 287g program made five recommendations including: (1) a clear objective be made for law enforcement agencies partnering with ICE; (2) clarification of local law enforcement and ICE jurisdictions; (3) clarification of the role of ICE officers in supervisory positions; (4) clarification of information to be collected by officers; and (5) establishment of performance measures of Section 287g. Stana (2009) reported that DHS and ICE acknowledged these problems were legitimate and needed reform. This report and the acknowledgement by DHS of the deficiencies in the Section 287g program suggest that the devolution of immigration authority from the federal government to local law enforcement may not necessarily be the best solution and should be examined more thoroughly.

Recently, illegal immigration has again been placed in the national spotlight, as a number of states have made drastic steps to crack down on undocumented immigrants. Arizona, a hotbed state for immigration controversy, set off the issue with Arizona Senate Bill 1070 (2010). The law initially *required* local law enforcement to inquire about immigration status if an officer had reasonable suspicion to believe the person was undocumented. States adopting these new tactics for enforcement could "single out Latinos, force them to demonstrate citizenship in the guise of 'securing' the border, and... accelerate attempts to seek deportation for minor or civil offenses even for those attached to native-born Americans in blended families" (Martinez 2010, 709). In addition, the law would more strictly target enforcement at day labor locations and target those who hire or transport illegal immigrants. Other states have made moves to adopt similar legislation targeting undocumented immigrants, including Alabama, Georgia, and Indiana (Fausset 2011; Lacayo 2011).

The devolution of authority from federal to local law enforcement gained increased momentum when the Bush and Obama administrations approved the "Secure Communities" initiative in 2009 (U.S. Immigration and Customs Enforcement 2009). Secure Communities is an evolving program that allows ICE agents access to Federal Bureau of Investigation databases containing identification information of those booked in local jails. Currently active in about half of local law enforcement agencies in the country, it was estimated that all local jurisdictions would be in cooperation by 2013 (U.S. Immigration and Customs Enforcement 2011b). Similar to Section 287g, Secure Communities has been publicized as a means to deport serious criminal aliens, yet many have criticized the program as targeting minor offenders and crime victims for deportation (Homeland Security Advisory Council 2011).

18.2.1 Pressures on Local Police for Immigration Enforcement

To further explore how local police respond to pressures to enforce federal immigration laws, a nationwide survey of police chiefs in the United States was conducted in 2007 (Decker et al. 2009). Decker and colleagues found that police chiefs are subject to a variety of influences when making decisions about immigration enforcement, including residents in their localities and officers in their departments. Two important considerations for local police in maintaining community safety are that they are able to gain the trust of residents and address issues that residents feel are important. It is apparent that the attitudes of police and residents are not always in line concerning immigration issues. For example, 51 percent of chiefs reported that their officers were concerned with gaining the trust of undocumented immigrants, but only 24 percent reported their localities felt similarly. Officers also appeared to be more concerned with victimization of undocumented immigrants, as their victimization was viewed as a serious problem in 31 percent of departments, but only in 23 percent of localities. Law enforcement executives felt pressure from their communities to police immigration, even when it was not viewed as their responsibility. Nearly 75 percent of departments reported that immigration enforcement was the responsibility of the federal government, while less than 60 percent reported that residents held this same view.

Local police chiefs are influenced to some extent by federal law enforcement; however, it is apparent that local police operate largely independently from federal authorities in immigration enforcement (Decker et al. 2009). About half of chiefs reported that federal law enforcement did not influence their ability to interact with immigrants. Furthermore, formal agreements with ICE to manage incarcerated inmates (a Section 287g agreement) were uncommon, with only 3 percent of departments maintaining such an agreement. This does not mean that local police do not actively work with ICE. The majority of respondents (73 percent) reportedly contact ICE when a suspected undocumented immigrant has committed a crime, while only 14 percent did not cooperate with ICE at all.

As local law enforcement agencies have revamped their immigration policies, so too have local governments. Localities are now being forced to balance the integration of immigrants into their communities with the removal of undocumented immigrants (Varsanyi 2008). In response, some local governments are adopting official and unofficial policies of "don't ask, don't tell" to provide protection to unauthorized immigrants where city employees cannot be questioned about their citizenship status and citizenship information cannot be given to government officials (Nyers 2010). Other localities have created policies to encourage local law enforcement to participate with federal authorities. Decker and colleagues (2009) found that 46 percent of local governments had no official policy regarding immigration, while 4 percent were deemed "sanctuary cities" (i.e., places where policies protect unauthorized immigrants from local police in non-criminal situations), and 15 percent had "don't ask, don't tell" policies. On the other hand, 11 percent of local governments expected local law enforcement to actively police immigration offenses and 17 percent were developing policies to encourage partnerships between local and federal police.

Consistent with the multi-jurisdictional patchwork described above, the policies of local governments are not always consistent with local police policies. For example, some localities may adopt a policy welcoming immigrants, while local police may be actively policing undocumented immigrants. These findings demonstrating the challenges faced by local police in enforcing immigration offenses have also been backed by national organizations. For example, a report by the Major Cities Chiefs declared that "local law enforcement of federal immigration laws raises many daunting and complex legal, logistical and resource issues for local agencies and the diverse communities they serve" (Major Cities Chiefs 2006, 3). At the same time that local police are confronted with the complexities that arise from the multi-jurisdictional patchwork of enforcement, their roles are further complicated as they are increasingly faced with balancing their conflicting responsibilities of maintaining community relationships and immigration enforcement.

18.3 Conflicting Roles of Officers and Challenges For Law Enforcement

Local law enforcement agencies have increasingly adopted the philosophy of community policing, a policing strategy that promotes partnerships between residents and police (Greene 2000; U.S. Department of Justice 2009; Reisig 2010). Based on the notion that local police are dependent on strong relationships with communities to protect residents and solve crimes, effective community policing relies on establishing and maintaining relationships with all residents, including undocumented immigrants. Law enforcement relationships with the community are vital to reducing the fear that immigrants may have of crime (Torres and Vogel 2001). The following section reviews how local police agencies are currently struggling with creating a balance between departmental goals of maintaining strong community relations and their newfound responsibilities to crack down on undocumented immigrants residing in their communities.

18.3.1 Enforcement of Immigration Laws in Communities

Limited research has examined how local police are adapting in the field to the authority placed on them by the federal government, especially regarding the responses of officers who deal with limited training and policies. Under Section 287g of the IIRIRA, local police departments that enter into agreements granting them power to enforce illegal immigration are required to receive training on detection, apprehension, and detention of undocumented immigrants (Newton and Adams 2009). Nevertheless, many agencies have yet to partner with ICE and therefore lack proper training. In fact, one study found that about 45 percent of departments reportedly do not offer training for officers when they are confronted with incidents dealing with unauthorized immigrants (Decker et al. 2009). Furthermore, only about half of law enforcement agencies provide policies to guide their officers in the field. In fact, the International Association of Chiefs of Police (2005, 16) "has never adopted a resolution or policy position" regarding immigration enforcement, as it recognizes the competing interests of local police who want to establish relationships in immigrant communities and those who view undocumented immigrants as criminals. Findings that policies and training for officers are frequently non-existent suggest that officers are not always prepared to deal with such issues.

Tenuous relationships between officers and immigrant communities are further complicated when a language barrier exists (Culver 2004; Hoffmaster et al. 2010). While officers reportedly find ways to "muddle through" communications with non-English speakers by using others for translation (Herbst and Walker 2001), this is not a best practice in policing. Culver's (2004) interviews with officers revealed frustrations with time delays because of language barriers and leniency towards Hispanics when officers believed they were non-English speaking. One officer stated, "I know there are times when I am tired and have had a bad day and I see a Hispanic commit a traffic violation and I think 'Oh I am not going to be able to communicate with them anyway.' Whereas with someone White, I would pull them over" (336). This sentiment was repeated by multiple officers who participated in the study (Culver 2004).

One important method of establishing relationships in immigrant communities has been increasing the ability of officers to communicate effectively with residents. To accomplish this, departments are increasingly hiring bilingual officers, interpreters, and volunteers to provide assistance (International Association of Chiefs of Police 2007). Local law enforcement agencies generally believe that having enough officers proficient in foreign languages is effective at maintaining community relations (89 percent), yet only 40 percent of departments reported they actually had enough officers who spoke a foreign language to be effective in their communities (Decker et al. 2009). Increasing the language competency of officers is particularly important for protecting immigrant victims of domestic violence, as officers may not be able to communicate directly with victims and instead rely on offenders' stories (Orloff et al. 2003).

18.3.2 Inconsistencies in Enforcing Immigration Laws

Both the DHS and ICE have acknowledged that there are inconsistencies in the enforcement of immigration offenses when local law enforcement agencies partner with federal authorities through Section 287g agreements (Stana 2009). For example, the removal of violent undocumented immigrants for the sake of community safety has been inconsistent. Because minor offenders are instead being arrested and deported when local law enforcement agencies take on federal responsibilities, resources are wasted and communities are not necessarily any safer.

Relationships between local law enforcement and ICE have been characterized as having unclear and limited communication. Stana's (2009) review of all law enforcement agencies collaborating with ICE as of 2007 revealed that the Memorandums of Agreements providing the devolution of authority were inconsistent across agencies. He notes that "a potential consequence of not having documented program objectives is misuse of authority" (4). Furthermore, many of the jurisdictions were required to report to ICE a variety of information regarding program implementation. Agencies reported confusion as to what information they were to relay to ICE, with many being unsure if they needed to report any data at all. Nearly half of law enforcement agencies report that useful information flows equally between them and ICE, with about a third reporting they have little or no communication with ICE (Decker et al. 2009). These findings suggest that the responsibility being placed on local police is, in many cases, lacking the proper support from the federal government for proper implementation.

Even though officers are not always guided by policies or training, they are still responsible for making difficult decisions posed by immigration issues, especially when confronted with serious and violent offenders. Decker and colleagues (2009) explored typical officer responses for a variety of situations when confronted with a potential undocumented immigrant. When confronted with more serious offenses (e.g., violent crime, parole violation, domestic violence), officers are the most likely to contact ICE or check immigration status. Officers who had stopped suspected undocumented immigrants for a traffic violation or who dealt with victims or witnesses were less likely to take formal action. This suggests that officers are more concerned about illegal immigrants when they are involved in more serious crimes, while at the same time valuing the importance of maintaining community relations.

It is clear that there is much variation in responses of local police to their new immigration enforcement responsibilities. Questions remain as to how best achieve community safety, whether it is through active enforcement of illegal immigration or establishing bonds within immigrant communities. Whereas some departments are using their authority to remove undocumented immigrants who have committed serious and violent crimes, others have used their power to target undocumented immigrants unnecessarily, including those charged with traffic offenses and victims of crimes. In many cases, individual officers now have unrestrained discretion to apply the law as they see fit. The social costs of the multi-jurisdictional patchwork of enforcement are just beginning to be explored. However, it is clear that with the ever-growing population of immigrants, there are bound to be adverse effects to the devolution of authority.

18.4 SOCIAL COSTS OF IMMIGRATION ENFORCEMENT

Partnerships between local and federal law enforcement may result in adverse social costs in border towns and localities with high concentrations of illegal immigrants. Under the guise of immigration enforcement, legal immigrants and U.S.-born Latinos may be similarly targeted by the police (Romero 2006). A small body of literature addresses how documented and undocumented immigrants are impacted when local law enforcement actively engages in the enforcement of illegal immigration offenses. However, it should be noted that a clear understanding of these impacts is limited because studies rarely distinguish between documented and undocumented immigrants (Wu 2010). A deeper understanding of undocumented immigrants' responses to the police is vital, especially because they directly influence the ability of local police to effectively uphold their responsibilities. The following section examines some of the adverse consequences that have been identified because of increased policing in immigrant communities including: the racial profiling of all Latino and minority residents, negative perceptions of law enforcement by undocumented immigrants, the vulnerability that victimized immigrants face, and the breakdown of community ties through deportation.

18.4.1 Risks of Racial Profiling in the Enforcement of Immigration Laws

Concerns have been raised that officers increasingly faced with the task of immigration enforcement will racially profile in order to carry out their responsibilities (Romero 2006; Sullivan 2008). Post-9/11 policies implemented to assist with investigations were criticized for their imposition on civil liberties, with policies being perceived as specifically targeting Arabs and Muslims (Wishnie 2004). It became apparent that racial profiling, which was once condemned in the law enforcement community, was slowly being legitimized as an appropriate mechanism to deal with terrorism. While some studies have demonstrated that Latinos in general experience racial profiling at a high rate (Reitzel, Rice, and Piquero 2004), very limited research has explored how Latino and non-Latinos, as well as all immigrants, are impacted by profiling (Martinez 2007).

Research has shown that Latinos, both immigrants and native-born, and other minorities are impacted when officers make decisions based upon the appearances of residents, which could potentially lead to increased profiling of immigrants (Reitzel, Rice, and Piquero 2004; Vidales, Day, and Powe 2009). Blacks and Hispanics reportedly feel that they experience racial and ethnic biases, but these perceptions of bias increase after minorities have had contact with law enforcement (Weitzer and Tuch 2005). While Hispanics appear to have more positive perceptions of law enforcement than blacks, these perceptions have been negatively influenced by recent changes in immigration enforcement. Latinos, both immigrants and U.S.-born, now report that they feel they are stopped more frequently, think more negatively of the police, and are less likely to report crimes than they had been before immigration enforcement became a politicized issue (Vidales, Day, and Powe 2009). Despite such negative feelings towards the police, Latinos reportedly are less likely to have their cars searched or have their records checked by law enforcement than other racial and ethnic groups (Alpert, Dunham, and Smith 2007). Of the few studies directly examining racial profiling among immigrants, Menjivar and Bejarano (2004) found that the opinions of undocumented immigrants regarding racial profiling are influenced by their perceptions of law enforcement in their own countries, direct experiences with American law enforcement, and their contacts at home.

In some localities, concerns over racial profiling are being raised as officers are now given the authority to detain suspected illegal immigrants based solely on the probable cause of being in the country illegally. The problem with this type of officer discretion is the difficulty that officers have in determining if an immigrant is illegal without consulting with ICE first. Although portions of Arizona's SB1070 are currently under an injunction, during the height of the furor over the law, Governor Jan Brewer's response when pressed on the criteria by which local police could identify undocumented immigrants during a national press conference was "I do not know what an illegal immigrant looks like." Clearly local law enforcement officers do not either. Nearly 60 percent of police chiefs stated that it is not easy for officers to determine who is in this country without authorization (Decker et al. 2009). The use of racial profiling in a post-9/11 society has since contributed to the deterioration of undocumented immigrants' perceptions of local law enforcement (Wishnie 2004).

18.4.2 Immigrant Cooperation with Local Law Enforcement

As local law enforcement has become increasingly allied with federal immigration officers, immigrants reportedly feel isolated and lack confidence in the police when they are victimized or witness crimes. Because undocumented immigrants fear they will have immigration status checked or will be deported if they contact law enforcement, they rarely request assistance from the police (Carter 1985; Bucher, Manasse, and Tarasawa 2010). For example, Skogan's (2006) evaluation of community policing in Chicago found that immigrants are fearful of police because of the misperception that contact with law enforcement could lead to deportation. These fears also contributed to immigrants not participating in community policing meetings, as immigrants were fearful that "their immigration status might be revealed at a beat meeting" (154). These fears persisted even after police departments went to great lengths to inform the public of their intentions with the community.

Similar findings were reported by law enforcement and court officials across the United States who believed that recent immigrants were less likely to report being victimized than the rest of the population (Davis and Erez 1998; Decker et al. 2009). About 70 percent of criminal justice officials in large cities believe that immigrants were less likely to contact law enforcement than the general population when they were victims of or witnesses to crimes. This is not surprising considering that over 15 percent of departments stated they would check immigration status or contact ICE when interviewing persons who were either victims or witnesses. The survey of police executives also showed that only 40 percent of departments had enough officers fluent in a foreign language to work with immigrant communities. Such a finding is concerning, especially considering the unique circumstances surrounding immigrants and their unwillingness to report.

A limited number of studies report that documented and undocumented immigrants are not always more hesitant to contact law enforcement (see, e.g., Ong and Jenks 2004). Correia's (2010) examination of 172 immigrants residing in Reno, Nevada revealed that immigrants in some localities actually have more positive views of local police than do native residents. Because this finding is in stark contrast to much of the previous research on relationships between immigrants and the police, Correia speculated that strong negative attitudes towards the police in immigrants' native countries led them to have more positive views of local police in the United States. Davis, Erez, and Avitabile (1998) came to similar conclusions, finding that both documented and undocumented immigrants had similar experiences with law enforcement as native-born citizens after they had been victimized.

When undocumented immigrants are fearful of contacting law enforcement, they become particularly at risk of victimization because they have nowhere to turn for legal recourse when victimized. As stated above, the limited reporting by immigrants in some Latino communities then gives the perception to the police that crime rates are fallaciously low in Latino neighborhoods (Skogan 2006), which could compromise the effectiveness of community policing. Vulnerabilities are especially heightened for female immigrant victims who are influenced by both their male abusers and immigrant status (Davis, Erez, and Avitabile 2001; Erez 2002).

18.4.3   Effects of Local Law Enforcement Involvement on Communities

Communities where undocumented immigrants reside are also harmed as a result of local law enforcement partnerships with the federal government, especially with regard to increased deportations. The removal of family members results in "fear, stress, family separation, and economic hardship" for those who remain in the United States (Hagan, Castro, and Rodriguez 2010, 1810). "Mixed-status" households, where some family members are illegal and others are U.S.-born, further complicate the effects of deportation, as U.S.-born citizen children may face one or both parents being deported (Brabeck and Xu 2010). The resulting effects are that children are separated from their deported parents, Latino businesses experience declines, immigrants will spend less money in the United States, and established ties to employment and social institutions are weakened (Hagan, Eschbach, and Rodriguez 2008; Hagan and Phillips 2008).

Interviews with undocumented immigrants in the 1990s and 2000s (Hagan et al. 2010) revealed the extent to which this population lives in fear. Nearly 16 percent reported being questioned by immigration officials over citizenship status. Some stated they had been questioned while walking to work or school, with about 40 percent reporting being arrested. Fears of confrontations with local and federal law enforcement have led undocumented immigrants to avoid contact with the general public. As a result, immigrants will avoid health services, government projects, schools, and driving to work. Immigrants in one county stated they were concerned that local police had adopted ICE responsibilities and felt they were unable to contact law enforcement as a result.

The consequences of deportation have grown in recent years as the number of removals has soared. In 2011, ICE Director John Morton announced that during the fiscal year, the agency had deported more immigrants than any other year (Morton 2011). Fifty-five percent of the nearly 400,000 deportees had committed either a felony or misdemeanor, suggesting that a large number of low-level offenders or non-criminals (45 percent) are being deported. A shortcoming of current immigration enforcement is highlighted by the fact that despite a record number of deportations, nearly 50 percent of deportees remain committed to returning to the United States (Hagan, Eschbach, and Rodriguez 2008; Hagan, Castro, and Rodriguez 2010). The potential for arrest and deportation by local police appears to not be a deterrent for re-entry, suggesting that merely deporting immigrants may not be the solution for effective immigration reform.

18.5 CONCLUSION

The presence of immigrants, both documented and undocumented, has been rising at unprecedented rates in the United States. Public and political pressures to crack down on undocumented immigrants have led to mixed responses from localities. On the one hand, a large portion of localities recognize the value and importance of promoting trust in law enforcement by local residents. As Decker and colleagues (2009) have shown, about one-fifth of large cities surveyed were either "sanctuary" or "don't ask, don't tell" cities. This means local law enforcement agencies can then formulate their own policies when tackling immigration issues. As has been recognized by national police organizations (Major Cities Chiefs 2006; Police Executive Research Forum 2008), negative consequences for public safety can result (e.g., diversion of resources, lack of immigrant cooperation, erosion of community policing) when local law enforcement takes on the role of "La Migra."

On the other hand, pressures placed on local police to actively participate in immigration enforcement complicate the roles of officers. Because of the controversy surrounding appropriate responses to immigration and the reluctance of municipal officials to create policies, officers are frequently left to carry out their duties without guidance. In other words, *de facto* immigration policies are made based on the individual practices of local police. As a result, officer responses are varied and are a reflection of their own individual values, not based on departmental guidance.

DHS and ICE both have acknowledged that the role served by local police in enforcing immigration enforcement is unclear. Police and sheriff's departments are not consistently told about their responsibilities under Section 287g, or given a clear purpose as to what the amendment was specifically created for, creating unfettered discretion when dealing with suspected undocumented immigrants. Such practices are even unattractive to ICE given its limits on detention space and capacity for carrying out deportations. A lack of clear direction and the focus on non-serious offenders has led to widespread fear in immigrant communities, increased risks of racial profiling, damage to communities through deportation, and an overall inability of local law enforcement to meet the goals of ICE.

A limited body of research to this date has considered the challenges of local police in handling immigrants, both documented and undocumented. Future research should continue to consider the complexities that documented and undocumented immigrants add to community relations and policing practices. Serious consideration needs to be given to the unique experiences of undocumented immigrants apart from documented immigrants. It is recognized that there are inherent difficulties faced by researchers in distinguishing between documented and undocumented immigrants (e.g., fear to come forward, failure of national statistics to report this distinction). However, in order to more thoroughly understand how undocumented immigrants are impacted by changes in policing practices, studies need to consider the unique experiences of each.

Future research should also focus on the impact of nationwide immigration reform since Arizona first introduced Senate Bill 1070. As policy changes in Arizona and states like Alabama, Florida, Georgia, Indiana, and North Carolina have been proposed, the potential for both support and backlash by residents is inevitable. The true impact of policy reforms, from changes in the cooperation of undocumented immigrants with law enforcement to the further devolution of power to local police, is not fully clear. In some states, local police could potentially be *required* to check immigration status if they suspect an individual is undocumented. The manner in which local police would deal with such a policy change is questionable, as some officers may disapprove of a new form of racial profiling and others may see it as an effective tool to provide increasing community safety. Furthermore, it is currently unclear how states would use such newfound power. Both ICE and President Obama have declared that the primary purpose of federal and local law enforcement partnerships is to allow local police to root out serious and violent criminals. Questions remain as to how changing state policies would impact these stated goals.

Finally, a greater focus should be given to the multi-layered, multi-jurisdictional patchwork that emerged as a result of the devolution of immigration enforcement authority from the federal government to local police. Effective policing tactics can frequently conflict with priorities imposed by the federal government, states, and, in some cases, communities. Police responsibilities are further complicated when local governments and police do not have policy or training in this area. Local police who have partnered with federal authorities are then placed in an awkward position where they must carry out the roles and responsibilities of *both* local and federal law enforcement. Tasked with both maintaining strong community relations to achieve public safety and participating in immigration enforcement, local police who have partnered with federal authorities are now burdened by these two competing goals.

NOTES

1. In 2003 DHS absorbed the Immigration and Naturalization Service, which previously was responsible for enforcement of immigration offenses.
2. The terms "Hispanic" and "Latino" are used interchangeably in this essay.
3. Arizona State Senator Russell Pearce was the author of the immigration bill, SB 1070, which initially required local police to check immigration status of suspected undocumented immigrants.

REFERENCES

Alpert, Geoffrey, Roger Dunham, and Michael Smith. 2007. "Investigating Racial Profiling by the Miami-Dade Police Department: A Multimethod Approach." *Criminology and Public Policy* 6(1): 25–56.

Bingham, Theodore. 1908. "Foreign Criminals in New York." *The North American Review* 188(634): 383–94.

Brabeck, Kalina, and Qingwen Xu. 2010. "The Impact of Detention and Deportation on Latino Immigrant Children and Families: A Quantitative Exploration." *Hispanic Journal of Behavioral Sciences* 32(3): 341–61.

Brownell, Peter. 2005. *The Declining Enforcement of Employer Sanctions.* Washington, DC: Migration Policy Institute.

Bucher, Jacob, Michelle Manasse, and Beth Tarasawa. 2010. "Undocumented Victims: An Examination of Crimes Against Undocumented Male Migrant Workers." *Southwest Journal of Criminal Justice* 7(2): 159–79.

Burns, Peter, and James Gimpel. 2000. "Economic Insecurity, Prejudicial Stereotypes, and Public Opinion on Immigration Policy." *Political Science Quarterly* 115(2): 201–25.

Caesar, Stephen. 2011. "Author of Arizona Immigration Law Pearce Loses Recall Fight." *Los Angeles Times*, November 8. http://articles.latimes.com/2011/nov/08/news/la-pn-pearce-arizona-election-20111108.

Carter, David. 1985. "Hispanic Perception of Police Performance: An Empirical Assessment." *Journal of Criminal Justice* 13:487–500.

Correia, Mark. 2010. "Determinants of Attitudes toward Police of Latino Immigrants and Non-Immigrants." *Journal of Criminal Justice* 38:99–107.

Culver, Leigh. 2004. "The Impact of New Immigration Patterns on the Provision of Police Services in Midwestern Communities." *Journal of Criminal Justice* 32:329–44.

Davis, Robert, and Edna Erez. 1998. *Immigrant Populations as Victims: Toward a Multicultural Criminal Justice System.* Washington, DC: National Institute of Justice.

Davis, Robert, Edna Erez, and Nancy Avitabile. 1998. "Immigrants and the Criminal Justice System: An Exploratory Study." *Violence and Victims* 13(1): 21–30.

——. 2001. "Access to Justice for Immigrants Who are Victimized: The Perspectives of Police and Prosecutors." *Criminal Justice Policy Review* 12(3): 183–96.

Decker, Scott, Paul Lewis, Doris Provine, and Monica Varsanyi. 2009. "On the Frontier of Local Law Enforcement: Local Police and Federal Immigration Law." In *Immigration, Crime and Justice*, edited by William F. McDonald. Bingley, 261–276. Bingley, UK: Emerald.

Decker, Scott H., Frank Van Gemert, and David C. Pyrooz. 2009. "Gangs, Migration and Crime: The Changing Landscape in Europe and the USA." *Journal of International Migration and Integration* 10(4): 393–408.

Erez, Edna. 2002. "Migration/Immigration, Domestic Violence and the Justice System." *International Journal of Comparative and Applied Criminal Justice* 26(2): 277–99.

Fausset, Richard. 2011 "Alabama Enacts Anti-Illegal-Immigration Law Described as Nation's Strictest." *Los Angeles Times*, June 10.

Greene, Jack. 2000. "Community Policing in America: Changing the Nature, Structure, and Function of the Police." In *Criminal Justice 2000: Policies, Processes, and Decisions of the Criminal Justice System*, edited by Julie Horney, 299–370. Washington, DC: National Institute of Justice.

Hagan, Jacqueline, Brianna Castro, and Nestor Rodriguez. 2010. "The Effects of U.S. Deportation Policies on Immigrant Families and Communities: Cross-Border Perspectives." *North Carolina Law Review* 88:1799–1823.

Hagan, Jacqueline, Karl Eschbach, and Nestor Rodriguez. 2008. "U.S. Deportation Policy, Family Separation, and Circular Migration." *International Migration Review* 42(1): 64–88.

Hagan, John, Ron Levi, and Ronit Dinovitzer. 2008. "The Symbolic Violence of the Crime-Immigration Nexus: Migrant Mythologies in the Americas." *Criminology and Public Policy* 7:95–112.

Hagan, John, and Alberto Palloni. 1998. "Immigration and Crime in the United States." In *The Immigration Debate: Studies on the Economic, Demographic, and Fiscal Effects of Immigration*, edited by James P. Smith and Barry Ednomston, 367–387. Washington, DC: National Academy Press.

Hagan, Jacqueline, and Scott Phillips. 2008. "Border Blunders: The Unanticipated Human and Economic Costs of the U.S. Approach to Immigration Control, 1986–2007." *Criminology and Public Policy* 7:83–94.

Herbst, Leigh, and Samuel Walker. 2001. "Language Barriers in the Delivery of Police Services: A Study of Police and Hispanic Interactions in a Midwestern City." *Journal of Criminal Justice* 29(4): 329–40.

Hoffmaster, Debra, Gerard Murphy, Shannon McFadden, and Molly Griswold. 2010. *Police and Immigration: How Chiefs are Leading Their Communities through the Challenges.* Washington, DC: Police Executive Research Forum.

Homeland Security Advisory Council. 2011. *Task Force on Secure Communities: Findings and Recommendations*. Washington, DC: U.S. Department of Homeland Security.

International Association of Chiefs of Police. 2005. *Enforcing Immigration Law: The Role of State, Tribal, and Local Law Enforcement*. Alexandria, VA: International Association of Chiefs of Police.

———. 2007. *Police Chiefs Guide to Immigration Issues*. Alexandria, VA: International Association of Chiefs of Police.

Kanstroom, Daniel. 2007. *Deportation Nation: Outsiders in American History*. Cambridge, MA: Harvard University Press.

Lacayo, Elena. 2011. *One Year Later: A Look at SB 1070 and Copycat Legislation*. Washington, DC: National Council of La Raza.

Lopez, Mark, and Michael Light. 2009. *A Rising Share: Hispanics and Federal Crime*. Washington, DC: Pew Research Center, Pew Hispanic Center.

Major Cities Chiefs. 2006. "M.C.C. Immigration Committee Recommendations for Enforcement of Immigration Laws by Local Police Agencies." http://www.houstontx.gov/police/pdfs/mcc_position.pdf.

Martinez, Ramiro. 2007. "Incorporating Latinos and Immigrants into Policing Research." *Criminology and Public Policy* 6(1): 57–64.

———. 2010. "Economic Conditions and Racial/Ethnic Variations in Violence: Immigration, the Latino Paradox, and Future Research." *Criminology and Public Policy* 9(4): 707–13.

Martinez, Ramiro, and Matthew Lee. 2000. "Comparing the Context of Immigrant Homicides in Miami: Haitians, Jamaicans, and Mariels." *International Migration Review* 34(3): 794–812.

Martinez, Ramiro, Jacob Stowell, and Matthew Lee. 2010. "Immigration and Crime in an Era of Transformation: A Longitudinal Analysis of Homicides in San Diego Neighborhoods, 1980–2000." *Criminology* 48(3): 797–829.

Martinez, Ramiro, and Abel Valenzuela. 2006. *Ethnicity, Race, and Violence*. New York: New York University Press.

Menjivar, Cecila, and Cynthia, Bejarano. 2004. "Latino Immigrants' Perceptions of Crime and Police Authorities in the United States: A Case Study." *Ethnic and Racial Studies* 27:120–48.

Morton, John. 2011. "International Association of Chiefs of Police General Assembly." http://www.ice.gov/doclib/news/library/speeches/111028morton.pdf.

Newton, Lina, and Brian Adams. 2009. "State Immigration Policies: Innovation, Cooperation, or Conflict?" *Publius: The Journal of Federalism* 39(3): 408–31.

Nyers, Peter. 2010. "No One Is Illegal between City and Nation." *Studies in Social Justice* 4(2): 127–43.

Olson, Christa, Minna Laurikkala, Lin Huff-Corzine, and Jay Corzine. 2009. "Immigration and Violent Crime: Citizenship Status and Social Disorganization." *Homicide Studies* 13(3): 227–41.

Ong, Marcos, and David Jenks. 2004. "Hispanic Perceptions of Community Policing: Is Community Policing Working in the City?" *Journal of Ethnicity in Criminal Justice* 2(3): 53–66.

Orloff, Leslye E., Mary A. Dutton, Giselle A. Hass, and Nawal Ammar. 2003. "Battered Immigrant Women's Willingness to Call for Help and Police Response." *UCLA Women's Law Journal* 13(43): 43–100.

Passel, Jeffrey, and D'Vera Cohn. 2008. *U.S. Population Projections: 2005–2050*. Washington, DC: Pew Research Center.

Police Executive Research Forum. 2008. *Police Chiefs and Sheriffs Speak Out on Local Immigration Enforcement*. Washington, DC: Police Executive Research Forum.

Reisig, Michael D. 2010. "Community and Problem-Oriented Policing." *Crime and Justice: A Review of Research* 39:1–53.

Reitzel, John, Stephen Rice, and Alex Piquero. 2004. "Lines and Shadows: Perceptions of Racial Profiling and the Hispanic Experience." *Journal of Criminal Justice* 32(6): 607–16.

Romero, Mary. 2006. "Racial Profiling and Immigration Law Enforcement: Rounding Up of Usual Suspects in the Latino Community." *Critical Sociology* 32(2): 447–73.

Sampson, Robert. 2006. "Open Doors Don't Invite Criminals: Is Increased Immigration Behind the Drop in Crime?" *New York Times*, March 11.

Sampson, Robert. 2008. "Rethinking Crime and Immigration." *Contexts* 7:28–33.

Sampson, Robert, and Lydia Bean. 2006. "Cultural Mechanisms and Killing Fields: A Revised Theory of Community-Level Racial Inequality." In *The Many Colors of Crime: Inequalities of Race, Ethnicity and Crime in America*, edited by Ruth Peterson, Lauren Krivo, and John Hagan, 8–38. New York: New York University Press.

Sampson, Robert, Jeffrey Morenoff, and Stephen Raudenbush. 2005. "Social Anatomy of Racial and Ethnic Disparities in Violence." *American Journal of Public Health* 95(2): 224–32.

Shaw, Clifford, and Henry McKay. 1942. *Juvenile Delinquency and Urban Areas.* Chicago: University of Chicago Press.

Skogan, Wesley. 2006. *Police and Community in Chicago: A Tale of Three Cities.* New York: Oxford University Press.

Spiro, Peter J. 1997. "Learning to Live with Immigration Federalism." *Connecticut Law Review* 29:1627–46.

Stana, Richard. 2009. *Immigration Enforcement: Controls over Program Authorizing State and Local Enforcement of Federal Immigration Laws Should be Strengthened* (#GAO-09-381T). Washington, DC: Government Accountability Office.

Stowell, Jacob, Steven Messner, Kelly McGeever, and Lawrence Raffalovich. 2009. "Immigration and the Recent Violent Crime Drop in the United States: A Pooled, Cross-Sectional Time-Series Analysis of Metropolitan Areas." *Criminology* 47:889–928.

Sullivan, Abby. 2008. "On Thin ICE: Cracking Down on the Racial Profiling of Immigrants and Implementing a Compassionate Enforcement Policy." *Hastings Race and Poverty Law Journal* 6:101–45.

Torres, Sam, and Ronald Vogel. 2001. "Pre and Post-Test Differences Between Vietnamese and Latino Residents Involved in a Community Policing Experiment: Reducing Fear of Crime and Improving Attitudes Towards the Police." *Policing: An International Journal of Police Strategies and Management* 24(1): 40–55.

U.S. Census Bureau. 2010. *American Community Survey 2008–2010.* Washington, DC: U.S. Census Bureau.

U.S. Department of Justice. 2009. *Community Policing Defined.* Washington, DC: U.S. Department of Justice, Office of Community Oriented Policing.

U.S. Immigration and Customs Enforcement. 2009. *Secure Communities: A Comprehensive Plan to Identify and Remove Criminal Aliens.* Washington, DC: Department of Homeland Security.

——. 2011a. "Fact Sheet: Delegation of Immigration Authority Section 287g Immigration and Nationality Act." http://www.ice.gov/news/library/factsheets/287g.htm#signed-moa.

——. 2011b. "Activated Jurisdictions." http://www.ice.gov/doclib/secure-communities/pdf/sc-activated.pdf.

Varsanyi, Monica W. 2008 "Rescaling the 'Alien,' Rescaling Personhood: Neoliberalism, Immigration and the State." *Annals of the Association of American Geographers* 98(4): 877–96.

Varsanyi, Monica, Paul Lewis, Marie Provine, and Scott Decker. 2012. "A Multilayered Jurisdictional Patchwork: Immigration Federalism in the United States." Law and Policy 34(2): 138–58.

Vidales, Guadalupe, Kristen Day, and Michael Powe. 2009. "Police and Immigration Enforcement: Impact on Latino(a) Residents' Perceptions of Police." *Policing: An International Journal of Police Strategies and Management* 34(4): 631–53.

Weitzer, Ronald, and Steven Tuch. 2005. "Racially Biased Policing: Determinants of Citizen Perceptions." *Social Forces* 83(3): 1009–30.

Wishnie, Michael. 2004. "State and Local Police Enforcement of Immigration Laws." *Immigration and Nationality Law Review* 25:741–72.

Wu, Yuning. 2010. "Immigrants' Perceptions of the Police." *Sociology Compass* 4(11): 924–35.

PART V

VARIETIES OF POLICE RESEARCH

CHAPTER 19

POLICE ADMINISTRATIVE RECORDS AS SOCIAL SCIENCE DATA

MATTHEW J. HICKMAN

THE present essay considers the use of police administrative records as a form of social science data. In particular, I focus on two somewhat interdependent areas: (1) systematic data collection from police departments (via establishment survey); and (2) the unsystematic ways in which police departments collect data about themselves. I specifically exclude police-generated crime statistics, as there have been several comprehensive studies of those data, their validity and reliability, and utility for social science research (e.g., Maltz 1999).

With regard to systematic data collection, I focus on the most systematic and comprehensive source of administrative data about the police in the United States: the Law Enforcement Management and Administrative Statistics (LEMAS) program, administered by the Bureau of Justice Statistics (BJS), the statistical agency of the U.S. Department of Justice. The LEMAS program has a deep and rich history and has contributed greatly to our macro-level understanding of law enforcement operations in the United States. Yet it is safe to say that LEMAS has not yet been exploited or leveraged to its full utility. LEMAS is also not without its flaws, some of which are very serious and may well lead to its demise if not addressed. In discussing these areas, I hope to shed some light on police administrative records as a form of social science data, through the lens of the LEMAS experience in particular.

With regard to the unsystematic ways in which police departments collect data about themselves, I focus on one particularly important issue for the police in a democracy: data concerning police use of force. Why would I focus on this particular issue? As Fyfe (2002, 99) remarked, "we still live in a society in which the best data on police use of force come to us not from the government or from scholars, but from the *Washington Post.*" Likewise, Kane (2007, 776) noted that "it is both ironic and unacceptable that in American democratic society, the police, which function as the most visible representatives of the crime control bureaucracy, collect data on members of the public in the form of arrest and complaint reports without systematically distributing comprehensive data on their own activities that produced those crime statistics."

This essay is organized in five sections. Section 19.1 reviews a variety of systematic data collections focused on police administrative data, paying particular attention to the genesis of the LEMAS program so that one can appreciate the need for attention and fidelity to its foundational goals. Section 19.2 tackles the problem of determining the scope of national law enforcement data collections, some of the realities of managing various "data constituencies," and discusses a recent National Academy of Sciences (NAS) review of BJS's law enforcement data collections. Section 19.3 deals with issues of validity and reliability in police administrative records collection. In Section 19.4, the essay turns to unsystematic data collection about the use of force. Finally, Section 19.5 offers some discussion of the future of LEMAS and related administrative data collections, as well as some key areas for potential improvement.

A number of conclusions can be drawn:

- Despite multiple efforts to refine the purposes of the LEMAS survey program, it continues to exist without a well-defined scope and is therefore subject to influences of different interest groups.
- The limitations of LEMAS notwithstanding, the survey remains the most systematic and comprehensive data collection program for obtaining information on police department administrative and management functions/activities.
- Given the unsystematic nature of use of force reporting, the field knows very little about the prevalence of use of force, let alone factors that might explain it.
- Many U.S. police departments still collect use of force information via hardcopy records as opposed to using automated record keeping systems. As a result, most of what we know about the use of force in U.S. police departments comes from studies of individual agencies, which measure use of force differently and produce a very large prevalence range.
- To develop the capacity to use police records as social science data, police departments should implement a standardized automated data collection system that can support the systematic data collection goals of validation, timeliness, core-supplement design, standardization, and context to ensure reliability and validity of the information.

19.1 SYSTEMATIC DATA COLLECTION

The LEMAS program owes intellectual debt to a variety of earlier efforts to capture police administrative records on a systematic basis. Most worthy of note are the efforts of the International City/County Management Association (ICMA), the Kansas City

Police Department (KCPD) in conjunction with the Police Foundation and the Police Executive Research Forum (PERF), the Division of Governmental Studies and Services (DGSS) at Washington State University, and preliminary work for BJS by the Institute of Criminal Justice and Criminology at the University of Maryland.

The ICMA began collecting data in the 1930s for its *Municipal Yearbook*, which reports information drawn from a variety of surveys (Uchida, Bridgeforth, and Wellford 1984; Langworthy 2002; Maguire 2002). The most recent ICMA data available are for 2009, pertaining to police and fire personnel, salaries, and expenditures. Unfortunately, the response rates are fairly low and seem to have been in a steady decline over the past couple of decades (see Maguire 2002). The 2009 data were collected from 1,263 of 3,279 municipalities with populations of 10,000 or greater (a 38.5 percent response rate). While the ICMA data have the longest history (perhaps on par with the Uniform Crime Reports) they are fairly limited in scope and do not really permit much in the way of meaningful analysis about police organizations or operations.

From 1951 to the early 1970s, the Kansas City Police Department (KCPD) conducted its *General Administrative Survey of Police Practices*, targeted at large police departments (Uchida, Bridgeforth, and Wellford 1984). The series was discontinued in 1973 due to lack of funding, but re-initiated with assistance from the Police Foundation in early 1977, and with additional data collection by PERF in late 1977 as the *Survey of Police Operational and Administrative Practices*. The Police Foundation and PERF jointly repeated the survey in 1981 (Uchida, Bridgeforth, and Wellford 1984). The survey collected data on a broad range of administrative measures, including salaries, benefits, uniforms, sidearms, vehicles, calls for service, firearm discharges, and other topics. The data were used in at least one analysis of large agency organizational characteristics (Langworthy 1986), and summary reports were issued by both the Police Foundation and PERF.

The Division of Governmental Studies and Services (DGSS) at Washington State University conducted national surveys of police departments every three years from 1978 to 2003 (see Maguire 2002). This data series collected a broad range of information about police agency characteristics, including a variety of policies and practices and emerging issues such as the adoption of new technology. The sample of approximately 300 agencies remained stable over the course of the series. However, the program was discontinued due in part to a lack of graduate students who wanted to work on the data collection, as well as declining response rates in more recent iterations (Zhao, personal communication). But the data series generated a substantial amount of important research on police organizations (e.g., Zhao 1996).

In 1983, BJS awarded a grant to the University of Maryland for the purpose of reviewing law enforcement data collections of the past and present, the quality of the data, and perhaps most important, the utility of the data to the police, research, and policy making communities. In order to address the latter task, two user surveys were conducted: A survey of 152 large police departments, and telephone interviews of police, researchers, and policy makers. The survey yielded a useful catalog of the availability and desirability of various input, process, and output data items among the surveyed police departments. The interviews pointed to an interesting difference in the perceived utility of data items for the police, as compared to academics and policy makers.

Police rated the following as the highest utility data items:

- calls for service
- salary by department
- salary by rank
- availability of incentive pay for education
- information on promotion

In contrast, *academics* and *policy makers* indicated an interest in:

- deadly force
- officer characteristics
- arrests and offenses
- spatial indicators
- cities as units of analysis
- personnel figures
- victimization and self-reported crime

The final report, *Law Enforcement Statistics: The State of the Art* (Ucihda, Bridgeforth, and Wellford 1984), concluded that existing data collection efforts were "inconsistent at best and non-existent at worst" (75) and recommended that BJS continue to develop a national-level data collection. The report additionally recommended a series of eight steps toward this goal: setting priorities for specific data elements; establishing uniform definitions and classifications; determining appropriate data collection instruments (suggesting a long-form every three years and a short-form used in the in-between years); research into efficient sampling strategies; a focus on the timeliness of the data; feedback mechanisms within the instrument; extensive pre-testing; and the launch of a national-level data collection.

The basic structure that emerged included two parts: (1) a Census of State and Local Law Enforcement Agencies (CSLLEA) to be conducted roughly every four years, and to serve to collect a limited and essential core set of measures regarding police agencies as well as to provide an accurate sampling frame for (2) a more detailed Sample Survey of Law Enforcement Agencies (SSLEA) conducted in years in between the census years. Also under the LEMAS umbrella are special data collections focused on campus law enforcement agencies, law enforcement training academies, and other law enforcement entities. Historically, the LEMAS data were collected for BJS by the U.S. Census Bureau. While the Census Bureau and its procedures delivered high response rates, they came with an ever-increasing cost that ultimately led BJS to open the data collection contract to private competition. The LEMAS sample survey data collection was awarded to PERF, and the agency census was awarded to the National Opinion Research Center, both of which were able to match or exceed Census Bureau performance at lower cost.

Finally, it is important to mention a more recent systematic effort that was funded by the National Institute of Justice in 2009. The *National Police Research Platform* seeks to collect information about individual officers as well as police organizations, and is intended to provide timely data of importance to both practitioners and researchers that is not presently available via LEMAS or other data collection efforts. The project is directed by Dennis Rosenbaum at the University of Illinois–Chicago, and includes a consortium of policing scholars at other universities. The project was designed with two phases: Phase 1 (2009–2011) was designated as a testing phase with a limited number of agencies from across the country; and Phase 2 (2012–2014) is to focus on a larger, national sample of agencies. The scope of data collection to date has included organizational surveys, community-based studies of police performance, and longitudinal studies of supervisors and new officers. These efforts are detailed in overview reports describing major data collection initiatives, and topical reports on police stress, innovation, training, supervision, job satisfaction, and integrity and discipline. The success of the platform's national data collection efforts remains to be seen, but the evidence from the smaller methodological studies is quite promising.

19.2 Determing Scope

As an omnibus survey, LEMAS has been perhaps unfairly criticized for its broad scope. Part of the problem is that the core purpose of LEMAS (description, explanation, evaluation, or all of the above) has not been articulated. In general, these larger purposes structure the methodology and define the types of data to be collected. The LEMAS data series provides longitudinal information on everything from the agency's core functions and policies, to the caliber of sidearm authorized, to the number of horses and dogs maintained, if any. While some may question the value of such detailed or specific data, one must keep in mind that there was an advocate for each and every item included on the questionnaire at some point in the history of the program. Horses, for example, have numerous benefits to law enforcement in terms of relations with the public, access to difficult parts of a city, and crowd control. They may also be part of a broader strategy or approach to policing in urban environments. But horses are also somewhat expensive to maintain and difficult to justify in tight budget climates. LEMAS provides the information necessary to approach these types of resource questions rationally, so that departments can make informed decisions based on what other similarly sized departments are reporting.

In addition, due to the fact that LEMAS is a government funded research endeavor, BJS receives continuous input from various data constituencies, such as the International Association of Chiefs of Police, National Sheriffs Association, and the like. This input is of great value, especially in rapidly changing areas of law enforcement such as technology and equipment. But there are also more "special interest" data constituencies, such as groups or organizations representing mounted horse patrol units, law enforcement aviation concerns, or those concerned with police abuse, all of whom can be very effective at lobbying BJS for additional or broadened data collection. Despite claims of total objectivity, the influence of data constituencies can be seen throughout all government data collections, for better or for worse.

The current scope of LEMAS is a reflection of the groundwork laid by Uchida, Bridgeforth, and Wellford (1984), with enhancements over time due to changes in policing theory and practice, technological developments, and the wants and needs of various data constituencies. BJS staff members are also generally experts in their areas of assignment, and regularly read the literature, attend professional conferences, and liaise with relevant agencies to ensure they stay on top of the latest research findings, directions, and issues. Part of their job is not only to maintain current data collections, but to determine where gaps in data coverage exist and to try to design new studies or enhancements to existing studies to address those gaps. In this vein, LEMAS also serves a purpose as a platform for methodological research and development.

As an example, in my previous career at BJS I became interested in different possible methods for collecting national data on police use of force, as required of DOJ by 42 U.S.C. 14142. I was motivated by the dearth of national data but more so by Fyfe's (2002) paper on the lack of data on the use of deadly force, which led me to informally consult with him on a number of occasions. In the course of our conversations it became clear that one less-than-perfect, but viable, option was to harness the LEMAS survey. After extensive discussions with Fyfe and other policing scholars, items were incorporated into the LEMAS survey instrument to collect departmental data on citizen complaints about police use of force (Hickman 2006). These data were collected from large agencies as a type of pilot study that, if successful, might lead to broader collection efforts (for example, the collection of available demographic information about complainants). It was also viewed as a necessary exploratory step toward the eventual long-term goal of collecting administrative records of use of force incidents on a national scale. This initial effort was indeed successful, providing evidence that police departments were in fact willing and able to provide this type of "sensitive" information to the Federal government, with some caveats regarding data quality. Additional development is necessary to establish the validity and reliability of these data. But you have to start somewhere; one can only conduct studies on paper for so long before one stops making progress. Eventually, you just have to try it out and see what you get.

Yet the prevailing wisdom at the time was that LEMAS was becoming too broad and needed some "trimming" as opposed to any expansion. There has always been a kind of hydraulic effect with the LEMAS instrument—if a new item is coming in, something else is going out—but additional pressure to reduce the overall size of the collection was brought to bear beginning with the 2007 LEMAS. It was again time to return to the scope question. In addition to re-visiting the foundational Uchida, Bridgeforth, and Wellford (1984) piece, one source of guidance was the Governmental Accounting Standards Board (GASB). The GASB identified several service efforts and accomplishments (SEA) indicators for law enforcement agencies (Drebin and Brannon 1992) that may assist in focusing police administrative data collection efforts. While not comprehensive, the recommended indicators are helpfully grouped by *inputs* (measures of service efforts), *outputs* (the quantity of services delivered), *outcomes* (degree to which objectives have been met), *efficiency* (ratios of outputs and outcomes to inputs), and *explanatory* variables (information relating to demand for police services and workload). Certainly every data item in LEMAS should be able to address one of these five areas; if not, then legitimate questions might be raised about its inclusion in the data collection. Table 19.1,

Table 19.1 Police Department SEA Indicators

Indicator	Rationale for Selecting Indicator
Inputs:	*To provide a measure of...*
Budget expenditures	... financial resources used to provide services
Equipment, facilities, vehicles	... non-personnel resources used to provide services
Number of personnel; hours expended	... the size of the organization and the human resources used to provide services
Outputs:	*To provide a measure of...*
Hours of patrol	... the quantity of patrol service provided
Responses to calls for service	... the quantity of response service provided
Crimes investigated	... the quantity of services provided by investigation units
Number of arrests	... the success of police efforts in apprehending criminal offenders
Outcomes:	*To provide a measure of...*
Deaths and injuries resulting from crime	... the effectiveness of police efforts in reducing the incidence of personal harm attributed to criminal activity
Value of property lost due to crime	... the effectiveness of police efforts in reducing the incidence or property loss due to criminal activity
Crimes committed per 100,000 population	... the effectiveness of police efforts in reducing criminal activity
Percentage of crimes cleared	... the effectiveness of police efforts in detection of criminal activity and apprehension of criminal offenders
Response time	... the quality of police response to calls
Citizen satisfaction	... the overall effectiveness of police efforts in meeting citizen needs
Efficiency:	*To provide an indication of...*
Cost per case assigned; cost per crime cleared	... the cost efficiency of police efforts
Personnel hours per crime cleared	... the productivity of personnel in providing police services
Explanatory variables:	*To provide information on...*
Population by age group, unemployment rate, number of households and businesses, land area, dollar value of property within jurisdiction, calls for service, cases assigned	... factors that are likely to affect the incidence and effects of criminal activity so that measures of output, outcome, and efficiency may be viewed in proper context

Source: Adapted from Drebin and Brannon (1992)

adapted from the GASB study, lists some examples of these types of indicators, and provides basic guidance for police administrative data collection.

In 2009, the National Academy of Sciences released its report on the data collection programs of the Bureau of Justice Statistics: *Ensuring the Quality, Credibility, and Relevance of U.S. Justice Statistics* (Groves and Cork 2009). In discussing BJS's law enforcement data collections, the reviewing panel noted that

> BJS's work in *law enforcement* is hindered by a sharp and overly restrictive focus on management and administrative issues; its analysis of law enforcement generally lacks direct connection to data on crime, much less providing the basis for assessing the quality and effectiveness of police programs. It is also in the area of law enforcement, with the proliferation of numerous special-agency censuses and little semblance of a fixed schedule or interconnectedness of series, where the need for refining the conceptual framework for multiple data collections is most evident. (133)

The NAS panel recommended that LEMAS should be reconceived as a core-supplement design, not unlike the National Crime Victimization Survey (NCVS). On the issue of a connection to crime or the quality and effectiveness of police programs, the problem is that these essentially research and development roles—which speak on some level to the utility of the data—cannot be fully realized due to lingering (and legitimate) concerns about the validity and reliability of the core methodology and the resulting data.

19.3 CONFRONTING ISSUES OF VALIDITY AND RELIABILITY

One of the major concerns about the LEMAS program is that BJS invests very little in validation research. There are data quality checks in place to ensure that survey responses are internally consistent, and substantial differences in quantitative data from previous iterations (among large agencies) are manually checked. Yet these checks are no match for true validation studies that assess the degree to which the data reported by agencies in LEMAS reflects reality.

For example, Walker and Katz (1995) conducted an exploratory study of bias crime units in sixteen municipal police departments in the central region of the United States (including ten states, with agencies as large as Chicago, Illinois, and as small as Boulder, Colorado). These sixteen agencies were selected in part because they had reported having a bias crime unit on the 1990 LEMAS survey. Walker and Katz conducted telephone interviews with the officers in charge of the bias crime units in those agencies. However, they found that only four of these agencies actually had such a unit, six other agencies had designated officers in other units to handle the bias crime function as needed, and the remainder had no unit, designated officers, or special procedures for bias crimes.

Some have raised concerns about the basic agency and employee counts (Maguire et al. 1998; Uchida and King 2002). Maguire et al. (1998), for example, noted discrepancies between the number of agencies and officers enumerated across the UCR, LEMAS, and data collected by the Office of Community-Oriented Policing Services, suggesting that LEMAS substantially undercounted agencies and officers in the mid-1990s.

Langworthy (2002) raised concerns about the reliability of data items pertaining to the number of patrol beats (asked in three different formats and four different instructions over four waves of surveys; these items have since been discarded as unreliable), as well as low item response rates for calls for service data (response rates too low to impute missing values reliably; subsequently not collected). The number of patrol beats in a jurisdiction speaks to spatial decentralization and police presence, while the total number of calls for service is a useful contextual variable for making comparisons of output, outcomes, and efficiency across departments.

The consistency of items and the influence of data constituencies is a major concern. One particularly gruesome example of this is with regard to measuring the number of community policing officers in the United States. The COPS office provided financial support for a special off-year iteration of the LEMAS survey (in 1999). In the 1997 LEMAS, a question concerning community policing officers read: "Of the total number of FULL-TIME sworn personnel working in field operations (2b(1) above), enter the number of uniformed officers whose regularly assigned duties included serving as a Community Policing Officer." For the 1999 LEMAS, the question was re-worded by the COPS office as follows: "As of June 30, 1999 enter the number of full-time sworn personnel serving as Community Policing Officers, Community Resource Officers, Community Relations Officers or others regularly engaged in community policing activities." Big surprise that a comparison of the two years revealed a dramatic increase in the number of officers so designated: from 21,000 in 1997 to 113,000 in 1999. Quite a change in just two years! BJS reported the findings in a publication titled, "Community Policing in Local Police Departments, 1997 and 1999" (Hickman and Reaves 2001) and included a methodological note that clearly stated the differences in the questionnaire items. But it is plainly clear that a comparison of the number of community policing officers in the two years is not meaningful.

LEMAS of course suffers from the common problems of self-administered questionnaires (such as memory, socially desirable responding, fatigue, indifference) but also those relatively unique to establishment surveys, such as inadequate record keeping or the "force fitting" of agency records to match the criteria of survey items, and error attributable to an individual's response to less quantitative items on behalf of the organization. On the front-end of the process, BJS invests in pre-testing of instrumentation, generally combined with focus groups comprised of law enforcement representatives or something of the like. PERF was especially helpful in this regard when that organization was collecting LEMAS data for BJS, ensuring that the providers (and in many cases, end users) of the data understood and could provide the data being requested and weigh in on the utility of the data. On the tail-end of the process, a random sub-sample of agencies selected for intense verification would yield a bona fide quality estimate. But BJS has largely relied on the research community for assessments of validity and reliability. BJS both learns from and responds to this research. For example, in direct response to Walker and Katz (1995), BJS modified LEMAS survey items concerning special units to incorporate expanded response options that did not force an agency into an "either-or" situation. Whether this is the most efficient means of accomplishing the larger goal is another question.

19.4 UNSYSTEMATIC DATA COLLECTION: POLICE USE OF FORCE

What do we know about the nature and extent of police use of force in the United States, and how do we know it? In a recent review of the literature conducted as part of an effort to construct an improved national estimate of police use of nonlethal force (Hickman, Piquero, and Garner 2008), we found that the majority of studies producing an incident-based rate of police use of force were based on data from a single jurisdiction, and the methods were quite diverse (including arrest reports, household surveys, independent observations, police surveys, suspect surveys, and official use of force forms), as were the units of analysis (arrests, contacts, citizen encounters, disputes, police stops, potentially violent mobilizations, suspect encounters, and calls for service). Somewhat unsurprisingly, across 36 studies reporting on the amount of nonlethal force used by the police, rates varied from about a tenth of 1 percent up to almost 32 percent (see Figure 19.1).

Is it any wonder, given the diversity of methods, units of analysis, and inherent instability of single agency foci, that the reported rates of police use of force range from roughly 1/1,000 to almost 1/3? While recognizing the value of different methodological approaches, Engel (2008) succinctly summarized the key issues that we can all agree upon: (1) scholars have failed to adequately conceptualize and measure police use of force; (2) it is a statistically infrequent event; (3) we know even less about excessive force, which is perhaps the most important aspect of police use of force; and (4) current approaches to understanding force on a national level are not achieving those goals, if precision is a worthwhile goal (e.g., see Klinger 2008; Smith 2008).

Perhaps more interesting for present purposes is the fact that only 8 of the 36 studies referred to above relied upon police-generated administrative data, in the form of official use-of-force reporting forms. Within this group of studies, use-of-force rates based upon arrests ranged from 0.9 percent to 18.0 percent of arrests (the highest figure was based on a definition of force that included handcuffing). Why only 8 studies using official use-of-force reporting forms? There are several issues, but the three most significant categories are: access, automation, and quality (where quality refers to the comprehensiveness of the data, accuracy of the data, and the extent to which useful data are being collected that actually speak to the key questions).

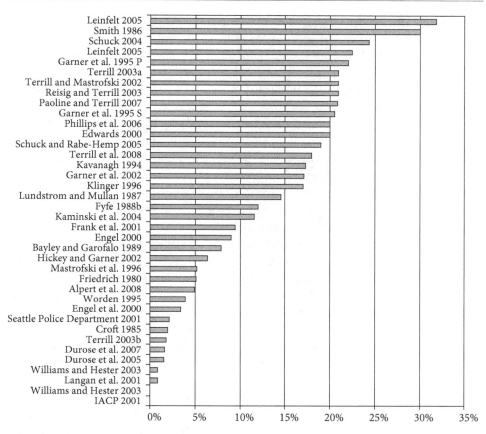

FIGURE 19.1 Reported rates of physical force in 36 studies

Note: P = Police Surveys; S = Suspect Interviews

Source: Adapted from Hickman et al. (2008)

Access to use-of-force data has been a long-running issue for social scientists. For a variety of legal (fear of lawsuits), administrative (inability to produce records), and political (desire not to make the city look bad) reasons, police agencies are often unable or unwilling to provide researchers with even the most basic data. Trust is a significant concern. To some extent, this is a warranted concern on the part of police departments due to enthusiastic and often self-serving researchers who prefer to obtain the data and uncritically analyze it without the benefit of interactions with departments. Understandably, the police executive would prefer to learn about use-of-force research from the researcher, and have an opportunity to comment (frequently pointing out misinterpretations, inaccuracies, or outright errors in the researcher's methods and/or analysis), as opposed to finding out the results from the front page of the local newspaper. One can generally obtain records through public disclosure requests, but it is a lot easier to forge relationships, find common research interests, and work with the department rather than against it, even if the latter is purely perceptual on the part of the department. The current trend in policing, with motivation from the DOJ Civil Rights Division, seems to be toward an understanding of the importance of transparency in democratic policing. However, this does not guarantee that the data will be in optimal format, or have the necessary content in order to answer a particular question.

Automation is a strange issue to discuss in an era of hand-held computing devices that can outperform the tasks once marginally performed by mainframe computing environments occupying hundreds of square feet and requiring a maintenance staff to change-out vacuum tubes. It was not that long ago. At any rate, I was surprised to discover that my own local police department, the Seattle Police Department, did not as of this writing have automated records concerning officer use of force. For sure, officers complete an electronic form with standard data-entry fields and blocks for signatures, but the data are not presently captured in a database that would permit analysis. The automated form is simply printed, routed for review and signatures, and physically filed. It should be noted that, as of this writing, the City of Seattle has agreed to the terms of a federal memorandum of understanding and letter of agreement resulting from a recent DOJ "pattern or practice" investigation of the Seattle PD. One good thing to come of this process is that the Seattle PD is presently, of its own accord, designing an automated database for use of force reporting.

What are the barriers to automation? One commonly cited barrier is cost, both in terms of the financial cost of automation, as well as the resource costs of maintaining such a database. The latter aspect is the most often ignored; in my experience I have encountered many automated reporting systems that have been left to gather dust for several years with no human "owner" of the data to ensure that the system is actually being used as designed. Legal concerns are another commonly cited barrier. This can be a very real barrier, since city attorneys will typically want the last word on any type of systematic data collection regarding officer use of force. They are operating from a legal framework and they are obviously concerned about the city's potential exposure. Kane (2007) does a good job, I think, of explaining why it is probably better to collect the data than not, since his experience with use-of-force litigation has revealed that the data tend to exonerate agencies more often than condemn them. Litigation often exposes the appearance of poor or misguided record keeping, and the data obtained through litigation are always less than desirable and rarely adequate to answer the questions at issue. Finally, police unions can be a barrier only to the extent that they are not included in the process of automation. Rest assured that just springing a new automated use of force reporting system on the rank-and-file without involving the union will result in disaster. But if the union is allowed to participate in the process in a real sense, so that the interests of the rank-and-file can be represented, a successful automation process is more likely.

Data quality is another reason why we see fewer use-of-force studies relying on official records. Here, I am referring specifically to the comprehensiveness of the data (i.e., whether use-of-force reports are being filed consistently and without street-level filtration), the accuracy of the data, and the extent to which the data that are being collected are actually useful for answering questions about use of force. This latter category is a big problem with racial profiling research, wherein agencies have simply presumed that if they collect race data it will be adequate for answering the racial profiling question (see Smith 2008). It is perhaps the most significant data quality problem. What data should be collected and why? This is where researchers can be most helpful. As an example, here in Seattle, I have informally consulted with the department to help identify what types of data should be collected in order to position themselves so that they can provide timely answers to questions about how often force is used, where, by whom, upon whom, with what degree and level of resistance, and in the context of *Graham* factors.[1] They can analyze these data for internal purposes in order to understand emerging problems and tailor their responses, as well as for public reporting purposes. Time will tell if they are successful in implementing such a scheme. Now we just need all other agencies to do it as well.

19.5 THE FUTURE OF POLICE ADMINISTRATIVE DATA

There are five areas of improvement that should be prioritized for systematic police administrative data collections, and by extension, unsystematic data collection at the agency level: validation, timeliness, core-supplement design (for systematic data collections only), standardization, and context. The first is to seriously invest in validation studies. There is not much point in moving forward if we are not very certain about where we stand. Self-administered establishment questionnaires have inherent limitations that deserve serious attention. This does not mean we have to be concerned with new or alternative methodologies (all methodologies have limitations); rather, we need to do the job of documenting and addressing these inherent limitations. BJS is very careful to report standard errors and other indicators of precision in estimation, but these are of course contingent on a comprehensive understanding of the quality of measurement. It would not be prohibitively expensive to conduct routine validation studies, and these should be incorporated into the overall data collection program. Likewise, at the agency level, validity checks in the form of routine audits would be beneficial and consistent with a democratic model of policing.

A second issue is to address the timeliness of the data. To be sure, it is no small task to execute national-level data collections, but the fact that the 2007 LEMAS data were released in December 2010, roughly three years after the reference period, is simply unacceptable to everyone (including BJS). Yet only BJS can answer questions about these delays and their sources, as most of it is internal to the organization and most of it is post-data collection. Whether the delays are in the analysis, report writing, or publication processes, they need to be identified and remedied if these data collections are to maintain their relevance. Rosenbaum's *National Police Research Platform* may well take over as the premier source of national-level police administrative data, if only because it seems to be able to get a report out in a timely fashion. Likewise, at the agency level, the public is not likely to accept data that is greater than one year old.

Third, a core-supplement platform (as suggested by the NAS panel) may help to achieve the goals of timeliness and high data quality for systematic data collection. This could take the form of a core of critical data elements such as those collected in the agency census (or perhaps focused on the management and administrative issues the NAS panel seemed to lament), with scheduled rotating supplements addressing special topics. This format would also provide for the flexibility to field items on rapidly changing or emerging topics, as well as to conduct methodological research and development. Enhanced electronic response options would greatly facilitate this type of framework. There is nothing more frustrating than fielding an instrument and discovering shortly thereafter that something has changed to the degree that the data you are about to collect will be obsolete by the time they arrive.

A fourth area of improvement is to seek and incentivize the standardization of record keeping across departments. BJS can effectively lead such an effort. When asked about why they respond to the survey, LEMAS respondents would often remark that they actually appreciated going through the process of collecting the data from their records because it helps them to organize their records as well as to prepare their own reports (for example, annual reports to the public or to municipal administrators). Some degree of standardization already exists for many types of data elements, but it is also important to lead the charge in other areas where departments may not be actively or effectively keeping and reporting records. As an example, one area in particular—data on the use of deadly force by the police—cries for leadership in standardization of record keeping and systematic reporting. This is an example of an absolutely essential data element for democratic policing.

Finally, I believe one of the most important areas for future work is to recognize that there are very compelling arguments to invest in the development and understanding of the geo-spatial context of policing. For example, the geographic component of LEMAS has not been fully exploited. There is a mechanical benefit in that geo-locating police administrative data would make it unnecessary to develop the onerous and quickly outdated "crosswalk" files in which BJS presently invests. Instead, all of the data could be tied to geography, which would greatly facilitate meaningful data merges with census and UCR data. If we want to get the biggest bang for the taxpayer dollar, LEMAS could be significantly leveraged by focusing on the geo-spatial context of policing in the United States. At the agency level, investing in Geographic Information System (GIS) data architecture has tremendous up-front costs that pay off over time, especially to the extent that the design and costs can be shared with other municipal and state entities.

Much can (and has) been learned from studies of police administrative data. However, there is an old adage in the research industry that "What you get depends on what you ask, who you ask, and how you ask it." The single most pressing need is to develop a research agenda around the validity and reliability of police administrative data so that we can move forward from a rational basis. It makes no sense to try and build knowledge about policing absent this foundation. This could, in turn, provide the leadership necessary to move individual departments toward more systematic data collection about themselves. Achieving consensus around a core set of critical, concrete police data elements for the nation, reserving a capacity to adapt to changes in the field and new research evidence, and being flexible with the need to accommodate supplemental data elements as well as methodological research and development would (surprisingly) not require any additional resources, and I cannot formulate a single argument against it.

Note

1. In Graham v. Connor, 490 U.S. 286 (1989), the Supreme Court distilled excessive force in the form of a three-prong test to be judged from the perspective of a reasonable officer at the scene with the information available to the officer at the time of action, and without the benefit of hindsight: the severity of the underlying offense, the immediate threat posed to officers and/or the public, and fleeing or active resistance to arrest. In assessing the "totality of circumstances," relevant issues may include the perception of suspect impairments, psychological threats, outnumbering of officers by suspects, physical size, and other considerations. Collectively, these are often referred to as Graham factors.

References

Drebin, Allan, and Marguerite Brannon. 1992. *Police Department Programs*. GASB Research Report GR 17. Norwalk, CT: Governmental Accounting Standards Board.

Engel, Robin. 2008. "Revisiting Critical Issues in Police Use-of-Force Research." *Criminology and Public Policy* 7:557–61.

Fyfe, James. 2002. "Too Many Missing Cases: Holes in Our Knowledge about Police Use of Force." *Justice Research and Policy* 4:87–102.

Groves, Robert, and Daniel Cork. 2009. *Ensuring the Quality, Credibility, and Relevance of U.S. Justice Statistics*. Washington, DC: National Academy of Sciences.

Hickman, Matthew. 2006. *Citizen Complaints about Police Use of Force*. Washington, DC: Bureau of Justice Statistics.

Hickman, Matthew, Alex Piquero, and Joel Garner. 2008. "Toward a National Estimate of Police Use of Nonlethal Force." *Criminology and Public Policy* 7:563–604.

Hickman, Matthew, and Brian Reaves. 2001. *Community Policing in Local Police Departments, 1997 and 1999*. Washington, DC: Bureau of Justice Statistics.

Kane, Robert. 2007. "Collect and Release Data on Coercive Police Actions." *Criminology and Public Policy* 6:773–80.

Klinger, David. 2008. "On the Importance of Sound Measures of Forceful Police Actions." *Criminology and Public Policy* 7:605–17.

Langworthy, Robert. 1986. *The Structure of Police Organizations*. New York: Praeger.

———. 2002. "LEMAS: A Comparative Organizational Research Platform." *Justice Research and Policy* 4:21–38.

Maguire, Edward. 2002. "Multiwave Establishment Surveys of Police Organizations." *Justice Research and Policy* 4:39–59.

Maguire, Edward, Jeffrey Snipes, Craig Uchida, and Margaret Townsend. 1998. "Counting Cops: Estimating the Number of Police Departments and Police Officers in the United States.: *Policing* 21:97–120.

Maltz, Michael. 1999. *Bridging Gaps in Police Crime Data*. Washington, DC: Bureau of Justice Statistics.

Smith, Michael. 2008. "Toward a National Use-of-Force Data Collection System: One Small (and Focused) Step is Better than a Giant Leap. *Criminology and Public Policy* 7:619–27.

Uchida, Craig, Carol Bridgeforth, and Charles Wellford. 1984. *Law Enforcement Statistics: The State of the Art*. College Park, MD: Institute of Criminal Justice and Criminology, University of Maryland.

Uchida, Craig, and William King. 2002. "Police Employee Data: Elements and Validity." *Justice Research and Policy* 4:11–19.

Walker, Samuel and Charles Katz. 1995. "Less than Meets the Eye: Police Department Bias-Crime Units." *American Journal of Police* 14:29–48.

Zhao, Jihong. 1996. *Why Police Organizations Change: A Study of Community-Oriented Policing*. Washington, DC: Police Executive Research Forum.

CHAPTER 20

....

USING COMMUNITY SURVEYS
TO STUDY POLICING

....

WESLEY G. SKOGAN

SURVEYS of the community have become a key police research tool. Police form the "front line" of the criminal justice system. During the course of the day they primarily interface with the general public rather than with hard-core offenders or other system professionals, and they draw more attention from voters and taxpayers than any other aspect of local government. Some of what they do and many of the consequences of their actions are best examined from the point of view of the public rather than via agencies' internal records, and these issues shape the content of police-community surveys.

A few early studies established topics which remain a staple of survey research on the police. The first major national study of the police-public interface was conducted for the Presidential Crime Commission in 1966, and Richard Block (1974) used this survey to examine decisions by crime victims to report their experiences to the police. The possibility that changes in victim reporting rather than true changes in its volume produce spikes in crime that influence public opinion and policy has kept this topic on the research agenda ever since. Charles Bahn's (1974) influential dissection of what he dubbed "the reassurance factor" in policing argued that visible patrolling signals the strength of authoritative control in an area and increases citizens' confidence that they will be protected as they navigate through public space. Ever since, questions such as whether this reassurance is best provided by officers on foot rather than by motorized patrols have been addressed using police-community surveys. Smith and Hawkins (1973) were the first to report on the impact of fear of crime on views of the police, and the relationship between the quality of service rendered to victims and their global satisfaction with the police. As the section below on police encounters with the public illustrates, this is today one of the most active topics on the police research agenda. Herbert Jacob (1971) showed readers the world of policing through the lens of race, a perspective that has had as much staying power as any in the policing field (see, for example, Weitzer and Tuch 2006). Finally, David Bordua and Larry Tifft (1971) pioneered thinking about the routine use of surveys by police departments themselves in order to gather "customer feedback," rather than just using them to provide an outsider's one-time peek into the world of police-community relations. Monitoring trust and confidence in the police remains the rationale for many local survey projects because the views of voters and taxpayers matter.

Section 20.1 of this essay reviews briefly the purposes of police-community surveys, which include assessing public concerns, monitoring the routine delivery of police services, evaluating innovative programs, and deepening our understanding of the relationship between police and the community in democratic societies. Section 20.2 then addresses the substance of the surveys. This section reviews the key concepts that have been examined using police-community surveys, how they have been measured, and some of what the surveys have found. Section 20.3 discusses selected methodological issues that need to be considered when planning a survey. These include how respondents will be selected and interviews conducted, the size of the survey samples that are required, and whether cross-sectional or longitudinal surveys are more appropriate for the task at hand. Section 20.4 concludes with a few practical recommendations for addressing the key issues raised in the essay.

Several observations and conclusions emerge from this review:

- Research suggests that there is a long list of potential benefits for the police where they are seen as effective and legitimate, and a great deal of new research is focusing on how they can build that support.
- Surveys are an effective tool for monitoring the quality of police-citizen contacts. This is particularly appropriate when crime victims' experiences are in question, because they are one of the core customers of the police. However, there are methodological problems in identifying crime victims that need to be considered carefully. A full-fledged victimization survey is probably beyond the range of most police-community research efforts.
- Many of the most important determinants of people's views of the police and fear of crime are not strongly influenced by what the police do. Negative contacts do have a great deal on influence on global attitudes toward police, but positive ones do not have much of an effect. Perceptions of neighborhood conditions have a much stronger influence on both fear and ratings of police effectiveness.
- Neighborhood-oriented policing calls for opening new channels of communication between police and the public, but many in the community may not get this message, and fewer still will actually get involved with them. Ironically, research indicates that those who do get involved may be the least likely to actually need better communication, and the most likely to already be satisfied with the service they are receiving.
- The issue of how respondents can be selected and interviews conducted is perhaps the biggest hurdle to conducting a quality police-community survey; the collapse of traditional survey methodologies near the end of the twentieth century presents daunting challenges to the twenty-first-century police researcher.

20.1 The Uses and Users of Police-Community Surveys

Police-community surveys can be used by planners and practitioners to identify public concerns and to monitor the quality of service that their organizations are delivering. When new programs are developed, surveys can be among the tools that can be used to monitor their implementation and evaluate their effectiveness.

Public satisfaction surveys are conducted by police departments across the United States, most on an occasional basis. The latest national survey of agencies conducted by the Bureau of Justice Statistics (BJS) found 15 percent of local police departments reporting they had carried out "a survey of citizens on crime, fear of crime, or satisfaction with the police." In the BJS survey these projects were more common in larger agencies. Only 9 percent of agencies serving cities less than 10,000 in size had conducted a survey in the past 12 months, but that figure was 60 percent for agencies in cities over 250,000. About 30 percent of the largest sheriff's offices also reported conducting surveys. Among both local departments and sheriff's offices, surveys were more common in the West and least common in the Northeast.

While one-time studies of public satisfaction and concern can be informative, a long-term commitment to monitoring trends in service quality and satisfaction is more likely to influence routine operations. The longest-running big city survey in the United States may be that conducted by the Boston Police Department, which has been reporting figures for fear of crime and public satisfaction with police services since 1999 (Boston Police Department 1999). However, the Metropolitan Police Service, the agency serving London, England, conducts the most impressive service monitoring survey. Each month their interviewers question 3,200 residents selected to represent their local boroughs. Police headquarters reports quarterly trends in confidence among residents of each borough. The surveys also monitor the quality of encounters between police and the public, questioning those who contact the police or are stopped by them about what took place. (For a discussion of the origins and purposes of this project, see Stanko et al. 2012.)

Academic researchers are routinely involved in monitoring and evaluation projects, as partners with police agencies. In addition, their research can push the envelope surrounding our understanding of modern policing by raising new questions and challenging old assumptions—sometimes in ways that make practitioners uncomfortable. These research projects may not have immediate operational utility, but they are fundamental to developing the field of crime science. For example, Weisburd et al. (2011) evaluated the impact of a crackdown on crime hotspots in three mid-sized California cities. What distinguished this from a routine evaluation was its focus on the possible "backfire" of intensive enforcement programs. While promising effective crime control, hot-spot policing threatens to alienate ordinary residents of the neighborhoods that are targeted for attention. Critics of hot-spot, zero-tolerance and other hard-nosed policing strategies have long feared that they undermine rather than build support for the police. In this evaluation, community surveys were used to monitor perceived fairness and the public's respect for the police, as well as perceptions of crime and disorder. The authors found that support for police did not decline in the face of increased police activity. They interpreted this as welcome news that hot-spot policing may not badly damage police legitimacy in targeted communities.

20.2 POLICE-COMMUNITY SURVEY TOPICS

This section addresses the substantive content of police-community surveys. It reviews the key concepts that have been examined, how they have been measured, and some of what the surveys have found.

20.2.1 Confidence in Police

Assessing public confidence in the police has been a goal since the earliest days of police-community surveys, for having the support and confidence of the voters and taxpayers is important to any segment of democratic government. In an evaluation of community policing in Chicago, I focused on several confidence dimensions (Skogan 2006b). The first was police *demeanor*, or views of how police treat people in the community. The specific elements of police demeanor examined were fairness, helpfulness, and expressions of concern about people's problems. Other studies have asked if police "treat people professionally and respectfully," and looked at the perceived extent of police use of force and verbal abuse. In a national survey, Weitzer and Tuch (2004) asked, "How often do you think police officers, when talking to people in your neighborhood, use insulting language against them?"

The Chicago surveys also assayed popular views of police *effectiveness*, in this case how good a job" they were doing in preventing crime, keeping order and "helping people out after they have been victims of crime. Other research has added questions about how promptly police responded when called for assistance. Some studies rely on very general questions about the quality of service; for example, one could choose to respond, "Overall I am satisfied with the service provided by the police in my community" (Kochel, Parks and Mastrofski 2011). The British Crime Survey (BCS) asks ten of thousands of Britons each year, "How good a job do you think the police are doing in their local area?" However, neither of these questions seems very promising for the purpose of improving police operations, given their very nonspecific character.

Finally, because it was a study of community policing, the Chicago surveys included several measures of perceived police *responsiveness* to community concerns; for example, residents were asked "how good a job" police were doing "working together with residents in your neighborhood to solve local problems?" In London, the Metropolitan Police Service asks residents, "Do you agree that the police in this area can be relied on to be there when you need them," and if the police "understand the issues that matter to people in the community" (Stanko and Bradford 2009).

Measures of confidence have also proven to be effective in tracking changes in public opinion that are associated with innovative programs. For example, before community policing began, Chicagoans were most negative in their views of police effectiveness. But over the course of a decade, the index measuring this aspect of confidence in police improved significantly, with the percentage of respondents averaging in the positive range rising from 36 to 50 percent (Skogan, 2006b).

However, it is important to note that many of the most important determinants of people's views of the police are not on the list of policy levers that police managers can directly pull. Race, age, and social standing are among the personal characteristics that most strongly color views of the police (Weitzer and Tuch 2006). Neighborhood-level factors such as concentrated poverty and social disorganization are also important. The views of family members and friends affect people's attitudes as well. Reisig and Parks (2000) found that assessments of the quality of life and neighborhood disadvantage far outweighed other determinants of general satisfaction with police. Finally, there is doubtless a strong effect of the mass media on popular images of the police, and this is yet another factor that the police can do little about (Rosenbaum et al. 2005). As a result, analyses of the findings of police-community surveys usually need to take this long list of factors into account. In the Chicago study, it was an important finding that all major racial groups in the city grew more positive about the police. The opinions of whites grew more positive by about 10 percentage points, while among African Americans and Latinos support rose by about 15 percentage points. On the other hand, after a decade of community policing the gulf between whites and others was almost as great as it was near the beginning.

As this illustrates, one approach to the deeply rooted nature of opinions about the police is to shift the focus from levels of confidence to changes in confidence over time, leaving the effects of all of the confounding factors listed above in the initial, benchmark level of confidence. In particular, focusing on changes in confidence reflects the logic of evaluations of innovations in policing, which typically gather "before" measures that provide benchmarks for assessing shifts in "after" measures, because the first-wave measures incorporate the many potentially confounding causes of confidence. Note that this recommendation is not low-cost. It has implications for sample size, which need to be large enough to reliably identify over-time change (see the section below, "Sampling and Surveying"). For example, the BCS tracks area-level changes in confidence in police for each of that nation's 42 police forces. However, the BCS involves more than 50,000 respondents each year, with at least 1,000 sampled from each policing area.

20.2.2 Police Legitimacy

Among academic researchers, studies of confidence in the police have been superseded by a somewhat broader and theoretically important line of inquiry into police legitimacy. Legitimacy is a topic of great interest, and news of the findings is beginning (in the 2010s) to percolate among criminal justice practitioners. The National Research Council's review of police research (Skogan and Frydl 2004) described legitimacy as one of the most socially and politically important outcomes of policing. Legitimacy is typically defined as the perceived obligation to obey police and the law. People may choose to go along because they calculate from the expected costs and benefits of doing so that there would be a net benefit from compliance with the law or cooperation with the police. On the other hand, following the dictates of the law and its representatives is not simply instrumental in nature. People also comply because of a sense of obligation toward authority and institutions. Democratic societies depend upon this latter, voluntary source of compliance with the law and the authorities. Among other things, this allows the police to do their jobs while applying coercion sparingly and respecting people's liberty and privacy. Voluntary compliance is driven by a belief in the legitimacy of police actions.

As an example, in a New York City study, Tyler and Fagan (2008) measured legitimacy of the police by multi-item scales representing three of its dimensions: the obligation to defer to police directives and to the law, trust and confidence in the police, and identification with the police. Obligation was assessed by responses to ten questions probing how much respondents agreed with the idea that they *ought* to obey the police (e.g., "You should accept the decisions made by police, even if you think they are wrong"). *Trust* in the police was scored from responses to seven questions (e.g., "I trust the leaders of the NYPD to make decisions that are good for everyone in the city"). Respondents were classified as *identifying* with the police when they responded affirmatively to ten items asking if they shared values with the police and respected them as people (e.g., "You can usually understand why the police who work in your neighborhood are acting as they are in a particular situation").

The "policy propositions" in the research literature—many of which are credible but the evidence for them is still thin—assert that enhancing their legitimacy will have a long list of benefits for the police. Increasing legitimacy should reduce unwarranted fear of crime; build support for the police among taxpayers and voters; encourage reporting crime and stepping forward as witnesses; spark participation in community-policing and crime-prevention projects; encourage compliance with police directives and willingness to obey the law; and increase confidence in the legitimacy of governmental institutions more generally. Many of these assertions are described in more detail in Hough et al. (2010), and they are the subject of a number of recent and ongoing research projects.

20.2.3 Satisfaction with Encounters

A presumption that is shared by police researchers and practitioners alike is that satisfactory personal experiences with the police are one of the foundations of legitimacy. As Tom Tyler notes:

> The perceived fairness of police procedures depends, for example, on the manner in which street stops are conducted, whether the police are neutral and transparent

in their application of legal rules, whether they explain their actions and seek input from community members before making decisions, and whether they treat people with dignity and respect. (Tyler, Schulhofer, and Huq 2010, 367)

Importantly, the work of Tyler and others has provided both a theoretical and empirical basis for evaluating the character of police encounters with the public, in order to assess how effectively they are being conducted. As the checklist enumerated by Tyler in the quotation above indicates, there is an emerging inventory of the features of encounters that have been demonstrated to deliver "procedural justice" in the eyes of the community, even among those judged to have done wrong.

Identifying encounters and assessing their character is a fairly straightforward survey procedure. It is a "recall task." That is, the questioning sequence first jogs respondent's memories with a series of "yes-no" screening items asking about possible recent contacts they may have had with the police. The best strategy is to provide them with a broad variety of cues that will expand the scope of their memory scan. For example, the BCS asks about seventeen possible reasons why respondents might contact the police, and fourteen different situations in which they may have been stopped by them. After completing each of these screening sequences, interviewers return to the contacts that respondents recalled and ask follow-up questions about what happened and their perceptions of how they were treated.

In my surveys respondents were presented with nine screening questions to establish whether they had contacted the police during the twelve months preceding the interview. This included calling the police to report a crime (26 percent of all respondents did so), followed in frequency by reporting an accident or some other emergency (19 percent) (Skogan 2006b). Other frequent types of contact were to report suspicious persons, suspicious noises, or "things that might lead to a crime." Twelve percent of the respondents called to give the police information, and 15 percent asked for advice or information. Taking into account overlap among contacts, 52 percent of Chicagoans recalled initiating contact with the police. The survey also asked respondents about their involvement in police-initiated encounters using several questions. Almost 20 percent of those who were interviewed recalled having been stopped by police during the past year, either while driving or while they were on foot. These are interestingly large percentages of the population, and they indicate that encounters are capable of affecting public opinion in short order.

Having identified survey respondents with recent contact with the police, the next step is to find out what happened. In the BCS, respondents who recall contacting the police are asked if the length of time they had to wait for them to arrive seemed reasonable; how polite the police were; how much interest police showed in what they had to say; and how much effort they felt the police put into dealing with the matter. The London police also ask if callers received any follow-up information about their case. BCS respondents who are stopped are questioned about police politeness and interest in what they had to say. In addition, they are asked how fairly they were treated, if they were given a reason for being stopped, and if they thought this was a good enough reason. Research also indicates that contact satisfaction plummets when officers make unproductive and apparently uncalled-for searches, a rationale for economy in police aggressiveness (Myhill and Quinton 2010). A promising line of research emphasizes the gap between what the public *expects* of the police and the service members of the public believe they actually *received*, treating both as empirical questions rather than making assumptions about what the targets of police efforts think they will encounter (Reisig and Chandek 2001).

A focus on encounters seems promising because they are to a significant degree in the hands of police themselves. As noted above, a great deal of scholarly research on attitudes toward the police does not focus on factors that police managers can directly influence, including race, concentrated poverty, and stories told by family members and friends. The actual experiences that people have with the police are another matter. Through recruitment, training, supervision, and even separation, agencies can hope to ensure professionalism in their dealings with the public. To the extent to which this makes a difference in popular confidence in the police, they can hope to profit from the policy propositions outlined above.

20.2.4 Awareness and Involvement in Programs

Police-community surveys are also commonly used to evaluate the effectiveness of police efforts to engage with the public in community policing and related programs. Two broad issues are important in this regard. The first is the extent to which police effectively get their message out. That is, does the public know it is being invited to participate? Modern policing is defined in part by its efforts to develop partnerships with groups and individual community members. These are intended to help the police better listen to the community, enhance constructive information sharing, build trust with the public, and involve them in setting public safety priorities. To accomplish this, departments hold community meetings and form advisory committees, establish storefront offices, survey the public, and create interactive websites. Awareness of such opportunities for participation is the key first step in building citizen involvement. However, it is a goal that will not be attained easily. To succeed, these programs require aggressive marketing on a variety of fronts, from mass media campaigns to appearances by the chief of police before church congregations. It is necessary to broaden awareness of new opportunities for participation that are being created and to actively encourage residents to get involved (Skogan 2006b).

The second questions is, do neighborhood residents actually turn out, or get involved in the programs on offer? Police can measure their own successes with regard to this question by counting heads at meetings or signatures on sign-up sheets. However, surveys can reveal important aspects of the dynamics of participation. Unlike headcounts, they can identify who attends and why, giving police a clearer picture of the representativeness of participants and the issues that they are hoping to bring to the table. Importantly, surveys can also identify who did not participate, and why. Knowing why residents choose not to get involved when they could be should be a topic of particular interest.

Police-community surveys routinely include measures of program awareness and participation. If police have opened a new office, residents can be asked if they know about it and if they have had an occasion to drop by. In two of my projects, awareness of a storefront office in their area stood at 65 percent in Houston, Texas, and 90 percent in Newark, New Jersey. In Newark, police working out of their storefront distributed newsletters door-to-door in one targeted area, and 40 percent of area residents interviewed remembered receiving one (Skogan 1990a). In Chicago, after a decade of aggressive marketing and community organizing efforts, 80 percent of residents knew of their city's community policing program, and 62 percent were aware that police-community meetings were being held regularly in their neighborhood. However, as a reminder that participation is not automatic, only 16 percent reported that they or someone from their household had actually attended a meeting (Skogan 2006b). Nonparticipants who knew about the program were different from those who attended on a number of dimensions. They were younger, less rooted in the community, and tended to be less educated than their immediate neighbors. Importantly, they were less likely than participants to have a positive view of the police.

Note that the relevant analytic unit for program participation is the household, not the individual. Some members will attend, while others will be represented. In Chicago, attendance at the city's monthly public beat meetings was greatly affected by household dynamics. Few residents of one-adult households participated, but members of two- (or more) adult households showed up regularly. Households with children living at home were very thinly represented, as were families in which all the adults were working. Instead, the meetings were dominated by retired home owners (Skogan 2006b).

It is wise generally to expect a strong establishment bias in involvement in police-community projects. A key issue that surveys can monitor is the *distribution* of involvement. There has been a great deal of research on government programs that rely on voluntary participation by the public, and these studies typically find that the opportunities for involvement they create advantage better-off neighborhood residents and those who may need the program least. Voluntary programs disproportionately attract better educated and informed people and households already well connected to public agencies and institutions. They prosper in neighborhoods that are already well organized and politically connected, where residents are already favorable toward the police, and in neighborhoods where residents do not fear retaliation for associating with police. Many of the benefits of these programs flow disproportionately to better-off home owners, long-term residents, and racial majorities. My evaluation of community policing projects in Houston during the 1980s found that the way in which programs in various areas were run favored whites, homeowners, and established interests in the community. Police worked well with members of those groups, but less affluent residents did not hear about the programs and did not participate in them. The positive effects of community policing also turned out to be confined to whites and homeowners; across two waves of neighborhood surveys, African Americans, Latinos, and renters reported no visible changes in their lives (Skogan 1990a).

20.2.5 Victimization

Police-community surveys can also be used to monitor the extent and change in criminal victimization over time. There are important reasons for doing so, including the sensitivity of officially recorded crime to changes in both victims' reporting practices and how police record the information the public supplies. However, survey measures of victimization are equally fragile, and are subject to a range of methodological problems that present their own challenges to gathering and interpreting the data.

The independent measurement provided by surveys is important because of the possibility that a program will influence the rate at which neighborhood residents report crimes to the police, as well as affecting the crime rate itself. In my experience police can be quick to argue that an unexpected increase in crime reflects well on them, because—they claim—it signals that the community has more confidence in them, and is therefore reporting more crime! (Of course, when crime goes down police never argue the opposite case, which is that their standing in the community is going down.) Only one study has directly addressed and documented this community effect (Schneider 1976), so it is certainly handy if an evaluator can introduce an independently-measured crime number into this discussion. A potentially darker problem would be deliberate manipulation on the police side of the crime-reporting-and-recording process, with the goal of making a department initiative look better than it really is. Because many critical community activists will anticipate this possibility, an independent measure of victimization is doubly handy.

However, the methodological problems associated with properly assessing the extent of victimization in a community are legion. They are documented in Skogan (1990b), which describes how the National Crime Victimization Survey tries to accommodate them. The key is that victims are people. They may forget, make mistakes, or lie about their experiences. They can be highly selective about what they tell interviewers, failing to report incidents that are embarrassing, when they might themselves be seen as at fault, or which are "none of the interviewer's business." Victims significantly under-report rape, domestic violence, and incidents of all kinds when there is a kin or continuing relationship between the parties, although reporting of sexual assault has been rising (Baumer and Lauritsen 2010; Tarling and Morris 2010). They are also very incomplete when it comes to reporting the victimization experiences of others in their household, so surveys must focus just on the respondent. Victims tend to forget incidents from the past; research indicates that victim recall is most accurate when they are asked only about events that occurred during the previous three months (Skogan 1990b). At the same time, there is a strong tendency to bring serious crimes which occurred in the more distant past into the conversation, and erroneously describe them as recent events. Comparing police and victims' reports of crimes reveals that, in later interviews, victims describe crimes as being more serious and their losses greater than they did at the time of the incident. They also describe the police as arriving on the scene much more slowly than was originally recorded.

In addition, victimization surveys typically report the counterintuitive result that personal assaults are more frequent among better-educated respondents. This is because more educated respondents are more "productive"—they are generally more at ease in an interview, they readily recall less serious incidents, and they are more able to recall the details of events (Skogan 1986, 1990b). This strong methodological regularity can be very hard to explain to policy makers and the media.

Further, violent assaults and household burglary are two crimes for which a relatively small number of victims often are involved in many repeated incidents. There is thus a potential disjuncture between the prevalence of victimization in an area (the percent of survey respondents victimized) and the rate of victimization there, which is based on the number of crimes they recall. Reports of repeat victimization easily drive up an area's crime rate, hopefully accurately because this small group weighs heavily in the findings. A final, ironic, point is that the prevalence of some crimes that are the focus of public concern and police programs is simply low for conventional data analysis, even in "high crime" neighborhoods. Often special statistics are required to analyze them, and it can be hard to document a reliable program effect when the pre-intervention base rate turns out to be low. In practice, self-reported victims of various sorts of crimes end up be combined together into a few generic categories. Otherwise, they are often too few in number to be analyzed in any detail.

Crime victims are among the primary "customers" of the police; as we have seen, victimization is the number one reason why people contact the police. Follow-up questions concerning how their case was handled are thus of particular importance. Thirty years of research on the views of crime victims have documented the importance of satisfaction with police demeanor at the scene. Satisfaction is higher when officers take adequate time to inform victims how they are going to handle their complaint and what could be expected to come of their case. It is higher when investigating officers are courteous, businesslike, and friendly (Reisig and Chandek 2001). Victims who later receive a follow-up contact from police are more favorable as a result, regardless of the news they receive. Highly-rated officers are those who are thought to have made a thorough examination of the scene, informed victims about their situation, offered advice, listened to the parties involved, and showed concern for their plight (Chandek and Porter 1998). Satisfaction is very consistently linked to perceived response time as well, although we have seen that this can be recalled inaccurately. The more of these details that can be included in monitoring surveys, the more easily police managers can make use of the data to identify areas of practice which may be engendering dissatisfaction with the quality of police service.

20.2.6 Neighborhood Disorder and Crime Problems

A key role for many police-community surveys is to gauge the extent of social disorder and physical decay problems. A survey is a good instrument for doing so, for many of the problems that concern neighborhood residents are not captured by official record-keeping system or are very poorly recorded when they are. For example, street drug dealing appears in official statistics only when arrests are made, and arrest numbers sometimes do not reflect the wide-open street drug markets that plague troubled neighborhoods. Graffiti is only rarely reported to police, and many people probably do not connect it with making an emergency 911 call. In addition to drugs and graffiti, the list of disorder problems relevant to a neighborhood or study could include public drinking, street prostitution, rowdy teenagers, verbal harassment of women passing on the street, abandoned cars, and trash on the streets and sidewalks.

These problems and more are of great interest to policy makers and researchers because they have a long list of documented consequences for individuals, communities, and cities. These include undermining the stability of urban neighborhoods, undercutting natural processes of informal social control, discouraging investment and commercial development, and stimulating fear of crime (Skogan 2012). Also, the survey evidence from Britain is that concern about neighborhood disorder and the inability of police and local residents to counter neighborhood decline are more important drivers of public confidence in the police than is fear of crime (Jackson et al. 2009).

In a neighborhood-focused survey, respondents typically are asked "how much of a problem" they consider each on a list of events or conditions. The response categories could include "a big problem" and other seriousness categories. A few studies have asked instead if respondents have observed or experienced the problems on the list, or for their estimates of the volume or frequency of each, rather than calling for an assessment of their impact. However, exactly how these questions are asked seems to have little practical effect on the findings (Sampson and Raudenbush 2004).

In any study the lists should be tailored to the issues and communities being examined; there is no standard list of disorders. Some appear in very situational contexts; an example would be squatters living in abandoned buildings. Graffiti appears disproportionately on schools or other public buildings and on untended and anonymous surfaces, and much less frequently on private residences (Skogan 1990a). Researchers conventionally subdivide the list, distinguishing between "social" and "physical" disorders. Social disorders are unsettling or potentially threatening and perhaps unlawful public behaviors. To measure the effectiveness of its antimonial behavior initiative, the British Home Office focuses on a list of sixty such activities. They add to the inventory presented above behaviors like making false calls to the fire service and setting cars on fire (Home Office 2004). Physical disorders include the overt signs of negligence or unchecked decay as well as the visible consequences of malevolent misconduct. In addition to the examples listed above, these could also include collapsing garages, loose syringes and condoms lying on the pavement, and illegal dumping of construction rubble.

Measures like these would be appropriate for evaluating community-oriented programs that take a wide view of the problems police can help to take responsibility for. When officers meet with neighborhood residents in park buildings and church basements to discuss neighborhood problems, residents bring up all manner of problems, for they don't make fine bureaucratic distinctions. When I surveyed residents of one of Chicago's highest-crime neighborhoods, one of the most highly ranked problems there was abandoned buildings; in another rough area, two of the top four problems were graffiti and vandalism of parked cars (Skogan and Hartnett 1997). Successful community policing takes seriously the public's definition of its problems, and this inevitably leads departments to get involved in a wide range of problem-solving efforts. This does not mean that they are going to do it all themselves. Rather, police need to form partnerships with other public and private agencies that can join them in responding to residents' priorities. These could include the schools and agencies responsible for health and housing codes, as well as the "housekeeping" agencies that tow cars, clear trash, and clean up graffiti.

Disorder is also important because it engenders fear of crime. A long list of studies indicates that the impact of disorder on fear is large. Unlike many crimes, disorder is visible to all, and can be observed on a frequent, even daily basis. In surveys, residents of disorderly areas are more likely to fear that they or other family members will be victimized, they more frequently report being afraid to leave their home, and they worry that their home will be broken into. Where people report high levels of disorder, they also are more likely to perceive higher levels of crime and increasing neighborhood crime. There is also evidence that perceived disorder has a special effect on fear in less affluent areas, where residents appear to take them more seriously than most as signs of danger. (For a detailed review of disorder issues, see Skogan 2012.) If police plan to confront the issue of fear, they have to take ownership of disorder as well.

20.2.7 Fear of Crime

Fear is a frequent topic of police-community surveys. However, although fear is an important term in everyday discourse, in research terms it can mean a number of different things. A "concern" definition of fear focuses on people's assessments of the extent to which *crime is a serious problem* for their community or society. Concern is a judgment about the seriousness of events and conditions in one's environment. To measure this aspect of fear, surveys sometimes ask whether respondents would place crime on their list of their community's most important problems. More frequently, researchers ask "how big a problem" respondents think that each of a list of conditions are in the immediate area and include various crimes as well as disorders on it. A second common meaning of fear is the perception that one is *likely to be victimized*. Respondents may be asked to rate "how likely" they are to be attacked or burglarized, on a scale ranging from not very likely to very likely. "Threat" definitions of fear emphasize the *potential* for harm that people feel crime holds for them *if they exposed themselves to risk*. The concept of threat of crime is distinct from risk and concern, for people frequently adopt routine tactics that reduce their vulnerability to victimization, and as a result they may not rate their risk as particularly high. However, they might rate the threat of crime as high if they were exposed to it. Threat is measured by questions that ask, "How safe would you feel if you were out alone on the street of your neighborhood at night?" or "How would you feel if you were approached by a stranger on the street or heard footsteps in the night?" Finally, fear of crime can be measured by *what people do* in response to perceived threat. From this perspective, fear is manifested in the frequency with which people fortify their homes, refrain from going out after dark, restrict their shopping to safer commercial areas, and avoid contact with strangers. (For a recent review of conceptualizations of fear, see Gray, Jackson, and Farrall 2011).

In addition to its differing meanings, there are important limits to the utility of fear in assessing (for example) the effectiveness of policing programs. The vast majority of variation in fear—perhaps 90 percent of the total—is attributable to differences between people rather than due to their immediate environment (Whitworth 2012). Age and gender are the two most important individual factors, followed by race. As a result, in practical terms, fear changes in response to changes in the environment only at the margin. It is firmly rooted in personal vulnerabilities which do not change and which profoundly affect people's views. A further implication of this is that the demographic distribution of the sample of people actually interviewed in a survey is a major determinant of its aggregate level of fear, so when it is off the mark (say, for example, because the survey has too many female respondents) so are the results. This also means that any analysis of the data will have to control for such personal factors (and the actual list is a longer one), which in turn means that the survey sample needs to be large enough to support a great deal of subgroup analysis. Fear is a politically and socially important phenomenon, and it is responsive to policing interventions. Many people (but not all racial and age groups) feel safer when they see police on patrol in their neighborhood; visible foot patrol reduces fear; and more responsive, community-oriented policing reduces fear. It is, however, a survey topic that needs to be considered carefully.

20.3 SAMPLING AND SURVEYING

This section considers some of the procedural issues involved in fielding a police-community survey. One of the most difficult issues facing the research community today is that of how to conduct a survey. This has become an issue because the traditional ways in which they have been carried out—personal interviews at sample addresses and phone interviews at sample telephone numbers—are no longer feasible in many circumstances. This section also reviews some of the sample requirements that police-community surveys face, and it addresses the issue of cross-sectional versus longitudinal surveys.

20.3.1 Interview Mode and Respondent Selection

Well into the 1980s, it was feasible to conduct police-community surveys in person. Interviewers knocked on the doors of randomly selected households and requested to meet with a randomly selected adult inside. The resulting data had a number of very valuable features. With repeated visits to catch selected respondents who were not often at home, the surveys could be highly representative. Interviewers could show respondents visual aides, including printed material they may have seen, and lists of questions and response categories answers for complicated questions. For example, in my study of community policing in Houston, interviewers presented respondents with a map of the area we were calling "your neighborhood" in the survey, and made clear its scope and boundaries. Establishing these personal contacts at sample addresses helped to make it quite feasible to return to the same households in the future for follow-up interviews, resulting in multi-wave or longitudinal data on the same individuals or households (see the section below on survey design). Finally, these interviews could be lengthy; it was not unusual for them to last 60 minutes or more, for many respondents felt uncomfortable showing their interviewer the door before they were able to complete the survey.

But by the end of the 1980s, the halcyon days of the address-sample personal interview survey were over. They had become too expensive for routine use, and surveys in this mold are now largely confined to a few lavishly-funded federal projects. In cities, crime and fear were driving down response rates as well. Residents were becoming wary of letting strangers into their home, and it could be dangerous to dispatch interviewers to doorsteps during the evening hours when people could more reliably be found at home. Households were getting smaller, most adults by then were in the labor force, and finding anyone at home and willing to be interviewed was getting harder.

This led to the widespread adoption of a new survey approach, the random digit dialing (RDD) telephone survey. Calling people on the phone was decidedly more cost-effective than driving to their home, and it could be done safely well into the nighttime hours. Because many Americans unlisted their telephone numbers in order to avoid unwanted calls (another growing trend), researchers generated pseudo telephone numbers that incorporated the prefixes and early digits of ranges of numbers known to be in active use by telephone companies. Their computers then added a final, random component to the number and passed the result to the call center. These numbers did not all work, but those that did reached both listed and unlisted households in the correct proportion, and the result could be treated as a random sample of the population. Telephone survey data quality could be good. Interviewers could actually be more closely supervised and their response rates verified more easily than they ever were out in the field. The data had some liabilities as well. The interviews had to be short, because people could easily hang up if the survey became too burdensome. The questions had to be simple, offering only a few response categories, because respondents had to keep it all in their head. But the data were relatively cheap, and telephone numbers that rang but were not answered could be called again and again until someone did so, because call-backs were easy. Like in-person surveys, telephone-based studies could recontact households later, although it can be difficult to be completely sure that you were talking to the same respondent, and recontact rates by telephone tended to be lower than those based on earlier personal home visits.

Alas, those days are gone as well. Representative survey data are very difficult to obtain through RDD telephone surveys. Voicemail enables people to screen out unwanted calls, privacy concerns have heightened, and surveys of all kinds have ended up in the junk-call category. By the early 2000s, RDD response rates had dropped to 20 percent or less. More fundamentally, they were based on the assumption that virtually every household was served by a primary telephone number. Like the personal visit, a telephone survey began with selecting a single household respondent from the list of persons living there. Now the norm is increasingly—but very far from completely—one telephone per person, a growing number of households have no fixed-line phone at all, and the surveyor does not know in advance what is at the other end of any call (Messer and Dillman 2010). This proliferation is due to the widespread adoption of wireless telephones, but the rules regarding who pays for cellular calls has led to an effective ban on random calling. Now, it is virtually impossible to assemble a high-quality RDD survey sample.

The jury is still out on the question of what to do in the face of these developments. The Internet is an attractive mechanism for surveying individuals, but (a) no one has developed an adequate approach to developing representative Internet samples, and (b) Internet "locations" are completely divorced from the cities or neighborhoods where respondents live and their experiences with crime and the police are rooted (Couper and Miller 2008). The collapse of telephone surveys has led to renewed interest in mail surveys, and they present a number of advantages. For sampling, the U.S. Postal Service's Delivery Sequence File can be purchased, and it lists every functioning residential delivery point in the county (Link et al. 2008). Each potential household can be reached cheaply, and as with telephone surveys, non-responding households can affordably be recontacted several times. Knowing exactly who fills out the questionnaire is a problem, because the process cannot control respondent selection very effectively. Paper questionnaires are a clumsy technology when it comes to asking respondents to skip across ensuing questions based on their responses to earlier ones, and it is impossible to keep them from going back to change earlier answers to questions. In the past, mail surveys were criticized for achieving only modest response rates, but as telephone survey response rates degraded, they began to look competitive (Messer and Dillman 2010).

20.3.2 Sample Size

A survey's sample size sets an important limit on the kinds of conclusions that can be drawn from it. To evaluate the impact of an intervention, the survey must be large enough to confirm a program effect of realistic size. To conclude that two groups—say, non-victims and those relatively rare victims—are reliably different, the sizes of each group must be large enough relative to the magnitude of the difference between them and the variability within each. One way to kill a program is to measure its effects with a survey that is too small, and then conclude that it "has no significant effect." Choosing a sample size is in part a technical matter, but it also involves substantial criminological knowledge and seasoned judgment on the part of planners and evaluators.

Before an evaluation survey is fielded, statistical techniques (a "power analysis") can be applied to calculate the minimum sample size required so that the analyst can reasonably expect to confirm that a program effect of a planned-for size is statistically significant. (Free power calculators can be found on the Internet.) However, sample size decisions are importantly substantive and involve criminological expertise. They are driven in part by an advance estimate of what the likely effect of a program (or a difference among groups of interest) will be. For example, if it seems likely that a program might actually produce a 10 percent decline in burglary, power calculations will reveal how large a survey needs to be in order to responsibly assess the planned intervention. To put this in obverse fashion, other things being equal, the smaller the sample size, the larger any changes in reports of, say, policing quality would need to be in order for them to be statistically reliable. Small samples can create an impossibly high bar for police to jump, so this is an important consideration in any study.

20.3.3   Cross-sectional or Longitudinal?

In contrast to the "one off" survey, multiple waves of interviews provide a much stronger basis for identifying causal processes and making plausible inferences about the impact of events and programs. Multiple waves of surveys can be organized in two different ways: as separate, "cross-sectional" snapshots of a community that are conducted independently, or as repeated "longitudinal" surveys of the same individuals over time. Each has advantages and disadvantages.

Among the advantages of longitudinal surveys is their ability to directly measure individual change. The analyst can control for each respondent's earlier reports of his or her attitudes and experiences, in order to clearly highlight how these have shifted. Longitudinal surveys are commonly conducted as part of long-term evaluations of programs, because of this interest in change. In addition, it is also possible to examine the impact of events that affect respondents between the waves of a survey, using the analytic power of a longitudinal survey to tease out the effects of those experiences. Finally, when resources are tight, longitudinal surveys yield more statistical power for the same sample size, when compared to cross-sectional studies.

For example, as part of an extended evaluation of community policing in Chicago, I conducted a two-wave longitudinal survey designed to gauge before-after changes in program awareness and the impact of community policing on crime, fear, and neighborhood problems (Skogan and Hartnett 1997). The survey was conducted by telephone, using a mixed-mode sampling strategy that was driven by the fact that we had to reach residents of selected police districts. Half of the respondents were selected at random from telephone directory listings of households that fell in a targeted area, while the other half were contacted by calling randomly generated telephone numbers and determining where they lived. The second approach ensured that households that did not have listed phone numbers would be included in the data. Fourteen months later we attempted to recontact respondents to the first wave of the survey. The re-interview rate was 59 percent. The 41 percent of respondents who were lost were far from a random group. Men, Hispanics, younger respondents, those with less education, and renters were less likely than others to be recontacted successfully. We responded by weighting the actual data so that the distribution of those key groups matched their numbers in the first wave. This was, of course, a stopgap measure, but a better choice than inferring from data with large known biases.

As noted earlier, an advantage of longitudinal surveys is that they directly measure individual-level change. Analysis of the Chicago examined "before-and-after" data separately for the experimental districts in which the program was being fielded and matched comparison areas where policing was continuing as usual. When there was a change in an experimental area but no comparable shift in its comparison area—or vice versa—we took it as evidence that the program made a difference, when we could reasonably link it to specific elements of the program that was in place. Importantly, the fact that we questioned individuals twice also gave us the capacity to look at the impact of events or experiences that they had between the two waves of interviews. For example, we looked at the impact of being stopped by police during the period between the interviews on changes in people's attitudes between the interviews.

But there are advantages in conducting pairs (or more) of separate, cross-sectional surveys instead. For example, it is quite likely that each independent wave of interviews will be more representative of the population. Despite attempts to recontact households, there is invariably a fair amount of attrition in longitudinal studies. These combine with biases in the representativeness of the first wave to produce second-wave samples which can be noticeably unlike the general population they are to represent. On the other hand, because each wave of a cross-sectional survey is a new sample survey, each is subject to separate sampling errors. In combination, in order to infer a reliable change from wave one to wave two requires many more survey interviews.

20.4 CONCLUSION

This essay reviewed the concepts and methods that have made community surveys a key police research tool. Surveys serve a number of purposes, such as assessing public concerns, monitoring the routine delivery of police services, evaluating innovative programs, and deepening our understanding of the relationship between police and the community in democratic societies. The essay reviewed the key concepts that make up the substance of this research. These included confidence in the police, perceptions of their legitimacy, satisfaction with encounters, public awareness and involvement in programs, victimization, neighborhood disorder problems and fear of crime.

In particular, surveys are an effective tool for monitoring the quality of police-citizen contacts. This is a determinant of the legitimacy of the police, and it is something that is in the hands of the police themselves. It is a place to look for disparate treatment of individuals by race, class and—very importantly—neighborhood status. Neighborhood context affects how police view its residents, how many are assigned there, the aggressiveness of their patrolling strategies, and the opportunities that open up for corruption and abuse of power. These increase the frequency of police-citizen contacts and the potential for acrimonious encounters (Weitzer, Tuch, and Skogan 2008; Terrill and Reisig 2003; Reisig and Parks 2000). Research suggests a list of things police can do to counter this tendency. However, it also indicates that positively-rated encounters have only a small effect on overall satisfaction with the police. Poor performance, on the other hand, greatly affects people's global assessments of the police (Skogan 2006a; Reisig and Parks 2000). Avoiding the downside of encounters that go awry is the best defense that police managers can mount against backfire from overly aggressive police actions.

I also recommend focusing on the quality of service that is delivered to crime victims. They are core customers of the police, albeit one group that is often not well served. In our Chicago surveys, "helping people out after they have been victims of crime" was the lowest-rated aspect of perceived police effectiveness, and public opinion was right. As I noted above, there are a raft of methodological problems in properly estimating the rate of victimization in the community. However, identifying crime victims who have been in contact with the police in order to question them about what happened at the time, and what the aftermath of their experience has been, is a far more straightforward matter.

Some daunting methodological issues were reviewed. How respondents should be selected and how the interviews should be conducted were the toughest of these. The collapse of traditional survey methodologies near the end of the twentieth century presents daunting challenges to the twenty-first-century police researcher. What is my advice? If a police-community survey is focused on a relatively small and densely built-up area, I would return to personal interviews. Interviewers can be turned loose for hours at a time in such areas, to knock on many preselected doors in rapid succession. They can easily return to unopened doors or unanswered buzzers while they work their sample list. In cities, the modal American household now includes only one adult resident, so respondent selection can often be conducted quickly (but this also means it is harder to find them at home). I would keep the interviews short, or have a brief fallback version, so they can be completed at the doorstep if respondents are unwilling to let the interviewer into their home. A prepaid mail questionnaire could be dropped at doors that never open; these will not pick up many respondents, but they would otherwise go completely unrepresented, and this is a cheap procedure. On the other hand, if targeted areas are relatively large and low-density, mail surveys are probably the only option today. With aggressive marketing supported by the police, repeated re-mailings, and a cash incentive for completing the questionnaire, a researcher can hope for a 45 percent response rate or so, which is now better than the alternatives (Dillman, Smyth, and Christian 2009; Messer and Dillman 2010).

How big should the sample be, taking response rates into consideration? As I noted, a responsible study—not one intent on killing a program—needs to be large enough to reliably confirm a difference of reasonable size. For example, a sample of about 160 completed interviews in each of two waves of surveys should be sufficient for detecting a 10 percentage point shift in confidence in the police working in a targeted area. I picked a 10 percent shift in confidence over a multi-year timeframe as plausible based on prior knowledge: the average year-to-year (upward) shift in confidence in Chicago police during my study in the 1990s was about 5 percentage points. Of course, if analysts are interested in the views and experiences of population subgroups, the sample requirements would be the same at that level. In Chicago, the smallest subgroup that we needed to track closely was recent immigrants—Hispanics who could not speak English and had to be interviewed in Spanish. These non-English speakers constituted about 16 percent of the overall population. Based on the quality of service power analysis described above, to interview enough recent immigrants in the course of conducting a citywide random sample survey would require a general population sample of about 1,000 respondents. In any survey, subgroups that are targeted to be of analytic interest will have to be chosen judiciously.

As for longitudinal versus repeated cross-sectional surveys, if budgets are tight, do longitudinal surveys. They may be less representative, but they directly measure change, and realistic program effects or subgroup differences are more likely to be statistically significant with a more modest (but still large enough) longitudinal sample.

References

Bahn, Charles. 1974. "The Reassurance Factor in Police Patrol." *Criminology* 12:338–45.

Baumer, Eric P., and Janet L. Lauritsen. 2010. "Reporting Crime to the Police, 1973–2005: A Multivariate Analysis of Long-Term Trends in the National Crime Survey (NCS) and National Crime Victimization Survey (NCVS)." *Criminology* 48:131–85.

Block, Richard. 1974 "Why Notify the Police: The Victim's Decision to Notify the Police of an Assault." *Criminology* 11:555–69.

Bordua, David J., and Larry L. Tifft. 1971. "Citizen Interviews, Organizational Feedback, and Police-Community Relations Decisions." *Law and Society Review* 6:155–82.

Boston Police Department. 1999. *The 1999 Boston Public Safety Survey*. Boston: Office of Research and Evaluation, Boston Police Department.

Chandek, Meghan Stroshine, and Christopher O. L. H. Porter. 1998. "The Efficacy of Expectancy Disconfirmation in Explaining Crime Victim Satisfaction with the Police." *Police Quarterly* 1:21–40.

Couper, Mick P., and Peter V. Miller. 2008. "Web Survey Methods: Introduction." *Public Opinion Quarterly* 72:831–35.

Dillman, Don A., Jolene D. Smyth, and Leah Melani Christian. 2009. *Internet, Mail and Mixed-Mode Surveys: The Tailored Design Method*. Hoboken, NJ: John Wiley and Sons.

Gray, Emily, Jonathan Jackson, and Stephen Farrall. 2011. "Feelings and Function in the Fear of Crime: Applying a New Approach to Victimisation Insecurity." *British Journal of Criminology* 51:75–94.

Home Office. 2004. *Defining and Measuring Anti-Social Behaviour*. Home Office Development and Practice Report no. 26. London: Research, Development and Statistics Directorate.

Hough, Mike, Jonathan Jackson, Ben Bradford, Andy Myhill, and Paul Quinton. 2010. "Procedural Justice, Trust, and Institutional Legitimacy." *Policing: A Journal of Policy and Practice* 4:1–8.

Jackson, Jonathan, Ben Bradford, Katrin Hohl, and Stephen Farrall. 2009. "Does the Fear of Crime Erode Public Confidence in Policing?" *Policing: A Journal of Policy and Practice* 3:100–11.

Jacob, Herbert. 1971. "Black and White Perceptions of Justice in the City." *Law and Society Review* 6:69–90.

Kochel, Tammy Rinehart, Roger B. Parks, and Stephen D. Mastrofski. 2011. "Examining Police Effectiveness as a Precursor to Legitimacy and Cooperation with Police." *Justice Quarterly* 29:1–31.

Link, Michael W., Michael P. Battaglia, Martin R. Frankel, Larry Osborn, and Ali H. Hokdad. 2008. "A Comparison of Address-Based Sampling (ABS) Versus Random-Digit Dialing (RDD) for General Population Surveys." *Public Opinion Quarterly* 72:6–27.

Messer, Benjamin L., and Don A. Dillman. 2010. *Using Address Based Sampling to Survey the General Public by Mail vs. "Web plus Mail."* Report Prepared for The National Science Foundation Division of Science Resources Statistics. Pullman, WA: Social and Economic Sciences Research Center.

Myhill, Andy, and Paul Quinton. 2010. "Confidence, Neighbourhood Policing, and Contact: Drawing Together the Evidence." *Policing: A Journal of Policy and Practice* 4:1–9

Reisig, Michael D., and Meghan Stroshine Chandek. 2001. "The Effects of Expectancy Disconfirmation on Outcome Satisfaction in Police-Citizen Encounters." *Policing: An International Journal of Police Strategies and Management* 24:88–99.

Reisig, Michael D., and Roger B. Parks. 2000. "Experience, Quality of Life, and Neighborhood Context: A Hierarchical Analysis of Satisfaction with Police." *Justice Quarterly* 17:607–30.

Rosenbaum, Dennis P., Amie M. Schuck, Sandra K. Costello, Darnell F. Hawkins, and Michael K. Ring. 2005. "Attitudes toward the Police: The Effects of Direct and Vicarious Experience." *Police Quarterly* 8:343–65.

Sampson, Robert J., and Stephen W. Raudenbush. 2004. "Seeing Disorder: Neighborhood Stigma and the Social Construction of 'Broken Windows'." *Social Psychology Quarterly* 67:319–42.

Schneider, Anne L. 1976. "Victimization Surveys and the Criminal Justice System." In *Sample Surveys of the Victims of Crime*, edited by Wesley G. Skogan, 135–150. Cambridge, MA: Ballinger.

Skogan, Wesley G. 1986. "Methodological Issues in the Study of Victimization." In *From Crime Policy to Victim Policy*, edited by Ezzat Fattah, 80–116. London: Macmillan.

——. 1990a. *Disorder and Decline: Crime and the Spiral of Decay in American Cities.* New York: The Free Press.

——. 1990b. "The National Crime Survey Redesign." *Public Opinion Quarterly* 54:256–72.

——. 2006a. "Asymmetry in the Impact of Encounters with Police." *Police and Society* 6:99–126.

——. 2006b. *Police and Community in Chicago: A Tale of Three Cities.* New York: Oxford University Press.

——. 2012. "Disorder and Crime." In *The Oxford Handbook on Crime Prevention*, edited by Brandon C. Welsh and David P. Farrington, 173–188. New York: Oxford University Press.

Skogan, Wesley G., and Kathleen Frydl. 2004. *Fairness and Effectiveness in Policing: The Evidence.* Washington, DC: National Academies Press.

Skogan, Wesley G., and Susan M. Hartnett. 1997. *Community Policing, Chicago Style.* New York and London: Oxford University Press.

Smith, Paul E., and Richard O. Hawkins. 1973. "Victimization, Types of Citizen-Police Contacts, and Attitudes toward the Police." *Law and Society Review* 8:135–52.

Stanko, Elizabeth A., and Ben Bradford. 2009. "Beyond Measuring 'How Good a Job' Police Are Doing: The MPS Model of Confidence in Policing." *Policing: A Journal of Policy and Practice* 3:322–30.

Stanko, Elizabeth A., Jonathan Jackson, Ben Bradford, and Katrin Hohl. 2012. "A Golden Thread, a Presence amongst Uniforms, and a Good Deal of Data: Studying Public Confidence in the London Metropolitan Police." *Policing and Society*. DOI: 10.1080/10 439463.2012.671825.

Tarling, Roger, and Katie Morris. 2010. "Reporting Crime to the Police." *British Journal of Criminology* 50:474–90.

Terrill, William, and Michael D. Reisig. 2003. "Neighborhood Context and Police Use of Force." *Journal of Research in Crime and Delinquency* 40:291–321.

Tyler, Tom R., and Jeffrey Fagan. 2008. "Legitimacy and Cooperation: Why Do People Help the Police Fight Crime in Their Communities?" *Ohio State Journal of Criminal Law* 6:231–75.

Tyler, Tom R., Stephen Schulhofer, and Aziz Z. Huq. 2010. "Legitimacy and Deterrence Effects in Counterterrorism Policing: A Study of Muslim Americans." *Law and Society Review* 44:365–401.

U.S. Department of Justice. 2011. *Law Enforcement Management and Administrative Statistics (LEMAS), 2007.* Office of Justice Programs. Bureau of Justice Statistics. [Computer file]. ICPSR31161-v1. Ann Arbor, MI: Interuniversity Consortium for Political and Social Research [distributor], 2011-07-07.

Weisburd, David, Joshua C. Hinkle, Christine Famega, and Justin Ready. 2011. "The Possible 'Backfire' Effects of Hot Spots Policing: An Experimental Assessment of Impacts on Legitimacy, Fear and Collective Efficacy." *Journal of Experimental Criminology* 7:297–320.

Weitzer, Ronald, and Steven A. Tuch. 2004. "Race and Perceptions of Police Misconduct." *Social Problems* 51:305–25.

——. 2006. *Race and Policing in America: Conflict and Reform.* New York: Cambridge University Press.

Weitzer, Ronald, Steven A. Tuch, and Wesley G. Skogan. 2008. "Police-Community Relations in a Majority Black City." *Journal of Research in Crime and Delinquency* 45:398–428.

Whitworth, Adam. 2012. "Sustaining Evidence-Based Policing in an Era of Cuts: Estimating Fear of Crime at Small Area Levels in England." *Crime Prevention and Community Safety* 14:48–68.

CHAPTER 21

....

SYSTEMATIC SOCIAL OBSERVATION OF THE POLICE

....

ROBERT E. WORDEN AND
SARAH J. MCLEAN[*]

POLICE discretion was "discovered" many decades ago through direct observation of police at work, with William Westley's (1970) study of Gary, Indiana, and the American Bar Foundation "survey" in the 1950s (Walker 1992). Other observational studies, of an anthropological or ethnographic kind, were conducted in the 1960s (Skolnick 1966; Bittner 1967; Rubinstein 1973), 1970s (Van Maanen 1974; Manning 1977; Muir 1977), and recently (Moskos 2008). *Systematic social observation* (SSO) of the police was conducted first in 1966, and it has made very substantial contributions to our understanding of what the police do, the discretionary choices that they make, and the forces that influence those choices.

Like other forms of observation, SSO provides for in-person observation of patrol officers as they perform their work in its natural setting, as researchers accompany selected officers during their regular work shifts. Unlike other forms of observation, SSO is systematic in two respects. First, the selection of officers to be observed is subject to probability sampling, so that inferences from analytic results can be drawn with the benefit of known statistical properties. Second, observers are all guided in their observation by a single structured coding protocol that is formulated prior to the field research, and which directs observers' attention to specified features of police work; thus their observations are captured in the form of standardized measurement categories, which are quantifiable and replicable.

In Section 21.1 of this essay, we describe each of the five major SSO studies and several more focused SSO projects, and we summarize their principal features of research design. In Section 21.2, we explain the main strengths of SSO relative to other methodologies, in terms of operationalizing key constructs. Then in Section 21.3, we assess the principal limitations of SSO. Section 21.4 concludes with a brief consideration of the prospects for future SSO studies of the police. The main points of the essay are:

- SSO is a method that is compatible with many theoretical perspectives and analytic foci.
- SSO yields data that are in important respects more valid and reliable than any of the conventional alternatives.
- The potential drawbacks of SSO have probably been overstated in some accounts and can be minimized when SSO is conducted properly.

21.1 PREVIOUS SSO-BASED STUDIES OF THE POLICE

When in 1966 Albert J. Reiss, Jr. used SSO to examine patterns of interaction between citizens and patrol officers, his pioneering study established SSO as one of the principal methods of studying police behavior and produced one of five large-scale sets of observational data that have together formed the basis for a substantial body of empirical evidence on the police. The other large-scale SSO projects are the Midwest City Study; the Police Services Study; the Project on Policing Neighborhoods; and the Policing in Cincinnati Project. Each of these data sets has been grist for the mill of numerous analyses. The number and substantive diversity of these analyses is testimony to the breadth and richness of the data sets. Some analyses have examined the functions that police perform and how their time and effort is distributed across those functions. Many studies have examined the exercise of police authority: arrest, the use of force, stops, and searches. Some analyses have focused on police interactions with particular subsets of citizens, such as suspects, complainants, and juveniles. Others have focused on police responses to particular kinds of incidents, such as interpersonal disputes, domestic conflicts, drunk-driving, and traffic violations generally. In addition to these large-scale projects, several smaller-scale and/or more focused data collection efforts have also formed the basis for a number of analyses. All of these studies focus on police patrol, although the method could be adapted to the study of other police functions or units.

21.1.1 The President's Commission Study

As the research director for President Lyndon Johnson's Commission on Law Enforcement and the Administration of Justice, and building on his exploratory field work in Chicago and Detroit in 1963 and 1964, Reiss undertook an SSO-based study of police-citizen encounters. He deployed observers in Boston, Chicago, and Washington, DC, for six to seven weeks during the summer of 1966. These cities' police departments were selected to represent different organizational styles: Boston was at the time considered a "traditional" department whose administration was "personalized" rather than bureaucratic; Chicago was an example of a more professional, bureaucratized department; Washington was in a transition from personalized to bureaucratic (Reiss 1971a, xi–xii).

Eight precincts—four in Washington and two in each of Boston and Chicago—were selected for study; most of the precincts were higher-crime areas, with correspondingly higher levels of police activity that maximized opportunities to observe police-citizen encounters. Thirty-six observers were recruited locally, selected equally from among those with backgrounds in law, law enforcement, and social science, but trained according to a single curriculum and subject to similar supervision.[1] Observations were conducted at all times of the day, although the presumptively busier tours were oversampled. In the field, observers kept a "log" of police-citizen encounters and later completed an observation "booklet" about each encounter that included forty-eight sets of items (Reiss 1968b, 355–56). They also recorded summary information about the tour, and as events allowed they administered an interview instrument to the observed officer(s). The study was presented to police as one of citizens' behavior toward the police, deemphasizing the extent to which police behavior was a focus, and observers were trained to build rapport with the officers, each of whom was observed (on average) on 2.5 tours.

Reiss, who passed away in 2006, was a sociologist, and the project was guided by a theory that holds that the police-citizen encounter is a *social* transaction. More specifically, the premise was that police action is influenced by a citizen's social status (sex, age, race, class) and situational status (as complainant, suspect, witness, etc., in the encounter), and by the citizen's "capability to undermine the means the police use to attain their goals" (Black and Reiss 1967, 8–9). Thus for each of up to five citizens in an encounter, observers coded sex, age, race, and social class, the citizen's role in the encounter, demeanor (civil, antagonistic, very deferential), emotional state (agitated, calm, detached), and sobriety, as well as the requests that citizens made of police. Observers also coded police "manner" (e.g., "nasty," "bossy," or "business-like") and specific actions toward each citizen, including formal actions such as arrests or tickets, and informal actions such as threats and admonishments. Across the three cities observers collected data on 840 8-hour tours and 5,391 mobilizations of the police, 3,955 of which eventuated in encounters with 11,422 citizens (Friedrich 1977, 211). The project also provided for 100 interviews with citizens who had been complainants in an observed encounter, and in each precinct surveys of or interviews with 200 residents, business representatives, and 50 officers (Reiss 1968b, 356).

21.1.2 The Midwest City Study

Sociologists Richard Sykes and John Clark directed the Midwest City study, which began in 1969. Observations were conducted in five departments that, to our knowledge, have never been identified; two were major city departments and the rest were suburban agencies in the Midwest (Sykes and Brent 1983). The most remarkable feature of the project was its attention to the "utterance" (i.e., "all [that] one person says during his or her turn at speaking"; Sykes and Brent 1983, 3). From a social behaviorist perspective that emphasizes police-citizen interaction through verbal communication, or symbolic interaction, the "utterance" is the fundamental unit of analysis. Officers handle or "regulate" situations mainly by talking: asking questions, making suggestions, making accusations, and issuing commands. They solicit information and establish identities. Citizens answer, evade, or decline to respond to questions, accept or deny accusations, follow or disobey commands (Sykes and Brent 1980, 1983). Observers captured data on such utterances in real time in the field with a portable device developed for the project and called MIDCARS (Minnesota Interaction Data Coding and Reduction System).

During the project's first phase, which extended over 15 months in 1970 to 1971, 365 patrol shifts were observed, and data on almost 2,000 police-citizen encounters were coded (Lundman 1996). During the second phase, in the summer of 1973, 1,622 encounters were observed (Sykes and Brent 1980). In all, 12 observers were deployed across all shifts and all patrol units, but busier shifts were oversampled and, in the second phase of the study, busier patrol units were also oversampled, with a view toward observing "non-routine" activities (Sykes and Brent 1983, xvii).

21.1.3 The Police Services Study

In 1977, the Police Services Study (PSS) put SSO to use in addressing different questions that have very different theoretical and disciplinary roots. Directed by Elinor Ostrom, Roger Parks, and Gordon Whitaker, all of whom are or were political scientists, the PSS approached police as a municipal service, the organizational fragmentation of whose delivery had prompted calls for consolidation. American policing was—and still is—provided mainly by thousands of local police agencies, many of which are quite small, with a median size of ten sworn officers (Reaves 2010, 9). Analyzing this police "industry," Ostrom, Parks, and Whitaker had previously found, in a series of matched neighborhood studies, that the residents of neighborhoods served by small to medium-sized agencies rated their police services more favorably than their counterparts served by big-city departments (Ostrom, Parks, and Whitaker 1973; Ostrom and Whitaker 1973). In the first phase of the PSS, they found across eighty SMSAs (standard metropolitan statistical area) a high degree of coordination among the numerous agencies in a metropolitan area (Ostrom, Parks, and Whitaker 1978). The second phase, which provided for SSO, was designed to deepen our understanding of how these institutional arrangements affect the effectiveness, efficiency, equity, and responsiveness of police service delivery (Ostrom, Parks, and Whitaker 2001).

The PSS examined policing in 60 neighborhoods spread across 24 jurisdictions in three metropolitan areas: Rochester, New York; St. Louis, Missouri; and Tampa-St. Petersburg, Florida. Among the 24 agencies were the 4 major city departments, but also county sheriff's departments and a number of small and medium-sized municipal agencies, including the "Lilliputs" of municipal policing (Ostrom and Smith 1976)—agencies with as few as 10 to 25 sworn officers. Neighborhoods served by different agencies were matched in strata defined by median household income and racial composition.

The PSS used an observation instrument much like that used by Reiss, capturing for each of up to 5 citizens their characteristics and actions, and police actions toward each citizen. Observations were conducted on 15 patrol shifts in each of the 60 neighborhoods, oversampling shifts that were presumptively busier. Across 7,200 hours of observation, observers recorded information on 5,688 encounters.

The PSS also administered a separate survey of officers, including but not limited to those who were observed, and which could be linked to observational data by an anonymous identifier. In addition, the PSS surveyed 200 sampled residents in each of the 60 neighborhoods, conducted a follow-up survey of people whose encounters with police were observed, and conducted interviews with police executives, elected officials, and representatives of community organizations. The breadth, depth, and scale of data collection for the PSS is truly remarkable.

21.1.4 The Project on Policing Neighborhoods

Nearly twenty years after the PSS was in the field, the Project on Policing Neighborhoods (POPN) began, directed by Stephen Mastrofski, Roger Parks, Robert Worden, and Albert Reiss, Jr. (Mastrofski et al. 2007). In the years since the PSS, policing had (arguably) entered the "community era" (Kelling and Moore 1988), and POPN was designed to describe community policing at the street level. POPN examined policing in two cities, Indianapolis and St. Petersburg, which were selected because their police departments had made substantial progress in implementing community policing, albeit different variants of community policing: the former more a broken-windows style, and the latter emphasizing problem-solving. But POPN was also intended to serve as the foundation for numerous replications, using POPN's instruments, so that comparable data across many sites could economically accumulate and support cross-jurisdictional analysis.

POPN concentrated on twelve police beats in each city, selecting (and matching across the sites) beats that were in the top three quartiles on a measure of socioeconomic distress—that is, beats other than those in which a minimum of police-citizen contact would be observed (Parks et al. 1999, 492–93). Observations were conducted during the summers of 1996 (Indianapolis) and 1997 (St. Petersburg), using an SSO instrument much like that used by Reiss and the PSS, but with provisions to capture data on any number of citizens (not a maximum of five), and benefiting from Mastrofski's Richmond project with the addition of items designed to tap behaviors that may be a part of community policing (e.g., whether the encounter was part of a long-term plan or project to deal with the problem and how officers responded to specific citizen requests). In addition, POPN provided for sampling both the patrol generalists and the community policing specialists who were assigned to the sampled beats. Like the PSS, POPN administered a separate survey of officers, data from which could be linked to observational data, as well as a survey of one hundred sampled residents in each of the twenty-four beats. POPN also conducted SSO of field supervisors.

Moreover, POPN added two forms of qualitative data to the coded observational data: *detailed* narrative accounts of encounters, and "debriefings" of officers. Observers were instructed to describe every encounter they observed in details sufficient to enable someone to stage a reenactment of the event. PSS had written narratives of some but not all events, and they tended to be fairly brief, so they were seldom used as a source of systematic information.[2] The POPN narratives, as we discuss below, have enabled researchers to supplement the coded data in key respects.

The "debriefings" were added in order to gain insight into how officers made discretionary choices. Immediately (or as soon as practicable) after an encounter, the observer invited the officer to share what s/he was thinking as s/he handled the situation. Data of this kind have been used to learn more about how decision makers attend to and process information and make choices; as a supplement to the conventional analysis from which we draw inferences about decision making (i.e., associations between observed choices and features of the decision context such as the nature of the offense and the deference of the suspect), the analysis of debriefings promises to more directly illuminate officers' decision making (Mastrofski and Parks 1990; Worden and Brandl 1990; Bonner 2012). Mastrofski had piloted debriefings in his Richmond project.

21.1.5 The Policing in Cincinnati Project

While POPN was still in the field, the Policing in Cincinnati Project (PCP) got underway, with field research stretching across thirteen months in 1997 and 1998. Directed by James Frank, the PCP used POPN's observation instruments adapted to the Cincinnati context.[3] Like POPN, the goal of the PCP was to describe the contours of community policing, and in Cincinnati, that meant observing both the specialized community policing (COP) officers and the "beat" officers who performed conventional patrol duties. Thus the PCP took as a sampling frame only the beats and patrol shifts on which COP officers worked (thus excluding two overlapping shifts that began between 7:00 and 11:00 PM). Ultimately, 32 COP officers and 131 beat officers were observed in 18 of Cincinnati's beats. As POPN did, PCP administered a separate survey of observed officers, using an instrument of its own design, as well as a survey of 613 residents.

In a companion project, observations were also conducted in 21 small agencies serving suburban jurisdictions and small towns in the greater-Cincinnati area (Liederbach 2002). These agencies ranged in size from 9 to 56 sworn officers. Over nearly 14 months from 1999 to 2000, 602 patrol shifts of 228 officers were observed. Only dates and shifts were sampled for observations, since 10 of the agencies did not divide their jurisdictions into geographic patrol beats, and in the remaining 11 agencies, deployment to beats varied with manpower availability.

21.1.6 Smaller-Scale SSO Studies

The five major SSO projects all drew broad boundaries around police functions and tasks to be observed and recorded, capturing a wide range of police behaviors and the contexts in which they are taken, and enabling a correspondingly wide range of analyses. Other SSO-based studies have been conducted with more focused inquiry into particular kinds of situations and/or police activity or behaviors. Some of the projects also used a different sampling scheme, based on individual officers rather than space and time. We briefly describe several of those projects.

21.1.6.1 *Denver*

In 1982, David Bayley (1986) deployed observers on eighty-five rides in Denver. The purpose of the project was to inventory the tactics that officers use in handling "problematic situations"—those "in which experience is most important in avoiding mistakes and enhancing useful outcomes" (331), with a view toward determining the tactics that are effective. Observations focused on two types of encounters: disturbances (i.e., interpersonal conflicts) and traffic stops. Observations were done only during the evening tours, when problematic situations are more numerous; and though observation was conducted in every patrol unit, those that were more likely to become involved in such encounters were observed with disproportionate frequency. In order to capture the "flow" of officers' tactical choices, the coding of police actions was segmented into three encounter stages: contact, processing, and exit.

21.1.6.2 *Metro-Dade Police-Citizen Violence Reduction Project*

At the request of the Metro-Dade Police Department, James Fyfe developed and evaluated a training program with the objective of reducing unnecessary violence by police (Fyfe 1988). Officers were sampled from the three busiest districts and, within those districts, from treatment and control groups to which officers had been assigned randomly. Observations focused on potentially violent situations (PVs), generally "incidents in which officers become aware that they are likely to confront citizens in adversarial contexts" (Fyfe 1988, 1), and more particularly disputes, traffic stops, and crimes in progress. Systematic observations of sampled officers were conducted prior to the delivery of the training, when trained observers observed 502 8-hour tours (or 5 per officer on average), and 1,148 PVs; post-training observations covered 375 tours and captured data on 994 PVs.

21.1.6.3 *New York City*

Building on Bayley's research in Denver, Bayley and Garofalo (1987, 1989) conducted systematic observation of two sets of New York City police officers: 20 officers who had been nominated by their peers as "especially skilled at handling potentially violent situations" (1989, 2); and 26 comparison officers who had not been so nominated. Study officers were drawn from 3 NYPD precincts, selected because they were "busy, mixed in ethnicity, and characterized by a diverse mixture of crime and calls for police service" (1989, 3). Although the original design provided for observations of each officer on 10 tours of duty, observations were conducted on "about 350" tours, with a focus on "potentially violent mobilizations" defined operationally as "police-citizen encounters involving disputes, intervention by the police to apply the law against specific individuals, and all police attempts to question suspicious persons" (5). Like Bayley's Denver study, this project was concerned with identifying police actions that are effective by analyzing differences between the skilled officers and others.

21.1.6.4 Richmond

Mastrofski conducted SSO in Richmond during the spring and summer of 1992, the third year of Richmond's 5-year plan to implement community policing. Field researchers observed, in each patrol beat on all 3 shifts and with members of the SEU in each precinct as well, a total of 125 ride-along sessions with 120 officers; data on 1,100 encounters with more than 1,600 citizens were coded. This was the first SSO study of community policing, from which POPN was an outgrowth.

21.1.6.5 Savannah

In the wake of public concerns about racial profiling by police, Geoffrey Alpert and Roger Dunham fielded an observational study to examine how officers form suspicion and decide to stop motorists or pedestrians. Analyses of the stop data that many police agencies collect confront the challenge of forming a baseline against which to compare the composition of the stopped population, so that inferences about police bias can be drawn. Alpert and Dunham circumvented this problem by not only observing and debriefing officers, but also querying officers when "they seemed to take notice of something but not act on it" (Alpert et al. 2004, 2–8). In 2002, 132 shifts of Savannah police were observed, with a particular focus on occasions on which officers formed suspicion; many police-citizen encounters, such as those in which no suspect was present, were not encompassed by the observational protocol. In all, officers were coded as having formed suspicion on 174 occasions resulting in 103 stops.

21.1.7 Overview

In general, the large-scale observational projects have sampled spatially and temporally, assigning observers to patrol units on selected shifts in selected beats/neighborhoods but oversampling the busier beats and shifts. The observer accompanies the officer(s) assigned to a sampled beat on a sampled police tour of duty from start to finish. Data collection has been organized mainly around police-citizen encounters, providing for the coding of the characteristics and actions of citizens, the actions of the police (including the officer to whom the observer is assigned and any others who may be at or come to the scene), and other features of the interaction, such as the nature of its location. Observers record information at each of several levels, including: (1) the shift or "ride," such as the beat to which the observed officer was assigned, the time of day, and the officer's assignment (district/beat officer or community policing specialist); (2) the encounter, such as how the encounter was initiated (e.g., a dispatched call, or officer-initiated), the type of location in which the encounter transpired (such as a private residence, a commercial business, or a parking lot), and actions taken by police that were not directed at individual citizens (such as searching the premises); and (3) the citizen, including traits such as race, sex, and age, as well as demeanor, requested actions by police, and actions taken by police toward the citizen. POPN also provided for another level, the "activity," which was anything that the observed officer did outside of the context of a police-citizen encounter, such as motor patrol. The PSS also captured these kinds of phenomena, albeit in less detail, as a part of the shift-level information (e.g., minutes spent on mobile patrol).

The notable exception to these more general rules of research design was the Midwest City study, with its in-field coding of "utterances." Capturing data at that level of detail leads to some burdensome data collection in the field, and utterances as units of analysis lead to some very complicated analysis, such as Markov chain models (see Sykes and Brent 1983).

Many of the more focused SSO studies did not provide for the same breadth of coding, confining themselves to particular kinds of encounters that suit their more focused purposes. Some of them also provided for sampling based not on shift or beat but on individual officer.

Observers were recruited from among mainly graduate students and undergraduates, and trained in the observation instruments and procedures. Observers were supervised on a day-to-day basis, with quality-control checks of the data that they collected.[4] PSS and POPN did not recruit observers who were local to the observation sites, but rather housed the observers (and other field research staff) at the sites for the duration of a summer of field work. PCP, by contrast, recruited students from the University of Cincinnati (the PI's home institution) to conduct observations locally, and hence conducted observations throughout the calendar year.

Observational data were in many instances supplemented with other forms of data. Four of the five large-scale studies provided for surveys of officers, which could be linked by an identifying number to rides on which officers had been observed, respectively. Four of the studies also provided for surveys of the residents of the beats or neighborhoods in which observations were conducted, such that the character of the neighborhoods could be described and analyzed in conjunction with the description and analysis of beat or neighborhood patterns of police behavior. The President's Commission study and the PSS also provided for follow-up surveys of citizens who had been involved in observed encounters. POPN observed not only patrol officers but also field supervisors, which researchers were subsequently able to link to the rides on which their respective subordinates were observed.

Finally, it is clear that SSO projects have had different theoretical underpinnings, serving somewhat different purposes, with some important variations in designs, but also sharing some common components. Broadly or more narrowly focused, SSO data also have some common strengths, and some common weaknesses.

21.2 Virtues of SSO Data

From four-plus decades of research using observational data, scholars have formulated, refined, and tentatively answered some basic questions about policing in America, including the role and functions of the police, the discretionary use and abuse of police authority, and the forces that shape officers' exercise of discretion. With respect to each set of findings, we discuss the virtues of observational data as an evidentiary foundation.[5] Answers to these questions do not rest solely on observational data, but observational data are on many scores superior to the alternatives—police records, citizen surveys, and police surveys—and at a minimum, findings based on observational data enable researchers to triangulate on empirical reality. Researchers have also learned about and further refined SSO as they have learned about policing, and one might expect still greater pay-offs from further SSO of police, as the application of better developed and more widely accepted protocols means that findings are still more likely to cumulate across studies.

21.2.1 Role and Functions of the Police

Analyses of observational data have contributed to our understanding of the role of police in society—the nature of the incidents that officers handle, how those incidents come to police attention, and the respects in which these elements of the police role have changed with the advent of community policing. Observational data are of unparalleled utility in describing these patterns (Whitaker 1982). Police dispatch records tend to omit or underrepresent proactive work, and officer activity logs are susceptible to reporting biases born of the organizational uses for which their completion is mandated.

Reiss (1971a, 70) showed that in the 1960s, police work was predominantly reactive, performed in response to a citizen's request for police assistance, rather than "proactive," at the officer's initiative.[6] Police dealt mainly with problems that citizens defined as police business, as 87 percent of police mobilizations were initiated by citizens. In the 1970s, PSS data showed that only 10 percent of officers' *unassigned* or discretionary time was spent on officer-initiated encounters (Whitaker 1982, 16). Later research revealed somewhat different patterns in the community era. In Indianapolis and St. Petersburg, even patrol generalists initiated on their own authority about one-third of their encounters, while community policing specialists initiated 50 to 60 percent of their encounters with the public (Parks et al. 1999, 507)—far more than the officers observed by Reiss in 1966. In Cincinnati, beat officers initiated nearly 60 percent of their activities (including but not limited to encounters) (Frank, Novak, and Smith 2001, 51–52).

The time and effort that officers devote to order maintenance would presumably increase with the move to community policing. Whitaker (1982) found that officers observed for the PSS in 1977 spent only about 15 to 20 minutes per shift on neighborhood disorders. Twenty years later, in Indianapolis and St. Petersburg, patrol generalists spent nearly an hour of the typical shift on "public disorders," while community policing specialists spent about 40 minutes (Parks et al. 1999, 503), though in Cincinnati, beat officers and COP officers spent only 14 minutes and 10 minutes, respectively, on order maintenance during the typical shift.[7]

21.2.2 The Use and Abuse of Police Authority

Coercive authority is the unique occupational prerogative of police and at the heart of the police role (Bittner 1974). Officers exercise their authority in the form of several different behaviors: arrest; physical force; verbal "force," including commands, threats/warnings, questioning/interrogation; and searches. Officers have been observed to infrequently make arrests and even more seldom use physical force, relying far more routinely on verbal coercion or persuasion, cajoling, or negotiation to maintain order and provide services. The tendency to "underenforce" the law that Wilson (1968) noted decades ago appears to have held over time.

Observational data have some clear advantages relative to other sources of data in analyzing the use of police authority. With respect to the arrest decision, the advantages stem mainly from the observational accounting of the situational circumstances, to which we turn below. But with respect to the use of physical force and other forms of police authority, observation offers advantages in measuring both police authority and the circumstances of its use. The use-of-force reports that many agencies require can be usefully analyzed, but we can have more confidence in the results when they are corroborated by findings based on observations, because the force reported by officers, and their reports of the situational conditions under which they used force, are subject to the same reporting biases that afflict activity logs. Even self-reports for only research purposes (Garner, Maxwell, and Heraux 2002) are subject to misreporting that stems from officers' perceptual biases. The same concerns apply to police records of stops, the underreporting of which requires administrative auditing, and searches. Furthermore, some elements of the situations, such as citizens' demeanor toward the police, either do not appear (at all or systematically) in self-reports, or they are subject to concerns about the content and consistency of the definitions that officers apply.

Be that as it may, observational data on police use of force have sometimes left something to be desired, and the more recent SSO projects have surely done better in measuring the use of force. For example, PSS observers coded officers' use of physical force in one of three items: (a) used force to restrain or make the person come along; (b) used (other) force, to be coded (according to a coding memo) in "instances where the officer is 'kicking ass' "; and (c) hit or swung at with a weapon. POPN improved on the coding of force, providing for a wider range of discrete coding options that more nearly match the forms of force that officers might use, such as a "firm grip or nonpain restraint," hand-cuff, "pain compliance," and "impact or incapacitation methods"; moreover, observers were instructed to merely describe and not make judgments about whether the force used was necessary or justified. Verbal force and other techniques of influencing citizens' behavior were also captured: suggestions, requests, persuasion, negotiation, commands, and threats. In addition, coded and narrative data on citizens' actions enable researchers to analyze both police coercion and citizen resistance (e.g., Terrill 2005), from which inferences may be drawn (for research purposes) about the propriety of the force used.

21.2.3 Police Support, Responsiveness, and Community Policing

Some research has examined actions that are often conceived as comprising a wholly different dimension of police behavior: support (Cumming, Cumming, and Edell 1965). These actions include offering comfort (DeJong 2004) and/or sympathy (Myers 2002), fulfilling citizens' requests for assistance, or providing information or physical assistance on the officer's initiative (Myers 2002). It can also take the form of counseling or mediation in disputes (Black 1980; Worden 1989). Such behaviors are valued by citizens, and they are certainly not well-documented by police records, so observation is the only way to examine such behavior.

Neither are many behaviors that are prescribed for community policing well-documented in police records, including good-will contacts with citizens and any of a variety of actions relating to problem-solving; for these, observation can be useful. Observation has some unfortunate limits in describing officers' efforts in problem-solving, however, since problem-solving may stretch over days, weeks, or even months, only some of which is captured through sampled shifts. Thus analyses of observed problem-solving concerns aggregate effort in this activity domain rather than sustained work on sampled problems (DeJong, Mastrofski, and Parks 2001; Engel and Worden 2003).

21.2.4 Situational Influences on Police Behavior

A large volume of research has dwelled on the situational patterns exhibited by officers' use of their authority, that is, with what circumstances and citizen characteristics the use of police authority is associated. Much of this research has examined officers' use of their arrest authority (e.g., Black 1971; Lundman 1974; Smith and Visher 1981; Mastrofski, Worden, and Snipes 1995), their use of physical force (Reiss 1968a; Friedrich 1980; Worden 1995), or their use of coercive authority more generally—including not physical force but also commands, warnings, or threats (e.g., Black 1980; Worden 1989; Terrill 2005). While officers infrequently make arrests and still less frequently use physical force, the gravity of these actions—and the prospects for abuses—attract the attention of scholars and police mangers alike. In their search for situational patterns, researchers have examined the degree to which these behaviors are associated with a number of situational elements, including the seriousness of the offense, the location of the encounter, citizens' race, sex, age, sobriety, and demeanor toward police. We focus on those in connection with which SSO has been of particular significance.

The seriousness of the offense (if any) and the strength of evidence are legal factors that have a significant bearing on police officers' choices, as one would expect, and sound measures of these factors are consequently important in holding legal factors constant so that inferences can be drawn about the impacts of extra-legal factors. Independent coding of both of these factors by observers obviates questions about what officers record and why; indeed, for the least serious offenses, no documentary record might exist.[8]

Evidence also affects officers' behavior, but evidence does not determine it. Officers frequently do not invoke the law even when they have the legal authority to do so. Reiss's study captured primarily information on citizen testimony as evidence, police witnessing illegal acts and/or finding physical evidence. The PSS did not provide for coded data on evidence. Richmond and, hence, POPN did the best, capturing discrete types of information that has evidentiary value (e.g., another citizen observed the illegal act, the suspect fit the description of a person wanted by the police, the suspect gave a partial confession, the officer observed the suspect perform an illegal act or observed the act and circumstantial evidence) that can be combined to form a scale (Mastrofski, Worden, and Snipes 1995). No other source of data offers such rich, systematic information on this important factor.

Research has also found that officers' decisions to arrest are strongly influenced by the preferences of complainants, especially (but not only) when the offense is a less serious one, and especially when the preference is for leniency. Complainants do not always articulate a clear preference for or against legal action, but when they do, police tend to comply. This is a pattern that has been observed in domestic incidents (Worden and Pollitz 1984), and it is one that recent pro-arrest statutory and policy changes have sought to alter. Again, it is better not to rely on police reports. But given the demonstrated importance of this factor, it is essential to measure it.[9]

Both ethnographic and SSO-based research has with few exceptions found that the demeanor of suspects toward police affects the likelihood that they will be subjected to police authority (e.g., arrest or the use of physical force). Given the tendency of the police to underenforce the law (Wilson 1968; also see LaFave 1965; Black 1971), this means that disrespectful suspects are less likely to get a break—to avoid justifiable arrest, or to receive the benefit of an evidentiary doubt. Officers are more likely to take punitive action against those who flunk the "attitude test."

David Klinger (1994) called these findings into question, arguing that demeanor had been measured improperly, and that the analyses failed to control adequately or at all for citizens' criminal behavior. His analysis of observational data on Metro-Dade police officers' behavior in 245 interpersonal disputes, using what he regarded as a proper measure and more adequate controls, indicated that demeanor had no effect on the likelihood of arrest. Re-analyses of the Midwest City data (Lundman 1994, 1996) and the Police

Services Study data (Worden and Shepard 1996) showed that the original findings hold, and Klinger's (1995a, 1996) later analyses of Metro-Dade data showed that demeanor affects both arrest and the use of force. But Klinger's critique made it clear that previous SSO-based studies left room for improvement in the coding of citizens' demeanor, and that empirical analyses of those data should rest on both a more carefully specified conceptual definition of demeanor and correspondingly judicious operationalizations.

Subsequent studies have exhibited the greater care that Klinger's critique demanded. This progress has not—and could not—resolve some conceptual and theoretical ambiguities: now research isolates "resistance" from "demeanor," yet many forms of (especially passive) resistance are entirely legal, and we have reason to believe that they are interpreted by police as failures of the attitude test, such that we should interpret their effects as the effects of demeanor (Worden, Shepard, and Mastrofski 1996). In any case, observational data are very useful in allowing researchers to examine the possibilities, and debriefing/protocol analysis could further add to our understanding of how officers interpret various forms of citizen behavior.

We might add that demeanor is an important analytical ingredient in studies of police behavior not only for its own sake but also to control for effects that could otherwise be confounded with those of other important factors, such as citizens' race. Some of the earliest inquiries into police-citizen interactions reported disparities in the treatment of white and African American suspects, to the (expected) disadvantage of the latter, but these disparities were attributed to causal factors other than race itself: to the more frequently disrespectful demeanor of African American (or other minority) suspects (Black 1971), or to the more frequently pro-arrest preferences of African American complainants (Black and Reiss 1970). The findings on race effects are quite mixed, and it may be that the effects of race are contingent on other factors (Smith, Visher, and Davidson 1984), but properly specified models are essential for reaching sound conclusions.

21.3 LIMITATIONS OF SSO DATA

SSO data, relative to the alternatives, have strengths but they also suffer limitations. Studies based on observational data routinely raise questions about whether officers behave normally when observers are present, and so we first address this important issue. But SSO also raises other issues: what kinds of questions SSO is well-suited to address; how far the findings based on SSO can be generalized beyond the sites of the research; and the static nature of coded observations. We address each of these issues in turn

21.3.1 Reactivity

Observational data have clear advantages over alternatives for many purposes, but they are of course subject to the potential for bias that stems from "reactivity"—the reactions of officers to the presence of observers. Officers may behave differently than they normally do, engaging in some behaviors more frequently, and refraining from other behaviors. For example, officers might be more proactive than they are typically, to show the observer police work, and to demonstrate their skills and work ethic. They might be more civil in their interactions with citizens than is normal for them. They might run fewer personal errands, and "coop" less often or not at all. They might be more restrained in their use of physical force. Insofar as any of these reactions to observation contaminate observational data, the data will yield misestimates of the prevalence or frequency of the affected behaviors, and biased estimates of the effects of explanatory variables in an analysis.

Several efforts to assess the bias introduced by reactivity suggest that the validity of observational data, in general, is quite high (Mastrofski and Parks 1990), and some evidence has shown that the relationships between police behavior and other variables (such as characteristics of the situation) are unaffected by reactivity (Worden 1989, 8n). In general, as Reiss (1971b, 24) observes, "it is sociologically naive to assume that for many events the presence or participation of the observer is more controlling than other factors in the situation." With respect to his analysis of police brutality, which is one behavior that would presumably be among the more susceptible to reactivity, Reiss maintains that "the use of force by the police is situationally determined by other participants in the situation and by the officer's involvement in it, to such a degree that one must conclude the observer's presence had no effect" (Reiss 1971b, 24; also see Reiss 1968a, 1968b).

Richard Spano's (2003, 2005, 2006, 2007) is the most extensive examination of reactivity. Spano exploited measures of reactivity prospectively built into POPN data, including the observer reports of reactivity at the ride and encounter levels, examining reactivity with respect to proactivity (2007), the arrest decision (2003, 2005), and use of force (2006). He also examined the forces that shape officer behavior and provided descriptive accounts of the motivations to alter behavior (2007). His findings indicate that officers are more proactive when with observers than they might normally be, and that this is particularly pronounced when the observer is female; the arrest decision is similarly influenced by observer gender; the use of force decision is influenced by observer helping behavior, though the arrest decision is not. However, these effects diminish over the course of field work, and reactivity as a behavioral change is not universal.

In evaluating findings based on observational data, one should not assume that biases produced by reactivity are pervasive any more than one should assume that they are absent. It is much more reasonable to begin with the premise that some forms of behavior are more susceptible to reactivity than others are, and also with the premise that steps can be taken (a) during the field research to minimize reactivity, and (b) during analysis to test the sensitivity of results to reactivity. Prospective steps can be taken to minimize and assess reactivity, including training observers prior to beginning fieldwork, documenting observers' inferences about reactivity (Spano suggests that observers use field diaries), extending periods of observation, more fully exploiting the potential for unobtrusive social observation (cameras), training observers to build rapport, and respecting pledges of confidentiality.[10]

21.3.2 Micro-Social Focus

SSO is especially well-suited to inquiry that is sociological in nature, and particularly the kind of theoretical perspectives that Black and Reiss adopted.[11] We believe that SSO could be adapted to empirical investigations that are oriented to other perspectives, including psychological and organizational frameworks. There is some evidence that individual officers exhibit "styles" of policing (White 1972; Muir 1977; Brown 1981), which in principle could be operationalized with observational data. Such an effort would quickly confront the question: how many cases for any one officer are needed to estimate an individual style or pattern, given the heterogeneity of police tasks and decision contexts? It might depend on the nature of the behavior in question. Some "tactical choices" (Bayley 1986) are shaped so strongly by the situation and the context that many cases would be needed, while some behavioral tendencies—such as an officer's "manner" or level of proactivity—might be more stable across situations that vary in their task and social structure. For behaviors that exhibit greater stability especially, we might expect SSO would be useful in estimating individual propensities.

Organizational and other institutional influences on the exercise of police discretion are of long-standing interest, and some research based on observational data has analyzed the effects of the formal structures of police organizations, including the degree of bureaucratization and the nature of administrative expectations, on officers' discretionary choices. Much of this research is based on James Q. Wilson's (1968) seminal study, which posited that in "professional," bureaucratic departments one tends to find "legalistic" patterns of policing (meaning that officers tend to be more proactive and to rely more on their legal authority), while in "fraternal," nonbureaucratic departments one tends to find "watchman" patterns of policing (meaning that officers tend to be reactive and to infrequently invoke the law). This research has been limited, however, by the very small number of police agencies (twenty-four for the PSS but only three in the Black-Reiss data, and two in POPN) and the rather crude indicators of organizational structure that could be devised. Perhaps as a result, the research reports either null or countertheoretical findings (Friedrich 1980; Smith 1984; Worden 1989, 1995). If and when SSO using the same protocol is undertaken across a number of agencies, then we may learn much more about the organizational patterns of police behavior, and if it is accompanied by further development of the analytic constructs, then we may learn much more about how organizational structures influence officers' behavior.[12]

21.3.3 Infrequent Events

SSO is not appropriate for the analysis of phenomena that occur rarely, either as a rate per time observed or as a fraction of all police-citizen encounters. The use of deadly force is an obvious example. In over 7,200 hours of observation for the PSS, "[a] gun was *drawn* by one or more officers in each of 53 encounters, and in one of those the gun was fired (albeit at a rattlesnake)" (Worden 1995, 17n). But deadly force is not the only infrequent event that we would like to be able to analyze.

We would like to understand how officers behave in "critical incidents" (Muir 1977), which test their judgment, insight, and skills more than routine day-to-day encounters, but such incidents may occur too seldom to study them economically through SSO. Bayley and Garofalo (1989, 8) concluded that "the opportunity to display superior skill in defusing conflicts occurs relatively rarely in patrol work." Worden (1990), finding in an analysis of PSS data that college-educated officers perform no better than less educated officers do, speculated that the benefits of education for patrol performance might manifest themselves mainly in critical incidents, but such presumptively critical incidents were so infrequent that he could not test this proposition with PSS data.

21.3.4 Generalizability

Any original empirical inquiry will pose some inconvenience for the police agencies that are the sites for the research, but SSO places a particularly onerous burden on the agencies that agree to host such research. Thus we should consider the claim of Fyfe, Klinger, and Flavin (1997, 468–69):

> Since 1968, police research… typically has been conducted in a few progressive jurisdictions that have closely regulated officers' conduct and that, presumably, have had little to fear from publication of what researchers might find in their observations and archival searches. As a consequence, and regardless of the sophistication of the methodologies they have employed, police researchers generally have provided information concerning the operations of a small, self-selected, and therefore, non-representative sample of police agencies that probably most closely approximate Wilson's more professional "legalistic" and "service" styles of policing.

Fyfe et al. referred particularly to research on how police handle incidents involving spousal violence, but we can contemplate their concern as a more general proposition.

Let us consider the agencies in which SSO-based research has been conducted. When Reiss studied it in 1966, Boston's police department was not regarded as "professional," even compared with Chicago or Washington. For the PSS, the selection of metropolitan areas turned on the need to represent agencies that varied in size, and within metropolitan areas, the study agencies included all four of the main city departments and a number of small to medium-sized agencies that together arguably represented a cross-section of urban police departments. Richmond, Indianapolis, and St. Petersburg were selected for study because they were reputed to represent community policing. Cincinnati, we can see in retrospect, was not a department that exhibited exemplary compliance with the rule of law, inasmuch as by 2002, it had entered into an agreement with the Justice Department pursuant to an investigation into a pattern or practice of civil rights violations.[13]

Let us now consider the agencies in which other studies of police have been conducted. Officer self-reports of the use of force were collected in seven agencies: first

Phoenix (Garner et al. 1995) and later Charlotte-Mecklenburg, Colorado Springs, Dallas, St. Petersburg, San Diego, and the San Diego Sheriff's Office (Garner, Maxwell, and Heraux 2002). Terrill and Paoline (forthcoming) used police records to examine the use of force in eight agencies: Columbus; Charlotte-Mecklenburg; Portland; Albuquerque; Colorado Springs; St. Petersburg; Knoxville; and Fort Wayne. Deadly force has been analyzed in Chicago, Los Angeles, Memphis, Philadelphia, and New York City. It is not obvious to us that SSO-based research is by its nature less representative of American police than research based on other approaches; indeed, SSO has been more successful in including smaller agencies. Police research confronts a daunting challenge in representing the approximately 17,000 police agencies in the United States, but observational research is not of inferior external validity compared to other forms of research.

21.3.5 Temporal Dynamics

For the most part, the data collected in early SSO studies provided a snapshot of police-citizen encounters: actions that citizens and officers take, respectively, but with few exceptions, not when in the encounter these actions were taken. Many police-citizen encounters unfold over time. Other than the Midwest City Study, SSO projects have not captured these temporal dynamics well; Bayley parsed out three encounter phases of police actions, but citizens' actions were not similarly differentiated. We should not forget that how officers approach a situation, and how they act during a police-citizen encounter, could contribute to the development of situational conditions to which they must then respond; situational factors are not in all instances exogenous forces to which police react.

The narratives of police-citizen encounters prepared by POPN observers have been put to good use in supplemental coding that recovers these features of police-citizen interactions. Terrill (2001, 2005) exploited the narrative data to code instances of suspect resistance and police force during police-citizen encounters, and to differentiate sequences of resistance and force; the originally coded data would not suffice for that purpose. Similarly, McCluskey (2003) used the narrative data to code police requests for compliance and citizen responses in temporal order, and also the procedural justice with which police acted in these encounters. Thus the narratives have made it feasible to reconstruct the "transaction"-level of police-citizen encounters, and to execute much richer analyses of police behavior.

21.4 THE FUTURE OF SSO OF POLICE

The costs of SSO are considerable, so we have to carefully consider whether the marginal benefit of further SSO is worth the cost even of further studies using the POPN instruments. What can we learn from further SSO studies? And might we find a way to further economize, adapting SSO to take advantage of advances in technology?

The three most compelling lines of inquiry into police behavior to which SSO could contribute concern: (1) efforts to identify, describe, and understand craftsmanship, or "good" police work; (2) efforts to better understand officers' decision making; and (3) further efforts to understand the influences of organizational and institutional environments. Moreover, two or all three of these questions could be addressed together, so that we might better understand how "good" officers make choices, and how organizations or other institutions (such as citizen oversight) contribute to (or detract from) officers' performance.

Most police research describes and analyzes what officers do—arrest or not, use or refrain from using force—but cannot say whether what they do represented good police work. We are not the first to lament this shortcoming in police scholarship (see Bittner 1983; Bayley 1986; Fyfe 1997). SSO could play a role in filling this hole. Research could follow the lead of Bayley and Garofalo (1989), soliciting nominations of exceptionally skilled officers from among their peers and observing them in the field. Or other means might be used to identify exemplary officers (e.g., officers who score well in citizen satisfaction or ratings of procedural justice). However they are identified, it seems unlikely that we will learn much about what they do that marks them as skilled by looking only in police records.

As useful as the (SSO and other) research on police has been in illuminating the forces that shape police behavior, much of the variation in behavior remains unexplained. Most analysis of SSO data rests on what amounts to a stimulus-response model, in which situational factors are the hypothesized stimuli to which police decision makers respond, and inferences are drawn from the empirically estimated relationships about how officers perceive and interpret the situations and make choices among alternative courses of action. This approach has been scientifically rigorous, but it is limited to factors that are of a priori significance, and we know that these factors fall far short of explaining police decisions. Moreover, this approach treats the process by which informational inputs are interpreted and judgments are made to reach decisions as a "black box."[14] A different approach, that of "protocol analysis" or "process tracing," promises to shed further light onto decision making by opening the black box of police officers' cognitive processes (Ericsson and Simon 1984; Ford et al. 1989; Worden and Brandl 1990). For research based on protocol analysis, decision makers are asked to think aloud as they perform decision tasks, or they might be asked to recount their thinking as soon as possible after performing a decision task. Research subjects' verbal reports of their thinking are data on their decision processes. Protocol analysis does not require direct observations (cf. Stalans and Finn 1995), but debriefings of officers as part of SSO could be put to use for this purpose. Alpert et al. (2004) illustrate how protocol analysis can be incorporated into SSO (also see Bonner 2012).

Finally, we believe that further SSO could be instrumental in developing a deeper understanding of how organizational environments affect behavior, for the better and for the worse. Extant research hints at the role of organizational policies (Fyfe 1979; Hirschel et al. 2007), the role of supervision (Engel 2001), and the implications of organizational structure (Brown 1981; Whitaker 1983). More and better evidence will require a better developed theoretical framework, but it will also require data on officer behavior that is not contained in police records. No one study is likely to produce the data from which such findings will emerge; it is more likely that the accumulation of multiple data sets will be necessary.

It is quite possible that advances in technology will permit the adaptation of SSO to a form of post-hoc observation, by taking advantage of video and audio recordings of police-citizen encounters. The digital "footage" from in-car or body cameras allows for "observation" after the fact and at a fraction of the expense. Moreover, this would make it feasible and cost-effective to collect observation-like data on critical incidents, or to collect data on samples of individual officers. In-car cameras are best suited to capturing the video of traffic stops, but even with dash-mounted equipment, the audio recordings can tell us much about police-citizen encounters. Cincinnati traffic stops were analyzed using video and audio recordings from CPD police units (Riley et al. 2005), and we are now using similar recordings in one agency to examine the procedural justice of police in sampled encounters (about which we also have survey data). Better still, a number of agencies are deploying body cameras; Albuquerque, for example, requires that its officers wear a personal video camera, and Austin is moving in the same direction (Police Executive Research Forum 2012). A next step for SSO research might be a hybrid approach, using both conventional SSO and, for the same incidents that in-field observers code, independent post-hoc video coding, with a comparison of the two sets of data to assess their congruence.

Notes

* We gratefully acknowledge the favor of reviews and comments on an earlier draft by Stephen Mastrofski, Gordon Whitaker, Roger Parks, James Frank, Geoffrey Alpert, and David Bayley.
1. Some differences in coding patterns were detected across the three backgrounds (Reiss, 1968b, 362).
2. Narratives were to be completed for selected types of encounters, e.g., domestic disturbances and juvenile problems, encounters with violence between officer and citizen, encounters in which officers from other police agencies participate, and encounters that the observer believed were too complex to adequately portray in coded data. Observers were advised to "[t]hink of the narrative as telling another observer what happened in a particular encounter. Write it similarly to the way you would tell someone about it verbally."
3. They did not, however, include debriefings of officers.
4. For more on the mechanics of administering an SSO study, see Mastrofski et al. (1998) and Mastrofski, Parks, and McCluskey (2010).
5. For an authoritative statement about the strengths and weaknesses of SSO data, see National Research Council (2004, 111–13).
6. Reiss is credited with coining the term "proactive," which is of course widely used in many contexts today. So innovative was the concept in 1965 that the *American Sociological Review* refused to print Reiss and Bordua's article that used the term, because the word was not

a part of the English language. The article was subsequently published by the *American Journal of Sociology*.

7. We caution, however, that these temporal comparisons may be confounded by other differences across police departments, across projects (i.e., sampling of beats and patrol shifts), and across analyses (which use somewhat different analytic categories).

8. Observation-based measures of these constructs have arguably left room for improvement. Offense seriousness has often been framed simply as a dichotomy: more serious and less serious (e.g., felony/misdemeanor). Klinger (1994) found fault with such measures as failing to capture much of the variation in seriousness, and the addition of other binary variables for weapons and injuries, in his estimation, did not adequately complement the more/less serious dichotomy. Klinger suggested instead a 5-point, ordinal scale of offense seriousness: no crime; minor property crime; minor violent or major property crime; moderate violent crime; major violent crime. His advice has not been consistently heeded, and at this time, it is not clear how much difference it makes; some previous research has found that a binary measure captures much of the variation in the 5-point scale (Worden and Shepard 1996).

9. Analyzing data drawn from police reports, Fyfe, Klinger, and Flavin (1997) come to the conclusion that police in Chester, Pennsylvania, were less likely to make arrests in cases of male-on-female assaults than in other cases, but their inability to measure and control for complainant preference casts doubt on this inference (but cf. Klinger 1995b).

10. Most SSO-based research has been federally funded, and federally funded research on crime control is, statutorily, immune to legal process, such that observers cannot be compelled to testify to what they have seen or heard in a criminal, civil, or administrative proceeding (Boruch et al. 1991). This immunity has not been tested in state courts (Lowman and Palys 2001). SSO that is not federally sponsored does not enjoy the same statutory privilege, but may be eligible for a certificate of confidentiality. Be all that as it may, the more prosaic challenge to confidentiality comes in the field from other officers and patrol supervisors in casual or not-so-casual conversations with observers; observers must be trained to maintain confidentiality from one ride to the next, and vis-à-vis field supervisors.

11. According to the National Research Council (2004, 113), "[o]bservational studies are best suited to inform judgments regarding the proximate and immediate influences at work during a police-citizen encounter."

12. But care must be exercised in drawing these comparisons across projects because sampling plans may differ (e.g., POPN and PCP).

13. See http://www.cincinnati-oh.gov/police/pages/-5122-/, and the documents available there.

14. Researchers thereby assume that police decisions, like the structural regression models, are a weighted sum of the postulated decision cues: legal seriousness, strength of evidence, complainant preference, suspect demeanor, and the like. We think it unlikely that the process of police decision making resembles this computational model, however. And the models seldom explain more than a small fraction of the variation in behavior. Process models, which resemble flow charts, are probably more accurate representations of how people make complex decisions, especially under conditions of ambiguity and uncertainty.

References

Alpert, Geoffrey P., Roger G. Dunham, Meghan Stroshine, Katherine Bennett, and John MacDonald. 2004. *Police Officers' Decision Making and Discretion: Forming Suspicion and*

Making a Stop. Report to the National Institute of Justice. Columbia: University of South Carolina.

Bayley, David H. 1986. "The Tactical Choices of Police Patrol Officers." *Journal of Criminal Justice* 14:329–48.

Bayley, David H., and James Garofalo. 1987. *Patrol Officer Effectiveness in Managing Conflict During Police-Citizen Encounters*. Albany, NY: Hindelang Criminal Justice Research Center.

——. 1989. "The Management of Violence by Police Patrol Officers." *Criminology* 27:1–25.

Bittner, Egon. 1967. "The Police on Skid-Row: A Study of Peace-Keeping." *American Sociological Review* 32:699–715.

Bittner, Egon. 1974. "Florence Nightingale in Pursuit of Willie Sutton: A Theory of the Police." In *The Potential for Reform of Criminal Justice*, edited by Herbert Jacob, 17–44. Beverly Hills, CA: Sage.

——. 1983. "Legality and Workmanship: Introduction to Control in the Police Organization." In *Control in the Police Organization*, edited by Maurice Punch, 1–11. Cambridge, MA: MIT Press.

Black, Donald. 1971. "The Social Organization of Arrest." *Stanford Law Review* 23:1087–111.

——. 1980. *The Manners and Customs of the Police*. New York: Academic Press.

Black, Donald, and Albert J. Reiss, Jr. 1967. "Patterns of Behavior in Police and Citizen Transactions." *Studies of Crime and Law Enforcement in Major Metropolitan Areas*, Volume II, Section I. Washington, DC: U.S. Government Printing Office.

——. 1970. "Police Control of Juveniles." *American Sociological Review* 35:63–77.

Bonner, Heidi S. 2012. *How Patrol Officers Make Decisions: Comparing a Structural Model to a Process Model*. PhD dissertation, University at Albany, State University of New York, School of Criminal Justice.

Boruch, Robert F., Albert J. Reiss, Jr., Joel Garner, Kinley Larntz, and Sally Freels. 1991. "Sharing Confidential and Sensitive Data: The Spouse Assault Replication Program." In *Sharing Social Science Data: Advantages and Challenges*, edited by Joan E. Sieber, 61–86. Beverly Hills, CA: Sage.

Brown, Michael K. 1981. *Working the Street: Police Discretion and the Dilemmas of Reform*. New York: Russell Sage.

Cumming, Elaine, Ian Cumming, and Laura Edell. 1965. "The Policeman as Philosopher, Guide, and Friend." *Social Problems* 12:276–86.

DeJong, Christina. 2004. "Gender Differences in Officer Attitude and Behavior: Providing Comfort to Citizens." *Women and Criminal Justice* 15:1–32.

DeJong, Christina, Stephen D. Mastrofski, and Roger B. Parks. 2001. "Patrol Officers and Problem Solving: An Application of Expectancy Theory." *Justice Quarterly* 18:31–61.

Engel, Robin S. 2001. "Supervisory Styles of Patrol Sergeants and Lieutenants." *Journal of Criminal Justice* 29:341–55.

Engel, Robin Shepard, and Robert E. Worden. 2003. "Police Officers' Attitudes, Behavior, and Supervisory Influences: An Analysis of Problem-solving." *Criminology* 41:131–66.

Ericsson, K., Anders, and Herbert A. Simon. 1984. *Protocol Analysis: Verbal Reports as Data*. Cambridge, MA: MIT Press.

Ford, Kevin, Neil Schmitt, Susan Schechtman, Brian M. Hults, and Mary Doherty. 1989. "Process Tracing Methods: Contributions, Problems, and Neglected Research Questions." *Organizational Behavior and Human Decision Processes* 43:75–117.

Frank, James, Kenneth Novak, and Brad W. Smith. 2001. *Street-level Policing in Cincinnati: The Content of Community and Traditional Policing and the Perceptions of Policing Audiences*. Final Report to the National Institute of Justice. Cincinnati: University of Cincinnati.

Friedrich, Robert J. 1977. *The Impact of Organizational, Individual, and Situational Factors on Police Behavior*. PhD dissertation, University of Michigan, Department of Political Science.

Friedrich, Robert J. 1980. "Police Use of Force: Individuals, Situations, and Organizations." *Annals of the American Academy of Political and Social Science* 452:82–97.

Fyfe, James J. 1979. "Administrative Interventions on Police Shooting Discretion." *Journal of Criminal Justice* 7:309–23.

———. 1988. *The Metro-Dade Police/Citizen Violence Reduction Project: Final Report*. Washington, DC: Police Foundation.

———. 1997. "Good Policing." In *Critical Issues in Policing: Contemporary Readings*, 3d ed., edited by Roger G. Dunham and Geoffrey P. Alpert, 194–213. Prospect Heights, IL: Waveland.

Fyfe, James J., David A. Klinger, and Jeanne Flavin. 1997. "Differential Police Treatment of Male-on-Female Spousal Violence." *Criminology* 35:455–73.

Garner, Joel H., Christopher D. Maxwell, and Cedrick Heraux. 2002. "Characteristics Associated with the Prevalence and Severity of Force Used by the Police." *Justice Quarterly* 19: 705–46.

Garner, Joel H., Thomas Schade, John Hepburn, and John Buchanan. 1995. "Measuring the Continuum of Force Used By and Against the Police." *Criminal Justice Review* 20:146–68.

Hirschel, David, Eve Buzawa, April Pattavina, and Don Faggiani. 2007. "Domestic Violence and Mandatory Arrest Laws: To What Extent Do They Influence Police Arrest Decisions?" *Journal of Criminal Law and Criminology* 98:255–99.

Kelling, George L., and Mark H. Moore. 1988. "From Political to Reform to Community: The Evolving Strategy of Police." In *Community Policing: Rhetoric or Reality*, edited by Jack R. Greene and Stephen D. Mastrofski, 3–25. New York: Praeger.

Klinger, David A. 1994. "Demeanor or Crime? Why 'Hostile' Citizens are More Likely to be Arrested." *Criminology* 32:475–93.

———. 1995a. "The Micro-Structure of Nonlethal Force: Baseline Data from an Observational Study." *Criminal Justice Review* 20:169–86.

———. 1995b. "Policing Spousal Assault." *Journal of Research in Crime and Delinquency* 32:308–24.

———. 1996. "More on Demeanor and Arrest in Dade County." *Criminology* 34:61–82.

LaFave, Wayne. 1965. *Arrest: The Decision to Take the Suspect into Custody*. Boston: Little, Brown.

Liederbach, John. 2002. *Policing Small Towns, Rural Places, and Suburban Jurisdictions: Officer Activities, Citizen Interactions, and Community Context*. PhD dissertation, University of Cincinnati, Department of Criminal Justice.

Lowman, John, and Ted Palys. 2001. "The Ethics and Law of Confidentiality in Criminal Justice Research: A Comparison of Canada and the U.S." *International Criminal Justice Review* 11:1–33.

Lundman, Richard J. 1974. "Routine Police Arrest Practices: A Commonweal Perspective." *Social Problems* 22:127–41.

———. 1994. "Demeanor or Crime? The Midwest City Police-citizen Encounters Study." *Criminology* 32:631–56.

———. 1996. "Demeanor and Arrest: Additional Evidence from Unpublished Data." *Journal of Research in Crime and Delinquency* 33:306–23.

Manning, Peter K. 1977. *Police Work: The Social Organization of Policing*. Cambridge, MA: MIT Press.

Mastrofski, Stephen, and Roger B. Parks. 1990. "Improving Observational Studies of Police." *Criminology* 28:475–96.

Mastrofski, Stephen D., Roger B. Parks, and Jogn D. McCluskey. 2010. "Systematic Social Observation in Criminology." In *Handbook of Quantitative Criminology*, edited by Alex Piquero and David Weisburd, 225–247. New York: Springer-Verlag.

Mastrofski, Stephen D., Roger B. Parks, Albert J. Reiss, Jr., Robert E. Worden, Christina DeJong, Jeffrey B. Snipes, and William C. Terrill. 1998. *Systematic Observation of Public Police: Applying Field Research Methods to Policy Issues.* Washington, DC: National Institute of Justice.

Mastrofski, Stephen D., Roger B. Parks, Robert E. Worden, and Albert J. Reiss, Jr. 2007. *Project on Policing Neighborhoods in Indianapolis, Indiana, and St. Petersburg, Florida, 1996–1997.* Computer File. Ann Arbor, MI: Inter-university Consortium for Political Social Research, ICPSR03160.v2.

Mastrofski, Stephen D., Robert E. Worden, and Jeffrey B. Snipes. 1995. "Law Enforcement in a Time of Community Policing." *Criminology* 33:539–63.

McCluskey, John D. 2003. *Police Requests for Compliance: Coercive and Procedurally Just Tactics.* New York: LFB Scholarly Publishing.

Moskos, Peter. 2008. *Cop in the Hood: My Year Policing Baltimore's Eastern District.* Princeton, NJ: Princeton University Press.

Muir, William Ker, Jr. 1977. *Police: Streetcorner Politicians.* Chicago: University of Chicago Press.

Myers, Stephanie M. 2002. *Police Encounters with Juvenile Suspects: Explaining the Use of Authority and Provision of Support.* PhD dissertation, University at Albany, State University of New York, School of Criminal Justice.

National Research Council. 2004. *Fairness and Effectiveness in Policing: The Evidence.* Committee to Review Research on Police Policy and Practices, edited by Wesley Skogan and Kathleen Frydl. Washington, DC: National Academies Press.

Ostrom, Elinor, Roger B. Parks and Gordon P. Whitaker. 1973. "Do We Really Want to Consolidate Urban Police Forces? A Reappraisal of Some Old Assertions." *Public Administration Review* 33:423-32.

———. 2001. *Police Services Study, Phase II, 1977: Rochester, St. Louis, and St. Petersburg.* Computer file. Ann Arbor, MI: Inter-university Consortium for Political and Social Research, ICPSR08605v3.

———. 1978. *Patterns of Metropolitan Policing.* Cambridge, MA: Ballinger.

Ostrom, Elinor, and Dennis C. Smith. 1976. "On the Fate of 'Lilliputs' in Metropolitan Policing." *Public Administration Review* 36:192–200.

Ostrom, Elinor, and Gordon P. Whitaker. 1973. "Does Local Community Control of Police Make a Difference? Some Preliminary Findings." *American Journal of Political Science* 27:48-76.

Parks, Roger B., Stephen D. Mastrofski, Christina DeJong, and M. Kevin Gray. 1999. "How Officers Spend Their Time with the Community." *Justice Quarterly* 16:483–518.

Police Executive Research Forum. 2012. *How Are Innovations in Technology Transforming Policing?* Washington, DC: Author.

Reaves, Brian A. 2010. *Local Police Departments, 2007.* Washington, DC: Bureau of Justice Statistics.

Reiss, Albert J., Jr. 1968a. "Police Brutality: Answers to Key Questions." *Trans-action* 5:10–19.

———. 1968b. "Stuff and Nonsense about Social Surveys and Observation." In *Institutions and the Person*, edited by Howard S. Becker, Blanche Geer, David Riesman, and Robert S. Weiss, 351–367. Chicago: Aldine.

——. 1971a. *The Police and the Public*. New Haven, CT: Yale University Press.

——. 1971b. "Systematic Observation of Natural Social Phenomena." In *Sociological Methodology 1971*, edited by Herbert L. Costner, 3–33. San Francisco: Jossey-Bass.

Riley, K. Jack, Susan Turner, John MacDonald, Greg Ridgeway, Terry L. Schell, Jeremy M. Wilson, Travis L. Dixon, Terry Fain, Dionne Barnes-Proby, and Brent D. Fulton. 2005. *Police-Community Relations in Cincinnati*. Santa Monica, CA: RAND.

Rubinstein, Jonathan. 1973. *City Police*. New York: Ballantine.

Skolnick, Jerome. 1966. *Justice Without Trial: Law Enforcement in Democratic Society*. New York: John Wiley.

Smith, Douglas A. 1984. "The Organizational Context of Legal Control." *Criminology* 22:19–38.

Smith, Douglas A., and Christy A. Visher. 1981. "Street-Level Justice: Situational Determinants of Police Arrest Decisions." *Social Problems* 29:167–77.

Smith, Douglas A., Christy A. Visher, and Laura A. Davidson. 1984. "Equity and Discretionary Justice: The Influence of Race on Police Arrest Decisions." *Journal of Criminal Law and Criminology* 75:234–49.

Spano, Richard. 2003. "Concerns about Safety, Observer Sex, and the Decision to Arrest: Reactivity in a Large-Scale Observational Study of Police." *Criminology* 41:909–32.

——. 2005. "Potential Sources of Observer Bias in Police Observational Data." *Social Science Research* 34:591–617.

——. 2006. "Observer Behavior as a Potential Source of Reactivity: Describing and Quantifying Observer Effects in a Large-Scale Observational Study of Police." *Sociological Methods and Research* 34:521–53.

——. 2007. "How Does Reactivity Affect Police Behavior? Describing and Quantifying the Impact of Reactivity as Behavioral Change in a Large Scale Observational Study of Police." *Journal of Criminal Justice* 35:453–65.

Stalans, Loretta J., and Mary A. Finn. 1995. "How Novice and Experienced Officers Interpret Wife Assaults: Normative and Efficiency Frames." *Law and Society Review* 29:287–321.

Sykes, Richard E., and Edward E. Brent. 1980. "The Regulation of Interaction by Police: A Systems View of Taking Charge." *Criminology* 18:182–97.

——. 1983. *Policing: A Social Behaviorist Perspective*. New Brunswick, NJ: Rutgers University Press.

Terrill, William. 2001. *Police Coercion: Application of the Force Continuum*. New York: LFB Scholarly Publishing.

——. 2005. "Police Use of Force: A Transactional Approach." *Justice Quarterly* 22:107–38.

Terrill, William, and Eugene A. Paoline, III. Forthcoming. "Examining Less Lethal Force Policy and the Force Continuum: Results from a National Use-of-Force Study." *Police Quarterly*.

Van Maanen, John. 1974. "Working the Street: A Developmental View of Police Behavior." In *The Potential for Reform of Criminal Justice*, edited by Herbert Jacob, 83–130. Beverly Hills, CA: Sage.

Walker, Samuel. 1992. "Origins of the Contemporary Criminal Justice Paradigm: The American Bar Foundation Survey, 1953–1969." *Justice Quarterly* 9:47–76.

Westley, William A. 1970. *Violence and the Police: A Sociological Study of Law, Custom, and Morality*. Cambridge, MA: MIT Press.

Whitaker, Gordon P. 1982. "What Is Patrol Work?" *Police Studies* 4:13–22.

——. 1983. "Police Department Size and the Quality and Cost of Police Services." In *The Political Science of Criminal Justice*, edited by Stuart Nagel, Erika Fairchild, and Anthony Champagne, 185–196. Springfield, IL: Charles C. Thomas.

White, Susan O. 1972. "A Perspective on Police Professionalization." *Law and Society Review* 7:61–85.

Wilson, James Q. 1968. *Varieties of Police Behavior: The Management of Law and Order in Eight Communities.* Cambridge, MA: Harvard University Press.

Worden, Robert E. 1989. "Situational and Attitudinal Explanations of Police Behavior: A Theoretical Reappraisal and Empirical Assessment." *Law and Society Review* 23:667–711.

———. 1990. "A Badge and a Baccalaureate: Policies, Hypotheses, and Further Evidence." *Justice Quarterly* 7:565–92.

———. 1995. "The 'Causes' of Police Brutality: Theory and Evidence on Police Use of Force." In *And Justice for All: Understanding and Controlling Police Abuse of Force,* edited by William A. Geller and Hans Toch, 31–60. Washington, DC: Police Executive Research Forum.

Worden, Robert E., and Steven G. Brandl. 1990. "Protocol Analysis of Police Decision Making: Toward a Theory of Police Behavior." *American Journal of Criminal Justice* 14:297–318.

Worden, Robert E., and Alissa A. Pollitz. 1984. "Police Arrests in Domestic Disturbances: A Further Look." *Law and Society Review* 18:105–19.

Worden, Robert E., and Robin L. Shepard. 1996. "Demeanor, Crime, and Police Behavior: A Reexamination of Police Services Study Data." *Criminology* 34:83–105.

Worden, Robert E., Robin L. Shepard, and Stephen D. Mastrofski. 1996. "On the Meaning and Measurement of Suspects' Demeanor toward the Police." *Journal of Research in Crime and Delinquency* 33:324–32.

CHAPTER 22

USING EXPERIMENTAL DESIGNS TO STUDY POLICE INTERVENTIONS

LORRAINE MAZEROLLE, CYNTHIA LUM, AND ANTHONY A. BRAGA

FIELD experimentation in policing occupies a relatively small, yet important, field of inquiry within criminology and criminal justice. As of the start of 2012, 29 randomized police experiments have been documented (see Lum, Koper, and Telep 2011). These policing experiments answer important questions about the effectiveness and efficiencies of different types of police interventions and help to advance our theoretical understandings as to the crime control and prevention role of police in modern society. Field experimentation in the area of policing, however, is challenging in that it demands police to alter their routine operations to accommodate adherence to random allocation and implementation of the experimental and control conditions.

Despite the complexities of field trials in policing, past and present experiments in policing have significantly shaped crime control policies and practice both in the United States and around the world. The Minneapolis Hot Spots experiment (Sherman and Weisburd 1995), for example, addressed lessons learned from the Kansas City Preventive Patrol Experiment and helped shape the way police agencies now direct patrol units to police hot spots of crime during "hot" times of the day or night. The cluster of Drug Market Analysis Program (DMAP) experiments (Sherman and Rogan 1995; Weisburd and Green 1995) applied field experimental methods to better understand police responses to drug problems, shaping the shift in drug law enforcement from reactive, arrest-oriented approaches to being problem-oriented in efforts to clean up open-air drug market activities. The most recent crop of second-generation experiments in policing have tested the effectiveness of foot patrols (see Ratcliffe et al. 2011), police legitimacy (see Mazerolle et al., 2012), compressed work schedules in policing (see Amendola et al. 2011), and hot spots policing that targets crime and disorder (Braga and Bond 2008), shaping the future of police operational practice and policy.

Section 22.1 of this essay provides a brief historical look at the key policing experiments that shape current police practice. The patrol and foot patrol policing experiments in the 1970s (Kansas City, Newark), primarily led by the Police Foundation, are described. The push for experimentation in the mid-1980s, led by Lawrence Sherman and David Weisburd, that altered patrol and drug law enforcement practice are reviewed. Finally, the surge in police experiments in the 1990s that has shaped many of the current operational police practices is also discussed. Section 22.2 focuses on the evidence-based policy agenda of governments throughout the world, along with the establishment of the Campbell Collaboration and the Academy of Experimental Criminology in the late 1990s to early 2000s. This period of consolidation led to the current mainstreaming of criminal justice experiments in general and policing experiments in particular. Section 22.3 introduces the Lum-Koper-Telep Evidence-Based Policing Matrix, identifying different types of policing experiments and their findings. In Section 22.4, we discuss the trials and tribulations of conducting randomized field trials with police, including a discussion about the complexities of randomizing police officers, police patrols, police organizational units and practices under field trial conditions. Section 22.5 concludes by reviewing the key points outlined in the essay.

A number of take-home messages emerge from the essay:

- Field experiments in policing are challenging, both for the police and researchers.
- The dearth of experimentation across many areas in policing offers clear opportunities for more field trials and for scholars to use experimentation to assess police effectiveness.
- The public policy impacts of police experiments are, arguably, greater than those generated using other types of inquiry—a factor that both police and police scholars might take into account when considering the pros and cons of conducting a field experiment.
- Police agencies throughout the world are now much more open to the idea of field experimentation than ever before.
- The use of experimental designs to study police and policing occupies an important place in the advancement of evidence-based practice in policing.

22.1 A BRIEF HISTORY OF POLICE EXPERIMENTS

The historical development of randomized experiments in criminology in general and in policing in particular cannot be disentangled from the history of evidence-based crime policy and the "what works" movement. The Martinson Report (Martinson 1974; Lipton, Martinson, and Wilks 1975) is widely recognized as starting the "what works" movement and the push for rigorous evaluation to discern the effectiveness of policies. Martinson's report, as well as other studies such as the

Kansas City Preventive Patrol Experiment (Kelling et al. 1974a, 1974b), set the stage for policy maker demands for effective interventions and better evaluation of new, innovative programs. Thus, the mid-1970s emerged as the starting point for reform in criminal justice practice and policy making, with demands for methodological rigor in evaluation research of criminal justice (including policing) interventions. In this section, we examine four key policing policies—patrolling, foot patrols, drug law enforcement, and policing domestic violence—and the contributions made by police experiments, both past and present.

22.1.1 Preventive Patrolling

Starting with the Kansas City Preventive Patrol Experiment (Kelling et al. 1974a, 1974b)—widely regarded as the first ever true, randomized police field experiment— policing experiments have led to major reform in the public policy arena. With preventive patrolling the cornerstone of professional policing during the 1970s, observers of the Kansas City experiment expected results to show that preventive patrolling was an effective and efficient use of police resources. The experiment sought to vary the dosage of police patrols across fifteen randomly allocated patrol beats and to test whether or not preventive patrolling—increasing the amount of patrol time across police beats—could deter crime. The results, however, "shook the theoretical foundations of American policing" (Sherman and Weisburd 1995, 625), finding no statistically significant differences between the three test conditions—emergency response only, standard levels of patrolling, and the elevated, omnipresent preventive patrolling beats—in the level of crime, citizen attitudes toward police services, citizen fear of crime, police response time, or citizen satisfaction with police response time (see Kelling et al. 1974b).

The public policy response to the Kansas City experiment heralded a major turning point for policing, police research, and field experimentation in policing, resulting in major reductions in public spending on police and a widely held view that the police could do little to deter crime (Moore, Trojanowicz, and Kelling 1988). The late 1970s and early 1980s subsequently became a very difficult period for policing where resources started to shift from police agencies to fund the rise of the community corrections movement.

It was not until the mid-1980s that the preventive value of police started to receive renewed recognition. In 1988, Lawrence Sherman and David Weisburd launched the Minneapolis Hot Spots Experiment. Dealing with the design flaws of the Kansas City Preventive Patrol Experiment (e.g., lack of statistical power, lack of dosage, lack of focus into high crime places), Sherman and Weisburd (1995) led the experimental evaluation of a test of directed patrols in high crime places. They randomly allocated 110 crime hot spots, where 55 hot spots received on average twice as much observed patrol presence as the 55 control hot spots. They concluded that "substantial increase in police patrol presence can indeed cause modest reductions in crime and more impressive reductions in disorder within high crime locations" (Sherman and Weisburd 1995, 625).

The public policy implications of the Minneapolis Hot Spots Experiment led police departments across the world to adopt patrol policies that direct police to hot spots during hot times. Further, for those agencies serious about gaining the best value from directed hot spots patrols, adoption of the "Koper Curve" augments the optimal deployment of patrol units such that patrol units stay in the hot spots for about fifteen minutes (see Koper 1995). Thereafter, the deterrent effects of hot spots policing decays.

Hot spots police patrols are now well established as an effective approach to crime control. Braga's (2007) systematic review of the effects of hot spots policing on crime and the National Academy of Sciences panel (see Skogan and Frydl 2004) both conclude that focusing police resources at high-crime places is an effective approach to preventing and controlling crime and disorder. A recent experiment, however, conducted in Jacksonville, Florida by Bruce Taylor, Christopher Koper, and Daniel Woods (2010) provides a cautious note to the otherwise chorus of evidence in favor of hot spots policing. Their study tested the crime control effects, under field trial conditions, of a problem-oriented policing (POP) strategy, directed-saturation patrol or a control condition. While they found some reductions in the hot spots receiving POP treatment, the changes in violence and property crime between the three types of experimental conditions were not statistically significantly different (see Taylor et al. 2010). While this Taylor trial is important and cannot be dismissed, the Braga (2007) systematic review evidence showing seven of the nine experimental evaluations of hot spots policing reporting crime and disorder reductions suggests that the body of evidence continues to favor police operational deployment of directed patrols to hot spots of crime.

22.1.2 Foot Patrols

Foot patrols have been a fundamental crime control tactic of police for as far back as the "rattle watches of the 1700s" (see Ratcliffe et al. 2011, 796). The first ever randomized field trial that tested the deterrent value of foot patrols was the Newark Foot Patrol Experiment, conducted from 1978 to 1979 (Kelling et al. 1981; Police Foundation 1981; Pate et al. 1986). Funding for the Newark Foot Patrol Experiment came quickly to the Police Foundation after the publication of the Kansas City experiment results. The foot patrol experiment varied foot patrol levels across twelve beats in Newark, New Jersey and, like the Kansas City experiment, found no significant differences between the treatment and control beats for changes in recorded crime or arrest rates. Yet despite a lack of evidence to support the deterrent effects of foot patrols, they became—and still occupy—a central part of community policing interventions throughout the world.

One of the reasons for the popularity of foot patrols continuing beyond the published findings of the experiment is due to the widely-acclaimed publication of the "Broken Windows" article by James Q. Wilson and George Kelling in the influential magazine *The Atlantic Monthly*. Using Kelling's field experiences during the Newark Foot Patrol experiment in Newark, the Broken Windows piece was a précis of the inter-connectedness of crime and disorder, fear of crime, and the role of order maintenance policing, particularly foot patrols. The central thesis of the article is that low-level street disorder (the "unchecked panhandler")—if left untended—leads to fear and a breakdown in community controls which gives rise to a spiral of decline and the vulnerability of an area to criminal invasion and serious crime (Wilson and Kelling 1982). They argued that foot patrol had a particular role to play in those neighborhoods at the "tipping point" of spiraling into decline (see Wilson and Kelling 1982). The Broken Windows thesis prevails today as one of the most highly cited (see Harcourt 1998; Parks 2008) and influential pieces of work that has shaped policing policies and practices since its publication in 1982. Interestingly, the longevity of foot patrols as a feature of urban police practices has prevailed through to the present day, despite the National Research Council (2004) finding that foot patrols offered only weak to moderate evidence of effectiveness in reducing fear of crime. The recent Philadelphia foot patrol experiment by Jerry Ratcliffe and his colleagues (Ratcliffe et al. 2011) arguably reverses this National Research Council summary, finding that intensive foot patrol efforts in violent hot spots do indeed have deterrent value when they increase certainty of disruption, apprehension, and arrest.

22.1.3   Policing Places with Drug Problems

The proliferation of drugs during the late 1980s and 1990s created unprecedented pressure on police and other law enforcement agencies to wage a "War on Drugs" and to control the violence and harms associated with open-air drug markets. In response to the drug problem, federal and state legislators enacted and implemented policies that were generally oriented toward enforcement activities (see Caulkins et al. 2004). It was against this policy backdrop that the National Institute of Justice launched the multi-site Drug Market Analysis Program (DMAP) in 1990. DMAP funded five sites and teams of researchers to develop plans to evaluate and analyze operational best practice in drug law enforcement. Funding was provided to teams of researchers and police agencies in Jersey City (see Weisburd and Green 1995), Kansas City (see Sherman and Rogan 1995), Hartford (see Tien et al. 1993), Pittsburgh (see Cohen, Gorr, and Olligschlager 1993), and San Diego (see Eck and Wartell 1998). From this DMAP program of funding, three field trials (in Kansas City, Jersey City, and San Diego) emerged that tested whether or not the arrest-focus on drug law enforcement was the best approach for dealing with open-air drug market activity.

The Kansas City "raid" experiment came at the height of the War on Drugs (see Caulkins et al. 2004), and police resources were largely focused on response tactics using SWAT-like teams to arrest and close down crack houses. At the time, court-authorized raids were legal where police had received at least five calls for service about a problem property in the preceding thirty days. The Kansas City experiment tested the block-level deterrent effects on crime of uniformed police court-authorized raids on 98 drug house properties. The control condition included 109 properties that received no treatment. Sherman and Rogan (1995) reported that the experimental blocks, compared to the control sites, showed reductions in both calls for service and offense reports, but effects were quite small and decayed in two weeks. The main policy implication of the study was that alternative police methods were likely to be far more cost effective than raids (Sherman and Rogan 1995).

The Jersey City DMAP experiment sought to test two types of drug law enforcement: the experimental treatment operationalized the basic steps of problem-oriented policing (POP) where experimental teams of narcotics officers had to identify and analyze the dynamics of the problem in each street drug market assigned to them, develop tailored responses to the problem, and then work to maintain the crime control gains. The control teams of narcotics officers did what was common at the time amongst drug law enforcement officers: surveillance and then enforcement action to arrest known users and dealers in high-activity street locations (Weisburd and Green 1995). The research team randomly allocated 56 drug markets to either the experimental condition (i.e., POP) or the control condition (i.e., business as usual). Using community surveys, police administrative data, and field observations, Weisburd and Green (1995) found consistent and strong effects of the experimental strategy on disorder activities with very little evidence of displacement of the crime control benefits to areas surrounding the experimental hot spots. The experimental study provided early evidence about the ineffective use of arrests as the cornerstone of drug law enforcement activity during the height of the drug epidemic in the United States. Alternatively, the field trial suggested that a better strategy, for even serious street drug market locations, was a more considered, analytic approach that matched the response to the dynamics of the problem.

The San Diego experiment tested the theoretical link between the effectiveness of place management and the likelihood of drug dealing and criminal behavior at places (see Eck and Wartell 1998). Using a case control design, Eck and Wartell (1998) identified 121 rental properties that had already been targeted by drug enforcement and then randomly assigned the properties into two approximately equal-sized treatment groups or a third control group that received no further police action. The Drug Abatement Response Team (DART) sent two types of letters to the equal-sized treatment groups: one letter informing the owner about the fines associated with drug dealing properties, but with no enforcement follow-up; the other group of properties received a similar letter informing them of the legal consequences of drug dealing on their properties, coupled with a request to the property owner to work with the DART. Using police agency records and environmental surveys, the experimental findings found large reductions in crime in the DART/letter group, providing strong support for the policy of having police and code enforcement officials meet with property owners following drug law enforcement (Eck and Wartell 1998).

The DMAP experiments, taken as a group, made large policy strides toward reforming the approach of street-level drug law enforcement from being reactive and arrest-oriented to taking a more considered, analytic approach to matching responses to the underlying social and environmental dynamics that allowed some street corners to attract drug market activity and others not. The DMAP experiments also set the foundations for police to better understand the link between crime and place (see

Braga and Weisburd 2010; see also Green 1995) and tailoring their crime control activities accordingly.

22.1.4 Policing Domestic Violence

Like patrols, foot patrols and drug law enforcement, the Minneapolis Domestic Violence Experiment (Sherman and Berk 1984a, 1984b), along with at least five replications of the original policing trial (see Dunford 1990; Dunford, Huizinga, and Elliott 1990; Berk et al. 1992; Hirschel, Hutchison, and Dean 1992; Pate and Hamilton 1992; Sherman et al. 1992; Garner, Fagan, and Maxwell 1995; Maxwell, Garner, and Fagan 2001; Weisz 2001), has similarly influenced policing policy and practice for decades. As a result of Sherman and Berk's initial experiment in Minneapolis in 1981–1982, police agencies throughout the world actively pursued "mandatory arrest" policies (and in some jurisdictions, legislation) in police call outs to misdemeanor domestic violence incidents (see Sherman 1992), a policy subsequently found to be flawed. Despite the replications of the Minneapolis trial raising concerns about mandatory arrest policies (see Berk et al. 1992; Hirschel, Hutchison, and Dean 1992), some jurisdictions in the world continue to mandate arrest as the preferred policing response.

In summary, police experimentation, or the "gold standard" of research, comprises a small segment of policing research relative to studies of police and policing using other methods of inquiry. Yet, despite the small number of policing experiments, the public policy impacts of these policing experiments have been enormous. As we have shown, we can point to experimental research that has shaped and altered police approaches to patrol policies, foot patrol interventions, drug law enforcement and policing domestic violence. The question begs to be asked: why are there not more field trials? And might there be more in the future? The next section describes a number of key initiatives designed to institutionalize the use of experimental research in criminal justice in general and in policing in particular.

22.2 INSTITUTIONALIZING EXPERIMENTAL RESEARCH IN POLICING

The institutionalization of experimental research in policing began in 1997 when Lawrence Sherman and his colleagues at the University of Maryland launched another Martinson-like review of criminal justice interventions. Known as the Maryland Report, Sherman and his colleagues (1997) carefully recorded the methodological rigor of evaluation studies (including evaluations of policing interventions), in order to make claims about interventions based on the strength of the science behind the evaluations (this review was updated by Sherman et al. 2002). The Maryland Report was tabled to the U.S.

Congress and emphasized the importance of putting more weight on interventions with high internal validity, principally experimental evaluations (see also Weisburd, Lum, and Petrosino 2001).

Shortly after the release of the Maryland Report, a group of international social scientists and decision makers formed the Campbell Collaboration in February 2000. The Campbell group is modeled on the Cochrane Collaboration, an organization in the health science field born in the early 1990s in the United Kingdom from a desire on the part of researchers and policy makers to review the state of the research evidence in medicine. Similarly, the Campbell Collaboration focuses on examining the state of evaluation research in the social sciences (Petrosino et al. 2001). The use of systematic reviews and meta-analyses is an important component in the activities of Campbell which, like the Maryland Report, highlight methodological rigor of evaluations as an important goal in developing evidence-based policies.

In addition to the Campbell Collaboration, other organizations advocating for more experimentation, as well as government changes in policies, have helped spur the growth of randomized controlled experiments in criminal justice and policing. In 1999, the Academy of Experimental Criminology (AEC) was established to recognize and encourage the efforts of scholars who had conducted experiments in the field through its Academy Fellows distinction. Specifically, Weisburd, Mazerolle, and Petrosino (2007) explain that the academy was developed to "create synergies" among experimental criminologists to facilitate communication around design, implementation, management, and outcomes of experimental research. The further prominence and importance of experiments was reflected in the rising prestige of a new journal, the *Journal of Experimental Criminology*, the first issue of which came out in 2005. Later, in 2007, members of the AEC formed a division within the American Society of Criminology called the Division of Experimental Criminology. The momentum behind experimental criminology in academe is now mirrored in governments around the world. For example, the U.S. Department of Justice's Office of Justice Programs and the National Institute of Justice (NIJ) actively fund experiments.

22.2.1 Systematic Reviews of Experimentation in Policing

Today, we know of twenty-nine policing experiments (Lum, Koper, and Telep 2011), with a growing number of systematic reviews of policing interventions emerging. These reviews help to draw generalizations from the research as a whole, especially in the cases of studies on similar subjects. Early reviews include Clarke and Hough's (1980) compilation of papers on police effectiveness, a series of reviews by Sherman (1983, 1986, 1990, 1992), and a special issue of *Crime and Justice: A Review of Research* (Tonry and Morris 1992). Farrington (1983) and Farrington and Welsh (2006) reviewed experiments more specifically, including some policing experiments.

The most comprehensive reviews prior to the Matrix are the University of Maryland Report to Congress (Sherman et al. 1997) and its update (Sherman et al. 2002) in which

Sherman (1997), and then Sherman and Eck (2002) conducted the policing reviews for these comprehensive examinations of criminal justice evaluation literature. Sherman and Eck reviewed fifteen policing experiments scoring a "5" on the Maryland Scientific Methods Scale, indicating that a randomized experiment was used. Subsequent to the Maryland Report, there have also been a number of specific reviews of evaluations of policing interventions that have highlighted experimental research as a gold standard for policing evaluations. Many of these have been conducted for the Campbell Collaboration, as mentioned above. These systematic reviews include hot spots policing (Braga 2007), problem-oriented policing (Weisburd et al. 2008), neighborhood watch (Bennett, Farrington, and Holloway 2009), suppression of gun carrying (Koper and Mayo-Wilson 2006), drug enforcement (Mazerolle, Rombouts, and Soole 2007), second responder programs for family abuse (Davis, Weisburd, and Taylor 2008), and community policing (Weisburd et al. 2012). These reviews, and the specific studies they include, generally point to problem-oriented, place-based, hot spot policing as being especially effective policing measures (National Research Council 2004; Weisburd and Eck 2004).

22.3   THE EVIDENCE-BASED POLICING MATRIX

The most comprehensive and consistently updated systematic review of evaluations of the range of police crime-control interventions is the Evidence-Based Policing Matrix (Lum 2009; Lum, Koper, and Telep 2009, 2011). The Evidence-Based Policing Matrix (shown in Figure 22.1) is a web-based tool that houses all police crime-control intervention research of moderate to high quality (evaluations must at least include a comparison unit of analysis that did not receive an intervention). Rather than focus only on one particular area of police crime-prevention research, the Matrix classifies all police intervention research on three very common dimensions of crime-prevention strategies: (1) the nature and type of target; (2) the degree to which the strategy is reactive or proactive; and (3) the strategy's level of focus (i.e., the specificity of the prevention mechanism it used). The appeal of the Matrix is that not only is it updated every year, but by "mapping" studies using these three dimensions, generalizations regarding the effectiveness of interventions with these characteristics also can be visualized more easily. Further, the visualization allows for multiple aspects of an evaluation to be seen simultaneously with other evaluations, including the type of intervention studied, the finding of the intervention, and the methodological rigor of the study.

Notice how clusters of studies appear in different areas of the Matrix. For example, a large number of evaluations showing significant effective findings appear clustered in the Micro Places, Focused, and Highly Proactive intersection of the Matrix. This indicates that there are a number of moderate- to high-quality evaluations that seem to indicate that interventions sharing those characteristics have positive effects. On the other hand, studies that are more general in nature and that focus on individuals, even if highly proactive, do not show as much consistent promise. The Matrix is essentially a visual systematic review, which allows in a quick glance numerous characteristics of studies to be grouped and examined together.

Figure 22.1 shows all experimental and quasi-experimental studies in the matrix. As noted earlier, there were 29 experiments in the Matrix, out of the 104 studies that appear in Figure 22.1. While this is almost a doubling of the number of experiments since the Maryland Report was published in 1997, the total proportion of policing experiments compared to other experiments has not increased notably. In the Maryland report, 22 percent (n = 15) of the 67 studies of moderate to high rigor were experiments, whereas today, 28 percent (n = 29) of the 104 evaluations in the Matrix are experiments (Lum and Mazerolle, 2014).

Selecting only experimental studies in the Matrix might also provide some insight into which intersecting dimensional areas of the Matrix experiments are clustered (and also what those clusters say about those general dimensions). Figure 22.2 shows only those studies appearing in the Matrix that are experiments. The bulk of experimental studies in policing (either in number or proportion) are conducted either on individuals or very small "micro places" as units of analyses. Almost half (48 percent) of all experiments focus on individual people as the unit of random assignment that test, for example, arrests of repeat offenders, or victim-centric interventions (such as secondary responders to domestic violence or restorative justice). A large proportion (41 percent) of the experiments have been conducted on interventions that target crime hot spots at small places, either using problem-oriented schemes, community remedies, or just saturated patrol. It should also be noted, compared to all other types of targets, the micro-place slab of the Matrix has the greatest proportion of studies, more generally, that are experiments in the Matrix. This is likely due to the connection of many of these authors to the original authors of the Minneapolis Hot Spots Experiment (Sherman and Weisburd 1995). Three (10 percent) of the experiments study neighborhood-based interventions, two of which show non-significant effects (on crime reduction) of police use of information-dissemination tools such as community newsletters (Pate et al. 1986), and one of which focuses on community approaches to high-risk juveniles (Weisburd, Morris, and Ready 2008).

Comparing Figures 22.1 and 22.2 shows that the nature and findings of experimental research in police interventions are even more pronounced, and it highlights the advantage that the Matrix has over non-visual reviews. For example, the most obvious difference is that certain areas of police research entirely "disappear," most notably research on groups (e.g., gangs and co-offenders), and "jurisdiction" level interventions (e.g., city-wide interventions). Additionally, almost all of the "neighborhood" based interventions disappear, since most community-oriented approaches in policing have yet to be rigorously evaluated. Given the high demand for evidence on whether gang and neighborhood interventions "work," evaluators may consider focusing their attention on these areas.

Further, Figure 22.2 shows that 38 percent of the 29 experiments show statistically significant positive results, 38 percent show non-significant results, 14 percent showed

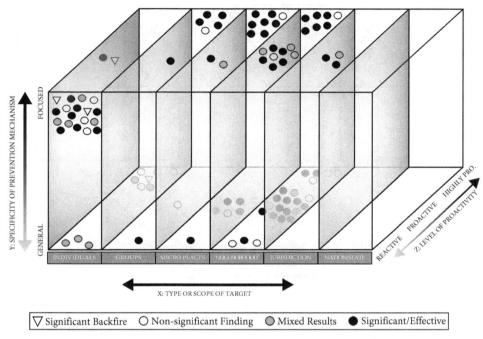

FIGURE 22.1 The evidence-based policing matrix

Source: Lum, Koper, and Telep (2009, 2011)

mixed results, and 10 percent show backfire effects of the interventions. In addition, the Matrix also visually indicates where these finding types are dispersed. For instance, 7 of the 13 interventions on individuals that have been evaluated using experimentation show non-significant, or even negative effects (i.e., the intervention *increased* offending or crime). In contrast, while many interventions at micro places have been evaluated using experimentation, the findings are more positive, with 8 out of 12 evaluations showing significant reductions in crime. This confirms the National Research Council's conclusion, highlighted by Weisburd and Eck (2004), that proactive, place-based, and multi-agency/problem-solving approaches at hot spots of crime seem to be the most effective approaches in policing *of which we are aware*. Of course, there are many interventions that may be effective that remain, as yet, unevaluated.

Overall, the Matrix suggests important findings with regards to police experiments. While there are relatively more experiments now compared to fifteen years ago, we still have very little experimental evidence on many types of crime prevention interventions (as indicated by the less populated intersecting dimensions in the Matrix). We also know, from experimental studies of them, that the most common policing interventions—reactive methods that focus on individuals—have not shown too much promise.

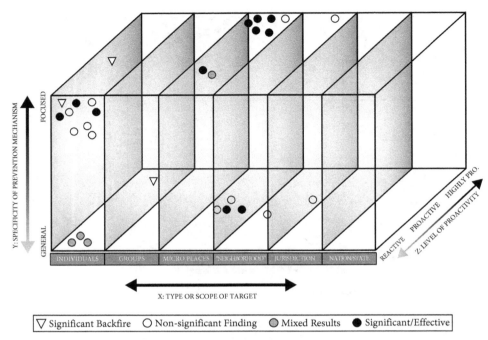

▽ Significant Backfire   ○ Non-significant Finding   ◐ Mixed Results   ● Significant/Effective

FIGURE 22.2 The evidence-based policing matrix (experiments only)

Source: Lum, Koper, and Telep (2009, 2011)

While there are many experiments indicating that highly proactive, micro-placed and focused interventions can reduce crime, these types of approaches are not often practiced (Weisburd et al. 2008; Lum 2009). One of the reasons why there are such a small number of randomized field trials in policing is because the "doing" of these trials is not exactly easy. In the next section, we examine the complexities of randomized field trials in policing and describe the range of factors that both police and researchers take into account both at the planning and implementation phases.

22.4 Doing Police Experiments

Randomized experimental designs allow researchers to assume that the only systematic difference between the control and treatment groups is the presence of the intervention; this permits a clear assessment of causes and effects (Campbell and Stanley 1966; Cook and Campbell 1979; Sechrest and Rosenblatt 1987). The classical experimental design involves three major pairs of components: (1) independent and dependent variables;

(2) treatment and control groups; and (3) pre-testing and post-testing. It is important to note that experiments sometimes do not include pre-test measurement. Some experimental designs simply randomize subjects to treatment and control groups and then measure outcomes for each group in the post-test period only.

Experiments essentially examine the effect of an independent variable on a dependent variable. The independent variable usually takes the form of a treatment stimulus that is either present or not. For instance, an experiment could examine the effect of a police foot patrol program (the independent variable) on crime (the dependent variable) in crime hot spots. The key element of an experiment is the random allocation of subjects or units of analysis to treatment and control groups. This randomization allows the researcher to determine with confidence what would have happened if the treatment stimulus or intervention was not applied to the treatment group (often referred to as the "counterfactual"). The treatment group (sometimes called the "experimental" group) receives the stimulus or intervention to be tested and the control group does not. During the pre-test period, treatment and control groups are both measured in terms of the dependent variable. After the stimulus or intervention is administered to the experimental group, the dependent variable is measured again in the post-test period. Differences noted between the pre-test and post-test period on the dependent variable are then attributed to the influence of the treatment.

Randomization provides a simple and convincing method for achieving comparability in the treatment and control groups. After subjects are recruited by whatever means, the researchers randomly assign those subjects to either the treatment or control group. If randomization is done correctly, the only systematic difference between the two groups should be the presence or absence of the treatment. Experiments that use randomization to create equivalent groups are often called "randomized controlled trials." Randomized controlled trials are generally considered the gold standard in evaluation research due to the design's high internal validity in assigning causation to the treatment applied.

While randomized field experiments are generally recognized as the most rigorous way to estimate causal effects, these designs are limited by the fidelity with which they are implemented (Berk 2005). There is a large and ever-growing body of literature on field experiment implementation problems; many well-known policing field experiments have experienced and successfully dealt with methodological difficulties. For instance, the landmark Kansas City Preventive Patrol Experiment had to be stopped and restarted three times before it was implemented properly because the patrol officers did not respect the boundaries of the treatment and control areas (Kelling et al. 1974b). Likewise, the design of the Minneapolis Spouse Abuse Experiment was modified to a quasi-experiment when randomization could not be achieved because officers chose to arrest certain offenders on a nonrandom basis (Berk, Smyth, and Sherman 1988).

In addition to implementation issues, an unwillingness of practitioners and policy makers to randomly allocate people or places to treatment and control conditions for political, ethical, or practical reasons has limited the use of field randomized experiments to evaluate crime and justice interventions (Weisburd 2003). In reality, few police departments are willing to play host to the more intrusive research designs such as randomized controlled trials. As Eck (2002) describes, there are many reasons why police departments may not be willing to play host to an experiment: the evaluator may not ask whether or not the department would be willing to conduct an experiment, the department may have other pressing business, or the department's leadership may not want to test a new approach to policing, among other reasons. Even when a police department is willing to engage in a more rigorous design, the external validity of the findings may be called into question because the host departments and their contexts are not considered to be representative of all agencies or contexts that use the intervention. Drawing on Campbell and Stanley (1966), Eck (2002, 104) identifies this as the problem of the "interaction of selection and treatment."

In a description of her experiences as an "embedded" criminologist in the State of California's prison reform efforts, Joan Petersilia (2008) notes that "timing is *everything*" when working with policy makers and criminal justice practitioners. Her observation is particularly salient when considering the inherent legal, political, institutional, and resource constraints in the successful execution of randomized controlled trials in criminal justice agencies. While there are undoubtedly other important factors, ongoing collaborative relationships between police executives and academics create opportunities to conduct rigorous evaluations of police programs (Braga 2010). In these collaborative relationships, academics can be more sensitive to broader operational environments and propose experiments that fit better with police department needs and constraints.

Researchers will often need to develop credibility with a particular police department before its executives feel comfortable in collaborating on a randomized controlled trial. Less ambitious research projects, such as the strategic analysis of persistent crime problems, may naturally lead to conversations about testing varying interventions to address identified problems. For instance, the now well-known observation that some 5 percent of addresses in a city generate roughly 50 percent of citizen calls for service to the police (Sherman, Gartin, and Buerger 1989) could spark interest in designing an experiment to test the most efficient and effective way to deliver patrol services to these high-activity crime places (Sherman and Weisburd 1995). Experience with less rigorous evaluation designs, such as quasi-experimental evaluations, may also strike interest in more rigorous tests. For instance, the Lowell, Massachusetts Police Department gained a tremendous amount of practical crime control knowledge through its support and participation in a quasi-experimental evaluation of an innovative, police-led gang violence reduction initiative (Braga et al. 2008). Former Lowell Police Chief Edward F. Davis was so enthused by the experience that he collaborated with Harvard University researchers on the design and implementation of a subsequent randomized controlled trial to test the effects of problem-oriented policing on crime and disorder hot spots (Braga and Bond 2008).

It is good practice to include police executives in the development of randomized controlled trials. Developing transparency in design decision making by providing police managers with the opportunity to voice and address concerns will garner considerable *a priori* support for the experiment. It is critical for police managers to feel that the randomized controlled trial is "their project" rather than an inconvenience imposed on them for unclear reasons by external academics. At the outset, police executives and academics should jointly decide on the research hypotheses to be tested. There should then be agreement on the units of analysis in the randomized controlled trial. For instance, in the Lowell problem-oriented policing experiment (Braga and Bond 2008), the Harvard research team worked with Lowell Police crime analysts on the initial identification of the crime and disorder hot spots and then considered the observations of police officers when drawing the final boundaries around the hot spots before inclusion in the experiment. The inclusion of police officers and civilian staff in this exercise demystified the development of the units of analysis and ensured that these locations "made sense" to the officers who would eventually be charged with implementing problem-oriented policing in these hot spot areas.

The randomization of units to treatment and control conditions should also be transparent. While the researcher must always control the actual randomization of units in the experiment, police executives should be included in the process. In the Lowell experiment, the 34 crime hot spots were matched into 17 like pairs (Braga and Bond 2008). In a meeting with then-Chief Davis and members of his command staff, the Harvard research team flipped a coin to randomly allocate hot spots within each pair to treatment and control conditions. The meeting atmosphere was light hearted as the officers present joked about hoping for "heads" or "tails" when particularly pernicious places were up for allocation. The experience seemed to strengthen the connection of the command staff to the experiment.

Researchers should work with police executives to develop a set of processes to ensure that the randomized controlled trial is being implemented as intended. It is critical to make certain that the treatment is being delivered with integrity and in sufficient dosage, and equally important that control conditions are also being maintained. In the Lowell experiment, captains were held accountable for the implementation of the problem-oriented policing interventions in treatment hot spots through monthly problem-solving meetings with the command staff (Braga and Bond 2008). Researchers monitored conditions at the control hot spots by attending bi-monthly CompStat meetings. Careful notes on the implemented interventions discussed in these meetings and observed at study hot spot locations during weekly researcher ride-alongs with police officers were maintained by the research team. The research team met with Chief Davis on a monthly basis to review study implementation and develop remedies for problems that arose over the course of the experiment.

The extensive documentation of the implementation of an experiment also facilitates the completion of a high-quality process evaluation. In any research and development project, it is important to conduct both process and impact evaluations (Rossi and Freeman 1993). In police crime-control projects, an *impact evaluation* focuses on questions of crime reduction effectiveness (e.g., Did the problem decline? If so, did the treatment cause the decline?), while a *process evaluation* focuses on questions of accountability and integrity in experiment implementation (e.g., Did the treatment occur as planned? Did all the treatment components work?). Even with a rigorous experimental design, without adequate monitoring it is difficult to determine whether treatments are efficacious. Given the well-known challenges of implementing randomized controlled trials in complex field settings described earlier, randomized controlled trials should include process evaluations to determine whether impact evaluation findings were affected by faulty or incomplete implementation. More generally, process evaluations create a detailed record of the treatment that can facilitate replications and proper adoption of effective practices by other police departments.

22.5 CONCLUDING COMMENTS

This essay provides an introduction to the use of experimental methods in policing. The historical account reviewed some of the key experiments that shaped changing policies over time in regards to preventive patrols, directed patrols, foot patrols, policing the hot spots of crime, drug law enforcement, and policing domestic violence problems. Specific projects, such as the Police Foundation's Kansas City Preventive Patrol Experiment and Newark Foot Patrol Experiment during the 1970s, the Minneapolis Hot Spots and Domestic Violence experiments of the 1980s, the Spousal Assault Replication experiments and the Drug Market Analysis Program experiments of the 1990s, and the more recent crop of hot spots, problem-oriented policing and foot patrol experiments in the 2000s have had a major impact. In short, policing experiments have "punched above their weight," significantly shaping police policies and operational practices for some forty years.

With the push for evidence-based policy agendas of governments throughout the world, along with the establishment of the Campbell Collaboration and the Academy of Experimental Criminology, the institutionalization of police experiments is now firmly established. Although conducting a policing experiment is a complex undertaking, opportunities for doing so are probably as frequent as they have ever been.

There are many trials and tribulations associated with conducting randomized field trials with police, including randomizing police officers, police patrols, police organizational units and practices under field trial conditions. While field experiments in policing are challenging, both for the police and researchers, policing offers clear opportunities for more field trials and for scholars to use experimentation to assess police effectiveness. The public policy impacts of police experiments are greater than those generated using other types of inquiry—a factor that both police and police scholars might take into account when considering the pros and cons of conducting a field experiment. Police agencies throughout the world are now much more open to the idea of field experimentation than ever before.

REFERENCES

Amendola, Karen L., David Weisburd, Edwin E. Hamilton, Greg Jones, and Meghan Slipka. 2011. "An Experimental Study of Compressed Work Schedules in Policing: Advantages and Disadvantages of Various Shift Lengths." *Journal of Experimental Criminology* 7(4): 407–42.

Bennett, Trevor, David Farrington, and Katy Holloway. 2009. *The Effectiveness of Neighborhood Watch*. Campbell Systematic Reviews no. 2009-18. Oslo: The Campbell Collaboration.

Berk, Richard A. 2005. "Randomized Experiments as the Bronze Standard." *Journal of Experimental Criminology* 1(4): 417–33.

Berk, Richard A., Alec Campbell, Ruth Klap, and Bruce Western. 1992. "A Bayesian Analysis of the Colorado Springs Spouse Abuse Experiment." *Journal of Criminal Law and Criminology* 83(1): 170–200.

Berk, Richard A., Gordon K. Smyth, and Lawrence W. Sherman. 1988. "When Random Assignment Fails: Some Lessons From the Minneapolis Spouse Abuse Experiment." *Journal of Quantitative Criminology* 4(3): 209–23.

Braga, Anthony. 2007. *The Effects of Hot Spots Policing on Crime*. Campbell Systematic Reviews no. 2007-01. Oslo: The Campbell Collaboration.

——. 2010. "Setting A Higher Standard For the Evaluation of Problem-Oriented Policing Initiatives." *Criminology and Public Policy* 9(1): 173–82.

Braga, Anthony A., and Brenda J. Bond. 2008. "Policing Crime And Disorder Hot Spots: A Randomized Controlled Trial." *Criminology* 46(3): 577–607.

Braga, Anthony A., Glenn L. Pierce, Jack McDevitt, Brenda J. Bond, and Shea Cronin. 2008. "The Strategic Prevention of Gun Violence Among Gang-Involved Offenders." *Justice Quarterly* 25(1): 132–62.

Braga, Anthony A., and David Weisburd. 2010. *Policing Problem Places*. New York: Oxford University Press.

Campbell, Donald T., and Julian C. Stanley. 1966. *Experimental and Quasi-Experimental Designs for Research*. Chicago: Rand McNally.

Caulkins, Jonathon, Peter Reuter, Martin Iguchi, and James Chiesa. 2004. *How Goes the "War on Drugs?" An Assessment of US Drug Programs and Policy*. Santa Monica, CA: RAND Corporation.

Clarke, Ronald V. G., and J. M. Hough, eds. 1980. *The Effectiveness of Policing*. Aldershot, UK: Gower Press.

Cohen, Jacqueline, William Gorr, and Andreas Olligschlager. 1993. *Computerized Crime Mapping: Pittsburgh Drug Market Analysis Program (P-DMAP)*. Pittsburgh, PA: Carnegie-Mellon University.

Cook, Thomas D., and Donald Thomas Campbell. 1979. *Quasi-Experimentation: Design and Analysis Issues for Field Settings*. Boston: Houghton Mifflin.

Davis, Robert C., David Weisburd, and Bruce Taylor. 2008. *Effects of Second Responder Programs on Repeat Incidents of Family Abuse*. Campbell Systematic Reviews no. 2008-15. Oslo: The Campbell Collaboration.

Dunford, Franklyn W. 1990. "System Initiated Warrants for Suspects of Misdemeanor Domestic Assault: A Pilot Study." *Justice Quarterly* 7:631–53.

Dunford, Franklyn W., David Huizinga, and Delbert S. Elliott. 1990. "The Role of Arrest in Domestic Assault: The Omaha Experiment." *Criminology* 28:183–206.

Eck, John E. 2002. "Learning From Experience in Problem-Oriented Policing and Situational Prevention: The Positive Functions of Weak Evaluations and the Negative Functions of

Strong Ones." In *Evaluation for Crime Prevention. Crime Prevention Studies*, vol. 14, edited by Nick Tilley, 93–118. Monsey, NY: Criminal Justice Press.

Eck, John, and Julie Wartell. 1998. "Improving the Management of Rental Properties with Drug Problems: A Randomized Experiment." In *Civil Remedies and Crime Prevention: Crime Prevention Studies*, vol. 9, edited by Lorraine Green Mazerolle and Jan Roehl, 161–185. Monsey, NY: Criminal Justice Press.

Farrington, David P. 1983. "Randomized Experiments on Crime and Justice." In *Crime and Justice: A Review Of Research*, vol. 4, edited by Norval Morris and Michael Tonry, 257–308. Chicago: University of Chicago Press.

Farrington, David P., and Brandon C. Welsh. 2006. "A Half Century of Randomized Experiments on Crime and Justice." In *Crime and Justice: A Review of Research*, vol. 34, edited by Michael Tonry, 55–132. Chicago: University of Chicago Press.

Garner, Joel, Jeffrey Fagan, and Christopher Maxwell. 1995. "Published Findings from the Spouse Assault Replication Program: A Critical Review." *Journal of Quantitative Criminology* 11(1): 3–28.

Green, Lorraine. 1995. *Policing Places with Drug Problems*. Thousand Oaks, CA: Sage.

Harcourt, Bernard E. 1998. "Reflecting on the Subject: A Critique of the Social Influence Conception of Deterrence, the Broken Windows Theory, and Order-Maintenance Policing New York Style." *Michigan Law Review* 97(2): 291–389.

Hirschel, J. David, Ira W. Hutchison, and Charles W. Dean. 1992. "The Failure of Arrest to Deter Spouse Abuse." *Journal of Research in Crime and Delinquency* 29(1): 7–33.

Kelling, George L., Tony Pate, Duane Dieckman, and Charles E. Brown. 1974a. *The Kansas City Preventive Patrol Experiment: A Summary Report*. Washington, DC: Police Foundation.

——. 1974b. *The Kansas City Preventive Patrol Experiment: A Technical Report*. Washington, DC: Police Foundation.

Kelling, George L., Antony Pate, Amy Ferrara, Mary Utne, and Charles E. Brown. 1981. *The Newark Foot Patrol Experiment*. Washington, DC: Police Foundation.

Koper, Christopher. 1995. "Just Enough Police Presence: Reducing Crime and Disorderly Behavior by Optimizing Patrol Time in Crime Hot Spots." *Justice Quarterly* 12(2): 649-71.

Koper, Christopher, and Evan Mayo-Wilson. 2006. "Police Crackdowns on Illegal Gun Carrying: A Systematic Review of Their Impact on Gun Crime." *Journal of Experimental Criminology* 2(2): 227–61.

Lipton, Douglas, Robert Martinson, and Judith Wilks. 1975. *The Effectiveness of Correctional Treatment: A Survey of Treatment Evaluation Studies*. New York: Praeger.

Lum, Cynthia. 2009. "Translating Police Research into Practice." *Ideas in American Policing*, no. 11. Washington, DC: Police Foundation.

Lum, Cynthia, Christopher Koper, and Cody W. Telep. 2009. "Evidence-Based Policing Matrix. http://gemini.gmu.edu/cebcp/matrix.html.

——. 2011. "The Evidence-Based Policing Matrix." *Journal of Experimental Criminology* 7(1): 3–26.

Lum, Cynthia, and Lorraine Mazerolle. 2014. "The History of Randomized Controlled Experiments in Criminology and Criminal Justice." In *The Encyclopedia of Criminology and Criminal Justice*, edited by Gerben Bruinsma and David Weisburd, 2227–2239. New York: Springer-Verlag.

Martinson, Robert. 1974. "What Works? Questions and Answers About Prison Reform." *Public Interest* 35:22–54.

Maxwell, Christopher, Joel H. Garner, and Jeffrey A. Fagan. 2001. *The Effects of Arrest on Intimate Partner Violence: New Evidence From the Spouse Assault Replication Program*. Washington, DC: U.S. Department of Justice.

Mazerolle, Lorraine, Sarah Bennett, Emma Antrobus, and Elizabeth Eggins. 2012. "Procedural Justice, Routine Encounters and Citizen Perceptions of Police: Main Findings from the Queensland Community Engagement Trial (QCET)." *Journal of Experimental Criminology* 8:343–367.

Mazerolle, Lorraine, Sacha Rombouts, and David W. Soole. 2007. *Street-Level Drug Law Enforcement: A Meta-Analytic Review*. Campbell Systematic Reviews no. 2007-02. Oslo: The Campbell Collaboration.

Moore, Mark H., Robert C. Trojanowicz, and George L. Kelling. 1988. "Crime and Policing." *Perspectives on Policing* no. 2. Washington, DC: National Institute of Justice.

National Research Council. 2004. "The Effectiveness of Police Activity in Reducing Crime, Disorder and Fear." In *Fairness and Effectiveness in Policing: The Evidence. Committee to Review Research on Police Policy and Practices*, edited by Wesley G. Skogan, Kathleen Frydl, and Committee on Law and Justice Division of Behavioral and Social Sciences and Education, 217–251. Washington, DC: The National Academies Press.

Parks, Roger B. 2008. "Broken Windows and Broken Windows Policing." *Criminology and Public Policy* 7(2):159–61.

Pate, Anthony M., and Edwin E. Hamilton. 1992. "Formal and Informal Deterrents to Domestic Violence: The Dade County Spouse Assault Experiment." *American Sociological Review* 57(5): 691–97.

Pate, Antony M., Mary Ann Wycoff, Wesley G. Skogan, and Lawrence W. Sherman. 1986. *Reducing Fear of Crime in Houston and Newark: A Summary Report*. Washington, DC: Police Foundation.

Petersilia, Joan. 2008. "Influencing Public Policy: An Embedded Criminologist Reflects on California Prison Reform." *Journal of Experimental Criminology* 4(4): 335–56.

Petrosino, Anthony, Robert F. Boruch, Haluk Soydan, Lorna Duggan, and Julio Sanchez-Meca. 2001. "Meeting the Challenges of Evidence-Based Policy: The Campbell Collaboration." *Annals of the American Academy of Political and Social Science* 578:14–34.

Police Foundation. 1981. *Newark Foot Patrol Experiment*. Washington, DC: Police Foundation.

Ratcliffe, Jerry H., Travis Taniguchi, Elizabeth R. Groff, and Jennifer D. Wood. 2011. "The Philadelphia Foot Patrol Experiment: A Randomized Controlled Trial of Police Patrol Effectiveness in Violent Crime Hotspots." *Criminology* 49(3): 795–831.

Rossi, Peter H., and Howard E. Freeman. 1993. *Evaluation: A Systematic Approach*. 5th ed. Thousand Oaks, CA: Sage.

Sechrest, Lee, and Abram Rosenblatt. 1987. "Research Methods." In *Handbook of Juvenile Delinquency*, edited by Herbert C. Quay, 417–450. New York: John Wiley and Sons.

Sherman, Lawrence W. 1983. "Patrol Strategies for Police." In *Crime and Public Policy*, edited by James Q. Wilson, 145–164. San Francisco: Institute for Contemporary Studies Press.

——. 1986. "Policing Communities: What Works?" In *Communities and Crime*, edited by Albert J. Reiss Jr and Michael Tonry, 343–386. Vol. 8 of *Crime and Justice: A Review of Research*. Chicago: University of Chicago Press.

——. 1990. "Police Crackdowns: Initial and Residual Deterrence." In *Crime and Justice: A Review of Research*, vol. 12, edited by Michael Tonry and Norval Morris, 1–48. Chicago: University of Chicago Press.

———. 1992. "Attacking Crime: Policing and Crime Control." In *Modern Policing*, edited by Michael Tonry and Norval Morris, 159–230. Vol. 15 of *Crime and Justice: A Review of Research*. Chicago: University of Chicago Press.

———. 1997. "Policing for Crime Prevention." In *Preventing Crime: What Works, What Doesn't, What's Promising*, edited by Lawrence W. Sherman, Denise Gottfredson, Doris MacKenzie, John Eck, Peter Reuter, and Shawn Bushway, Part 8. Washington, DC: U.S. Department of Justice.

Sherman, Lawrence W., and Richard A. Berk. 1984a. *The Minneapolis Domestic Violence Experiment*. Washington, DC: Police Foundation.

———. 1984b. "The Specific Deterrent Effects of Arrest for Domestic Assault." *American Sociological Review* 49(2): 261–72.

Sherman, Lawrence W., and John E. Eck. 2002. "Policing for Crime Prevention." In *Evidence-Based Crime Prevention*, edited by Lawrence W. Sherman, David P. Farrington, Brandon C. Welsh, and Doris Layton MacKenzie, 295–329. New York: Routledge.

Sherman, Lawrence W., David P. Farrington, Brandon C. Welsh, and Doris Layton MacKenzie, eds. 2002. *Evidence-Based Crime Prevention*. New York: Routledge.

Sherman, Lawrence W., Patrick R. Gartin, and Michael E. Buerger. 1989. "Hot Spots of Predatory Crime: Routine Activities and the Criminology of Place." *Criminology* 27(1): 27–55.

Sherman, Lawrence W., Denise Gottfredson, Doris MacKenzie, John Eck, Peter Reuter, and Shawn Bushway, eds. 1997. *Preventing Crime: What Works, What Doesn't, What's Promising*. Washington, DC: U.S. Department of Justice.

Sherman, Lawrence W., and Dennis P. Rogan. 1995. "Deterrent Effects of Police Raids on Crack Houses: A Randomized Controlled Experiment." *Justice Quarterly* 12(4): 755–82.

Sherman, Lawrence W., Janell D. Schmidt, Dennis P. Rogan, Douglas A. Smith, Patrick R. Gartin, Ellen G. Cohn, J. Collins, and Anthony R. Bacich. 1992. "The Variable Effects of Arrest on Criminal Careers: The Milwaukee Domestic Violence Experiment." *Journal of Criminal Law and Criminology* 83(1): 137–69.

Sherman, Lawrence W., and David Weisburd. 1995. "General Deterrent Effects of Police Patrol in Crime Hot Spots: A Randomized Controlled Trial." *Justice Quarterly* 12(4): 625–48.

Skogan, Wesley, and Kathleen Frydl, eds. 2004. *Fairness and Effectiveness in Policing: The Evidence*. Washington DC: National Academies Press.

Taylor, Bruce, Christopher S. Koper, and Daniel J. Woods. 2010. "A Randomized Controlled Trial of Different Policing Strategies at Hot Spots of Violent Crime." *Journal of Experimental Criminology* 7:149–81.

Tien, James, Thomas Rich, M. Shell, Richard Larson, and J. Donnelly. 1990. "COMPASS: A Drug Market Analysis Program (DMAP)." Final report to the National Institute of Justice.

Tonry, Michael, and Norval Morris, eds. 1992. *Modern Policing. Crime and Justice: A Review of Research*, vol. 15. Chicago: University of Chicago Press.

Weisburd, David. 2003. "Ethical Practice and Evaluation of Interventions in Crime and Justice: The Moral Imperative for Randomized Trials." *Evaluation Review* 27(3): 336–54.

Weisburd, David, Trevor Bennett, Charlotte Gill, and Cody Telep. 2012. *Community-Oriented Policing to Reduce Crime, Disorder, and Fear and Increase Legitimacy and Citizen Satisfaction in Neighborhoods*. Campbell Systematic Reviews. Oslo: The Campbell Collaboration.

Weisburd, David, and John E. Eck. 2004. "What Can Police Do to Reduce Crime, Disorder, and Fear?" *The ANNALS of the American Academy of Political and Social Science* 593(1): 42–65.

Weisburd, David, John E. Eck, Joshua C. Hinkle, and Cody Telep. 2008. *The Effects Of Problem-Oriented Policing On Crime and Disorder*. Campbell Systematic Reviews no. 2008-14. Oslo: The Campbell Collaboration.

Weisburd, David, and Lorraine Green. 1995. "Policing Drug Hot Spots: The Jersey City Drug Market Analysis Experiment." *Justice Quarterly* 12(4): 711–35.

Weisburd, David, Cynthia M. Lum, and Anthony Petrosino. 2001. "Does Research Design Affect Study Outcomes in Criminal Justice?" *Annals of the American Academy of Political and Social Science* 578:50–70.

Weisburd, David, Lorraine Ann Mazerolle, and Anthony Petrosino. 2007. "The Academy of Experimental Criminology: Advancing Randomized Trials in Crime and Justice." *The Criminologist* 32(3): 1–7.

Weisburd, David, Nancy A. Morris, and Justin Ready. 2008. "Risk-Focused Policing at Places: An Experimental Evaluation." *Justice Quarterly* 25(1): 163–200.

Weisz, Arlene. 2001. *Spouse Assault Replication Program: Studies of Effects of Arrest on Domestic Violence*. National Online Resource Center on Violence against Women. http://www.vawnet.org/applied-research-papers/print-document.php?doc_id=394.

Wilson, James Q., and George L. Kelling. 1982. "Broken Windows: The Police and Neighborhood Safety." *Atlantic Monthly* 249:29–38.

CHAPTER 23

....

ETHNOGRAPHIES OF
POLICING

....

PETER K. MANNING

ETHNOGRAPHY, or the close-up study of culture and how meaning is produced, distributed, and understood, has a long history in social science, criminology, and criminal justice. It has been the primary technique used to establish the foundational work in the field of police studies. Yet, there is apparently less ethnography cited now, other than the "classic" studies done some years ago. Discussing changes in the role of ethnography in criminology and criminal justice requires a brief discussion of the origins of what might be called ethnographies of the police as an occupation and the police organization.

In the late 1940s, armed with the sponsorship of Joseph Lohman, a faculty member at the University of Chicago and later sheriff of Cook County, a young graduate student undertook an ethnographic study of the police in Gary, Indiana. This was to be the basis for his PhD dissertation in sociology at the University of Chicago. This student, William Westley, wrote two brief, now classic articles on the police and violence (Westley 1953) and police and secrecy (Westley 1955). When interest in policing surfaced in the late 1960s, his dissertation, *Violence and the Police*, was published by MIT Press (Westley 1970). This research defined many of the central questions addressed by scholars for more than fifty years. Westley's ethnography, with a handful of other monographs (Banton 1964; Whitaker 1964; Skolnick 1966; Cicourel 1967; Wilson 1968; Bittner 1970; Laurie 1970; Rubinstein 1972; Cain 1973; Van Maanen 1973; Alex 1976; Manning 1977), set the stage and the questions of concern for several generations of young scholars.

There were others of importance, as is discussed below, but the classics have not been forgotten unlike Rock's (2005) assessment of "chronocentrism," the favoring of more recent publications, in a study of citations in the *British Journal of Sociology*. Rock's generalization apparently does not hold for the police ethnography literature. While the classics in criminology developed by Sutherland, Thrasher, Shaw and McKay, and later Cressey have lost their momentum and became more distinctively differentiated from sociology, their works were foundational for the multi-disciplinary field that emerged in the 1970s as "criminal justice."

This essay considers the ways in which this ethnographic foundation was elaborated, specified, and clarified over the following years. It identifies the key works in ethnography published in the last sixty-plus years. The virtues of ethnography are also noted in reference to these key works. In order to accomplish this, it is necessary in the first few sections of the essay to consider the context within which various kinds of policing were established and the emergence of policing as a governmental function. The police mandate is then discussed. It is then possible to consider ethnography and fieldwork as a research strategy and establish its relevance to police studies. Key ethnographies of the police and the police organization, in monographs, chapters, and articles, are discussed by decades and the continued strength of ethnography noted. The essay concludes by reflecting on the fate of ethnographic work.

23.1 POLICING

The study of policing is relatively new in the Anglo-American world, but analysis of the role and function of "police" has a long tradition in continental and English philosophy and in political philosophy (Jobard, 2014). Implicitly at least, empirical research on Anglo-American policing has assumed the "Peel model" unreflectively and assumed that police refers exclusively to public formal policing that is visible, preventive, reactive and responsive, uniformed, and politically neutral. This concept of policing, cast in the shadow of the utilitarianism of Bentham and Chadwick, and the early innovation of Patrick Colquhoun on the London docks, has obscured other traditions and modes of policing and narrowed the range of studies of policing. The range includes the constabulary mode of security policing, a model for the Gendarmerie and the U.S. State police; high policing, notably connected to central government agencies and divisions; non-democratic policing agencies and functions; and mixed systems such as those in Scotland, Quebec, and Ireland that blend features drawn from the continental and common-law systems. There are variations in the cultural and social bases of the legitimation of policing, including religious systems, the common law, and the continental legal systems. In addition to *ad hoc* and unofficial policing bodies, there are semi-formal and part-time bodies. There is also a long tradition of formally organized policing: police reserves, auxiliaries, military policing, and private policing that has been little researched. These are analytic distinctions that bear on the parochial nature of modern empirical research which has a singular focus on the visible, public police.

The importance of these historically-based distinctions is that police research has been very narrowly defined almost from the beginning of empirical work on policing. While early work in the United States on police was done by reformers such as Arthur Woods, Raymond Fosdick, and Bruce Smith and analysts who contributed to the Wickersham Report, the empirical work was done by sociologists, such as William Westley, Egon Bittner and others; political scientists such as W. Kerr Muir, George Berkley, and James Q. Wilson; a journalist who trained as an historian, Jonathan

Rubinstein; and an anthropologist, Michael Banton. This work was focused on the police but *assumed* a lively democratic governance system with viable civil liberties. The definition of police, albeit tacit, was drawn from this model (Cain 1979; Reiner 1992). The Peel model of policing, reflecting these attributes of governance, is the context for current research—it assumes the political neutrality of the police; a democratic and elected citizenry with rights and obligations in part defined by law; an insulation of the police organization from abrupt changes in the economy, polity, or socio-cultural environment; an overt rhetorical commitment to crime control; and some accountability to the public for actions and policies. These continue to be the threads linking the Peel model with present ideas about the police mandate. This positioning of the police in the state, the web of governance, has focused a great deal of police research on the relationships between the police and the public, whether this information is sought via interviews, surveys, documents, or fieldwork, and has left to modest investigation the role of the police in national security the role of national security agencies, and federal police agencies generally; private policing; and those agencies that lie at the edges of formal, public policing (Liang 1992).

While there has been some challenge to this conventional focus, or lack thereof (Ericson and Haggerty 1997; Aas 2007; Brodeur 2010; Bowling and Sheptycki 2012), the research in this tradition is limited in scope and largely done via social surveys—officially collected, unaudited, police constructed and officially recorded data (ORD)—or by using police records of various sorts. It is perhaps no longer necessary to point out that no single source of data has been subjected to more pointed, devastating, and revealing critiques than the ORD. It is necessary, then, to step back and reflect on the context within which fieldwork-based studies have been undertaken and published.

23.2 Contingency, Mandate, Strategy, Tactics, Theme, And Focus

All occupations are in some way directed to a fundamental contingency or uncertainty in a social system. These are analytically a basis upon which an occupational mandate may be constructed. Uncertainties are matters that are neither soluble by gathering facts (who won the 1944 World Series? How many police office are employed by the Denver department in 2012? What is the cost of a gallon of gas?) nor completely impossible to know (Can terrorists strike the Democratic convention? How might they do it?). Some uncertainties are matters which groups seek to control in spite of their universality—sin, disease, property, ignorance, and crime, or deviance (perhaps more generally social order and formal ordering processes), and they assemble institutions to cope with them. These are socially developed means of coping with the uncertainty; but the uncertainty remains. The license claimed by occupations, the right to define the nature of the work, if validated, leads to further claims to circumscribe the tasks and duties associated with that validated claim in the shape of a mandate (Hughes 1958). The mandate extends to defining the proper attitude toward the work and its practitioners—respect, deference, compliance. This seeking of confirmation and validation is a dialectical process. The mandate in effect is an occupation's rendering of the societal uncertainty or contingency, an elaboration of their connection to the central concerns of the society. It is a sign of the moral division of labor as well as the division of tasks and duties in any society. However, the mandate (a valid or accepted moral claim to carry out work) and license (delimited tasks and duties) are always in some dynamic tension in a democratic society. Once a mandate is granted, however, occupations sustain their claims variously: by appeals and control of a market, by association with the sacred and holy remnants thereof in Western industrialized societies, or they can claim expediency—someone needs to do it. The ability of an occupation to control to its practices and the costs of its services are indications of its power and authority, or indices of the strength of its mandate.

The primary uncertainty of concern to the police, it might be said, is negative, unwanted risk. This is the basis, as Bittner (1970) forcefully argues, for "calling the cops." They claim to supply security and political ordering in the face of uncertainty. At best, police rely on the trust of their publics, the publics' trust of the police, and this trust, binding in theory, extends public trust of each other in their civic roles. The police also select and perhaps have cast upon themselves a theme. A theme is a matter of how the work is defined to the public in general terms. A theme refers to how the occupation carries out its tasks and what it does to render its services consumable, needed, and indeed necessary. Policing has touted a responsiveness theme in this last century and refined it conspicuously—the police are a 24-hour full-service occupation. Given this contingency of negative, unwanted risk, the mandate, license, and the responsiveness theme, the police have narrowed their focus or strategies and related tactics, the ways in which the strategies are carried out. These strategies are: random patrol, responding to calls for service and investigating crime. Research has followed this definition of the mandate and studies now "crime management" and its converse, community policing. The diverse symbolic, representational and miscellaneous services rendered are studied only as inadvertent adjuncts to the role.

This framework, the claim and the validation by the public of a quasi-open organization that serves local publics, has meant a relative openness to police research in the United States since the 1980s; it has led to interest of governmental agencies and foundations in police research and related funding; it has stimulated research and evaluation of police policies and practices, especially since the establishment of the Office of Law Enforcement Assistance (OLEA), later the Law Enforcement Assistance Administration (LEAA) and still later the National Institute of Justice (NIJ) and the Office of Community Oriented Police Services (known as COPS); it has led to increased interest by the Home Office and the Association of Chief Police Officers (ACPO) in police research in the United Kingdom; and it has facilitated consultations between academics, practitioners of big-city agencies and government civil servants and a greater degree of reflexivity or mutual understandings. Increasingly, in other words, there is a mutual ongoing dialogue between these interested parties and the research that is funded and supported by access, tolerance, sponsorship, and cooperation. The findings of ethnography have been critical to understanding of modern patterns of policing.

23.3 Fieldwork and Ethnography

Fieldwork is a way of finding detailed and nuanced material that explains behavior in a given setting. This means observing and experiencing the setting, group, or organization; interpreting the meaning to participants of what is seen; and then presenting an argument about the coherence, logic, and emotional tone obtained in that environment. In many respects, ethnography has a literary aspect, and the voice or representational work required is essential in making the case for the analysis presented (Van Maanen 2011, xv).

Ethnographic research has a significant history beginning in the mid-nineteenth century with the work in London and Henry Mayhew and Charles Booth, but it took root in the United States through the efforts of sociologists at the University of Chicago. Beginning with the Polish peasant project of Thomas and Znaniecki (1918), and the students of Robert Park in particular, the aim of these studies was to describe the city in respect to its regions, neighborhoods, functions, and residents' occupational pursuits. This grand project was organized around the concentric zones of the city and their dynamics. The city was imagined as a rich variegated sort of social mosaic that was composed of the social worlds of the city. This work, which included studies of occupations (deviant and otherwise), areas, groups, and crimes, was framed in two ways simultaneously—the dynamics of the growth of the city and the functional adaptation of groups to these changes. It was the latter that required ethnographic work—making observations, doing interviews, seeking records, and drawing inferences from these to build a coherent story (Manning 1972; Van Maanen 2011). These ethnographies gave life to the city and informed policy; they were linked analytically and provided windows into the underside of the city as well as its prosperous and modest lifestyles.

Surprisingly, although the many studies in this early period in Chicago were done on delinquency and crime, there were no published studies of the police or of policing. It was William Westley that brought the lens of the Chicago School to bear on the police in the late 1940s, and Michael Banton in England who successfully depicted in great detail policing in rural areas and the police role. This of course was another example of the impact of the Peel model of policing, for interest in the police ethnographically was late in beginning on the continent for many reasons, but the Anglo-American concern for the individual and individual rights under law propelled and still propels much ethnographic research. For this reason also one can argue that the most common trope, or style, of police ethnographers is "irony" or a focus on the contrasts and contradictions; between the ideal and the real, or the expected and the observed (Manning 1979). Regardless of style, ethnographers who achieve fame are writers with exceptional style that swerves into poetic-like writing. Fortunately, these stylistic variations led to the charge that this sort of skill "can't be learned" and other dismissive phrases. Of course, there is much pedestrian and dull ethnography; perhaps as much as there are pedestrian and dull ethnographers.

The rationale for fieldwork—work that includes document gathering and analysis; observation in one or more roles (observer, participant as observer, participant observer); interviewing and perhaps use of a video or camera to record events—is that it facilitates the readings of culture and its constraints. Ethnography is, technically speaking, writing about culture, and it is about the phase(s) of field research in which the writing up takes place. In effect it is a form of persuasive communication between observer-observed and the reader. Fieldwork contrasts with other, qualitative approaches such as content analysis, visual sociology, or historical-archival research, and with quantitative research. There are many clear statements of the merits of ethnographic field work (see, e.g., Van Maanen 2011). These authors also discuss the issues that are often problematic: inference and proof based on field data; the validity of field data; the degree to which it is reliable and cumulative; and the relationship between the embodied researcher and his/her data, those observed and the broader public (including IRBs [Institutional Review Board], lawyers, and courts). In many respects, and in a very complex fashion, the self of the fieldworker is the research tool, the source of reflections, doubts, efforts to make sense and clarify emotions and data; and he or she is unavoidably the producer of things expressed or given off and things stated, done, and written about (Goffman 1959, 2). Ethnographic work is punctuated by difficulties, moral quandaries, and dilemmas (Punch 1989).

This brings us to culture, a debated concept, and it is the base the fieldworker seeks to explicate such that the examples, vignettes, tables, pictures, charts, or figures make sense. It usually includes reference to not only beliefs, cognitions, rituals, and ceremonies, but the taken for granted assumptions that shape and make sensible what the observer sees, records, smells, touches, hears, and photographs. As Van Maanen (2011, 3) writes poetically, "Culture is not visible, but is made visible only through its representation." In addition, there are variations within culturally defined groups that may emphasize or de-emphasize aspects of the culture in which they are embedded—thus one finds reference in policing studies to subcultures, or segments within the organization that differ in their emphases and explanations for what they do and why they do it.

There is a general consensus reflected in Lofland (2006) that fieldwork proceeds as a kind of phased natural history—a beginning, middle, and end, with the "end," the writing up, being the most problematic for many fieldworkers (Wolcott 1990). Having said this in defense of fieldwork, it must be said that most fieldwork begins with an open-ended text, a series of questions or hunches, rather than a theoretically rationalized set of propositions, hypotheses, or ideas tightly linked to a theory. This animates the work but often confounds and confuses young fieldworkers who cannot, when they sit down to write, identify the problem on which they have spent this time working. Having been fascinated by the field and the experiences, many fieldworkers have trouble in seeing what the data are all about, and their theoretical rationale is unexplored or unstated. Often this soul-searching for a problem is less salient to new fieldworkers than trying to find a site and determine or explain the merits of a research project—this may be an internal dialogue or a group exercise such as a grant proposal or a PhD proposal.

Ethnography has been most visible in studies of the police occupation and organization. Police occupational subculture is the focus of a great deal of police research, and has been since the beginning of police studies in North America and in the United Kingdom (Reiner 1992). In the abstract, the term references here all those means by which the members of the occupation cope with, manage, define, ignore, and otherwise experience the fundamental contingencies and uncertainties of the job as they see it. The culture includes material, symbolic, and rhetorical resources, as well as an oral tradition, rules of thumb about how to do the job, and cautionary tales—major mistakes and their consequences. To some extent, the ideas that are packaged as an occupational culture are occasioned or used to explain or rationalize what has been done. Since the kinds of uncertainties experienced vary within the occupation, the content of the subculture takes on nuances within and between or across the divisions or segments of the occupation. It is essential to bear in mind that there is no single occupational culture in policing or any other occupation, but rather a cluster of segments, and that emphases and attitudes, for example, vary within the segments by such matters as race, gender, and age. On the other hand, the police organization has been viewed as exceptional and studied statistically, and very little theorizing has been undertaken. In part because of the unique history of policing as a governance function, and in part because of the interest in organization theorists in business and manufacturing organizations, speculation about the relationship between the police organization as a rational actor and its environment remains an open question.

23.4 Occupational and Organizational Ethnographic Studies: Monographs, Chapters, and Articles

It is important to discuss briefly the classics and near-classics that have an ethnographic or interpretative component. Included also are those studies that contain qualitative materials based on experience, interviews, and observations and in which the data are not restricted to survey, interview, and/or attitudinal data. The selected and strategic sample shown here is a combination of my assessment, a search of the bibliographies of all the books listed for cross-referencing, and a check of the citation index of a few of the best known monographs in Google Scholar. I did not trawl through dissertation abstracts, and clearly there are a large number of PhDs who have both advanced and sharpened our understandings. Considered are published materials, not dissertations and theses. A full check of impact, citation indexes, and the rest was unfortunately beyond the time frame permitted for this writing. What is presented is in some sense an impressionistic assemblage rather than a sample based on impact, citation, or a survey of scholars' assessments of important sources. It should be said also that the number of PhD students and PhD programs in criminal justice and criminology, and the number of journals have increased considerably over the last forty years. Thus, making any firm generalizations about the growth or decline in police ethnographies remains somewhat moot. In some sense, then, this is an overview of the salient and significant ethnographies in the field of police studies and in some indirect way, a measure of their impact on scholarship. I take the tables that follow as illustrative. I did query a few respected colleagues for their impressions, but I advance this as a modest framework for further analysis and solicit tolerance if a deserving monograph, chapter, or article has been omitted.

The books listed can be roughly divided into those that analyze the *occupation* and its features, and those that analyze the police as an organization. The police organization is composed of many occupations—janitors, cooks, lawyers, biochemists, computer repair people, clerks, and baby-sitters—but is dominated by the ideology of the police as an occupation. About 25 percent of the organization are not sworn officers, and in this sense, as a result of union contracts, traditions of employment, and growing expertise on which the organization depends, analysis of the occupation differs from an analysis of the dynamics of the organization. The police engage in the practice of policing, which is the public face of the organization. Ethnographic work has been both inward looking, describing the organizational and occupational tensions and cultures, as well as outward, charting the relationships between the police and their publics. The studies of relevance here are organizational and occupational, and include those that focus on the ways in which the organization and its occupations shape what is done and how it is explained and rationalized. The analysis that follows arrays and takes up first occupationally-focused ethnographies. It then considers interpretative organizationally-focused analyses. Finally, chapters and articles that encompass the organization and the occupation that shapes and defines it are set in a table and discussed. The topics are relatively few in fact.

It is useful from a commonsense point of view to sort the works by decade, bearing in mind that this may gloss important features but capture similarities that reflect the events and intellectual trends of the decade. It is also true that this classification scheme may be misleading in some cases in which the actual fieldwork was done in previous time. The Westley (1970) book, which is based on work done more than twenty years before its publication, is a dramatic example.

Table 23.1 reveals a number of important facts and suggests some inferences from these. (The works are cited by last name and the details of the publication are found in the references.) Let us consider the general points first, prior to a discussion of the intellectual trends revealed. Among the books listed are among those one might consider as foundational to the field of criminal justice and police studies. They are frequently cited and used as the basis for further exploration of concepts and ideas, and this is true for statistical studies as well as ethnographic and interpretative studies. Here are some highlights. Clearly, there is a trend if one considers Westley as the first known work (although not published until 1970) to six works in the 1960s, ten in the 1970s, eleven in

Table 23.1 Ethnographic monographs with a police occupation focus

1960s	1970s	1980s	1990s	2000s
Banton (1964)	Bittner (1970)	Black (1980)	Foster (1990)	Glaeser (2000)
Whitaker (1964)	Westley (1970)	Ericson (1981)	Brewer and Magee (1991)	Innes (2003)
Skolnick (1966)	Laurie (1970)	Ericson (1982)	Guyot (1991)	Loader and Mulcahy (2003)
Cicourel (1967)	Cain (1973)	Martin (1982)	Simon (1991)	Manning (2003)
Niederhoffer (1967)	Rubinstein (1973)	Holdaway (1983)	Young (1991)	Jackall (2005)
Alex (1969)	Alex (1976)	Reuss-Ianni (1983)	Reiner (1992)	Herbert (2006)
	Manning (1977)	Leinen (1985)	Leinen (1993)	O'Neill (2006)
	Sanders (1977)	Smith and Gray (1985)	Sheptycki (1993)	Huey (2007)
	Reiner (1978)	Grimshaw and Jefferson (1987)	Young (1994)	Moskos (2008)
	Muir (1979)	Fielding (1988)	Fielding (1996)	Wender (2008)
		Hobbs (1988)	Chan (1997)	Loftus (2009)
			Herbert (1997)	Bowling (2010)
			Jackall (1997)	Glaeser (2011)
			Choongh (1998)	Huey (2012)
			Barker (1999)	
			Miller (1999)	

the 1980s, and sixteen in the 1990s. The turn of the century now runs to almost thirteen years rather than ten, but it appears that since 2000, some fourteen monographs have been published.

Perhaps because of their precedence, many of the earlier works, those published through the 1970s, remain highly visible, often cited and seen as essential in literature reviews. No one would dispute the salience and influence of Michael Banton (1964), Jerome Skolnick (1966), Aaron Cicourel (1967), Egon Bittner (1970), William Westley (1970), Maureen Cain (1973), Jonathan Rubinstein (1973), and Peter K. Manning (1977) on research and publication. However, the subtle rather prescient and insightful work of Ben Whitaker (1964) and Peter Laurie (1970) are not frequently cited in the United States. The 1980s brings a tighter focus on aspects of the job divisions within the job; socialization to the job; gender influences (Martin 1982); and the first full-scale studies in London (see, e.g., Smith and Gray 1985). Donald Black's (1980) *Manners and Customs of the Police* is a powerful Durkheimian conceptualization of policing as governmental social control.

By the 1990s, more diversity on questions asked, data gathered, and analyses appears. Here, one can find studies carried out in Northern Ireland (Brewer and Magee 1991), England (Foster 1990; Fielding 1996), and Australia (Chan 1997), as well as studies done in the United States. Reiner's (1992) classic study and Young's (1991) open for the first time the world of top command. Gender and race are considered (Leinen 1993; Barker 1999; Miller 1999). Simon's (1991) work on homicide detectives, arguably journalistic, is brilliant, insightful, and touching, and there was also a closely done study of rural policing (Young 1994). In the years following 2000, it is more difficult to generalize about the works. There is a more international flavor (Glaeser 2000, 2011; Huey 2007; Bowling 2010), works on policing football in Scotland (O'Neill 2006) and the north of England (Loftus 2009), contentious ethnographies (Jackall 2005), and a treatment of street policing (Moskos 2008). The earlier works remain visible and frequently cited as a required prefatory to any contemporary study, especially those that outline the occupational culture of patrol officers. On the other hand, the later studies are more diverse as to topic and less general in their scope and contentions, and apply the ethnographic art or craft in more diverse settings.

At least from this somewhat informal gathering of data, it does not appear that ethnographic studies of the occupation of policing are becoming less prevalent. Perhaps newer works have not achieved the notoriety, impact, citation power, and visibility of works done some forty or more years ago. Why this is the case is an open question given the changes in the composition of cities, changes in the economy, the recruitment of other than white, heterosexual males to the work, and the increase of college educational achievement and higher degrees in policing, especially among the top command. It is likely that for better or worse, the earlier works set of a kind of paradigm and as such must be cited, while the later works are establishing variations or nuances on the basic pattern. The marginalization of minorities in policing has not been reduced. Reading the recent works specifically on the occupational culture reveals that it is criticized almost uniformly and seen as negative by ethnographers, with Robert Jackall's (1997) *Wild Cowboys* being one of the few exceptions. Young's (1991) work contains a consistently ambivalent ironic tone in description of both the resilience and anomalous character of the police organization and its management.

There are no discussions of the role of the culture in promoting and sustaining discipline, uniformity, morale, and solidarity in the face of criticism, not to speak of pride, honor, self-esteem, and bonding amongst individuals. There are few studies of careers over time, top command, networks of sponsorship and promotion (i.e., the politics of the police organization and the work of middle managers). How does the complex stratification system of the police organization maintain itself? Through what actions and agency does this take place? The role of deviance as a positive source of social solidarity, the Durkhemian theme that essentially produced modern criminology, seems unappreciated, especially as a result of the crime control frenzy of the experimentalists. The almost poetic work of Loader and Mulcahy (2003) on the culture of policing, that is, the culture in which policing as an organization resides and in which it is embedded, is too little studied.

Three further points can be made before advancing to a discussion of ethnographic-organizational studies. It is ironic that the most context-sensitive strategy of research, ethnography, is most rooted in the past and past observations and inferences; one would have guessed that detailed, fine-grained observations would have altered and refined the earlier paradigm-setting ideas. This apparently has not happened. One of the most recent ethnographies, done in the North of England, affirms the relevance of the classic studies of the occupational culture, what the author calls "the orthodox account" (Loftus 2010). The complexity and nuance of the organizational culture remains unexplored, as what has been studied is talk, often talk designed to dramatize, idealize, and mystify the work. A second point is that the craft of ethnography is still developing, and the techniques are debatable or even "primitive" (Van Maanen 2011, 24); the standards for judging merit are problematic, unlike statistical arguments that can be judged by conventional rules of thumb about significances, sample size, techniques of analysis, and so on. Finally, given the prevalence of cell phones, cameras, and computers for car aural and videotaping capacity in police cars, when will the first visual ethnography be published? Will it be available as a collection of CDs available on Amazon or through Kindle?

Turning now to interpretative organizational studies, as shown in Table 23.2, there is a similar pattern to that found in Table 23.1. There are a few that arguably are now classics in the field—James Q. Wilson (1968), Michael Brown (1969), and the works of Wesley Skogan and colleagues (1997, 1999). Brodeur's (2010) effort at synthesis may become a classic, but it is too early to assess its impact. A few very early works are followed by

Table 23.2 Ethnographic monographs with a police organizational focus

1960s	1970s	1980s	1990s	2000s
Wilson (1968)	Lambert (1970)	Manning (1980)	Bayley (1991)	Ellison and Smyth (2000)
Bayley (1969)	Reiss (1971)	Scheingold (1984)	Scheingold (1991)	Websdale (2001)
Berkley (1969)	Sherman (1978)	Sykes and Brent (1983)	Ackroyd (1992)	Rigakos (2002)
Brown (1969)		Bayley (1985)	Kemp et al. (1992)	Sheptycki (2002)
Rex and Moore (1969)		McClure (1985)	Brogden and Shearing (1993)	Wakefield (2003)
		Manning (1988)	Hunt and Mageneau (1993)	Deflem (2004)
		Shapland and Vagg (1988)	Nadelmann (1993)	Goold (2004)
			Waddington (1993)	Altbeker (2005)
			Skolnick and Fyfe (1994)	Marks (2005)
			Ericson and Haggerty (1997)	Mulcahy (2006)
			Skogan and Hartnett (1997)	Skogan (2006)
			Jones and Newburn (1998)	Manning (2008)
			Lyons (1999)	Hunt (2010)
			Silverman (1999)	Bowling (2010)
			Skogan et al. (1999)	Brodeur (2010)

some organizational analyses in the 1960s, and a flurry in the 1990s. A promising and diverse group of publications appeared after the turn of the century. Like the ethnographies of the occupation, the numbers by decade advance from five studies prior to 1970, excluding the early administratively-oriented works of Raymond Fosdick, Arthur Woods, and Bruce Smith, to three in the 1970s, seven in the 1980s, and fifteen in the 1990s. There have been fifteen published thus far since 2000. Certainly, James Q. Wilson (1968) and Albert Reiss (1971) continue to be widely cited, and the publications resulting from Skogan's research in Chicago is generally considered the most systematic and valid work on community policing (see, e.g., Skogan 2006).

There is a tendency toward more diversity studies being done outside the United States or the United Kingdom, including in Japan (Bayley 1991), Canada (Ericson and Haggerty 1997), South Africa (Brogden and Shearing 1993), and cross-border policing (Nadelmann 1993). In the next decade, new published studies were set in the Caribbean (Bowling 2010), Northern Ireland (Ellison and Smyth 2000; Mulcahy 2006), and South Africa (Altbeker 2005; Marks 2005), and investigations of transnational policing (Sheptycki 2002) and the first systematic studies of private policing (Rigakos 2002; Wakefield 2003) also appeared. There is no central theme except perhaps a more international vision. In many respects, it is more difficult to generalize about themes in these studies because the topic of "organization," indeed even the concept and its definition, is broad and contentious. Perhaps the most enduring works remain those of Albert Reiss (1971), James Q. Wilson (1968) and David Bayley (1985), while Ericson and Haggerty (1997) have been seen as challenging much of the past police organization studies because they see the organization more as an information-processing system than an enforcement entity, and officers as "knowledge workers."

The key published sources in this area appear to be articles and chapters rather than monographs, as is discussed below, and they are more theoretical in nature than empirical. One might venture that the shifting focus to comparative work and transnational policing is a reflection of the general consensus that the study of "policing" must include the study of more than formal policing and more than public policing; that private policing is a major force; that some metaphor like the "policing web" or the "surveillant assemblage," with emphasis on mentalities, practices, and interconnections of organizations, is needed; and that some of the fundamental assumptions of the Bittner (1970) model may require rethinking given comparative, cross-cultural research. Perhaps with the exception of rethinking the impact of technology on the police organization, crime mapping, crime analysis, and CompStat-like meetings (Silverman 1999; Manning 2008), there is little rethinking of the basic model of the police organization outlined by Wilson (1968), although its place in the political economy has been discussed (Deflem 2004). Two abiding questions might be advanced.

Over time, it appears that the vision of scholars is broadening and taking into account other models of policing other than the Peel model, looking at transnational policing, and the role of antiterrorism and terrorism (seen more in recent articles than in monographs). Nevertheless, there are no studies of federal agencies, national security-focused agencies (ICE and its component organizations, or in particular the CIA, FBI, and DEA).

More studies are investigating specialized units. What is the role, if any, of the political, economic, and cultural context of the police organization's operations? It has been sold as an apolitical, neutral "law enforcement" agency, evidence to the contrary notwithstanding, and its members cast as loyalty, dutiful, dogged in their determination, and only occasionally excessively violent, corrupt, venial, or stupid. Only through comparative studies that look at several organizations over time can these influences be identified and sorted out as to effect. The New Orleans Police Department's behavior during and after Hurricane Katrina and the flooding of the city (Sims 2007; Deflem and Sutphin 2009), for example, is suggestive.

Turning now to salient chapters and articles in the ethnographic tradition that have shaped research, it is clearly more difficult to discern their impact—admittedly, it will be a combination of citation, recognition, and durability in the field, and a role in an ongoing question or set of questions that animate the field. This grouping is perhaps the most contentious.

The articles and chapters in Table 23.3 are not, strictly speaking, comparable with the monographs on the organization and occupation, since they are refereed in a different manner and articles tend to be more visible, numerous, and cited. In addition, the number of journals, including some that are seen as prestigious, has increased exponentially. There are many ways one could argue for "significance," such as reprinting, citation, role in the references of works that are themselves cited, scope, and topic. Clearly general works are more salient, and are more likely to be cited than more specialized works (e.g., works on community policing, detective work, or technology). Thus, this grouping is a kind of imaginative exploration of topics and importance rather than a detailed content or impact analysis. As far as an overview of these listed, note the isolation of Westley's (1953, 1955) publications in the 1950s, and the similar trajectory of articles and studies to the pattern shown in Tables 23.1 and 23.2. In the 1960s, nine key articles appeared, including those by Egon Bittner (1967a, 1967b), Cumming and associates (1965), and David Bordua and Albert Reiss (1966, 1967), which are still much cited. The 1970s saw thirteen still-influential papers, such as those by John Van Maanen (1973, 1974, 1978), Egon Bittner (1974), Herman Goldstein (1979), and Peter K. Manning (1979). The 1980s saw thirteen trend-setting articles including those by Jean-Paul Brodeur (1983), Peter Manning (1983), Clifford Shearing and Philip Stenning (1983), and Lawrence Sherman and colleagues (1984, 1989). It would be difficult to underestimate the importance of the Sherman articles, even though they have a modest ethnographic component, not only in respect to citations but with regard to their influence on increasing the popularity of quasi-experimental methods.

In the 1990s, twelve important and influential statements shaped the development of the field. These include articles about private policing (Shearing and Ericson 1991), socialization (Chan 1996) and patrol tactics (Herbert 1996, 1998; Klinger 1997), militarization (Kraska and Cubellis 1997) and the occupational culture (Shearing and Ericson 1991; Waddington 1999). The last twelve years have seen only a handful of noteworthy articles and chapters. It is difficult in fact to discount the chapters in the Weisburd and Braga (2006) collection based on diverse data, including ethnographic materials, as

Table 23.3 Salient ethnographic chapters and articles on policing

1950s	1960s	1970s	1980s	1990s	2000s
Westley (1953)	Clark (1965)	Black (1970)	Waegel (1981)	Shearing and Ericson (1991)	Meehan and Ponder (2002)
Westley (1955)	Cumming et al. (1965)	Punch and Naylor (1973)	Waegel (1982)	Sherman et al. (1991)	Marks (2004)
	Bordua and Reiss (1966)	Van Maanen (1973)	Wilson and Kelling (1982)	Crank and Langworthy (1992)	Beckett et al. (2006)
	Bittner (1967a)	Bittner (1974)	Brodeur (1983)	Reiss (1992)	Weisburd and Braga (2006)
	Bittner (1967b)	Marx (1974)	Manning (1983)	Chan (1996)	Carr et al. (2007)
	Bordua and Reiss (1967)	Reiss (1974)	Shearing and Stenning (1983)	Herbert (1996)	Willis et al. (2007)
	McNamara (1967)	Van Maanen (1974)	Van Maanen (1983)	Jones et al. (1996)	
	Reiss and Bordua (1967)	Van Maanen (1978)	Sherman and Berk (1984)	Klinger (1997)	
	Black and Reiss (1969)	Cain (1979)	Van Maanen (1984)	Kraska and Cubellis (1997)	
		Chatterton (1979)	Bayley and Bittner (1986)	Herbert (1998)	
		Goldstein (1979)	Bayley and Garafolo (1989)	Kennedy (1998)	
		Guyot (1979)	Foster (1989)	Meehan (1998)	
		Manning (1979)	Sherman et al. (1989)	Braga et al. (1999)	
				Waddington (1999)	

they address the contours of the field in precise and penetrating fashion. I have counted this as one work, even though it contains three parts and seventeen chapters including an advocate's statement and a critic's response.

The lack of focus on conceptual matters, a concern of ethnographic work that connects concepts with practices, is revealed in the findings of a panel appointed by the National Research Council (2004). The experts chosen were unable to identify what makes policing fair, just, efficient, or effective. In many respects although they are not ethnographic, the chapters published in the edited volume of Weisburd and Braga (2006) summed up the concerns of the decade and the absence of a strong ethnographic presence. What is known about police practices in the present century based on articles and chapters has to be inferred because there are few ethnographically-oriented studies except those by Marks (2004) on special units of the South African police; Willis, Mastrofski, and Weisburd (2007) on CompStat; and Carr, Napolitano, and Keating (2007) on calling the police.

Taking the three sets of publications, it can be argued that the impression of the diminution of ethnographies is revealed most vividly in the articles and chapters that have been cited and used in research publications. There are no comparable chapters or articles with the impact of those by David Bordua and Albert Reiss (1966, 1967), or John Van Maanen (1973, 1974, 1978), or Herman Goldstein's outline of "problem-solving" (1979), and Egon Bittner's articles (1967a, 1967b). But there are many that describe new innovations like CompStat, community policing, and specialized units such as bomb squads. Let us review some of the salient findings of police ethnographic work before returning to the question of "ethnographic fade."

23.5 Fieldwork with the Police

The virtues of ethnographic work have been well described by Van Maanen (2011) and connected to the classic police studies, but his concern is with "voice," or genre or style of presenting the materials gathered, rather than the findings themselves. There are a number of important contributions of ethnographic work that can be identified and linked to future research questions.

Ethnographic work with the police brings together a secretive, violent, complex, and traditionally organized occupation in an organizational context with a researcher or a research team. Let's set aside in this context the difficulties encountered in carrying out the fieldwork itself and focus on the merits of such a research strategy. This discussion, and these citations and examples are not meant as a way of minimizing other modes of research, but rather to state the aims of such research in the context of studying policing and how they facilitate discovery of the phenomenon of "policing" as a social object—something that has social meaning, durability, and constraint, and is a social fact. Consider the following examples of the virtues and findings of fieldwork on the police as an introduction to the classic works.

When doing fieldwork, one encounters the ways in which the problematics of the occupation are described, defined, reacted to, and managed. This is nicely described in Bittner's (1967b) study on policing on skid row, which shows how the tacit understandings of the police shape what is done and why. As Bittner shows, the tactics officers use reveal their preferences and their skills in managing outcomes (see also Kemp, Norris, and Fielding 1992). These differences and how they reflect citizens' preferences in less than felony encounters are elegantly captured in the work of Black and Reiss (1969). As Bittner has pointed out, the job of the officer is to size up the problem not in the natural habitat of the citizen, but through the occupationally shaped lenses of the officer—the aim is to manage complexity quickly and to manage the outcomes with a minimum of paperwork, supervision, and "hassle." In other words, the situation cannot be described outside the dynamics as defined in the here and now, thus making ethnographic analysis essential to any attempt at comparison across situations and over time and across organizations. If one thinks of the organization as a kind of label that refers to the constraints of action in an organizational role, then the "organization" looks different if one is looking down from a top command position, from the middle as a supervisor, or from the view of an investigator or a patrol officer. This perspectival difference is well reflected in the classic studies of the occupational culture of the police, as well summarized by Loftus (2009). This proposition is perhaps revealed in studies of attitudes, but more dramatically as a result of close observations and interviews revealing the views and the practices of officers on the job (Hunt 2010). "Looking different" refers to the ways in which patrol officers view the organization as a punitive bureaucracy (Gouldner 1954; Manning 1977) that is dangerous to them and their careers, and arbitrary and capricious; how sergeants must act as mediators to sustain their power and authority (Van Maanen 1983; Moskos 2008); and how top command views rules as tools to keep the troops in line (Reuss-Ianni 1983).

Enforcement of rules is a primary source of power, and, as Bittner observes as a result of his lengthy and detailed observations, this is often unrelated to good performance which is left undefined (Bittner 1970, 55). The authority of sergeants is demonstrated by the ways in which "output" is shaped by their decisions, not the nature of the behavior of citizens (Moskos 2008). Of course, the actions of officers produce unanticipated negative and positive consequences, which are revealing of the ways in which deciding must be observed to discern the dynamics of the situation as it unfolds. From a praxis perspective, in what people do one sees the nature of "rules," "laws," "norms," and "values." It is through their actions that the meaning and consequences of these social facts are revealed (Manning 1977). Police work is always at least in theory "team work" in the sense that officers share secrets and act in concert in situations from time to time. They speak of themselves as part of a "police family" (Van Maanen 1974), and this metaphor variously applies. They maintain clear boundaries between what is public or front stage at any given time and what is private or "back stage" (Holdaway 1983), and this itself requires cooperation to sustain a definition of the situation (Goffman 1959). The ability of a fieldworker to move back and forth between "stages" and to share team secrets, back-stage knowledge, and the nature of mistakes at work is the usufruct of good fieldwork and established trust. For example, as a result of being a trusted quasi- or "limbo member" of a group of police officers, Jennifer Hunt was able to elicit a number of lies told by police to cover their mistakes as well as lies told in court (Hunt and Manning 1991).

As Bittner first noted and Marks amplified, it is often the case the police do not articulate at the time their reasons for acting as they did—they are pragmatists who act first and rationalize later. But the willingness to explore reasons and accounts after the fact is again a function of trust, more likely to be granted to female fieldworkers than male. These accounts (Mills 1940) are related to the "multiple realities" of policing—the view from the streets and from the desk produce quite different socially constructed viewpoints. Like all occupations, the police are segmented by rank, by specialty, and by gender and race, and these segments tend to produce different attitudes and beliefs about the nature of the job, its purposes, rewards, satisfactions, and merits (Alex 1969; Leinen 1985, 1993; Miller 1999). As Marks (2004) and others have argued, continuous contact with an organization is considered ideal, on the model of anthropologists who spent many months in an isolated site, learned the language, and lived the lifestyle of those they studied (Malinowski 1989). In fact, the time spent in the field and what aspects of the field were studied varies among anthropological studies from a few weeks to years of intermittent contact. It is considered a requirement to state how long one has worked in the field, where and with what purpose and types of data gathering. It is most likely that due to time, costs, patience, and practical constraints such as family, end of an academic degree period, or other crisis, that most fieldwork is relatively brief, a matter of a few months, rather than taking the years associated with the anthropological golden age. All police research exposes one to dilemmas, to violence, to unethical behavior and frightening events and scenes. The unpredictable, variable and uneven practices of IRB committees certainly have been of no value to serious fieldwork.

Perhaps the enduring tension noted in all these works is between the individualistic, entrepreneurial motifs and self-designations of patrol officers and their view of the organization as a loose aggregation of quasi-rational actors, and descriptions of the organization as "paramilitary." This tension is captured in the rationalization that is going on inside the police organization, especially in regard to information systems. Ethnographic work reveals that the enduring pressures, largely from politicians and public demand, have led police organizations to create and adapt ever more elaborate rules and legalistic procedures, management information systems, strategic plans, management by goals and objectives, career planning schemes, computerized dispatching systems, Internet websites, media relations offices, and activities on social media (Manning 2008, 36–39). The most significant of these is the combination of computer-assisted dispatching with other electronic means of record keeping, processing, storing, and retrieving data. These in turn are linked to the increasing use of non-sworn personnel (which make up somewhere between 25 to 30 percent of modern departments in the United States).

These modest innovations are refining the means of policing, and the basic Peel model has been little changed structurally with the exception of the addition of investigation divisions, and the basic strategies are frozen in place. Many tactical changes, such as community policing and team policing, have been tried and abandoned. The core of the work remains the officer working alone, taking on and shaping work as he or she defines it, subject to very little active supervision (except after the fact), taking low visibility, and unreviewed decisions. Even though the educational level of police officers has risen appreciably in the last forty years, the police organization still presents itself as a "lean, mean, crime-fighting machine," and it trains young officers in a stilted, unimaginative style in brief academies (Moskos 2008). There remains a conflict between the dramaturgical presentation of the job in recruiting efforts and the media and the incoming idealism of young officers, and the cynical core of attachment to extrinsic values of the work, such as pay, security, and retirement and pension schemes, and little emphasis on the skills, tasks, and competencies that are intrinsic to the job. The modern officer clearly has access to more information, faster and more efficiently, but the basic policing practices are remarkably similar over time, and across organizations in the Anglo-American (Canada, New Zealand, Australia, the United States, and the United Kingdom) policing world. And as Bittner (1970, 64) remarks, "no one [in a police department] tells anybody more than he absolutely has to."

While one could lay out an analytic scheme to identify needed research (see Reiner 1992, 458), the missing piece in regard to studies of the organization and the police occupation is some sense of the internal dynamics within and across the segments. The early studies were quite clearly sociological. They depict the occupational culture in classic Chicago School terms—the ways in which the occupation defines its central interests as they relate to those they deal with, and its role within the moral division of labor. This focus includes elaborating a sense of the occupation's vested interests, license and mandate, its etiquette, or how to cope with the demands of its audiences, the salient identities of those who practice, and the occupational segments into which it is divided. Clearly, the inherited dominant imagery is derived from the role and practices of the street officer in large cities, and it is layered with the oppositional, negative, even defensive aspects of that segment of the occupational culture. Arguably, there are at least five segments—patrol officers, supervisors, top command, specialized units, and investigators—and each has a dynamic internal character as well as a role in the hierarchy of power interests within the organization. It is this dynamic, psycho-social aspect, internal to the segments and between the segments, that is not well captured in the literature of police studies and the sociology of the police. In order to consider this position, it is necessary to see the self and body in some moralistic, holistic connection such that the connections between and among groups of people are emotionally loaded, and to see that these connections have holistic, moral, political, economic, and social consequences for members of the occupation. A shorthand for these considerations is the social identity of the member of a segment and its relationship to other identities, gender, age, rank, ethnicity, and perhaps religion. Being in the world is in organizational terms a sense of social location, a combination of these identities.

There are some generalizations to be made concerning the occupation and the organization of policing using this framework for consideration in future ethnographic research. Think of the police occupation in big cities in the Anglo-American world and consider these propositions to be further explored. It appears that rather than regarding the occupational culture of the patrol officer as a part that reflects or reveals the whole, it is better to conceive of the organization as peopled by segments. If the occupation is segmented or based on the degree of interaction that is greater with members of the same segment than the sum of interactions with other segments in the occupation, this is a mosaic rather than a unified "culture." The key to understanding the segment and its role in the organization is to identify the sorts of contingencies that characterize the segment. These segments have vested interests in the hierarchy of power relationships within the organization. These interests include respect, career advancement, sponsorship of protégés for niches, positions and rank promotion, pay (including over-time and special assignments), and protection from punishment or investigation (inter-nal affairs). This is one way in which the segment reproduces itself over time.

The segments seek to maintain their power relationships with various publics they serve (e.g., the perks of office such as meals, deals, consideration for services, and other informal benefits). These are webs of exchange, reciprocated and institu-tionalized to some degree. These are not static relationships based on norms, values, or mini-ideologies, but are sanctified practices. There is a dynamic tension based on competition within and between members of segments for organizational resources and career options, social, symbolic, and material capital. Nevertheless, all segments are affected by the contingencies of the job. However, each segment endures specific and proximal contingencies (matters with consequences, positive and negative, with unknown and not easily controlled outcomes), and copes stylistically and character-istically with them. Segment members endure both objective contingencies, such as demotion, risks of accidents and on-the-job-violence, and subjective, emotional con-tingencies. While the objective contingencies are relatively well-studied, the emotional costs and benefits are less well understood. There are insights gathered from studies of police suicide, alcoholism and drug use, divorce and depression, especially that which results from a trauma such as a shooting or being shot. The stresses associated with death and injury studied by a few (Young 1991; Brandl and Stroshine 2003; Henry and Lifton 2004) remain powerful in part because they are so consistently denied by iconic male officers.

Emotions animate the segments and create conflicts between segments. These emo-tions include, for example, envy (wishing for the perceived advantages of others), jealously (anger at a formal or final advantage being lost or taken away), rage, embar-rassment (on the job failure or personal malady or difficulty), or ressentiment—a French word—(deeply felt feelings of resentment, frustration and hostility combined with a feeling of inability to alter the circumstances that created such feelings). The segments are not equal in power or authority. In crude terms, one might distinguish three levels within the organization: officers of whatever rank and specialty, middle level-supervisors, and top command or "management cops." The occupational culture, seen as a bundle of segments in some kind of equilibrium, is shaped by crises and turn-ing points, especially succession of top management that differentially affects them. These succession crises in turn have career ramifications. The police organization is not constituted solely by rank distinctions in part because it is a personalistic bureaucracy and thus vacillates from a punitive to a mock bureaucratic form (Gouldner 1954). Thus, downward mobility is not revealed in the rare rank demotion or being fired or forced to resign. It comes through degrees of shaming and transfer, working without a gun, being banished to an organizational Siberia, and losing political clout as a result of a succes-sion crisis.

While the boundaries between segments are in part sacred and marked by symbols such as weapons, uniforms or lack thereof, audiences, and career interests, within each segment are those marked for exclusion—marginalized members. They differ either by race, ethnicity, age, or long-term on-the-job "troubles" or differences, bad reputation, or work level. They are the deviants who set out the contours of "good careers" and "good police work." Management or supervisory changes in style or enforcement practices, especially at the middle level, have ramifications in all segments. These dynamics of supervision typically create a kind of iconography of rules (i.e., enforcing the rule becomes a miniature version of the relationships between the segments and the organization as a whole). Patterns of resistance to the actions of other segments and to the top command become institutionalized in game-like fashion.

So, what holds the police, organization, occupation, and practice, together? Why is the ensemble glossed as the occupational culture of policing? There are integrating strands. Everyone enters at the bottom; they were all trained in some combination of an academy and apprentice relationships, first with a field officer and later with a more senior partner; they take their first position in patrol; they share a common notion about "the job" and what it means and needs—"common-sense"—and does not mean-intellectualized pondering and cumbersome weighing up of situations; they share tacit notions about what is "good police work" and "bad police work;" they are wrapped in a network of cliques and personalized loyalties that overlap and compete for power; they celebrate occasionally together—at funerals, weddings, and parades—and work together as a team in riots, demonstrations, and large public gatherings. There are a myriad of exchanges based on mutual reciprocity, teamwork, partnerships past and present, exchanges of information between the uniformed and investigative units, shared secrets, covering for each other when workload is high, and overlooking errors and "screw-ups." Absent changes in recruitment, training, rewards, and the political economy of risks, police practices will little change.

23.6 THE FADING OF ETHNOGRAPHY

Is there a fading of salient ethnography? Is it still a viable technique? There is a history that bears on the role of ethnographies in police studies. The fame of individual ethnographers in sociology has never been equivalent to that in anthropology. The figures who developed anthropology through the idea of ethnographic work, Bronislaw Malinowski, Margaret Mead, Gregory Bateson, Alfred Radcliffe-Brown, and later Raymond Firth, Edmund Leach, and Claude Levi-Strauss, remain key figures in anthropological studies. The work styles of those who dominated the early days of sociology, members of the Chicago School such as William I. Thomas, Florian Znaniecki, Robert E. Park, and Ernest Burgess, are not regarded as methodological models for young students. The exceptions are Clifford Shaw, Henry McKay, and Frederick Thrasher who remain prominent not for their style, but for their development of studies of mapping, social disorganization theory, and juvenile-gang crime. The ethnographic strand seems to have lost its visibility especially in the case of known and cited peer-reviewed articles. This is where the fade is dramatic. It is not for lack of opportunity or access. Given that access to police departments in the Anglo-American world has been increasing since the 1980s, the growth in available funding for social research until the last few years, and the abundance of new PhD programs in criminal justice in the Anglo-American world, let us consider a number of possible explanations for this. Recall that qualitative research is time consuming, depends upon an ability to infer from complex and confusing materials, is often truncated by organizations or events (this is unlikely once one has a data set for secondary analysis), and is engaging if not engulfing.

- PhD programs are heavily weighted to statistical techniques and measurement. Qualitative methods are seen as less relevant and valuable from a career perspective.
- Few faculty members can and do teach qualitative methods. Like most social science research, it is ideally learned in an apprentice relationship. Many ethnographers are self-taught.
- Young students are encouraged to finish higher degrees quickly, publish articles while in graduate school, pick publishable and currently popular topics, and align themselves with professors who do the same.
- Young faculty members are given the same encouragement; they are increasingly rated on formal impact or citation scores designed to assess published peer-reviewed articles; assessed for tenure on these grounds; subject to external expert reviewers whose opinion may be valued more than their local colleagues (who may be more familiar with their teaching and student mentorship skills); and dissuaded from working on or seeking to publish books or longer monographs.
- The field is dominated by statistical reports that reward atheoretical, brief, and snappy styles. Long, wordy and often complex studies are not only difficult to produce; they are difficult to get published.
- Fieldwork is a young person's craft, in part because of the energy, patience, and endurance that are involved, even if the study is done in the industrialized Western world, and done "at home." At best it is emotionally draining, frustrating, and problematic (Punch 1989).
- Many major projects require long and detailed field notes and are not easily compressed. Very few ethnographers in the police field have returned repeatedly to a site and written publications (Burawoy 2005).

In summary, one might argue that ethnography is a setting-specific craft suited to developing societies, best done by the young, and a skill taught in few graduate schools, and now has few well-known successful role-models for younger scholars. It is also true that several important, large-scale studies, such as the one run by Sampson (2012) in Chicago, have gathered some kinds of ethnographical data.

If, on the other hand, one looks at several other bits of data that arise from the three tables, a number of less negative inferences can be drawn. There is a continuing interest in the occupation and organizational culture that spans now some sixty-plus years of research and writing, and this research has continued to raise questions pursued in non-Anglo-American contexts including work published in English about policing in Germany (Glaeser 2000), South Africa (Altbeker 2005; Marks 2005), and France (Fillieule and Jobard 1998; Ferret 2004, Mouhanna 2008). There are a number of new studies of policing now underway in Taiwan, Hong Kong, Macan and mainland China. The interest in understanding crime and reducing it has not been translated into ethnographic studies of crime with rare exceptions. The ethnographic classics still set the questions asked with the exception of the studies of gender roles and race in police context. It is fascinating, at least, to observe that the deluge of crime control studies, those claiming to have understood how crime is reduced (by police actions *ceteris paribus*) report no fieldwork data in their studies, and thus tell us little about crime. This is of course amplified by the claims of experimental criminologists that they have the answers not only to crime reduction using official figures but to understanding the causes, dynamics, and complexity of what is called crime.

The paradigm set early remains, elaborated topically, rather than theoretically; the high status journals, perhaps because of the differentiation of the professions of sociology, criminology, and criminal justice, rarely if ever publish ethnographic work of any kind. Interest in policing as an occupation and organization has been trumped to some degree by statistical and some experimental studies of crime control. These of course have absolutely no ethnographic basis, and touting their success absent an explanation for why and how this took place means it is a form of scholarly magic.

23.7 Conclusion

The tradition that casts police research in the Anglo-American world into the Peel model, ignoring the structural conditions that make such policing possible, the alternative modes of policing present in the industrialized world, and the ironic theme of crime control over prevention, has long narrowed the scope of ethnographic research. This Peel-model approach now has a developed body of knowledge to which researchers can refer, and a number of works that can be viewed as classic and foundational. The early works in many respects became visible and powerful indicators of "the literature" in policing, even as they were done forty or more years earlier. They were threads woven together into what Loftus (2009) correctly calls the "the orthodox account" and as she also notes, citing Waddington, a quite negative account of policing. The ethnographies done in the past twenty-plus years, ethnographies of the occupation and or the organization, have modified marginally this orthodox picture. Perhaps the most striking variations in ethnographies have been the broadening of the settings in which the studies are done, including rural venues; the close examinination of transnational and cooperative policing arrangements; and the detailed studies of aspects of private policing and new kinds of policing technology. A strain of classic ethnography remains. Some unconventional phenomenological studies of organization have appeared. It is in the articles and chapters that the touch of ethnography is less apparent. Trends in funding, career prospects, and governmental evaluation systems do not favor more ethnographies.

REFERENCES

Aas, Katja Franko. 2007. *Globalization and Crime*. Thousand Oaks, CA: Sage.

Ackroyd, Stephen. 1992. *New Technology and Practical Police Work: The Social Context of Technical Innovation*. Berkshire, UK: Open University Press.

Alex, Nicholas. 1969. *Black in Blue: A Study of the Negro Policeman*. New York: Appleton-Century Crofts.

——. 1976. *New York Cops Talk Back: A Study of a Beleaguered Minority*. New York: Wiley.

Altbeker, Antony. 2005. *The Dirty Work of Democracy: A Year on the Streets with the SAPS*. Johannesburg and Cape Town, South Africa: Jonathan Ball.

Banton, Michael. 1964. *The Policeman in the Community*. London: Tavistock.

Barker, Joan C. 1999. *Danger, Duty, and Disillusion: The Worldview of Los Angeles Police Officers*. Prospect Heights, IL: Waveland Press.

Bayley, David, H. 1969. *The Police and Political Development in India*. Princeton, NJ: Princeton University Press.

——. 1985. *Patterns of Policing: A Comparative International Analysis*. New Brunswick, NJ: Rutgers University Press.

——. 1991. *Forces of Order: Policing Modern Japan*. Berkeley: University of California Press.

Bayley, David H., and Egon Bittner. 1986. "The Tactical Choices of Police Patrol Officers." *Journal of Criminal Justice* 14:329–48.

Bayley, David H., and James Giarofalo. 1989. "The Management of Violence by Police Patrol Officers." *Criminology* 27:1–26.

Beckett, Katherine, Kris Nyrop, and Lori Pfingst. 2006. "Race, Drugs, and Policing: Understanding Disparities in Drug Delivery Arrests." *Criminology* 44:105–38.

Berkley, George E. 1969. *The Democratic Policeman*. Boston: Beacon Press.

Bittner, Egon. 1967a. "Police Discretion in Emergency Apprehension of Mentally Ill Persons." *Social Problems* 14:278–92.

——. 1967b. "The Police on Skid-Row: A Study of Peace Keeping." *American Sociological Review* 32:699–715.

——. 1970. *The Functions of the Police in Modern Society: A Review of Background Factors, Current Practices, and Possible Role Models*. Washington, DC: National Institute of Mental Health.

Bittner, Egon. 1990 "Florence Nightingale in Pursuit of Willie Sutton: A Theory of the Police." In *Aspects of Police Work*, edited by Egon Bittner, 233–268. Boston: Northeastern University Press.

Black, Donald. 1970. "Production of Crime Rates." *American Sociological Review* 35:733–48.

——. 1980. *The Manners and Customs of the Police*. New York: Academic Press.

Black, Donald, and Albert J. Reiss. 1969. "Police Control of Juveniles." *American Sociological Review* 35:63–77.

Bordua, David, and Albert J. Reiss. 1966. "Command, Control and Charisma: Reflections on Police Bureaucracy." *American Journal of Sociology* 72:68–76.

Bordua, David, and Albert, J. Reiss. 1967. "Law Enforcement." In *The Uses of Sociology*, edited by Paul Lazerfeld, William H. Sewell, and Harold L. Wilensky, 275–303. New York: Basic Books.

Bowling, Ben. 2010. *Policing the Caribbean: Transnational Security Cooperation in Practice*. Oxford and New York: Oxford University Press.

Bowling, Ben, and James Sheptycki. 2012. *Global Policing*. Thousand Oaks, CA: Sage.

Braga, Anthony, David Weisburd, Elin Waring, Lorraine Mazerolle, William Spelman, and Francis Gajewski. 1999. "Problem-Oriented Policing in Violent Crime Places: A Randomized Controlled Experiment." *Criminology* 37:541–80.

Brandl, Steven, and Megan Stroshine. 2003. "Toward an Understanding of the Physical Hazards of Police Work." *Police Quarterly* 6:172–91.

Brewer, John D., and Kathleen Magee. 1991. *Inside the RUC: Routine Policing in a Divided Society*. Oxford and New York: Oxford University Press.

Brodeur, Jean-Paul. 1983. "High Policing and Low Policing: Remarks about the Policing of Political Activities." *Social Problems* 30:507–20.

——. 2010. *The Policing Web*. Oxford and New York: Oxford University Press.

Brogden, Michael, and Clifford Shearing. 1993. *Policing for a New South Africa*. London: Routledge.

Brown, Michael K. 1969. *Working the Street*. New York: Russell Sage Foundation.

Burawoy, Michael. 2005. "2004 ASA Presidential Address: For Public Sociology." *American Sociological Review* 70:4–28.

Cain, Maureen. 1973. *Society and the Policeman's Role*. London: Routledge.

——. 1979. "Trends in the Sociology of Police Work." *International Journal of the Sociology of Law* 7:143–67.

Carr, Patrick, Laura Napolitano, and Jessica Keating. 2007. "We Never Call the Cops and Here Is Why: A Qualitative Examination on Legal Cynicism in Three Philadelphia Neighborhoods." *Criminology* 45:445–80.

Chan, Janet. 1996. "Changing Police Culture." *British Journal of Criminology* 36:109–134.

——. 1997. *Changing Police Culture: Policing in a Multicultural Society*. Cambridge, UK: Cambridge University Press.

Chatterton, M. R. 1979. "Supervision of Patrol Work Under the Fixed Points System." In *The British Police*, edited by Simon Holdaway, 83–101. London: Arnold.

Choongh, Satnam. 1998. *Policing as Social Discipline*. Oxford: Clarendon Press.

Cicourel, Aaron. 1967. *The Social Organization of Juvenile Justice*. New York: Wiley.

Clark, John. 1965. "Isolation of the Police: A Comparison of the British and American Situations." *Journal of Criminal Law and Criminology* 56:307–19.

Crank, John, and Robert Langworthy. 1992. "Institutional Perspective on Policing." *Journal of Criminal Law and Criminology* 83:338–63.

Cumming, Elaine, Ian Cumming, and Laura Edell. 1965. "Policeman as Philosopher, Guide and Friend." *Social Problems* 12:276–86.

Deflem, Matthew. 2004. *Policing World Society: Historical Foundations of International Police Cooperation*. Oxford and New York: Oxford University Press.

Deflem, Matthew, and Suzanne Sutphin. 2009. "Policing Katrina: Managing Law Enforcement in New Orleans." *Policing: A Journal of Policy and Practice* 3:41–49.

Ellison, Graham, and Jim Smyth. 2000. *The Crowned Harp: Policing Northern Ireland*. London: Pluto Press.

Ericson, Richard. 1981. *Making Crime: A Study of Detective Work*. Toronto: Butterworths.

——. 1982. *Reproducing Order: A Study of Police Patrol Work*. Toronto: University of Toronto Press.

Ericson, Richard, and Kevin Haggerty. 1997. *Policing the Risk Society*. Toronto: University of Toronto Press.

Ferret, Jérôme. 2004. "The State, Policing and "Old Continental Europe": Managing the Local/national Tension." *Policing and Society* 14:49–65.

Fielding, Nigel. 1988. *Joining Forces: Police Training, Socialization, and Occupational Competence.* London and New York: Routledge.

Fielding, Nigel. 1996. *Community Policing.* Oxford and New York: Oxford University Press.

Fillieule, Olivier, and Fabien Jobard. 1998. "The Policing of Protest in France: Toward a Model of Protest Policing." *Policing Protest: The Control of Mass Demonstrations in Western Democracies,* edited by Donatella della Porta and Herbert Reiter, 70–90. Minneapolis, MN: University of Minnesota Press.

Foster, Janet. 1989. "Two Stations: An Ethnograpic Study of Policing in the Inner City." In *Crime and the City: Essays in Memory of John Barron Mays,* edited by David M. Downes, 128–153. Hampshire: Macmillan.

——. 1990. *Villains: Crime and Community in the Inner City.* London: Taylor and Francis.

Glaeser, Andreas. 2000. *Divided in Unity: Identity, Germany, and the Berlin police.* Chicago: University of Chicago Press.

——. 2011. *Political Epistemics: The Secret Police, the Opposition, and the End of East German Socialism.* Chicago: University of Chicago Press.

Goffman, Erving. 1959. *The Presentation of Self in Everyday Life.* New York: Doubleday.

Goldstein, Herman. 1979. "Improving Policing: A Problem-Oriented Approach." *Crime and Delinquency* 25:236–58.

Goold, Benjamin. 2004. *CCTV and Policing: Public Area Surveillance and Police Practices in Britain.* Oxford and New York: Oxford University Press.

Gouldner, Alvin. 1954. *Patterns of Industrial Bureaucracy.* Glencoe: Free Press.

Grimshaw, Roger, and Tony Jefferson. 1987. *Interpreting Policework: Policy and Practice in Forms of Beat Policing.* London and Boston: Allen and Unwin.

Guyot, Dorothy. 1979. "Bending Granite: Attempts to Change the Rank Structure of American Police Departments." *Journal of Police Science and Administration* 7:253–84.

——. 1991. *Policing as Though People Matter.* Philadelphia: Temple University Press.

Henry, Vincent, and Robert Lifton. 2004. *Death Work: Police, Trauma, and the Psychology of Survival.* Oxford and New York: Oxford University Press.

Herbert, Steve. 1996. "Morality in Law Enforcement: Chasing Bad Guys with the Los Angeles Police Department." *Law and Society Review* 30:799–818.

——. 1997. *Policing Space: Territoriality and the Los Angeles Police Department.* Minneapolis: University of Minnesota Press.

——. 1998. "Police Subculture Reconsidered." *Criminology* 36:343–70.

——. 2006. *Citizens, Cops, and Power: Recognizing the Limits of Community.* Chicago: University of Chicago Press.

Hobbs, Dick. 1988. *Doing the Business: Entrepreneurship, the Working Class, and Detectives in the East End of London.* Oxford and New York: Oxford University Press.

Holdaway, Simon. 1983. *Inside the British Police: A Force at Work.* Oxford: Blackwell.

Huey, Laura. 2007. *Negotiating Demands: The Politics of Skid Row Policing in Edinburgh, San Francisco, and Vancouver.* Toronto: University of Toronto Press.

——. 2012. *Invisible Victims: Homelessness and the Growing Security Gap.* Toronto: University of Toronto Press.

Hughes, Everett. 1958. *Men and Their Work.* New York: Free Press.

Hunt, Jennifer. 2010. *Seven Shots: An NYPD Raid on a Terrorist Cell and Its Aftermath.* Chicago: University of Chicago Press.

Hunt, Jennifer, and Peter K. Manning. 1991. "The Social Context of Police Lying." *Symbolic Interaction* 14:51–70.

Hunt, Raymond, and John Magenau. 1993. *Power and the Police Chief: An Institutional and Organizational Analysis.* Thousand Oaks, CA: Sage.

Innes, Martin. 2003. *Investigating Murder: Detective Work and the Police Response to Criminal Homicide.* Oxford and New York: Oxford University Press.

Jackall, Robert. 1997. *Wild Cowboys: Urban Marauders and the Forces of Order.* Cambridge, MA: Harvard University Press.

——. 2005. *Street Stories: The World of Police Detectives.* Cambridge, MA: Harvard University Press.

Jobard, Fabien. 2014. "The Concept of Police." In *Encyclopedia of Criminology and Criminal Justice*, edited by Gerben Bruinsma and David Weisburd. New York: Springer.

Jones, Trevor, and Tim Newburn. 1998. *Private Security and Public Policing.* Oxford and New York: Oxford University Press.

Jones, Trevor, Tim Newburn, and David Smith. 1996. "Policing and the Idea of Democracy." *British Journal of Criminology* 36:182–98.

Kemp, Charles, Clive Norris, and Nigel Fielding. 1992. *Negotiating Nothing: Police Decision-Making in Disputes.* Brookfield, VT: Avebury.

Kennedy, David. 1998. "Pulling Levers: Getting Deterrence Right." *National Institute of Justice Journal* 236:2–8.

Klinger, David. 1997. "Negotiating Order in Patrol Work: An Ecological Theory of Police Response to Deviance." *Criminology* 35:277–306.

Kraska, Peter, and Louis Cubellis. 1997. "Militarizing Mayberry and Beyond: Making Sense of American Paramilitary Policing." *Justice Quarterly* 14:607–30.

Lambert, John. 1970. *Crime, Police, and Race Relations: A Study in Birmingham.* Oxford and New York: Oxford University Press.

Laurie, Peter. 1970. *Scotland Yard: A Study of the Metropolitan Police.* New York: Holt, Rinehart, and Winston.

Leinen, Steven H. 1985. *Black Police, White Society.* New York: New York University Press.

——. 1993. *Gay Cops.* New Brunswick, NJ: Rutgers University Press.

Liang, Hsi-Huey. 1992. *The Rise of Modern Police and the European State System from Metternich to the Second World War.* Cambridge, UK: Cambridge University Press.

Loader, Ian, and Aogan Mulcahy. 2003. *Policing and the Condition in England: Memory, Politics, and Culture.* Oxford and New York: Oxford University Press.

Lofland, John. 2006. *Analyzing Social Settings: A Guide to Qualitative Observation and Analysis.* Belmont, CA: Wadsworth/Thomson Learning.

Loftus, Bethan. 2009. *Police Culture in a Changing World.* Oxford and New York: Oxford University Press.

——. 2010. "Police Occupational Culture: Classic Themes, Altered Times." *Policing and Society* 20:1–20.

Lyons, William. 1999. *The Politics of Community Policing: Rearranging the Power to Punish.* Ann Arbor: University of Michigan Press.

Malinowski, Bronislaw. 1989. *A Diary in the Strict Sense of the Term.* Palo Alto, CA: Stanford University Press.

Manning, Peter K. 1972. "Observing the Police." In *Research on Deviance*, edited by Jack D. Douglas, 213–268. New York: Random House.

——. 1977. *Police Work: The Social Organization of Policing.* Cambridge, MA: MIT Press.

——. 1979. "Metaphors of the Field: Varieties of Organizational Discourse." *Administrative Science Quarterly* 24:660–71.

——. 1980. *The Narcs' Game: Organizational and Informational Limits on Drug Law Enforcement.* Cambridge, MA: MIT Press.

——. 1983. "Community Policing." *American Journal of Police* 3:205–27.

——. 1988. *Symbolic Communication: Signifying Calls and the Police Response.* Cambridge, MA: MIT Press.

——. 2003. *Policing Contingencies.* Chicago: University of Chicago Press.

——. 2008. *The Technology of Policing: Crime Mapping, Information Technology, and the Rationality of Crime Control.* New York: New York University Press.

Marks, Monique. 2004. "Researching Police Transformation The Ethnographic Imperative." *The British Journal of Criminology* 44:866-88.

——. 2005. *Transforming the Robocops: Changing Police in South Africa.* Scottsvile, South Africa: University of KwaZulu-Natal Press.

Martin, Susan Ehrlich. 1982. *Breaking and Entering: Policewomen on Patrol.* Berkeley and Los Angeles: University of California Press.

Marx, Gary T. 1974. "Thoughts on a Neglected Category of Social Movement Participant: The Agent Provocateur and the Informant." *American Journal of Sociology* 80:402–42.

McClure, James. 1985. *Cop World: Inside an American Police Force.* New York: Pantheon Books.

McNamara, John H. 1967. "Uncertainties in Police Work: The Relevance of Police Recruits' Backgrounds and Training." In *The Police: Six Sociological Essays,* edited by David Bordua, 163–252. New York: Wiley.

Meehan, Albert J. 1998. "The Impact of Mobile Data Terminal (MDT) Information Technology on Communication and Recordkeeping in Patrol Work." *Qualitative Sociology* 21:225–54.

Meehan, Albert J., and Michael C. Ponder. 2002. "Race and Place: The Ecology of Racial Profiling African American Motorists." *Justice Quarterly* 19:399–430.

Miller, Susan L. 1999. *Gender and Community Policing: Walking the Talk.* Boston: Northeastern University Press.

Mills, C. Wright. 1940. "Situated Actions and Vocabularies of Motive." *American Sociological Review* 5:904–13.

Moskos, Peter. 2008. *Cop in the Hood:My Year Policing Baltimore's Eastern District.* Princeton, NJ: Princeton University Press.

Mouhanna, Christian. 2008. "A Critical Appraisal of Support for Community Policing in France." In *The Handbook of Knowledge Based Policing: Current Conceptions and Future Directions,* edited by Tom Williamson, 79–94. New York: Wiley.

Muir, William Ker. 1979. *Police: Streetcorner Politicians.* Chicago: University of Chicago Press.

Mulcahy, Aogan. 2006. *Policing Northern Ireland: Conflict, Legitimacy and Reform.* Devon: Willan.

Nadelmann, Ethan A. 1993. *Cops Across Borders: The Internationalization of US Criminal Law Enforcement.* University Park: Pennsylvania State University Press.

National Research Council. 2004. *Fairness and Effectiveness in Policing: The Evidence.* Washington, DC: National Research Council.

Niederhoffer, Arthur. 1967. *Behind the Shield: The Police in Urban Society.* New York: Doubleday.

O'Neill, Megan. 2006. *Policing Football: Social Interaction and Negotiated Disorder.* Hamshire, UK: Palgrave Macmillan.

Punch, Maurice. 1989. "Researching Police Deviance: A Personal Encounter with the Limitations and Liabilities of Field-Work." *The British Journal of Sociology* 40:177–204.

Punch, Maurice, and Trevor Naylor. 1973. "The Police: A Social Service." *New Society* 17:358.

Reiner, Robert. 1978. *The Blue-Coated Worker: A Sociological Study of Police Unionism.* Cambridge, UK: Cambridge University Press.

——. 1992. *Chief Constables: Bobbies, Bosses, Or Bureaucrats?* Oxford and New York: Oxford University Press.

Reiss, Albert J. 1971. *The Police and the Public.* New Haven, CT: Yale University Press.

——. 1974. "Discretionary Justice." In *Handbook of Criminology*, edited by Daniel Glaser, 679–699. Chicago: Rand-McNally.

——. 1992. "Police Organization in the 20th Century." In *Crime and Justice, Volume 15, Modern Policing*, edited by Michael Tonry and Norval Morris, 51–97. Chicago: University of Chicago Press.

Reiss, Albert J., and David J. Bordua. 1967. "Environment and Organization: A Perspective on the Police." In *The Police: Six Sociological Essays*, edited by David J. Bordua, 25–55. New York: Wiley.

Reuss-Ianni, Elizabeth. 1983. *Two Cultures of Policing: Street Cops and Management Cops.* New Brunswick, NJ: Transaction.

Rex, John, and Robert Samuel Moore. 1969. *Race, Community and Conflict: A Study of Sparkbrook.* Oxford: Oxford University Press for the Institute of Race Relations.

Rigakos, George S. 2002. *The New Parapolice: Risk Markets and Commodified Social Control.* Toronto: University of Toronto Press.

Rock, Paul. 2005. "Chronocentrism and British Criminology." *The British Journal of Sociology* 56:473–91.

Rubinstein, Jonathan. 1973. *City Police.* New York: Farrar Straus and Giroux.

Sampson, Robert J. 2012. *Great American City: Chicago and the Enduring Neighborhood Effect.* Chicago: University of Chicago Press.

Sanders, William B. 1977. *Detective Work: A Study of Criminal Investigations.* New York: Free Press.

Scheingold, Stuart A. 1984. *The Politics of Law and Order: Street Crime and Public Policy.* London: Longman.

——. 1991. *The Politics of Street Crime: Criminal Process and Cultural Obsession.* Philadelphia: Temple University Press.

Shapland, Joanna, and Jon Vagg. 1988. *Policing by the Public.* London: Routledge.

Shearing, Clifford D., and Richard V. Ericson. 1991. "Culture as Figurative Action." *The British Journal of Sociology* 42:481–506.

Shearing, Clifford D., and Philip C. Stenning. 1983. "Modern Private Security: Its Growth and Implications." In *Crime and Justice: An Annual Review of Research*, vol. 3, edited by Michael Tonry and Norval Morris, 193–245. Chicago: University of Chicago Press.

Sheptycki, J. W. E. 1993. *Innovations in Policing Domestic Violence: Evidence from Metropolitan London.* Brookfield, CT: Avebury.

——. 2002. *In Search of Transnational Policing: Towards a Sociology of Global Policing.* Hampshire, UK: Ashgate.

Sherman, Lawrence W. 1978. *Scandal and Reform: Controlling Police Corruption.* Berkeley, CA: University of California Press.

Sherman, Lawrence W., and Richard Berk. 1984. "The Specific Deterrent Effects of Arrest for Domestic Assault." *American Sociological Review* 49:261–72.

Sherman, Lawrence W., Patrick R. Gartin, and Michael E. Buerger. 1989. "Hot Spots of Predatory Crime: Routine Activities and the Criminology of Place." *Criminology* 27:27–56.

Sherman, Lawrence W., Janell D. Schmidt, Dennis P. Rogan, Patrick R. Gartin, Ellen G. Cohn, Dean J. Collins, and Anthony R. Bacich. 1991. "From Initial Deterrence to Long-Term

Escalation: Short-Custody Arrest for Poverty Ghetto Domestic Violence." *Criminology* 29:821–50.

Silverman, Ely. 1999. *NYPD Battles Crime: Innovative Strategies in Policing*. Boston: Northeastern University Press.

Simon, David. 1991. *Homicide: A Year on the Killing Streets*. Boston: Houghton Mifflin.

Sims, Benjamin. 2007. "The Day after the Hurricane: Infrastructure, Order, and the New Orleans Police Department's Response to Hurricane Katrina." *Social Studies of Science* 37:111–18.

Skogan, Wesley. 2006. *Police and Community in Chicago: A Tale of Three Cities*. Oxford and New York: Oxford University Press.

Skogan, Wesley, and Susan M. Hartnett. 1997. *Community Policing, Chicago Style*. Oxford and New York: Oxford University Press.

Skogan, Wesley, Susan M. Hartnett, Jill DuBois, Jennifer T. Comey, Marianne Kaiser, and Justine H. Lovig. 1999. *On the Beat: Police and Community Problem Solving*. Boulder: Westview Press.

Skolnick, Jerome H. 1966. *Justice without Trial: Law Enforcement in Democratic Society*. New York: Wiley.

Skolnick, Jerome H., and James J. Fyfe. 1994. *Above the Law: Police and the Excessive Use of Force*. New York: Free Press.

Smith, David J., and Jeremy John Gray. 1985. *Police and People in London: The PSI Report*. Brookfield, VT: Gower.

Sykes, Robert E., and Edward E. Brent. 1983. *Policing: A Social Behaviorist Perspective*. New Brunswick, NJ: Rutgers University Press.

Thomas, William I., and Florian Znaniecki. 1918. *The Polish Peasant in Europe and America: Monograph of an Immigrant Group*. Chicago: University of Chicago Press.

Van Maanen, John. 1973. "Observations on the Making of Policemen." *Human Organization* 32:407–18.

——. 1974. "Working the Street: A Developmental View of Police Behavior." In *The Potential for Reform in Criminal Justice*, edited by Herbert Jacobs, 83–130. Beverly Hills: Sage.

——. 1978. "The Asshole." In *Policing: A View from the Street*, edited by Peter K. Manning and John Van Maanen, 221–238. New York: Random House.

——. 1983. "The Boss: First-line Supervision in an American Police Agency." In *Control in the Police Organization*, edited by Maurice Punch, 275–317. Cambridge, MA: MIT Press.

——. 1984. "Making Rank: Becoming an American Police Sergeant." *Journal of Contemporary Ethnography* 13:155–76.

——. 2011. *Tales of the Field: On Writing Ethnography*. Chicago: University of Chicago Press.

Waddington, P. A. J. 1993. *Calling the Police: The Interpretation of, and Response to, Calls for Assistance from the Public*. Brookfield, VT: Avebury.

——. 1999. "Police (Canteen) Sub-culture. An Appreciation." *British Journal of Criminology* 39:287–309.

Waegel, William. 1981. "Case Routinization in Investigative Police Work." *Social Problems* 28:263–75.

——. 1982. "Patterns of Police Investigation of Urban Crimes." *Journal of Police Science and Administration* 10:452–65.

Wakefield, Alison. 2003. *Selling Security: The Private Policing of Public Space*. Devon, UK: Willan.

Websdale, Neil. 2001. *Policing the Poor: From Slave Plantation to Public Housing*. Boston: Northeastern University Press.

Weisburd, David, and Anthony A. Braga. 2006. *Police Innovation: Contrasting Perspectives*. Cambridge, UK: Cambridge University Press.

Wender, Jonathon. 2008. *Policing and the Poetics of Everyday Life*. Urbana: University of Illinois Press.

Westley, William. 1953. "Violence and the Police." *American Journal of Sociology* 59:34–41.

——. 1955. "Secrecy and the Police." *Social Forces* 34:254–57.

——. 1970. *Violence and the Police: A Sociological Study of Law, Custom, and Morality*. Cambridge, MA: MIT Press.

Whitaker, Ben. 1964. *The Police*. London: Eyre and Spottiswoode.

Willis, James J., Stephen D. Mastrofski, and David Weisburd. 2007. "Making Sense of COMPSTAT: A Theory-Based Analysis of Organizational Change in Three Police Departments." *Law and Society Review* 41:147–88.

Wilson, James Q. 1968. *Varieties of Police Behavior*. Cambridge, MA: Harvard University Press.

Wilson, James Q., and George Kelling. 1982. "The Police and Neighborhood Safety: Broken Windows." *Atlantic Monthly* 249:29–38.

Wolcott, Harry F. 1990. *Writing Up Qualitative Research*. Thousand Oaks, CA: Sage.

Young, Malcolm. 1991. *An Inside Job: Policing and Police Culture in Britain*. Oxford: Clarendon Press.

——. 1994. *In the Sticks: Cultural Identity in a Rural Police Force*. New York: Oxford University Press.

PART VI

....

POLICING INTO THE FUTURE

....

CHAPTER 24

POLICE LEGITIMACY IN ACTION: LESSONS FOR THEORY AND POLICY

BEN BRADFORD, JONATHAN JACKSON, AND MIKE HOUGH

POLICE require legitimacy if they are to function effectively, ethically, and legally (Tyler 2003, 2011a). When citizens consider the police to be legitimate, they are more likely to cooperate with officers, defer to them in moments of crisis, and obey the laws they enforce and to a certain extent embody (Tyler 2004, 2006a, 2006b, 2011b). Absent voluntary consent of the public, police would be forced to turn to ever more repressive, force-led styles, undermining their claim to be acting on behalf of and in cooperation with those they police (Tyler 2009; Schulhofer, Tyler, and Huq 2011).

It is well recognized that legitimacy is a vital aspect of the relationship between police and citizens. Some of the potential sources of police legitimacy—and the mechanisms of its reproduction—are also increasingly well understood. Arguably less attention has been paid to the policy implications of current knowledge about the construction and maintenance of legitimacy in criminal justice settings. Policy makers and politicians have been slow to pick up on some of the challenges, and possibilities, offered by studies into the quality, correlates, and distribution of police legitimacy.

This essay explores exactly these aspects of police legitimacy. Concentrating on the perspective of the policed, we ask, on what basis is police legitimacy established, maintained, and undermined? What are the implications of the extant body of empirical evidence for policing policy and practice? We concentrate in particular on what might be added to our understanding of police legitimacy by thinking not just about Tom Tyler's procedural justice model but about some of the other social processes that might shape or influence people's legitimating beliefs and actions. In doing to, we hope to outline some as yet unanswered theoretical, as well as policy-oriented, questions.

The essay proceeds in five parts. Section 24.1 introduces a working, empirical definition of legitimacy. It summarizes two sources of police legitimacy as viewed from the perspective of the policed: (a) experiences of the activity of police officers, and (b) experiences of the wider activity, and perceived success of, policing. Section 24.2 considers current evidence in relation to the legitimacy implications of the activity and actions of police officers and organizations. Section 24.3 shifts the focus to the wider context of policing, asking, what other factors may be related to individuals' legitimacy judgments as these relate to the public police? Section 24.4 considers the theoretical implications of broadening our understanding of police legitimacy, while Section 24.5 concentrates on the policy implications. We take an international perspective on these questions as is currently possible, although the bulk of the extant evidence pertains to what Manning (2010) has called Anglo-American Democratic Policing (AADP) contexts.

A number of main points emerge:

- To confer legitimacy on the police is to (a) recognize the authority of the police to dictate appropriate behavior (via a felt positive obligation to obey), and (b) justify the power and influence on the police (via beliefs about the moral validity of police power and influence).
- Tyler's work on procedural justice states that one of the surest ways of building legitimacy is for justice officials to treat people fairly and respectfully, to listen to what they have to say, to make fair decisions—in other words, to demonstrate procedural fairness and justice.
- Police legitimacy may also be shaped by the wider social "field" of policing, specifically the strength of informal social control processes operating at the neighborhood level.
- Recognizing that a wide range of factors influence people's legitimacy judgments, we conclude that policy attempts to enhance legitimacy should concentrate on factors that police can control and be realistic in terms of scope and ambition. The notion that each encounter between officer and citizen is a "teachable moment" (Tyler 2011a) suggests that enhancements to police legitimacy can be best secured at the level of everyday interaction between officer and citizen. Such enhancements are likely to be incremental, but built on firmer ground than more ambitious programs.

24.1 POLICE, POLICING, AND LEGITIMACY

Our interest in this essay is on an empirical or subjective concept of legitimacy (Tyler 2006a; Hinsch 2008), in which legitimacy is a characteristic of the relationship between police and public (Tyler 2006b; Bottoms and Tankebe 2012), particularly in relation to the question as to whether people believe that the police have a valid right to power and influence, and the types of opinions and actions such a belief engenders (Jackson et al. 2012a; Tankebe 2013; Tyler and Jackson 2013). We assume, following ongoing pan-European work (Jackson et al. 2011; Hough, Jackson, and Bradford

2013a, 2013b), that the police can be considered to be legitimate when individuals perceive that police officers act in morally valid ways, when individuals believe that the police abide by the rules and procedures intended to govern their behavior, and when individuals voluntarily offer their consent to police activity. Our measures of legitimacy thus reference two connected psychological states: first, people's assessment of the normative justifiability of possessed power (and consequent degree of identification with the police and the group that the police represent); and second, people's belief that the police have a positive right to dictate appropriate behavior (with a corresponding and positive sense of duty to obey officers, abide by their decisions, and so on).

The empirical account of legitimacy of focus here is somewhat distinct from those offered by legal philosophers or political theorists, who may be more concerned with those characteristics of the police or police activity that make it actually legitimate in some objective or normative sense (Hinsch 2008, 2010). Such accounts are vital to any proper understanding of the role of the police. They are also likely to be correlated with the legitimating beliefs of members of the public. We set aside such concerns, however, to concentrate instead on the sources and implications of individuals' legitimating beliefs and actions.

Legitimacy can, from an empirical perspective, be seen as partly dependent on people's assessments of the behavior of the police (e.g., citizens make assessments of whether or not the police follow the rules and act in normatively justifiable ways) and partly dependent on their motivations or behavior in relation to the police (e.g., citizens act in ways that indicate their consent to the role of the police). Given this, a number of implications follow. First, this is a fluid notion of legitimacy. Citizens make active assessments of police behavior that may change over time or vary depending on context. People may assign the police more or less legitimacy in different places or at different times, and legitimacy is a continuous, rather than dichotomous, variable. Second, and concomitantly, the actions of the police, and interactions between officers and citizens, are key moments in which legitimacy is generated, reproduced, or undermined (Tyler 2011a). Third, the emphasis on individuals' beliefs and motivations for action implies that factors beyond assessments of police officers or organization will also be in play. The sources of legitimating perceptions and behaviors are likely to be complex and varied, so, a wider range of factors needs to be considered in order to arrive at a fully rounded understanding of the phenomenon.

Bottoms and Tankebe (2012) offer one avenue toward such an understanding. Stressing the dialogic nature of legitimacy, they underline the extent to which police organizations are involved in the discursive creation of legitimacy by, among other things, making claims about their actual and ideal roles in society, their success in fulfilling these roles, and so on. The way the public(s) served by the police react to such claims comprises the other voice in the dialogue, but equally as important is the "power-holder's" (i.e., the police's) sense of their own legitimacy (cf. Tyler et al. 2007). This idea seems to us to be worthy of much further study. In this essay, however, we will limit our discussion to only the public side of the dialogue, primarily on the pragmatic grounds that this is where most of the empirical evidence in relation to police legitimacy is currently to be found.

24.1.1 Sources of Legitimacy

Two broad sets of experiences can be identified as potential sources of legitimacy as viewed from the perspective of those subject, at least nominally, to the power of the police. Both are explored in more depth below. The first is people's relationship with the police as an organization, and their understandings of the behavior of police officers and of policing styles and processes, whether via personal, vicarious, or mediated exposure; here the emphasis is on assessments of the police itself. The second set of experiences is wider, and is emergent from the social context within which both police and citizen operate. At issue here is a broader consideration of the knowledge or experiences that people draw upon when making legitimacy judgments. We describe this set of experiences below as relating particularly to processes of social ordering that are not limited to the concrete activities of the uniformed police.

To anticipate the discussion, we argue that people judge the success of the police—and the extent to which they believe its behavior, power, and influence are justified—on the basis not only of the behavior of the organization but also on the perceived success (or failure) of more general processes of social ordering and control. When these are seen to be successful and achieving normatively justifiable ends, so are the police, and legitimacy is consequently bolstered. But when social order is lacking, and the processes generating it appear threatened, the police appear unsuccessful and police activity appears misdirected, and legitimacy is undermined (Jackson et al. 2012b). We stress below that local concerns appear key—the quality of people's immediate social and physical environment has an important influence on the way they think about the police. Importantly, instrumental concerns about crime and risk do not seem to drive people's sense that their neighborhood lacks social control (and therefore that the police lack authority and moral validity); rather it is more relational concerns about the weakness of social bonds and collective efficacy that appear to be the important factors (Jackson and Sunshine 2007; Jackson and Bradford 2009).

24.2 Police Activity and Legitimacy

At the heart of people's experiences of the police is the way in which officers exercise their power and authority. "Procedural justice" refers to impartial service to the law, as well as fair, respectful and even-handed use of power. Numerous studies show how the exercise of authority via the application of fair process strengthens the social bonds between individuals and authorities (Tyler and Huo 2002; Sunshine and Tyler 2003; Tyler 2006a). Individuals establish connections even in groups with only tenuous bases for group identification (Tajfel and Turner 1986; Lind and Tyler 1988; Tyler and Lind 1992; Mulford, Jackson, and Svedsater 2008); they are sensitive to signs and symbols that communicate information about their status and position within a group (de Cremer and Tyler 2005); and how the police treat people communicates their status within the group that the police represent (Tyler and Blader 2003), which has been jointly and variously characterized as the nation, state, or community (Waddington 1999; Reiner 2010; Loader and Mulcahy 2003; Jackson and Bradford 2009).

Fostering the idea that the individual and the police are "on the same side," procedural justice is marked and demonstrated by neutrality and transparency, by fair, equitable and respectful treatment, and by a feeling of control (or "voice"; see Hirschman 1970). The experience of procedural justice or injustice communicates status within the group, and of particular relevance in this context is the idea that procedural injustice can communicate stigmatization by legal authorities resulting from their application of negative stereotypes (Tyler and Wakslak 2004). If people perceive that the way police officers treat them is based not on what they are doing, but on their race, gender, or age, police behavior carries negative identity implications, raising critical questions about whether those on the receiving end are accorded rights pertaining to membership of the superordinate group (or the rights accorded to group members in good standing):

> The example of racial profiling illustrates the risks a person undertakes when merging one's sense of self into a group. If people are drawing their sense of self from a superordinate group membership, then demeaning and disrespectful treatment from that superordinate group will undermine their feelings of favorable self-esteem and self-worth. It will communicate marginality and exclusion from important protections that are extended to most other group members—for example, "freedom from arbitrary arrest and seizure." (Tyler and Blader 2003, 359)

In other words, procedural injustice erodes legitimacy in part because of the profound importance, to subordinates, of the manner in which power holders exercise their power. Tyler and Blader's (2003) group engagement model predicts that people identify strongly with groups that provide favorable status evaluations. Feeling pride and respect via their connection to the group, they gain confidence in their identity through their association with that group; they also cooperate with organizations when those organizations serve the social function of providing individuals with a favorable identity and a positive sense of self (Blader and Tyler 2009). If people feel pride in the group, and if they believe that they are accorded respect, then their motivations will be transferred from the personal to the group level. Defining themselves in terms of their group membership, they will be more willing to act cooperatively on behalf of that group: in the current context, the goals of the police become their own goals.

Increased identification with the group that the police represent generates legitimacy, encouraging a belief that one should obey the police as an important group representative. Kelman and Hamilton (1989) refer to legitimacy as "authorization." To hold an authority legitimate within some social context involves both authorizing it to determine appropriate behavior within that context and accepting an obligation to conform to the expected behavior. When someone feels obligated to follow the directives or rules that legitimate authority establishes, he or she internalizes the value that it is morally just to obey the police. Believing that it is the right thing to do to respect police directives subjectively precludes (or at least inhibits) the possibility of disobeying officers. Furthermore, under such conditions the authorization of actions by authorities carries automatic justification for them—legitimate authority is empowered to determine right and wrong behavior, and behavior becomes right or wrong because it is determined as such by the authority.

On the other hand, identification with the police, which is strengthened by fair use of authority, helps to create a sense of the moral validity of police possession of power (Jackson et al. 2012a, 2012b; Bradford et al. 2013). When police treat us in procedurally fair ways they indicate to us that they share and act on a set of values we ourselves share. This "moral alignment" with the police assists the process of transitioning goals or motives from the individual to the group, encouraging people to place greater emphasis on the outcomes of the group as a whole and to confer moral validity on the power and influence that the police hold (Turner 1975; Turner, Brown, and Tajfel 1979; Tajfel and Turner 1986; Tyler and Blader 2003; Blader and Tyler 2009). Identifying with the group in these ways generates role and expectation involvement: if people accept a reciprocal-role relationship (the law-abiding and upstanding citizen), they feel a corresponding need to meet the expectations of that role, and they engage in reciprocal behaviors, such as cooperation with police officers.

Most of the available evidence shows the importance of procedural justice in driving legitimacy and, conversely, the relative unimportance of police effectiveness; however one or two recent studies have suggested that people's perceptions of the effectiveness of the police may be important in certain contexts. In a Ghanaian study, Tankebe (2009, 1275) found that perceived police effectiveness was just as strongly correlated with felt obligation to obey the police as perceived procedural fairness. In a South African study, Bradford et al. (2013) similarly found that perceived effectiveness was just as strongly correlated with felt obligation and moral alignment with the police as was perceived procedural fairness (indeed, in multivariate analysis, effectiveness emerged as more important than procedural fairness). In both studies the argument was that the police in Ghana and South Africa have not yet demonstrated basic levels of effectiveness; that citizens are not yet convinced that public policy can provide security; and that there are specific social and political histories that complicate matters considerably.

In assessing the relationship between instrumental effectiveness and legitimacy, we agree with Bottoms and Tankebe (2012, 127) that effectiveness is a necessary but not a sufficient condition of legitimacy. In countries such as Ghana and South Africa, this necessary condition has not been established, and police need to demonstrate a baseline of effectiveness before the possibility of a broader sense of legitimacy is opened up, and certainly before justice judgments come to the fore. It is interesting to note, however, that in the South African study, which used a nationally representative sample, people who believed the police to be more effective were both more likely to believe they had a duty to obey the instructions of police officers and to feel a sense of "moral alignment" with the police. That is, beliefs about (or trust in) the effectiveness of the police seemed to be being used as a basis for judgments about the moral justifiability of police power.

It may thus be that the association between effectiveness and legitimacy, from the perspective of the policed, may not be purely instrumental (if this was the case, effectiveness would simply "purchase" a duty of obedience in a transactional sense and have little to do with judgments about the moral character of police), as theories of "eudaemonic legitimation" (Chen 1997; see Bottoms and Tankebe 2012) might have it, but rather have an important affective or relational component. People may feel a stronger sense of identification and pride in relation to groups they feel are successful (Tyler and Blader 2009)—most pertinently, here, groups that are effective in protecting their members— and thus feel more closely aligned with group representatives, particularly those charged with providing such protection. Conversely, a lack of an effective police service seems likely to signal abandonment and exclusion to those forced to live under such conditions, thus weakening their sense that police are "on their side" and share their values.

24.3 The Social Context of Police Legitimacy

Despite the apparent importance of procedural justice, and police behavior more widely, in determining the legitimacy of the police in AADP contexts it would seem naïve to suggest that it is the only source of legitimacy upon which police may draw. There are likely to be multiple causes of people's ideas about and actions in relation to the police, encompassing such potentially important predictors as the strength of the democratic process, state legitimacy, and historical-institutional context. We concentrate here, however, on those at least nominally proximal to the activity of the police: namely, processes of social control as these function and play out, particularly in local areas.

There are two accounts of the relationship between police legitimacy, on the one hand, and processes of social ordering and control, on the other. According to the first account, the bonds of trust and cohesion necessary for people to take collective action to address issues of social order flow from trusted, legitimate policing (thus implicating the claim that procedural justice strengthens ties within social groups): such processes may work at both macro- and micro-levels.

Loader and Walker's (2001, 2006, 2007) notion of "thick" security provides one way to conceptualize the association between police legitimacy and the social bonds between citizens at a wide, societal level. Here, a strong, deep sense of public security comprises three dimensions that help to constitute the "cultural conditions" of democratic political community. The first of these dimensions is maintenance of a baseline level of instrumental safety that secures individual freedom. The second is recognition of the social dimension of security (that the security of any one citizen implicates the security of all).

The third dimension concerns the constitutive aspects of security, specifically, the role a sense of security plays in generating notions of shared group membership, ontological security and "a sense of dignity and authenticity, of ease with one's social environment" (Loader and Walker 2006, 192). Legitimate policing, on this account, both provides security and generates bonds between citizens, and between citizens and state, thus enabling the maintenance and reproduction of plural, democratic polities.

At the micro-level, authors have noted that a legitimate police service, with which citizens are willing to cooperate (and which is itself more likely to act on their behalf), may be one element that comprises, or builds up, processes of social control in local areas, and particularly those that are related to the idea of collective efficacy. Research in the United States has shown that social cohesion and collective efficacy are closely associated with social control processes (Sampson and Bartusch, 1998), and, for example, that opinions of and orientations toward the police predict people's willingness to engage in informal social control activities (Silver and Miller 2004; Wells et al. 2006; Kochel 2012). The argument here is that trustworthy, legitimate policing enables collective responses to local problems of crime and disorder and/or constitutes a structure of stable norms and values toward which people orient their behavior (LaFree 1998), although some studies have failed to identify a link between opinions of the police and willingness to engage in social control activities (e.g., Warner 2007).

According to the second account of the link between police legitimacy and social ordering, police legitimacy may flow from assessments of quotidian, and local, processes of social control. In line with work on procedural justice, this account begins by questioning the basis of people's legitimacy judgments—why do we hold the opinions of and orientations toward the police that we do? The key suggestion is that people's understanding of local social control processes provides a proximate measure of the behavior and success of the police that they then draw on when making their legitimacy judgments (Jackson et al. 2012a). Such social and environmental cues are likely to be relevant because, for all the importance of procedural justice and other elements of actual police behavior, many people will have little or no direct contact with officers from one year to the next. Other sources of "direct" experiences of policing are, furthermore, either highly unevenly spread through the population or have complex and often untested associations with people's views, meaning that, overall, their relationship with legitimacy is unclear and possibly weak.

To give just two brief examples of what we mean here, direct experience of crime is, first, rather rare: while certainly pervasive (Garland 2001) in many countries, it is not often a daily reality for a majority of citizens in ADDP contexts. Furthermore, the extent to which people "blame" the police for crime is uncertain—compare Jackson and Bradford (2009) with Sindall, Sturgis, and Jennings (2012)—and studies tend to find only relatively modest, and inconsistent, links between perceptions of or concerns about crime and opinions of the police (Brown and Reed Benedict 2002; Skogan 2009). Second, while mediated experiences of police may be important in shaping long-term trends in opinion (Reiner 2010), the evidence of short-term "media effects" on public trust in the police, for example, is thin (Miller et al. 2004; Jackson et al. 2012b).

Rather, given that it seems unlikely that the empirical legitimacy of the police is solely about procedural justice or other direct or indirect experiences of police activity, we contend that legitimacy (i.e., people's perceptions of the police's right to dictate appropriate behavior and hold power and influence) is also shaped by the strength of social control processes operating at the local level, including those that operate largely outside of the ambit of formal police mechanisms. We posit, in other words, that people recognize and justify police power not only when the police wield this power in a fair way (i.e., procedural justice), nor indeed simply when the police itself seems effective in an instrumental sense (e.g., that it prevents and deters crime, that officers respond promptly to calls for service), but also when social order in their local neighborhood seems to be adequately maintained; that is, when the broader activity of "policing" appears successful. Crucially, the quality of such policing extends beyond formal institutions of social control to include those informal social control mechanisms that underpin collective efficacy—the willingness of local people to intervene on behalf of the collective good. When such processes are active and strong, local disorder is likely to be lower and the need for the police reduced: the less the police are needed, the more effective they seem (Reiner 2010). Conversely, when social order seems to be weak, people may question police power and authority; they begin to doubt the desirability of conferring it power and authority in exchange for the regulation of social order.

From a sociological point of view, we can think of policing as both an institution (a social structure or set of practices) and a field (Bourdieu 1993; Emirbayer and Johnson 2008) (i.e., a structured social space, oriented toward a specific set of ends, within which a variety of actors occupy positions and roles; Bourdieu 1993, 72). Actors within the field of policing comprise citizens, police, and other organizations, each embedded in a set of social relations with others in the field. Yet, not all such actors are equal and, in the case of policing, the uniformed (or formal) police have been characterized as an institutionalized organization that represents, indeed embodies, the field within which it operates (Crank 2003). We might also note that for many people in AADP countries "the police" simply dominate "policing" in a more mundane sense, leading to considerable conceptual slippage between the two (Girling, Loader, and Sparks 2000).

Institutionalized organizations may be legitimated not only on the basis of their own behavior but also on the basis of external and ceremonial factors. In particular, they may gain legitimacy from their social fitness, the extent to which their form is regarded to fit the environment in which they operate (Scott 2001). It seems to us that the "isomorphism" of organization and field (Meyer and Rowan 1977) in the context of policing may mean that to perceive no need for intervention from formal policing agents—to perceive that local informal social control processes are strong—may also be to perceive that the police are justified in their power and role in society. When people's social and physical environment seems to be adequately policed—however this is actually achieved—the formal structures of policing seem to fit well, and the police garner legitimacy. But when social order seems weak or conflictual, the formal structures of policing seem a poor fit to the field within which they operate, and legitimacy is undermined.

This argument can be stated, more parsimoniously, as a version of Locke's social contract. People grant the police power in exchange for social order; they cede power and authority to the police in exchange for social regulation and justice; and this conferral of power and consent to police authority to some degree depends upon the strength of social order at a local level. Because of the "fit" of the police to the activity of policing, the police organization may garner legitimacy from the extent to which the establishment and reproduction of normative social order is strong (cf. Jackson and Sunshine 2007; Jackson and Bradford 2009). People feel more obligated to obey officers when the local community seems well policed, and are more likely to feel that the police share their values when the neighborhood seems orderly and well-regulated.

24.3.1 Implications for Empirical Legitimacy

In counter-posing two accounts of the relationship between police legitimacy and social ordering processes outlined above—that, on the one hand, police legitimacy is pre-condition of and factor in the creation of social order while, on the other hand, such order can act as a source of legitimacy for the police—we do not wish to argue for the ascendancy of one over the other. Police legitimacy and wider mechanisms of social control will comprise a complex, iterative set of social, cultural, and political relationships, wherein police legitimacy both produces and is reproduced by processes of social ordering (which we have characterized here as "policing" in its widest sense). Our key claim is more restricted: if the aim is to understand how and why people come to hold the police legitimate, particularly if we wish to move "beyond procedural justice" (Bottoms and Tankebe 2012), it may make more sense to prioritize the latter account over the former. What this means in practical terms is that people use their assessments of social cohesion and collective efficacy, and their perception of the extent of disorder in their neighborhood (the extent of shared ability and effort in maintaining order and the success of such endeavors) as heuristics when making judgments about the police. When order is apparent and social cohesion and collective efficacy are strong, the police are more likely to be judged as operating according to a common set of values, to be following the rules, and to be worthy of deference: that is, to be judged legitimate. When disorder is apparent and cohesion and collective efficacy weak, the police are more likely to be judged as failing to work toward shared ends in a normatively justifiable manner, and to be not worthy of deference or respect.

In sum, people's judgments about and actions in relation to the police are likely to be informed by their assessments of their communities and neighborhoods; by their daily, lived experience of social order and its maintenance. Naturally, these are probabilistic not deterministic associations. Living in a disorderly area with weak social ties between residents will not cause an individual to necessarily de-legitimize the police—rather, all else being equal, we would expect police legitimacy to be lower on average among individuals living in such areas than among those living in more orderly areas with stronger ties between residents (Gau et al. 2012; Jackson et al. 2012b). Any general association among perceptions of disorder, the quality of social bonds between local residents, and police legitimacy is also likely to be cut across with countervailing trends in particular times or social spaces (it may be, for example, that in some areas strong collective ties are maintained in the face of, and possibly even drawing from, negative orientations toward the police).

24.4 THEORETICAL IMPLICATIONS

The argument laid out above, if it has any purchase, has some interesting theoretical implications. First, if people base their legitimacy judgments in part on the perceived quality of order maintenance and informal social control, this may go some way toward explaining why the legitimacy of the police does not collapse as a result of an accrual of personal experiences. The net negative (i.e., asymmetrical) effect of contact with officers in individual's trust and legitimacy judgments is one of the most reliably replicated findings in criminology (Skogan 2006; Bradford, Jackson, and Stanko 2009), although the precise extent of the asymmetry is open to significant question (Tyler and Fagan 2008; Myhill and Bradford 2012). Why does this asymmetry not add up over time to severely undermine police legitimacy across the population, the vast majority of whom will have some contact with the police over their lifetimes (with a significant proportion having rather frequent contact)? It could be that as the memories of contact experiences fade, more available experiences take their place in providing triggers for belief and action in relation to the police. Most people, most of the time (in AADP countries at least) experience their neighborhoods as at least moderately orderly and cohesive; for example, only 17 percent of respondents to the 2007–2008 British Crime Survey perceived a high level of anti-social behavior in their local area (Moon et al. 2009). This lived experience, in as much as it is one of relative order and cohesion, may serve as a well-spring of police legitimacy among significant sections of the population.

Second, since the factors that influence police legitimacy are not exhausted by police behaviors, there remains a proportion of the empirical legitimacy of the police that must be explained in other ways; concomitantly, only a proportion of this legitimacy is amenable to change as a result of public experiences of police and police activity. Furthermore, processes of social ordering and control are much "bigger" than direct, individual experience of police activity, and indeed are influenced by factors far beyond those that pertain simply to the bonds between people living in local areas. At one level this is little more than a claim that the police, as is any other state institution, are caught up in the various legitimacy crises (Habermas 1976) that have afflicted all such institutions since the 1960s, as well as the general process of de-subordination (Miliband 1978) and related phenomena over the same timespan. Yet, the links between disorder, cohesion, collective efficacy, and legitimacy outlined above provide a way of envisaging how such processes play out at the level of individual experience. Police legitimacy has undoubtedly declined since the 1960s (Loader and Mulcahy 2003; Reiner 2010; Bradford 2011), and this may be as much as a result of the fragmentation of local communities and the individualizing consequences of late or liquid modernity (Giddens 1991; Beck 1992;

Bauman 2002) as it is a result of revelations of police malpractice, inefficiency, and so on. However police legitimacy has not collapsed, and this may, in part, be precisely because revelations of corruption, ineffectiveness and so on are somewhat offset by the fact that despite the level of social change that has occurred since the 1960s, most people still experience their communities as relatively orderly and cohesive.

We do not wish to claim, of course, that the legitimacy of the police is a structurally determined constant, but simply that this legitimacy is only partly shaped by police behavior, at least as this is narrowly understood. Even limiting the discussion to mechanisms of social ordering in local areas, as we have here, it is therefore possible to suggest many possible configurations of the relationship among police activity, legitimacy, and wider social processes. To take just two possible cases, on the one hand we might suggest that in areas where social order is fragile or threatened, and that are marked by high levels of disorder and concomitantly low levels of collective efficacy, police legitimacy may be constantly undermined, whatever the efforts made in relation to, for example, improving the procedural fairness of police activity. On the other hand, we can envisage situations wherein change in local areas, either positive or negative (e.g., as a result of inward investment or disinvestment by government or major employers), result in changes to the extent of police legitimacy in those areas, again regardless of actual police activity.

Third, and encapsulating both points above, we would underline that many other factors must also have an effect on the empirical legitimacy of the police. A key idea here may be the extent to which the police are mandated or authorized by government and other state agencies (Zelditch 2001; cf. Manning 2010); a lack of trust in the government, for example, might undermine its ability to mandate the police (to make and support a claim to the public that the power vested in the police is justified; see Bradford et al. 2013). By contrast, many individual, indeed psychological, factors might also promote, or inhibit, a sense among citizens that the police are legitimate. One interesting recent suggestion is that system justification theory offers a way to understand why people who are reliant upon, but often "let down" by, systems of governance continue to support them. For example, Van der Toorn, Tyler, and Jost (2011, 128) argue that "dependence on authorities for desired resources activates system justification motivation, and this contributes to the legitimation of power holders. The idea is that when an individual is dependent on a powerful other, he or she is motivated to perceive the powerholder as relatively legitimate in order to rationalize the system of authority relations and to feel better about the status quo." People who, perhaps due to low levels of social or economic capital, are dependent on the police to provide assistance at times of need may, as a result of this dependence, be motivated to perceive them as legitimate.

24.5 POLICY IMPLICATIONS

What, in the light of the discussion above, can and should the police do to enhance trust and legitimacy? The imperative to act in a procedurally fair manner seems to be ever-strengthened by current research, and we certainly would not wish to resile from this position. In particular, we support placing measures of trust and legitimacy at the center of policy assessments of police actions and behaviors. What people think of the police is important, and their orientations toward potential acts of cooperation (that are likely to be correlated with their legitimacy judgments), for example, should be an important aspect of police performance monitoring (European Social Survey 2012). Furthermore, there is some experimental evidence that, despite some of the obvious difficulties and challenges, improving the procedural fairness of police activity can be associated with increased legitimacy and some of the rewards it might bring (Paternoster et al. 1997; Mazerolle et al. 2013); a range of cross-sectional and other studies imply much the same (Tyler and Wakslak 2004; Hinds and Murphy 2007; Tyler and Fagan 2008; Hasisi and Weisburd 2011; Hough et al. 2013a, 2013b).

What we might suggest, however, is that there are important limits or boundaries to the fairness-legitimacy nexus that might usefully focus policy efforts to improve the empirical legitimacy of the police and, to reiterate, access some of the benefits in terms of cooperation and compliance that might flow from such legitimacy. Most critically, and most obviously, procedural justice does not provide a magic wand. While the fairness of police behavior in almost any context we can think of can and should improve for any number of reasons (e.g., ethical, moral, legal), in only a proportion of cases is this likely to result in a significant increase in legitimacy in the short or medium term. Paradoxically, and rather unfortunately, areas where there are significant problems of crime and disorder, which would benefit most from increased cooperation between police and public, may be the most difficult nuts to crack, since the social and structural characteristics of those areas militate against the idea that changes to police behavior might increase legitimacy. Policy interventions, when they occur, need therefore to be both tailored to local conditions and to work toward realistic targets.

If, furthermore, the legitimacy of the police is embedded in the quality of social ordering in local areas, efforts to enhance legitimacy must also be considered alongside and in conjunction with other policy interventions. An important factor in enhancing police legitimacy may be programs aimed at fostering productive relationships between neighborhood residents, at least to the extent that this bolsters cohesion and collective efficacy. Police legitimacy in these terms may be a by-product of other processes, and it may be enhanced by policies that have little or no relationship with "policing" and "crime" at all. One might question, of course, what such programs might look like, particularly in times of fiscal austerity, and what precisely they would be targeted at, but it is at least an open possibility that they may have some influence on the legitimacy of the police.

Another important lesson is that change in levels of police legitimacy is likely to be slow. In relation to direct efforts to enhance legitimacy via improving the procedural fairness of officers' activity, the asymmetry in the effect of contact on people's opinions and judgments means improvements are likely to be incremental, at best. Turning to wider policy interventions that might affect police legitimacy, it takes time to build the types of relations that promote effective social ordering, and it is likely to take even longer for these to filter through to people's attitudes and orientations toward the police.

Unfortunately there is a lengthening tradition in the United Kingdom of policy makers ignoring these arguments and attempting to encourage police to act in legitimacy-enhancing ways by instituting performance target regimes that either (a) apply at the population level and/or (b) are unrealistic in terms of the goals set. The last Labour government's "confidence target," that set all police across England and Wales an over-arching target to increase public confidence in the police was in many ways admirable, in that it placed center stage the idea that what people think of the police is important and a suitable area of policy concern (Jackson and Bradford 2009). However the target measure was badly conceptualized (FitzGerald 2010) and, worse, established as a blanket measure that took no account of local particularities and ignored the other factors that might influence the survey responses against which the police were being assessed. Similarly, the Mayor of London's 20:20:20 "challenge" for policing, established in late 2012, set the Metropolitan police the target of increasing public confidence by 20 percent by 2016, something which, given the arguments above and all available evidence concerning the way public opinion in relation to the police changes over time (Jackson et al. 2012b; Sindall, Sturgis, and Jennings 2012), seems virtually unachievable.

It might be tempting, given the association between police legitimacy and broader processes of social ordering, for police organizations tasked with enhancing public opinion to attempt policies aimed not so much at improving legitimacy directly as by affecting change via addressing issues of disorder, collective efficacy and so on. After all, it seems that police garner legitimacy when disorder is low and collective efficacy high. Of course, many police policies are already aimed at the first half of this equation, and quality of life or "broken windows" policing is now a mainstay of both the literature and police practice. However, not only is the effectiveness of such policies contested (Kelling and Coles 1996; Harcourt 2001; Johnson, Golub, and McCabe 2010), but there is evidence that such techniques can have significant negative effects on certain population groups (Howell 2009, Geller and Fagan 2010), particularly in terms of their relationships with the police (Brunson and Miller 2006), and, thus, the extent to which they hold it legitimate (although see Weisburd et al. 2011 for evidence that aggressive policing strategies, when properly targeted, need not necessarily undermine legitimacy). In terms of legitimacy, quality of life or order maintenance policing may be something of a double-edged sword, increasing legitimacy among some sections of the population while undermining it among others; often, of course, those where police legitimacy is both already most contested and where the cooperation it garners most needed.

It is rather more difficult to identify policing policies that address not the relationship between police and citizens but relations between citizens themselves; that is, policies that address the relationship between legitimacy and collective efficacy seek to exert police influence to strengthen the social ties between people living in local areas, and aim to garner legitimacy in a more distal sense. Indeed, what would police activity that explicitly aims to encourage social ties among citizens look like? Is it the job of the police to engage in "social engineering" of this type? Yet, it may be that the group engagement elements of the procedural justice model offer the possibility of just such a process. Recall that people value procedural fairness in part because it indicates inclusion and status within the group the police represent, a group frequently characterized as the nation or the 'community' (Lind and Tyler 1988; Tyler and Lind 1992; Tyler and Huo 2002; Sunshine and Tyler 2003; Tyler 2006a). Police activity, in as much as it is experienced as fair, may strengthen people's sense that they are members of a valid social group that is worth supporting and which includes within it others around them (Bradford 2012). What is perhaps most important here is that, if it does indeed occur, this process will happen as a result of everyday interactions between police officers and members of the public. What is needed, arguably, is not a grand scheme for police "community building" but simply greater emphasis on improving the quality of interactions between officers and citizens, coupled with a set of realistic expectations concerning the likely timescale of any benefits such improvements might bring.

24.5.1 In Conclusion

It seems to us that, taken together, the set of theoretical and policy concerns described above point toward the relevance for attempts to enhance police legitimacy of what has been variously termed "minimal" (Marks and Wood 2010) or "fire-brigade" (Reiner 2012) policing, which is oriented toward providing for a "narrow but deep" (Loader and Walker 2007) sense of security and belonging among the policed (see also Steinberg 2011). That is, rather than instituting ambitious programs that seek new ways to achieve short-term public opinion targets, police should concentrate on their core tasks—dealing with issues of crime and disorder, responding to emergency calls—while always trying to interact with citizens in as procedurally fair a way as possible. In particular, the notion that each encounter between officer and citizen is a "teachable moment" (Tyler 2011a) suggests that enhancements to police legitimacy, whether induced directly via experiences of procedural fairness, or indirectly via long-term processes that strengthen feelings of social inclusion and people's sense that social order is appropriately maintained, can be secured at the level of everyday interaction, a possibility that seems both normatively and practically preferable to the idea that there is a police response to many of the much wider social issues outlined above.

References

Bauman, Zygmunt. 2002. *Society under Siege*. Cambridge: Polity Press.
Beck, Ulrich. 1992. *Risk Society: Toward a New Modernity*. London: Sage.
Blader, Steven L., and Tom R. Tyler. 2009. "Testing and Expanding the Group Engagement Model." *Journal of Applied Psychology* 94:445–64.
Bottoms, Anthony, and Justice Tankebe. 2012. "Beyond Procedural Justice: A Dialogic Approach to Legitimacy in Criminal Justice." *Journal of Criminal Law and Criminology* 102:119–70.
Bourdieu, Pierre 1993. *The Field of Cultural Production*. Cambridge: Polity.

Bradford, Ben, Jonathan Jackson, and Elizabeth A. Stanko. 2009. "Contact and Confidence: Revisiting the Impact of Public Encounters with the Police." *Policing and Society* 19(1):20–46.

Bradford, Ben. 2012. "Policing and Social Identity: Procedural Justice, Inclusion and Cooperation Between Police and Public." *Policing and Society*. iFirst, doi: 10.1080/10439463.2012.724068.

Bradford, Ben, Aziz Huq, Jonathan Jackson, and Benjamin Roberts. 2013. "What Price Fairness When Security Is at Stake? Police Legitimacy in South Africa." *Regulation and Governance*. iFirst, doi: 10.1111/rego.12012.

Brown, Ben, and W. M. Reed Benedict. 2002. "Perceptions of The Police: Past Findings, Methodological Issues, Conceptual Issues and Policy Implications." *Policing: An International Journal of Police Strategies and Management* 25:543–80.

Brunson, Rod K., and Jody Miller. 2006. "Young Black Men and Urban Policing in the United States." *British Journal of Criminology* 46:613–40.

Chen, Feng. 1997. "The Dilemma of Eudaemonic Legitimacy in Post-Mao China." *Polity* 29(3):421–39.

Crank, John P. 2003. "Institutional Theory of the Police: A Review of the State of the Art." *Policing: An International Journal of Police Strategies and Management* 26:186–207.

de Cremer, David, and Tom R. Tyler. 2005. "Am I Respected or Not?: Inclusion and Reputation as Issues in Group Membership." *Social Justice Research* 18:121–53.

Emirbayer, Mustafa, and Victoria Johnson. 2008. "Bourdieu and Organizational Analysis." *Theoretical Sociology* 37:1–44.

European Social Survey. 2012. *Policing by Consent: Understanding the Dynamics of Police Power and Legitimacy*, ESS Country Specific Topline Results Series Issue 1 UK. By Jackson, Jonathan, Mike Hough, Ben Bradford, Katrin Hohl, and Jouni Kuha. Available at http://ssrn.com/abstract=2168702.

FitzGerald, Marian. 2010. "A Confidence Trick?" *Policing: A Journal of Policy and Practice* 43(3): 298–301.

Garland, David. 2001. *The Culture of Control*. Oxford: Oxford University Press.

Gau, Jacinta M., Nicholas Corsaro, Eric A. Stewart, and Rod K. Brunson. 2012. "Examining Macro-Level Impacts on Procedural Justice and Police Legitimacy." *Journal of Criminal Justice* 40:333–43.

Geller, Amanda, and Jeffrey Fagan. 2010. "Pot as Pretext: Marijuana, Race and the New Disorder in New York City Policing." *Journal of Empirical Legal Studies* 7:591–633.

Giddens, Antony. 1991. *Modernity and Self-Identity*. Cambridge: Polity Press.

Girling, Evi, Ian Loader, and Richard Sparks. 2000. *Crime and Social Change in Middle England: Questions of Order in an English Town*. New York: Routledge.

Habermas, Jurgen. 1976. *Legititmation Crisis*. London: Heinemann.

Harcourt, Bernard E. 2001. *Illusion of Order*. Cambridge, MA: Harvard.

Hasisi, Badi, and David Weisburd. 2011. "Going Beyond Ascribed Identities: The Importance of Procedural Justice in Airport Security Screening in Israel." *Law and Society Review* 45:867–92.

Hinds, Lyn, and Kristina Murphy. 2007. "Public Satisfaction With Police: Using Procedural Justice to Improve Police Legitimacy." *Australian and New Zealand Journal of Criminology* 40:27–42.

Hinsch, Wilfried. 2008. "Legitimacy and Justice." In *Political Legitimation without Morality?* Edited by Jörg Kühnelt, 39–52. London: Springer

——. 2010. "Justice, Legitimacy, and Constitutional Rights, Critical Review of *International Social and Political Philosophy*." 13:39–54.

Hirschman, Albert O. 1970. *Exit, Voice, and Loyalty: Responses to Decline in Firms, Organizations, and States*. Cambridge, MA: Harvard University Press.

Hough, Mike, Jonathan Jackson, and Ben Bradford. 2013a. "The Governance of Criminal Justice, Legitimacy and Trust." In *The Routledge Handbook of European Criminology*, edited by Sophie Body-Gendrot, Mike Hough, Klara Kerezsi, Réne Lévy, and Sonja Snacken, 243–265. Oxford: Routledge.

——. 2013b. "Legitimacy, Trust and Compliance: An Empirical Test of Procedural Justice Theory using the European Social Survey." In *Legitimacy and Criminal Justice: An International Exploration*, edited by Justice Tankebe, and Alison Liebling, 326–352. New Haven: Yale University Press.

Howell, K. Babe. 2009. "Broken Lives from Broken Windows: The Hidden Costs of Aggressive Order Maintenance Policing." *New York University Review of Law and Social Change* 33: 271–329.

Jackson, Jonathan, and Ben Bradford. 2009. "Crime, Policing and Social Order: On the Expressive Nature of Public Confidence in Policing." *British Journal of Sociology* 60:493–521.

Jackson, Jonathan, Ben Bradford, Mike Hough, Jouni Kuha, Sally Stares, Sally Widdop, Rory Fitzgerald, Maria Yordanova, and Todor Galev. 2011. "Developing European Indicators of Trust in Justice." *European Journal of Criminology*. 84:267–85.

Jackson, Jonathan, Ben Bradford, Mike Hough, Andy Myhill, Paul Quinton, and Tom R. Tyler. 2012a. "Why Do People Comply with the Law? Legitimacy and the Influence of Legal Institutions." *British Journal of Criminology* 52:1051–71.

Jackson, Jonathan, Ben Bradford, Elizabeth A. Stanko, and Katrin Hohl. 2012b. *Just Authority? Trust in the Police in England and Wales*. Oxford: Routledge.

Jackson, Jonathan, and Jason Sunshine. 2007. "Public Confidence in Policing: A Neo-Durkheimian Perspective." *British Journal of Criminology* 47:214–33.

Johnson, Bruce D., Andrew Golub, and James McCabe. 2010. "The International Implications of Quality-of-Life Policing as Practiced in New York City." *Police Practice and Research* 11:17–29.

Kelling, George L., and Catherine M. Coles. 1996. *Fixing Broken Windows: Restoring Order and Reducing Crime in our Communities*. New York: Free Press

Kelman, Herbert C., and V. Lee Hamilton. 1989. *Crimes of Obedience*. New Haven: Yale University Press.

Kochel, Tammy R. 2012. "Can Police Legitimacy Promote Collective Efficacy?" *Justice Quarterly* 29:384–419.

LaFree, Gary. 1998. *Losing Legitimacy*. Boulder, CO: Westview Press.

Lind, E. Allen, and Tom R. Tyler. 1988. *The Social Psychology of Procedural Justice*. New York: Plenum Press.

Loader, Ian, and Neil Walker. 2001. "Policing as a Public Good: Reconstituting the Connections between Policing and the State." *Theoretical Criminology* 5(1):9–35.

Loader, Ian, and Neil Walker. 2006. "Necessary Virtues: The Legitimate Place of the State in the Production of Security." In *Democracy, Society and the Governance of Security*, edited by Jennifer Wood and Benoît Dupont, 165–195. Cambridge: Cambridge University Press.

——. 2007. *Civilising Security*. Cambridge: Cambridge University Press.

Loader, Ian, and Aogan Mulcahy. 2003. *Policing and the Condition of England: Memory, Politics and Culture*. Oxford: Clarendon Press.

Manning, Peter K. 2010. *Democratic Policing in a Changing World*. Boulder, CO: Paradigm Publishers.

Marks, Monique, and Jennifer Wood. 2010. "South African Policing at a Crossroads: The Case for a 'Minimal' and 'Minimalist' Public Police." *Theoretical Criminology* 14:311–29.

Mazerolle, Lorraine, Emma Antrobus, Sarah Bennett, and Tom R. Tyler. 2013. "Shaping Citizen Perceptions of Police Legitimacy: A Randomized Field Trial of Procedural Justice." *Criminology* 51:33–63.

Meyer, John W., and Brian Rowan. 1977. "Institutionalized Organizations: Formal Structure as Myth and Ceremony." *American Journal of Sociology* 83:340–63.

Miliband, Ralph. 1978. "A State of Desubordination." *British Journal of Sociology* 29:399–409.

Miller, Joel, Robert C. Davis, Nicole, J. Henderson, John Markovic, and Christopher, W Ortiz. 2004. *Public Opinions of the Police: The Influence of Friends, Family, and News Media.* New York: Vera Institute of Justice.

Moon, Debbie, Alison Walker, Rachel Murphy, John Flatley, Jenny Parfremont-Hopkins, and Philip Hall. 2009. *Perceptions of Crime and Anti-Social Behavior. Supplementary Volume to Crime in England and Wales 2008/09.* Home Office Statistical Bulletin 17/09. London: Home Office.

Mulford, Matthew, Jonathan Jackson, and Henrik Svedsater. 2008. "Encouraging Cooperation: Revisiting Group Identity and Cooperative Norm Effects in Prisoners' Dilemma Games." *Journal of Applied Social Psychology* 38:2964–89.

Myhill, Andy, and Ben Bradford. 2012. "Can Police Enhance Public Confidence by Improving Quality of Service? Results from Two Surveys in England and Wales." *Policing and Society* 22:397–425.

Paternoster, Raymond, Robert Brame, Ronet Bachman, and Lawrence W. Sherman. 1997. "Do Fair Procedures Matter? The Effect of Procedural Justice on Spouse Assault." *Law and Society Review* 31:163–204.

Reiner, Robert. 2010. *The Politics of the Police.* Oxford: Oxford University Press.

——. 2012. *In Praise of Fire Brigade Policing: Challenging the Role of the Police.* London: The Howard League for Penal Reform.

Sampson, Robert J., and Dawn Jeglum Bartusch. 1998. "Legal Cynicism and (Subcultural?) Tolerance of Deviance: The Neighborhood Context of Racial Differences." *Law and Society Review* 32:777–804.

Scott, W. Richard. 2001. *Institutions and Organizations.* Thousand Oaks: Sage.

Schulhofer, Stephen, Tom R. Tyler, and Aziz Huq 2011. "American Policing at a Crossroads: Unsustainable Policies and the Procedural Justice Alternative." *Journal of Criminal Law and Criminology* 101:335–75.

Silver, Eric, and Lisa L. Miller. 2004. "Sources of Informal Social Control in Chicago Neighborhoods." *Criminology* 42:551–83.

Sindall, Katy, Patrick Sturgis, and Will Jennings. 2012. "Public Confidence in the Police: A Time Series Analysis." *British Journal of Criminology* 52:744–64.

Skogan, Wesley G. 2006. "Asymmetry in the Impact of Encounters with the Police." *Policing and Society* 16:99–126.

——. 2009. "Concern About Crime and Confidence in the Police: Reassurance or Accountability." *Police Quarterly* 12:301–18.

Steinberg, Jonny. 2011. "Establishing Police Authority and Civilian Compliance in Post-Apartheid Johannesburg: An Argument from Egon Bittner." *Policing and Society* 22:481–95.

Sunshine, Jason, and Tom R. Tyler. 2003. "The Role of Procedural Justice and Legitimacy in Shaping Public Support for Policing." *Law and Society Review* 37:555–89.

Tajfel, Henri, and John C. Turner. 1986. "The Social Identity Theory of Inter-group Behavior." In *Psychology of Intergroup Relations*, edited by Stephen Worchel and William Austin, 7–24. Chicago: Nelson-Hall.

Tankebe, Justice. 2009. "Public Cooperation with the Police in Ghana: Does Procedural Fairness Matter?" *Criminology* 47:1265–93.

———. 2013. "Viewing Things Differently: The Dimensions of Public Perceptions of Legitimacy." *Criminology* 51:103–35.

Turner, John C. 1975. "Social Comparison and Social Identity: Some Prospects for Intergroup Behavior." *European Journal of Social Psychology* 5:5–34.

Turner, John C., Rupert J. Brown, and Henri Tajfel. 1979. "Social Comparison and Group Interest in Ingroup Favoritism." *European Journal of Social Psychology* 9:187–204.

Tyler, Tom R. 2003. "Procedural Justice, Legitimacy, and the Effective Rule of Law." *Crime and Justice: A Review of Research* 30:431–505.

———. 2004. "Enhancing Police Legitimacy." *The Annals of the American Academy* 593:84–99.

———. 2006a. "Legitimacy and Legitimating." *Annual Review of Psychology* 57:375–400.

———. 2006b. *Why People Obey the Law*. Princeton: Princeton University Press.

———. 2009. "Legitimacy and Criminal Justice: The Benefits of Self-regulation." *Ohio State Journal of Criminal Law* 7:307–59.

———. 2011a. "Trust and Legitimacy: Policing in the USA and Europe." *European Journal of Criminology* 8:254–66.

———. 2011b. *Why People Cooperate: The Role of Social Motivations*. Princeton: Princeton University Press.

Tyler, Tom R., and Stephen Blader. 2003. "Procedural Justice, Social Identity, and Cooperative Behavior." *Personality and Social Psychology Review* 7:349–61.

Tyler, Tom R., and Jeff Fagan. 2008. "Legitimacy and Cooperation: Why do People help the Police Fight Crime in their Communities?" *Ohio State Journal of Criminal Law* 6:231–75.

Tyler, Tom R., and Yuen J. Huo. 2002. *Trust in the Law: Encouraging Public Cooperation with the Police and Courts*. New York: Russell Sage Foundation.

Tyler, Tom R., and Jonathan Jackson. 2013. "Future Challenges in the Study of Legitimacy and Criminal Justice." In Legitimacy and Criminal Justice: An International Exploration, edited by Justice Tankebe and Alison Liebling, 83–104. New Haven: Yale University Press.

Tyler, Tom R., and E. Allan Lind. 1992. "A Relational Model of Authority in Groups." In *Advances in Experimental Social Psychology*, edited by Mark P. Zanna, 115–191. San Diego, CA: Academic Press.

Tyler, Tom R., Lawrence Sherman, Heather Strang, Geoffrey C. Barnes, and Daniel Woods. 2007. "Reintegrative Shaming, Procedural Justice, and Recidivism: The Engagement of Offenders' Psychological Mechanisms in the Canberra RISE Drinking-and-driving Experiment." *Law and Society Review* 41:553–86.

Tyler, Tom R., and Cheryl J. Wakslak. 2004. "Profiling and Police Legitimacy: Procedural Justice, Attributions of Motive, and Acceptance of Police Authority." *Criminology* 42:253–81.

Van der Toorn, Jojanneke, Tom R. Tyler, and John Jost. 2011. "More than Fair: Outcome Dependence, System Justification, and the Perceived Legitimacy of Authority Figures." *Journal of Experimental Social Psychology* 47:127–38.

Waddington, P. A. J. 1999. *Policing Citizens: Authority and Rights*. London: University College Press.

Warner, Barbara D. 2007. "Directly Intervene or Call the Authorities? A Study of Forms of Neighborhood Social Control Within a Social Disorganization Framework." *Criminology* 45: 99–129.

Weisburd, David, Josh Hinkle, Christine Famega, and Justin Ready 2011. "The Possible 'Backfire' Effects of Broken Windows Policing at Crime Hot Spots: An Experimental Assessment of Impacts on Legitimacy, Fear and Collective Efficacy." *Journal of Experimental Criminology* 7:297–320.

Wells, William, Joseph A. Schafer, Sean P. Varano, and Timothy S. Bynum. 2006. "Neighborhood Resident's Production of Order: The Effects of Collective Efficacy on Responses to Neighborhood Problems." *Crime and Delinquency* 52:523–50.

Zelditch Jr., Morris. 2001. Theories of legitimacy. In *The Psychology of Legitimacy: Emerging Perspectives on Ideology, Justice, and Intergroup Relations*, edited by John T. Jost and Brenda Major, 33–53. Cambridge, MA: Cambridge University Press.

....

CHAPTER 25

PRIVATE POLICING IN PUBLIC SPACES

....

ALISON WAKEFIELD AND MARK BUTTON

THE concept of private policing has come to be well used in contemporary police studies but belies clear definition. This is due to the definitional complexities associated with both the notion of privacy or private matters and the activity of policing (Jones and Newburn 1998; Wakefield 2003). What is evident is that, since the late 1970s, a growing body of policing scholarship has demonstrated that in order to explore policing fully, one has to investigate a much wider range of policing agents than simply the police. Public space is also difficult to define: it may reflect who owns the space, and/or who is permitted to use it (Wakefield 2003). It is indisputable, however, that agents of policing other than the police are today so ubiquitous as to be almost taken for granted in urban life, as one enters and exits one's workplace, seeks directions in a shopping mall, or submits to a baggage or body search when entering a tourist venue or progressing through an airport. We place our trust in those individuals who supervise our office or apartment blocks, employ technologies to survey us as we move through shopping malls and other large complexes, maintain order in the busy social venues that we sometimes frequent, or even patrol our neighborhoods.

A number of studies in the 1970s and 1980s investigated the increasing significance of private security in the United States (Kakalik and Wildhorn 1971, 1977; Cunningham and Taylor 1985); Canada (Farnell and Shearing 1977; Shearing, Farnell, and Stenning 1980; Shearing and Stenning 1981, 1983, 1987) and the United Kingdom (Draper 1978; South 1988). Private security, as Shearing and Stenning (1981) were quick to recognize, comprises not only a substantial commercial security industry; its corporate in-house dimension also reflects organizations' often substantial investment in internal security systems. In the 1990s, a second wave of research demonstrated an increasing recognition that policing is undertaken by a wide range of voluntary, private sector, public sector and quasi-public sector organizations (Johnston 1992; Jones and Newburn 1998, 2006; Crawford et al. 2005) and, through ethnographic research, began to shed light on how private forms of policing were delivered (McManus 1995; Noaks 2000; Rigakos 2002; Hobbs et al. 2003; Wakefield 2003). Such has been the change in the focus of policing studies that much of the contemporary literature considers the "pluralization," "multilateralization," or "fragmentation" of policing (Bayley and Shearing 1996, 2001; Johnston 2000). It is recognized, therefore, that policing is undertaken by the "public" police, other public policing bodies, "hybrid" policing bodies, private security, and by voluntary organizations. The fashion for what has been termed "late modern policing" has generated a growing literature on the many categories of policing agents and organizations that are now present today.

In this essay we provide a review of research on private policing. Section 25.1 begins with the historical development of private policing within the modern period. Section 25.2 considers contemporary forms of private policing, employing a typology by Brodeur (2010) in order to examine the variety of objectives and activities that can be placed under such a heading: the private penetration of the public sphere, the public penetration of the private market, and the private funding of public police organizations. Section 25.3 looks to the future of private policing, with reference to a range of underlying trends.

25.1 THE HISTORY OF PRIVATE POLICING

Historically, policing in most countries has been largely dominated by private and voluntary forms of policing. It is only with the emergence of modern industrial economies towards the end of the nineteenth century that the police became the dominant model in the delivery of policing (Johnston 1992). Private and voluntary forms of policing did not disappear, but rather were eclipsed by the dominant public arrangements. The emergence of commercial private security companies, however, is relatively new. In the United States such companies can be traced to the late nineteenth century and the rapid emergence of company towns surrounding the coal, iron, and steel industries—developments that are discussed by critical scholars as inevitable consequences of the crisis of capitalism whereby the state draws on the private sector to strengthen its legitimacy (Spitzer and Scull 1977; Weiss 1978; Couch 1987). The development of the coal, iron, and steel industries took place in rural areas in which the state was not well established. Industrial militancy threatened the corporations of the time and, as a result, companies resorted to private policing to maintain control. These measures went well beyond keeping the peace. Private groups were employed to ensure the working classes remained obedient. The companies would draw upon their own private forces but also made use of contractors for investigations and policing industrial disputes.

The most famous of the commercial security companies was Pinkerton, a firm still in operation today across a range of countries as part of the Securitas group of companies. As documented by Weiss (1978), they provided a range of services that included general property protection services and strike-breaking services such as labor espionage, strike-breakers, strike-guards, and strike missionaries (those who were paid to convince strikers to go back to work). The policing practices that emerged, particularly during industrial action in this period, led to serious confrontations between the forces of capital and labor. Pinkerton's chequered history culminated in the Homestead Riots in 1892, when its guards were hired to challenge an employee siege of the Carnegie Steel Plant, resulting in twelve deaths. Such were the problems throughout this period that private police systems were the subject of many Congressional reports (see United States Committee on Education and Labour 1971, a publication of a 1931 report). As the 1931 Congressional report argued:

> The use of private police systems to infringe upon the civil liberties of workers has a long and often blood stained history. The methods used by private armed guards have been violent. The purposes have usually been to prevent the exercise of civil rights in the self-organisation of employees into unions or to break strikes either called to enforce collective bargaining or to obtain better working conditions for union members.

This passage is typical of a widespread view in the United States at the time that conceived of private security as involving private armies/spies, and viewed this as a threat to the public interest, as dangerous to society, and as a phenomenon that should be restricted in the roles it undertook. Private industrial policing went into decline in the United States following legislation in 1935 that substantially increased labor rights and, according to Weiss (1986, 106), led to labor discipline functions shifting to conservative trade unions employing the same tactics hitherto used by employers: "espionage, black-listing, use of strike breakers during 'outlaw' or 'wildcat' strikes, fines, intimidation, red baiting, etc."

It is the post-World War II period, however, that witnessed the emergence of the modern private security industry and its expansion to the extent that many countries now have more private security officers than police officers. This growth, described by Johnston (1992) as the "rebirth of private policing," has been underpinned by a variety of social, political, and economic factors (see CoESS/Uni-Europa 2004; CoESS 2008; Prenzler 2009). Increased prosperity with more private property and consumer goods to protect coincided with rising crime in many countries, especially from the 1970s to the 1990s. Improvements in security technology (especially alarms and closed-circuit television) have led to better, and cheaper, security products as companies, public institutions, and private individuals have become more security conscious. The expansion of privately controlled, publicly accessible spaces ranging from hypermarkets to airports has increased the demand for dedicated private security teams which can cost effectively be employed to meet the specific policing needs of such sites. Public spending restrictions have led to governments' increased outsourcing of non-core tasks to the private sector. Additionally, there has been a general growth in the subcontracting of security functions within both the public and private sectors as organizations have found it more economical to concentrate on their core business and expertise, while dedicated providers of ancillary services (such as cleaning, catering, and maintenance, as well as security) deliver these much more cost effectively.

25.2 Private Policing Today

The variety of activities that might be placed under the heading of "private policing" demonstrate that this is not so much a discernible activity as a reflection of the complexity of interest groups and actors that define and undertake policing today. In this section we outline the definitional challenges associated with the concept of privatization, and the many forms of contemporary private policing that are now in operation.

25.2.1 Defining Privatization

Privatization is described by Saunders and Harris (1990, 58) as "a confused concept which carries many different meanings." Variants include "outsourcing," "commercialization," "user pays," and "deregulation". Most simply, it refers to a process in which government-owned assets or services are wholly or partially transferred to private companies, yet it is seen by a number of commentators as having evolved to embrace a range of actions whereby the delivery of public services is exposed to market forces. Pirie (1988) identifies twenty-one different types of privatization, while Saunders and Harris (1990) summarize these diverse forms in a four-fold classification. They categorize actions according to the locus of responsibility (producers or consumers) and the change in the government's role (change of ownership or change of control). Changes of ownership comprise "denationalization" (i.e., the selling of a state-owned agency to a private service provider) and "commodification" (i.e., the selling of state-owned resources to those who consume them). Changes of control consist of processes of "liberalization," where responsibility for providing or financing a good or service is retained by the state, and non-state agencies are partially or fully responsible for its delivery; and "marketization": the provision of allowances to consumers to purchase goods and services previously delivered by the state.

According to Pirie (1988), the concept was seldom used before 1979. As a product of the managerialist movement that has swept through industrialized countries since the 1980s in the drive for greater efficiency in public sector management, privatization has been a key feature of political economies, spreading internationally following a rigorous privatization program in the United Kingdom. Thus, most countries have seen government-owned institutions, such as banks and monopoly services (e.g., railways and electricity) sold to private companies. The justification has been that commercial competition and the profit motive provide powerful incentives for more efficient and better quality services to the public. There has also been a decisive shift to "user-pays" principles, based on the idea that competition promotes efficiency and the whole cost of the product, resources can be allocated more efficiently when consumers bear in policy areas such as education and health.

Equally subject to tightening financial accountability, such principles have been applied to police services, albeit in a significantly more limited way. Brodeur (2010) provides three meanings of policing privatization that may be applied to the visible forms of policing that occur in public settings: the private penetration of the public sphere, the public penetration of the private market, and the private funding of public police organizations. These three dimensions are examined in depth in the following sections.

25.2.2 The Private Penetration of the Public Sphere

Operational policing has been largely immune from deliberate policies of privatization. Profit making is generally seen as being incompatible with the ideals of impartial justice and universal service intrinsic to modern policing, while police numbers are also always a politically charged issue and perceived threats to the police are commonly considered to be an electoral liability. Outright privatization of the police, the transfer of government-owned assets or services to private companies either wholly or in part, looks likely to remain the stuff of fantasy and fiction. The 1987 film *Robocop*'s offering of a dystopian vision of neoliberal measures taken to extremes at a time when such policies were gaining momentum in the United States under Ronald Reagan's presidency is an example of this fantastical privatization. A *de facto* privatization of policing is happening to varying degrees around the world, however, resulting in a revolution in how policing is being done (Wakefield and Prenzler 2009).

The rise of alternative forms of policing to the police has taken two main forms, described by Johnston (1992) as "load shedding" and "contracting out" or "outsourcing." The former category refers to the supplementation or replacement of certain areas of policing by commercial or voluntary provision, but Johnston also employed the term to include the active encouragement by police of third-party provision. His examples ranged from police initiated neighborhood watch schemes to situations whereby some police functions were effectively being "usurped" by voluntary action such as street patrol initiatives. An especially visible example is that of street patrol, carried out by community groups on a voluntary basis (such initiatives are particularly developed in New Zealand where they are represented by a national body, the Community Patrols of New Zealand Charitable Trust) or private security firms hired by residents' collectives. The most substantial element of "load shedding," however, has been the growing recourse of organizations and individuals to commercial security, resulting in the sector's phenomenal growth as discussed above.

Notably, the diversification of policing has also occurred *within* police forces, and Jones (2009) identifies three distinct kinds of auxiliary policing. The first comprises volunteer police officers who work on an unpaid basis within police forces. As he observes, volunteer auxiliaries in police forces have a long history with, for example, the New York City auxiliary police dating back to 1916, and the special constabulary having been established in England and Wales in the Special Constabulary Act 1831. A second category comprises civilian patrol personnel with more limited training and powers than regular police officers, including the Dutch *politiesurveillanten* or "police assistants," which were introduced in the 1990s, and police community support officers (PCSOs) established in English and Welsh police forces early in the new millennium. A third dimension includes the policing tasks delivered by personnel employed by local municipalities, including the *stadtswachten* (city guards) in the Netherlands, neighborhood and street "wardens" in the United Kingdom, and the *polices municipales* in France.

Such diversification trends have much to do with the organization and the use of urban space. It has been argued that the growth of publicly accessible forms of "mass private property," often policed by security officers, has substantially raised the profile of the private security industry in policing (Shearing and Stenning 1981, 1983). The owners of shopping centers, leisure parks, and other major commercial facilities have frequently drawn on private security services in exercising their legal rights to maintain control of the policing of their territories (Shearing and Stenning 1983; Caldeira 1996; Davis 1998: Abaza 2001). Rather than relying on traditional policing methods based on apprehending offenders during or after the commission of offenses, property owners are able to initiate a more proactive, pre-emptive approach to policing by drawing on teams of private security officers. As a result, the commercial environments they create can be carefully managed to maximize custom and, naturally, profit-making.

Common areas of urban space have become subject to further controls through attempts to manage retail districts of town centers in a manner that in many ways mirrors the operation of privately owned shopping centers, by means of the Business Improvement District (BID) and Town Centre Management (TCM) models. BIDs first emerged in Canadian and US towns and cities in the 1970s, and spread to New Zealand, South Africa, and parts of Europe, specifically Albania, Germany, Ireland, Serbia, and the United Kingdom (Cook 2009; Cook and Ward 2012). TCM developed in England in the late 1980s and is mirrored by TCM-like schemes in Australia and several European countries including France, Italy, Sweden, and Spain (Cook 2009). Both models, outlined more fully by Cook (2009), are based on partnerships between local municipalities and business communities in order to provide local improvements to boost the trading environment, and address competition from mass private property retail developments and rival urban centers. These may include additional street cleaning, landscaping, and safety and security measures such as closed circuit television systems and security patrols.

The second trend identified by Johnston was the rise of contracting out or outsourcing, whereby police forces enter into contracts with third parties to purchase goods or services. This has been especially notable in the United Kingdom, indeed, such has been the scale of these developments that it is described in a report by the Confederation of European Security Services (CoESS 2008) as a special case within Europe to the extent that it has delegated public services to the private security sector. UK police organizations have seen such practices extended from uncontroversial functions within the police organization such as the procurement of goods ranging from stationery to police equipment, and of ancillary services such as cleaning, catering, and maintenance, to "back office" elements of policing, specifically custodial and prisoner escort services, and technically specialized areas including forensic services and information technology development and delivery.

25.2.3 The Public Penetration of the Private Market

Brodeur's (2010) second and third categories of policing privatization, by contrast, see the police engaging in a growing marketplace for policing. His second category comprises active competition by police agencies against their private sector counterparts whereby, he notes, "they are privatizing themselves" (257). The widespread practice of "moonlighting" by police within the United States was well documented by Reiss (1988, 2), who found that in many police departments the actual number of off-duty uniformed officers performing police duties (i.e., paid by private individuals) exceeded by a substantial number those officially on duty (i.e., funded through the taxation system). Thus, police officers have long been able to supplement their pay by providing uniformed security sometimes equipped with firearms at special events and private establishments such as bars and nightclubs, banks, apartment complexes, and retail outlets. US police forces also provide such services directly for private hire. Similar practices apply overseas: Brodeur notes that the marketing of police services has been a long-standing practice in mainland Europe (Malochet 2007, cited in Brodeur 2010, 257), while Gans (2000) reviews such practices in Australia and especially the United Kingdom, where this has been permissible since the Police Act 1964.

25.2.4 Private Funding of Public Police Organizations

Linked to the charging of fees and selling of services, Bryett (1996) has identified four methods in which privately owned non-police resources have been extended to the police. At its simplest level, monies and physical resources have been given to the police. Clearly the donation of large sums of money or resources raises concern over the independence of the police should an investigation into the donor ever become necessary. At a second level, another donation is that of space, which can also be a form of physical resource. Bryett provides one example from the United States where the McDonalds food chain gave part of one of its stores as premises for a police station. Brodeur (2010) provides a Canadian example comprising elements of both, noting proposals by a bankers' association to subsidize an economic crime unit staffed by investigators from the Montreal Police Department, with its office located within a building owned by one of the association's members.

A third type of private sector aid is giving time. This most frequently takes the form of private individuals offering their time as police auxiliaries, termed "special constables" in the United Kingdom. At another level it might be helping the police in a search for a missing person or for evidence. The pursuit of cooperative ventures between the public and private sectors is the fourth means of cooperation. For instance, in Montgomery County in the United States, the local police department cooperated with IBM to produce a sophisticated computer disaster and security capability. In the United Kingdom, some police forces have contracted with the private sector to design, finance, build, and manage police facilities. Some of these have included police stations and firearms ranges (Button and Wakefield 2013).

25.3 THE FUTURE OF PRIVATE POLICING

These developments reflect a general, worldwide trend whereby law enforcement and crime prevention services are expanding and diversifying (Wakefield and Prenzler 2009), and there is no reason why such trends should not continue. Demand by citizens and corporations for a variety of forms of policing and security is likely to grow, and the supply of different forms of policing is certain to evolve. In considering these factors, we now look to the future of private policing with reference to seven broad trends, referred to under the headings of "privatization," "diversification," "technologization," "globalization," "territorialization," "professionalization," and "harmonization."

25.3.1 Privatization

Austerity budgets in the United States, Canada, the United Kingdom, and elsewhere have placed enormous pressure on police funding, already challenged by the spiralling costs of policing a high crime, interconnected, post-9/11 world. These difficulties are explored in detail with regard to UK policing in a report by Boyd, Geoghegan, and Gibbs (2011). Pressures on police are likely to promote increasing recourse by citizens to private security services, in a way that is already commonplace in middle class life in high crime societies such as South Africa and Brazil, and may become a driver for new forms of police outsourcing. For a short period in 2012, it appeared that UK policing was facing a new wave of privatization of police functions until recent events shifted the prevailing public mood towards the policy, from one of quiet acceptance to unrest over the prospect of its further substantial growth. Following the UK government's announcement in late 2010 that central government police funding will be reduced by 20 percent in real terms by 2014–2015, two police forces, the West Midlands and Surrey, invited bids for the largest ever police outsourcing contract at a value of £1.5 billion (*Guardian* 2012a), invoking a brief media storm in the spring of 2012. Surrey, however, suspended its plans a few months later following a considerable furor over G4S, the world's largest security company, which failed to meet the terms of its substantial contract to provide the security officers for the London Olympics, with respect primarily to the number but also to the quality of personnel they were able to mobilize for such a large event (*Guardian* 2012b). The West Midlands force followed in pulling out of the arrangements, and the temptation to rely on outsourcing as a means of doing more with less has proven politically difficult for UK police forces to realize, at least in the immediate aftermath of these events.

25.3.2 Technologization

The political problems with outright privatization may, therefore, inhibit such measures at least in the short term, but a continuing *de facto* privatization as demand for private services grows appears highly likely. Technological advancement favors a security industry that is constantly developing newer, more sophisticated, and more cost effective technologies. Thus, in the United States, it has been estimated that the market for security products and systems will increase 6.3 percent annually to reach $19.9 billion in 2016, a trend associated with rebounds in construction and capital investment spending, perceived high risks of crime, and improvements to security technology, with an underlying shift from manned security towards automated security functions (Freedonia 2012). Shearing and Stenning (2012) note how policing in general has become increasingly technology-intensive as opposed to labor-intensive, and reiterate their observation nearly thirty years earlier that private security has always enjoyed an enormous advantage to the police in their access to technological resources (Shearing and Stenning 1983).

25.3.3 Diversification

Today there are few functions undertaken by police forces that the commercial security industry does not also fulfill. What might be termed "security goods and services companies" represent the most substantial as well as visible sector of the commercial security industry. These are companies selling manned and/or physical security goods and services, as summarized in Table 25.1.[1] They tend to be multi-functional and indeed the larger security goods and services companies are increasingly becoming "one-stop shops" for security products and services.

It is, however, what is known as the "manned guarding" sector of the industry, and its growing profile as well as scale, that most visibly demonstrates the industry's growing ubiquity (in practice it is impossible to distinguish clearly between the guarding companies and other market sectors, given the wide range of security products and services being offered by many firms in response to the growing market for integrated security solutions). Given the aggressive expansion of the larger companies, discussed next, and their penetration of new areas of business, there is no reason to anticipate that these trends will not continue.

Table 25.1 Services Provided by the Security Goods and Services Sector

Goods and Services	Examples
Cash handling services	Cash-in-transit (CIT) Cash processing ATM maintenance
Crowd management	Event security Door supervision
Electronic security	Alarms Access control Closed-circuit television (CCTV)
Guarding	Static Mobile Security checks Close protection Alarm response Reception Key holding
Information security	ICT security Document security ID security
Monitoring and alarm receiving	Alarm receiving (and dispatching) Electronic surveillance and positioning Operational remote control Guard safety control CIT remote control
Physical/mechanical security	Locks Barriers Seals Lighting Safes Strong rooms/vaults
Security consultancy and training	

25.3.4 Globalization

Today's so-called guarding companies range from small, locally oriented firms to the global operators, the largest of which are the Swedish firm Securitas, operating in 51 countries and dominating the US and European markets (Securitas 2013a); and the Anglo-Danish firm G4S (2013), which operates in a wider spread of countries, stated to number over 125 at the time of this writing. Both of these major players have expanded globally through acquisition and merger, Securitas having been one of the fastest growing companies in the last two decades. G4S has, however, rivaled Securitas in size since 2004, when it was formed through the merger of Group 4 Falck and Securicor. Securitas was established in 1935 by Erik Philip-Sörensen, and for many years restricted its operations to Sweden, until one important landmark event in 1981 when it was divided between Sörensen's two sons, with the international operations (eventually to become part of G4S) being led by Sven Philip-Sörensen, while the Swedish business continued under his brother Jørgen, which retained the Securitas name (Securitas 2013b).

In the last decade of the twentieth century Securitas began its massive expansion program, penetrating markets in numerous European countries through acquisition. It then consolidated its position as one of the leading global players by purchasing the long-established American firm Pinkerton in 1999. The reach of Securitas is reflected in its range of services as well as the national markets in which it is based; the acquisition of Pinkerton allowed the company to combine its core activities of alarm systems, cash-in-transit services, and security guarding with Pinkerton's expertise in pre-employment screening, risk assessment, and integrated security systems. G4S has had a more stilted evolution, involving numerous acquisitions and mergers, as the company timeline shows (G4S 2013), with the G4S brand having been launched in 2006.

Shearing and Stenning (2012) note how, despite the considerable-and growing-global presence of the larger transnational security companies, police studies scholarship on transnational policing has been predominantly focused on cooperation between different countries' police forces and assistance missions to post-conflict and transitional states. They observe that the limited research into transnational private policing has focused mainly on activities in hostile environments, implying that this has presented a biased, unsystematic and incomplete picture, and emphasized the problems associated with transnational private policing with little attention to the benefits. Yet they conclude that "there is every reason to believe…that, as is the case domestically, they employ far more people than their international policing counterparts" (276). As these authors outline, this aspect of private policing is ripe for research.

25.3.5 Territorialization

The globalization of commercial products and services, as well as social policy models, is evident in the global expansion of forms of mass private property such as the shopping mall, the gated community, or the sports stadium, and successful service delivery models such as the BID or TCM scheme. The former have an important social function in an increasingly insecure, anonymous world: Bottoms and Wiles (1994) observed some twenty years ago that modern social systems will try to offer us "locations of trust"—spaces that serve as "bubbles" of security—such as the shopping mall—in an otherwise insecure world, and they drew attention to the proliferation of "defended locales," that is, the multiplication of facilities such as the chain store, restaurant, or hotel, as well as the car, across the world, so that one may find familiar and seemingly safe settings no matter how foreign the location. Visitors to such spaces readily place their trust in the proprietors of such settings, and security is an important element of the service on offer.

BID and TCM schemes have flourished globally as municipalities in conjunction with local business communities have sought to compete with privatized sites of retail and leisure. As Cook and Ward (2012) observe, global policy transfer is now more readily achieved than ever, as urban policy makers and practitioners can readily access information on new developments around the world by means of the numerous Internet-based and other information resources available, which in turn inform the establishment of models of good practice. The apparent success of such managed spaces, and the ongoing opportunities to learn from the most successful models, will surely promote such schemes further, in which private policing once again plays a key part.

26.3.6 Professionalization

Likely improvements in the professionalization of private policing should be a further driver of growth. Private security suffers from frequent public portrayals of it as unprofessional. Briggs (2005) describes the security community as "secretive and closed," operating on a "strictly need-to-know basis." Consequently, she argues, they are held back by security practitioners' general lack of engagement with public debates, so that "non-security experts have set the tone of debates and their perceptions and assumptions have been allowed to go unchecked" (34). The activities of the private sector, as a result, tend to gain most attention in the media and politics when something goes wrong. The shortage of security officers and the low caliber of many of those employed by G4S in its poor handling of the security guarding contract for the London Olympics (*Guardian* 2012b) cast the UK commercial security sector in an extremely negative light in a media story that played out for some time, while the government's arguably equally poor management of the procurement arrangements gained relatively little attention. Similarly, the most extreme cases of misconduct concerning armed private security personnel operating in hostile environments overseas, such as the Blackwater shootings of Iraqi civilians or the drunken shooting by a British Armourgroup contractor of two of his colleagues following an altercation (*Guardian* 2012a) have intensified social concern about this segment of private security and the need for its regulation.

Despite these common concerns that, by virtue of the profit motive, private security services are vastly inferior to those of public security agencies, private security is very much a sister discipline to its public sector counterparts. Former police, military, and intelligence personnel have traditionally made up a large proportion of security managers, and they continue to do so. Research studies carried out in the United Kingdom (Hearnden 1993) and the United States (Cavanagh and Whiting 2003) suggest that somewhere between 60 and 75 percent of security managers are derived from these public sector disciplines. Consequently, as White and Gill (2013) discuss, the cultural divide between them is not so great and is marked by blurred, not sharp, boundaries. A drawback of this close relationship is that security employers rely on the wealth of training and experience that those with public security backgrounds have gained elsewhere, possibly limiting the investment in education and training, the appetite for professional development, and opportunities for recruiting others from a more diverse range of backgrounds. Yet, as we have argued elsewhere, the security profession itself, through its associations including the global body ASIS International, does much on a collective basis to promote standards, training, education, and research (Button and Wakefield 2013), suggesting that developments are moving in the right direction.

With respect to the front line of security work, it should be noted that the compulsory training standards in the United States and United Kingdom, in comparison to most European countries and some Canadian and Australian states, are considerably lower (see Sarre and Prenzler 2005; Button 2007; Prenzler and Sarre 2008; Palmer and Button 2011). Furthermore, there are a number of countries that do not regulate private security, or do not regulate all the private security activities in an industry, or where the enforcement of regulation is minimal. As a consequence, in some countries there are problems with individuals of inappropriate character, namely significant criminal records, working in the private security industry. Other notable problems on a global level include the penetration of security companies by organized crime, and abuse and excessive force (Button and Wakefield 2013). The variability of standards internationally highlights the need for effective regulation and control of the private security industry, although good models do exist. In many European countries the minimum standards for entry occupations such as security officers are in the hundreds of hours of training before working in the industry is allowed (CoESS 2011), and there are also usually standards for specialist roles, supervisors, and managers in these regimes (Prenzler and Sarre 2008).

25.3.7 Harmonization

This final category refers to the prospects for a more fruitful partnership between public and private policing agencies. It is now well recognized that today's interconnected world is inhabited by diverse and complex risks that defy national and agency boundaries, and that partnership working has become a critical aspect of the delivery of security. The deficiencies in the security architecture of the United States prior to 9/11, particularly the barriers to effective communication between agencies, were well documented in the 9/11 Commission (2004) report, and led to significant strategic and operational changes to national security provision. This increased emphasis on partnership working has extended to the local delivery of policing, with one notable example of a public-private partnership being NYPD Shield, a program to promote counterterrorism information sharing and training. A similar model launched in London in 2004, called Project Griffin, has been extended across most of the United Kingdom and exported to a number of other countries including Canada and Australia.

Some time ago, Stenning (1989) presented a typology of reactions by the Canadian police service to the growth of private security, presenting seven distinguishable stages which can equally be applied to the situation in the United States and elsewhere. Progressing through (1) denial, (2) grudging recognition, (3) competition and open hostility, (4) calls for greater controls, (5) mutual suspicion and ambivalence, (6) active partnership, and (7) equal partnership, it can be said that the shift towards stage six is getting increasingly close as the value of public-private partnership is increasingly recognized through the success of strategies such as BIDs and NYPD Shield/Project Griffin. A useful insight into current and prospective future relations between the two sectors in the United Kingdom is provided in a study by Gill, Owen, and Lawson (2010), in which the authors emphasize the growing size and status of private security, and today's mounting challenges for policing, ranging (at the time of this writing) from countering terrorism to planning the security for the 2012 London Olympics. Their research suggests that there remains a lack of mutual understanding between the police and business community, the former prioritizing the prevention, detection, and prosecution of crime, and the latter treating crime as a risk to be managed to the degree and in the manner that makes most economic sense, even if this allows a certain amount of crime to be tolerated. The study participants emphasized the need for better quality interactions between the two sectors to enhance understanding and trust, and allow for better sharing of resources and expertise. With respect to relations between the police and the commercial security sector, it is similarly suggested that a better police understanding of its private sector counterparts needs to be fostered if the police are to make more effective use of them. This aspect of the research focused on the possibilities for more police outsourcing of functions to the private sector, and uncovered a range of barriers relating to the types of roles that might be suitable, lack of knowledge about the capabilities of the private sector as well as its regulation, concern about the possible threat to policing associated with its profit-making orientation, and lack of police confidence in how to undertake effective procurement.

Gill and his colleagues (2010) see opportunities for much more effective partnership working between the two sectors. They relate this not only to the new crime and security imperatives referred to above, but also to the pressures on police forces associated with a continued rising demand for service, and the need to find new efficiencies in the face of reductions in public spending. Their recommendations propose some of the steps needing to be taken for the UK's police to move closer to realizing Stenning's (1989) sixth stage of acceptance of private security more fully, and to shift closer to that of equal partnership, likely to be equally applicable to inter-agency workings within the United States.

25.4 CONCLUSION

The increased reliance on privatized forms of policing, most substantially the *de facto* privatization that has occurred as the private security industry has expanded in size and profile, has a number of implications. First, it is important to note the significant contribution that private security makes, providing services that are essential to public safety and which, if the private sector did not provide them, would in many cases not be supplied at all. The private security industry can be a strong partner to the state to enhance the overall resilience to crime and terrorism, as in the case of NYPD Shield and Project

Griffin. There is also a compelling argument, based on the established practices of outsourcing that are especially prevalent in the United Kingdom, that in some circumstances the private sector can supply an equal or even better service to the state at a lower cost. This brings benefits to society as a whole, particularly in an era of fiscal constraint.

At the same time, it would be wrong to ignore some of the challenges associated with private security. Globally, standards vary considerably and are associated with vastly different degrees of regulation. At its worst, private security is blighted by criminal infiltration, little or no training for security personnel, abuses of authority including the excessive use of force, and generally low standards of professionalism. Yet it must also be acknowledged that such problems are also entrenched in many countries' police forces and, in the absence of effective state policing, for many citizens around the world private security offers a far better alternative.

What is certain is that both public and private policing are rapidly evolving against a backdrop of significant and ongoing political and economic change. Neither the providers of security nor those who study them can stand still. Police studies scholars need to recognize the changes and their implications in terms of the functions of policing and who delivers these, which will vary from one jurisdiction to the next. They must also take into account the ramifications for the oversight and accountability of policing agencies, both public and private, as well as the partnerships they are entering into. Private interests and private actors have become an important dimension of the character of contemporary policing, and their role is likely only to grow.

Notes

1. Table 25.1 is adapted from Hakala (2010).

References

9/11 Commission. 2004. *The 9/11 Commission Report*. Washington, DC: National Commission on Terrorist Attacks upon the United States.

Abaza, Mona. 2001. "Shopping Malls, Consumer Culture and the Reshaping of Public Space in Egypt." *Theory, Culture and Society* 18: 97–122.

Bayley, D., and C. Shearing. 2001. *The New Structure of Policing: Description, Conceptualization and Research Agenda*. Washington, DC: National Institute of Justice.

Bayley, David H., and Clifford D. Shearing. 1996. "The Future of Policing." *Law and Society Review* 30:585–606.

Bottoms, Anthony E., and Paul Wiles. 1994. "Crime and Insecurity in the City." Paper presented at the International Society of Criminology International Course on Changes in Society, Crime and Criminal Justice in Europe, Leuven, Belgium (May).

Boyd, Edward, Rory Geoghegan, and Blair Gibbs. 2011. *Cost of the Cops: Manpower and Deployment in Policing*. London: Policy Exchange.

Briggs, Rachel. 2005. *Joining Forces: From National Security to Networked Security*. London: Demos.

Brodeur, Jean Paul. 2010. *The Policing Web*. Oxford: Oxford University Press.

Bryett, Keith. 1996. "Privatization-Variation on a Theme." *Policing and Society* 6:23–37.

Button, Mark. 2007. "Assessing the Regulation of Private Security Across Europe." *European Journal of Criminology* 4:109–28.

Button, Mark, and Alison Wakefield. Forthcoming, 2013. "Police or Policing? The Privatization of Policing in an International Context." In *Encyclopedia of Criminology and Criminal Justice*, edited by Gerben Bruinsma and David Weisburd. New York: Springer Verlag.

Caldeira, Teresa P.R. 1996. "Building Up Walls: The New Pattern of Spatial Segregation in San Paolo." *International Social Science Journal* 48:55–66.

Cavanagh, Thomas E., and Meredith Whiting. 2003. *Corporate Security Management: Organization and Spending since 9/11*. New York: The Conference Board.

CoESS. 2008. *Private Security and Its Role in European Security*. Paris: Confederation of European Security Services/Institut National des Hautes Études de Sécurité.

———. 2011. *Private Security Services in Europe: COESS Facts and Figures 2011*. Wemmel, Belgium: Confederation of European Security Services.

CoESS/UNI-Europa. 2004. *Panoramic Overview of Private Security Industry in the 25 Member States of the European Union*. Wemmel, Belgium: Confederation of European Security Services (CoESS) and UNI-Europa.

Cook, Ian R. 2009. "Private Sector Involvement in Urban Governance: The Case of Business Improvement Districts and Town Centre Management Partnerships in England." *Geoforum* 40:930–40.

Cook, Ian R., and Kevin Ward. 2012. "Conferences, Informational Infrastructures and Mobile Policies: The Process of Getting Sweden 'BID ready.'" *European Urban and Regional Studies* 19:137–52.

Couch, Stephen R. 1987. "Selling and Reclaiming State Sovereignty: The Case of Coal and Iron Police." *The Insurgent Sociologist* 4:85–91.

Crawford, Adam, Stuart Lister, Sarah Blackburn, and Jonathan Burnett. 2005. *Plural Policing: The Mixed Economy of Visible Patrols in England and Wales*. Bristol, UK: Policy Press.

Cunningham, William Clay, and Todd H. Taylor. 1985. *The Hallcrest Report: Private Security and Police in America*. Portland, OR: Chancellor.

Davis, Mike. 1998. *City of Quartz: Excavating the Future in Los Angeles*. London: Pimlico.

Draper, Hilary. 1978. *Private Police*. Markham, Ontario: Penguin Books.

Farnell, Margaret B., and Clifford D. Shearing. 1977. *Private Security: An Examination of Canadian Statistics, 1961–1971*. Toronto: Centre of Criminology, University of Toronto.

Freedonia. 2012. *Security Products to 2016*. Cleveland, OH: Freedonia.

G4S. 2013. "Where We Operate." http://www.g4s.com/en/.

Gans, Jeremy. 2000. "Privately Paid Policing: Law and Practice." *Policing and Society* 10:183–207.

Gill, Martin, Katy Owen, and Chappell Lawson. 2010. *Private Security, the Corporate Sector and the Police*. Leicester, UK: Perpetuity Research and Consultancy International.

Guardian. 2012a. "Blackwater Guards Lose Bid to Appeal Charges in Iraqi Civilian Shooting Case" (June 5). http://www.guardian.co.uk/world/2012/jun/05/blackwater-guards-lose-appeal-iraq-shooting.

———. 2012b. "G4S Boss Discovered Olympic Security Guard Shortfall Only a Few Days Ago" (July 14). http://www.guardian.co.uk/sport/2012/jul/14/london-2012-olympic-security-g4s.

Hakala, Jorma. 2010. *Definition of Private Security Services*. Wemmel, Belgium: Confederation of European Security Services.

Hearnden, Keith. 1993. *The Management of Security in the UK*. Loughborough, UK: University of Loughborough.

Hobbs, Dick, Philip Hadfield, Stuart Lister, and Simon Winlow. 2003. *Bouncers: Violence and Governance in the Night-time Economy*. Oxford: Oxford University Press.

Johnston, Les. 2000. *Policing Britain: Risk, Security and Governance*. Harlow, UK: Longman.

——. 1992. *The Rebirth of Private Policing*. London: Routledge.

Jones, Trevor. 2009. "Auxiliary Police." In *The Sage Dictionary of Policing*, edited by Alison Wakefield and Jenny Fleming, 8–10. London: Sage.

Jones, Trevor, and Tim Newburn. 1998. *Private Security and Public Policing*. Oxford: Clarendon Press.

——. 2006. *Plural Policing: A Comparative Perspective*. London: Routledge.

Kakalik, James S., and Sorrel Wildhorn. 1971. *Private Security in the United States*. Santa Monica, CA: Rand Corporation.

——. 1977. *The Private Police: Security and Danger*. New York: Crane Russak.

Malochet, Virgina. 2007. *Les Policiers Municipaux. Paris: Le Monde, Partage du Savoir*. Paris: Presses Universitaires de France.

McManus, Michael. 1995. *From Fate to Choice: Private Bobbies, Public Beats*. Aldershot: Avebury.

Noaks, Lesley. 2000. "Private Cops on the Block: A Review of the Role of Private Security in Residential Communities." *Policing and Society* 10:143–61.

Palmer, Robin W., and Mark Button. 2011. *Civilian Private Security Services: Their Role, Oversight and Contribution to Crime Prevention and Community Safety*. Expert Group on Civilian Private Security Services. Vienna: United Nations Office on Drugs and Crime.

Pirie, Madsen. 1988. *Privatization*. Aldershot: Wildwood House.

Prenzler, Tim. 2009. "Private Security." In *The Sage Dictionary of Policing*, edited by Alison Wakefield and Jenny Fleming, 241–243. London: Sage.

Prenzler, Tim, and Rick Sarre. 2008. "Developing a Risk Profile and Model Regulatory System for the Security Industry." *Security Journal* 21:264–77.

Reiss, Albert J. 1988. *Private Employment of Public Police*. Washington, DC: U.S. Department of Justice, National Institute of Justice.

Rigakos, George S. 2002. *The New Parapolice: Risk Markets and Commodified Social Control*. Toronto: University of Toronto Press.

Sarre, Rick, and Tim Prenzler. 2005. *The Law of Private Security in Australia*. Pyrmont, NSW: Thomson.

Saunders, Peter, and Colin Harris. 1990. "Privatization and the Consumer." *Sociology* 24:57–75.

Securitas. 2013a. "About Securitas" (April 1). http://www.securitas.com/en/.

——. 2013b. "Our History" (April 4). http://www.securitas.com/en/.

Shearing, Clifford D., Margaret B. Farnell, and Philip C. Stenning. 1980. *Contract Security in Ontario*. Toronto: Centre of Criminology, University of Toronto.

Shearing, Clifford D., and Philip C. Stenning. 1981. "Modern Private Security: Its Growth and Implications." In *Crime and Justice: An Annual Review of Research*, edited by Michael Tonry and Norval Morris, 193–245. Chicago: University of Chicago Press.

——. 1983. "Private Security: Implications for Social Control." *Social Problems* 30:493–506.

——. 1987. *Private Policing*. Santa Monica, CA: Sage.

——. 2012. "The Shifting Boundaries of Policing: Globalization and its Possibilities." In *Policing: Politics, Culture, and Control*, edited by Tim Newburn and Jill Peay, 265–284. Oxford: Hart Publishing.

South, Nigel. 1988. *Policing for Profit*. Newbury Park, CA: Sage.

Spitzer, Steven, and Andrew T. Scull. 1977. "Privatization and Capitalist Development: The Case of Private Police." *Social Problems* 25:18–29.

Stenning, Philip C. 1989. "Private Police and Public Police: Toward a Redefinition of the Police Role." In Future Issues in Policing: Symposium Proceedings, edited by Donald J. Loree, 169–192. Ontario, Canada: Police College.

U.S. Committee on Education and Labour. 1971. *Private Police Systems*. New York: Arno Press and the New York Times.

Wakefield, Alison. 2003. *Selling Security: The Private Policing of Public Space*. Cullompton, Devon: Willan.

Wakefield, Alison, and Mark Button. Forthcoming, 2013. "New Perspectives on Police Education and Training: Lessons from the Private Security Sector." In *International Perspectives on Police Education and Training*, edited by Perry Stanislas. London: Routledge.

Wakefield, Alison, and Tim Prenzler. 2009. "Privatization." In *The Sage Dictionary of Policing*, edited by Alison Wakefield and Jenny Fleming, 243–246. London: Sage.

Weiss, Robert P. 1978. "The Emergence and Transformation of Private Detective and Industrial Policing in the United States, 1850–1940." *Crime and Social Justice* 1:35–48.

——. 1986. "Private Detective Agencies and Labour Discipline in the United States, 1855–1946." *The Historical Journal* 29:87–107.

White, Adam, and Martin Gill. 2013. "The Transformation of Policing: From Ratios to Rationalities." *British Journal of Criminology* 53:74–93.

CHAPTER 26

THE POLICING OF SPACE: NEW REALITIES, OLD DILEMMAS

STEVE HERBERT

ON a sunny weekday afternoon in August of 2010, Ian Burk, an officer with the Seattle Police Department, was alone in his patrol car, cruising the streets just north of the downtown core. Stopped at a traffic light, Burk witnessed a middle-aged man, John Williams, crossing the street in front of him. Williams had a piece of wood in one hand, a small carving knife in the other. Intent on his carving, Williams walked with his head down.

Concerned about the knife, Officer Burk exited his car. As he crossed in front of his car walking toward Williams, his gun was already drawn. He barked three quick demands to Williams to drop his knife. A split second after his last such command, he shot Williams four times. Only seven seconds elapsed between Burk's initial shout of "Hey" to Williams and the fatal bullets.

Unsurprisingly, the case ignited controversy. Williams, it turned out, was a common figure on downtown's streets. A chronic alcoholic, he frequented several locations around the downtown core, most notably Victor Steinbrueck Park, located next to Seattle's iconic Pike Place Market. There he commonly gathered with other American Indians, many of whom shared his passion for wood carving. At the moment of his death, in fact, he was walking to that park to join his brother for a carving session, both of them intent on preserving a family tradition.

Other Seattle Police Department (SPD) officers indicated in press reports that they knew Williams, given his ubiquity on the streets. They described him as a gentle individual, one unlikely to threaten the police. And, indeed, the SPD's internal investigation of the shooting ruled it unjustified. Burk was found in violation of department policy on several counts: a failure to request backup before handling a potentially dangerous situation; a failure to properly identify himself to Williams; a failure to allow Williams to respond; and a premature exercise of deadly force.

Burk, however, did not face criminal charges for conduct that Seattle Police Assistant Chief Clark Kimmerer, a 30-year police veteran, described as "the most egregious failings that I have seen." That is because Washington state law requires that officers only be charged with murder or manslaughter if they act with demonstrable malice. Given this legal hurdle, the King County District Attorney declined to press charges against Burk. Unhappily for Burk, news of the prosecutor's decision was followed quickly by release of the results of the SPD investigation. Aware that he was likely to be fired, Burk immediately resigned.

These events strongly impacted Seattle. Street protests of the decision not to charge Burk erupted in the days following the announcement. The City of Seattle settled a lawsuit filed against it by the family of John Williams, paying out a reported $1.5 million. Members of the carving community spent the summer of 2011 creating a totem pole in Williams's honor along the Seattle waterfront. The Seattle Police Department made several promises to improve its training procedures, the better to avoid similar outcomes in the future.

In one view, the case of Ian Burk is an anomaly. Deadly force is rarely used by police officers. Even rarer are instances where officers so blatantly violate expected procedure, and incur the level of public shame directed at Burk. If anything, police misconduct is arguably too rarely punished, in Seattle and elsewhere, given the manifold difficulties that attend to police accountability measures (Walker 2001, 2005).

Yet Burk's case illustrates many of the central tensions that unavoidably adhere to the police's role in modern society. In his mobile police car, Burk represented the now-expected insertion of state authority into the flow of everyday life. Burk was amply endowed to exercise the capacity for violence that normally lies hidden behind the law. This violence should be exercised sparingly, else the legitimacy of law will wither. The outcry that accompanied the shooting illustrates the public expectation that police coercion will be wisely deployed. In this instance, Burk's recourse to violence was widely denigrated.

Yet it is not entirely surprising that state law prevented a prosecution. That is because the police are more typically heralded for their willingness to embrace danger (Manning 1977; Herbert 1996). They are regularly viewed as society's protectors, as the "thin blue line" separating order from chaos. In deference to this moral authority and to the reality that officers can find themselves in quickly-developing situations that require instantaneous and sometimes imperfect decisions, legislators understandably seek to protect the police from criminal prosecutions that can too easily rely on hindsight. In short, the public alternately fears, respects, and celebrates the deadly force that officers can deploy as they insinuate themselves into the fabric of urban space.

These conflicting views of police violence are mirrored by conflicting views about police technology. Again, Burk's case is illustrative. In his patrol car, Burk was able to access extensive databases of criminal records. He was able to communicate immediately with a dispatcher and his fellow officers, in a fashion that enabled a swift response to the scene after the shooting. And many of his actions were captured by a video camera mounted on his dashboard. It was that video that showed Williams crossing the street and Burk's initial approach, with his gun drawn. Although the shooting was off-camera, the audio captured his commands to Williams and the fatal shots.

This technological sophistication is now commonplace and enables policing to be more efficient and coordinated. It also enables the police to be more easily held accountable. In the absence of the video and audio record of Burk's behavior, his narrative of the extreme danger he faced might have escaped rigorous challenge. At the same time, more sophisticated technology furthers the project of enhanced surveillance, and hence amplifies concerns about an overly-intrusive government. Burk, like other police officers, was not only equipped for violence but existed as a component of an increasingly intensive web of networked communications that can track individuals to an unprecedented degree. As with police violence, the technological sophistication of contemporary policing can alternately soothe and frighten the population.

These concerns about violence and technology raise profound and intractable questions about where to locate the police, both literally and figuratively. In literal terms, we can ask just where we want the police to be in physical space. How ever-present should they be? Should they be in some neighborhoods more frequently than others? What barriers should exist between them and the population? How extensive should be their technological reach? In figurative terms, we can ask how we should situate the police in social space. Can Officer Burk be faulted for not knowing more about the character of John Williams? Should we expect officers to know their beats intimately, as adherents of community policing would expect? Or should officers be more detached and hence presumably be less tempted to violate standardized norms of professionalism? And who gets to determine the basic parameters of police practice? The citizenry, through community forums, civilian review boards, or even street protests? Elected officials? The police themselves?

I use this essay to explore intractable questions such as these, ones inextricably connected to the policing of space. These questions possess a long historical legacy, emerging alongside the first officers walking their beats. They persisted throughout the various waves of police reform movements. And they will invariably linger well into the future, even as policing threatens to become yet more technologically-sophisticated and as various police reforms promise to come and go. The police possess a series of social roles characterized by an ambivalence that resists resolution.

Importantly, all of these questions about the proper role of the police in urban space are shaped by underlying issues about how that space is defined. Most notably, the ways in which officers understand the spaces they oversee often contrast sharply with those of the citizens they police. This is especially the case when police rely on technology, which often implicitly views space largely in technocratic terms, as an empty series of coordinates. This can differ quite notably from how residents view space. Connected to place through daily patterns of use and often-deep attachments, residents can chafe when the police intrude in brusque and seemingly insensitive fashion. As the officers organize themselves to fulfill their sense of mission, they sometimes can run afoul of localized meanings of space, and thereby amplify the tensions inherent in modern policing.

I explore these issues through three sections. In Section 26.1, I discuss the key historic dynamics that most critically shaped the role of the police in physical space, from the emergence of uniformed beat officers to contemporary deployments of sophisticated cartographic capabilities. In Section 26.2, I review how the intractable dilemmas that flare in debates about the proper role for the police in urban neighborhoods are made more tangled by differing conceptions of urban space. In Section 26.3, I examine some interesting new arenas where modern policing is emerging, most notably in its increased roles in the regulation of immigration and of behavior on the oceans. Yet here, again, the dilemmas of policing follow officers like a shadow. Ambivalent attitudes will orbit around the use of the police to regulate space and guarantee a politics of the geography of policing that can be inflamed quickly and robustly.

The essay draws several conclusions about the processes or policing space:

- The control of geographic territory, both through delineating boundaries and managing people within geographic locations, remains central to the police function.
- The public is necessarily ambivalent about the coercive power of police and their capacity for surveillance, and hence a complicated politics attends to efforts to regulate the police.
- The politics of the spatial regulatory tactics of the police are often underwritten by conflicting views of place.
- The inherent tensions of the policing of space can be seen in new arenas where spatial regulation is increasingly common, such as efforts to control immigration and to control behavior on the oceans.

26.1 Approaches to the Policing of Space

The regulation of space is central to the modern state. Through various mechanisms—such as mapping and grid making (Johnson, 1976; Anderson 1991; Blomley 2003), census taking (Hannah 2000) and immigration regulation (Nevins 2001; Coleman 2007; Varsanyi 2008a)—the modern state creates itself as it delimits the spaces it claims to rule. Indeed, the modern state is unimaginable absent such spatial demarcations (Giddens 1987; Mann 1988; Murphy 1996); its legitimacy rests centrally upon its ability to control its territory (Herbert 2008). The state's capacity to exercise coercive power enables it to secure its territorial claims with violence, if necessary (Weber 1964; Cover 1986).

The police are vital to the internal regulation of the modern state. As societies became more industrialized and urbanized in the late 1700s and early 1800s, the resultant class divisions and general chaos motivated efforts to generate order. The police were one critical component of these efforts to create order, with the bobbies of London emerging as symbols of the modern state (Miller 1977). Although the legitimacy of the police was something of a tenuous accomplishment in the early years, especially in the tyranny-fearing United States, uniformed officers were eventually accepted. As Silver (1967, 8) puts it, the police ultimately became an institution that carried a power that can be "widely diffused throughout civil society in small and discretionary operations that are capable of rapid concentration."

Of course, the legitimacy of the state—and its coercive power—is never a settled matter. As a consequence, any concerns about the power of the state on the part of the citizenry are often projected onto the police. This general concern about state power has frequently been magnified by particular concerns about police performance. In the United States, for instance, the police of the urban political machines of the mid- to late-1800s were especially scorned. This was because of their tendencies to treat their bosses' friends rather better than their bosses' enemies, and their general organizational inefficiencies (Fogelson 1977; Walker 1977). These critiques of the police helped motivate Progressive Era reforms to make the police better organized and more insulated from politics. These reforms came eventually to coalesce into the Professional Movement. As epitomized by William Parker's Los Angeles Police Department, and the paradigmatic TV detective Sgt. Joe Friday, the professional police sought "just the facts," when they encountered citizens, and otherwise kept themselves aloof from community affairs. This presumably allowed the police to be less corruptible and more beholden to professionalized norms of proper and effective practice (Woods 1973; Gazell 1976).

Effective police practice in the Professional era came not just from greater loyalty to bureaucratic procedures but also more ardent use of technology. With ample numbers of patrol cars available for quick dispatch, and increasingly sophisticated detection capacities, such as fingerprint and ballistic analysis, the professional police were touted as a force able to notably reduce crime. Perpetrators would either be caught in the act or apprehended after the fact to a degree that would allegedly deter future criminality. In this fashion, a strong connection between police performance and state-of-the-art technology was forged, a connection that remains robust.

Although popularized by the TV show *Dragnet*, the technologically-sophisticated professional ideal for police organization and practice did not lack for critics. The professional police were sometimes seen as too detached, unable and unwilling to understand life inside urban neighborhoods. Some of the citizenry were arguably less willing to engage with the police and hence to share detailed information about street-level dynamics. This attitude was arguably more present in disadvantaged neighborhoods, where often brusque policing was rarely counterbalanced with public relations efforts, a reality that likely contributed to much urban unrest in the 1960s (Stark 1972). Trapped inside their patrol cars, and perhaps overeager to look to technology rather than the simple art of conversation, the police were sometimes seen as something of an occupying force rather than an integral part of the social fabric. When much of Los Angeles was engulfed in unrest following the acquittals of the four officers accused of deploying excessive force while apprehending the motorist Rodney King, the Professional movement was arguably over.

In its stead came community policing (Greene and Mastrofski 1988; Skolnick and Bayley 1988; Kappeler and Gaines 2009). This reform model encouraged the police to actively pursue stronger connections within urban neighborhoods. Officers would walk foot beats, ride bicycles and horses, staff mini-stations, and otherwise get out of their patrol cars to mingle more freely with the populace. Those on patrol would be assigned to beats for extended periods of time, the better to know a given neighborhood and its residents. Officers would no longer ignore issues they previously considered trivial, such as loud neighbors and stray litter, but instead would work cooperatively with the citizenry and other city agencies to solve whatever problems captivated a neighborhood's attention. The aloof "just the facts" officer would become more friendly and versatile.

Yet community policing became no more a political panacea for the police than any other model for police organization. The police demonstrated stubborn difficulties in listening closely to the citizens and maintained an allegiance to the serious crime-fighting ideal (Lyons 1999; Skogan and Hartnett 1999; Herbert 2006). Indeed, the rise of community policing was accompanied by the emergence of broken-windows policing (Kelling and Coles 1998; Harcourt 2001), which in its more testosterone-fueled versions became zero-tolerance policing, as epitomized by New York City during the 1990s (Bratton and Knobler 1998; Silverman 1999). Although sometimes mistakenly conflated with community policing (Herbert 2001), broken-windows and zero-tolerance policing demanded a more intrusive and often heavy-handed police presence. As behaviors such as sitting, sleeping, and begging became criminalized through civility codes (Mitchell 1997; Gibson 2004), the police became more active in making arrests and otherwise inserting themselves into the lives of the downtrodden. In cities like Seattle, the police are now able to make arrests quite easily, due to the rise of various forms of spatial exclusion (Beckett and Herbert 2010). Thousands of individuals are barred from particular spaces. All an officer needs to do to make an arrest is simply observe a banished individual in the wrong place. Easier arrests are hard to imagine.

These broken-windows-justified techniques were accompanied, as well, by the more regular use of sophisticated geographic information systems. With these cartographic tools, the police are presumably better able to map where crime is occurring and hence to deploy their officers more thoughtfully (Paulsen and Robinson 2008; Ratcliffe 2008; Paynich and Hill 2009). Again, New York City was paradigmatic, with its use of CompStat, a practice that required that police commanders be held accountable for shifts in crime patterns in their areas of supervision, patterns more easily tracked through geo-coded data. This process was soon emulated elsewhere (Willis, Mastrofski, and Weisburd 2007).

In this way, the quest for the best technological means to pursue the police mission continues unabated. It is further fueled by the use of ever more sophisticated means to conduct surveillance. These techniques continually develop. The contemporary police car is laden with various means of communication and information retrieval. Most cars include a computer terminal that allows the quick acquisition of data regarding an individual's criminal history and the specifics of any outstanding warrants. Similar data about automobiles and their owners are also easily available. In this way, officers are able to speedily ascertain whether a given individual or car might be an object of concern.

But police surveillance can be more intrusive and omnipresent. Police sometimes seek to use monitors that they attach to the car of a criminal suspect. Such a monitor would enable the police to track the suspect's movements, and hence presumably to ascertain his/her involvement in alleged criminal enterprises. Recently, the US Supreme Court ruled that such monitors cannot be attached without a search warrant, a reflection of widespread anxiety about overly intrusive police watchfulness. Similar concern sometimes arises from the implementation of Closed Circuit Television (CCTV) in public areas. By now ubiquitous in cities in the United Kingdom and popular elsewhere, CCTV cameras make possible the continual surveillance of frequently-used public spaces. CCTV proponents argue that cameras can help create more secure public environments by detecting and deterring crime. This, in turn, makes people feel safer and thus more likely to make consumption-oriented visits to city centers (Coleman and Sim 2000; Coleman, Tombs, and Whyte 2005). Whether CCTV actually deters crime is another story. Evidence suggests that CCTV is most effective at controlling not serious crimes, but low-level crimes like car prowls (Welsh and Farrington 2009) or at reducing activities which are not always illegal, such as loitering (Williams and Johnstone 2000). Much as is the case with the simple presence of the police, the insertion of surveillance mechanisms into everyday life can be reassuring to some and frightening to others, all the while demonstrating a questionable degree of effectiveness.

Thus, as various reform movements come and go, and as technology shifts, regnant questions persist about the policing of space. As officers make themselves a ubiquitous presence in the city, ambivalence about their coercive authority travels with them. An aloof professional officer arguably resists corruptibility but slaps too few backs to understand local dynamics. A community police officer shares ice cream at a social but implicitly challenges the crime fighter ideal embraced within the subculture. A technologically-sophisticated officer can learn much about criminal suspects in a given area but may know more than is Constitutionally—or morally—permissible. In short, there is no resolution to long-standing questions about how the police should be structured, how they should exercise their authority, and how they should be regulated. Advances in technology and other shifts only exacerbate the challenges of finding the right balance between police power and citizen sovereignty. To make matters more complicated, debates about these issues are often fueled by disagreements about how to best define urban space, disagreements which are often submerged. In the next section, I seek to bring them to light.

26.2 Regulating The Policing of Space

Even if the presence of officers in the fabric of everyday life is now an accepted part of modern society, the symbolic significance of the police's power remains contested. At some times and in some places, the police are avidly welcomed and heartily celebrated. Yet other situations may birth rather less enthusiasm. In minority-dominated neighborhoods, in particular, police presence may magnify social tensions more than minimize them (Skogan 2006; Weitzer and Tuch 2006). The generalized tensions surrounding the coercive capacities of the police can take compelling shape in specific places.

There are multiple factors at play here, all of which contribute to the politics of the policing of space. A useful way to capture many of these factors is to consider how space is being socially constructed. Of special significance are views of space developed by the police, on the one hand, and by urban residents, on the other. If these contrast, then tensions between the police and the citizenry are likely to perpetuate. Matters become even more complicated when one considers the implicit view of space inherent in the technologies upon which the police increasingly rely. Especially notable here are the epistemologies that underlie the geographic information systems used to generate the crime maps that are meant to determine police behavior. Here, space becomes an abstract plain upon data are projected. This more technocratic and scientific vision of space may not cohere with visions possessed by either the police or the citizenry.

For the police, their views of space are most significantly shaped by the internalized norms and regularized practices of their somewhat insular and particularistic culture. These norms and practices are clearly as important to the police's spatial constructions as the realities of the neighborhoods through which they cruise (Herbert 1997). For instance, officers are socialized to value safety highly, and hence are trained to take manifold measures to protect themselves. For this reason, when they are in areas where police-community relations are tense, they are more likely to take precautionary steps to minimize the possibility of harm, including "pat down" searches of those whom officers suspect of bearing arms. They are also socialized to value the courage required to insert themselves into dangerous situations, particularly in neighborhoods where tensions with the police are strong. In these "anti-police" areas, officers are more likely to engage in regular surveillance and to approach citizens with more caution. These normative emphases on safety and courage can become exaggerated, to the point where officers are overly aggressive and thereby worsen tensions with the citizenry (Chemerinsky 2005). When such questionable tactics are used, and police excesses occur, officers often protect each other through collective silence (Independent Commission on the Los Angeles Police Department 1991).

Bureaucratic routines also condition police constructions of space. Where one sits in the bureaucracy often conditions where one goes, and what one notices. A patrol officer may be confined to a particular area and be on the lookout for any evidence of criminal wrongdoing. A narcotics officer, by contrast, may focus solely on particular areas hoping to witness illegal commerce. One's bureaucratic place will also determine the types of interactions one has with citizens, from episodic encounters by patrol officers to attendance at public forums by command staff. For commanders, these expected public interfaces leave them more aware of the politicized environment in which the police operate and provide them opportunities to attempt to demonstrate accountability to the public.

Yet just whether and how the police choose to respond to public input is never straightforward. Evidence from studies of community policing, for instance, demonstrate that the police are not as responsive as residents might ideally like (Lyons 1999; Skogan and Hartnett 1999; Herbert 2006). This illustrates, in significant part, the stronghold that entrenched norms and regularized practices exert on the police. It also illustrates how residents might see space differently from the police. For starters, urban residents do not typically evince much interest in creating strong community bonds with their neighbors, as advocates of community policing might ideally hope. That is why there is rarely a solid foundation within an alleged community upon which the police could build stronger practices of informal social control (Herbert 2005). Beyond this, urban residents develop more particularized attachments to particular areas, and oftentimes quite nuanced understandings of local dynamics. In this fashion, they can be said to see their areas of frequent use more as places than as spaces (Tuan 1977; Entrikin 1991). They are not nodes on a Euclidean grid, but repositories of symbolic connection and rich personal experience. As residents' time-space patterns become regularized, their connections to place intensify. As a consequence, strong-armed police intrusions into an area can rankle residents. If officers display an insensitivity to the particularities of place and fail to make adequate distinctions between the criminally-intent and the merely annoying, then residents might ardently question police practice.

Take, as an example, the practices of banishment in Seattle. As interviews with those who are excluded from large swaths of downtown demonstrate, police efforts at exclusion mostly backfire. Even if individuals are homeless and thus seemingly transient, they still develop strong connections to the neighborhoods they frequent. Indeed, for some people, their geographic ranges can be as small as the eight square block area where they can regularly find the resources necessary to meet their needs for food, shelter, and health care. The lack of permanent shelter, in other words, does not mean that people lack a deep attachment to place (Herbert and Beckett 2010). Even if legally excluded, they persist in place, a reality that seems to escape serious police understanding.

Thus, police views of space often contradict those held by urban citizens, further inflaming the persistent tensions that accompany the modern police. These tensions are made even more notable by any presumed police reliance on technology. As noted, this reliance is increasing, most significantly by the more regular use of sophisticated geographic information systems (GIS). These enable the cartographic display of extensive databases. For the police, this means that they can presumably track crime patterns in greater detail and with greater accuracy. This could then enable departments to target their resources on particular "hot spots" (Braga 2005; Braga and Weisburd 2010).

In theory, GIS enable multiple layers of data to be mapped onto a particular space. It is therefore feasible that more sophisticated and comprehensive views of space can be developed by the police through the use of these technologies. However, at its core, a GIS constructs space as a set of abstract grids onto which data are projected (Curry 1998; Miller and Wentz 2003; Graham 2005). This is essentially a view of space as a container, one that can be filled or emptied (Sack 1986). To embrace GIS is thus implicitly to embrace a largely technocratic and thin vision of space. Only certain variables about an area are selected for mapping, and projected onto a grid. The lived, place-based experience of residents, constructed over years and through countless street-level experiences and interactions, cannot be captured in this fashion.

Further, this reliance on GIS-mapped data can legitimate geographically-differentiated police practice. Police can largely ignore some areas, and mobilize intensive operations in others. Indeed, this is the central focus of "intelligence-led" policing (Ratcliffe 2008). That this practice can lead to robust justifications for geographic profiling (Rossomo 1999) illustrates how tensions between the police and particular neighborhoods might only intensify through reliance on geo-spatial technologies. This will especially be the case where the police fail to consult neighborhood residents before deploying them in more intensive fashion. One potential, if unintended, consequence of this approach to deploying police resources could well be the intensification of already well-entrenched racial disparities in the criminal justice system (Beckett, Nyrop, and Pfingst 2006).

So, the abstract view of space inherent in GIS may contrast notably with the more nuanced and rich views of place developed by neighborhood residents. But it may contrast just as much with police views of space. Evidence from some studies, for instance, suggests that the implementation of CompStat and problem-oriented policing changes very little in police practice (Cordner and Biebel 2005; Willis, Mastrofski and Weisburd 2007; Manning 2008). Such programs can be resource- and labor-intensive, and they can compete with other legitimate demands for police service. These are considerable obstacles, to be sure. Perhaps even more significant is the fact that how the police choose to view and patrol space is largely determined by their well-established routines and cultural systems of meaning. New approaches to policing require a culture of innovation to work effectively. This runs against ingrained practices of following orders and abiding by well-worn bureaucratic routines (Willis, Mastrokski, and Weisburd 2003). No matter how much academics might wish for more rational and ostensibly scientific approaches to guide police decision making, departments may find it too easy to simply repeat past practice.

Part of this perpetuation of past practice, according to Peter Manning (2008), lies in the simple repetition of routines, most notably routines that emphasize immediate experience. In his comparison of three police departments' use of computer-based mapping, Manning detected little change in police behavior as a consequence of new technologies. As he summarizes it (2008, 260): "The entire organization is shadowed by the incident focus of the patrol division and the salience of the here and now. This makes gathering systematic needed information that reflects past decisions, aggregated materials, or future planning something of a crisis." In other words, the processes of pattern detection and long-range planning so necessary to make effective use of crime mapping remain alien to most police departments, and hence the potential promise of new technology remains unrealized.

In sum, then, many of the persistent issues and tensions that accompany the policing of space stem from just how different spaces might be defined. Officers construct space through the ongoing use of cultural norms institutionalized through routine practices; residents use daily patterns of use and often deep senses of attachment; mapping software packages construct abstract grids onto which various data points are projected. That these constructions often fail to cohere means that the inherent tensions that attach to police power resist any easy resolution. That these tensions are so entrenched is further illustrated by focusing on the work of the police in two arenas attracting increasing attention—in regulating migration, and in regulating behavior on the oceans.

26.3 New Policing Frontiers, Same Old Issues

The policing of immigration is a very contentious issue at present, and very much so in the United States. Increasingly defined in terms of their illegality (Nevins 2001), undocumented migrants attract notable scorn from many quarters. Efforts to deter them include more intensive formal and informal patrolling at the border, efforts sometimes enhanced by more extensive walling. These efforts along borders, however, are increasingly augmented by policing efforts in the interior. Most of these occur inside the borders of the United States, although some efforts occur inside the countries of origin of the migrants, like Mexico (Coleman 2007).

Yet even if this policing is welcomed in many places, it remains contentious. Much of the controversy concerns police power. For many, the presumed scourge of undocumented migration means that all available police resources should be devoted to the apprehension of those without formal permission to migrate. That means doing everything possible to empower local police agents to monitor and detain anyone suspected of improper migration. This might mean passing ordinances that restrict gatherings that attract undocumented individuals, such as day laborer sites (Varsanyi 2008b). It also might mean enabling police officers to seek documentation whenever they encounter anyone they suspect of being undocumented. Provisions enabling these practices are central components of recent law in some states, most notably Arizona and Alabama.

Such provisions are quite controversial, largely because they seem to displace authority for immigration enforcement from the federal government to local police agencies. But they also raise the perennial questions that attach to debates about just what role we wish the police to play. Should the police be this intrusive? Should they use something like a routine traffic stop as a means to determine immigration status (Coleman 2012)? Might such police presence lead migrant communities to avoid any interaction with the police, and hence restrict police awareness of criminal activities (Skogan 2006)? Once again, we are left wondering just where to situate the police, in both physical and political space.

We are also left recognizing how the brute assertion of police presence can obliterate more capacious understandings of those who are policed. Undocumented migrants possess stories that are richer than the blunt category of "illegal" can capture. They are in the United States or any other locale for a wide variety of reasons, including impoverishment that may well stem from globalized dynamics from which the United States principally benefits (Nevins 2007). They occupy jobs that citizens may well shun, such as the brutal work in meat-packing plants. And they hardly prosper from the lack of documentation, instead inhabiting a shadowy world of rights-less invisibility (Coutin 2000). In short, the connections to place forged by many migrants are more multi-faceted than the police seem to understand.

Similar ambiguities about the nature of policing attend to the increasing role of regulation on the open sea. For centuries, oceans have resisted easy political categorization. As a consequence, it has not always been clear just who can or should assume authority for regulating sea-based activities (Steinberg 2001). In recent years, a growing trend has emerged to make ocean governance more clear and effective, alternately termed "marine spatial management" or "ocean zoning." The central idea is simple: if zoning is a beneficial governmental project on land, so can it be on water. Ocean zoning, like land-based zoning, could help to separate different activities and to generate greater efficiencies (Norse 2010). Because ocean spaces invite a diversity of potentially-incompatible uses—from resource extraction to recreation to transit—the segregation of these activities might reduce conflict (Osherenko 2006; Lorenzen 2010; Sanchirico 2010). Because of international interest in the seas, the effort is often cast as a means to inspire multi-state cooperation to better manage ocean space and ocean resources (Douvere and Ehler 2009). Internationally-recognized marine reserves, for instance, are said to enable the perpetuation of various threatened species whose survival depends upon uninterrupted use of a particular area (Halpern and Warner 2002; Lubchenco 2003).

Yet my ongoing investigations of the implementation of zoning-based regulation on the open waters reveal that the tensions that attend to land-based policing are no less trenchant on the water. In the case that I am examining, the US federal government is seeking to provide more defined spatial buffers between boats and a group of orca whales in the waters of the Pacific Northwest. These orcas are listed as endangered under the Endangered Species Act. They are also the focus of an extremely large whale watching industry, one that attracts more than 500,000 paying customers per year to board boats aimed at viewing these charismatic animals (Milstein 2011). Yet an emerging consensus amongst many marine scientists suggests that the orcas and other cetaceans behave differently in the presence of boats. In particular, the orcas are said to spend less time foraging (Lusseau 2009; Noren 2009). For an endangered population that lacks abundant prey, any distraction from feeding arguably increases their vulnerability to extinction (National Oceanic and Atmospheric Administration 2008). Given this, the federal government proposed regulations that would create a 200-yard buffer around the whales at all times, creating a "no-go zone" in one particularly popular whale-foraging area.

These proposed regulations generated a massive level of controversy, one very much fueled by underlying concerns about the assertion of police power in a place open to multiple uses and multiple social constructions. Some of the debate focused on simply accepting the idea that the water was a space susceptible to regulation. When asked in an interview whether he was surprised by the level of controversy generated by the proposed vessel regulations, the local prosecuting attorney said:

> No, no, no, are you kidding? The water is still a frontier for laws and regulations, and it attracts people who believe that, and have that kind of frontier attitude about things. It's a real frontier. It's like you're dealing with cattle ranchers out there. You don't need a license or a set age to drive a boat, there are no speed limits out there, there are no safety checks for your vessels. That exists here, today, in northwest Washington. So, that's a different mentality.

Beyond this, many boaters, in interviews, expressed considerable fear about the potential misuse of police power. These boaters argued that ocean dynamics are continually shifting, based on the movements of the whales, the currents, and other boats. For this reason, they suggested, boaters could run afoul of the law even when trying to be conscientious. Even those boaters who recognized the need for law enforcement—indeed, some of them welcomed it—were afraid of excessive police power.

This controversy over a sea-based policing of space illustrates more broadly the tensions that follow officers wherever they go. Their coercive power is welcomed by some, resisted by others. Even individuals who are happy to see the police simultaneously fear coercive power exercised with inadequate understanding of local dynamics. With different users of that space—fishers, commercial whale watchers, kayaks, recreational boaters, ferry operators, commercial transportation companies—all viewing the space in particular ways, they necessarily do not react in unison to the insertion of the police into an evolving and uncertain dynamic. In this space, as all others, the role of the police attracts notice and concern.

26.4 Conclusion

This essay is hardly an exhaustive catalogue of the inherent dilemmas that attend to the role of the police in regulating the spaces of common human use, most notably urban spaces. Yet any thoughtful examination of the police's work in space—for the present or the future—must recognize the intractable nature of the issues I explore here. Even if the presence of the police in everyday life is an accepted component of modern life, their coercive capacity and their technological sophistication serve as sources of both comfort and controversy. We can never know for certain just how to situate the police in either physical or social space. That the police develop a strong internal culture by which they construct their social roles and the spaces they patrol makes this challenge all the more pronounced.

Ian Burk is no longer a police officer. But the aftershocks of his lethal use of force still reverberate in Seattle. Indeed, his actions helped motivate the decision of the US Department of Justice (DOJ) to investigate uses of force within the Seattle Police Department. The DOJ team discerned a pattern of excessive force that it found troubling and is, at this writing, working with the SPD to develop new training mechanisms. The citizens of Seattle undoubtedly hope that these training techniques reduce unjustified uses of force. Yet it is too much to hope that the dilemmas that inhere to the police's presence in space can ever be definitively resolved. Debates about the police's role in the regulation of space may not always be as inflamed as those that occurred in Seattle after the shooting of John Williams, but they will most certainly persist.

REFERENCES

Anderson, Benedict. 1991. *Imagined Communities: Reflections on the Origin and Spread of Nationalism.* London: Verso.

Beckett, Katherine, and Steve Herbert. 2010. *Banished: The New Social Control in Urban America.* Oxford and New York: Oxford University Press.

Beckett, Katherine, Kris Nyrop, and Lori Pfingst. 2006. "Race, Drugs and Policing: Understanding Disparities in Drug Delivery Arrests." *Criminology* 44:105–38.

Blomley, Nicholas. 2003. "Law, Property, and the Geography of Violence: The Frontier, the Survey and the Grid." *Annals of the Association of American Geographers* 93:121–41.

Braga, Anthony. 2005. "Hot Spots Policing and Crime Prevention: A Systematic Review of Randomized Trials." *Journal of Experimental Criminology* 3:317–42.

Braga, Anthony, and David Weisburd. 2010. *Policing Problem Places: Crime Hot Spots and Effective Prevention.* New York and Oxford: Oxford University Press.

Bratton, William, and Peter Knobler. 1998. *Turnaround: How America's Top Cop Reversed the Crime Epidemic.* New York: Random House.

Chemerinsky, Erwin. 2005. "An Independent Analysis of the Los Angeles Police Department's Board of Inquiry Report on the Rampart Scandal." *Loyola of Los Angeles Law Review* 34: 545–657.

Coleman, Mathew. 2007. "Immigration Geopolitics beyond the Mexico-US Border." *Antipode* 38:54–76.

———. 2012. "The Local Migration State: The Site-Specific Devolution of Immigration Enforcement in the U.S. South." *Law and Policy* 34:159–90.

Coleman, Roy, and Joe Sim. 2000. "'You'll Never Walk Alone': CCTV Surveillance, Order, and Neoliberal Rule in Liverpool City." *British Journal of Sociology* 51:623–39.

Coleman, Roy, Steve Tombs, and David Whyte. 2005. "Capital, Crime Control and Statecraft in the Entrepreneurial City." *Urban Studies* 42:2511–30.

Cordner, Gary, and Elizabeth Biebel. 2005. "Problem-Solving Policing in Practice." *Criminology and Public Policy* 4:155–80.

Coutin, Susan. 2000. *Legalizing Moves: Salvadoran Immigrants' Struggle for U.S. Residency.* Ann Arbor: University of Michigan Press.

Cover, Robert. 1986. "Violence and the Word." *Yale Law Journal* 95:1601–29.

Curry, Michael. 1998. *Digital Places: Living with Geographic Information Technologies.* London: Routledge.

Douvere, Fanny, and Charles Ehler. 2009. "New Perspectives on Sea Use Management: Initial Findings from European Experience with Marine Spatial Planning." *Journal of Environmental Management* 90:77–88.

Entrikin, Nicholas. 1991. *The Betweeness of Place: Towards a Geography of Modernity.* Baltimore: Johns Hopkins University Press.

Fogelson, Robert. 1977. *Big City Police.* Cambridge, MA: Harvard University Press.

Gazell, James. 1976. "William H. Parker, Police Professionalization and the Public: An Assessment." *Journal of Police Science and Administration* 4:28–37.

Gibson, Timothy. 2004. *Securing the Spectacular City: The Politics of Revitalization and Homelessness in Downtown Seattle.* Lanham: Lexington Books.

Giddens, Anthony. 1987. *The Nation-State and Violence.* Berkeley and Los Angeles: University of California Press.

Graham, Stephen. 2005. "Software-Sorted Geographies." *Progress in Human Geography* 29:562–80.

Greene, Jack, and Stephen Mastrofski. 1988. *Community Policing: Rhetoric or Reality?* New York: Praeger.

Halpern, Ben, and Robert Warner. 2002. "Marine Reserves Have Rapid and Lasting Effects." *Ecology Letters* 5:361–66.

Hannah, Matthew. 2000. *Governmentality and the Mastery of Territory in Nineteenth-Century America.* New York: Cambridge University Press.

Harcourt, Bernard. 2001. *The Illusion of Order: The False Promise of Broken Windows Policing.* Cambridge, MA: Harvard University Press.

Herbert, Steve. 1996. "Morality in Law Enforcement: Chasing 'Bad Guys' with the Los Angeles Police Department." *Law and Society Review* 30(4): 799–818.

——. 1997. *Policing Space: Territoriality and the Los Angeles Police Department.* Minneapolis: University of Minnesota Press.

——. 2001. "Policing the Contemporary City: Fixing Broken Windows or Shoring up Neo-liberalism?" *Theoretical Criminology* 5:445–66.

——. 2005. "The Trapdoor of Community." *Annals of the Association of American Geographers* 95:850–65.

——. 2006. *Citizens, Cops, and Power: Recognizing the Limits of Community.* Chicago: University of Chicago Press.

——. 2008. "Coercion, Territoriality, Legitimacy: The Police and the Modern State." In *The Sage Handbook of Political Geography*, edited by Kevin Cox, Murray Low and Jennifer Robinson, 161–181. London: Sage.

Herbert, Steve, and Katherine Beckett. 2010. "'This Place is Home to Us': Questioning Banishment from the Ground Up." *Social and Cultural Geographies* 11:231–45.

Independent Commission on the Los Angeles Police Department. 1991. *Report of the Independent Commission on the Los Angeles Police Department.* Los Angeles: City of Los Angeles.

Johnson, Hildegard. 1976. *Order Upon the Land: The U.S. Rectangular Land Survey and the Upper Mississippi Valley.* New York: Oxford University Press.

Kappeler, Victor, and Larry Gaines. 2009. *Community Policing: A Contemporary Perspective.* New York: Anderson.

Kelling, George, and Catherine Coles. 1998. *Fixing Broken Windows: Restoring Order and Reducing Crime in Our Communities.* New York: The Free Press.

Lorenzen, Kai. 2010. "The Spatial Dimensions of Fisheries: Putting it All in Place." *Bulletin of Marine Science* 86:169–77.

Lubchenco, Janet. 2003. "Plugging a Hole in the Ocean: The Emerging Science of Marine Reserves." *Ecological Applications* 13:53–7.

Lusseau, David. 2009. "Vessel Traffic Disrupts the Foraging Behavior of Southern Resident Killer Whales (*Orcinus orca*)." *Endangered Species Research* 6:211–21.

Lyons, William. 1999. *The Politics of Community Policing*. Ann Arbor: University of Michigan Press.

Mann, Michael. 1988. *States, War and Capitalism*. Oxford: Basil Blackwell.

Manning, Peter. 2008. *The Technology of Policing: Crime Mapping, Information Technology and the Rationalization of Crime Control*. New York: New York University Press.

——. 1977. *Police Work*. Cambridge, MA: MIT Press.

Miller, Wilbur. 1977. *Cops and Bobbies: Police Authority in New York and London, 1830–1870*. Chicago: University of Chicago Press.

Miller, Harvey, and Elizabeth Wentz. 2003. "Representation and Spatial Analysis in Geographic Information Systems." *Annals of the Association of American Geographers* 93:574–94.

Milstein, Tema. 2011. "Nature Identification: The Power of Pointing and Naming." *Environmental Communication* 5:3–24.

Mitchell, Don. 1997. "The Annihilation of Space by Law: The Roots and Implications of Anti-Homeless Laws in the United States." *Anitpode* 29:303–35.

Murphy, Alexander. 1996. "The Sovereign State System as Political-Territorial Ideal: Historical and Contemporary Considerations." In *State Sovereignty as Social Construct*, edited by Thomas Biersteker and Cynthia Weber, 81–120. Cambridge: Cambridge University Press.

National Oceanic and Atmospheric Administration. 2008. *Recovery Plan for Southern Resident Killer Whales*. Seattle: National Marine Fisheries Services, Northwest Regional Office.

Nevins, Joseph. 2001. *Operation Gatekeeper: The Rise of the "Illegal Alien" and the Remaking of the U.S.-Mexico Border*. New York: Routledge.

——. 2007. "Dying for a Cup of Coffee? Migrant Deaths in the U.S.-Mexico Border Region in a Neoliberal Age." *Geopolitics* 12: 228–47.

Noren, Dawn. 2009. "Close Approaches by Vessels Elicit Surface Active Behaviors by Southern Resident Killer Whales." *Endangered Species Research* 8:179–92.

Norse, Elliott. 2010. "Ecosystem-Based Spatial Planning and Management of Marine Fisheries: Why and How?" *Bulletin of Marine Science* 86:179–95.

Osherenko, Gail. 2006. "New Discourses on Ocean Governance: Understanding Property Rights and the Public Trust." *Journal of Environmental Law and Litigation* 21:317–81.

Paulsen, Derek, and Matthew Robinson. 2008. *Crime Mapping and Spatial Aspects of Crime*. New York: Allyn and Bacon.

Paynich, Rebecca, and Bryan Hill. 2009. *Fundamentals of Crime Mapping*. New York: Jones and Bartlett Publishers.

Ratcliffe, Jerry. 2008. *Intelligence-led Policing*. New York: Willan.

Rossomo, Kim. 1999. *Geographic Profiling*. New York: CRC Press.

Sack, Robert. 1986. *Human Territoriality: Its Theory and History*. Cambridge: Cambridge University Press.

Sanchirico, James. 2010. "Comprehensive Planning, Dominant-Use Zones, and User Rights: A New Era in Ocean Governance." *Bulletin of Marine Science* 86:273–85.

Silver, Allen. 1967. "The Demand for Order in Civil Society." In *The Police: Six Sociological Essays*, edited by David Bordua, 12–24. New York: Wiley.

Silverman, Eli. 1999. *NYPD Battles Crime: Innovative Strategies in Policing*. Boston: Northeastern University Press.

Skogan, Wesley. 2006. *Police and Community in Chicago: A Tale of Three Cities*. Oxford and New York: Oxford University Press.

Skogan, Wesley, and Susan Hartnett. 1999. *Community Policing: Chicago Style*. Oxford and New York: Oxford University Press.

Skolnick, Jerome, and David Bayley. 1988. *The New Blue Line: Police Innovation in Six Cities*. New York: Free Press.

Stark, Rodney. 1972. *Police Riots: Collective Violence and Law Enforcement*. Belmont, CA: Wadsworth.

Steinberg, Phillip. 2001. *The Social Construction of the Ocean*. Cambridge: Cambridge University Press.

Tuan, Yi-Fu. 1977. *Space and Place: The Perspective of Experience*. Minneapolis: University of Minnesota Press.

Varsanyi, Monica. 2008a. "Rescaling the 'Alien,' Rescaling Personhood: Neoliberalism, Immigration, and the State." *Annals of the Association of American Geographers* 98:877–96.

——. 2008b. "Immigration Policing through the Back Door: City Ordinances, the 'Right to the City,' and the Exclusion of Undocumented Day Laborers." *Urban Geography* 29:29–52.

Walker, Samuel. 1977. *A Critical History of Police Reform*. Lexington, MA: Lexington Books.

——. 2001. *Police Accountability: The Role of Citizen Oversight*. Belmont, CA: Wadworth.

——. 2005. *The New World of Police Accountability*. Thousand Oaks, CA: Sage.

Weber, Max. 1964. *The Theory of Social and Economic Organization*. New York: Pantheon.

Weitzer, Ronald, and Steven Tuch. 2006. *Race and Policing in America: Conflict and Reform*. Cambridge: Cambridge University Press.

Welsh, Brandon, and David Farrington. 2009. "Public Area CCTV and Crime Prevention: An Updated Systematic Review and Meta-Analysis." *Justice Quarterly* 26:716–45.

Williams, Katherine, and Craig Johnstone. 2000. "The Politics of the Selective Gaze: Closed Circuit Television and the Policing of Public Space." *Crime, Law and Social Change* 34:183–210.

Willis, James, Stephen Mastrofski, and David Weisburd. 2003. *Compstat in Practice: An In-depth Analysis of Three Cities*. Washington, DC: Police Foundation.

——. 2007. "Making Sense of Compstat: A Theory-Based Analysis of Organizational Change in Three Police Departments." *Law and Society Review* 41:147–88.

Woods, Joseph. 1973. "The Progressives and the Police: Urban Reform and the Professionalization of the Los Angeles Police." PhD dissertation: University of California, Los Angeles.

CHAPTER 27

POLICING IN CENTRAL AND EASTERN EUROPE

Past, Present, and Future Prospects

GORAZD MEŠKO, ANDREJ SOTLAR, AND
BRANKO LOBNIKAR

IN terms of land mass, Central and Eastern Europe are quite large. Their area includes Switzerland to the west, Germany to the north, and Poland to the east, and stretches south to Greece. Although the region has historically shared several common developments, the last century has been characterized by turbulence rather than stability. For example, this geographic area has witnessed the rise and fall of nations, the succession of political regimes, democracy in action, and the worst manifestations of totalitarianism. Against this historical backdrop, this essay provides a descriptive account of police and policing in several Central and Eastern European countries.

The essay is divided into four topical areas. Section 27.1 discusses the historical development of police organizations in Central and Eastern Europe. Section 27.2 identifies the characteristics and trends of contemporary policing. Section 27.3 provides an overview of significant policing research, while Section 27.4 discusses some of the challenges policing researchers face in Central and Eastern Europe. Finally, the essay concludes with a discussion of the future of policing in this part of the world.

This essay emphasizes several conclusions:

- Traditionally the police in Central and Eastern Europe were influenced by the Napoleonic gendarmerie military model; however, following World War II the influence of Sir Robert Peel's approach to policing has become more influential.
- Since the aftermath of World War II, police organizations in countries under the influence of the Soviet Union have struggled to regain public trust.
- Following the collapse of the Soviet Union, many Central and Eastern European countries either fired or retired police personnel who were closely linked to the Communist party or who had cooperated with the secret police.

- Although the democratic processes associated with police reform have varied across the countries of Central and Eastern Europe, the structure of police organizations and the tasks they perform are very similar.
- The private security industry has grown considerably. In some Central and Eastern European countries the number of private security officers now exceeds the number of public police officers.
- CEPOL (European Police College) has made an attempt to form linkages between colleges and EU member states as a way to enhance the educational and training programs for police officers.
- Much more policing research is necessary to understand and enhance the level of policing in the multicultural societies of Central and Eastern Europe. EU requirements in both legislation and police operations should be extended to include policing research to better understand the dynamics of these transitional policing efforts.

27.1 The Development of Police Organizations in Central and Eastern Europe: A Historial Overview

Even though it is difficult to find a common definition of Central European countries, Central Europe has historically been defined by the areas of the German Empire (1871–1918) and the Weimar Republic (1918–1933), the Habsburg Monarchy (1562–1804) and its successors, and the Austrian (1804–1867) and the Austro-Hungarian Empire (1867–1918) (Johnson 1996). In addition, Switzerland is also considered a Central European country. The influence of outsiders, namely the English and French, is an important part of the history of policing in this part of the world. The historical development of police forces in Central Europe has also been influenced by the division of this geographic area into the democratic West (e.g., West Germany, Austria, and Switzerland) and the non-democratic East (e.g., East Germany, Poland, Hungary, Czechoslovakia, and Yugoslavia) following World War II. The historical development of policing in Central Europe as a result of these two factors is discussed below.

27.1.1 English and French Influences

The English influence is characterized by decentralized and demilitarized police services with a strong emphasis on public supervision. Even today the English police are said to be acting in accordance with the principles set forth by Sir Robert Peel, who as England's Home Secretary established a non-repressive professional police organization whose underlying motto was to respect and protect the rights and freedoms of citizens.

Sir Robert Peel's motto was portrayed by the unarmed London police, whose uniforms were much different than those worn by the armed military forces. In addition, supervisory boards, established as early as 1835, were used as a method to control police work. These boards included members from local community councils and representatives of the judicial branch of the government (Mawby 1999). Peel's influence can still be found throughout Europe. For example, the Council of Europe's European Code of Police Ethics (2001) embodies many of his principles. Organizational patterns and especially his policing philosophy in England significantly influenced the development of policing in the United States and, more recently, in continental Europe. Such examples can be observed in the decentralized organization of the Dutch police after 1990, the cantonal organization of the police in Switzerland, and the organization of the police in West Germany following World War II.

Another important influence on policing in Central Europe originates from its Napoleonic France heritage. The "Napoleonic" police structure refers to national- (or state-) level police organizations that are centralized and responsible to different state ministries. The contemporary organization of the police in France is based on the historical heritage of the gendarmerie (*Gendarmerie Nationale*), a military police organization that is active primarily in rural areas, and the activities of the national police (*Police Nationale*), which mostly operates in urban areas. The gendarmerie, established in 1791, is the oldest police organization in France. Joseph Fouche, Napoleon's police minister, established a police organization with centralized leadership to protect the state (Tupman and Tupman 1999).

The influence of the French heritage can be seen throughout Europe and specifically in Central European countries where, for example, the Austro-Hungarian Empire and many German provinces until the end of World War II (e.g., Prussia) practiced the Napoleonic style of the police organization. The division into the national (civil) police and (military) gendarmerie was also typical of Austria until 2005, when the gendarmerie was integrated into the state police (Edelbacher and Norden 2013). The gendarmerie also operates as a police organization in the French-speaking Swiss cantons, and the Napoleonic style of the police organization also shaped the Slovene police when Slovenia was a part of the Austro-Hungarian Empire, as well as later when it was in the Kingdom of Serbs, Croats, and Slovenes after World War I. After World War II, the gendarmerie in socialist Yugoslavia was replaced by the people's militia, which maintained many of the characteristics of the Napoleonic gendarmerie military model (Kolenc 2003). It was also typical of Hungary until the end of the World War II that police activities in rural areas were performed by gendarmes, whose organization was set up in 1881 (Szikinger 2000).

27.1.2 The Period Following World War II

The development of the German police was of key importance to the evolution of policing in Central Europe. Individual German provinces adopted the Napoleonic model until the Nazis came into power in 1933. The police in Germany, however, became more centralized after 1938. After World War II, the occupation forces (i.e., Great Britain, the United States, France, and the Soviet Union) reformed the police following the 4 Ds— denazification, demilitarization, decentralization, and democratization (Reinke 2004; Paun 2007). Though differences in respective occupation zones emerged, the Western Allies were successful in limiting police powers in post-war Germany. Prior to that, the German police possessed numerous powers, including some legislative and judicial competences, which were abolished following World War II. Great Britain tried to set up the English system of local organization and responsibilities in its occupation zones, but German politicians insisted on the centralization of the police after the establishment of the Federal Republic of Germany in 1949. Ultimately, Germany established police organizations for each state that were autonomous from the central government. The police in East Germany (*Volkspolizei*—DVP) were organized in accordance with the Soviet model and shared many of the characteristics of police organizations in authoritarian countries. The situation changed with German reunification on October 3, 1990. The West German police adopted an organizational approach similar to that of Switzerland. There, police activities are organized at the cantonal level and in some cases even at the municipal level.

The development of the police in eleven federal states of West Germany after 1950 was characterized by the transition to a professional and democratic style of policing that emphasized responsibility, professionalization, and legitimacy. What is more, the West German police, which was comprised of personnel that reflected the population, exercised a high degree of political independence, worked to provide transparency, and established civilian supervision, demilitarization, and the minimal application of force (Caparini and Marenin 2004). However, the same cannot be said for the police in East Germany. The *Volkspolizei* were one of the pillars of national defense. It was organized in military style and under the influence of the General Committee of the Communist Party. The *Volkspolizei* were supervised directly by the East German political police, *Staatssicherheit*, better known as "Stasi," with the main tasks of ensuring public security and supervising events in local communities (Jobard 2004). This type of subordination to the secret police was also common in other countries of the Warsaw Pact (e.g., Hungary, Poland and Czechoslovakia) and in the countries that belonged to the non-aligned block (e.g., Slovenina and Croatia, then part of Yugoslavia).

The East German policing model could also be observed in other Central European countries that were either under the direct supervision of the Soviet Union (e.g., Czechoslovakia, Poland, and Hungary) or under its ideological influence (e.g., Slovenia and Croatia). Kratcoski (2000) reports that the police in Poland, which operated until the end of World War II, was replaced by the new people's militia. The name of the new police organization in Poland (i.e., militia) reflected the Soviet Union's influence. Militia, which as a word stems from the Latin origin (*miles, militis*—soldier), is a people's army, a kind of armed citizens' organization with the purpose of ensuring order, peace, and protecting the heritage of the socialist revolution (Kutnjak Ivković 2004).

Following World War II, it was typical of Central and Eastern European countries to have centralized police organizations whose primary purpose was to serve the communist or socialist governments. These organizations were based on obedience, their operations were not subjected to public scrutiny, and it was not unusual for the militia to operate on the basis of secret legislation (such examples could be found in Hungary and Yugoslavia). Consequently, it is not surprising that such police organizations were associated with quite a high level of illegitimacy or distrust among citizens. Widespread distrust toward the police in Central and Eastern Europe continued well into the twenty-first century (Kratcoski 2000; Jenks 2004; Jobard 2004). However, in Slovenia and Croatia, the northernmost republics of the former Socialist Federal Republic of Yugoslavia, the militia actively participated in the independence processes and protected the development of democracy. Following the transition from socialist to democratic government, the police in these two countries enjoyed higher levels of trust (Pagon 2004; Vukadin Kovčo, Borovec, and Ljubin Golub 2013; Meško et al. 2013). Prior to independence, the police in the former Yugoslavia were perceived as uneducated and unprofessional (Kutnjak Ivković 2004).

27.1.3 Democratization in Central and Eastern Europe

Police resistance to the democratic process was not met with public approval in Central and Eastern European countries formerly under Soviet influence. A well-known case of violent repression of the democratic process was in Poland, where special militia forces (*Zmotoryzowane Odwody Milicija Obywatelska*), which represent as much as one-fifth of the whole Polish militia force, repressed protests organized by the Solidarność Trade Union (Paun 2007). A similar event took place in East Germany, where the police in East Berlin brutally acted against the protesters during Mikhail Gorbachev's visit in October of 1989. Participation in repressing that protest served as a criterion to refuse employment to police officers following German reunification (Jobard 2004). Other criteria were also put in place, resulting in the refusal to hire police officers who closely cooperated with the communist regime, especially its secret police, such as the East German *Stasi*, the Czechoslovakian *Statni Bezspecnost* (STB), or the Polish *Sluzba Bezpieczenstwa*. A great number of experienced police officers were not retained for service in the Czech Republic (Jenks 2004) and in unified Germany (Jobard 2004). Haberfeld (1997) reports that as many as half of Polish police officers lost their jobs during the transition to the new political system for having cooperated with the secret police.

Following democratic reforms, participation in politics by the police has also been limited in Central and Eastern Europe. For example, the 1991 Slovenian Constitution prohibits police officers from being members of political parties. Similar prohibitions are still in place in the Czech Republic and Hungary. Forced retirement was another approach used to depoliticize the police following the fall of the communist regimes. For example, after unification, every former East German police officer 50 years or older was forced to retire (Jobard 2004). In Slovenia, the new government sent 480 Ministry of Interior staff to early retirement immediately after the Independence Act, most of whom were staff of the State Security Service (*Služba državne varnosti*), a Slovenian version of secret police. Also, in 1998 the Police Act was passed which retired some 504 police officers (Meško and Klemenčič 2007).

After the fall of the Berlin Wall, nearly every Central European country under the influence of Soviet ideology initiated police reforms (e.g., attempts to democratize and decentralize the police) and adopt standards similar to those of West Germany, Switzerland, and Austria. The process has not always been smooth. Paun (2007) reports that the Polish police are in a continuous state of reform. Caparini and Marenin (2004) observe that, in comparison with the Eastern European and Balkan countries, the process of democratizing police organizations in Central Europe has progressed. In the countries that entered social transition after changes in their political system (e.g., Slovenia, Slovakia, Poland, Hungary, and the Czech Republic), this process has come closer to the standards that are in place in the Central European countries that went through a similar transition after World War II (e.g., West Germany and Austria).

27.2 CONTEMPORARY POLICE ACTIVITIES IN CENTRAL AND EASTERN EUROPE: CHARACTERISITCS AND TRENDS

27.2.1 Organizational Patterns in the Police and Police Tasks

With the exception of the police in Switzerland, most police organizations in Central and Eastern Europe were put in place after the fall of totalitarian political regimes. For example, Austria and Germany had to set up new police organizations after World War II. In many parts of Central and Eastern Europe the process of democratization did not narrowly focus on police reform, but focused also on the introduction of political and economic systems and the establishment of new nations (e.g., Bosnia and Herzegovina, Croatia, the Czech Republic, Slovenia, Slovakia, Serbia, and Macedonia).

Although the democratic process has varied across the countries of Central and Eastern Europe, a high degree of similarity can be observed in police organization and tasks. Generally speaking, state/national police organizations are subordinated to governments, mostly either to a Ministry of Interior or a Ministry of Justice. They are centralized and hierarchical organizations with their branches in regions (i.e., headquarters and directorates) and in municipal units or towns and villages (i.e., police stations and inspection units). In Switzerland the responsibility for policing lies exclusively in the hands of twenty-six cantons while only limited tasks are carried out at the confederation level (Federal Department of Justice and Police 2013). In most larger countries, where the police are organized at the level of federal states, there are also central federal units that predominantly deal with prosecuting crime and ensuring security at the national level such as the Federal Criminal Police Office in Austria or the Federal Criminal Police Office (*Bundeskriminalamt*) and the Federal Police in Germany (Edelbacher and Norden 2013; Feltes, Marquardt, and Schwarz 2013). After Austria abolished the gendarmerie in 2005 (Edelbacher and Norden 2013), gendarmerie units could only be found in French-speaking Swiss cantons (Federal Department of Justice and Police 2013) and in Serbia (Kešetović 2013). The evolution of the demilitarization of the police organization doubtlessly presents significant progress for the region for the decades following World War II (Pagon 2004; Meško et al. 2013; Sergevnin and Kovalyov 2013).

Police tasks are largely consistent across Central and Eastern European countries. Such tasks include ensuring security, protecting the public and their property, promoting public order and safety, preventing, detecting and investigating crimes, border control, traffic regulation, anti-terrorism activities (Reitšpís et al. 2013), fighting organized crime and corruption, and expanding the effort to fight cybercrime (Edelbacher and Norden 2013; Foltin, Rohál, and Šikolová 2013).

27.2.2 Plural Policing and Privatization

Plural policing, which first started in the West and gradually spread to other countries, involves transferring typical police activities to private security companies and other governmental agencies (Jones and Newburn 2006). Regarding the latter, many of these agencies were not set up to perform police duties. These new agencies, however, were defined as "new police forces," whether at the state level (e.g., customs, judiciary police, and financial police) or the city/local level (e.g., city traffic wardens, private security firms, and private detectives). In regards to ensuring security, these local public and private organizations have more authority than those of the common citizens (Wakefield 2005; Button 2007; Sotlar 2010).

As part of the decentralization process of police and security functions, there is also a trend in city/local police or traffic wardens subordinated to mayors or local authorities. They primarily deal with ensuring public order and safety, and they supervise traffic (Czapska 2013). Apart from that, there is also the Civil Guard in Hungary, which is an organization of unarmed, uniformed citizens that perform certain police tasks, such as patrolling residential areas in marked civil cars (Leyrer 2013).

If private security in the West was already developed in the past (in Austria and Germany as well) and then "reborn" in the 1990s (Johnston 1992), it was the changes in political, economic, and social systems that enabled the emergence and expansion of the private security sector in Central and Eastern European countries. Since 2008, the economic and financial crisis led to austerity measures in almost every country of the region. Such measures adversely affected the budgets that fund the public police, thus forcing difficult decisions regarding the priorities of police work. Private security firms assumed many of the tasks traditionally performed by the police. In the Czech Republic and Serbia, private security officers now outnumber public police officers. In Poland

and Hungary, the number of security officers is between two and three times more than the number of public police officers (Coess 2011).

The growth of private security has necessitated greater cooperation between the public police and these private organizations. Private security organizations have also become an important factor in post-conflict societies (e.g., Croatia, Serbia, Bosnia and Herzegovina, and Macedonia), both in terms of ensuring security and in terms of providing employment opportunities for demobilized soldiers and police officers (Sotlar 2009).

27.2.3 Europeanization of Policing

There is one more process that should be mentioned that has influenced policing in Central and Eastern Europe—that is, Europeanization. This is primarily reflected through the establishment of common European police agencies. The European Police Office (EUROPOL) supports national police organizations of European Union (EU) member states in fighting serious international crime and terrorism. EUROPOL has also signed operative and strategic agreements with non-EU countries in the region (e.g., Switzerland, Macedonia, and Serbia), thus enabling police cooperation and information exchange across the continent (Europol 2012).

The Frontex Agency (European Agency for the Management of Operational Cooperation at the External Borders of the Member States of the European Union) was established by the EU with the purpose of strengthening coordination among the member states' border police. The agency operates in several areas, such as training, risk assessment, and information exchange. Moreover, Frontex cooperates with the countries that are not part of the Schengen Agreement. This is especially true for countries of origin or transit for illegal migration, such as the Western Balkan countries, and EU candidate countries or potential candidate countries that benefit from this relationship in order to achieve the standards of managing and supervising existing EU borders (Frontex 2012).

The educational and training programs for senior police officers play an important role as well. This is one of the objectives of the European Police College (CEPOL), which links together police colleges and academies from the EU member states and Switzerland. Although most European countries still demand secondary education as an entry criterion for new police officers, at least four of them require undergraduate education, and fifteen require undergraduate or graduate degrees for middle- and senior-staff positions. In 2010, twenty-one countries listed seventy-three accredited Bologna programs with police curriculum in three study cycles—undergraduate, postgraduate, and PhD (Ferreira et al. 2010).

The Association of European Police Colleges (AEPC) plays a similar role to CEPOL by aligning fifty police colleges from forty-two European and neighboring countries. AEPC has helped ten EU candidate countries to achieve European policing standards and has also supported judicial reforms in Western Balkan countries. AEPC also carried out the Regional Police Training Initiative to serve the needs of the Stability Pact for Southeastern Europe (Bistiaux 2011). Last but not least, eight countries from Central and Eastern Europe (i.e., Switzerland, Germany, Austria, the Czech Republic, Slovakia, Hungary, Poland, and Slovenia) established the Central European Police Academy (*Mitteleuropäische Polizeiakademie*) where police officers and detectives from the region can acquire practical knowledge, which enables more efficient cross-border cooperation (MEPA 2012).

The Europeanization of policing itself has had a significant effect on the organization, tasks, ethics and other important aspects of police organizations in Central and Eastern European countries. Namely, if countries want to become members of EU, they must enact legislation and establish regulations in a variety of fields, including justice and internal security. This is part of the reason why some of the most important features of policing in contemporary Central and Eastern European counties are so similar.

27.3 POLICING RESEARCH IN CENTRAL AND EASTERN EUROPE

The nature of policing research conducted in Central and Eastern Europe over the last two decades is quite diverse. In the period before 1990 the research on policing was mainly in the form of literature reviews followed by discussions, while empirical research on policing started later (Meško 2007). Policing does not play a leading role in crime and justice research activities, but the area has been developing quite intensely lately (Meško 2007). In this section, selected policing research conducted in Central and Eastern European counties that appears in international publications is discussed.

Joutsen (1995) highlighted numerous judiciary issues in Central and Eastern Europe as a starting point to study social control. These issues included beliefs that crime pays, that the police are inefficient at investigating criminal offenses, that judges are too permissive, that courts are too slow, that the staff turnover in institutions of formal social control is too high, and that there are numerous problems with training police officers. The above research findings suggest that policing should be viewed as one facet of a system of formal social control.

Research projects on policing that went beyond simple internal analyses for government agencies started to expand in Central and Eastern European countries during the early part of the twenty-first century. Many studies were presented at international conferences and published in international journals (Meško 2007). Among the more prominent topics included the public image of the police with emphasis on the challenges of professional and democratic policing in developing democracies (Centre for Democracy and Human Rights [CEDEM] 2004; GFk 2009; Klekovski, Nuredinoska, and Stojanova 2010; Centar za slobodneizbore i demokratiju [CESID] 2011). Studying media presentations of police activities also gained importance (Bučar-Ručman and Meško 2006).

The expansion of the EU and the accession process of new member states has intensified research on policing, especially regarding the international cooperation among police organizations in investigating serious forms of crime, extreme violence, and terrorism.

Organizational research has focused on the transition from paramilitary to democratic policing, obstacles in the development of policing, organizational changes in the police (Harris 2005), and the level of professionalism, ethics and integrity (Pagon and Lobnikar 2004; Meško and Klemenčič 2007), basic and on the job training, career development, trust and organizational support, legality and professionalism, and police cynicism (Lobnikar and Pagon 2004). Research on police training and education (Kordaczuk-Was and Sosnowski 2011; Nalla, Rydberg, and Meško 2011) has shown that on-the-job training is more respected than training in police academies. Research also shows the need for more professional management and addresses the role that middle and top management should play in building more professional police organizations (Ljubin and Grubišić-Ilić 2002; Gilinskiy 2011; Zernova 2012). Additionally, prior research has assessed police corruption as a consequence of professional (sub) culture, opportunities, and internal and external control (Kutnjak Ivković et al. 2002; Veić and Cajner Mraović 2004; Kutnjak Ivković, Cajner-Mraović, and Ivanušec 2004; Cheloukhine and Haberfeld 2011).

Community policing is still in the developing stages in Central and Eastern Europe. Cooperation with local residents and other institutions is still lacking. Factors such as poor police-public relationships, discontinuity in community policing implementation, financial problems, and organizational culture all influence police work in the community and have been found to contribute to the lackluster implementation of community policing initiatives (Gilinskiy 2005; Meško and Lobnikar 2005; Vejnović and Lalić 2005; Deljkić and Lučić-Ćatić 2011; Czapska 2013).

Another important topic is the perceived legitimacy of the police (Meško and Klemenčič 2007). Research in this area shows that the factors that shape police legitimacy and public cooperation in the West (e.g., the United States and Australia) are also salient in Central and Eastern European countries (e.g., Slovenia; Reisig, Tankebe, and Meško 2012).

Research using victimization survey data underscores the importance of crime investigation, especially in the prevention of secondary victimization (Cajner Mraović, Cerjak, and Ivanušec 2002). Fear of crime and policing studies show the importance of understanding fear of crime and the role police play in fear reduction strategies (e.g., reassurance policing; Meško et al. 2007). Related research emphasizes the importance of efforts to improve social cohesion, strengthen social networks, respond to social and physical disorder, and build trust in public institutions (e.g., the police; Meško 2012a, 2012b).

Research on crime investigation has evolved in two distinct directions—the investigation of crime as an important police activity and the utility of modern scientific methods (forensics) to collect and analyze evidence (Maver 2009). Other, mainly internal research of the Ministries of the Interior on policing has dealt with issues of criminal investigation techniques, police interviews and interrogation techniques, police evidence, and the use of modern technologies in criminal investigation (e.g., DNA, fingerprinting, polygraph testing, and crime pattern analysis). This type of research has also investigated the role of police clubs in youth crime prevention.

Although the volume and quality of policing research in Central and Eastern Europe has improved considerably over the past two decades, it is still conducted sporadically and with few follow-ups when compared to Western nations.

27.4 Conducting Policing Research In Central and Eastern Europe

Much more policing research in Central and Eastern Europe is needed. Among the topics in need of further attention include policing in a multicultural society, migration management, depoliticization, demilitarization and support to police reforms, trust in the police, decreasing cross-cultural ethical conflicts, accountability, respecting human rights, and preventing police abuse of authority.

Policing research is conducted at various institutions, including research institutes, universities, Ministries of Interior, and non-governmental organizations (Meško 2007; Amnesty International 2013). For example, policing research in Slovenia is being conducted at universities and research institutes, whereas in many other countries research on police and policing is done within Ministries of Interior and associated research institutes. Interest in publishing the results from policing research projects varies significantly. Internal research is rarely published in international or national journals and other scientific publications (with the exception of research reports), whereas research findings from studies conducted at universities can generally be found in publicly accessible publication outlets. If we assume that policing science exists merely as a consequence of accumulated (applied) research and theory, then the direction of future policing research will be shaped primarily by the activities of educational and research institutions.

Apart from research, it also needs to be emphasized that most Central and Eastern European countries have a tradition of publishing scientific and professional papers in native languages, and some publications have gained international significance (e.g., Collection of Scientific Papers on Policing in Central and Eastern Europe). Leading scholarly journals in the area of policing include *Kriminalistik* (Germany), *Journal of Criminal Justice and Security* (*Varstvoslovje*, Slovenia), and the *Journal of Criminal Investigation and Criminology* (*Revija za kriminalistiko in kriminologijo*, Slovenia). In addition to the aforementioned journals, policing research is also published in the *SIAK Journal* (Austria), *Police and Security* (*Policija i sigurnost*, Croatia), *Criminal Justice*

Issues (*Kriminalističke teme*, Bosnia and Herzegovina), and the *Journal of Criminalistics and Law* (*Žurnal za kriminalistiku i pravo*, Serbia). Policing research from this part of the world also appears in national and international criminology and criminal justice journals of general interest (e.g., *European Journal of Criminology*).

The internationalization and Europeanization of criminal justice and policing research and the contributions of Central and Eastern European researchers opens new opportunities for comparative policing research (see, e.g., the Composite 2012 and Corepol 2012 projects) on police organizations, police activities, and the professionalization and legitimacy of police operations in Europe. The ongoing European projects Urbis (2012) and Eemus/Ecus (2012), which focus on urban security management, also emphasize the role of policing in urban areas. The European research project Euro-Justis demonstrates the importance of trust to police and criminal justice in Europe (Hough and Sato 2011). A new EU research project, Fiducia (2013), focuses on "trust based" policy and related policy recommendations in relation to emerging forms of criminality to be addressed to EU member states and EU institutions.

27.5 THE FUTURE OF POLICING IN CENTRAL AND EASTERN EUROPE

EU requirements for unification in the fields of legislation and police operations have played an important role, especially in countries that have recently joined or are in line to join. The same can be said for policing research in these countries.

The CEPOL created a network platform for police training, education, and research. There has been no evaluation of police and policing research so far but it is unclear whether the results from applied research actually impacts police practice. Evidence-based practices are still in the early development stage in many Central and Eastern European countries. The capacity to carry out rigorous police research projects also varies across nations too.

The European Commission facilitates comparative research in the field of security, which includes research on police and policing. Significant changes have happened in the last ten years as more researchers and police forces from Central and Eastern Europe have partnered in European policing research projects. In this framework, it would be necessary to go beyond working groups in professional societies (e.g. European Society of Criminology's working group on policing) and establish a European network of police researchers.

The postgraduate policing programs at Ruhr University Bochum (Germany), German Police University in Muenster (Germany), Neustadt University of Applied Sciences in Vienna (Austria), the Faculty of Criminal Justice and Security of the University of Maribor (Slovenia), and their international partners will continue to shape the direction of future police research in Central and Eastern Europe and elsewhere.

From an organizational standpoint, the police in Central and Eastern Europe are slowly adopting several common characteristics, including democratization, accountability, and legitimacy linked to citizens. In the last decade, state police organizations in the region, particularly those from Eastern Europe, have accepted the fact that they no longer occupy a monopolistic position in policing due to the development of plural policing. The pluralization of social control institutions, which encompasses state police organizations, local community police organizations, and private security organizations, has created competition in policing with individual police (state) organizations being forced to constantly prove themselves and justify their existence. The response of state police organizations at present is reflected in strengthening the professionalization of policing, more transparency, increased public relations, better educated police officers, and the use of modern technologies in police work.

The development of police sciences, supported by research activities, and the increased academic demands in the police education process are merely an outside manifestation of such efforts. All of these are essential for police officers to be able to address the demands of modern society. However, some differences can be observed. If the countries of the eastern part of Central Europe (e.g., Slovenia, Croatia, and Hungary) are addressing the issues related to the appropriate response to the growth of organized crime (which was more easily suppressed under totalitarian rule because non-democratic standards of the police were tolerated), the police organizations in the western part of Central Europe (e.g., Austria, Switzerland, and Germany) are facing challenges related to the increasing internal violence, originating from cultural conflicts due to migration flows in the common EU territory. Consequently, all police organizations in Central and Eastern Europe are faced with a dual challenge in terms of organizing policing. First, they need to cultivate reliable and effective cooperative relationships with other European police organizations to deal with cross-border crime. Second, they should focus time and energy on operations in the local environment (e.g., through community policing), as citizens are becoming more demanding in terms of the expected results from police services.

References

Amnesty International. 2013. http://www.anesty.org/.

Bistiaux, Gaëlle. 2011. "Association of European Police Colleges: Brief History of Association." http://www.aepc.net/wp-content/uploads/2010/11/20120308AEPC_history.doc.

Bučar-Ručman, Aleš, and Gorazd Meško. 2006. "Presentation of Police Activities in the Mass Media." *Varstvoslovje* 8:223–34.

Button, Mark. 2007. "Assessing the Regulation of Private Security Across Europe." *European Journal of Criminology* 4:109–28.

Cajner Mraović, Irena, Andreja Cerjak, and Dražen Ivanušec. 2002. "Policing Sexual Assaults: The Women's Point of View." In *Policing in Central and Eastern Europe: Deviance, Violence and Victimization: Conference Proceedings*, edited by Milan Pagon, 239–251. Ljubljana, Slovenia: College of Police and Security Studies.

Caparini, Marina, and Otwin Marenin. 2004. *Transforming Police in Central and Eastern Europe: Process and Progress.* Munster: LIT Verlag.

Centar za slobodneizbore i demokratiju [CESID]. 2011. "Attitude of Serbia's Citizens Towards the Police Work." http://www.mup.rs/cms/resursi.nsf/Public%20Opinion%20Research%20 2011.doc.

Centre for Democracy and Human Rights [CEDEM]. 2004. "Public Perception Surveys: Local Community and Uniformed Police." http://www.cedem.me/index.php?IDSP= 1248&jezik=lat.

Cheloukhine, Serguei, and Maria. R. Haberfeld. 2011. *Russian Organized Corruption Networks and Their International Trajectories.* New York: Springer.

Coess. 2011. "Private Security Services in Europe: Facts & Figures 2011." http://www.coess.eu/ _Uploads/dbsAttachedFiles/Private_Security_Services_in_Europe-CoESS_Facts_ and_Figures_2011%281%29.pdf.

Composite. 2012. http://www.composite-project.eu/index.php/european_partners.html.

Corepol. 2012. http://www.corepol.eu/team/siak/index.php.

Council of Europe. 2001. The European Code of Police Ethics. http://legislationline.org/ documents/action/popup/id/8007.

Czapska, Janina, ed. 2013. *Policje i strażemiejskie w Europie [Municipal Policing in Europe].* Krakow: Jagellonian University Press.

Deljkić, Irma, and Marija Lučić-Ćatić. 2011. "Implementing Community Policing in Bosnia and Herzegovina." *Police Practice and Research* 12:172–84.

Edelbacher, Maximilian, and Gilbert Norden. 2013. "Policing in Austria: Development Over the Past Twenty Years, Present State and Future Challenges." In *Handbook on Policing in Central and Eastern Europe*, edited by Gorazd Meško, Charles B. Fields, Branko Lobnikar, and Andrej Sotlar, 15–31. New York: Springer.

Eemus/Ecus. 2012. http://masterinurbansecurity.eu/index.php?id=31814.

Europol. 2012. "International Relations." https://www.europol.europa.eu/content/page/ international-relations-31.

Federal Department of Justice and Police. 2013. "Structure of the Swiss Police." http://www.ejpd. admin.ch/content/ejpd/en/home/themen/sicherheit/ref_polizeistruktur.html.

Feltes, Thomas, Uwe Marquardt, and Stefan Schwarz. 2013. "Policing in Germany: Developments in the Last 20 Years." In *Handbook on Policing in Central and Eastern Europe*, edited by Gorazd Meško, Charles B. Fields, Branko Lobnikar, and Andrej Sotlar, 93–115. New York: Springer.

Ferreira, Eduardo, Hans-Gerd Jasche, Harry Peters, and Rosana Farina. 2010. "Bologna Process: Survey on European Police Education and Bologna—SEPB." *Cepol.* https://www. cepol.europa.eu/fileadmin/website/TrainingLearning/Publications/SEPEB_Final_Report. pdf.

Fiducia. 2013. http://www.fiduciaproject.eu/page/21.

Foltin, Pavel, Andrej Rohál, and Mária Šikolová. 2013. "Policing in the Czech Republic: Evolution and Trends" In *Handbook on Policing in Central and Eastern Europe*, edited by Gorazd Meško, Charles B. Fields, Branko Lobnikar, and Andrej Sotlar, 57–81. New York: Springer.

Frontex. 2012. "Missions and Tasks." http://www.frontex.europa.eu/about/mission-and-tasks.

GFk. (2009). "National Public Opinion Survey: On Citizen Perception of Safety and Security in the Republic of Croatia. 2009." http://www.undp.hr/upload/file/230/115095/FILENAME/ Survey_on_safety_and_security_E.pdf.

Gilinskiy, Yakov. 2005. "Police and the Community in Russia." *Police Practice and Research* 6:331–46.

———. 2011. "Torture by the Russian police: An Empirical Study." *Police Practice and Research* 12:163–71.

Haberfeld, Maria R. 1997. "Poland: The Police are Not the Public and the Public Are Not the Police: Transformation from Militia to Police." *Policing: An International Journal of Police Strategies and Management* 20:641–54.

Harris, Frank. 2005. "The Role of Capacity-Building in Police Reform." *Pristina: Organization for Security and Cooperation in Europe.* http://www.osce.org/kosovo/19789?download=true.

Hough, Mike, and Mai Sato. 2013. *Trust in Justice: Why It Is Important for Criminal Policy, and How It Can Be Measured: Final Report of the Euro-Justis Project.* Helsinki: European Institute for Crime Prevention and Control.

Jenks, David A. 2004. "The Czech Police: Adopting Democratic Principles." In *Transforming Police in Central and Eastern Europe*, edited by Marina Caparini and Otwin Marenin, 23–45. Münster: LIT Verlag.

Jobard, Fabien. 2004. "The Lady Vanishes: The Silent Disappearance of the GDR Police after 1989." In *Transforming Police in Central and Eastern Europe*, edited by Marina Caparini and Otwin Marenin, 45–65. Münster: LIT Verlag.

Johnson, Lonnie R. 1996. *Central Europe: Enemies, Neighbors, Friends.* Oxford: Oxford University Press.

Johnston, Les. 1992. *Rebirth of Private Policing.* Routledge: London.

Jones, Trevor, and Tim Newburn, eds. 2006. *Plural Policing.* New York: Routledge.

Joutsen, Matti. 1995. "Crime Trends in Central and Eastern Europe." In *Crime Policies and the Rule of Law—Problems of Transition.* Ljubljana, Slovenia: The Institute of Criminology.

Kešetović M., Želimir. 2013. "Serbian Police: Troubled Transition from Police Force to Police Service." In *Handbook on Policing in Central and Eastern Europe*, edited by Gorazd Meško, Charles B. Fields, Branko Lobnikar, and Andrej Sotlar, 217–239. New York: Springer.

Klekovski, Sašo, Emina Nuredinoska, and Daniela Stojanova. 2010. *Trust in Macedonia: General Trust and Trust in Institutions Trust in Civil Society Knowledge and Opinion About Civil Society Organizations.* Skopje, Macedonia: Macedonian Center for Cooperation.

Kolenc, Tadeja. 2003. *The Slovene Police.* Ljubljana: Ministry of the Interior of the Republic Slovenia, Police, General Police Directorate.

Kordaczuk-Was, Marzena, and Sebastian Sosnowski. 2011. "Police In-Service Training and Self-Education in Poland." *Police Practice and Research* 12:317–24.

Kratcoski, Peter C. 2000. "Policing in Democratic Societies: An Historical Overview." In *Challenges of Policing Democracies. A World Perspectives*, edited by Dilip K. Das and Otwin Marenin, 23–44. Amsterdam: Gordon and Breach Publishers.

Kutnjak Ivković, Sanja. 2004. "Distinct and Different: The Transformation of the Croatian Police." In *Transforming Police in Central and Eastern Europe*, edited by Marina Caparini and Otwin Marenin, 195–221. Münster: LIT Verlag.

Kutnjak Ivković, Sanja, Irena Cajner-Mraović, and Dražen Ivanušec. 2004. "The Measurement of Seriousness of Police Corruption." In *Policing in Central and Eastern Europe: Dilemmas of Contemporary Criminal Justice*, edited by Gorazd Meško, Milan Pagon, and Bojan Dobovšek, 300–309. Ljubljana, Slovenia: Faculty of Criminal Justice.

Kutnjak Ivković, Sanja, Carl Klockars, Irena Cajner-Mraović, and Dražen Ivanušec. 2002. "Controlling Police Corruption: The Croatian Perspective." *Police Practice and Research* 3:55–72.

Leyrer, Richard. 2013. "Finding the Right Path of Policing In Hungary." In *Handbook on Policing in Central and Eastern Europe*, edited by Gorazd Meško, Charles B. Fields, Branko Lobnikar, and Andrej Sotlar, 115–129. New York: Springer.

Ljubin, Tajana, and Mirjana Grubišić-Ilić. 2002. "Some Factors Related to Police Cadets' Perceptions of Deviant Police Behavior." In *Policing in Central and Eastern Europe: Deviance, Violence and Victimization: Conference Proceedings*, edited by Milan Pagon, 387–394. Ljubljana, Slovenia: College of Police and Security Studies.

Lobnikar, Branko, and Milan Pagon. 2004. "The Prevalence and the Nature of Police Cynicism in Slovenia." In *Policing in Central and Eastern Europe: Dilemmas of Contemporary Criminal Justice*, edited by Gorazd Meško, Milan Pagon, and Bojan Dobovšek, 103–111. Ljubljana, Slovenia: Faculty of Criminal Justice.

Maver, Darko. 2009. "Criminal Investigation/Criminalistics in Slovenia: Origins, Development and Trends." *Journal of Criminal Justice and Security* 11:493–519.

Mawby, Robert I. 1999. *Policing Across the World: Issues for the 21st Century*. London: UCL Press.

MEPA. 2012. "Objectives and Tasks." http://www.mepa.net/Englisch/ueberuns/Pages/Ziele.aspx.

Meško, Gorazd. 2007. "The Obstacles on the Path to Police Professionalism in Slovenia: A Review of Research." In *Policing in Emerging Democracies—Critical Reflections*, edited by Gorazd Meško and Bojan Dobovšek, 15–55. Ljubljana, Slovenia: Faculty of Criminal Justice and Security.

———. 2012a. "A Reflection on Selected Fear of Crime Factors in Ljubljana, Slovenia" *Journal of Criminal Justice and Security* 4:422–34.

———. 2012b. "Policing in Central and Eastern Europe—An Overview of Recent Research and Future Challenges." *A Paper Presented at the 2012 CEPOL Police Research and Science Conference*. Lyon: CEPOL.

Meško, Gorazd, Marte Fallshore, Mojca Rep, and Aletha Huisman. 2007. "Police Efforts in the Reduction of Fear of Crime in Local Communities: Big Expectations and Questionable Effects." *Sociologija. Mintis ir veiksmas* 2:70–91.

Meško, Gorazd, and Goran Klemenčič. 2007. "Rebuilding Legitimacy and Police Professionalism in an Emerging Democracy: The Slovenian Experience." In *Legitimacy and Criminal Justice*, edited by Tom R. Tyler, 84–114. New York: Russell Sage Foundation.

Meško, Gorazd, and Branko Lobnikar. 2005. "The Contribution of Local Safety Councils to Local Responsibility in Crime Prevention and Provision of Safety." *Policing: An International Journal of Police Strategies and Management* 28:353–73.

Meško, Gorazd, Branko Lobnikar, Andrej Sotlar, and Maja Jere. 2013. "Recent Developments of Policing in Slovenia" In *Handbook on Policing in Central and Eastern Europe*, edited by Gorazd Meško, Charles B. Fields, Branko Lobnikar, and Andrej Sotlar, 263–287. New York: Springer.

Nalla, Mahesh, K., Jason Rydberg, and Gorazd Meško. 2011. "Organizational Factors, Environmental Climate, and Job Satisfaction Among Police in Slovenia." *European Journal of Criminology* 8:144–56.

Pagon, Milan. 2004. "A Study of a Police Reform in Slovenia" In *Transforming Police in Central and Eastern Europe*, edited by Marina Caparini and Otwin Marenin, 115–131. Münster: LIT Verlag.

Pagon, Milan, and Branko Lobnikar. 2004. "Police Integrity in Slovenia." In *The Contours of Police Integrity*, edited by Carl. B. Klockars, Sanja Kutnjak Ivković, and Maria. R. Haberfeld, 212–231. Thousand Oaks, CA: Sage.

Paun, Christopher. 2007. Democratization and Police Reform. Berlin: Freie Univerzizät.

Reinke, Herbert. 2004. "The Reconstruction of the Police in Post-1945 Germany." In *The Impact of World War II on Policing in North-West Europe*, edited by Cyril Fijnaut, 133–151. Leuven: Leuven University Press.

Reisig, Michael D., Justice Tankebe, and Gorazd Meško. 2012. "Procedural Justice, Police Legitimacy, and Public Cooperation with the Police Among Young Slovene Adults." *Journal of Criminal Justice and Security* 14:147–64.

Reitšpís, Josef, Libor Gašpierik, Kamil Boc, and Miroslav Felcan. 2013. "Policing in the Slovak Republic: The Organization and Current Problems of Police Work." In *Handbook on Policing in Central and Eastern Europe*, edited by Gorazd Meško, Charles B. Fields, Branko Lobnikar, and Andrej Sotlar, 239–263. New York: Springer.

Sergevnin, Vladimir, and Oleg Kovalyov. 2013. "Policing in Russia." In *Handbook on Policing in Central and Eastern Europe*, edited by Gorazd Meško, Charles B. Fields, Branko Lobnikar, and Andrej Sotlar, 191–217. New York: Springer.

Sotlar, Andrej. 2009. "Post-Conflict Private Policing: Experiences from Several Former Yugoslav Countries." *Policing: An International Journal of Police Strategies and Management* 32:489–507.

——. 2010. "Private Security in a Plural Policing Environment in Slovenia." *Cahiers polities-tudies* 3:335–53.

Szikinger, Istvan. 2000. "The Challenges of Policing Democracy in Hungary." In *Challenges of Policing Democracies. A World Perspectives*, edited by Dilip K. Das and Otwin Marenin, 3–22. Amsterdam: Gordon and Breach.

Tupman Bill, and Alison Tupman. 1999. *Policing in Europe: Uniform in Diversity*. Exeter: Intelect Books.

URBIS. 2012. http://www.urbisproject.eu/index.php/en/obiettivi.html.

Veić, Petar, and Irena Cajner Mraović. 2004. "Police Training and Education: The Croatian Perspective." *Police Practice and Research* 5:137–48.

Vejnović, Duško, and Velimir Lalić. 2005. "Community Policing in a Changing World: A Case Study of Bosnia and Herzegovina." *Police Practice and Research* 6:363–73.

Vukadin Kovčo, Irma, Krunoslav Borovec, and Tajana Ljubin Golub. 2013. "Policing in Croatia: The Main Challenges on the Path to Democratic Policing." In *Handbook on Policing in Central and Eastern Europe*, edited by Gorazd Meško, Charles B. Fields, Branko Lobnikar, and Andrej Sotlar, 31–57. New York: Springer.

Wakefield, Alison. 2005. "The Public Surveillance Functions of Private Security." *Surveillance and Society* 2:529–54.

Zernova, Margarita. 2012. "Coping with the Failure of the Police in Post-Soviet Russia: Findings from One Empirical Study." *Police Practice and Research* 13:474–86.

CHAPTER 28

....

LOCAL POLICE AND THE "WAR" ON TERRORISM

....

BRIAN FORST[*]

> The task we have set for ourselves is to elucidate the role of the police in
> modern American society by reviewing the exigencies located in practical
> reality which give rise to police responses, and by attempting to relate the
> actual routines of response to the moral aspirations of a democratic polity
>
> (Bittner 1970, 5).

> A great deal of the responsibility for preparing for and responding to ter-
> rorist events rests with local police departments
>
> (Scheider and Chapman 2003).

WE ask much of the police. The familiar mission statement—"to protect and serve"—
is rich in possibility, but loaded in ambiguity and doomed to leave in its wake a sea of
unfulfilled expectations.[1] The general public expects its local police to protect and serve
in ways both profound and mundane, from solving serious felonies to removing cats
from trees and giving directions.

The September 11, 2001 terrorist attack on New York and Washington, DC gave new
meaning to the notions of protection and service. The police were the first line of security after the attacks and, together with the fire and rescue personnel, the first line of
emergency response. Sixty officers from the New York Police Department (NYPD)
and Port Authority who participated in rescue operations were lost in the World Trade
Center. In the aftermath, the police were placed on varying levels of terrorism alert;
they provided unprecedented levels of security at public places and events; worked in
partnerships with federal and other local law enforcement and intelligence agencies;
investigated several thousands of people identified as "suspicious"; collected, analyzed,
and shared information on such people; worked to protect vulnerable infrastructure
resources; and developed relationships with key members of the community to prevent future such attacks and aid in response in ways both unprecedented and unfamiliar. Following the guidance of officials at the US Department of Justice, such as that of
Scheider and Chapman in the second of the pair of quotes that open this chapter, the

police have assumed considerably more responsibility for counterterrorism than before, some of it supported with federal funds.

The police, in short, have become a central component of homeland security in the War on Terror. This "war"—more rhetorical than legitimate—nonetheless imposed new demands on local police departments, both real and substantial. To accommodate these demands, the NYPD created a Deputy Commissioner for Counter Terrorism; Washington, DC created the Homeland Security and Emergency Management Agency (HSEMA), with a chief responsible to plan for, coordinate, and respond to man-made or natural disasters ranging from bad storms to nuclear bombs. HSEMA's chief played a central role in planning for the 2008 presidential inauguration and responding to a fatal 2009 Metro subway accident, the back-to-back blizzards in 2010, and the city's brush with Hurricane Irene in 2011. Los Angeles Police Department Chief William Bratton collaborated in the creation of a National Counter Terrorism Academy to train local law enforcement officers in tools of counterterrorism; former White House officials created the Center for Policing Terrorism, a think tank in New York City; joint task forces were created throughout the United States to coordinate local and federal counterterrorism plans and interventions; and police officers from every state began attending training sessions on counterterrorism. Similar projects have been created outside the United States.[2]

Largely missing from these developments, however, has been the sort of serious deliberation encouraged by Egon Bittner in the opening quote of this chapter on the proper role of police in society. Should the police regard terrorism primarily as a problem of national security or primarily as a local public safety problem? To what extent are these two perspectives in tension? How, precisely, should local police departments exercise responsibility for rhetorical wars on crime, drugs, and now terrorism? Stripping away the rhetoric, what are the legitimate responsibilities of local police to the serving of national interests?

This essay attempts to reconcile the activities of local police done in the name of the War on Terror with the moral aspirations of our democratic polity. Section 28.1 attempts to come to terms, literally, with terrorism and counterterrorism, discussing the criminal dimensions of domestic terrorism and the implications for local policing. Section 28.2 addresses the issues of jurisdictional conflict associated with counterterrorism operations. Specifically, this section asks about the responsibility of local police for terrorists and activities associated with terrorism, taking into account the multiple and often mutually conflicting goals of policing. Section 28.3 confronts the tension that American police departments face when assuming a counterterrorism role while still attempting to remain responsive to the local community that authorizes them. This section also focuses on the problems and prospects of coordinating local police with federal officials responsible for what has come to be known as "homeland security"—an expression that, like the War on Terror, has been used largely to galvanize political support for the expansion of counterterrorism engagements by local police.[3] Section 28.4 of the essay highlights many emerging issues that arise when local police agencies assume an increasingly paramilitary posture when taking on a counterterrorism role. This section also identifies the slippery slope of too much security as an added risk of increased paramilitarization, noting that the use of military symbols and rank insignia can undermine legitimacy, particularly in Muslim communities. Section 28.5 describes the importance of police departments learning to effectively manage the demands made on their time as the result of widening the scope of the function to include counterterrorism. Section 28.6 points out that as a counterbalance to the increased para-militarization, police departments might adopt community policing as a widespread deployment philosophy to effectively mitigate the potential for decreased community trust at both local and national levels. Section 28.7 concludes by considering a research and political agenda that can satisfy Bittner's classic call for more thoughtful and coherent considerations of police practice, police legitimacy, and the proper role of police in counterterrorism operations and national security. The focus will be on the prevention of terrorism, recognizing that emergency response falls squarely within the domain of responsibility of local police, including training and equipping local police and coordinating with other responsible agencies—federal, state, and local.

The perspectives offered here lead to several conclusions:

- In the post-9/11 era, it is clear that local police departments will be asked to further assume counterterrorism functions, making their role in society increasingly complex.
- Local police agencies should be careful not to alienate certain communities—particularly Muslim communities—as they take on an increasingly paramilitary role.
- Just as community policing has done much over the past few decades to increase police legitimacy in marginalized communities, so too might it counterbalance the risks of increased paramilitarism.
- Local police agencies must adapt to an environment that may be characterized by conflicting goals: From one perspective, they are accountable to local communities through the mayor (or other local lead administrator), while from another, they are accountable to federal authorities who may ask for deployments that local government officials oppose.
- Police scholars should conduct research aimed at informing the best practices when it comes to policing counterterrorism. In particular, scholars might apply well-known crime control perspectives, such as routine activities theory, to the study of counterterrorism policing to guide police departments in the development of strategies to prevent terrorism.

28.1 TERRORISM AND THE ROLE OF POLICE

The law enforcement community can more coherently consider its proper role in countering terrorism, first, by coming to terms with basic definitions of terrorism and the implications. I offer the following, adapted from an earlier (Forst 2009) treatment on the subject:

> Terrorism is the premeditated and usually unlawful use or threatened use of violence against a noncombatant population or target having symbolic significance, with the aim of either inducing political change through intimidation and destabilization or harming a population identified as an enemy.

Under this and most other conventional definitions, terrorism committed in the United States is a crime, usually one involving both the use of violence and the destruction of property. It violates federal criminal statutes against terrorism. For local police, it almost always violates any of a variety of state and local criminal statutes: homicide, assault, arson or other malicious destruction of property, and others. In all jurisdictions—federal, state, and local—terrorism differs from conventional crimes in at least two important respects: (1) it is typically conducted in the name of an extremist cause—typically political or religious—that transcends immediate material gains to the individual, often designed to call attention to the cause; and (2) it aims to generate fear as a primary goal rather than merely as a means to achieve personal gain. Counterterrorism interventions are those that either prevent such attacks or respond to those that security organizations fail to prevent.

These distinctions should be important to the law enforcement community at all levels. Regardless of what one thinks of wars on terror, police would be foolish to treat individuals who commit crimes to promote extremist interests in precisely the same way that they do ordinary street offenders, even very serious ones. Terrorists aim to commit much more serious crimes, to do so after more planning—often aided by a network of external support—and to cause greater disruption to the community than those who commit more conventional street crimes. Because of their severity and their capacity to produce extreme fear and disruption, terrorism calls for greater preventive efforts, including coordination with federal and other local law enforcement agencies that may have information to help prevent such crimes. They call, no less, for efforts to detect and monitor extremist groups and behaviors within the community that may be unknown to law enforcement or intelligence authorities outside the community.

One might reasonably ask whether local police should bear primary responsibility for crimes much larger than the jurisdiction for which they are responsible. Acts of terrorism aim to achieve a political effect much larger than that associated with a town or city—usually a problem of national defense. The US Constitution was designed uniquely to create a system of federalism that would separate the responsibilities for national defense from those having to do with the local maintenance of order and safety, but terrorism raises questions not clearly addressed in the Constitution. How can our understanding of the proper role of police under constitutional authority inform our understanding of the responsibility of police for terrorism?

It might surprise the ordinary citizen to learn that the Constitution makes no specific reference to the police. While a law enforcement function is implicit in the need to enforce federal laws, the Tenth Amendment to the Constitution grants to the states the authority to regulate behavior and enforce order. The role of the police has evolved, accordingly, in ways that are unique to the needs of each state and community. The role of the police varies from place to place; there is no mandated role that applies universally across the fifty states.

It is nonetheless possible to identify a fundamental feature that the police in Alaskan villages and the Florida Keys share with those in Los Angeles and New York: the police are unique in their having a monopoly of authority to use non-negotiably coercive force.[4] Bittner (1970, 46) distinguishes this authority from that of a private security guard or citizen in suggesting a higher level of competence: the police should execute their authority to use force "in accordance with the dictates of an intuitive grasp of situational exigencies."[5] The police must exercise this discretion in order to overpower resistance, as the circumstances warrant (40). Effective screening and training policies and practices should aim to provide assurance that they will do so prudently.

Unfortunately, this distinction offers little guidance on terrorism to local police departments. The resulting ambiguity has made it easier to ask the police to play a prominent role in counterterrorism.

Preventing and responding to terrorism is clearly within the mandate of the police and consistent with the traditional role of police in society. The question of how much of the load the local police should bear cannot be answered in the abstract. It depends on factors both practical and political: the seriousness of a matter at hand involving a threat or actual instance of extremist violence, the other demands on all agencies with responsibility for the matter, and the resources available to each of the agencies that share responsibility. It depends also on standing arrangements for sharing responsibilities in such matters among cognizant agencies, a matter to which we now turn.

28.2 COORDINATION IN THE FACE OF OVERLAPPING RESPONSIBILITIES FOR COUNTERTERRORISM

As with many other criminal matters—including interstate crimes, bank robbery, organized crime, and others—acts of terrorism typically violate criminal laws at both local and federal levels, and often the laws of more than one state or local jurisdiction. Federal and local law enforcement often have both interest in and responsibility for criminal matters that simultaneously violate federal and state statutes, sometimes involving crimes committed in more than one state. A given act of terrorism is likely to violate federal laws that differ fundamentally from state and local statutes, which raises opportunities for complementary contributions to counterterrorism from each jurisdiction. The question of who bears primary responsibility for any particular criminal matter of potential interest to agencies when jurisdictions overlap gets answered differently from place to place and time to time, depending on resource availability within each of the overlapping agencies, established formal agreements among different agencies with overlapping authority, historical precedents and local conventions, and political considerations.

How does this play out today in the case of terrorism and counterterrorism? Because of the scale of typical counterterrorism operations, the need for coordination between the local police and federal law enforcement agencies is particularly acute, especially in large urban centers like New York, Washington, DC, Los Angeles, Chicago, Philadelphia, and Miami. The police in all metropolitan areas are concerned about serious crime, and many more lives were lost on US soil in two acts of terrorism—the Oklahoma City bombing in 1995 and the 9/11 attacks on New York and Washington—than in any other two single criminal acts on US soil in the history of the nation. Terrorism is usually very costly because the aftermath of security expenditures to prevent repeat occurrences and deal with fear-induced avoidance of activities previously enjoyed. The associated social costs, moreover, tend to be much greater than the immediate costs incurred in the original act itself. Local police have every reason to be concerned about acts of terrorism as a local matter, and every reason to pursue opportunities to work with other agencies—federal, state, and local—that can help to prevent such acts from occurring in the first place and, when prevention fails, to help bring terrorists to justice.

The case of "Beltway Snipers" John Allen Muhammad and Lee Boyd Malvo illustrates the value of cooperation when terrorism cases are prosecutable in more than one jurisdiction, as they usually are. Muhammad and Malvo paralyzed the Washington, DC area in October 2002 with the spree killings of ten people in Maryland, Virginia, and the District of Columbia, predominantly at gas stations and in shopping mall parking lots. In most of the killings, Muhammad drove the car, a blue 1990 Chevrolet Caprice, from which Malvo fired a .223-caliber Bushmaster rifle through a hole in the trunk. Over the three-week period during which the death count mounted, people throughout the region became increasingly afraid to leave their homes and put themselves at risk as targets in public places. The pair was eventually caught at a highway rest stop in Maryland and then prosecuted in courts in both Virginia and Maryland. One of the Virginia courts found Muhammad guilty of killing "pursuant to the direction or order" of terrorism. District attorneys from three counties in Virginia and one in Maryland, and federal prosecutors too, all shared a strong interest in prosecuting the pair. The opportunity to exercise discretion to prosecute the cases in either federal or state court—under dual jurisdiction authority—and in multiple state courts, gave all the prosecutors a wide range of options to ensure that the two would be brought to justice without violating the double jeopardy clause of the Fifth Amendment to the Constitution. They took full advantage of these opportunities: Muhammad was convicted in courts in both Maryland and Virginia and executed in Virginia on November 10, 2009; Malvo, just seventeen years old at the time of the killings, received a life sentence without the possibility of parole, a term he serves today in a Virginia prison.

In the Muhammad-Malvo matter, federal law enforcement authorities played a supportive role, helping local police by providing information needed to identify the offenders and thus enable their capture and prosecution. For terrorism matters generally and high-profile cases in particular, federal law enforcement officers are more likely to take the lead, operating within several line agencies that make up the Department of Homeland Security: United States Citizenship and Immigration Services, Customs and Border Protection, Immigration and Customs Enforcement, Secret Service, Transportation Security Administration, and Federal Emergency Management Agency. Federal law enforcement officers are responsible for protecting the nation against the threat of terrorist attacks. Their numbers are small relative to that of sworn local police officers,[6] but their role is important nonetheless. Much as local police discovered opportunities to leverage their small numbers by building bridges to the community in the 1980s through community policing, so too have federal law enforcement officials leveraged their relatively small numbers by building bridges to local police departments.

Much of the groundwork for such collaboration began in the 1980s, with the creation of joint drug task forces. The drug task forces provided a model for coordination and information-sharing centers among the federal and state-local components of a national counterterrorism system. These centers were launched in 2003 as "fusion centers," the product of a collaboration between the Department of Homeland Security and the US Department of Justice. The space and resources for the conduct of fusion center operations is typically provided by state and local police departments. The centers vary from state to state, depending on local circumstances and the players involved. Most operate tip hotlines from the public and from a variety of public and private agencies. Some fusion centers broaden the inclusion of members by including firefighters, sanitation workers, and other public employees; others restrict participation to law enforcement officials. Some centers focus more on Islamic extremists, others more on right-wing extremists, and those along the Mexican border focus more on narco-terrorists, and so on (Rittgers 2011). The seventy-two fusion centers operating in the United States in 2010—one in each state and another twenty-two serving urban centers—received about $425 million in federal support from 2004 through 2010 (*Los Angeles Times* 2010).

Fusion centers today perform a variety of functions. They process tips from local police departments on possible terrorist-related activities, run names through government and commercial databases to help local police investigate suspicious activity, and coordinate with the FBI and other federal agencies on a variety of issues. The fusion centers are not an independent investigative entity; they are, rather, a broker and conduit of information among various law enforcement and prosecution agencies—federal, state, and local.

Federal-local cooperation on domestic security can be extremely complicated, based not only on local precedents, but on basic asymmetries in the relationship. Federal agencies are responsible for intelligence on terrorist suspects, and local police are restricted from much of this information. Some chiefs do not want the burden of high levels of security clearance that would only compromise their abilities to serve local constituents. At the same time, however, local police have important roles to play in responding to federal intelligence requests and in mitigating terrorism events once they happen. At the margins, difficult decisions must be made by both federal and local authorities; in serious matters, they should be made by people whose judgment we can trust.

28.3 Allocating Finite Resources to Serve Multiple, Often Conflicting Goals

The fusion centers can provide vital information to local police departments on terrorism networks and suspects, but they impose information demands on those agencies as well. In expanding the role of local police as front-line defenders of national security against terrorism, the centers place a burden on local police that raises larger questions about the priorities of those departments. Local police agencies, already stretched thin by ordinary demands on police and the severe fiscal austerity that has been imposed on all public agencies since the "Great Recession" struck in 2008, are limited in their ability to take on counterterrorism as yet another responsibility. Each of the 17,000 police departments in the United States must answer first to its local community and to prosecution and court authorities of the county and state, not to the Department of Homeland Security or another federal authority. Under the US system of federalism, the police report typically to a mayor. This system is unique in that, unlike virtually every other national security system in the world, the nation's top executive officer is not at the apex of the policing hierarchy. If the community perceives the risk of terrorism to be small relative to that of other, more traditional problems confronting local police, the chief may not feel compelled to add a significant counterterrorism component to an already full plate of local policing responsibilities, and this lack of enthusiasm is likely to show up as weak or no participation at fusion centers in the region.

Police departments, like other public and private agencies, operate in a world of finite resources and fixed budgets. They cannot satisfy all demands for service. The public generally takes comfort in knowing that the stakes are higher with policing, that officers will be available to deal with what Bittner (1974, 30) describes as "something-that-ought-not-to-be-happening-about-which-something-ought-to-be-done-now." But it would take approximately 4.5 sworn officers each serving 2,000 hours per year to put a single officer on the street 24 hours per day, 365 days per year. Taking out time for training, officers in managerial and administrative capacities, medical and administrative leave, and so on, we end up with a multiple of some 10 sworn officers or more to allow a single officer to be on the street at all times—in normal times, without extreme problems and under ordinary economic conditions. Terrorist events satisfy Bittner's "about-which-something-ought-to-be-done-now" criterion, and some alarmists would have us believe that all potential threats of terrorism qualify, too. But in the real world only the most urgent and palpable threats receive significant attention by local police departments.

Even in normal times, the problem of resource scarcity is exacerbated by the problem of inflated public expectations. With or without the War on Terror, much of the same public that has come to expect the vast array of services associated with ordinary policing has grown increasingly reluctant to pay the taxes that permit the department to allocate resources to fulfill even the demands of dealing with street crime.

Of course, the post-9/11 era has been anything but normal. A decade after the attack on New York, the NYPD spends a considerable share of its budget on counterterror activities, and the share has increased. Over the 10 years since 9/11, the Department fielded some 84,000 calls involving suspicious packages or substances believed to be potentially associated with terrorism, with 10,567 in 2010 (Johnson 2011). In Washington, such calls to the Metropolitan Police Department jumped substantially in the four years after the campaign, "If You See Something, Say Something," was launched in 2006. The number of calls involving suspicious packages or substances in Washington is about one-tenth the level in New York,[7] which corresponds roughly to the respective populations of the two cities. These increases may correspond to increases in real terrorist threats, or they may correspond to reduced tolerance for the risk of terrorist strikes. Either way, they displace substantial resources available for conventional police work.

New York and Washington are, of course, quite atypical. They were the targets of the 9/11 strikes, and there is considerable reason to expect that they are more vulnerable to future attacks, not only because they are large cities and much larger metropolitan areas, but because of their symbolic importance to terrorists: New York is the world's financial capital, and Washington is the seat of US federal power and headquarters to about half of the world's military resources. It makes sense for these two cities to be more vigilant than others. In both cities, the local police and federal law enforcement agencies alike consume substantially more counterterrorism resources than in other cities, large and small.

It should surprise only the naïve that federal support of local homeland security initiatives has been largely unrelated to the risk of terrorist strikes, more political than threat-related. In 2005, North Pole, Alaska, was awarded over a half million dollars for homeland-security rescue and communications equipment (Lowry 2005). Wyoming received $38 per capita in federal homeland security grants, while New York received $5 per capita (de Rugy 2005). Beyond these dubious allocations of federal resources, it is very difficult to parse the local priorities and practices on terrorism across police departments in the United States. According to Jack Greene (2011, 224):

> Looking for terrorism in traditional police information systems might be likened to drinking from a fire hose; you will get some water, but you are also going to get very, very wet. Even with advanced data-mining techniques, scaling down police information to the subset that might be more useful than others is a difficult task, and not yet conceptualized or validated.... How the police will integrate data from several sources to address terrorism is yet an unresolved question.

In all cities, police departments must determine how much of their resource pool should be allocated to terrorism relative to all other demands on those limited resources. There is no magic formula for making this determination. How, after all, should the police chief weigh the risk of failing to stop a serious terrorist attack against the problems of crime and disorder in a public housing complex or a rapist terrorizing the area? How much can the department actually do to prevent a terrorist attack? There are no formulas and not nearly as large a body of historical evidence on which to base answers to questions about terrorism as there is for crime.

Many, perhaps most, of the new burdens associated with counterterrorism are readily achieved through conventional policing. This is true not only because acts of terrorism are also acts of crime at the local level—violations of state criminal codes—but also because terrorists often sustain themselves and finance their extremist activities through illegitimate activities: creating and using forged documents, trafficking in cigarettes, drug dealing, profiting from identity theft and other frauds, and engaging in ordinary street crime. When the police make arrests for these crimes, they can use the arrest as a lawful basis for searches of the arrestee's computers and telephone records to uncover terrorist connections and crimes. When the police have reliable prior information about terrorist ties or activities, the commission of new, more conventional crimes by terrorist suspects can thus serve as a lawful basis for making arrests and assisting in the prevention of terrorism.

28.4 Paramilitarization of the Police, Reification of Fear, and Other Slippery Slopes

Using terrorism as a basis for departing from conventional policing practices is not a riskless venture, however. Two related risks appear to be especially dangerous: the slippery slope problem and the problem of excessive paramilitarization of the police motivated by war rhetoric. The slippery slope problem involves the risk that police will go overboard in preventing terrorism through hyper-vigilance, not only by wasting resources that could be more productively allocated elsewhere, but in applying them in a manner that actually aggravates the threat of terrorism by alienating citizens and groups disproportionately burdened as targets of surveillance and disruption (Greene 2011). The same "can-do" spirit of enthusiasm and slogans of "zero tolerance" for terrorism that can help to protect the community can also lead to overly aggressive practices, especially when competitive juices flow among ambitious young warriors.

Policing Muslim communities is an especially slippery slope. The United States is fortunate in having a large Muslim population—about 7 million—that is, by all appearances, more integrated into a secular and predominantly non-Muslim society than any other in the world (Ahmed 2010; Pew Research Center 2011). Community policing has done much to build on this integration at the neighborhood level, as we note in a later section, but the challenges of maintaining and building on this are formidable. If the police are viewed as building ties with mosque leaders primarily to gain better intelligence rather than to treat Muslims as members of the community in equal standing to other groups, the relationship is sure to slide down the slope to a bad place for both Muslims and the larger community. In aiming first and foremost at bridge-building and community integration rather than at intelligence-gathering, the police are likely to do better on both fronts.

Concern about the related risk of excessive militarization of police was raised by Egon Bittner (1970, 52) over forty years ago:

> The conception of the police as a quasi-military institution with a war-like mission plays an important part in the structuring of police work in modern American departments. The merits of this conception have never been demonstrated or even argued explicitly. Instead, most authors who make reference to it take it for granted or are critical only of those aspects of it, especially its punitive orientation, that are subject of aspersion even in the military establishment itself.[8]

Several commentators have warned more recently that the War on Terror could induce the police to replace effective community policing programs with more hard-line traditional models that emphasize hierarchy over autonomy, rules over discretion, and toughness over civility (Murray 2005; Greene 2011; Mijares and Jamieson 2011). Long before 9/11, the police had adopted language and principles from the military model as a matter of practice. The police ranks of "captain," "commander," "lieutenant," "major," and "sergeant," with accompanying markings of rank on uniforms, and the language of "patrol" and "standard operating procedures" are some notable examples. Sir Robert Peel designed the modern police model specifically in such a way as to differentiate it from the military, with blue rather than red uniforms used by soldiers, armed with sticks and noisemakers rather than pistols, abandoning all ranks other than that of sergeant, and using a civil service model of management rather than the more rigid model of command and control used in the military. Jerome Skolnick and James Fyfe (1993, 115) have warned specifically of the dangers of reducing police officers to unquestioning soldiers: "The view of police officers as soldiers engaged in a war on crime not only diverts attention from more effective strategies for crime control but also is a major cause of police violence and the violation of citizens' rights." Skolnick and Fyfe see no small irony in "simple low-level grunts laboring in the trenches far removed from the sterile offices in which foolhardy wars are plotted" (133). These tendencies unfold in a bewildering variety of ways across the 17,000 police departments in the United States, depending on the size of the jurisdiction, the political environment, historical precedents, relationships with federal law enforcement officials in the area, and the unique styles of leadership among incumbent police executives.

A tendency for old-fashioned hierarchy and tough-minded action can snowball and feed on itself especially when it is imposed in response to media-fueled panic attacks facilitated by political pandering to overblown fears of terrorism (Forst 2009, 2011). Fear is a primary goal of most acts of terrorism; the word "terror" means fear in the extreme. To the extent that the police succumb to extreme fears by imposing harmful intrusions on the public that exceed the harms of the terrorist attacks themselves, the police will have not only wasted scarce public resources, but will have violated fundamental notions of proportionality put forth by Cesare Beccaria and Jeremy Bentham in the late eighteenth century. If the police lend support to the notion of warfare against terrorism, they could hand the terrorists a significant strategic victory.

The Australian criminologist John Braithwaite (2011) has argued compellingly that an antidote to engaging with terrorists on a rhetorical battlefield is to treat terrorism instead as a public health problem, much as we might a nasty influenza epidemic or an infestation of disease-carrying rodents or ticks. Braithwaite suggests that terrorism is a sort of societal inflammation and that we may be more effective in cooling the flames of emotion that feed it than by trying to retaliate with appeals to patriotism and use of overwhelming force. He argues that terrorism does not lend itself well to either the war model or the criminal justice deterrence model, which makes dubious assumptions about the incentives of people who commit acts of terrorism, ignoring the prospect that retaliatory strikes done in the name of deterrence are likely instead to stimulate defiance and blowback by the group targeted.

As a practical matter, no police chief cares to have a terrorist event that could be regarded as preventable occur on his or her watch. There can be little doubt that terrorist events can be prevented when the police build good relations with communities with large numbers of disenfranchise people, and there can be little doubt that the police can do more to obtain information about plans to commit acts of terrorism. These opportunities tend to be greater the less skillful the terrorist. Police in the United States, London, and elsewhere have managed to thwart several attempts by untrained, unsophisticated young men to commit acts of terrorism. They have also done much to build bridges to Muslim communities, so that competent and potentially productive people can be discouraged from moving down the path from alienation to extremism, and on to terrorism. Wars on terror are fundamentally inconsistent with enlightened policing.

28.5 PROBLEM OF NET WIDENING: CAN POLICE DEPARTMENTS FIGHT TERRORISM TOO?

As to the question of whether terrorism should be added to the demands on police even in the face of budget restraints, some say yes, absolutely. For example, George Kelling and William Bratton (2006) have written the following on the police role in the "war on terror":

> Local police can be leveraged in this war in three key ways. First, we can train police in the problem solving techniques that will make them effective first preventers of

terrorism. Second, we can use computer statistics (CompStat) and technology to enhance data sharing and to catalyze intelligence-led counterterrorist policing. Finally, and most vitally, the theory of order maintenance commonly called "broken windows," which police in New York City have used so successfully in the war on crime, can be adapted for the war on terror. Doing so will dramatically bolster our ability to disrupt terrorists before they strike.

Kelling and Bratton go on to say that the NYPD has indeed made this adaptation, that its intelligence operation is widely regarded as the gold standard. The department hired a cadre of intelligence and counterterrorism experts, including officers fluent in Arabic, Farsi, and Pashto. They monitor foreign news services and intelligence reports, and have stationed officers overseas. Of course, the NYPD has considerably more reason than other police departments to take such extraordinary measures against terrorism, as noted earlier, but posting officers abroad is really exceptional.

While one can question the usefulness of referring to such activities as elements of a War on Terror,[9] one cannot question the need for a police role in the national security against terrorists, especially in light of the genuine threat that terrorists pose even against mid-size communities and the fact that there are many more sworn police officers in the United States than federal agents with responsibilities for counterterrorism. Kelling and Bratton note that, given this imbalance, local police personnel are much more likely than federal officers to cross paths with terrorists. They are thus more inclined to receive and respond to citizen tips, more inclined to encounter terrorist activities on the ground, and more likely to know key members of local communities who can be helpful in deterring terrorism. It is entirely appropriate for local police departments to be formally involved in the nation's homeland security network.

At the same time, the police cannot ignore the real world of virtually limitless demands on finite resources in an era of shrinking budgets. The police have already been saddled with inflated expectations associated with new burdens: zero tolerance against drug kingpins in wars on drugs and crime, all-hazards policing, and so on (Greene 2011). There is a limit to what the police can realistically accomplish.

These burdens have been complicated by the new demands associated with homeland security. Effective counterterrorism usually involves a complex web of coordination, both within and between agencies. The mix of networks involved can be bewildering: horizontal and vertical; local, national, and international; public and private. Ed Maguire and William King (2011) conjecture that the explosion of interagency and intergovernmental task forces in law enforcement in the years since 2001 could represent a fundamental shift in the structure of American law enforcement, especially as local police are diverted to joint counterterrorism task forces and indoctrinated away from local community needs.

Finding the right balance is a matter of legitimacy. The police are the citizen's first point of contact with the criminal justice system, and typically the first contact that offenders, victims, and witnesses have with the criminal justice system. The public's perception of the legitimacy of the criminal justice system is shaped largely by these direct impressions. What the police do to shape these impressions matters. If the police treat the threat of terrorism as the genuine threat it is to public safety without abandoning their core responsibilities for more conventional matters of public safety—and if they fully respect the rights of minorities who may be targets of unfounded but widespread public resentments—they will maintain the legitimacy they need to operate effectively and as agents of justice.

28.6 Community Policing and Counterterrorism

Community policing—and its core principles of public safety through commitment to the community, respect for the public, and the idea of improving the quality of life in the community through partnerships that build social capital and contribute to neighborhood vibrancy—is one of the most promising arrows in the quiver of counterterrorism, both at home and abroad. If terrorism is usually borne of alienation, surely a more vibrant community can serve to remove the seeds of alienation and extremism that give rise to terrorists and insurgent violence in the first place. Community policing interventions have, indeed, been found to enhance counterterrorism efforts, largely by improving relationships with immigrant groups, especially in communities with sizable Muslim populations (Friedmann and Cannon 2007; Jones and Supinski 2010; Greene 2011). As noted in an earlier section, community policing can continue to keep these relations from sliding down the slippery slope of mutual alienation, if not to help to elevate the standing of Muslims in the larger community, as long as the community policing program aims primarily toward community-building rather than intelligence-gathering.

Informed people, however, sometimes disagree sharply over how the police should work to improve the quality of life in the community. One source of disagreement: There may be as many definitions and characterizations of community policing as there are of terrorism. Some emphasize community outreach and bridge-building; others emphasize fixing "broken windows" and other signs of crime to send a message to would-be offenders that the people here care about their neighborhood and are likely to take action against disorder and crime. Some emphasize police autonomy and organization, arguing for less centralized command and hierarchy; others emphasize accountability for improving measures of community order and stability and reducing complaints against the police.

Perhaps the most basic source of disagreement is ideological. Conservative ideology is stereotypically opposed to change and in favor of consistently tough approaches to attacks on the community, while liberal ideology is stereotypically opposed to tough sanctions and in favor of the reform of the day. These are cartoons, but as with other stereotypes, elements of empirically supportable realities often lie beneath the simplistic images. Core elements of community policing are bound to help to prevent terrorism, but they must be selected judiciously to serve situational nuances both within and across communities. Neither local communities nor the nation will be served by rigid adherence to simple formulas for the complex world in which we live. Just as community policing is no panacea, so is it the case that intolerance of minorities who bear only superficial resemblances to terrorists is bound to be not only counterproductive but also inconsistent with conventional standards of ethical policing.

28.7 ISSUES FOR FURTHER RESEARCH

A useful framework for thinking about what works to prevent and respond most effectively to terrorist threats is provided by the logic of routine activity theory (RAT). Developed by Cohen and Felson (1979), RAT holds that crimes are the product of three components: motivated offenders, suitable targets, and the absence of capable guardians to protect the targets from the offenders. Much as heat, oxygen, and fuel are required to produce fire, crime requires the presence of all three RAT elements to produce crime. The routine patterns of work, school, commuting, and leisure influence the convergence of these three components in time and place, and motivated, rational offenders are inclined to seize opportunities presented by such patterns. (It is no coincidence that the theory is alternately referred to as "opportunity theory.") The theory has been used to develop situational interventions to prevent crime through a more purposeful application of guardianship resources, and this idea may be applicable as well to homeland security strategies. Federal buildings have been made less accessible to street bomb attacks following the 1995 bombing of the Murrah Federal Building in Oklahoma City, and major monuments, bridges, buildings, and other targets in the United States that are known to have been targeted by jihadist terrorists have been similarly "hardened." Routine activities theory could help in the development of a system of weights to assign to the allocation of scarce screening and surveillance resources, to maximize their effectiveness.

The use of technology—closed circuit television networks, sound surveillance systems, high-altitude imagery intelligence, and other electronic intelligence devices—can be instrumental as counterterrorism tools available to the police, to provide both general and actionable intelligence. Following the logic of RAT, technology can be used to target extremists who present high risks to the community, to protect targets attractive to these individuals and groups, and to enhance guardianship. Still, we have much to learn about which combinations of these technologies can be most effective for dealing with various threats presented by extremists. Such information could be helpful in protecting communities throughout the land—at the local level to prevent crimes committed by extremists, and at the national level as more effective instruments of the network of domestic security agencies.

It will be especially important to improve the data and analytic capacities to use the data to "connect the dots" for intelligence and policy analysis purposes. Crime prevention strategies have been informed through "evidence-based" policing (Sherman 1998;

Lum 2009), and the general concept is likely to have relevance both to counterterrorism strategy generally and to specific threats posed by violent extremists. While the data on terrorism are extremely spare and the prospects of finding close parallels of evidence-based policing strategies for crime prevention to the threats posed by terrorism limited, the prospects are substantial for collecting and analyzing intelligence data on specific terrorist threats (Brodeur 2011). The challenge is to establish which dots are pertinent, how they relate to one another, and the implications of these associations. As with intelligence generally, the problem for police is to collect the data, establish its reliability, have competent people analyze it so that logical connections can be made among items of information and threats can be assessed, and then to share those assessments with the people on the ground who need the information and can act on it.

28.8 Conclusion

One of the enduring problems of policing is its susceptibility to politicization, its tendency to get moved from its central purpose of serving and protecting the community in the name of a politically invented war of the day: on crime in the late 1960s, on drugs in the 1970s, and on terrorism following the tragedy of September 11, 2001.

Terrorism has, rightfully, induced serious rethinking of national security in the United States, as it has in other nations. It has produced considerable changes in policing and even more monumental changes in the US military establishment, highlighted by major shifts in strategy—away from Cold War-era policies on nuclear deterrence, strategic air commands, and rapidly deployable fleets of warships, and towards War on Terror-era actions against insurgents in Iraq and Afghanistan and Homeland Security actions against prospective terrorists in the United States. Ironically, as community policing has provided a blueprint for the conversion of the military from storm troopers to bridge builders in hostile environments, with police officials serving effectively as trainers of new police departments and military peace-keepers abroad, so have the police changed domestically as well, with inducements to serve more as defenders of the homeland. Thus, the lines between the police and military have blurred. The police are likely to encounter further changes, both to prevent and respond to terrorism, over the coming years.

It would be most unwise—especially in light of a considerable record of achievements by the police in the decade following 9/11—to take seriously fervent demands for terrorism-induced shifts in either the role of police in society or the administration of policing. Terrorism is but the latest of an unending list of demands placed on the police over the decades. As with prior rhetorical wars on crime and drugs,[10] the police have been given neither sufficient resources nor clear battle instructions to permit anything resembling victory in a war on terrorism, nor have they been relieved from other considerable demands on their core mission.

Real war is the use of aggression by one sovereign nation against another, following a formal declaration by the nation's legitimate authority to do so, and ended by surrender and treaty (Forst 2009, 13). Wars on poverty and cancer, drugs and crime—and now terrorism—are not bona fide wars. They make use of the war metaphor to generate a sense of urgency in order to garner support for interventions that might otherwise be unprecedented and draw political resistance. Making such causes matters of "war" appeals to primitive human impulse, not reason. These wars cannot produce peace treaties; they are unwinnable. They may be effective in achieving short-term political aims; over the longer term, they create false hopes, unfulfilled expectations, discrimination against Muslims and other immigrants and, ultimately, public disappointment. The most powerful response to terrorism may be to avoid over-reacting to it. This might restore the United States' moral authority and lessen the prospect of future such attacks. Calling it war has achieved precisely the opposite result. The police do not distinguish themselves by collaborating in folly.

The police can "defend the homeland" most effectively—and without undermining their core legitimacy—by treating terrorism as crime, and leaving it to federal authorities to respond to it as a national security matter. The police can both prevent and respond to terrorist events in much the same way they do other serious crimes—by establishing and maintaining close relationships with key individuals and institutions in the community and by working closely with federal law enforcement and intelligence agencies and with other police departments in the sharing of information essential to the monitoring of extremists and prevention of terrorism.

The fires of terrorism are fueled principally by fear. The police have proven to be effective in reducing the public's fear of crime. They can be equally effective in defending against terrorism by treating it as serious crime, leaving it to federal officials to treat it as a national security problem. Public safety will not be served by continuing to elevate terrorism to a grand stage, or by rewarding fanatic criminals by making them celebrity martyrs. Nor should the police allow the atmosphere of political pandering in which they operate to keep them from protecting and serving the community effectively, efficiently, and fairly. The alternative—waging "war" on terrorists—hands victory to the terrorists by allowing them to turn our primal fears into self-inflicted wounds. The police can be the first line of defense against violent extremists by depriving them of any legitimate claim to "warrior" status and treating them instead as thugs.

NOTES

* The author wishes to thank Tom Brady, Ed Maguire, Stephen Tankel, and the editors of this volume for their helpful comments on earlier drafts.

1. This general problem is not unique to the police. Others have observed that we ask no less of prisons.

2. For example, a Centre for Policing, Intelligence and Counter Terrorism was created at Macquarie University in Australia in 2005 to promote research, deliver postgraduate

programs, and provide professional education and consultancy services in support of counterterrorism.

3. Linguist Geoffrey Nunberg, when asked about the word as used in "homeland security," responded:

   Americans don't usually think of themselves as having a "homeland" in that sense. It's like "fatherland" in German or "patris" in French. English and particularly American English doesn't have a word for that. We need some way to describe this part of America that's located here, and that's a very interesting usage. It has an Old World feel to it and it's not the sort of way we've thought about our country. I don't know if it augers a change in the way we think of America itself or if it's just a convenient or slightly awkward term that (President) Bush grabbed for, but it's certainly interesting. (Voice of America News, January 30, 2002; Language of Terror, Part 2, October 14, 2001)

4. The police monopoly on the use of force has been eroded in recent years by the authority that courts have granted to private citizens under "stand-your-ground" laws.

5. Bittner (1974) adds that while the core of the police role is the authority to use force, "the skill of policing consists in finding ways to avoid its use" (as quoted in Klockars and Mastrofski [1991], 269).

6. In 2004 there were approximately 100,000 federal law enforcement officers, many assigned to DHS, and some 600,000 sworn state and local officers.

7. Johnson (2011) reports 1,023 such calls to the Washington Metropolitan Police Department in 2010.

8. Bittner goes on to observe that the militarization of police served a useful purpose in the mid-twentieth century. It professionalized police by replacing the "flatfoot on the take" with "cadres of personally incorruptible snappy operatives working under the command of bureaucrats-in-uniform," and it introduced a modicum of internal discipline (1970, 53). On balance, however, he was negative about the militarization of policing: "as long as policemen will be treated like soldier-bureaucrats, they cannot be expected to develop professional acumen, nor value its possession" (61).

9. The White House officially ended its use of the phrase in 2009, directing the Department of Defense to replace it with "Overseas Contingency Operation" (Wilson and Kamen 2009).

10. Egon Bittner (1970, 48–49) said this about the War on Crime: "The rhetorical shift from 'crime control' to 'war on crime' signifies the transition from a routine concern to a state of emergency. We no longer face losses of one kind or another from the depredations of criminals; we are in imminent danger of losing everything!... But the conceit that they can be ultimately vanquished, which is the implicit objective of war, involves a particularly trivial kind of utopian dreaming."

References

Ahmed, Akbar. 2010. *Journey into America: The Challenge of Islam*. Washington, DC: Brookings Institute.

Bittner, Egon. 1970. *The Functions of the Police in Modern Society*. Rockville, MD: National Institute of Mental Health.

———. 1974. "Florence Nightingale in Pursuit of Willie Sutton: A Theory of Police." In *The Potential for Reform in Criminal Justice*, edited by Herman Jacob, 17–44. Beverly Hills, CA: Sage.

Braithwaite, John. 2011. "Regulating Terrorism." In *Criminologists on Terrorism and Homeland Security*, edited by Brian Forst, Jack R. Greene, and James P. Lynch, 383–408. New York: Oxford University Press.

Brodeur, Jean-Paul. 2011. "Go Analyze! (Connecting the Dots)." In *Criminologists on Terrorism and Homeland Security*, edited by Brian Forst, Jack R. Greene, and James P. Lynch, 245–272. New York: Oxford University Press.

Cohen, Lawrence E., and Marcus Felson. 1979. "Social Change and Crime Rate Trends: A Routine Activity Approach." *American Sociological Review* 44:588–608.

de Rugy, Veronique. 2005. "What Does Homeland Security Spending Buy?" Working paper no. 107. Washington, DC: American Enterprise Institute.

Forst, Brian. 2009. *Terrorism, Crime and Public Policy*. New York: Cambridge University Press.

——. 2011. "Managing the Fear of Terrorism." In *Criminologists on Terrorism and Homeland Security*, edited by Brian Forst, Jack R. Greene, and James P. Lynch, 273–299. New York: Oxford University Press.

Friedmann, Robert R., and William J. Cannon. 2007. "Homeland Security and Community Policing: Competing or Complementing Public Safety Policies." *Journal of Homeland Security and Emergency Management* 4(4). http://scholarworks.gsu.edu/cgi/viewcontent.cgi?article=1000&context=cj_facpub

Greene, Jack R. 2011. "Community Policing and Terrorism: Problems and Prospects for Local Community Security." In *Criminologists on Terrorism and Homeland Security*, edited by Brian Forst, Jack R. Greene, and James P. Lynch, 208–244. New York: Oxford University Press.

Johnson, Kevin. 2011. "Increased Citizen Vigilance Means More Work for Police." *USA Today*, September 11, A2.

Jones, Chapin, and Stanley B. Supinski. 2010. "Policing and Community Relations in the Homeland Security Era." *Journal of Homeland Security and Emergency Management* 7(1): ISSN (Online) 1547–7355; DOI: 10.2202/1547-7355.1633

Kelling, George L., and William J. Bratton. 2006. "Policing Terrorism." *Civic Bulletin* no. 43. New York: Center for Civic Innovation at the Manhattan Institute.

Klockars, Carl B., and Stephen D. Mastrofski. 1991. "Policing Everyday Life." In *Thinking About Police: Contemporary Readings*, 2n ed., edited by Carl B. Klockars and Stephen D. Mastrofski, 268–272. New York: McGraw-Hill.

Los Angeles Times. 2010. " 'Fusion Centers' at a Glance: Facts about Homeland Security's Regional Fusion Centers," November 15. http://articles.latimes.com/2010/nov/15/nation/la-na-fusion-centers-box-20101115.

Lowry, Rich. 2005. "Homeland Pork: 'Unless We Waste Money, the Terrorists Will Win.'" *National Review Online*, July 19. http://www.nationalreview.com/articles/214970/homeland-pork/rich-lowry#.

Lum, Cynthia. 2009. "Translating Police Research into Practice." *Ideas in American Policing* 11:1–16.

Maguire, Edward R., and William R. King. 2011. "Federal-Local Coordination in Homeland Security." In *Criminologists on Terrorism and Homeland Security*, edited by Brian Forst, Jack R. Greene, and James P. Lynch, 322–356. New York: Oxford University Press.

Mijares, Tomas C., and Jay D. Jamieson. 2011. "Soldiers and Spies, Police and Detectives." In *Criminologists on Terrorism and Homeland Security*, edited by Brian Forst, Jack R. Greene, and James P. Lynch, 183–207. New York: Oxford University Press.

Murray, John. 2005. "Policing Terrorism: A Threat to Community Policing or Just a Shift in Priorities?" *Police Practice and Research* 6(4): 347–61.

Pew Research Center. 2011. *Muslim Americans: No Signs of Growth in Alienation or Support for Extremism: Mainstream and Moderate Attitudes.* New York: Pew Research Center for the People and the Press.

Rittgers, David. 2011. "We're All Terrorists Now," Cato@Liberty, February 2. http://www.cato-at-liberty.org/we%E2%80%99re-all-terrorists-now/.

Scheider, Matthew C., and Robert Chapman. 2003. "Community Policing and Terrorism," Homeland Security Institute. http://www.homelandsecurity.org/journal/articles/Scheider-Chapman.html.

Sherman, Lawrence W. 1998. "Evidence-Based Policing." *Ideas in American Policing* 1:1–16.

Skolnick, Jerome H., and James J. Fyfe. 1993. *Above the Law: Police and the Excessive Use of Force.* New York: Free Press.

Wilson, Scott, and Al Kamen. 2009. "'Global War On Terror' Is Given New Name," *Washington Post*, March, A4.

Index

CPSIA information can be obtained
at www.ICGtesting.com
Printed in the USA
BVHW091141300120
570902BV00003B/4